THE COMPANION GUIDE TO
Southern Italy

THE COMPANION GUIDES

GENERAL EDITOR: VINCENT CRONIN

It is the aim of these Guides to provide a Companion, in the person of the author, who knows intimately the places and people of whom he writes, and is able to communicate this knowledge and affection to his readers. It is hoped that the text and pictures will aid them in their preparations and in their travels, and will help them remember on their return.

THE GREEK ISLANDS

PARIS

THE SOUTH OF FRANCE

LONDON

VENICE

ROME

FLORENCE

JUGOSLAVIA

TUSCANY

UMBRIA

THE WEST HIGHLANDS OF SCOTLAND

In preparation

EAST ANGLIA

GREECE

TURKEY

SOUTH-WESTERN FRANCE

SOUTHERN SPAIN

THE COMPANION GUIDE TO

SOUTHERN ITALY

PETER GUNN

Collins
ST JAMES'S PLACE LONDON
1969

The size of the area covered and its immense richness, scenically, historically and architecturally, have made it necessary for the Editors to abridge considerably the author's original manuscript in order to bring the volume within the scope of the Companion Guides. They have done so in the belief that nothing vital to the tourist has been omitted and that the high standards set himself by the author and consistent with those of the series have been fully maintained.

Maps by Charles Green

© *Peter Gunn, 1969*
Printed in Great Britain
Collins Clear-Type Press
London and Glasgow

Contents

Contents

Illustrations

Illustrations

Introduction

It is the four mainland regions of Southern Italy, and the islands administered from their provincial capitals, which form the subject of this guide. The regions, that is, of **Campania**, **Basilicata** (which is also known as **Lucania**), **Apulia** and **Calabria**. The most important of the islands included are **Capri**, **Ischia** and **Procida**, and the **Tremiti Islands**. The large islands of Sicily and Sardinia, the small Ponziane group and the Lipari (Aeolian) Islands fall outside our present scope.

The school-atlas image of Southern Italy as a tilted riding boot protruding deep into the Mediterranean towards Africa, with its well-defined 'toe' and 'heel' and also its 'spur', the Gargano peninsula, is a useful one. Through it runs the high range of the Apennines and their offshoots in a series of majestic peaks which continue beyond the narrow Strait of Messina into Sicily. Mountains and sea are the dominant features of the landscape, and the only plain of any size is the Capitanata around Foggia. These geographical facts largely determine communications in the South; roads and rail either follow the coastline or are compelled to cross high mountainous tracts. But they thereby reward the tourist with some of the most magnificent scenery in Europe.

If I had to make the decision which way to approach the South, I would unhesitatingly come by sea, through the Bay of Naples. As the ship enters the Bocca Grande between the islands of Ischia and Capri, the splendour of the natural amphitheatre in which Naples stands cannot fail to move even the most hardened, unromantic traveller. Ischia lies on our left, the vegetation on the lower slopes of Monte Epomeo a most brilliant emerald green. Beyond, over the blue waters of the channel, lies Procida, the castle a pale yellow against the brown cliffs of Cape Misenum. Behind Pozzuoli on its curving bay rise the thickly wooded hills of the Phlegraean Fields, which continue above the smoking stacks of the Ilva works at

9

Bagnoli, the high ground running on to join the pine woods on Posillipo. Naples appears a city of whites and pinks (flecked here and there with the green of gardens), rising in terraces from the water's edge to the skyline of Vomero, San Martino and Pizzofalcone.

From a distance Vesuvius seems strangely lacking in height but not in impressiveness; the perfect symmetry of its gently sloping cone is broken where the crater falls away to form Monte Somma. Inland the Apennines are the purest blue, differing only in tone from the sky and sea. To the right, beyond Torre del Greco and Torre Annunziata, the shoreline curves round towards Castellammare. Above Vico Equense the greens of the chestnut woods which cover the sides of Monte Faito are softened in a pale violet haze. On either side of Sorrento the colour deepens; sea merges with coast, as if the water's surface reflects the cliff face and lemon groves. The Sorrentine peninsula, running out to the Punta Campanella, hides from our view the beautiful Costiera Amalfitana. Opposite, over the narrow gap of the Bocca Piccola, the cliffs on the east end of Capri face the mainland. To the west of the island, under the summit of Monte Solaro, cluster the white villas of Anacapri.

However, there are also frequent air services between all the principal European centres and Naples's airport, Capodichino, and Italian domestic airlines, such as Alitalia, connect with the main towns. Mail steamers from the United Kingdom to Australia and the East call at Naples, and there are efficient rail services via Rome to Naples, through carriages going on to Reggio Calabria, and as far as Lecce in the heel of Italy. Overnight car-sleeper services run to Milan and Brindisi during an extended holiday season, and the magnificent new Autostrada del Sole is now complete from Milan as far as Naples. Beyond Naples a further stretch is already open as far as Battipaglia, with a break at Salerno, and work is progressing fast.

Once in the South there are also bus services which, when we take into account the often very difficult terrain to be traversed, are very good indeed. There are not many villages, even the most remote in the mountains of Calabria and Basilicata, that are not connected with neighbouring villages and the nearest town by buses at least twice a day. Although these buses are often crowded and noisy— and in the summer months uncomfortably hot—they are often amusing, and between them and the railways there are few parts of Southern Italy outside the reach of the ordinary tourist.

There is little doubt that more of the country can be seen, in less time, and perhaps with more comfort, in a car than by any other means, and on the whole the roads in Southern Italy are good, each year bringing an improvement. Main roads are maintained by the State (the *Strade Statali*, marked SS plus a number, e.g. SS 6) or by the Provinces (*Strade Provinciali*, SP plus a number); the former are normally superior in surface and upkeep.

Landslides—*frana*—tend to occur in the South after heavy rain, and even main roads can be seriously affected, though bad patches are usually well and quickly signposted. The motorist should also remember that distances on the map may in mountainous regions be little indication of the time it takes on the ground. These mountain roads are usually triumphs of engineering skill—the grading is excellent and the magnificent scenery is more than a recompense, but the number of hairpin bends makes driving necessarily slow, and often very fatiguing as well. Since petrol pumps may be few and far between, the motorist is advised always to start out with a full tank, or to carry an emergency petrol-can.

The quality of hotel accommodation in the South (another deterrent no longer valid) naturally varies greatly, but the improvement in recent years has been remarkable. The number of hotels has increased enormously (although there are still large towns like Aversa and Capua where provision is inadequate) and building continues; but the even greater relative increase in the number of visitors, especially to the seaside resorts, makes it essential to ensure previous booking, certainly in July and August. In spring and autumn, which are fortunately the best times for travelling in Southern Italy, things are considerably easier.

No strict consistency has been adopted in this guide as to the use of proper names. Where there is an obvious English usage, as in 'Naples' or the 'Apennines', this has been followed; otherwise the Italian form has been used.

NOTE

Map references, i.e. street names in Naples and names of towns and villages elsewhere, are given in bold type, thus: **Piazza del Mercato, Sorrento, Bari, Terlizzi.** Where several maps are referred to within one chapter, marginal map references are given.

Places of interest occurring within a map reference are shown thus: *cathedral church of S. Andrea, Castello, Grotte di Castellana.*

CHAPTER 1

Approaches to Southern Italy

Map: The Environs of Naples, pp.72–3

Aquino—Montecassino—Gaeta

From Rome to Naples the motorist has the choice of three principal
routes. Each of these roads has an excellent surface and each has
much that is of interest on the way. For those in a hurry the new
autostrada, opened completely as far as Naples in 1962, will be an
obvious first choice. For others with more time, either the Via
Casilina (which follows the route of the ancient Via Latina) or the
Via Appia (another Roman road, built by the censor Appius
Claudius Caecus in 312 BC) offers an opportunity to stop at places
less easily accessible from the autostrada.

Many of the towns that we pass will repay a visit, but with the
exception of two they fall outside the scope of this book. Aquino and
Montecassino, however, are inseparably connected with the history
of the Kingdom of Naples. Their inclusion in Lazio is the result of
changes in regional administrative borders since the unification of
Italy. For them we take the Via Casilina, which runs close to, at
places crossing, the autostrada, but it is part of the countryside as the
latter is not.

Aquino, which lies about a mile to the south of the Via Casilina,
has the appearance of a northern country village, with its orchards
and cottage-gardens. The family of Aquino, one of the most powerful
feudal houses in Angevin Naples, is remembered today chiefly for
St Thomas (1227–74), the 'Angelic Doctor', but it also produced at
about the same time as well as warriors the notable poet Rinaldo.
Remains of the Aquino castle stand on the bluff to the right of the
Romanesque church. Masonry from the Roman town of
Aquinium supplied much of the material for this remarkable
building, one of the most beautiful of the smaller churches south of
Rome. A wide flight of steps leads up to the entrance, the central
portal of which is constructed entirely of Roman carving. Above it

is a lunette in mosaic of the school of Montecassino. The sombre interior is severely basilican, with two rows of columns separating the aisles from the nave. The altar is formed of an ancient alabaster sarcophagus, depicting horses and horsemen with chariots.

At the entrance to **Cassino**, which was completely rebuilt after its destruction in the last war, a road on the left climbs to the famous Benedictine *Abbey of Montecassino*. Founded by St Benedict of Nursia at the beginning of the sixth century as a 'school for the service of the Lord', it was for centuries the chief centre of monastic life for Western Europe. The monastery has been destroyed in turn by Lombards, Saracens and lastly, in 1944, by the Allies. The rebuilding is now completed, and the form and decoration of the ancient monastery meticulously restored.

The school of painters, illuminators and mosaicists in the Byzantine tradition, who were brought together in the latter half of the eleventh century by the Abbot Desiderius (later Pope Victor III) to work on the monastery, influenced the art of all Central and Southern Italy. In the dissolution of the monasteries after the unification of Italy in 1860 the Abbey of Montecassino was spared (largely

14

through the efforts of English well-wishers) and became a national monument, with the monks as custodians. It is doubtfully claimed that St Benedict and his sister, St Scholastica, were buried here.

South-east of Cassino the Via Casilina passes from Lazio into Campania, skirts Roccamonfina and crosses the Volturno at Capua; then it passes through Aversa and approaches Naples to the west of Capodichino Airport.

The ancient Appian Way joined Rome to Brindisi and was the main route of the legions to Greece and the Eastern provinces. After crossing the Alban Hills it runs in a direct line through the now drained **Pontine Marshes** to the sea at Terracina, where it is advisable to fork right, leaving the Via Appia for the newly made Via Flacca, the SS 213, which skirts the sea and passes many Roman remains. To the right of the road, on its high cliff, stands **Sperlonga** which is becoming a fashionable resort.

At Serapo, a suburb of Gaeta, a road to the right leads down to the beach and to Gaeta's best hotels. Today **Gaeta** is a naval port— as it was under the Romans, with the name of Caietai Portus. On the promontory stands the mausoleum of Munatius Plancus, Mark Antony's lieutenant. Many fragments of Roman ruins are incorporated in walls and houses in the streets around the cathedral and in the remarkable campanile of the cathedral itself.

After Gaeta the road is joined again on the left by the Via Appia, and on the nearer bank of the River Garigliano, the boundary between Lazio and Campania, lie the extensive ruins of Minturniae, a Roman colony settled in 296 BC. Near by is the British War Cemetery.

Once in Campania, we take the right branch, the reconstructed Via Domiziana, which first crosses a fertile plain, then bears right past the site of the Roman colony of Sinuessa (where the road approaches the coast) to the **Bagni di Mondragone**, a seaside resort and spa. The road crosses the Volturno at Castel Volturno and runs for some distance parallel with the fine sandy beach. All this part is being rapidly developed but in Roman times it was a desolate waste of marshes and shifting sand dunes.

At the southern end of the Lago di Patria, close to the bathing beach of Lido di Patria, are the excavated ruins of Liternum. By the forum are remains of a temple, basilica and theatre, and at the entrance to the excavations is a modern memorial to Publius Cornelius Scipio Africanus, the conqueror of Hannibal, who died at Liternum in 182 BC, embittered and disgusted with the machinations of his enemies in Rome. On his tomb he had inscribed the words:

'My ungrateful country, you hold not even my bones—*Ingrata patria, ne ossa quidem mea habes.*' Pliny later recorded seeing the vines and myrtles that Scipio was said to have planted here with his own hand.

Ahead rise the hills of the **Phlegraean Fields** (see p. 70), a fantastic region—still actively volcanic—of extinct craters, lakes, hot springs, sulphurous exhalations and boiling mud. Near by is the *cave of the Cumaean Sibyl.* As the road descends towards Pozzuoli, on the right in a deep wooded hollow lies **Lake Avernus**, where the ancients placed the entrance to the underworld.

The road passes through the outskirts of Pozzuoli and at the Roman amphitheatre bends left and climbs among the hills, from which there are magnificent views over the Bay of Naples. Beyond the turning off to the Baths of Agnano we approach the modern suburb of Fuorigrotta. Here, in the Palazzina Funivia, the tourist authorities have set up a convenient information office, the Portierato della Città di Napoli. Thence by the tunnel under Posillipo we enter Naples via the suburb of Mergellina and the fashionable Sezione Chiaia. *Chiaia* is derived from the Latin *plaga*, a flat tract or beach, and thus has a family connection with the Italian *spiaggia* and the French *plage*. Who but an etymologist would imagine what a Neapolitan could do with language?

CHAPTER 2

Naples on the Sea

Map: Naples, pp.24–5

In his novel *The Skin*, Curzio Malaparte writes: 'Naples is the most mysterious city in Europe. It is the only city of the ancient world that has not perished . . . It is not a city: it is a world—the ancient pre-Christian world—which has survived intact on the surface of the modern world.'

Naples is all this; yet it is something more. It is as if each succeeding wave of conquerors (but especially the Spaniards) had deposited on the essential Greekness of Naples and Neapolitans unresolved layers of their own nationality—visible in the buildings and in the character of the people. Naples is confusing, stimulating, and utterly unlike any other city I know.

The **'old city'** stretches northwards from the port, its natural boundaries formed on the west by the spur on which stands the Castel S. Elmo and the line of hills that run north, then east, beyond the palace and park of Capodimonte, Capodichino and Poggioreale. **'Naples on the sea'** consists of the promontory of S. Lucia below the Castel S. Elmo; then to the west the suburbs (*sezioni, rioni*) of Chiaia and Amedeo, which lie behind the gardens of the Villa Comunale on the sweep of the bay bordered by the splendid Via Caracciolo, the esplanade which links S. Lucia with the little port and suburb of Mergellina. Above Mergellina rise the heights of Posillipo, the western extremity of **'Naples on the hills'**. Between Posillipo and the Castel S. Elmo, on the crest of the hill and expanding rapidly to the north, is the modern suburb of Vomero.

Hotels and pensioni

Close to the Central Station on the east of Naples, in the **Piazza**

Garibaldi and along the Corso Umberto I, there is a wide choice of hotels of all categories. These are convenient for travellers by train, but the fact that they are so far from the Bay means that you will miss one of the greatest pleasures of Naples. For this reason I would strongly advise an hotel in S. Lucia, or beyond it in Chiaia, Mergellina or on Posillipo. (For list of recommended hotels see Appendix 4.)

My own choice is perhaps Parker's on the Corso Vittorio Emanuele, an old-established hotel inseparably connected with late Victorian and Edwardian Naples.

S. Lucia and the Castel dell' Ovo

Traditionally a first meal in Naples should be eaten in **S. Lucia** (for restaurants in other parts of the city, see pp. 56-7), which takes us immediately to 'Naples on the Sea'. Here, at one of the restaurants on the Borgo Marinaro round the little port (formed by the causeway linking the Castel dell' Ovo with the mainland), at Zi' Teresa, the Bersagliera, Ciro or the Transatlantico, we can sit at water's level, literally among the moored yachts and all the animated movement of small boys diving for coins, fishermen at work in their boats, ambulant musicians, hucksters and idlers. Opposite are the exclusive *circoli nautici*, the waterside clubs, and behind them flows the incessant traffic of the Via Partenope. Above towers the shambling mass of the Castel dell' Ovo, the tricolor of United Italy flying from its walls.

The former S. Lucia of the song, picturesque and squalid, is gone. The de luxe Excelsior and the Vesuvio have replaced the old Albergo Roma. But the excitement of the place remains.

The 'island' on which we sit was known to the ancients as Megaris. Here, and on the headland of Pizzofalcone opposite, Lucullus built two of his several villas on the Bay of Naples, whose buildings, fishponds and gardens were famous for their luxury and magnificence. Two rows of columns from one of the villas are incorporated in the refectory of a seventeenth-century monastery in the **Castel dell' Ovo.** (The Castel is now a military establishment, but permission to visit it may be obtained from the Commando Territoriale Militare in the Piazza del Plebiscito.) It was either the Castel dell' Ovo, or another Lucullan villa at Misenum, that effectively saw the end of the Roman Empire, for in one or other of them Romulus Augustulus, the last Emperor of the West, was deposed and

18

imprisoned by the Scyrrian Odoacer in AD 476. Under the Normans and Hohenstaufens the Castel dell' Ovo became a royal residence. Giotto, who was court painter to the Angevin King Robert from 1329 to 1333, decorated the chapel with frescoes, but no trace of these remains. In 1799 the castle was seized by the people, but they were expelled shortly after when Cardinal Ruffo and his Sanfedisti put a bloody end to the ephemeral Parthenopean Republic (see Appendix 3).

Chiaia—Villa Pignatelli—the Aquarium—La Torretta—S. Maria di Piedigrotta and a festival

To the left, beyond the Castel dell' Ovo, stretches the esplanade of the Via Caracciolo, flanked on the right by the gardens of the Villa Comunale, and ending at the small port of **Sannazzaro** in Mergellina, where among the moorings for yachts and pleasure craft the *aliscafi* (hydroplanes) come and go for Capri and Ischia.

From the Piazza Vittoria the Villa Comunale is bounded on the north by the wide Riviera di Chiaia with its eighteenth- and nineteenth-century palaces, and behind them lies the quarter of **Chiaia,** fascinating for its mixture of 'the two Naples'.

The short Via Calabritto, a street of fashionable shops, joins the Piazza Vittoria with the neighbouring Piazza dei Martiri, so called from the column in its centre, raised in 1866 to the memory of Neapolitans who fell in the struggle against the Bourbons. On the right, just beyond where the Via Domenico Morelli enters the triangular piazza, a short cul-de-sac, the Vico S. Maria a Capella Vecchia, leads through a gateway (1506) to what was once the courtyard of an abbey. On the suppression of the monastery in the late eighteenth century, the building was acquired by the Marchese Sessa, who transformed it and let it to Sir William Hamilton, and it was here that Nelson first met Emma Hamilton in 1793.

Continuing northwards by the Via S. Caterina, we meet the Via Chiaia, and see above us the vast sixteenth-century *Palazzo Cellamare.* Beneath it is the largest cinema in Naples, the Metropolitan. But before reaching this, we shall turn left and follow the narrow Via Cavallerizza, which takes us through a most picturesque part of old Chiaia. This street, which widens into the Largo Vasto a Chiaia, runs roughly parallel with the Via Filangieri and its continuation, the Via dei Mille, the shopping-centre for the well-to-do Rione Amedeo. On the left are the rather derelict remains of the fifteenth-century *villa of Alfonso II of Aragon,* and opposite it the palace formerly owned by the Carafa Counts of Policastro.

The street is now crossed by several wide thoroughfares with blocks of expensive modern flats, and changes its name to the Via S. Teresa. A little farther on, to the right, it opens out in a piazzetta in front of the church of the *Ascensione a Chiaia*—very Neapolitan this, with living quarters and workrooms built into the front of the portico; washing lines and children, the true emblems of Naples. Originally of the fourteenth century, the church was rebuilt by Fanzago in 1622. From here, behind the gardens of the Villa Pignatelli, the street changes its name for the last time to Via S. Maria in Portico, after the church at the end on the right.

The entrance to the charming neo-classical *Villa Pignatelli* is from the Riviera di Chiaia. Set back in its gardens and green trees, it looks more like a modest but elegant country place of *villeggiatura* (summer escape) than a town house. It was built in 1826 by Pietro Valente for Sir John Acton, Ferdinand I and IV's prime minister, and was later acquired by a branch of the Rothschilds, who had Gaetano Genovese carry out some internal alterations. From them it passed to the family of Aragona Pignatelli and became at the end of the last century the centre of Neapolitan intellectual and social life. In 1952 it was given to the State, and it is now open to the public as the *Museo Principe Diego Aragona Cortes*. The main interest of the museum lies in its furnishing of the period (admission, weekdays 9.30 a.m.–4.0 p.m.; Sundays and holidays 9.30 a.m.–1.0 p.m.).

Almost opposite, across the Riviera di Chiaia, a cream stuccoed building among the holm-oaks of the Villa Comunale houses the *Zoological Station,* with its fascinating and world-famous *Aquarium.* Founded in 1872 by the German naturalist Anton Dohrn, it is now an international centre for the study of underwater life. (Admission to the Aquarium, winter 8.0 a.m.–6.0 p.m.; summer 8.0 a.m.–10.0 p.m.; Saturdays and holidays 8.0 a.m.–midnight.)

On the Riviera di Chiaia, farther west towards Piedigrotta, just before the Piazza Principe di Napoli, is the church of *S. Giuseppe a Chiaia,* where in 1818 Shelley took the mysterious child Elena Adelaide to be christened, giving her his own family name. The Shelleys were then living on the Riviera near by at No. 250. A little farther on, where the street broadens out in a kind of piazza at the junction of Via Mergellina and Via Piedigrotta, the scene has all the animation of parts of the 'old city'. This is the district called **La**

Torretta, from a tower which was built here in the sixteenth century as protection against the raids of Barbary corsairs. In the market on the left, opposite the church of S. Maria della Neve (Our Lady of the Snow), sellers of ices, roasted chestnuts and hot pizzas cry their wares above the shouts of children. The Via Piedigrotta, the right-hand fork, leads us to one of the most popular churches in Naples, **S. Maria di Piedigrotta,** at the entrance to the motor tunnel under Posillipo.

It is here that the ancient, probably pagan in origin, festival of Piedigrotta takes place on the night of September 7th. Under the Spaniards and the Bourbons the celebrations included a military parade; but since the latter part of the last century it has been associated with competitions for the best new songs, the popular *canzoni napoletane*. The lovely '*Te voglio bene assaie*' was one of the first winners at Piedigrotta, and in 1880 the opening of the funicular to Vomero brought forth the well-known '*Funiculì-funiculà*'. The festival is the most popular of all Neapolitan festivals, an orgy of noise and high spirits which goes on all night.

Behind the church, on the steep side of the hill, rises the Parco Virgiliano (see p. 71), but from here we descend the Via Mergellina under the plane trees to the Piazza Sannazzaro. At any of a number of small restaurants on the right of the piazza we can eat cheaply such typical Neapolitan dishes as pizza and *frutti del mare*, washed down with strong red Gragnano or the white wines of Ischia. The piazza derives its name from Jacopo Sannazzaro, the poet of *Arcadia* and loyal subject of the last Aragonese kings, for whom King Frederick built a villa near by—'*There where the sea waves drink up the stream from the rocks and surge against the walls of the little sanctuary.*' The villa has gone but the sanctuary remains and it is there that Sannazzaro is buried, in his own little church of **S. Maria del Parto.** The church, which is reached by following the Via Mergellina past the Porto Sannazzaro, stands high on the right. Steps lead up to a terrace in front of it, from which there is a fine view over the port of Mergellina to where the shoreline curves away towards Pizzofalcone and the Castel dell' Ovo.

Piazza del Plebiscito—Palazzo Reale

From the Porto S. Lucia the Via Partenope finishes to the east at the **fountain of the Immacolatella** (1601), a pleasant baroque structure in gleaming white marble, with statues by Bernini and

21

caryatids by Naccherino. From this point and along the Via Nazario Sauro, as the esplanade becomes after its turn to the left, we have magnificent views over the port and bay towards Portici and Torre Annunziata, with Vesuvius rising among the green foothills to its truncated summit. Running parallel with the Via Partenope is the Via Chiatamone (from the Greek *platamon*, a beach). On the site of the houses now numbered 26, 27, there stood in the mid-eighteenth century the famous inn of the Crocelle, much frequented by the *beau monde* of the time. Here Casanova used to recruit clients for the gambling-hall and brothel run by the beautiful Irishwoman Sara Goudar on Posillipo. Of the visiting Englishmen Casanova wrote discouragingly: 'The English are like a flock of sheep; they follow each other about, always go to the same place, and never care to show any originality . . .'

At the end of the short Via Nazario Sauro the Via Acton, bearing left, leads down to the port and to the Tunnel della Vittoria, which runs under the high ground of Pizzofalcone to the Piazza Vittoria. Just before the Via Acton, on the left of the statue of Augustus (one of the many bestowed on Italian cities by the munificence of Mussolini in 1936), the Via Cesario Console takes us into the Piazza del Plebiscito. The street is called after the Admiral who defeated the Saracens at Gaeta in 846, at the time of the autonomous Dukes of Naples.

The **Piazza del Plebiscito,** the focus of modern Naples, has become one vast car park. It is bounded on the west, towards Pizzofalcone, by the church of **S. Francesco di Paola,** with its semi-circular Doric colonnade, the latter built by Murat in 1810 and obviously inspired by Bernini's colonnade in the piazza of St Peter's. The church was begun in 1817 by Ferdinand I and IV of the Two Sicilies in fulfilment of a vow for the recovery of his kingdom. Inside, S. Francesco is coldly neo-classical in marked contrast with the usual Neapolitan church interiors, an effect increased by the confessionals which are all of marble (and in this are perhaps unique).

At the southern end of the piazza is the eighteenth-century Palazzo Salerno, now the headquarters of the Military Commandant, and opposite it, to the north, the Palazzo del Governo (1815). This is the work of the architect Laperuta, who also designed Murat's colonnade. The two equestrian statues in the centre of the square are of *Charles III* (Don Carlos) on the left, the first of the Neapolitan Bourbons, by Canova; and, on the right, the figure of *Ferdinand I and IV* by Calì. Ferdinand I and IV, '*il re lazzarone*', was an amiable poltroon whose eccentric behaviour became the diplomatic small-talk of Europe. He was adopted and loyally supported by Neapolitans of the lowest class, the *lazzaroni*, as their father-image. In the church of S. Ferdinando in the adjoining Piazza Trieste e Trento (Neapolitans persist in calling it Piazza S. Ferdinando), which was re-named after the King's patron saint, lies buried his morganatic wife, the Duchess of Floridia.

The east side of the Piazza del Plebiscito is closed by the Spanish-built *Palazzo Reale.* The palace was erected by Domenico Fontana for the viceroy, the Conte de Lemos, in 1601-2, and the original façade differed a little from that which we see today. The present roofing is higher, and each alternate arch of the portico has been filled in (on the advice of Vanvitelli in the eighteenth century) to form a series of niches, which now contain statues representing the eight dynasties which have reigned in Naples. From left to right: Roger the Norman, the Emperor Frederick II of Hohenstaufen, Charles I of Anjou, Alfonso I of Aragon, the Emperor Charles V, Charles III of Bourbon, Joachim Murat and Victor Emmanuel II of Savoy.

The Palazzo Reale suffered damage from a fire in 1837, and was restored by Gaetano Genovese; it also suffered from bombing in the last war, and even more seriously from occupation by Allied troops. (Admission, weekdays 9.30 a.m.–4.0 p.m.; Sundays and holidays 9.30 a.m.–1.30 p.m.; closed on Tuesday.) The *Staircase of Honour* was designed by Francesco Picchiatti in 1651, but it was also restored and the coloured marbles added by Genovese. These stairs lead to the *Historical Apartments,* which contain some pictures (the best have been removed to Capodimonte), tapestries, and *objets d'art*, but the whole collection is something of a jumble.

At the top of the stairs on the south side is the charming eighteenth-century *Court Theatre* (1768), designed by Fuga and now restored after war damage. The rooms which follow have frescoed ceilings mostly by Neapolitan painters. At the end of the south wing, in Room VI which was part of the private rooms of King 'Bomba's' first wife, Maria Cristina (known as the Saint for her piety), there is a painting (in rather poor condition) by Titian—a portrait of Benvenuto Cellini's arch enemy Pier Luigi Farnese in gala dress. Room X, which was *Murat's study,* contains some fine furniture of the style of the First Empire, held by connoisseurs to be the best of this period in Italy.

In the north wing the large Room XVII, known as the *Salon of Hercules,* which has been completely restored after bomb damage,

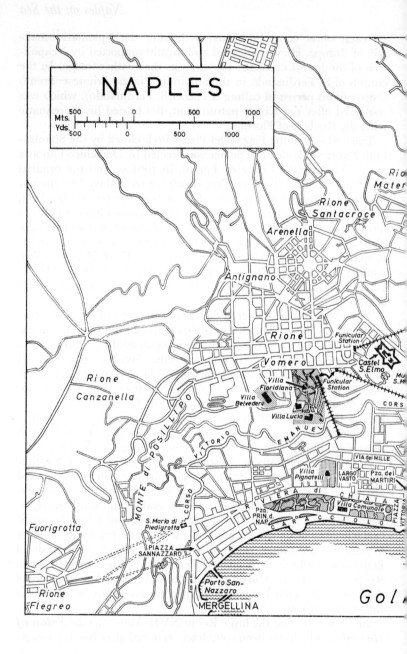

NAPLES

Mts. 500   0   500   1000
Yds. 500   0   500   1000

Rio Mater

Rione Santacroce

Arenella

Antignano

Rione Vomero

Funicular Station

Castel S.Elmo

Mu S.M

Villa Floridiana

Funicular Station

Villa Belvedere

Villa Lucia

CORS

Rione Canzanella

MONTE di POSILLIPO

VITTORIO

V. EMANUE

VIA del MILLE

Villa Pignatelli

LARGO VASTO

Pza. del MARTIRI

CORSO

ROVIERA di CHIAIA

PIAZZA VITTORIA

Villa Comunale

Fuorigrotta

S. Maria di Piedigrotta

Pza. PRIN. d. NAP.

V. A. CARACCIOLO

PIAZZA SANNAZZARO

Rione Flegreo

Porto San-Nazzaro

MERGELLINA

Gol

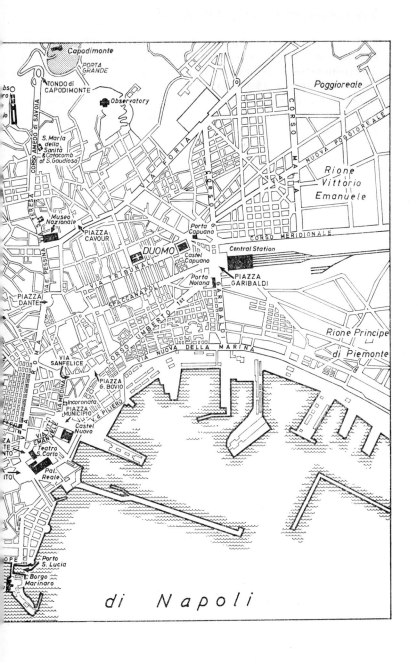

di Napoli

leads into the **Court Chapel.** This was built in 1660 by Cosimo Fanzago, and has been restored by Genovese, and again recently. The painting of the *Assunta* on the damaged ceiling by the academic Domenico Morelli (1826–1901) is being restored.

The second floor of the palace has been given over to the Biblioteca Nazionale (see p. 28), the entrance of which is in the Via Vittorio Emanuele III.

CHAPTER 3

Naples—The Old City

Maps: Naples, pp.24–5; The Old City, pp.40–1

Piazza Trieste e Trento—Teatro San Carlo—Castel Nuovo

The **Piazza Trieste e Trento** (or S. Ferdinando) is one of the busiest points in the city. On the east side, next to the Palazzo Reale, is the side of the Theatre of S. Carlo, and opposite it, the nineteenth-century Galleria Umberto. Next to it, on the left, is the church of **S. Ferdinando** (see also p. 23), built originally for the Jesuits at the beginning of the seventeenth century and much altered by Fanzago. The church later came into the hands of the Archconfraternity of the Addolorata, for whom Pergolesi composed his famous *Stabat Mater*. This is now performed here annually on Good Friday. Naples pp. 24-5

At S. Ferdinando begins the **Via Roma** (or the **Toledo**, as Neapolitans still call it), the most famous street in Naples, and once, in the eighteenth century, if we can accept Stendhal's word, 'the most populous and gayest street in the universe'. Every traveller to Naples wrote of the colour, bustle and gaiety of the Toledo, and at the Museo di S. Martino there is a fascinating painting of it early last century, seen from the Largo S. Spirito, by Giacinto Gigante (1806–76), the best-known of the 'School of Posillipo'. Naples pp. 24-5

On the left of the piazza is the entrance to the narrow Via Chiaia, off which, on the right, equally narrow, stepped streets—*gradini*—lead up steeply to the densely populated *quartieri*—the 'quarters' built by the Viceroy Toledo for his Spanish soldiers. On the corner of the piazza and the Via Chiaia is another remnant of old Naples, Gambrinus, the café and restaurant where in the last century the young bloods met to discuss the performances of the singers and ballet dancers at the S. Carlo across the way. Some sad vestiges of the charming decoration of the rooms can still be seen.

The **Theatre of S. Carlo,** whose entrance is in the Via Vittorio Emanuele III, was one of the many buildings with which Charles III

27

of Bourbon adorned his new kingdom. He called in as architect the Sicilian Medrano, who designed the royal palaces at Capodimonte and Portici. Work was begun on March 4th, 1737, and—incredible as it seems—was completed in time for the opening on November 4th, the King's birthday. The first performance was Metastasio's *Achille in Sciro*, with music by Sarro. The handsome façade, with its portico and loggia, was added by Niccolini in 1810, and six years later he rebuilt the theatre after a fire. From 1822 until 1861 the foyer was the gaming club of the aristocratic Accademia dei Cavalieri, and afterwards of the elegant but somewhat more democratic Casino dell' Unione. The auditorium and foyer may be visited daily, 9.0 a.m.–noon. The entrance is on the right of the theatre.

Neapolitan opera found a lasting home at S. Carlo. By the end of the seventeenth century Alessandro Scarlatti had produced at least five operas in the viceroy's private theatre at the Palace or at the Theatre of St Bartholomew (now demolished). The Neapolitan school of composers, singers, instrumentalists and librettists which followed him at S. Carlo was considered by Jean-Jacques Rousseau to lead all Europe. Rossini wrote several operas especially for S. Carlo. Bellini's *La Sonnambula* was produced there in 1831, and Donizetti's *Lucia di Lammermoor* in 1835.

From S. Carlo the Via Vittorio Emanuele III (sometimes also known as Via S. Carlo) leads past the Castel Nuovo to the Piazza del Municipio. Beside the theatre is the **garden of the Royal Palace.** The gates are supported by two bronze statues, *The Horsebreakers*, by the Russian sculptor Clodt, the gift of Czar Nicholas I to Ferdinand II, in remembrance of his visit to Naples in 1845. The entrance to the **Biblioteca Nazionale** (admission weekdays 9.0 a.m.–8.0 p.m.), which is housed, as we saw, upstairs in the Royal Palace, is through the gardens. This magnificent library has grown from the Farnese Collection brought from Parma by Charles III. Its present arrangement owes much to the advice of Benedetto Croce. Among the most precious of its possessions are the Herculaneum Papyrus, found in a villa excavated at Herculaneum in 1752; the *Valerius Probus*, a beautiful example of Irish copyists of the eighth century; many palimpsests and incunabula (including the *Divine Comedy* in an edition of 1485, with engravings designed by Botticelli); and autographs of St Thomas Aquinas, Tasso (including that of *Jerusalem Delivered*) and Leopardi.

The curious Neapolitan use of alternatives in their municipal nomenclature is again exemplified in the **Castel Nuovo.** 'Castel

Nuovo' (the new castle) was to distinguish it from the older castles of Ovo and Capuano; 'Maschio Angioino' (the Angevin Fortress), its other commonly used name, referred to its construction by Charles I of Anjou in 1279, though, save for its squat round towers, the building we see owes more to the Aragonese than to the Gothic builders brought by Charles from Provence. The Angevins were great builders and employed architects and sculptors from both France and other parts of Italy, as well as painters and mosaicists from all the leading Italian schools of painting at the time. The Castel Nuovo was one of the main royal palaces until the Spaniards built the Palazzo Reale.

The historical event most closely connected by popular imagination with the Castel Nuovo was the bloody suppression of the Barons' Revolt in 1486. The barons of Apulia, led by the powerful Sanseverino family, supporters of the Angevins against what they regarded as the Aragonese usurpation, conspired against Ferrante (Ferdinand I, 1458–94) at a meeting in the castle of Miglionico in Basilicata. Ferrante, a cunning Renaissance prince, heard of this and invited the feudal magnates to Naples to celebrate the pretended marriage of the son of the Conte di Sarno, one of the disaffected barons, with his own niece, the daughter of the Duke of Melfi. Here, in what is called the **Barons' Hall** (where the Municipal Council of Naples now sits), he then arrested the ringleaders, among them the Conte di Sarno. Later they were put to death. Only one of the principals escaped, the Sanseverino Duke of Salerno, who, before leaving for Rome, fixed a notice on the door of his palace, today the church of the Gesù, reading: 'An old sparrow does not enter the cage.'

In a crypt of the castle (known as the **crypt of the Barons' Conspiracy**) which is entered from the chapel of S. Barbara, can be seen the remains of four bodies, one of a prelate whose contorted face and bound hands seem to indicate that he was strangled. Ferrante liked to have his enemies near him, alive or dead. Alive, they were imprisoned in his palace so that he could have a look at them; dead, they were mummified in the clothes they wore when living.

The Renaissance Aragonese were also patrons of the arts and classical learning. Both Alfonso il Magnanimo and Ferrante, his illegitimate son, surrounded themselves with humanists and men of talent. The **Triumphal Arch** which forms the entrance to the Castel Nuovo was begun by Alfonso in 1454 to commemorate his capture of Naples from the French. His soldiers had entered the city on June 12th, 1442, by means of a tunnel under the city walls, which emerged in the well of a tailor's shop in the present Vico S. Sofia, just off the Via Carbonara.

(It is often claimed that the Triumphal Arch of Alfonso is the first Renaissance building in Italy to be constructed in direct imitation of antiquity; yet in Southern Italy alone we have two edifices—the Castel del Monte in Apulia and the Capuan Gate in Capua—built by the Emperor Frederick II two hundred years earlier, which show a conscious reference to Roman design and construction.)

The original design has been variously attributed, the strongest claimants being either Luciano Laurana (who rebuilt the famous ducal palace at Urbino) or the Spaniard Sagrera from Majorca, who is credited anyway with the carving of *the King in his triumphal chariot* in the relief above the lower arch. The two figures beside the chariot and the two panels on either side are by Francesco Laurana. Of the four Virtues above the upper arch (from left to right), *Temperance* is considered to be the work of Domenico Gagini, *Fortitude* is probably by Isaia da Pisa, *Justice* by Laurana; the sculptor of the fourth, *Magnanimity*, is not known. Above the niches appear *two large figures of rivers*, somewhat later in date; and the arch is surmounted by a statue of *St Michael*, with his right hand raised, the work of the Frenchman, Père Johan.

The **bronze doors,** with their six panels of low-reliefs showing episodes of Ferrante's struggles with the barons, were done by Guillaume le Moine of Paris and Pietro di Martino of Milan in 1462–8. Embedded at the foot of one door is a cannon-ball which failed to penetrate—the Aragonese had strengthened the Angevin castle to withstand artillery. This is thought to date from the invasion of Charles VIII of France in 1495.

In the courtyard the Barons' Hall faces us on the left with its external staircase. This is by Sagrera in the Catalan-Gothic style. Directly opposite us is the **chapel of S. Barbara,** one of the few remaining parts of the original Angevin structure. The beautiful Renaissance doorway is contemporary with the Triumphal Arch, and the charming *Madonna* in the niche above is by Francesco Laurana. Catalan sculptors for some reason replaced the Angevin rose window with this fine example of their carving. Giotto worked here in the chapel, and the remains of the frescoes have been attributed to one of his pupils. There are also a good fifteenth-century ciborium by Jacopo della Pila and a *statue of the Madonna*, the work of the Lombard Domenico Gagini (*ca.* 1420–92), whose descendants

30

were to become well-known as sculptors, especially of crucifixes, in Calabria and Sicily.

Piazza del Municipio—the Incoronata—Niccolò Pesce, the legendary fish-boy

The **Piazza del Municipio,** to the north of the Castel Nuovo, has been modernized by ruthlessly cutting down the beautiful holm-oaks which once stood there, and by the addition of some unimaginative fountains and lawns. At the west end of the piazza, from which one looks straight down on the liners berthed at the Molo Angioino (Nuova Stazione Marittima), is the *Palazzo Municipale,* built in 1819 by Ferdinand I and IV as offices for his ministries. On the right-hand side, incorporated in the building, is the church of *S. Giacomo degli Spagnoli,* which the great viceroy Pedro de Toledo erected in 1540. In spite of many damaging restorations, the church remains as a monument of the Spanish rule. In the apse is the tomb of Toledo and his wife, designed by Giovanni da Nola (1488–1558), which is perhaps of historical rather than aesthetic interest.

Naples pp. 24-5

On the left-hand side of the piazza, at the other end towards the port, is the *Teatro Mercadante,* built in 1778 but with its façade re-made in 1892. This is one of the city's principal theatres 'for prose', as the Italians express it. Beyond it, upstairs in the modern building on the corner of the Via del Piliero, is *Casale's bookshop,* known to all lovers of literary Naples. Gaspare Casale, until his death in 1963, was a bibliophile as well as bookseller and publisher, who numbered among his friends Anatole France, Di Giacomo, Croce, Pirandello, Malaparte and Norman Douglas. And close by is the 'characteristic' Neapolitan restaurant, Ai due Leoni.

From the Piazza del Municipio we take the Via Medina, which runs north from the centre of the piazza opposite the Castel Nuovo. On the left, well below street-level, is the church of S. Maria dell' Incoronata, or the *Incoronata,* as it is usually known. This was built in 1352 by Queen Giovanna I of Anjou, in memory, it is said, of her coronation, but perhaps rather as an act of atonement for the murder (of which she was later exonerated by the Pope) of her first husband, Andrew of Hungary, at Aversa in 1345.

Recent restoration has revived the Gothic form of the church, but the frescoes inside, which are important for the light they throw on early Neapolitan painting, have suffered from neglect, and some are difficult to see. In the vault on the left of the entrance the frescoes

31

representing the *Triumph of Religion* and the *Seven Sacraments* are by
Roberto Oderisi and assistants, followers of Giotto and Simone
Martini (both of whom were imported from northern Italy to work
at the court). Some have seen in the *Baptism* the laurel-crowned
figures of Petrarch and Laura, and this could be so since Petrarch
was well known in Naples, having visited King Robert in 1341 and
Queen Giovanna in 1344. The Queen herself is thought to be
portrayed in the *Communion, Confession* and *Marriage,* in the last
together with her cousin Louis of Taranto, whom she married. In
the chapel of the Crucifix, so called from the crucifix and the
grieving *Madonna* carved by Naccherino (1550–1622), are other
frescoes by a less sure hand.

As we walk up the Via Medina the quarter on our left, the Rione
di Carità, has been rebuilt almost entirely since the war with blocks
of offices and shops. At the busy corner of the Questura, we turn
right down the Via Sanfelice, which leads to the Piazza G. Bovio in
the Corso Umberto I, or the **Rettifilo,** as Neapolitans know it. This
straight, ugly thoroughfare was driven through the slum areas as
part of the *sventramento* or gutting of the old overcrowded Porto and
Mercato districts after the cholera outbreak of 1884. The *fountain
of Neptune* in the centre of the piazza was designed by Fontana at
the beginning of the seventeenth century, then rebuilt by Fanzago.
Naccherino carved the figure of Neptune; the marine monsters are
by Pietro Bernini.

Old City
pp. 40-1

We turn off the Via Sanfelice into the **Via Sedile di Porto,** on
the left, just before the Corso Umberto I. This is named after the
ancient Sedile, Seggio, or city-ward of Porto. At the end of the first
cross-street, we see again to the right the fountain of Neptune; and
on the left-hand side of this street running down to the Piazza G.
Bovio, is the *Bourse.* This is built around the chapel of S. Aspreno
al Porto, which was founded in the eighth century over the grotto
where the Saint lived. On our left, under a narrow arch between two
houses are the *Gradini di S. Barbara,* presenting a characteristic
picture of old Naples. The steps lead up to the Piazza Teodoro
Monticelli, where we shall arrive after a short detour (see p. 34).

Old City
pp. 40-1

Continuing along the Via Sedile di Porto we reach the **Via
Mezzocannone,** which is built on the western extremity of Graeco-
Roman Naples. The ancient city was laid out in straight streets
crossing at right angles, and in the portico of the cinema higher up
the Via Mezzocannone are some remains of the Graeco-Roman
walls. Facing us, on the other side of the street, is the left flank of the
University, which was established in 1224 by the Emperor

32

More than a hundred antique columns support the sixteen arches of the nave of the Naples Duomo, dedicated to S. Gennaro. His head is preserved in a chapel on the right. The liquefaction of his blood is attended with great popular rejoicing three times a year.

Above The cloister of the Museo di S. Martino in Vomero, a former Carthusian monastery, is a perfect example of the fusion of Renaissance and baroque. *Below* The Palazzo Reale, built originally for the Spanish viceroys, has a Staircase of Honour by Francesco Picchiatti (1651). It was restored in the last century and leads to the Historical Apartments.

Frederick II to train good Ghibelline clerks who could counter the influence of Popes and northern Guelfs. In the wall of the University building has been placed a doorway of the Durazzo period (*ca.* 1400) from the demolished Palazzo Pappacoda.

We turn left in the Via Mezzocannone. When the old buildings and archway over the Via Sedile di Porto were pulled down during the *sventramento*, a curious low-relief with an inscription was preserved and replaced on the wall of the house here. Antiquarians believed the figure to be of Orion, and to come from a Graeco-Roman temple which stood close to the old port. But from the time when it was found, in the reign of Charles I of Anjou, Neapolitans have obstinately held that it represented the mythological **Niccolò Pesce**. Gervase of Tilbury, who was in Naples in 1190, knew the tales of this wonderful fish-boy, who appears in conflicting mariners' legends from Sicily to as far west as Portugal.

Niccolò spent all his time in the water, until one day his mother, in exasperation, rashly prophesied that he would turn into a fish. And into a fish, or half-fish, he turned. He could pass an entire day under the sea without surfacing for breath. He would journey to Messina in the bowels of a large fish, cutting his way out with a knife which he always carried with him. The King set him various tasks, one of which was to enter the mysterious cavern under the Castel dell' Ovo. He returned to report that it was lined with jewels. Finally the King ordered Niccolò to perform a task which was beyond his half-human powers. He replied that only his duty as a loyal subject could require that he seek his own death. The King was insistent. So Niccolò dived down into the sea deeper than man had ever gone before. The waters turned to crystal about him, and he was never seen again.

S. Giovanni Maggiore—Palazzo Penna—Palazzo Gravina—S. Anna dei Lombardi—the Gesù Nuovo

Steps on the left of the Via Mezzocannone lead up to the church of **S. Giovanni Maggiore.** Like many Neapolitan churches, this has suffered over the centuries (particularly the last) from re-building after earthquakes, fires and general neglect. The original church was constructed in the sixth century, or even earlier, as a three-naved basilica with an arched apse and ambulatory, from the ruins of Hadrian's temple dedicated to Hercules and his favourite Antinoüs. Two Roman columns stand on either side of the high altar. On the wall of the left transept a marble tablet records the consecration (or perhaps a re-consecration) of the church at the time of Pope Sylvester II (999–1003). There is a terracotta crib (*presepio*) of the eighteenth century in the first chapel on the right, an example of a craft which became very popular at that period and is still carried on in Naples.

From a door in the right aisle we come out into the pleasant little Piazza S. Giovanni Maggiore. Adjoining the church is a chapel dedicated to the Saint (with the addition of the family name of its founder), *S. Giovanni Pappacoda,* erected by Artusio Pappacoda, Grand Seneschal to King Ladislaus of Anjou-Durazzo, in 1415. The high Gothic arched doorway with its deep-encrusted foliage and its angel musicians is the work of Antonio Baboccio (1351–1435), who also did the doorways of the Duomo.

On the other side of the square is the fine *Palazzo Giusso* which today houses the Oriental Institute of the University of Naples. The district of narrow streets and little squares that we are now entering retains much of its medieval aspect. On the right of the Palazzo Giusso the Via Candelora leads into the **Piazza Banchi Nuovi,** where, in the Middle Ages, stood the houses of bankers—Florentines for the most part, and among them members of the Acciaiuoli (one, Niccolò, was virtually prime minister under Giovanna I), Bardi and Peruzzi families. Boccaccio's father was sent by the Bardi as a representative to King Robert, and in two stories in the *Decameron* (those of Andreuccio of Perugia and of Peronella) and in his *Amorous Fiammetta* Boccaccio gives us a wonderfully close and lively picture of Angevin Naples.

From the piazza of the bankers we come to the Piazzetta Teodoro Monticelli, where stands one of the most remarkable of early private houses in Naples, the *Palazzo Penna,* built in 1406 by Antonio Penna, secretary to King Ladislaus. (Parts of his tomb, by Baboccio, saved from the wartime bombing of S. Chiara, may still be seen in that church, where there are also frescoes of his family, possibly also by Baboccio.) The façade of the palazzo is built of curiously raised piperno stone (*a bugne*), a local volcanic basalt, similar to that used to pave the streets, which shows the fleur-de-lys of Anjou, and the feather, the badge of the family. Note the depressed arch of the doorway (which we shall see again in Catalan portals) and the wooden door, which is original.

We continue in a westerly direction by the Via S. Maria la Nova (or alternatively by the Via Donnalbina), to the wide Via Monteoliveto. The church of *S. Maria la Nova,* with its Renaissance

Old City
pp. 40-1

façade, is raised above street level and approached by double-ramped steps. It was the church of a Franciscan monastery founded in 1279. The cloisters now house public offices. In the former refectory is a triptych by a painter of the Lombard school of about 1500, possibly a follower of Bramantino. The chapel of S. Giacomo della Marca was built by the 'Great Captain', Gonsalvo de Cordova, who won Naples for Ferdinand of Spain against the troops of Louis XII of France, in 1504. In 1550 his nephew, the Duke of Sveva, raised monuments beside the high altar to two of the French generals who died in the siege of 1528, when the French tried in vain to recapture the Kingdom.

Opposite us in Via Monteoliveto is the crude fascist building of the Palazzo delle Poste. On its right-hand wall, however, a charming baroque loggia in dark-coloured stone has been left. Steps from here lead up to the impressive *cloister of Monteoliveto* with its lofty porticoes, once part of the adjoining church and monastery.

A short way up the Via Monteoliveto, to the right, is one of the finest Renaissance palaces in Italy, the *Palazzo Gravina,* now occupied by the Faculty of Architecture of Naples University. This was built in 1539–41 for Ferdinand Orsini, Duke of Gravina. It is uncertain who the architect was, but it is close to the Roman architecture of the period. The doorway was designed by Mario Goffredo at the end of the eighteenth century. The palace survived an insurrection against the Bourbons in 1848, when the Swiss soldiers of the King set fire to the building to burn out the insurgents who had barricaded themselves inside. Within the court-yard the façade and the adjoining sides as far as the second window are parts of the original building, and are decorated with the arms and portrait medallions of members of the Orsini family.

Farther up the street, on the corner of the Piazza Monteoliveto, is a curious little baroque fountain (*ca.* 1668), surmounted by the statue of Charles II of Spain as a boy, the work of Donato Cafaro. But the fountain, like most Neapolitan fountains, is dry.

On the slight rise at the west end of the piazza is the former *Monastery of Monteoliveto,* today the barracks of the Carabinieri (the Caserma Pastrengo). In this building in 1799–1800 sat the Giunta di Stato which meted out death sentences on so many fine members of the Parthenopean Republic. And in 1848 Monteoliveto housed the ephemeral and ineffectual Neapolitan Parliament granted under the new Constitution. The monastery is not usually open to visitors. The guest-rooms were painted by Giorgio Vasari, better known for his *Lives of the Painters*, that quarry of information

35

and misinformation. Tasso was a guest of the monks in 1588, and here may have written his poem *Monte Oliveto*.

To the left is the church of **Monteoliveto** or **S. Anna dei Lombardi,** erected, together with the adjoining monastery and its four cloisters (one of which we have seen behind the Palazzo delle Poste), in 1411 by the Olivetan Benedictines. Church and monastery owed much to the lavish patronage of the Aragonese, and today S. Anna dei Lombardi is perhaps the richest repository of Renaissance sculpture in Naples.

We enter through an atrium under a simple depressed Catalan-Gothic arch. To the left is the restored tomb of Domenico Fontana (1543–1607), the architect of Pope Sixtus V, who completed the dome of St Peter's after Michelangelo's death and raised the famous obelisk in the piazza in front of St Peter's. Above the doorway is an early organ (1497) which has been decorated in the Neapolitan baroque style of the eighteenth century. The altar to the left (1524) is the work of Santacroce. That on the right was done by Giovanni da Nola (1532). The **Mastrogiudice chapel,** on the right, has some beautiful sculpture by the Florentine Benedetto da Maiano (1489). The exquisite relief of the *Annunciation*, one of his masterpieces, is above the altar between two statues.

In the **Piccolomini chapel** to the left of the entrance is Antonio Rossellino's beautiful *monument to Maria d'Aragona*. He was commissioned to raise a monument in the style of his tomb for the young Prince Cardinal of Portugal at S. Miniato al Monte in Florence; it was still unfinished at his death in 1478 and was completed by Benedetto da Maiano. The fine *Nativity with Saints and Prophets* in the same chapel is also by Rossellino. The mosaic floor is in the manner of the Cosmati.

Giovanni Marigliano da Nola, or Giovanni da Nola as he is usually known, dominated Neapolitan sculpture in the first half of the sixteenth century, and he is well represented here by the altar, the *tomb of Alfonso II of Aragon* in the apse, the *Baptist* in the fifth chapel on the left, and (perhaps) the *tomb of G. Nauclerio* in the third chapel on the right. Both he and Santacroce, whose *Pietà* is in the chapel with Giovanni's *John the Baptist*, were strongly influenced by Rossellino and Benedetto da Maiano.

One of the most popular pieces of sculpture in Naples is the remarkably realistic *Pietà* (1492) by Guido Mazzoni of Modena, at the end of the right transept. The eight terracotta figures (originally polychrome) gathered round the body of the dead Christ are usually considered to be lifesize portraits of the court of Ferrante—Joseph of

Arimathea, the King; Nicodemus, his son (Alfonso II); one, Pontano, the humanist; and the old man with the lock of hair protruding from under his cap was said by Vasari to be the poet Sannazzaro. Certainly Vasari was here in 1544, when, besides the guest-rooms in the monastery, he painted the frescoes which we see in the *old sacristy*. The beautifully inlaid stalls here, with their views of Naples and Rome, were done by Fra Giovanni da Verona and assistants in 1506–10.

On leaving S. Anna dei Lombardi we retrace our steps and, crossing the Via Monteoliveto, continue up the gentle rise of the Calata Trinità Maggiore to the Piazza del Gesù Nuovo. At this point there stands one of those architectural absurdities dear to the hearts of all lovers of Naples—the *Guglia dell' Immacolata*. A guide-book describes the baroque efflorescence of saintly effigies, surmounted by the gilded statue of the Virgin, as 'elegant and vivacious'; it is grotesque, and one would not have it otherwise.

Beyond it, on the north side of the square, is the popular Jesuit church of the *Gesù Nuovo,* constructed at the end of the sixteenth century out of a *quattrocento* palace of the Sanseverini, Princes of Salerno. The piperno façade is that of the original building, but little else of this remains. The main doorway is of 1685.

Inside, the Church Triumphant (and not least the Society of Jesus) is proclaimed in a paean of multicoloured marble, crystal candelabra, altars aflame with candles and bright with flowers, and enough paintings to fill a gallery: *S. Francis Xavier in Ecstasy, S. Francesco Borgia adores the Most Holy Sacrament, S. Ignatius in Glory, the Immaculate Virgin in Glory with Saints*, and above the main door, Solimena's huge fresco of *Heliodorus driven from the Temple* (1725). There are paintings by Neapolitan and other artists of the seventeenth century, among them, over the altar in the left transept, Ribera's *S. Ignatius in Glory* and *Pope Paul III approving his Rule*. The architects involved were Giuseppe Valeriano, who began the church; Lanfranco, whose cupola collapsed in the earthquake of 1688; Fanzago, and Fuga (who helped to design the Fountain of Trevi in Rome, but also spoilt the façade of the church of the Gerolomini on the Tribunali in Naples).

Spaccanapoli and S. Chiara

We now approach the very heart of the 'old city'. The street on which the Gesù stands (at this stage forming the north side of the

37

piazza) cuts ancient Naples in two, for which reason it is known as **Spaccanapoli.** Spaccanapoli in its course of little over a mile changes its name six times. At its western beginning under the hill of S. Martino it is Via Pasquale Scura, then successively Via Domenico Capitelli, Via Mariano Semmola (or Via B. Croce), Largo Corpo di Napoli, Via S. Biagio dei Librai, Via Vicaria Vecchia, and finally Via Forcella. Spaccanapoli corresponds to the lower *decumanus* of Graeco-Roman Naples.

On the south side of the Piazza Gesù Nuovo, at No. 20, is the entrance to the Angevin *Monastery of S. Chiara,* built in 1317 for the Friars Minor. King Robert and his devout Queen Sancia were great patrons of the Franciscans and they founded not only the royal church of S. Chiara and this monastery, but also, farther to the east, a convent for the Poor Clares, thus forming a great Franciscan enclave in the centre of Naples.

The monastery (to visit, apply to the porter) no longer houses the *frati minori*, who have moved to the former nuns' convent, but is of interest for the remains of its *trecento* architecture and frescoes. On either side of the entrance are small service cloisters; then, on the left, the *chapel* (formerly the chapter-house), and, on the right, the *choir* (the ancient refectory). Both rooms were frescoed; the large work in the choir, possibly by Lello da Roma, shows us *the Redeemer, the Virgin and SS. Louis of Toulouse* (an elder brother of King Robert who died in 1297), *Clare, John the Evangelist, Francis and Anthony of Padua.* The praying figures are *King Robert, Queen Sancia, Charles of Calabria* and *Giovanna I.* Beyond is the *great cloister,* its Gothic arches supported on columns from Roman buildings. Some of the capitals are Roman, others of the fourteenth century.

The entrance to the *church of S. Chiara* is in Spaccanapoli (here Via Semmola) through an original fourteenth-century gateway. The architect is said to have been the Neapolitan Gagliardo Primario, that mysterious personage who collaborated with Tino di Camaino on the tomb of Queen Maria of Hungary in S. Maria Donnaregina. The church is basilican in the Provençal-Gothic style. When King Robert first showed it to his son, Charles of Calabria, the latter remarked that it reminded him, with its stall-like chapels, of nothing so much as a stable.

In the 1740's the austere Angevin fabric was baroqued over by D. A. Vaccaro. However, a fire started by Allied incendiary bombs in 1943 burnt for forty-eight hours and completely gutted the building, causing irreparable damage to the Angevin monuments, some of the finest examples of Gothic sculpture in Southern Italy.

38

The superb low-relief *Scenes from the Life of St Catherine of Alexandria* by Giovanni and Pacio da Firenze (who were employed by Robert the Wise and Giovanna I to work on memorial sculptures between 1343 and 1345) were destroyed. But fortunately, another example of their work remains, though damaged, in the *tomb of King Robert* behind the high altar. As is usual at the period the sarcophagus is set in a Gothic tabernacle which, like the figures, was originally heavily pigmented. King Robert was represented four times: on the front of the sarcophagus, supported by figures of the six Virtues, he is shown with Queen Sancia and their family; above, where two angels draw back the curtains to reveal him in the habit of a Franciscan Tertiary, watched over by the Seven Liberal Arts; above this again he is seen seated on a faldstool over an inscription said to have been written by Petrarch—'*Cernite Robertum regem virtute refertum*—Behold King Robert crammed with virtue.' Finally, in a lunette (now gone) he was shown being presented by St Francis to the Virgin and Child.

Tino di Camaino worked on two monuments in S. Chiara. Of these only one remains, the *tomb of Mary of Valois*, the wife of Charles of Calabria, which is on the wall to the right of the main altar. The figures of *Charity* and *Faith* which support the sarcophagus are fine examples of his work, although very different in style from the beautiful *Charity* in S. Lorenzo (see p. 50).

The lateral chapels contain several interesting pieces of sculpture, some damaged, and to the right of the main doorway is Baboccio's monument to Agnese and Clemenza Durazzo. On the left of the entrance and in the second chapel on the right, are the remains of the Penna monuments, also by Baboccio (see p. 34).

A doorway to the right of the main altar leads to the **nuns' choir,** which retains its primitive Gothic form. Here are more remains of sculpture formerly in the church. Behind the choir is the beautiful **cloister of the Clarisse** (the usual entry is by a doorway outside and to the right of the church). Of all the monuments in the city this cloister and its rustic garden perhaps illustrate best the grace and charm of eighteenth-century Naples. The design for the refacing of the Angevin cloister was by Domenico Vaccaro and formed part of the baroque redecoration of the church. The lovely majolica tiles of the same period, with their gay scenes of country and town life, of fishing, carnivals and mythological events, are by the Neapolitans Giuseppe and Donato Massa.

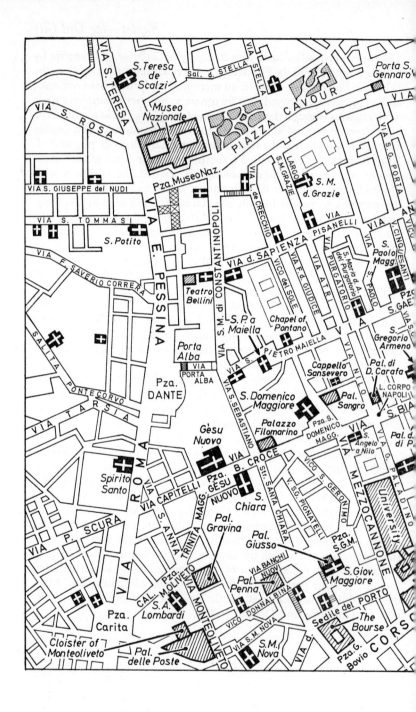

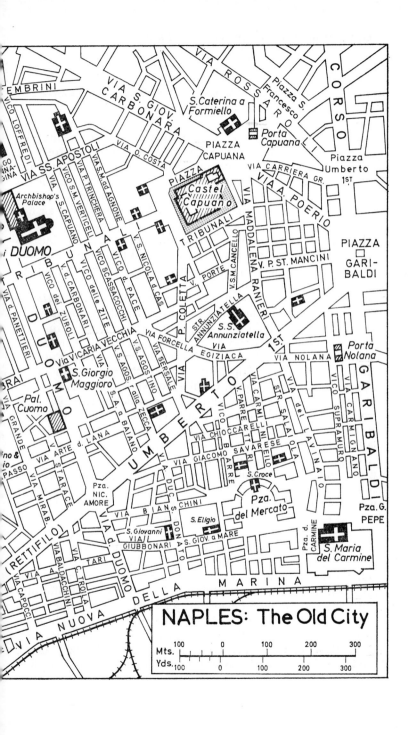

NAPLES: The Old City

Mts.
Yds.

100 0 100 200 300

Spaccanapoli—Palaces—Capella Sansevero—S. Domenico Maggiore—
S. Angelo a Nilo—More palaces

Once more in Spaccanapoli, we continue in an easterly direction
through increasing crowds and traffic towards the nerve-centre of the
'old city', the most ancient part of 'the two Naples'. The narrowness
of the streets which intersect at right angles, following the ancient
Graeco-Roman plan, prevents us from seeing properly the old
palaces which surround us. Some of these buildings, with their fine
courtyards, have been taken over and kept in repair by the municipal
authorities or by large firms such as the Bank of Naples, but too
many, since the aristocratic families who built them moved west to
more salubrious quarters, have degenerated into those insanitary
slums which are the shame of Naples.

On our left, just beyond Via S. Sebastiano, is the **Palazzo
Filomarino,** where Benedetto Croce lived until his death in 1952.
The palace was rebuilt in 1512 for the Sanseverino Prince of
Bisignano; the baroque doorway, however, was added by Ferdinando
Sanfelice at the beginning of the eighteenth century. In 1947 Croce
founded here the Italian Institute for Historical Studies and
bequeathed to it his magnificent library. Naples has had a proud
history of scholarship from her humanists, but Benedetto Croce must
be given a place apart. His resistance to fascism is well-known, and
for years he travelled to Rome for the sole purpose, as a Senator of
the Kingdom, of recording his vote against the government.

No. 45, on the right, is the baroque Palazzo Carafa della Spina.
Of the three C's—the ancient families of Caracciolo, Carafa and
Capece—who were said to rule Naples, the two first still flourish. A
number of family names well-known in Neapolitan history are to be
found as early as the records of the times of the Dukes of Naples
(763–1139). A short way on, and to our left there opens out the
Piazza S. Domenico Maggiore, in the middle of which stands
another *guglia*, raised to commemorate the plague of 1656.

On the north side of the square is the apsidal end (much restored)
of S. Domenico Maggiore, and next to it, on the left, the fifteenth-
century doorway to the Romanesque (possibly as early as the eighth
century) church of S. Angelo a Morfisa. Facing us, on the right-hand
side of the piazza, is the Sangro Palazzo Corigliano, with its early
eighteenth-century doorway. On its left stands the Palazzo Sangro,
built in the first half of the sixteenth century for the main branch of

Old City
pp. 40-1

42

the family. The baroque doorway was added by Vitale Finelli in 1621. Opposite these, on the left of the square, is the fifteenth-century Palazzo del Balzo, the exterior of which was rebuilt after the earthquake of 1688. (The del Balzo, the Provençal des Baux, accompanied Charles of Anjou on his conquest of the Kingdom, and one of the family married the King's daughter.) On our right, forming the south side of the piazza, is the Palazzo Cascacalenda, constructed for another branch of the Sangro family by Mario Goffredo (1766). In the courtyard part of the portico is formed of some Greek columns found on the site when the foundations were being dug.

There is a small pâtisserie and café here, owned by Signor Scaturchio, where we can drink the fiery *anice* and the best coffee in Naples, which means the best coffee in the world, as any Neapolitan will inform you. The excellence of the coffee is attributed, apart from the care in choosing and roasting the coffee beans, to the peculiar properties of the water, which comes from the springs of Serino in the Apennines near Avellino. The water-ices of Naples are famous too—those made on the spot, not those of the national firms.

Before we enter the church of S. Domenico Maggiore, we should pay a quick visit to one of the curiosities of Naples, the **Capella Sansevero,** the private burial chapel of the Sangro family. We take the narrow Vico S. Domenico, between the Palazzo Sangro and S. Domenico, and almost immediately turn to the right in Via Francesco de Sanctis, where the chapel stands facing the side wall of the palace. This was founded in 1590, but the extraordinary collection of monuments is owed chiefly to Raimondo di Sangro, Prince of Sansevero, the eighteenth-century eccentric. He boasted of performing at home the miracle of S. Gennaro (see p. 52), and his tastes and behaviour were both deliberately shocking.

Above the doorway, Cecco di Sangro, bored with his tomb by Francesco Celebrano (1766), is about to leave it, sword in hand. In the middle of the nave is the extraordinary *Veiled Christ* by the Neapolitan Sammartino (1753). Around the chapel are arranged statues with such illuminating titles as *Divine Love, Education, Self-control, Religious Zeal, Bashfulness, Sweetness of the Marriage Yoke, Liberality, Sincerity* and *Decorum,* by eighteenth-century masters of virtuosity. One of these, Queirolo, is responsible for another 'masterpiece' to the right of the altar, the group entitled *Disillusion,* in which a man extricates himself from a marble net with the gentle encouragement of a seated angel. From the ceiling, frescoes of the saints of the Sangro family by Russo (1799) look down on all the marble. In addition, the sacristan will be delighted to show visitors a gruesome skeleton, most realistically fitted up with hair, eyes, and even nerve fibres, which is lodged in a cupboard at the side of the chapel.

Returning to the Vico S. Domenico, we turn right, and a few yards farther on a doorway on the left brings us to the entrance of the church of **S. Domenico Maggiore.** Founded in 1289 by Charles II of Anjou, incorporating an older church, it and the monastery which lies behind it are inseparably connected with the great figure of St Thomas Aquinas, who studied here from his youth to his sixteenth year, and in 1272, at the request of Charles I of Anjou, returned as professor of theology. He taught in what is now a convent at the back of the church, and his cell on the first floor can be visited by applying to the Dominican fathers. It was here too, in 1563— S. Domenico Maggiore then forming part of the University—that Giordano Bruno from Nola read theology (he wrote an early thesis on Noah's Ark) and developed his angry opposition to Aristotle, the Dominican Order and the Catholic Church.

The church has suffered much from earthquakes and fires and, not least, from the hands of restorers. The last restoration—that carried out in the 1850's by Frederico Travaglini—is particularly deplorable, especially in the hideous stuccoing and gilding of the interior. Of the original façade only the Gothic-arched doorway and the wooden door remain.

The church, richly patronized by the Aragonese nobility, contains much of historical and aesthetic interest. Tino di Camaino has several works here. On the wall to the right of the main altar, at the entrance to the old church, is his front of the sarcophagus of Giovanni d'Anjou (d. 1335). The paschal candle to the left of the altar is supported by nine Virtues, which Tino carved for the tomb of the Angevin Philip of Taranto. The front of Philip's sarcophagus, also by Tino, is on the wall between the two chapels in the left transept.

Two early sixteenth-century works by Giovanni da Nola are particularly fine, the first a figure of *John the Baptist* in the fourth chapel on the left (the two pictures here are good examples of the work of Mattia Preti, 1613–99), and in the eighth chapel on the same side an exquisite altar (1536) with the figures of the *Virgin and Child, John the Baptist and St Matthew.* On the right wall of this chapel is the cenotaph of the Neapolitan poet G. B. Marino, who died in 1625. The licentious author of *Songs of Kisses* and *Adonis* may seem a far cry from the young Milton who visited Naples thirteen years later, but they shared the friendship of the erudite Neapolitan Marquis of

Villa, G. B. Manso, the friend and biographer of Tasso. And when he left Naples, Milton wrote for his host Manso some Latin verses in which he recalled the 'sweet-tongued Marino'.

At the altar end of the church, on the right, is a cluster of inter-connected rooms and chapels, near the entrance from the Piazza S. Domenico. Nearest the piazza is the ancient church of *S. Angelo,* consisting of two chapels; then the sacristy, and next the chapel of the Crucifix, entered from the seventh chapel in the right aisle. The floor of the old church is paved with fine eighteenth-century majolica tiles. Over the altar is the oldest existing *portrait of St Dominic* (first half thirteenth century), and to the right stands Jacopa della Pila's beautiful *tomb of Thomas Brancaccio* (1492).

On the ceiling of the **sacristy** is Solimena's *Triumph of the Catholic Faith* (1709). For some strange reason, the coffins of Aragonese royalty and notables have been placed above the vestment presses. Among them are those of Ferrante (1494), his grandson Ferrandino (1496), and G. A. Petrucci, whom Ferrante beheaded in 1486 for his part in the Barons' Conspiracy. A coffin with a sword on it contains the body of Ferrante d'Avalos, Marquis of Pescara, the beloved husband of Vittoria Colonna. The sword was the one surrendered to him by Francis I after the French defeat at the battle of Pavia in 1525.

The **chapel of the Crucifix** is usually kept closed, but will be opened on request to the sacristan or to one of the monks. It is named after the thirteenth-century painting of the crucifix over the altar, which is said to have spoken the famous words to St Thomas Aquinas: 'Well hast thou written of me, Thomas. What would'st thou have as a reward?' To which St Thomas replied: 'None other than Thee.' In the ante-chapel is the papal bull of 1567 proclaiming St Thomas Doctor of the Church. To the left of the altar of the Crucifix is a *Deposition* by an unknown Neapolitan follower of Roger van der Leyden (fifteenth century) and to the right the *Road to Calvary* by a Lombard disciple of Bramantino. The monumental tombs here and in the two little chapels on the left show some very good Renaissance carving. The tomb of Francesco Carafa (d. 1487) to the left of the altar is by Tommaso Malvito of Como (fifteenth to sixteenth centuries).

S. Domenico also possesses a signed *Annunciation* by Titian, in a small chapel off the left transept, and in the chapel just to the left of the apse is one of Caravaggio's best-known works, the *Flagellation* (1607). Near by is a copy by the seventeenth-century Andrea Vaccaro.

45

(The only other paintings by Caravaggio in Naples, which he visited at the end of his short, hectic life, to die there, aged thirty-eight, in 1610, are in the church of the Monte della Misericordia in the Via Tribunali near the cathedral—a large, disturbing canvas of the *Seven Acts of Mercy*—and the *St John the Baptist* at Capodimonte.)

As we leave the Piazza S. Domenico Maggiore following Spacca-napoli, to the right, on the corner of the Via Mezzocannone, stands the little church of **S. Angelo a Nilo.** (*Nilo,* corrupted by Neapolit-ans to *Nido,* was the old name of the *seggio* or city-ward, called after the ancient statue close by of the River Nile, which was erected by the Alexandrian colony who lived here from before the time of the Emperor Nero.) S. Angelo was built originally in 1385 as a chapel of the powerful Brancaccio family. The building is now unsafe and recently desultory efforts to repair it seem to have been made. It contains, to the right of the main altar, the only work in Naples of Donatello—the tomb of Cardinal Brancaccio, carried out in Pisa in the 1420's with the assistance of Michelozzo and Pagno di Lapo Portigiani. Donatello himself carved the right-hand angel who draws back the curtain, the head of the cardinal, and the low-relief of the Assumption on the sarcophagus.

Beyond the little Largo Corpo di Napoli, with the curious statue of the fecund River Nile, Spaccanapoli becomes the Via S. Biagio dei Librai, after the booksellers' shops which used to stand here. Immediately to our left is the **Palazzo Carafa di Montorio** where the Carafa Pope Paul IV was born in 1476; and a short way farther on, to the right, No. 121 is the interesting **Palazzo di Diomede Carafa** (or Palazzo Santangelo), built in 1466 by Diomede Carafa, first Count of Maddaloni, that ornament of the court of King Ferrante. Architecturally it is Catalan and Florentine Renaissance, and in the courtyard is a replica of the horse's head given to Carafa by Lorenzo il Magnifico in 1471. The original, which is today in the National Museum, is thought to be Roman work of the third century.

Farther on, again to the right, stands the massive **Palazzo del Monte di Pietà,** built to the plans of G. B. Cavagna in 1597. On the far side of the court is the chapel of the Pietà, its façade adorned with two statues by Pietro Bernini, and by Naccherino's *Pietà*, all done in 1601. The porter will show visitors the chapel, with its stucco decoration and paintings by Corenzio and Santafede. In the adjoin-ing sacristy is a lively example of the work of the eighteenth-century colourist Giuseppe Bonito.

At the intersection on the left of the Via S. Gregorio Armeno with Spaccanapoli, an inscription on the wall marks the site of Antonio

Vico's bookshop, where his son Gianbattista was born in 1668 and spent his youth. Of the three remarkable Neapolitan jurists of the age, Vico, Giannone and Gravina, Vico had the greatest originality; he was the first to apply the revolutionary notion of a progressive historical development to the concepts of law.

*Street-markets and the Porta Capuana—Piazza del Mercato—
S. Maria del Carmine*

Here, virtually in the centre of Naples, we may leave Spaccanapoli and penetrate north into the very heart of old Naples (see pp. 49 *et seq.*), but we will for the moment continue eastwards, for at this spot every building—every palace, church, *basso* (single-roomed dwelling on the street)—has its own fascinating history.

Close by, to the south of Spaccanapoli (towards the church and cloisters of SS. Severino and Sossio) stood the palace of the autonomous Dukes of Naples, who from 763 until the Normans finally gained possession of Naples in 1139, ruled over the most enlightened and civilized city in the West. In the near-by Via del Duomo, to the right, the Renaissance Palazzo Cuomo houses the **Filangieri Civic Museum** of pictures, sculptures and porcelain, which replaces the collection wantonly burnt by the Germans in 1943. On the other side of the street, on the corner of Spaccanapoli (which now becomes Via Vicaria Vecchia) is the church of S. Giorgio Maggiore, which retains an interesting palaeo-Christian apse of the fifth century. Farther along, the Via Forcella branches off to the right. This is the site of a notorious street market-place, a wonderful piece of 'local colour'. During the last war it was the centre of a fantastic black market; here, it is said, warships, aircraft, tanks, and Allied soldiers could all be bought at a price.

A short way on and the Via Pietro Coletta leads, on the left, to the **Castel Capuano** or **Vicaria**, originally a royal palace but now the law-courts of Naples, where the histrionic gifts of the Neapolitans find ample scope.

Behind the Castel Capuano on the other side of the piazza stands the Renaissance church of S. Caterina a Formiello (1519), and next to it the beautiful **Porta Capuana,** erected in 1484 to the design of Giuliano da Maiano, one of the finest Renaissance gateways in Italy. The piazza also has its market, and one can watch the gaily-painted Neapolitan carts arriving from the market gardens beyond Poggioreale. But perhaps the best market for fish from the Bay of Naples is

47

The Companion Guide to Southern Italy

the one near the Porta Nolana, the Aragonese gateway off the Corso Garibaldi. (From the Porta Capuana, take the Via A. Poerio to the adjacent Piazza Garibaldi. The Corso Garibaldi crosses the Piazza Garibaldi from north to south, and the **Porta Nolana** is a short distance along, south of the piazza.) The fishmarket is in the narrow Via Carmignano, which runs parallel to the Corso Garibaldi as far as the Piazza G. Pepe (behind the church of S. Maria del Carmine). Wooden pails are filled with black and blue-silver mussels and shell-fish, *frutti del mare*, like delicate Cosmati work, contrasting with the glowing yellows of lemons and fresh roses.

Old City
pp. 40-1
From the market it is but a step to the church of S. Maria del Carmine just off the **Piazza del Mercato.** Architecturally the square has been ruined, not only by war damage, but more particularly by the erection of hideous blocks of flats—yet for the historian no spot in Naples calls to mind so immediately the tragedy of Neapolitan history. At one time the piazza held in constant readiness a scaffold for members of the nobility, a gallows for plebeians and a gibbet for social dregs. In 1268 Charles I of Anjou beheaded here the young Conradin of Hohenstaufen, his friend Frederick of Baden and seven others. (A statue of Conradin, after Thorvaldsen, is in S. Maria del Carmine.) In 1647 this was the centre of Masaniello's rebellion against the Spanish domination. He was shot in the monastery attached to the Carmine and his grave is not known. In 1799 the leaders of the Parthenopean Republic were executed here on the orders of Ferdinand I and IV of Bourbon.

The church of *S. Maria del Carmine* still appears to be especially connected with the poor families of fishermen and mariners. In adjoining cloisters are hung as *ex-votos* some touching examples of popular art. A favourite scene is of a woman in an operating theatre, her viscera crudely exposed, successfully calling on the intervention of the Virgin. From the Carmine, the visitor can leave the Piazza del Mercato by the archway beside the little Gothic church of *S. Eligio* on the opposite side of the square. Bombing in the last war has exposed the beautiful Angevin structure (thirteenth century). Farther along the Via S. Giovanni a Mare, on the right, below the street level, is the church of *S. Giovanni*, another interesting little church, very English in its way, and frequented by the inhabitants of the port district near by. From here the Via Nuova della Marina to the left leads back along the docks to the Castel Nuovo and the Piazza del Municipio.

48

Above The Castel dell' Ovo in the S. Lucia quarter, now a military establishment, was a royal residence under the Normans and Hohenstaufen and contains columns from a villa of Lucullus on the site. *Below* A wayside shrine keeps watch over moments of relaxation, symbolized by the basket chair outside this house in the 'old city'.

Above The Porta Capuana, erected in 1484 to the design of Giuliano di Maiano, is one of the finest Renaissance gateways in Italy. Behind it lies a busy market. *Below* Wild rejoicing characterizes the Festa di Piedigrotta, a noisy Neapolitan festival which takes place annually on September 7th and goes on all night. It includes competitions for the best songs, the popular *canzoni napoletane*.

S. Gregorio Armeno—S. Lorenzo—the Duomo

The detour of the last section has been by way of paren-
thesis. We return now to the point on Spaccanapoli (here, the Via
S. Biagio dei Librai) where Via S. Gregorio Armeno leads north-east
up a slight hill towards the Via Tribunali. Here we can see most
clearly the appearance of these city streets before the *sventramento* of
the last century, when each craft had its own quarter—we have just
passed through the district of the book-traders. On the **Via S.
Gregorio Armeno** lived the makers of the traditional figures for the
Christmas cribs (*presepi*), those typically Neapolitan representations
which, beautifully carved, show the Infant Jesus born into a picturesque but essentially workaday—and Neapolitan—world.

Old City
pp. 40-1

The church of **S. Gregorio Armeno** (or S. Liguro, as Neapolitans
know him), on the left, is preceded by an atrium of dark piperno.
The interior is also dark, which prevents our picking out clearly
much of the decoration of this perhaps most typical example of
Neapolitan baroque, so that it first appears a sombre harmony of
browns and gold. On the right is the popularly venerated shrine of
S. Patrizia, the illuminated effigy of the Saint, positively ablaze with
the richness of her jewels and vestments, lying in a glass case below
the altar. The convent has a large collection of relics, among them a
phial of the Saint's blood, obtained from the extraction of a molar
one hundred years after her death, when it is reported to have 'bled
copiously'. This has the miraculous power of liquefying, like that of
the more celebrated S. Gennaro.

To visit the delightful **convent** of S. Gregorio Armeno, we
continue up the hill, taking the first turning on the left which leads
to the convent door. In the centre of the tranquil court, two stone
figures of *Christ* and the *Woman of Samaria* stand beside a baroque
fountain in the form of a well. The group is by the eighteenth-century
Neapolitan sculptor, Matteo Bottiglieri. Above the arcade and
balconies (on to which the nuns' cells open) rises the seventeenth-
century campanile with a cupola tiled in multi-coloured majolica.

Back in Via S. Gregorio Armeno, we see ahead the Piazza S.
Gaetano (an eighteenth-century statue of the Saint stands there),
which occupies part of the site of the Graeco-Roman forum. On the
right the open space is prolonged to form the angle between the
church and monastery of **S. Lorenzo Maggiore.** It was at mass in
the church of S. Lorenzo on Holy Saturday, March 30th, 1336, that

Giovanni Boccaccio at the age of twenty-three beheld 'the marvellous beauty of a young woman, come hither to hear what I too heard attentively'. Fiammetta is reputed to have been Maria, the natural daughter of King Robert of Anjou and Sibilla Sabran, the wife of a member of the same noble family as St Thomas Aquinas.

Petrarch also visited S. Lorenzo, and was a guest in the Franciscan monastery on the night of November 25th, 1345, when a fearful hurricane struck Naples. He wrote a graphic and detailed account of the storm, in which he described the waves scattering the survivors from a wreck against the rocks and 'smashing them like so many eggshells. The whole shore was strewn with crushed bodies, some still breathing, others from which the brains and entrails protruded . . .'

Work on the restoration of both church and cloisters of S. Lorenzo goes on slowly, but it has progressed far enough in the church for us to appreciate one of the finest examples of French Gothic architecture in Southern Italy. Through the wide-sprung pointed arch of the nave we can see the beautiful apse, with its ambulatory and radiating chapels, built by the Franciscans at the end of the thirteenth century. Excavations under the floor of the transept have revealed the apse and part of the pavement of the sixth-century church of Bishop Giovanni II, and beneath, at various levels, a paved Roman roadway, remains of shops, and large tufa blocks from the original Greek city.

Many of the church's works of art have still to be replaced, but the fine high altar by Giovanni da Nola (note the two panels with views of Naples) is there, and near by, on the right at the beginning of the apse, Tino di Camaino's *tomb of Caterina d'Austria* with its interesting caryatids. A doorway on the right leads to the cloisters of the monastery, which are still in a state of disarray. On the left is the fourteenth-century portal to the chapter-house, and at the end of the colonnade, the refectory, now housing the municipal archives, where the medieval parliaments of the Kingdom once sat, and later the meetings of the city *seggi* were convened. The badges of the *seggi* can be seen above the main doorway to the monastery in Piazza S. Gaetano. Re-crossing the church, a short passage leads to the Via Tribunali.

We turn right in the Tribunali, which soon widens out as the Piazza dei Gerolomini, with the **church of the Gerolomini** (or of S. Filippo Neri) on the left. The once aristocratic and studious order of Oratorians has fallen today on lean times. In the early 'fifties the few remaining members created something of a scandal by selling off chalices, candelabra, reliquaries, lamps, and even the organ pipes to delighted local dealers, who got them for a song. Some four hundred seventeenth-century *objets de vertu* in gold and silver—valued at more than £500,000—were melted down and sold as ingots.

The plan of the church—designed by G. A. Dosio in 1592—is interesting as a revival of the basilican form which spread from here to many churches in eastern Sicily. The façade was rebuilt by Fuga in 1780. The twelve columns of the nave are granite monoliths transported at vast expense from the island of Giglio. By a pillar at the far end of the church, on the left, is the tomb of G. B. Vico (see p. 47). The magnificent library is worth a visit (admission 9.0 a.m.–1.0 p.m.), as well as the two beautiful baroque cloisters of the attached monastery, entered from a doorway in the right-hand aisle or from an entrance in the Via del Duomo. Paintings from the monastery's collection, the oldest in Naples, are now on public view here (admission, 9.0 a.m.–12.0 noon and 4.0–8.0 p.m.).

If we leave the monastery by the door on the Via del Duomo, we see opposite us the neo-Gothic façade (in a lifeless pale grey stone) of the **Duomo,** the cathedral church dedicated to the city's patron, S. Gennaro. The present building was begun by Charles I of Anjou in 1272, replacing the primitive fifth-century cathedral church of the Stefania. (The basilica of S. Restituta and its baptistery from approximately the same period are fortunately preserved.) The Duomo, like most Neapolitan churches, has suffered over the centuries, the rebuilding of the façade (after 1877) being particularly deplorable, although Baboccio's original portals (1407) have been retained. Inside, the first impression is somewhat overwhelming. In form a Latin cross, the sixteen piers of the nave are composed of more than a hundred antique columns supporting pointed arches, above which, on walls and ceiling, Santafede, Forlì, Imparato and Luca Giordano have left us a lavish display of their talents.

There is so much to see (and even more to avoid) that I shall concentrate only on the more important works: the ancient church of S. Restituta and its baptistery, the chapel of the Treasure of S. Gennaro, the Cappella Minutolo, and the crypt of S. Gennaro.

A doorway opposite the fourth arch on the left leads down to the church of *S. Restituta.* (As you pass the first pier, notice the baptismal font, the lower section of which is of Egyptian basalt, with ancient Greek carving of bacchic masks; this is surmounted by seventeenth-century work in bronze and polychrome marble, which may be seen as symbolizing, as a Neapolitan remarked, the Old and New Testaments.) The church originally was built in the fourth century, and although subsequently much altered, was the first Neapolitan basilica. In the eighth century it was re-dedicated to S. Restituta when the body of the Saint was brought here from Ischia. The primitive building shared an atrium with the Stefania, but lost this when the present cathedral was erected.

At the altar end, on the left, are three side-chapels; the centre chapel contains a fine mosaic, *Virgin and Child between SS. Gennaro and Restituta* (1322), by Lello da Roma; and in the chapels on each side are beautiful examples of Italian low-reliefs of the early thirteenth century. To the right of the apse and main altar, an opening leads through to the baptistery. (Note the Roman sarcophagus with bacchantic relief in the chapel before the doorway.)

The **baptistery** (S. Giovanni a Fonte) was almost certainly built by Bishop Soter in the latter half of the fifth century, and is the oldest building in Italy (older than S. Vitale at Ravenna) to illustrate the use of squinches rather than pendentives in passing from square walls to the circular dome. There are also remains here of contemporary mosaics, showing early Christian iconography.

The **Cappella di Tesoro** (di S. Gennaro) lies on the south side of the Duomo, directly opposite the entrance to S. Restituta. It was built in tardy fulfilment of a vow made by the citizens to the Saint during the terrible plague of the 1520's; the work was not begun until 1608. The massive doors of gilded bronze open-work are by Fanzago (1668). Except for the *Paradise* in the cupola, by Lanfranco (1643), all the other frescoes are by the Bolognese Domenichino, who also painted four of the paintings over the seven altars. The commission for the decoration of the chapel led to intimidation, threats and open assault on the part of the so-called 'Cabal of Naples' (the painters Corenzio, Ribera—there is a painting of his over the central altar on the right—and Caracciolo), so that a succession of painters was offered the task. Domenichino used to turn up in the morning to find his painting of the previous day spoiled, and his servant was once nearly done to death by hired ruffians; but, after a temporary retirement to Rome, he returned to complete the work before his death in 1641.

Behind the high altar are preserved the *head of S. Gennaro*, encased in a silver bust of French fourteenth-century workmanship, and the two phials of his congealed blood, which miraculously liquefies three times a year—on the first Saturday in May, when the Saint is carried in state to S. Chiara, and on September 19th and December 16th. The safety of the city is said to depend on the speed with which the blood liquefies, and a delay is greeted with vociferous expostulations on the part of a section of the congregation known as the Saint's 'relatives'. In rooms off the right of the chapel is kept the Treasure of S. Gennaro, which includes forty-five silver busts of other saintly patrons of Naples, some of whom have at times been called in to act as first patron when the Neapolitans considered S. Gennaro dilatory in his guardianship of the city.

Though the first historical record of the liquefaction was in 1389, the tradition of S. Gennaro is very ancient. As Bishop of Benevento, he suffered martyrdom at Pozzuoli under Diocletian's persecution in 305. The blood of the martyr, collected by a man whose sight he had restored, was said to have first liquefied in the hands of the saintly Bishop Severus when the body of the Saint was brought to Naples and buried in the catacombs at the time of Constantine. Later it was removed to Benevento, thither in 1159 to Montevergine, and finally in 1497 back to Naples. S. Gennaro's birthplace is not known, but on an eighteenth-century house in the Via S. Gregorio Armeno an inscription nevertheless informs us that 'in this palace was born the most illustrious of all Neapolitans, S. Gennaro.'

On the farther side of the right transept, in the angle, is the *chapel of the Minutolo family,* opened on request to the sacristan. This gives us an excellent idea of the richness of the original Angevin church, with its mosaic floor depicting animals (late thirteenth century), its frescoes of Crusaders by the school of Pietro Cavallini (late fourteenth, early fifteenth centuries) and its contemporary tombs. That of Cardinal Filippo Minutolo ('of marble and very magnificent') is the one which the two thieves opened with the aid of Andreuccio da Perugia in Boccaccio's tale. The chapel of the Tocca family, to the left, has also been kept in its original Gothic form.

Two stairways in front of the choir descend to the *crypt of S. Gennaro* (or Cappella Carafa or the Succorso) beneath the main altar. The sacristan has the key to the beautiful bronze doors with their insignia of the Carafas. This chapel, built by Tommaso Malvito of Como between 1497 and 1508, is rightly considered the most elegant Renaissance work in Naples. The carving which decorates the chapel is crisp and clean, but a little cold.

S. Maria Donnaregina—Via Tribunali—Porta Alba

Once back in the Via del Duomo we turn right and right again almost immediately in the Largo Donnaregina. At Nos. 22–3 is the entrance to the Cardinal-Archbishop's Palace, with its doorway of the Durazzo period (early fifteenth century). On the opposite side of the little square steps lead up to the baroque church of S. Maria Donnaregina (1620—frescoes and paintings by Solimena and Luca Giordano), but it is an earlier church of the same name that brings us here. This is reached by the Vico Donnaregina on the right of the church.

S. Maria Donnaregina was built 1307–20 on the site of an early (pre-eighth century) basilican convent, largely with the aid of Maria of Hungary, wife of Charles II of Anjou. After the suppression of the convent in 1860 the buildings passed to the Municipality; it has now been restored to its *trecento* Gothic form (admission, daily; ring the bell; tip.) Entrance is through an eighteenth-century cloister, the work of Ferdinando Sanfelice, one of the most interesting Neapolitan architects of the period. The interior of the church has a severely simple polygonal apse and a nuns' choir which is like a dress-circle in a theatre and extends almost to the presbytery. Against the left wall is the fine Gothic *tomb of Maria of Hungary*, executed by Tino da Camaino and Gagliardo Primario in 1325. The queen is represented with the Virgin; below are the figures of her children, and the sarcophagus is supported by the four cardinal Virtues. Opposite, in the Cappella Loffredo, are the remains of some frescoes of the school of Giotto.

A staircase leads to the **nuns' choir,** with its wonderful frescoes (1310–20) by the Roman Pietro Cavallino and his assistants— among them Lello da Roma. Cavallino, like Lello, worked in fresco as well as mosaic, and he played an important part in the development of Byzantine conventions into more natural forms by infusing into them some of the sculptural qualities of early Christian (and thereby classical) art. He has been unfairly overshadowed by his greater contemporary Giotto, and it is worth comparing his work here with the mosaics in S. Maria in Trastevere and the frescoes at S. Cecilia in Trastevere. Part of his *Last Judgment* has been cut into by the sixteenth-century ceiling; the rest can be seen in the room above. There, too, are the apartments of the former abbesses.

Crossing the Via del Duomo, we take the narrow street between the sombre-looking church of S. Giuseppe dei Ruffi and one of the oldest cafés in Naples, where in the last century literary people foregathered. The street we are now entering was the *decumanus superior* of the Graeco-Roman city, and derives its name of Anticaglia from the 'ancient remains' of Roman brickwork which are visible in the walls of houses and the two arches that span it. These once joined the baths, which were on our right, to the theatre, where Nero used to perform to the applause of his hired Alexandrians. We turn left in the Vico Cinquesanti which brings us out again in the Piazza S. Gaetano, with the doorway and campanile of S. Lorenzo in front of us. On our right is the church of *S. Paolo Maggiore,* erected in 1583–1603 for the Theatine Fathers by Francesco Grimaldi, in place of a ninth-century church which incorporated parts of the Augustan temple of the Dioscuri. From the balustraded terrace in front of S. Paolo we can look down on the scene below. The statue of *S. Gaetano* appears from the rear, with its filigreed iron halo, like some inflated Tanagra figure. Behind us, attached to the façade of the church, two of the original Roman columns remain, part of the portico which was destroyed by the earthquake of 1688; and in the corner is the mutilated antique torso of Castor or Pollux.

We now follow the Via Tribunali to the right. Almost immediately on our left, beneath the piperno portico of the thirteenth-century palace of Philip of Anjou, Prince of Taranto, is a street-market, completely medieval in its colour, confusion and litter. Farther along, on the right is the little baroque church of *S. Maria delle Anime del Purgatorio,* built by Fanzago, *ca.* 1650, and restored and decorated further in 1717—remarkable for the bronze skulls and thigh-bones on stone pillars in front of it. The bronze is of a beautiful light colour from the constant rubbing of pious hands. And a little farther, on the same side, is the eleventh-century Romanesque campanile of a much earlier basilican church erected by Bishop Pomponio in 514. In its base can be seen pieces of Roman stonework and two columns of grey granite.

Here the Tribunali opens out in a piazzetta which is closed at the farther end by the Gothic portal and the campanile of S. Pietro a Maiella. But before this, standing in the square, is the charming Renaissance *chapel of the humanist Pontano* (1492). It has Latin epigraphs round the outside walls, expressing Pontano's own philosophy, and others are inscribed inside. The chapel is normally open only on Sundays, which is a pity, since there is a good contemporary triptych of the Virgin. The floor is covered with exquisite Florentine majolica tiles.

The church of *S. Pietro a Maiella* was built at the end of the thirteenth and beginning of the fourteenth centuries and was dedicated to S. Pietro Angeleri, the unsophisticated ascetic from the Maiella Mountains who became Pope Celestine V in 1294, and a puppet in the hands of Charles II of Anjou. Unable to control the factions among the cardinals and wishing to return to his own spiritual practices, he abdicated after six months' rule and was imprisoned by his successor, Boniface VIII, near Anagni, where he died in 1296. He was canonized in 1313. Celestine had an immense popular following in Naples, and a reformed order of Benedictines was later known as Celestines after him. Many of the paintings in the church depict episodes from his life, and those by Mattia Preti on the ceiling of the nave (1656–61) are worth mentioning, although in certain lights they are difficult to see. The circular paintings in the transept are also by Preti and show *Scenes from the Life of St Catherine of Alexandria.*

The adjoining monastery in Via S. Pietro a Maiella (as the Tribunali has become) now contains the **Conservatory of Music,** which, if we take its effective date of origin as 1537, is the oldest music school in existence. The Conservatory was a fusion at the beginning of the last century of four existing institutions: S. Maria di Loreto, Pietà dei Turchini, S. Onofrio and the Poveri di Gesù Cristo. Few musical establishments can rival its roll of honour, for as masters or pupils it can claim among many others Alessandro and Domenico Scarlatti, Pergolesi, Bellini and Donizetti. Although the library and museum are normally open only to scholars, permission to visit them will be given on request at the office. There is a most interesting collection of portraits, curios, musical scores and instruments.

Old City
pp. 40-1

Crossing Via S. Sebastiano we enter (under an arch) the **Via Porta Alba,** once the street of the *pizzerias*, now of bookshops. Notice the garden high up on the arch at the farther end, the **Porta Alba** proper. This gateway was erected by the Viceroy Antonio Toledo, Duke of Alba, in 1625, and rebuilt in 1797. Above

Old City
pp. 40-1

the coat of arms a statue of S. Gaetano surveys the crowded **Piazza Dante.** This spacious semi-circle, which has the Via Roma (Toledo) as its diameter, was designed by Vanvitelli in 1757, the statues on the balustrade representing the virtues (all twenty-six of them) of Charles III of Bourbon.

Restaurants

The standards of Neapolitan restaurants are very variable, but here are some that were good when I was last there: Le Arcate, 249 Via Aniello Falcone, on the Vomero. (The view from the terrace is magnificent, and the fish excellent. Try *spigola al forno*, one of the best of Mediterranean fish, cooked in the oven.) Near by, also in Via Falcone, at No. 203, is the old-established D'Angelo, which is also a *pizzeria*. Good fish can be had at Da Ciro a Mergellina, 18 Via Mergellina; at Giuseppone a Mare on Posillipo (13 Via F. Russo), and at two restaurants overlooking the Bay at Marechiaro—Fenestrella a Marechiaro and Terrazzino dei Fiori.

More centrally, in the Piazza dei Martiri in Chiaia, there is the *rosticceria* and *pizzeria* Da Gennaro; and in the streets off the piazza are Da Giovanni, 14 Via Domenico Morelli, which used to be a friendly bohemian haunt but now has become somewhat more sedate; and Da Umberto, 30 Via Alabardieri—this is also a *pizzeria*. In the Via C. de Cesare, which is one of the narrow streets in the *quartieri* to the west of the Via Roma, there are a number of good small restaurants, of which the Pappagallo, No. 14, can be specially recommended. (Next door is the town house built by Caffarello, the famous *castrato* singer.)

Farther up the Via Roma, around the Piazza Dante, there are several restaurants and *pizzerias*, among them Dante & Beatrice and Al 53. This district, with the Via Porta Alba which leads out of it, was once famous for its *pizzerias* and for being the meeting-place of composers of popular songs. Illiterate musicians would turn up here to have their songs transcribed on the spot. For those visitors who want to see some of the more 'characteristic' of Neapolitan types, there is a spot of local colour at Della Quercia, 5 Vico della Quercia. This little street is on the right of the Via S. Anna dei Lombardi as it enters the Via Roma (also on the right), a short distance before you reach the Piazza Dante.

Another characteristic restaurant is Da Giovanni il Ferroviere, 34 Via Carriera Grande, which is appropriately near the Central Station—just off the Piazza Garibaldi, on the north side towards the Piazza Principe Umberto. Da Giovanni is unassuming and is patronised almost entirely by Neapolitans. You can sit behind the pot-plants in this little terrace on the pavement and observe the clandestine street-trading which goes on all around you.

The Museo Nazionale

From the **Piazza Dante** the Via Roma is prolonged northwards as the Via E. Pessina. A short way up this street on the corner of the Piazza Museo Nazionale stands the great reddish building which houses the National Archaeological Museum, usually referred to

Old City pp. 40-1

57

simply as the **Museo Nazionale.** The building itself has served very different purposes: erected in 1586 as a cavalry barracks, it was converted in 1616 for the use of the University. In 1738 Charles III of Bourbon began the construction of the Palace of Capodimonte to receive the Farnese Collection of antiquities, paintings and books which he had inherited from his mother, Elizabeth Farnese. The excavations which were being carried on at the time in the buried cities of Herculaneum, Pompeii and Stabia had filled the Palace of Portici to overflowing with the valuable objects removed, so it was decided to bring together all the royal collections in the present building, and in 1777 the University went elsewhere. Since then, the Biblioteca Nazionale has been moved to the Royal Palace, and in 1957 the National Gallery was transferred to the Palace of Capodimonte.

The collection of Greek and Roman antiquities is one of the finest in the world. Until his death in 1963, the great archaeologist Amedeo Maiuri was in charge of both field excavation and the display of the collections at the Museo Nazionale, and nowhere else can we get so intimate a picture of ancient life as in these relics from the rich cities round the Bay of Naples. Admission to the museum is 9.30 a.m.–4.0 p.m. weekdays, 9.30 a.m.–1.30 p.m. Sundays, closed on Wednesdays. All I shall do here is give a general indication of what is to be seen, and point out only too arbitrarily some of the objects which, for one reason or another, have claimed my own attention.

In the entrance hall, the **Grande Atrio dei Magistrati,** with its colossal statues, most of which came from the Farnese Collection, there are realistic *family portraits of the Balbo family* from Herculaneum.

The **Gallery of the Tyrannicides** (Room 1) has good Roman copies of the famous early fifth-century bronze group by Critios and Nesiotes, and the beautiful Greek funeral stele is an original of the fifth century BC, from the Borgia collection.

In Room II, the **Gallery of the Great Masters,** there are *two statues of Aphrodite* from Herculaneum and Pompeii, the colossal *head of Artemis,* often called the Farnese Juno, the *statue of Athene,* and the lovely low-relief of *Orpheus, Eurydice and Hermes*—all Roman copies of the fifth-century BC originals.

In Room III is the *Javelin Thrower* (Doryphorus) from the Samnite Palaestra at Pompeii, the best-preserved copy of one of the most famous statues of the ancient world, by Polycleitus of Argos, *ca.* 440 BC, which became the paragon of the male form.

Rooms V and VI contain some of the finds made at Locri in

58

Magna Graecia, among them two identical fifth-century groups in Parian marble of the *Dioscuri*, with horses and tritons.

The long **Gallery of Flora** (Room VIII) takes its name from the colossal statue of the *Farnese Flora*, a Roman work of the second or third century AD, from the Baths of Caracalla.

Room X has, among other Aphrodite-Venuses, all of the Hellenistic period, the famous *Venus Callipyge* (Venus of the Beautiful Bottom), from Nero's Golden House in Rome. She was in fact probably not Venus but a hetaira. Note, too, the curious *head of Aphrodite*, with her black painted eyes, from the temple of Isis in Pompeii.

The colossal *Farnese Hercules* in the **Gallery of the Farnese Bull** is a copy of the bronze original by Lysippus from the Baths of Caracalla. There are also beautiful examples of Hellenistic sculptors' skill in the representation of the female form. The *Farnese Bull*, the huge group which dominates Room XVI, is again from the Baths of Caracalla. Originally carved in the first to second centuries AD from a single block of marble, the work has suffered from a series of restorations (Michelangelo is said to have had a hand in the first of these) after its discovery in 1546.

In the basement, reached from Room XVII, are the **Egyptian Prehistoric Collections** (admission is from 12.0 noon–2.0 p.m. or on request to the attendants). The Borgia collection of Egyptian antiquities, which came into the possession of the Museo in 1817, forms the basis of the collection. Room XXI contains the result of excavations and finds in Capri, the Gargano, Capua, Manduria and Cumae, and illustrates the early civilizations of the cities of Campania.

The **Gallery of Coloured Marbles**, Room XXIX, has the *statue of Artemis-Diana of Ephesus*, a Roman work of the time of Hadrian, representing the nature goddess worshipped in the temple of Ephesus; and the *statue of Anubis* from Pozzuoli, with its jackal's head on a Greek base. On the walls are eleven *votive reliefs to Apollo and the Nymphs* from Ischia, where the Nymphs formerly presided over the medicinal springs.

Rooms XXIV to XXVIII are devoted to decorative sculpture—statues, altars, herms, reliefs, tombs, fountains, etc., which once decorated houses and gardens in Pompeii, Herculaneum, Capri and elsewhere. Room XXX, the **Gallery of Herculaneum,** contains some of the Museum's unique collection of bronzes, including the reconstructed horse, one of the four which stood, drawing a bronze chariot, in front of the ancient theatre. This was patiently restored from a thousand fragments by order of Charles III of Bourbon.

In the **Gallery of the Emperors,** Room XLIV, is a seated statue thought to be of *Agrippina*, Nero's mother, whom he tried to drown at Baia, and subsequently had stabbed to death (see p. 79). There are two statues of *Antinoüs*, favourite of the Emperor Hadrian, one here, and another, a colossal representation of him as Bacchus, in Room XLII. Room XXXVI has the famous *bronze head of a horse*, given by Lorenzo il Magnifico to Diomede Carafa and formerly in the courtyard of the Palazzo Carafa on Spaccanapoli.

The **Gallery of Greek Portraits,** Room XLV, contains many old friends from our schooldays: the herm of *Socrates*, with its inscription from Plato's *Crito*; busts of *Euripides*, and the touching 'portrait' of the blind *Homer*.

Upstairs Rooms LVII–LXIV contain the **Pompeian Mosaics,** which include some of the finest examples of the mosaicist's art to have been preserved from the ancient world. In Room LVII the amusing *Drunken Silenus on an Ass* comes from the house of P. Paquius Proculus, whose portrait and that of his wife are among the paintings on the first floor. Dioscurides of Samos has left his signature on two fine mosaics from the so-called Villa of Cicero: *the Love-philtre* and *Wandering Musicians*. In the same room is a representation of *Plato in his Academy*, with the Acropolis in the background, and also an accurate and lovely study of fish, *Fauna Marina*. The celebrated *Battle of Issus* with *Alexander and Darius*, from the House of the Faun, is in Room LXI.

In the **Salone Grande** is the famous statue of the *Farnese Atalanta*, and the rooms on the right contain the best of the splendid collection of bronzes from Herculaneum and Pompeii, as well as furniture, glassware and utensils.

The **mural paintings** from Pompeii, Herculaneum and Stabia are really extraordinary. With few exceptions, they are the work of ordinary craftsmen, but the technical skill and imagination displayed are astounding. Most were painted directly on to the wet plaster, *al fresco*; a few are in *tempera*. In Rooms LXXI and LXXII there are the only examples we have from antiquity of coloured line-drawings on marble.

In Room LXXVII are the portraits of the Pompeians *P. Paquius Proculus and his wife*, and some landscapes and views of the coast. For a magnificent painting of a mythological subject there is *Hercules watching the young Telephus* in Room LXXI. In Room LXX two paintings of the *Three Graces* show the skill achieved in treatment of the female form. But what is perhaps most endearing in these Graeco-Roman artists is their choice of common scenes and objects of everyday life as subjects for painting. The still lifes here—especially in Room XCVI (where there is also a model of the excavations at Pompeii)—and at Herculaneum and Pompeii, are very appealing.

Other rooms on this floor, beginning at Room LXXXIII, display a fascinating collection of domestic and personal objects. A showcase in Room XCV contains surgical instruments, including some for specifically gynaecological uses. And on the ground floor, at the back of the main building beyond the courtyard, is an interesting technological collection showing the high development of tools and mechanical appliances.

Room LXXXIII also has the marvellous *Farnese Cup* in veined sardonyx, made in Alexandria at the time of the Ptolemies. Gladiators' arms are shown in Room LXXIX. And on the second floor are the magnificent collection of *figured vases* and an extensive collection of **Greek and Roman coins.**

CHAPTER 4

Naples on the Hills

Map: Naples, pp.24–5; The Environs of Naples, pp.72–3

The catacombs—Palace of Capodimonte—the National Gallery

From the Museo Nazionale the prolongation of the Via Roma northwards is known first as Via E. Pessina, then as Via S. Teresa degli Scalzi, and finally as the Corso Amedeo di Savoia. This latter portion, with the bridge over the district of the Sanità, was built by Joseph Bonaparte in 1809 to improve the access to the Palace of Capodimonte. To the right stands the church of S. Teresa, which gives its name to the street, and almost opposite, a winding alley, the Salità S. Raffaele, leads up to S. Gennaro a Materdei, where Don Mario Borrelli has the headquarters of his **Casa dello Scugnizzo,** known internationally for its work in rehabilitating the street-urchins (*scugnizzi*) of the Neapolitan slums. Father Borrelli is a busy man, but he (or his assistants) will welcome interested visitors.

It is in the **catacombs** of Naples, cut in the soft tufaceous rock in the hills to the north of the city, that we have some of the best-preserved remaining links with its Roman and early Christian past. Some of the underground passages run for great distances and have not yet been thoroughly explored. The most important of the catacombs are those of S. Gennaro and of S. Gaudioso. To reach the former, we descend the ramp and steps to the left of the Corso Amedeo di Savoia about half-way between the Ponte della Sanità and the oval piazzetta known as the Tondo di Capodimonte and turn right in Via S. Gennaro dei Poveri. After a short way we see, again on the right, the baroque façade (1667) of the Ospizio di S. Gennaro dei Poveri.

The **catacomb of S. Gennaro** lies behind the church of **S. Gennaro extra Moenia,** which is reached across the two courts of the Ospizio. This basilican church is very ancient, the foundations being of the fifth century, although the upper portions have been rebuilt several times. The remains of the fifth- or sixth-century frescoes in the right aisle were found beneath the church. The sacristan will show visitors round (admission, weekdays 9.0 a.m.–4.0 p.m.; Sundays 9.0 a.m.–12.0 noon; tip).

In origin this was possibly a family tomb of pagan patricians of the second century AD, which a little later became used as a Christian burial ground. A basilica was built in the third century above the tomb of S. Agrippino, a celebrated bishop of Naples, and this became a popular place of pilgrimage, especially after the body of S. Gennaro was brought here at the beginning of the fifth century. In 831 Sicone, the Lombard Prince of Benevento, carried off the Saint's relics, and the importance of the spot began to decline, but it was not until the thirteenth century that it was abandoned and fell to ruin.

The catacomb is on two levels, the lower floor being divided into two main sections, with many small adjuncts. The right-hand section is known as the Basilica Cimiteriale of S. Gennaro. There are remains of frescoes and mosaics in the *arcosolia* or arched burial vaults, and second-century frescoes on the ceiling of the left-hand section. This large hall was the original family burial place and in the centre of the floor is a baptismal font of the eighth century. There is also an ithyphallic goat which dances on the wall above the entrance, of the same period as the paintings on the ceiling. It is hard to imagine how its symbolism could be squared with the Christian symbols we see all round.

Over the door of the so-called crypt of S. Gennaro and Companions is a Greek cross and the inscription, 'Jesus Christ conquers'. Behind the little building with the goat, various cubicles show early paintings, and a further room has a marble column in the centre with the word 'Priapus' in Greek and Hebrew. This is thought to be the meeting-place of Jews, after the catacombs had been abandoned by the Christians in the thirteenth century. The floor above has a large basilican hall and remains of frescoes, among them the earliest (fifth-century) portrait of S. Gennaro, in an *arcosolium.*

The church of S. Maria della Sanità (a Dominican building of 1602, with a notable cupola of majolica tiles) on the site of the other important **catacomb of S. Gaudioso**, is reached by returning along the Via S. Gennaro dei Poveri, taking the Via S. Vincenzo on the left, and passing under the bridge of the Sanità, where we see the church immediately on our left. The sacristan will show visitors the catacomb.

The African S. Gaudioso was supposedly banished from Abitina by the Vandal King Genseric. Placed in an open boat, he and his companions were miraculously transported to Naples (a common occurrence in Neapolitan hagiography), where Gaudioso founded a monastery on this spot, and after his death in 451 the place became a centre of pilgrimage. But the fascination here lies in the macabre burial customs from the seventeenth century. The bodies were placed on a seat carved out of the tufa, which was then walled up so that only the head was showing. On the face of the wall was painted the rest of the skeleton and a symbol of its owner's human activity: a sword for the soldier Scipio Brancaccio, a skirt for the Prioress of Montesarchia, a brush and palette for the painter Balducci, and so on.

As we climb the hill from the Tondo di Capodimonte, with the modern church of the Madre di Buon Consiglio on our left (directly above the catacomb of S. Gennaro), a magnificent view of the city, bay and mountains unfolds itself. The **Palace of Capodimonte** stands in a lovely, bosky setting surrounded by its park. Charles III of Bourbon originally planned to build a hunting-lodge here: subsequently he called in the Sicilian architect Medrano to design him a palace which could also house the Farnese Collection. The present building, begun in 1738, was not completed until a hundred years later, when it became, with Caserta, one of the chief residences of King 'Bomba'. In the park were the porcelain works (the kilns still exist) with which Charles hoped to rival his father-in-law at Meissen. On the first floor many of the royal apartments have been kept as they were, but the second floor has been skilfully adapted to exhibit the pictures from the National Gallery, the collections of nineteenth-century Neapolitan painting formerly in the Accademia di Belle Arti and the gallery of the Banco di Napoli, the Farnese Collection of arms and armour, and porcelain from Capodimonte and elsewhere. (Admission, park 9.0 a.m.–dusk; art gallery and museum, weekdays 9.30 a.m.–4.0 p.m.; Sundays and holidays, 9.30 a.m.–1.0 p.m.; closed on Mondays.)

As in many of the churches in Naples, a number of unquestionable masterpieces are shown alongside a mass of third-rate work. And although some of the paintings are of historical or social interest, those on a short visit would be advised to concentrate on the paintings in rooms on the second floor, on the collection of porcelain in Rooms LXVIII–LXXI on the first floor, and on the charming little *chinoiserie* room (XCIV), decorated completely in china of Capodimonte.

On the second floor, **Rooms IV to VI** contain some interesting

Above The Castel Nuovo was built by Charles I of Anjou in 1294 – hence its other name, 'the Angevin fortress'. The towers are original, but it was largely rebuilt by the Spaniards. It was a royal palace until the building of the Palazzo Reale, and was the scene of the suppression of the Barons' Conspiracy in 1486. *Below left* The Triumphal Arch which forms the entrance was begun by Alfonso il Magnanimo in 1454 to commemorate his capture of Naples from the French. *Right* The main doorway (1685) of the church of the Gesù Nuovo, constructed out of the 15th c. Palazzo Sanseverino.

Two of the treasures of the National Gallery, now housed in the Palace of Capodimonte. *Above The Transfiguration* by Giovanni Bellini. *Below Danaë* by Titian.

fourteenth- and fifteenth-century Tuscan paintings, among them Simone Martini's *Crowning of Robert of Anjou by his brother S. Louis of Toulouse*; two *Madonnas* by Bernardo Daddi; *St James the Apostle* by Andrea Vanni. In Room VI there are a magnificent *Crucifixion* by Masaccio (1426) and two panels of a polyptych by Masolino.

Room VII is devoted to the Florentine school and includes an early *Madonna and Child* by Botticelli. **Rooms VIII and IX** have two paintings by Colantonio, the master of Antonello da Messina (*ca.* 1430–79), who influenced and was influenced by Giovanni Bellini. *The Mathematics Lecture* by an unknown (possibly Venetian) artist gives a portrait of the Franciscan Fra Luca Pacioli, the friend and mathematics teacher of Leonardo da Vinci. There are good Parmigianinos and Correggios in **Room XV**.

Venetians of the fifteenth and sixteenth centuries are well represented in **Room XVII** and include an early work (1465) by Mantegna, *S. Eufemia*, and his charming portrait of *Francesco Gonzaga*. The Vivarini, whom we shall meet again in many churches of Apulia, were a family of painters, like the Bellini. The *Transfiguration* here by Giovanni Bellini is one of his finest pictures, and Lorenzo Lotto's disquieting portrait of *Bernardo de' Rossi* is also very fine.

There is a single work by El Greco in **Room XVIII,** which also contains a Palma Vecchio. **Room XIX** is entirely devoted to Titian, a magnificent collection of paintings executed for the Farnese family, among them the lovely *Danaë* (1545) and the sinister group of *Pope Paul III Farnese with his Nephews*. In **Room XX** are two paintings, dated 1568, by Pieter Brueghel the Elder, one of them the marvellous *Blind Leading the Blind*; one by Cranach; and a *Winter Scene* by Jan (Velvet) Brueghel.

From the refreshment room a staircase leads up to the terrace and a splendid view. The three rooms which follow contain drawings by Michelangelo, Raphael, Tintoretto and Rembrandt. **Rooms XXV and XXVII** show the Bolognese school of the seventeenth century, and from then on Neapolitan painters, or those who directly influenced Neapolitan painting, like Ribera, predominate. In **Room XXXVIII** there is a *Landscape* by Claude Lorrain and a *Crucifixion* by Van Dyck; **Room XL** has works of the interesting Calabrian painter Mattia Preti (1613–99). Luca Giordano, called '*Fa presto*' from the speed at which he worked, and admired by Wordsworth, also has a room to himself (**XLI**). Of the Collection of the Banco di Napoli, we may single out the two Salvator Rosa's (**XLII bis**) and the two splendid portraits by Goya, *Charles IV of Spain* and *Maria Luisa of Parma*, in **Room XLV**.

On the first floor, the **Collection of Nineteenth-century Neapolitan Art** in Rooms XLVII to LXVI tells us much about Naples of the time. Besides the academic school with its romantic colouring, represented by Domenico Morelli (1826–1907), Naples produced in the last century two other important groups of painters, the 'School of Posillipo' and the 'Republic of Portici'. The Posillipo painters centred around the great figure of Giacinto Gigante (1806–76) and the four Palizzi brothers. The interesting group of rebels who styled themselves Republicans of Portici includes such different painters as De Gregorio, De Nittis, Rossano and Gaeta. We may also single out the landscape painter Fergola and Vincenzo Migliaro.

The **Porcelain and Majolica Collection** has beautiful examples of Sèvres, Meissen, Vienna and the Royal Factory at Capodimonte. In the **Royal Apartments,** Room LXXIX is furnished in the First Empire style by Murat, and in the two following rooms there are Bourbon portraits by Vigée Lebrun, Angelica Kauffmann and others. The **De Ciccio Collection** of porcelain and *objets d'art* is contained in Rooms LXXXII–LXXXV. Across the vast ballroom, **Room LXXXVII** has some beautiful bronzes, including a *bust of King Ferrante* by Guido Mazzoni and a precious *David* by Pollaiuolo. Then follow the rooms devoted to the **Farnese Armoury,** and the fine collection of **medals.**

The charming little **Salottino di Porcellana** (Room XCIV) is composed of more than three thousand pieces of Capodimonte porcelain. In the next room (XCV) is the famous **Farnese Casket,** one of the finest examples of the sixteenth-century goldsmith's art.

The belvedere of Camaldoli—a magnificent view

From Capodimonte there is a good drive of about seven miles westwards along the crest of the hills to the north of the city, with a series of views culminating in one of the most famous in Italy—the view from the **belvedere of the monastery of the Camaldoli.** (Bus No. 114 leaves from the Piazza Vanvitelli on Vomero for the little village of Nazareth, from which it is only a short walk.)

Environs
pp. 72-3

Midway between the Porta Grande and the Porta Piccola of the park of Capodimonte we take the Viale Colli Aminei. Behind the Hospital Cardarelli we turn left in the Via Pansini, where a right fork takes us to a junction of eight roads. Here we take the Via Leonardo Bianchi, and at the Sanatorium branch left into the Via

Orsolone for the villages of I Guantai and then Nazareth. It is deliciously fresh in this countryside of chestnuts and fruit trees after the heat of the city, and in the trattorias you can still sometimes hear the traditional Neapolitan melodies sung by the inevitable tenor to the guitar or mandoline.

The monastery of the Camaldoli was built in 1585, to replace a much earlier edifice. It is of no great interest and women are not admitted, but from the Belvedere Pagliarella, about ten minutes' walk along the path from the terrace outside the entrance to the monastery, we look out over the city towards Vesuvius and the fertile Campania. Beyond the Monti Lattari on the Sorrentine peninsula are the distant mountains of the Cilento; then the whole sweep of the Bay of Naples from Capri to Ischia and Procida, Point Misenum and Baia on the Bay of Pozzuoli. Below, on the right, rise the wooded cones of the volcanic region of the Phlegraean Fields, and beyond lies the Bay of Gaeta. Sunset on a clear day is the best time for this magnificent view.

Vomero—the Museo di S. Martino—Villa Floridiana

The return to **Vomero** was once through winding country roads and little villages. Now the whole area is becoming one built-up overspill for modern Naples. Vomero is not just a suburb of Naples, but a new city now with a life of its own. It is connected with Naples by three funicular services, and the Piazza Vanvitelli, in the heart of Vomero, is close to all three, as well as to the Castel S. Elmo and the Museo di S. Martino.

The huge mass of the ***Castel S. Elmo*** (which may be visited by permission of the Military Command in Piazza del Plebiscito) is in the form of a six-pointed star. It was rebuilt by the Valencian architect Pier Luigi Scrivà in 1537, on the orders of the Viceroy Toledo, to replace an earlier construction (1329) of King Robert of Anjou. Standing on a spur which dominates the city, its possession was essential to the defence of the city, and the surrender of its garrison of French and Neapolitan liberals in 1799 to the Sanfedist Cardinal Ruffo brought to a close the brief and tragic Parthenopean Republic. From the balustrade of the terrace in front of the entrance to the museum which adjoins the castello, there is a fine view over the 'old city', with Spaccanapoli cutting its narrow way clean through the centre.

The ***Museo di S. Martino*** is housed in a former Carthusian

Naples
pp. 24-5

67

monastery. The monks were finally expelled in 1866; during the French occupation they had already incurred Bourbon displeasure by holding a ball decorated with flags made from ecclesiastical vestments in the colours of the Parthenopean Republic. The original foundation was Angevin, but most of the present buildings were begun on the plans of the Florentine architect G. A. Dosio at the end of the sixteenth century, and continued by Fanzago. The Great Cloister, particularly, is an example of the perfect fusion of Renaissance and baroque.

The entrance to the museum (admission, weekdays 9.30 a.m.–4.0 p.m.; Sundays and holidays 9.30 a.m.–1.0 p.m.; closed Mondays) takes us through the seventeenth-century **Chiostro dei Procuratori.** It includes among its treasures an interesting collection of historical records of the Kingdom of Naples; the famous *Tavola Strozzi*, by an unknown painter of the fifteenth century, showing the return of the fleet of Ferrante of Aragon from the battle of Ischia in 1465; a fascinating section devoted to aspects of Neapolitan *Feste e Costumi*—the life and arts of the people; a collection of eighteenth-century figures for the Christmas cribs by well-known sculptors such as Sammartino and D. A. Vaccaro (including the wonderfully anachronistic *Presepe Cuciniello*). There are also some nostalgic records of famous Neapolitan theatres and actors.

We cross the lovely **Chiostro Grande** to reach the **art collections,** which include a typical landscape by Salvator Rosa. Fanzago is also responsible for some of the statues on the balustrade and in the little cemetery with its death's-head decoration. The florid decoration of the church and monastic rooms has been described as among the most important of the seventeenth century in Italy.

From the Piazza Vanvitelli it is only a short walk down the Via Bernini and right in the Via Cimarosa (past the funicular station for Chiaia) to the gateway to the park of the **Villa Floridiana.** The Villa, built 1817–19 in the neo-classic style by Niccolini, was Ferdinand I and IV's present to the dark-eyed Lucia Migliaccio, created Duchess of Floridia, whom he morganatically married a few months after the death of Maria Carolina. It is said that when the Hereditary Prince remonstrated with his aged father on his choice of partner, the King replied, 'Think of Mama, my son, think of Mama!' Niccolini also built the 'Pompeian' Villa Lucia next door, which was inhabited for a time by Lady Blessington, who complained of the noise from the animals in the zoo in the park grounds. The park (admission, 9.30 a.m.–sunset) is particularly beautiful in the late afternoon when one can look out from the lower belvedere over the bay towards Capri where everything is touched with gold. There are many fine specimen trees among the lawns and walks, and in spring there are most beautiful camellias.

The villa now houses the *ceramic collection of the Duca di Martina* and contains fine Italian and foreign porcelain, ivories, goldsmiths' work, etc. (admission, weekdays 9.30 a.m.–4.0 p.m.; closed Mondays).

A short way past the entrance to the Villa Floridiana in Via Cimarosa, we cross the Via Aniello Falcone, and a long avenue of holm-oaks on the left leads to the lovely Villa Belvedere. The house is private, but permission will be given to walk out on the terrace. This charming villa and its grounds are now entirely hemmed in by blocks of towering flats.

Returning to the Via Aniello Falcone, we follow its winding descent to two good restaurants already mentioned (pp. 56, 57), D'Angelo at No. 203 or Le Arcate at No. 249.

CHAPTER 5

The Environs of Naples:
the Phlegraean Fields

Map: The Environs of Naples, pp.72–3

Rich as Campania is in the material remains of Hellenistic antiquity, perhaps not even in Pompeii and Herculaneum does the spirit of Greece so persist as in the region to the west of Naples known as the Campi Flegrei, the **Phlegraean Fields.** The name is Greek, recalling to the earliest immigrants the burning (i.e. volcanic) plain of Pellene in the Chalcidice, where the giants were said to have warred against the Olympian gods. The Greeks brought their myths with them, and here in these hills, lakes, grottoes and woods they located much that was left vague in Homeric topography. Virgil was later to reinforce and add authority to the popular mythology with his *Aeneid*. Yet one does not have to be a classical scholar to feel the sense of mystery which hangs over this strange and beautiful landscape of extinct volcanoes, whose sides are now covered with woods and vineyards but whose waters still reveal their origin in active thermal springs and steaming fissures (*fumarole*).

Virgil's memorial—Posillipo—Pozzuoli—a Roman market-place and amphitheatre—Baia and Roman baths

In the summer months round bus tours of the Phlegraean hills are arranged by CIT or ATAN. But by far the most satisfactory method of visiting the region is by car—or on foot.

We will begin appropriately with a visit to Virgil's memorial. Virgil loved this countryside, and the *Georgics*, which were probably written in Naples, are full of Campanian references: to the Lucrine Lake, to Avernus and to the habit (still continued) of 'weaving the elms with the joyous vines'. Virgil returned ill from Greece and died

70

at Brindisi on September 21st, 19 BC. At his request, his ashes were placed in a tomb 'outside Naples, on the Via Puteolana, between the first and second milestones'. The burial-place became a place of pilgrimage, but was in time forgotten and was probably demolished during the Dark Ages. However, it was as a magician that Virgil's name lived on among Neapolitans, and his 'tomb' became popularly associated with one of his more striking magical achievements, the boring of the tunnel, the so-called Crypta Neapolitana, where the Via Puteolana passes through the hill of Posillipo. (This was in fact probably the work of the Roman engineer, Cocceius, who was employed by Agrippa in the great military works undertaken here for Augustus.)

The *Parco Virgiliano* lies behind the church of S. Maria di Piedigrotta at Mergellina near the entrance to the Galleria Quattro Giornate. A gateway leads up the wooded hillside through gardens planted with *flora virgiliana* to a Roman columbarium beside the now disused tunnel. Close by is a monument to the poet Leopardi, whose body was saved by his friend Antonio Ranieri from interment in the common grave of victims of the cholera outbreak of June 1837.

On Virgil's original tomb was inscribed the well-known distich:

> *Mantua me genuit, Calabria rapuere, tenet nunc*
> *Parthenope; cecini pascua, rura, duces.*

('Mantua bore me, Calabria carried me off, now Parthenope holds me; I sang of flocks, fields and heroes.')

Now another Latin inscription describes the solitude and beauty of the spot where Virgil was or was not buried:

> 'Ravaged the tomb, and broken the urn. Nothing remains.
> And yet the poet's name exalts the place.'

At the Porto Sannazzaro of Mergellina begins the magnificently panoramic **Via Posillipo,** conceived by Murat in 1812 and completed in 1823. As the road ascends, we see on the left the imposing pile of the *Palazzo di Donn' Anna,* begun in 1642 on the designs of Cosimo Fanzago for Anna Carafa, the Neapolitan wife of the Spanish viceroy, the Duke of Medina. Much of the building has now been restored, but the cavernous vaults beneath, into which the sea enters, have given rise to one of those lurid tales of Queen Giovanna II so delightful to Neapolitans. According to popular belief, the Queen was a nymphomaniac with a particular penchant for muscular fishermen who, after serving their purpose, were dropped into the sea below the palace. The stories that their ghosts haunted these

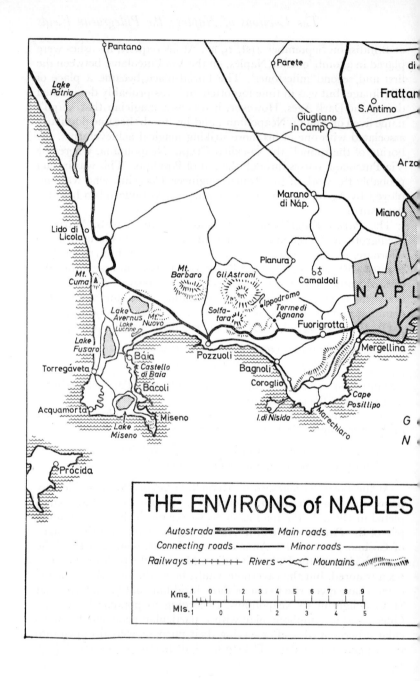

THE ENVIRONS of NAPLES

Autostrada	Main roads	
Connecting roads	Minor roads	
Railways +++++++	Rivers	Mountains

Kms. | 0 1 2 3 4 5 6 7 8 9

Mls. | 0 1 2 3 4 5

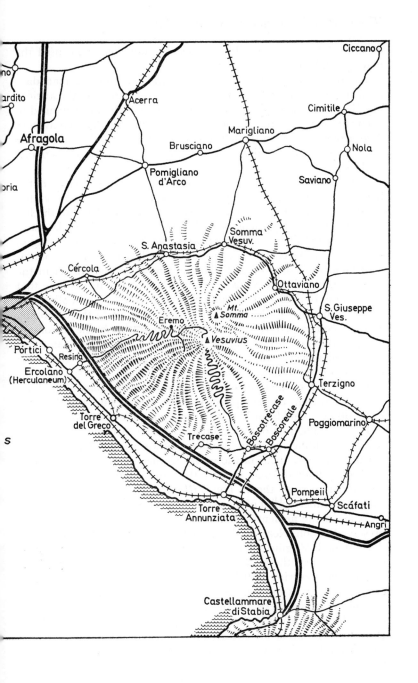

marine arcades were possibly fostered by smugglers, who used the place to land their contraband.

The delightful promontory of **Posillipo** has since Roman days been the setting for luxurious villas; the most famous of the ancient buildings, Vedius Pollio's Villa Pausilypon, which later belonged to Augustus, gave its name to the hill. Just beyond the Piazza Salvatore di Giacomo a road on the left, the Via F. Russo, leads down to the little bay of Capo Posillipo, and the popular restaurant, Giuseppone a Mare.

The Via Posillipo continues to rise, offering splendid views of the bay, to the Quadrivio del Capo. At this point there is a diversion that no visitor should forgo. Take the road that curves down to the left between villas and gardens, past the chiesetta of S. Maria del Faro, to the fishing village of **Marechiaro** (the Neapolitan rendering of *mare planum*). Marechiaro is very close to the hearts of all Neapolitans —di Giacomo's song of that name is almost as well-known in the popular repertoire as 'S. Lucia'—and traditionally it was here that the families of the *piccoli borghesi* came on feast-days and holidays to eat the fish taken fresh from the sea and to listen to the throbbing tenors accompanied by the mandoline and guitar. At the Ristorante la Fenestrella, or at the near-by Terrazzino dei Fiori, we can sit on the terraces overlooking the Lido delle Rose and eat *zuppa alla marinara*, or red mullet (*triglia*) fried in olive oil.

This stretch of the coast was once covered with Roman buildings —a column from the Temple of Fortune is built into a wall on the white piazza—and from Marechiaro we can hire a boat for the ruins of Pollio's villa. Just outside Marechiaro, beneath the water, lies a Roman building, perhaps a villa, known as the Palazzo degli Spiriti. The movement of the waves in the caves on the foreshore produces a hollow sound, whence the name—the Grotta dei Tuoni —of the largest of them. The **Villa Pausilypon** stands on the extreme southern point of the promontory. Excavations have revealed parts of the ancient buildings, including a theatre and a well-preserved odeon. Near by there are further Roman ruins known as the Scuola di Virgilio, from the medieval belief that the poet taught the magical arts there. Around the point lies the island of Nisida, and in the towering cliff-face a natural amphitheatre caused by erosion, known as the Cala di Trentaremi.

Nisida, called Nesis by the ancients, is formed by a volcanic crater. The tradition is that Lucullus had a palace on the island. If so, his reputation for extravagance was not unmerited, for he is also said to have had one where the Castel dell' Ovo now stands and one at Misenum. It was on Nisida that Brutus and Cassius planned Caesar's assassination, and Brutus is thought to have retired there after the event, where he was visited by Cicero. Certainly it was on Nisida that he took leave of his wife Portia before departing for Greece and the battle of Philippi.

Returning to the Quadrivio del Capo, we continue straight on (the Via Posillipo now becoming the Discesa di Coroglio) for about one hundred and fifty yards, and then take a left turn into the Via T. L. Caro, which brings us to the pillared entrance to the **Parco di Posillipo** and its magnificent belvedere. Retracing our steps to the Discesa di Coroglio, we turn to the left, pass under the viaduct and come to the Rotonda, another belvedere which overlooks the Phlegraean Fields and the Gulf of Pozzuoli. From the Rotonda the Via Napoli descends to skirt the shore and runs through rather dreary industrial suburbs to **Pozzuoli.** At the entrance to the town the remains of a Capuchin convent rise apparently out of the sea. This whole area, now submerged through subsidence, was once part of a great system of Roman docks, which may still be seen beneath the water from a boat on a calm day. The ancient monastery, where Pergolesi died in 1736, now contains a restaurant with the appropriate name (since the ground floor of the building is under water) of Vicienzo a Mare. Farther on we pass under the Porta di Città, and via the Corso Vittorio Emanuele come to the centre of the town, the Piazza della Repubblica.

Pozzuoli was founded about 529 BC by political refugees from the tyrannical rule which Polycrates had established in Samos; and it was with some reason that they named the new colony Dikaiarchia, 'Just Government'. Like near-by Cumae (now Cuma), it succumbed first, in 421 BC, to the Samnites. Under the Romans the port of Puteoli, as it was renamed, became the chief maritime entrepôt in Italy for the rapidly increasing trade with Greece and the Near East until the construction of the port of Ostia, begun by Claudius in AD 42 and completed by Nero. Puteoli continued to be the chief port for Campania until the barbarians overran Italy in the fifth century; and the remains we see today attest to its importance and wealth.

From the Piazza della Repubblica we continue past the church of S. Maria delle Grazie to the busy port where the modern mole incorporates remains of the Roman wharves and breakwater, one of the most impressive feats of ancient marine construction. To the right the Lungomare C. Colombo brings us past the fish-stalls and some small restaurants (which serve excellent *spaghetti a vongole*) to the Public Gardens. From here the Via Roma leads to the so-called

Serapeum, in reality a *macellum,* or market-place, of the first century AD (admission, 9.0 a.m.–4.0 p.m.; the ticket also admits to the adjacent Antiquarium). It was erroneously named after a statue of Serapis, discovered when excavations began in 1750. This circular type of market, with stalls opening alternately inwards and towards the outside, was common in the antique world; and since the *macellum* in Rome was converted into the church of S. Stefano Rotondo, the example we have at Pozzuoli is of the greatest archaeological interest.

In the centre of the market stood a domed circular *tholus,* supported by sixteen columns of *giallo antico,* which were removed and employed by Vanvitelli in the Palatine Theatre at Caserta. Some pieces of the sculptural decoration of the *macellum* are in the **Phlegraean Antiquarium** (which stands to the west of it and is entered from the Via del Serapeo), as well as other antiquities from Pozzuoli, Baia and Cuma.

From the Porta della Città we can make our way by the Via del Duomo to the populous and picturesque parts of the town, built over the site of the Graeco-Roman citadel which once successfully withstood the onslaughts of Hannibal. A short way along, a narrow street on the left brings us to the **Duomo,** dedicated to the Puteolan martyr St Proculus, built over and incorporating the temple erected in honour of Augustus by a rich citizen, L. Calpurnius, as we can read from an inscription. Of the temple there remain the top section of the Corinthian columns, the frieze and architrave on the east side of the church. Above the door another inscription tells us that L. Cocceius was the architect. Returning, we take the Via Marconi, which passes over the Porta della Città and becomes first the Via C. Rossini, then the Via Solfatara. On the left rise the external walls of the great **Flavian amphitheatre.**

The amphitheatre (admission, daily 9.0 a.m.–6.0 p.m.) is, after the Colosseum and amphitheatre of Capua, the largest in Italy, measuring 163 yards by 127. The arrangements for housing the wild beasts and presenting them in the arena are interesting; a diversion of the Campanian aqueduct would have supplied the arena with water for the staging of elaborate sea-fights (*naumachiae*). A subterranean chapel to the north of the amphitheatre, constructed in 1689, commemorates the imprisonment here of SS. Gennaro, Procolo and others in 305 under the edict of Constantine against the Christians. It appears that they were not exposed to the wild beasts, but had their sentence commuted to beheading, which took place near by on the Solfatara road.

For Baia we leave Pozzuoli by the Via Roma and its continuation in the Via Miliscola, passing through another dreary industrial area, parallel with the Cumana railway. Shortly after the station for Arco Felice we turn left, and the road runs between the sea and the slopes of Monte Nuovo. A pathway leads up to the summit and down into the crater of this most recent of the Phlegraean volcanoes. Between the years 1536 and 1538 earthquakes became increasingly frequent in the district, culminating in twenty shocks in the course of a single day on September 28th, 1538, when much damage was done to houses in Pozzuoli. Then at two o'clock in the morning of the 29th a terrific explosion opened a cleft between Monte Barbaro and the Lucrine Lake, and from this poured forth mud, ashes and stones which, within a period of only forty-eight hours, formed the mountain we now see.

The emergence of Monte Nuovo diminished the extent of the **Lucrine Lake,** so that its ancient appearance is completely altered. The lake was famous in antiquity for its oysters and for its *lupi*, mentioned by Horace. This fish is the excellent *spigola*, and both oysters and *lupi* still come from the lake, though the opening of a *fumarola* on the eastern shore in 1922 damaged the fishing. Of the many Roman villas which were built in the vicinity the most celebrated was Cicero's, known as the Academia, the remains of which were destroyed in the eruption of Monte Nuovo. Here he wrote several of his books, including the *De Republica*, and at a later date the villa became part of the imperial possessions. The Emperor Hadrian was buried there in AD 138.

To the east of the lake, at the road junction on the right, we may make a short diversion to visit **Lake Avernus.** This region, according to the ancients, was the land of the Cimmerians on whom the sun never shone, where Odysseus landed to conjure up the spirit of old Teiresias; and the earliest Greeks regarded this crater-lake, with its leaden surface and its noxious exhalations which were said to be fatal to all bird life, as the entrance to the under world.

During the struggle between Octavian and Mark Antony, the fleets of Sextus Pompeius held command of the seas, and it was to counter this threat that Octavian's lieutenant, Marcus Agrippa, constructed the system of naval fortifications, stretching from Cumae to Misenum and round the bays of Puteoli and Neapolis, that were one of the wonders of the age. He joined Lakes Avernus and Lucrinus to the sea by a ship-canal, built docks in the former, and had Cocceius construct tunnels to give direct access for the movement of chariots and soldiers between Cumae and Lake Avernus, and between the latter and the sea.

It is difficult today to locate all Agrippa's works. The tunnel in the hill on the south of the lake (now partly blocked and filled with water) was for long erroneously associated with the grotto of the Sibyl. The overgrown ruins of the western side of the lake were possibly the storage and ship-building yards. A little farther on (behind the modern building where refreshments are sold) is the entrance to Cocceius's tunnel which led to Cumae. During the last war this was used as an arms dump, and explosions have rendered it unsafe. It was formerly wide enough for two chariots to pass and was well illuminated by vertical light-shafts. On the eastern shores of the lake stand the ruins of the so-called Temple of Apollo, in reality a great thermal establishment built by the Romans over the mineral and thermal springs which once were plentiful on the spot.

The Baia road skirts the southern shore of the Lucrine Lake; to the left the railway separates us from the *stabilimenti di bagno* which somewhat untidily line the so-called Lido di Napoli. This causeway, part of the Via Herculanea, is held to have been built by Hercules as he returned from successfully completing his tenth labour, driving before him the oxen stolen from Geryon. At the curve of the road a path leads up to one of the many local thermal establishments, the **Stufe di Nerone** (the Stove of Nero), where among the ancient buildings there is a spring whose water rises at a temperature of over 170° F.

All this district between the Lucrine Lake and **Baiae,** as the Romans called it, was once covered with luxurious villas, among them those belonging to Marius, Julius Caesar and Pompey the Great. Eventually, in imperial times, the private villas of nobles and *nouveaux riches* fell almost entirely into the hands of the emperors, and the shoreline and hills about Baiae became virtually one great extended palace. Because of subsidence many of these buildings now lie some hundred yards out in the bay, ten to twelve feet below the present sea-level. Roman writers (Horace among them) praised Baiae for the beauty of its surroundings and the health-giving properties of its waters, but are almost unanimous in their censure of the depravity and extravagance of life there.

It is Nero whose name is most closely associated with ancient Baiae. He started on a project to have a covered bath surrounded by cloisters stretching from Misenum to Lake Avernus, and fed by all the hot springs in the district. Another plan was to build a ship canal from Lake Avernus to Ostia, a distance of 160 miles. Perhaps more

78

practical were the brothels he set up along the coast, each staffed by noblewomen, so that he could land at will. And it was at Baiae that he endeavoured to rid himself of his interfering mother, Agrippina, by drowning her. The attempt failed. She swam ashore. He finally arranged for her to be stabbed at her Lucrine villa, and afterwards arrived to survey the corpse, pointing out to the onlookers (between drinks) the good and bad points of her limbs.

Behind the railway station at the beginning of the town, on our right, stands the so-called Temple of Diana, like a great apse set against the hillside. This is in fact part of the vast complex of thermal baths, porticoes, swimming-pools and recreation rooms constructed at different periods from that of Augustus down to the reign of Alexander Severus (AD 222–34), now known collectively as the *Terme Baiane* (admission, daily 9.0 a.m. until sunset). The entrance may be reached either by the road to the right, leading over the Sella di Baia to Lake Fusaro, or by the footpath and steps to the left of the station. The excavations here have revealed the most extensive thermal establishment left us from antiquity. Detailed plans may be obtained at the entrance; in general plan the Terme consist of four principal sections each with an arcaded swimming-pool or a large hall. Two of these sections lie outside the excavated enclosure—the Temple of Diana, behind the station, and the so-called Temple of Venus, the rotunda to the left of the Baia–Bacoli road. From the Sella di Baia entrance an avenue leads to the third *terme*, known as the Temple of Mercury (from the top of a stairway here we have a splendid view of the baths and the Bay of Pozzuoli). The fourth, the largest and most architectonically integrated of the divisions, is called the Terme di Sosandra, from the marble copy of a Greek bronze of the fifth century BC, found there in 1953.

Bacoli—Cumae—the Sibyl's cave—Solfataro—Agnano and a modern thermal establishment

Leaving the picturesque little port and town of Baia, we climb the hill to the imposing landmark of the *Castello di Baia,* built in the sixteenth century by the great viceroy Pedro de Toledo against the corsairs. Today it is an orphanage, and permission to visit it may be obtained from the director. From the beginning of the ramp which leads up to the gateway there is a fine view of the coast towards Misenum. (The posts which one sees in the water off the foreshore all along the bay are for oyster culture.)

From Baia we go on to **Bacoli** (it is uncertain whether this is in fact the ancient Bacoli), and at the entrance to the town the Via Agrippina leads down on the left to a little port and the erroneously called Tomb of Agrippina. This is in fact a small odeon, possibly part of a Roman villa. Bacoli itself is a rambling town built on a hill overlooking the sea, the Lake and Bay of Misenum and the cape of the same name. It is best to leave one's car by the cab rank and public gardens, where the road splits to encircle Lake Misenum, and to take the steps on the left that lead up to the *Piscina Mirabile*, one of the most impressive remains of Roman waterworks. (The key to the gate is at the house just before the entrance; tip.)

The Piscina Mirabile was built as a reservoir, fed by the Augustan aqueduct, to supply the fleet at Misenum. (The latter port superseded the Portus Julius, whose channel early began to silt up.) Steps lead down to a subterranean building that has all the majesty of a great basilican cathedral. It is composed of five main aisles crossed at right-angles by thirteen others, and apertures in the vaulting allow the light to filter through hanging ferns and ivy.

From the gateway we turn right and go north up the Via Piscina Mirabile and its continuation, the Via A. Greco, to the parish church of S. Anna. At this point the Via Cento Camerelle brings us to the ruins of what was possibly the villa of Quintus Hortensius, the orator and friend of Cicero. It is called *Cento Camerelle* from the number of small rooms (some probably cisterns), which on two levels formed part of one of the most famous of all Baian villas. Later it became the property of Drusus's wife Antonina (who kept a pet eel with gold ear-rings), and from her the villa passed to Nero.

From the public gardens a road leads due south along the causeway which now separates the Lake from the Bay of Misenum. The naval port constructed by Agrippa in 41 BC consisted of the port proper in the bay and a shelter in the lake (also called the Mare Morto) which was entered by a canal. Beyond the causeway a road forks left to the village of **Miseno**, ancient Misenum. Besides having some interesting ruins (Marius had a villa on the promontory, later owned by Lucullus), Miseno is the starting-point for the rather arduous climb to the summit of the cape, with its magnificent view of the whole Bay of Naples.

The road to the right runs past the bathing establishments of the Spiaggia di Miliscola (a corruption of *Militis Schola*), skirts the western shore of Lake Misenum and then bears left for the village of Cappella in the wine-producing valley between Monte Grillo and Monte dei Selvatici. About a mile beyond Cappella we can turn left

Above The Via dell' Abbondanza, one of the main streets of Pompeii.

Below The Samnite Temple of Apollo. The statue of the god is a copy of that now in the Museo Nazionale, Naples. In the background, still smoking, the cause of the catastrophe: Vesuvius.

Below A fountain with a figure of Concordia Augusta holding a horn of plenty, from which the street takes its modern name.

Above Remains of the Greek city of Paestum. *Right*, the Doric Basilica, the earliest temple (*ca* 565 BC); *left*, the Temple of Poseidon, built a century later, the most perfect specimen of Doric temple architecture in existence. *Below* A delicate marble group showing a stag at bay from the so-called House of the Deer, one of Herculaneum's largest and finest houses.

to the small seaside village of Torregaveta, the terminus of the Cumana railway. (There is not much to recommend this as a bathing resort.) From here a winding road leads up through vineyards, among which are many ruins of Roman villas, to the little town of Monte di Procida, with splendid views over the Strait towards the islands of Procida and Ischia. The more indefatigable may descend from the town to the tiny bay of Acquamorta and visit the Scoglio di S. Martino.

Those who prefer to omit the diversion may take the right-hand fork at the junction beyond Cappella for the **Lago di Fusaro,** known to the ancients as the Acherusian Swamp, and renowned through the ages for its shellfish. The eccentric Ferdinand I and IV had Vanvitelli build him in 1782 a little casino in the lake near the eastern shore, now a marine biological station. The King used to auction his catch personally to his delighted subjects in Naples. The road skirts the eastern shores of the lake, where it meets that from the Sella di Baia, and continues roughly in a northerly direction to a junction, the Trivio di Cuma, with the road from Pozzuoli. A few hundred yards before the junction, as the road makes rather a sharp bend between vineyards and orchards, a gate on the right brings us in sight of the remains of the amphitheatre of **Cumae.**

The site of ancient Cumae (Greek *Kyme*) is now obscured by the peach orchards and vineyards which stretch northwards beyond the drained Lake of Licola, part of a great scheme of land-reclamation which has converted what were the royal hunting preserves into a luxuriant garden. To the right we see the narrow archway of the ***Arco Felice,*** built by the Emperor Diocletian when he constructed the coast road which takes his name, from the point where the Via Appia turns inland after crossing the River Garigliano, to give more rapid access to Pozzuoli and Misenum. And on the left, a rocky eminence rising abruptly from the plain, is the ***Monte di Cuma,*** the original acropolis of Kyme.

Although the traditional date for the founding of Cumae by migrants from Chalis and Kyme in Euboea is given as 1050 BC, thus making it the oldest Greek settlement in the western seas, there is in fact no proof that it was founded before Naxos and Syracuse, which date from 754 and 753 BC. However, it was the Cumaeans who introduced the use of their Chalcidian alphabet from which the Roman lettering is derived, and who, during the seventh and sixth centuries BC, dominated the whole Phlegraean region.

In 421 BC Cumae fell to the Samnites and later, with the rest of Campania, to the Romans. Unlike Capua, she remained faithful to

Rome against Hannibal, but as Pozzuoli rose in importance under the empire, she became something of a backwater, and was finally destroyed by the Saracens. Thenceforth the caverns and tunnels of the acropolis became dens of outlaws, robbers and pirates, until they were finally extirpated by the forces of Naples and Aversa led by Goffredo di Montefoscole in 1207. Even the locality of the grotto of the Cumaean Sibyl was forgotten, buried under debris and tangled vegetation.

A short way beyond the Trivio di Cuma a road on the left (opposite a ruin known, with little authority, as the Tomb of the Sibyl) brings us up to the entrance to the excavations of the **acropolis of Cumae** (admission, daily 9.0 a.m.–4.0 p.m. winter; 9.0 a.m. –5.0 p.m. summer). A path flanked by oleanders ascends to the entrance of the acropolis itself. On the right is some of the original stonework of the walls, the lower courses of which are Greek, the upper Roman. A tunnel hewn in the tufaceous rock traverses the hill and leads us to the **cave of the Cumaean Sibyl** (on the left), and opposite it, to a yawning chasm, at the bottom of which is the vestibule of the Roman crypt. Two stone inscriptions quote Virgil's description of the spot.

The evidence indicates that this cave, excavated only in 1932, is indeed that of the Sibyl. It consists of a trapezoidal-shaped corridor (*dromos*), 144 yds long, 8 ft wide and about 16 ft in height, similar to Mycenaean structures. Lateral openings on the western (sea) side give light to the *dromos* and to the galleries off it to the left, which are possibly of later, Roman, construction, and were used first as cisterns and later for Christian tombs. The *dromos* may have been cut as early as the sixth or fifth century BC, but the end room (the *oikos endótatos*), the holy of holies, where the Sibyl, possessed by the *numen*, uttered her cryptic prophecies, appears to have been enlarged and altered possibly two hundred years later.

A pathway leads down to the entrance of the vast Roman crypt, which was bored right through the Monte di Cuma from west to east and then carried on to make a turn to the right, which would place it on the axis of the tunnel built for Augustus by Cocceius to connect Cumae with Lake Avernus; a stupendous work for that time. Christian symbols (the palm, crown and crosses) carved in the walls show that this was used as a kind of catacomb by the early Christian community here.

Another pathway beside the Sibyl's cave leads up through the trees, forming a Via Sacra to the temples on the top of the acropolis. Half way up, on the right, is the **Temple of Apollo** which appears to have been of the Graeco-Samnite period, transformed in the sixth or seventh century AD into a Christian basilica. Farther on, the Via Sacra brings us to the **Temple of Jupiter,** built in a most beautiful position on the summit of the hill. This, too, was originally Greek (possibly fifth century BC), then rebuilt in Augustan times, and later also converted in the fifth or sixth century for use as a Christian church. The large circular piscina for baptism by immersion has survived almost complete.

Here, on the acropolis of Cumae we can hear the waves breaking on the shore where Aeneas beached his ships, and in the vineyards I have seen the vines being pruned and tended with implements which would have been familiar to the author of the *Georgics*.

From the Trivio di Cuma we take the road which leads up under the Arco Felice, where some of the original paving of Domitian's road remains, and over the crest of the hill we see below us on the right Lake Avernus and the Bay of Pozzuoli. Shortly after, we join the Via Domiziana Nuova which brings us quickly to the outskirts of Pozzuoli. At the Quadrivio dell' Annunziata we take the Corso Terracciano, pass the Flavian amphitheatre, and bear left in the Via Solfatara. After climbing gently for less than a mile we come to the semi-extinct volcano, the **Solfatara di Pozzuoli,** the entrance to which is on the left of the road. (Admission, 9.0 a.m. until sunset. A guide is obligatory. In summer the crater is sometimes illuminated in the evening.)

This volcano, whose elliptical crater measures some half a mile across at its widest, was known to the Romans as Forum Vulcani. Areas of its arid, lunar-like surface are hot and ring hollow beneath our tread; elsewhere it is broken by *fumarole*, jets of steam and sulphurous vapours that issue with great force emitting a sibilant sound; some of them (for example, the so-called Bocca Grande) reach temperatures as high as 350° F. Other cavities—known as *mofete*—exude hot mud and gases.

Shortly after the entrance to the Solfatara, on the other side of the road, a little piazza planted with holm-oaks leads to the church of **S. Gennaro,** with its attached Capuchin monastery, built in the sixteenth century on the traditional site of the Saint's martyrdom. Inside, in the first chapel on the right, is a stone which was splashed with the blood of S. Gennaro, and which is said miraculously to turn bright red at the time when the liquefaction takes place in Naples (see p. 52).

The road now runs along the flanks of Monte Spina and affords some splendid views. These hills above Bagnoli were called by the ancients the Colles Leucogaei, from the white earth which was used for bleaching barley. At the Quadrivio di Agnano the Via Domiziana curves right, and on our left is the road to the Ippodromo di Agnano (the racecourse). A little to the east of this another, older road, the Strada Comunale degli Astroni, leads to the **Terme Agnano**, the thermal establishment (the property of the State) built near the ruins of Roman baths on the site of the extinct volcanic crater of Agnano. In the eleventh century the crater became a lake, but this was drained in the 1860's by means of a tunnel through Monte Spina to the sea. The Terme, which are housed in Victorian buildings, are undergoing some reconstruction. In the Gran Salone and passages off it are statues found near by in the Roman baths. To the north-east of the main buildings are various springs and the curious cavity which emits the hot (rather smelly) mud (*fanghiera*) for the baths.

Opposite the main entrance to the Terme are the six-storeyed ruins of the Roman baths, the **Termae Anianae** (apply for admission at the office of the Terme). These are built into the hillside of Monte Spina, and were in active use from Roman times until the fifteenth century. The infamous **Grotta del Cane,** mentioned by Pliny, has now been closed to the public. In this deep cave carbon dioxide covered the floor to a height of some two feet—lighted torches held in it would be instantly extinguished, and unfortunate dogs were used to demonstrate its noxious effects.

Returning to the Quadrivio di Agnano, the Via Domiziana takes us past the Mostra d'Oltremare in Fuorigrotta, then through the tunnel to Chiaia and back to the centre of Naples.

CHAPTER 6

The Environs of Naples:
Vesuvius, Herculaneum and Pompeii

Maps: The Environs of Naples, pp.72–3; Herculaneum, p.89;
Pompeii, p.96

Since 1944 visitors to Naples have missed the characteristic plume of
smoke rising above the cone of **Mount Vesuvius.** Twenty years of
quiescence have blurred memories of the terror that periodic
eruptions aroused in the inhabitants of Naples and of the towns and
villages which cluster round the volcano's luxuriant foothills.
Vesuvius's appearance today is of a truncated cone; from east and
west the ancient crater appears as a saddle separating the two
highest points, Monte Somma to the north, from a smaller cone,
Vesuvius proper, to the south. It may have been the catastrophe
of AD 79, which overwhelmed Pompeii, Stabiae and Herculaneum, that accounted for the complete blowing-out of the central
section.

Before that date the sides of Vesuvius were cultivated with vines—
Vesuvian wine was famous—right to the lip of the crater, which was
covered with trees and scrub, the haunt of wild boars. A violent
earthquake in AD 63, which did much damage to the cities round the
Bay of Naples, heralded the eruption, but no one heeded it. Ten
years later Spartacus and his rebel slaves and band of gladiators
from Capua found an excellent refuge there from the Roman force
of 3000 men, under Clodius Pulcher, sent to root them out. Pulcher
placed his men to guard what he thought was the only exit, but
Spartacus had rope ladders plaited from the wild vines and, descending the precipitous slopes unseen, he fell on the Roman troops and
destroyed them.

A visit to Herculaneum may be combined conveniently with the
ascent of Vesuvius, but the excavations at Pompeii are far more

extensive and require at least an entire day. However, both towns may be reached from Naples by the Circumvesuviana railway, which leaves from the station in the Corso Garibaldi. Passengers descend at Pugliano-Resina for Herculaneum, and at Pompeii-Villa dei Misteri for Pompeii. Tourist agencies run frequent coach services, and for Herculaneum the ATAN bus No. 255 leaves every ten minutes from the Piazza del Municipio, and allows you to alight at Portici on the way. By car there is a choice of the autostrada or the SS 18. The latter is full of interest, and in spite of heavy traffic, this is the road we shall follow.

Portici—the Palazzo Reale—Vesuvius

The SS 18 leaves Naples by the quayside, along the Via Nuova della Marina and the Via della Marinella, and we get some idea of the poverty in which many of the Neapolitans still live from the hut-encampments (*baracche*) which are here so obvious. Through the populous industrial area of S. Giovanni a Teduccio, the dreary buildings obscure both sea and mountain until we draw near to **Portici.** In the eighteenth century the sea coast and the foothills of Vesuvius were adorned with charming villas of the Neapolitan aristocracy, partly because of the beauty and salubriousness of the place, but also to be near the King's palace at Portici.

In 1738 Charles of Bourbon, visiting the villa of the Prince of Elboeuf, was so taken with the site that he ordered Medrano to design him the **Palazzo Reale.** When his courtiers pointed to possible dangers from the proximity of Vesuvius, he is said to have replied, 'God, Mary Immaculate and S. Gennaro will see to that.' Yet, on the principle of trusting to God and keeping your powder dry, he did consult the best scientific opinion of the day, and subsequent lava flows have never reached the palace.

From the centre of the town of Portici the Via Università, as the road becomes here, rises gently between some interesting eighteenth- and early nineteenth-century villas with large gardens behind, and the two imposing barracks of the Royal Guard, and enters the octagonal courtyard-piazza around which the palace is built. To the right is the main entrance to the Faculty of Agriculture of Naples University, which has occupied the building since 1873. Visitors may apply to the porter for permission to see some of the former state rooms, with their decorations of the *settecento* and the time of Murat.

On the side of the building towards the sea is a terrace with a balustrade surmounted by sculptured busts. Before the war this stretch of the coast was a delightful place to wander in, but now new buildings have greatly altered the environs of Portici and Resina. However, some of the eighteenth-century country houses still remain—the Villa Elboeuf, the Villa Caravita, the Villa Meola and, on the 'Golden Mile' beyond Resina, so called from its *settecento* splendour, the royal residence of La Favorita.

In the centre of Resina, on the right, is the entrance to the excavations of Herculaneum. But for **Vesuvius** we shall turn left—just before the entrance—and take the narrow, crowded, colourful street which leads up to the autostrada and the station of Pugliano-Resina. Buses meet the Circumvesuviana trains and run from the station to the Stazione Seggiovia, high on the flank of Vesuvius, where a chair-lift takes visitors to the crater. The Vesuvius road begins near the exit-entrance to the Naples–Salerno autostrada. There are other roads to the summit, but the Pugliano road is more convenient for travellers from Naples.

The road climbs rapidly through olive groves and vineyards, which produce the well-known Lacrima Christi. The lava-flows eventually decompose into soil of extraordinary fertility, as we can see from the luxuriant vegetation around us. The first plant to gain a hold is the broom (*spartium junceum*), known here as 'the ginestra of Leopardi', from the famous poem *La Ginestra*, written in 1836 or '37 when the poet was a guest of Antonio Ranieri at a villa at the foot of Vesuvius. Past the church of S. Vito we cross the lava fields of 1767 and of 1858–60, leaving vegetation behind us as we enter this lunar world of volcanic slag heaps. To our right stretches the Piano delle Ginestre, and the curving road affords magnificent views over the whole expanse of the Bay of Naples. At the Trattoria da Rosa we can turn off to the right for the Albergo Eremo and the ***Osservatorio Vesuviano.*** This observatory was built by Ferdinand II in 1841 to enable volcanological studies to be carried out on the spot. Its position on a spur has saved it from the lava-flows. In 1872 the director, Luigi Palmieri, remained at his post during a violent eruption, and the reassuring messages he sent down prevented panic in the threatened towns below.

Returning to the road, we continue our ascent. On our left towards Monte Somma we can see the strange shapes formed in the huge hollow by the lava of 1944. At the crossroads, the road to the left, the **Strada Matrone Occidentale,** leads by the Colle Margherita, with views over the desolate Valley of the Giant, to the spot where we pick up the obligatory guides for the crater. The road to the right leads to the Stazione Inferiore della Seggiovia, where a chair-lift conveys you in six minutes of aerial trepidation, compensated for by the splendour of the view, to the beginning of the short path to the summit. Guides are again obligatory. It is an awe-inspiring sight, this huge well—600 ft deep and more than 600 yds across—which is the crater of Vesuvius. At the moment only steam issuing from some *fumarole* shows that the volcano is still active.

On our way down we may stop at the Eremo for lunch. There are small restaurants at Resina (and at the Albergo Ercolano, at Pugliano, on the Vesuvius road), but those near the excavations, although I have enjoyed my meals there, are perhaps too 'characteristic' for all tastes. And at the Eremo we can turn our backs on the gloomy Gustave Doré world of Vulcan and enjoy the unbelievable beauty of the scene below us.

Herculaneum

A visit to Vesuvius can bring us very close to the fearful catastrophe of August 24th, AD 79, which destroyed Herculaneum and Pompeii. At **Herculaneum,** however, it seems likely that almost all the citizens escaped; very few skeletons have been found there. But the town was overwhelmed by an avalanche of volcanic mud which covered it to a depth of some forty feet, and in 1631 a lava flow buried it still deeper, which has made excavation here infinitely more difficult than at Pompeii, since the mud entered everywhere and solidified into tufa. From the car park (admission to the excavation, daily 9.0 a.m.–4.0 p.m.) we look on to what was the town wall facing the ancient port. The sea has since retreated, but the luxurious villas which were built on the wall allowed their inhabitants a then uninterrupted view over the bay. The idyllic position of Herculaneum, a small town of some 4000–5000 inhabitants, made it an ideal place for secluded retirement or *villeggiatura*.

The name Herculaneum (Greek *Herakleion*) is derived from its legendary foundation by Hercules, but whatever its origin, it came under Greek influence from Cumae and Neapolis as early as the sixth century BC, and retained this Greekness throughout its history. Together with the other coastal towns, it fell to the Samnites at the end of the fifth century, and in 307 BC was taken by the Romans. In the revolt of the Italic cities against Rome, Herculaneum was

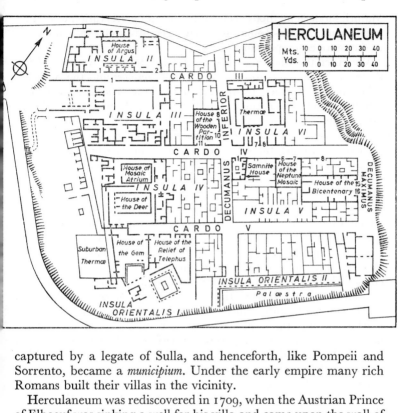

captured by a legate of Sulla, and henceforth, like Pompeii and Sorrento, became a *municipium*. Under the early empire many rich Romans built their villas in the vicinity.

Herculaneum was rediscovered in 1709, when the Austrian Prince of Elboeuf was sinking a well for his villa and came upon the wall of the stage of the Roman theatre. He cut shafts in the tufa, and found a quantity of precious marbles and statues. Charles of Bourbon took over the excavation soon after his accession, and between 1738 and 1765 archaeologists located the forum, the basilica and parts of the city we see today, and also the magnificent *Villa of the Papyri* near by (so called from the discovery there of the Epicurean papyri, now in the Biblioteca Nazionale in Naples). Many of the statues in bronze and marble in the Naples Museum come from this villa; but unfortunately the building itself was not uncovered and the shafts and tunnels were later filled in. In 1755 the Reale Accademia Ercolanese was founded, and produced eight volumes on the mural paintings, bronzes and other works of art discovered in Herculaneum. After several attempts in the last century, systematic digging was finally begun in 1927. Under the direction of the late Amedeo

89

Maiuri, modern methods of classification and preservation were used and a small Graeco-Roman town emerged, dissimilar in many ways to the more cosmopolitan Pompeii.

We enter the excavations by cardo III, the most westerly of the three cardinal streets to be cleared. (The *cardines* and the blocks—called *insulae*—formed by the crossing of the *decumani*, have been numbered, as well as the individual houses. Roman numerals are used for the *insulae* and Arabic for the houses.) On our left (II, 1–2) is the patrician **House of Argus**. From the handsome peristyle we can see in the tufa-face one of the tunnels which led to the Villa of the Papyri. Opposite (III, 1) is another patrician house, which must originally have been one of the most magnificent in the town.

Crossing the *decumanus inferior*, on our right are the **Town Baths**, which occupy half the entire insula VI. One of the two entrances to the men's section is a little way up the street (VI, 1). Men and women bathed separately, and the women's entrance is in cardo IV (VI, 8), next door to the second entrance for the men (VI, 7). A corridor brings us to the *palaestra*, with porticoes on three sides. On the left is the entrance to the men's changing-room (*apodyterium*), barrel-vaulted in fluted stucco with a floor of white, black and grey marble. Around three sides are seats and shelves for clothes; at the farther end, in an apse, is a *cipollino* basin or *labrum* for washing. A door to the left of the apse brings us to the circular *frigidarium* with a domed vault, painted to represent the sea-bottom, which would have been reflected in the transparent pale green of the bath, so that bathers had the illusion of being in a fishpond. On the farther side of the *apodyterium* we pass to the *tepidarium*, with a mosaic floor depicting Triton, a rudder in his hand, surrounded by dolphins, amorini, octopuses and fish; and thence to the *calidarium*, which has the customary plunge-bath, and a shell-shaped apse for another *labrum* of cold water. The women's section, though smaller, is similar in lay-out but is better preserved. These baths were built *ca.* 10 BC, but the decoration is somewhat later, possibly from the time of Nero.

In cardo IV, at the intersection with the *decumanus inferior*, stands the **Samnite House** (V, 1), architecturally one of the most interesting houses in Herculaneum. Here we can see some of the transformations of the earlier type of Italic house to meet the changed conditions of urban life. As in many other Herculaneum houses a further storey was added, possibly to lodge the servants, or more likely, to let to tenants. The height of the *atrium* (the square central court) has been raised by the addition of a blind gallery with elegant columns and balustrade of diamond trellis-work which seems to foreshadow the loggias of Renaissance palaces. In a number of instances (e.g. the **House of the Wooden Partition** (III, 8, 10, 11) and the **House of the Neptune Mosaic** (V, 6–7)) parts of the earlier house have been adapted to be let as shops. The *atrium* and peristyle (the colonnaded courtyard behind it) became restricted in area and served as light-wells to several self-contained flats, or simply as courtyards with stairs giving access to the flats on the first floor. In the *insula orientalis* (between cardo V and the *palaestra*) this architectural rationalism has been carried to its logical conclusion; the whole block appears to have been constructed of shops and workrooms on the ground floor, with small flats on the upper storey, similar in plan to the large-scale buildings of the imperial age in Ostia and Rome.

Both in the grander houses and in the more modest family rooms behind the shop we can see something of the sophisticated simplicity of life in ancient Herculaneum—in the frescoed rooms, the mosaics, the *nymphaea*, the enclosed courts and gardens, and the elegance of furniture, glass and jewellery—and we can imagine the presence everywhere of sculpture and delicate bronze work. But nowhere can we better recapture the leisurely refinement, the *dulce otium* of the rich, than in the four splendid houses built high on the bastions above the Marine Gate and the Suburban Baths—the **Houses of the Mosaic Atrium** (IV, 1, 2), **of the Deer** (IV, 21), **of the Gem** (*insula orientalis*, 1), and **of the Relief of Telephus** (*insula orientalis*, 2–3). Everything here is planned to exploit the advantage of the position on the walls, which themselves were built on the high ground overlooking the ancient port. But the sea has now retreated, so that it is only in imagination that we can picture the perfection of the original setting.

These villas show the architectural development of the Italic *domus* in conjunction with Hellenistic innovations, to produce a sophisticated dwelling. In the peristyle (which has sometimes become a windowed colonnade) were gardens, fountains and fish-ponds; off it were rooms designed to catch the sunlight and views of the sea. The terraces which completed the house on the sea side were formed into gardens, trellised loggias and rest-rooms.

Beneath these houses were the **Suburban Baths,** which have recently been excavated. Flooding from underground waters made this a difficult task, but pumps now keep the water in check. Behind them, on the east of the town, was the colonnaded *palaestra*, with a *crypto-portico* and loggia entered from the end of the *decumanus maximus* on the south of the still unexcavated forum.

At the farther end of the *decumanus maximus* recent digging has revealed the **Sacello degli Augustali,** the shrine of the official college of the cult of the imperial house. Vespasian had shown his patronage of the town in helping with its restoration after the earthquake of AD 63. However, it is essentially in its private dwellings that Herculaneum shows itself with such particular secluded intimacy—more so, in this respect, than Pompeii. This may be affected partly by our knowledge that fewer inhabitants met a violent death here; partly by the appearance of the houses, almost as if ready to receive their owners, with so many objects and domestic furnishings preserved (for instance, the beautiful beds and the very bed-covers). And upstairs in a room in the **House of the Bicentenary**—so called because it was excavated in 1938, two hundred years after the excavations began—there remains in the stucco a shape of a cross, possibly from a wooden one which once stood there. Below it is a kind of cupboard with a footstool, a primitive *prie-dieu*. This is thought to be the first evidence of the early use of the cross as a Christian symbol. It may have been the shrine of the first local Christians, for St Paul made converts at Pozzuoli when he landed there on his way to Rome in AD 61, eighteen years before the destruction of Herculaneum.

For visitors who wish to follow in more detail the fascinating results of these recent excavations—and also those of Pompeii—I can strongly recommend the little guides written by the late Amedeo Maiuri and published by the Italian State Bookshop.

Pompeii

Pompeii was a town of Oscan foundation of perhaps as early as the eighth century BC. Some time later it came under Hellenic influence from Cumae and Neapolis. Evidence of this is found in the remains of a Doric temple of the sixth century BC. After successive occupation by the Etruscans and the Samnites and an unwilling alliance with Rome, Pompeii sided with the Italic towns against Rome in the Social War, and successfully withstood a siege by Sulla in 89 BC, until after nine years the citizens had had enough of the struggle and opened their gates to him. A colony of Roman veterans was planted there, and from then on the town was increasingly Romanized, though many of the earlier elements in Pompeian culture seem to have been still strong at the time of the city's destruction—some of the *graffiti* are written in Oscan characters, and the scales for establishing the official weights and measures have been found in the forum, with the measurements inscribed in both Oscan and Latin.

Pompeii was a prosperous industrial and trading centre, built on the edge of a prehistoric lava-flow near the entrance of the River Sarno to the Bay of Naples. The city was roughly ovoid in shape, and was enclosed in a strong system of walls and towers. One export was a popular brand of fish-sauce, and the wine trade was also important. In its latter days Pompeii, like Herculaneum, became a resort for rich Romans. The life led there must have in many ways resembled that described by Petronius in his *Satiricon*; the population was cosmopolitan, pleasure-loving and volatile.

Of the fatal eruption of AD 79 we have an eye-witness's account in Pliny's famous letter to Tacitus, in which he describes how his uncle, Pliny the Elder, in command of the Roman fleet stationed at Misenum, took the triremes on a rescue expedition to the coastal towns directly below Vesuvius, and how he met his death at Stabiae, asphyxiated by the fumes.

About the middle of August, earth tremors were felt in Pompeii and in the towns around the Bay of Naples, and after the 20th these increased in intensity and frequency. On August 22nd they ceased. The sky was blue and cloudless; there was no wind to temper the sun's heat, and the air had a strange foreboding stillness, so that oxen stirred uneasily in their stalls and dogs howled for no apparent reason. The sea's surface at times became ruffled, unaccountably large waves breaking along the shore. The morning of the 24th was very hot, but the sky was serene and fears had subsided. The inhabitants went about their daily tasks and were preparing for lunch when a severe shock followed by what seemed like a terrific clap of thunder made everyone turn in the direction of Vesuvius. It looked as if the top of the mountain had burst open and was pouring forth glowing fire. The conflagration died down, and a large mushroom-shaped cloud of black smoke (Pliny likened it to a pine tree) quickly formed above the summit. Then began a series of explosions, each detonation hurling huge boulders high into the sky, where they disintegrated. Suddenly it began to rain, and mixed with the rain were cinders, small pumice stones, lumps of larger rock and dust which quickly turned to mud. Birds plummeted to earth. In a matter of minutes the sun was obscured and the bright day turned to blackest night, lit only by the lurid flashes of successive explosions. The darkness, Pliny wrote, 'was not as on a moonless and clouded night, but as in a completely sealed room'. The sea was in turmoil, retreating, then flooding in, with huge waves which pounded and inundated the coastline.

It was the hail of pumice stones and mud, followed by cinders and ashes, that buried Pompeii with such astounding rapidity. When rifts in the pall which overhung the countryside allowed a gradual return of daylight, only the roofs of the highest houses that had not collapsed under the weight showed above the white blanket of debris. Of the 20,000 inhabitants of Pompeii, more than 2,000 lost their lives in the town. Poignant evidence of their death-throes from suffocation or poisoning from the noxious vapours can be seen in the Pompeii Museum and in private houses, such as that of the Crypto-portico, for as the bodies decomposed, their original shapes were left as cavities in their beds of volcanic matter. When liquid plaster of Paris was poured into these moulds, remarkable casts were obtained. It is not known how many perished outside the walls in the darkness and confusion. Huge crevices were formed by the earthquakes, one large enough to swallow a flock of 600 sheep. The exhalations and fumes were lethal.

By the sixteenth century the site of Pompeii had become com-pletely obliterated—its position was much disputed by scholars—and although some marbles and coins, and even inscriptions with the name 'Pompeii' were turned up from time to time, it was not until 1748 that the archaeologist Mazzocchi proposed to the King that excavations be carried out; by great good fortune, within a week the workmen lighted on a fresco of garlands of fruit, flowers and vine-leaves. From that time the work has gone on, so that today more than half of the city has been laid bare.

The excavations are open daily from 9 a.m. until an hour before sunset. It is cheaper before 3 o'clock, but some buildings are closed on Sundays. From June 1st until September 30th it is also open from 8.0–11.0 p.m., and floodlit. English-speaking guides may be engaged by those who can support their patter, but a much better course is to buy Amedeo Maiuri's *Pompeii* which gives a wealth of fascinating detail. Incidentally, the custodians of those houses which are kept locked are supposed to open them free of charge, but a small tip is often welcome. It is well to remember that there is very little shade in Pompeii, and to plan one's visit accordingly. It can be very hot indeed.

The Environs of Naples: Herculaneum and Pompeii

Nowhere has archaeological excavation revealed more details of ancient life than in Pompeii. Some 20,000 *graffiti*, painted or scratched on walls, give us a most graphic and intimate picture of life at the time of Vespasian and Titus; schoolboys, prostitutes, soldiers, travellers, slaves and lovers have recorded their comments. The ithyphallus, too, is much in evidence in Pompeii—not merely a sign of physical love, but of the regenerative powers of Nature, and as such central to the rites of the Orphic Mysteries, the initiation ceremonies of which can be seen in the wonderful frescoes in the Villa of the Mysteries outside the Herculanean Gate. (The Senate's prohibition of these Dionysiac excesses seems to have been ignored here.) The phallus was also regarded as a charm to ward off the evil eye, as it still is in Naples. Other drawings illustrate industrial and commercial life or show scenes from the gladiatorial combats in the amphitheatre.

The itinerary which I suggest can be completed in a little more than two hours, but it would be wiser to allow considerably longer. However, it has the advantage of passing *en route* the well-equipped Posto di Restoro in the Via del Foro (Reg. VII, V), where a pleasant stop may be made.

Inside the Porta Marina, on the right, is the **Antiquarium** or Museum, where the exhibits allow us to follow the successive stages and sources of influence in the development of Pompeii. The Via della Marina leads up to the **Forum.** Next to the museum are the remains of the **Temple of Venus Physica Pompeiana,** which had suffered badly in the earthquake of AD 63 and was being repaired at the time of the final catastrophe. And beyond it stands the **Basilica,** the law-court. To the north, flanking the left side of the forum, is the **Temple of Apollo,** a Samnite building surrounded by a portico. The statues of Apollo and Diana are copies of those in the Naples Museum.

At the northern end of the forum stood the **Temple of Jupiter,** or the Capitolium, once flanked by two triumphal arches. The remaining three sides of the forum were enclosed by a colonnade of tufa faced with travertine, supporting a gallery for spectators of the shows which were held there before the amphitheatre was built. In front of the colonnade stood statues; the bases of some remain. On the west side, in the middle, rises the orator's tribune. To the right of the Temple of Jupiter is the *macellum*, the public market and business centre. Next to it (Reg. VII, VIII, 3) is the **Temple of the Lares,** then the **Temple of Vespasian** (VII, IX, 2), and on the corner of the Via dell' Abbondanza, one of the city's two *decumani*,

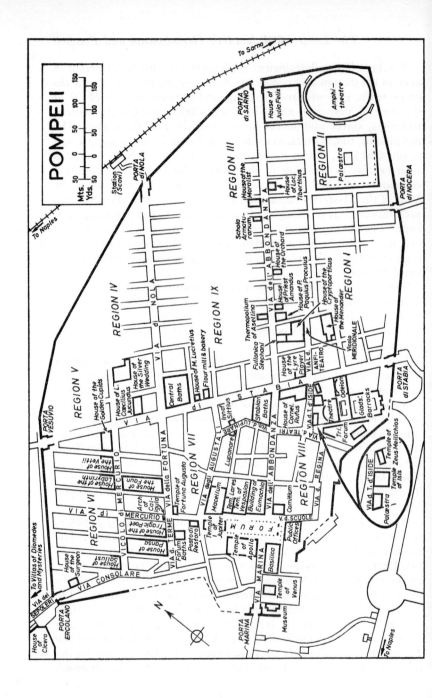

is the **Building of Eumachia,** built by the priestess Eumachia and dedicated to Concordia Augusta and Pietas; at the back of the building stood the statue of Eumachia now in Naples.

On the southern corner of the Via dell' Abbondanza is the *comitium* or municipal polling-booth. The forum is bounded on the south by public offices—the buildings for the town council, the mayors and the *aediles*. From here the Via delle Scuole runs south to the Via della Regina (on the left), with a fine view over the Valle del Sarno towards the Monti Lattari. At No. 23 Via della Regina is a small private *bagno* with a *palaestra* attached. At the end of the street we arrive at the Via dei Teatri, where on the right is the entrance to the **Triangular Forum,** through an Ionic portico. A Doric colonnade surrounds this triangular piazza, with its ruins of a sixth-century Doric temple, possibly dedicated to Hercules. Next door to the entrance to the forum, towards the Via del Tempio d'Iside, is the **Samnite Palaestra,** where the golden youth of Pompeii exercised. Here on a plinth on the south side stood the famous copy of Polycleitus's *Doryphoros*, removed now to Naples.

Much of the block to the south of this is occupied by the two theatres, and what was originally a grand foyer to them, later converted to the **Gladiators' Barracks.** In these barracks were found the gladiatorial arms in the Naples Museum, and sixty-three skeletons, one of which was of a woman whose rich jewellery suggests that she was there on a visit to her gladiator lover. The larger theatre, the **Teatro Scoperto,** which could hold 5000 spectators, was begun in the second century BC and added to under Augustus. An awning or *velarium* protected the audience from the sun. The **Teatro Coperto** (*ca.* 80 BC) was roofed in, and could seat 1000 persons. This may be entered from the Via Stabiana, one of the city's main *cardines*. We reach it by way of the Via del Tempio d'Iside, passing on the right the **Temple of Isis.**

On the corner of the Via del Tempio d'Iside and the Via Stabiana is the little **Temple of Zeus Meilichios** (Jupiter the Gracious), a Greek cult thought to have come from Sicily. From the Via Stabiana we turn right into the Via dell' Anfiteatro (Reg. I, III–IV). But first we should visit the elegant **House of the Lyre Player** (Reg. I, IV, 5) whose entrance is in the Via Stabiana. In this quarter were many houses of the upper classes. The Street of the Amphitheatre leads into the Vicolo Meridionale. On the left (Reg. I, IV, 15) is the **House of L. Ceius Secundus,** and next door is the back entrance to the fine **House of the Cryptoporticus** (Reg. I, VI, 2). Opposite (Reg. I, X, 4) is the imposing **House of the Menander,** where in 1930 was discovered the wonderful collection of silver plate to be seen in the Naples Museum.

We turn left at the end of the Vicolo Meridionale in the street between the House of the Cryptoporticus and the *House of P. Paquius Proculus* (Reg. I, VII, 1). The latter house (which is entered from the Via dell' Abbondanza), has, as befits the dwelling of one of Pompeii's leading citizens, some fine mosaic work.

Work on the Regions we are now entering was begun in 1911 and is not yet complete; but they are fascinating for the picture they give us of ancient life. As far as possible, the buildings are now left as they were, with the objects recovered placed *in situ*. (The numbering is being altered, and consequently some numbers given here may have been changed.) The Via dell' Abbondanza ends to the east at the Porta di Sarno. Opposite the House of P. Paquius Proculus is the *Thermopolium of Asellina* (Reg. IX, X), a tavern for the sale of hot food and drink. Farther on, to the south, the *House of the Priest Amandus* (Reg. I, VII, 7) has some paintings of the third Pompeian style. There follow middle-class houses and shops, many of great interest. The *House of the Orchard* (Reg. I, IX, 5) is an upper-class dwelling, named after the wall decorations in the bedrooms. On the left is the *Schola Armaturarum* (Reg. III, III, 6), the headquarters of a military body. Farther on, also on the north side of the street, is the *House of the Moralist* (Reg. III, IV, 2–3), so called after the maxims painted in the dining-room.

Beyond, on the right, is the fine patrician *House of Loreius Tiburtinus* (Reg. II, II, 5), with its charming garden. Farther along, on the same side, is a large and rich establishment, the *Villa of Julia Felix* (Reg. II, IV, 7), who—as we learn from a notice preserved in the Naples Museum—had converted parts of her house to be let as flats (with a communal bathroom) and as shops or inns.

At this point we turn right and enter the area occupied by the *Amphitheatre* and the *Great Palaestra*. The amphitheatre, begun in 80 BC (and thus one of the most ancient known to us) was completed at the time of Augustus, and accommodated some 20,000 spectators. A *velarium* gave protection against the sun. The *palaestra*, which lies to the west, was once shaded by plane-trees and surrounded by a colonnade. The facilities for the exercise of the Pompeian youth included a swimming-pool. From here we return to the Quadrivio di Olconio where the Via di Stabia crosses the Via dell' Abbondanza, noticing in the latter street as we pass, the *Fullonica Stephani* (Reg. I, VI, 7), which gives us a very complete example of an ancient laundry and dyer's.

Just beyond the Quadrivio di Olconio we enter the **Stabian Baths** (Reg. VII, I) which occupy almost half the insula, the largest of the three bathing establishments in Pompeii. Built originally in Samnite times and subsequently enlarged, they are grouped round a *palaestra* and show the customary division into men's and women's sections. Almost opposite the entrance to the baths is the patrician *residence of Cornelius Rufus* (Reg. VIII, IV, 15).

We turn off the Via dell' Abbondanza into the Vicolo del Lupanare, on the right. A little way along, on the right, is the **Inn of Sittius** (Reg. VII, I, 44–45), with his sign of the elephant; and opposite is the two-storeyed **Brothel** (*Lupanar*) **of Africanus and Victor** (Reg. VII, XII, 18), with most interesting pictures and *graffiti*. Continuing, we turn right in the Via degli Augustali, with its tradesmen's shops; and then left into the Via Stabiana. On the right-hand side of the street (Reg. IX, III, 12) is a restored **flour-mill and bakery** (*pistrinium*); and at No. 5 is the **House of Marcus Lucretius,** a priest of Mars and decurion of the city.

The next insula (Reg. IX, IV) is taken up with the **Central Baths,** built after the earthquake of AD 63 to meet the demand for even more sumptuous bathing facilities.

We follow the Via Stabiana over the Quadrivio di Orfeo towards the Porta Vesuvio. (From the ramparts at the gate there is an excellent view.) On the right stands the **House of L. Caecilius Jucundus** (V, I, 26) and opposite are **shops, workshops** and (Reg. VI, XIV, 28) a **gambling-den** and **brothel.** Beyond the next cross-roads, on the left, is the beautiful **House of the Gilded Cupids** (Reg. VI, XVI, 7), which belonged to the Pompeian family of the Poppaei, who had the doubtful distinction of providing a wife for Nero.

We return to the cross-roads and take the Vicolo di Mercurio, on the right. The first street, again on the right, the Vicolo dei Vettii, brings us to the entrance (on the left) of one of the best-preserved of the richer Pompeian dwellings, the **Casa dei Vettii** (Reg. VI, XV, 1). This should on no account be missed, for it gives us a delightful picture of life among the merchant classes of the Roman colony. Next door in the Vicolo di Mercurio is the **House of the Labyrinth** (Reg. VI, XI, 10), a Samnite building, with a mosaic of Theseus and the Minotaur which gives it its name.

Opposite the doorway of the House of the Labyrinth we may enter in the back way to the **House of the Faun** (Reg. VI, XII, 2–5), the largest (it occupies a whole insula) and one of the most interesting of Pompeii's patrician houses. It shows the modification in the construction of the Italic house under Hellenistic influences. The statue of the faun, whence comes the name, is a copy of that in the Naples Museum. Notice the 'Welcome' sign, '(H)*ave*', on the pavement at the main entrance in the Via di Fortuna.

From here we turn right and see on the corner opposite the *Temple of Fortuna Augusta*, built in 3 BC and restored after the earthquake. Turning left into the Via del Foro, we see behind us the *Triumphal Arch of Caligula.* On our right are the *Forum Baths,* constructed in the Sullan period, and at the farther end of them is the Posto di Restoro—and how appropriate is the derivation of our word restaurant!

After we have been restored, the stronger of us may care to take a half-mile walk to the fascinating Villa of the Mysteries. We take the Vico delle Terme behind the Posto di Restoro, which brings us to the Via delle Terme opposite the large *House of Pansa* (Reg. VI, VI, 1). To the right, on the corner, is the *House of the Tragic Poet* (Reg. VI, VIII, 5), famous as the dwelling of Glaucus in Lord Lytton's *Last Days of Pompeii*. But we shall take the street to the left of the House of Pansa and, bearing left, enter the Via Consolare. We pass on our right the Samnite *House of Sallust* (Reg. VI, II, 4). Again keeping to the left, we pass the *Salt Warehouse* (Reg. VI, I, 13), then (9–10) the *House of the Surgeon,* an excellent example of the older Italic-type dwelling of the fourth to third centuries BC. The surgical instruments in the Naples Museum came from here.

The *Porta Ercolano,* or Herculanean Gate, was built towards the end of the second century BC; it was known as the Porta Saliniensis (Salt Gate) to the ancients. To the right, the Pomerium road to the Porta Vesuvio gives one a good idea of the fortifications Sulla failed to break through in 89 BC. Outside, the Via dei Sepolcri, the Street of Tombs, with its funerary altars, seats, columbaria and monuments, leads past (on our left) the so-called *House of Cicero,* which was excavated in the eighteenth century and covered up again. A short way on, also on our left, we reach the suburban *Villa of Diomedes.* On the west side, where the main entrance was, stood a beautiful colonnaded garden (the largest in Pompeii) with fish ponds, fountain, and summer dining-room. The owner of the villa was found with the key of the garden door in his hand; near by was a slave with his money and valuables.

From the Villa of Diomedes we continue and, bearing left, meet the Viale alla Villa dei Misteri, which takes us to the famous *Villa of the Mysteries,* discovered in 1909, a vast complex dwelling of more than sixty rooms, built possibly in the mid-second century BC. It seems that its earlier patrician owners had disposed of it, possibly after the earthquake, to a farmer, who put it to more rustic uses, but fortunately left intact the series of mural paintings which show us the initiation of a maiden in the Orphic Mysteries. The young woman kneeling next to the winged figure with the flail keeps the phallus covered. Its discovery to the initiate is the climax of the ceremony.

CHAPTER 7

Northern Campania

Map: I, p.104

Northern Campania—today the administrative province of Caserta—is known also as the Terra di Lavoro. This was the *Campania felix* proper of the Romans, with its centre in ancient Capua. Pliny describes the countryside as 'so blest with natural beauties and riches that it is clear that when Nature formed it she took delight in accumulating all her blessings in a single spot'. And it is as true today (if we take the usual extension of the name 'Campania' to include the plain and foothills south of Naples as far as Salerno) that this is some of the richest agricultural land in Italy.

In the late eighteenth and early nineteenth century the towns and countryside of north-east Campania were part of the customary tour of the enchanting environs of Naples—ultimately preferred by foreigners to Naples itself.

The towns of Northern Campania are all within easy reach of Naples by car; Roccamonfina, one of the farthest, is only some fifty miles away, and the district is covered by a network of roads, so that there is a wide choice of interesting routes. But there are other, more centrally placed headquarters—Caserta and S. Maria Capua Vetere, for instance—although even today large centres like Capua and Aversa have no good hotels.

From Naples we shall follow the SS 7 *bis* to Caserta. This takes us through Aversa, and a pleasant way to join it begins at the Palace of Capodimonte, where we take the Via di Miano, which passes the Porta Piccola and skirts the wall of the royal park on our right. At the Trivio del Garittone we keep straight on, with a fine view over the park and, to the left, of the deep depression known as the Cavone, which our road crosses before the village of Miano. From there an avenue of plane trees brings us to the crossroads of Arzano, where we turn to our left in the SS 7 *bis*.

It was at **Aversa** in 1030 that the Normans gained their first territorial foothold in South Italy, when Duke Sergius IV of Naples assigned the county to Rainulf, who had married his sister, in return for his assistance against Pandolf IV, the Lombard prince of Capua, who was at that time perhaps the most powerful ruler in the South of Italy.

Rainulf took possession (his position between Naples and Capua making him a kind of lord of the marches), and removed from the ruins of Roman Atella much of the remaining stonework in order to build his town walls. Atella lies about two miles from Aversa but the paucity of its remains makes it hardly worth a visit. It was famous in classical times as the birthplace of the crude rustic farces in the Oscan language, the *fabulae atellanae,* which later became so popular in Rome.

The fertile countryside around Aversa produces the light straw-coloured wine known as Asprino or Asprinio, which sometimes has a slight natural sparkle. This is grown from vines introduced by King Joachim Murat. It goes pleasantly with fish.

We enter Aversa by the Porta Napoli, under the arch constructed in the seventeenth century by the architect Gentile di Aversa. To the left of the gate rises the ponderous unfinished campanile of the **Annunciata,** the church on the right. The campanile was begun in 1477, the upper storeys being added some hundred years later in early baroque style. A fine Renaissance doorway, with carvings in low relief of allegorical figures and *the End of the World* and *the Resurrection,* the work of Iacopo Mormile (1518), leads into the courtyard of the church and hospital of the Annunciata. This Angevin institution was founded before 1310. The baroque façade of the church is preceded by a portico, the arches of which are supported by four columns of *cipollino* from ancient Atella. If the church is not open, ask for the custodian at the porter's lodge of the hospital—to the right of the main entrance. The Annunciata contains some very beautiful fifteenth-century paintings, which should not be missed.

To the right of the entrance is the Renaissance tomb of L. Zurlo (1546), and beyond it two chapels which are usually kept locked but are opened on request to the sacristan. In the first chapel are two paintings by Angelillo Arcuccio of Naples (*ca.* 1464–92). In the *Madonna delle Grazie* over the altar the souls in purgatory call on the intercession of the Virgin who stands on a sickle moon—a reference to the Apocalypse: 'a woman that wore the sun for her mantle, with the moon under her feet and a crown of twelve stars about her head'. The other painting is of *St John the Evangelist.* Of the same period but

103

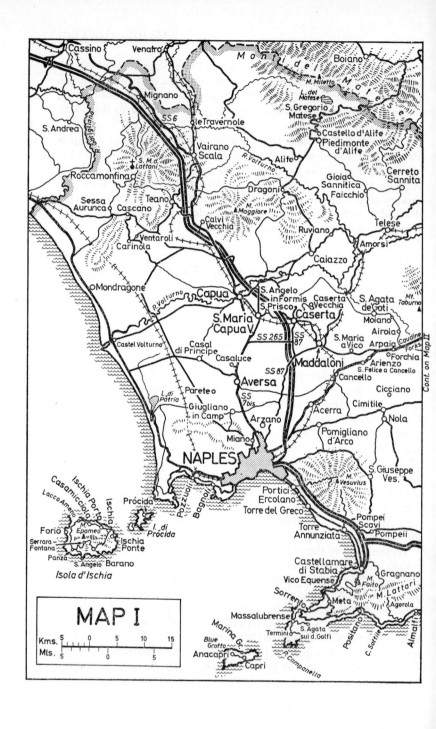

MAP I

Kms. 5 0 5 10 15
Mls. 5 0 5

by an unknown artist is the *Madonna and Child between St Catherine of Alexandria and Mary Magdalen*, which forms the altar-piece in the second chapel. In the space behind the high altar is a most beautiful fourteenth-century *Annunciation*.

From the Porta Napoli, the main street (the Corso Umberto) runs due north. A short way along it, on the right, is the church of the Madonna di Casaluce, and just before it a dark stone doorway leads into a Gothic courtyard. Much neglected and built over, this is said to be part of the Angevin castle in which Queen Giovanna I's husband, Andrew of Hungary, met his death. (Whether the murder took place here or in the other castello near the Duomo is a matter of dispute.)

From the Corso we follow (on the left) the Strada S. Paolo for the **Duomo.** This magnificent church dedicated to St Paul was begun by Count Richard I in 1053, but rebuilding after damage from fire and earthquake has left us only the eastern portion of the original structure, with a splendid Norman ambulatory and a cupola in the Norman-Sicilian style. (The latter can be best seen from the left of the church in the Piazza Normanna. Note here too the Romanesque doorway in the left transept, and in the building next door, the Seminario, fragments of Roman stonework from Atella and columns of Byzantine workmanship.) An arch joins the Duomo to the massive campanile, erected in 1499, which incorporates ancient marbles also from Atella, as well as the eight columns in the angles. An inscription commemorates Count Rainulf, founder of Aversa.

The western parts of the Duomo were rebuilt in the eighteenth century by C. Beratti. On the right wall of the right transept is a Renaissance altar (1563) with reliefs of *the Trinity, the Annunciation,* and *SS. Peter and Paul.* From here we enter the ambulatory, one of the earliest and purest examples of true Gothic to be found south of the Alps. The resemblance to the chevets (the term applied to a circular or polygonal apse when it is surrounded by an ambulatory off which are chapels) of the smaller churches of Auvergne and Poitou, suggests that the builders were Frenchmen brought in by Rainulf. Some of the carving is most impressive. Over the door on the right are bearded heads, very powerful in their formalized simplicity, and on the inner wall of the ambulatory are two remarkable pieces of early medieval carving, one of them showing *St George killing the Dragon.* Their origin is unknown but they appear to me to be older than the cathedral, and the design and carving suggest the nomadic art of the steppes. In the left transept is a stucco model of the House of Loretto, made for Bishop Carlo Carafa in 1630; and

The Companion Guide to Southern Italy

in the fourth chapel on the left is a wooden Crucifix carved in the Catalan style of the thirteenth century.

Leaving the Duomo by the Piazza Normanna, we take the Strada del Castello to the Piazza Trieste e Trento, where on the right stands the *castle,* rebuilt by Alfonso I of Aragon from the remains of Rainulf's construction, which was destroyed by an earthquake. Today it is an asylum for the treatment of criminal lunatics. Facing the castello is the graceful little *trecento* church of *S. Maria a Piazza.* (If it is shut, the key can be obtained from the custodian in the house opposite the main portal.) The beautiful fourteenth-century frescoes here are possibly by Andrea Vanni and his pupils. Particularly charming is the manger scene.

In the labyrinth of streets in the old town of Aversa are many churches and convents, some of Norman foundation, though most have suffered baroque restoration. But there is still much of the Middle Ages in the bustle and squalor of the streets themselves. There are no palaces such as one sees in Naples, but Aversa in the eighteenth century could boast as citizens two of the finest musicians in Italy—Niccolo Jommelli and Domenico Cimarosa.

Just over a mile north of Aversa on the SS 7 *bis* a road on the left leads to the small town of **Casaluce,** which has a castle (built by Rainulf and belonging later to the del Balzo family) and a church with a Gothic portal. In a room in the castle are some frescoes by the school of Andrea Vanni, and in the church there is a much venerated painting of the *Madonna and Child*, attributed to the hand of St Luke but more probably also by Vanni. For years the inhabitants of Casaluce and Aversa quarrelled over the possession of this painting, until in 1892 an ecclesiastical tribunal decided that from June 15th to October 15th it should go to Aversa and for the remaining eight months of the year it should stay in Casaluce.

The road now runs beside the railway line through fields of flax, tobacco, fruit trees and festooned vines, crossing over the Regi Lagni—the first land-reclamation carried out after 1539 by the Viceroy Pedro de Toledo to drain the swamps formed by the River Clanio (the Clanis of the ancients). We turn right at the junction with the SS 265 for Marcianise, a market town with little of architectural interest, and continue until we meet the SS 87, where we turn left for Caserta. This road was the traditional route for the royal visitors bound from Naples for the Palace of Caserta. It was planned as a broad shady avenue of plane trees and was designed so that the traveller could see the palace façade ahead, and behind, the cascade on the wooded hillside.

106

Caserta, the capital of the most fertile province of the Terra di Lavoro, was a small village known as La Torre when Charles III of Bourbon began building his Royal Palace in 1752. The King had confiscated the estate from the disaffected Gaetani Prince of Sermoneta, who was later paid the precise sum of 489,348 ducats for the property.

The *Royal Palace,* which has been described as 'the overwhelmingly impressive swan-song of the Italian baroque', was designed by the Dutchman Vanvitelli to rival Versailles. Its façade, however, is rather monotonous, since Vanvitelli's original design, which included raised sections with arches at each corner and a central cupola, was never completed. Charles intended that Caserta should be the administrative capital of his new kingdom, but the vast plans for blocks of administrative offices and the circular piazza (with barracks for the royal guard) in front of the palace were never carried out. The north wing of the palace, overlooking the park, was to have been the most magnificently furnished part of the building, but in fact only the south wing was lived in. (Admission: palace, weekdays 10.0 a.m.–4.0 p.m.; Sundays and holidays 10.0 a.m.–1.0 p.m.; park, daily 9.0 a.m. until an hour before sunset. Cars may drive into the park.)

Vanvitelli's skill as an architect can best be seen in the hexagonal vestibule and grand stairway in the centre of the four inner courts, which reveal his training as a theatrical designer. (Theatrical too is the construction of its double vaulting, in the space between which an orchestra was concealed to welcome the arrival of the royal party with triumphant strains of hidden music.) The visitor enters through the main doorway into a lofty atrium, which is continued past the central vestibule to the park doorway, so that one looks out over lawns, stretches of water and the play of fountains, to where the cascade gleams white among the greens of woods on the hillside two miles away. Something of the grandeur of Vanvitelli's conception can be gauged when we realize that all this water is brought from Monte Taburno, twenty-five miles away. In its course it traverses (by means of tunnels) five mountains and is carried over three valleys by aqueducts, one of which, the Ponte della Valle, is half a mile long and some 150 ft high.

In the left-hand corner of the first courtyard on the left is the *Court Theatre,* an excellent example of eighteenth-century theatre design, with its horseshoe shape of tiered boxes and the beautiful columns from the so-called Temple of Serapis at Pozzuoli. In the intimate surroundings of the little theatre Ferdinand I and IV entertained his guests with the comedies of Goldoni and light operas, especially those of his favourite Master of the King's Musick, Paisiello, whose operetta *Nina pazza per amore* was all the rage. (Emma Hamilton used to delight the visitors to Sir William's drawing-room in Naples by singing a song from it, with the charming title 'It's three days now that Nina's kept her bed'.)

At the top of the Stairway of Honour a doorway opens into the **Palatine Chapel,** richly decorated and with paintings by Bonito, Conca and Mengs. Passing through the large Saloni of the Halbardiers and of the Guard we reach the Salone di Alessandro, the centre of the southern façade, from whose windows the Bourbon courtiers could watch for the carriages and military escort bringing their Majesties to Caserta from Naples.

On the left of the Salone di Alessandro is the **Appartamento vecchio,** the first part to be inhabited, in 1780, the furnishings here being in the style of Louis XV and XVI. The Queen's boudoir and bathroom are particularly fine. The bathroom has a gilded bath and gold tap—very early for such sophisticated plumbing. Near by are the library and the Sala del Presepio. The figures of the crèche did not belong to the Bourbons but are beautiful examples of the work of eighteenth-century sculptors such as Bottiglieri and Sammartino. The King's bedroom is the one in which Ferdinand II (King 'Bomba') died of a contagious disease in 1859, his furniture and belongings being for this reason hastily burnt.

To the right of the Salone di Alessandro is the **Appartamento nuovo,** and the **Throne Room** which was decorated by Gaetano Genovese in 1844–5; but the main interest of the rooms here is in the elegance of the French furniture of the First Empire in the King's bedroom and that of Joachim Murat, and in the beautiful bathroom, with its stone bath adorned with lions' heads and its alabaster dressing-table which has a fountain for scent in the middle.

Although the main scheme for the **park** was Luigi Vanvitelli's, the woods and gardens which we see owe more to the Frenchman Martin Biancour, and are modelled on those of Versailles. The **fountains** were designed by Carlo Vanvitelli, who continued his father's work after his death in 1773. The rather crude statues were the work of contemporary Neapolitan sculptors. The charming **English garden,** with its exotic trees and shrubs (it has the first camellia tree to be introduced into Europe) and its pools and waterworks, was laid out by John Graefer for Queen Maria Carolina. Near the palace—to the left of the first stretch of lawns which precede the long lake—is the *Castelluccia,* a miniature castle built for the royal children, and beyond it lies the *Peschiera Grande.* Such was the eccentric Ferdinand I and IV's love of fishing and shooting that he stopped all work on the palace until the galley slaves and Mohammedan prisoners who were employed on the building had completed the fishpond.

It was in the Royal Palace at Caserta, as the headquarters of the Allied Command in Italy, that Field Marshal Alexander received the unconditional surrender of the German forces in 1945. Today part of the buildings is occupied by the Italian Air Force School for Specialists.

Caserta Vecchia—Maddaloni—the Caudine Forks—S. Agata de' Goti

From Caserta it is a short run to **Caserta Vecchia,** a most picturesque and fascinating old town, founded as early as the eighth century by the Lombards from Capua, but largely depopulated over the last hundred and fifty years in favour of new Caserta, so that now the visitor sees what is in effect a medieval hillside town.

From the centre of new Caserta, Piazza Dante, we follow the Corso Trieste to its end, then turn left into the Via Unità d'Italia, and then right into the Viale Medaglie d'Oro. A signpost shortly points to a turning on the left, which takes us past the military barracks, up a winding road, through the village of Casolla, and along the flank of a hill from which we have splendid views over the whole extent of the Terra di Lavoro. Just before we reach Caserta Vecchia, we see above us on the right the ruins, with a great circular tower, of the castello of the first counts (possibly eighth century), now partly adapted for use as a restaurant and bar.

It is better to leave one's car and to walk through the narrow streets with their curiously suspended street lamps to the central piazza. There are many interesting old houses—some of them ecclesiastical and feudal—but the pride of place goes to the magnificent Norman-Sicilian *cathedral of S. Michele,* built by Bishop Rainulf and his successor, Nicholas, between 1113 and 1153. The west front shows the Lombard design of high nave and lower aisles, which we shall see again as the form most frequently adopted by the Norman builders in the churches of Apulia. However, above the Lombard corbel-table the gable is faced with a blind arcade of interlacing arches in the Sicilian manner. The projecting animals (horses, centaurs and bull) we shall also meet again in Apulia. The bull (or ox) over the central doorway represents here the force and grandeur of the Church.

The lantern (it is best seen from the left flank of the building) is a marvellously successful blending of Norman-Sicilian and Byzantine elements, with two rows of interlacing arches in variegated stone and a shallow conical cap of warm-coloured tiles. Under the ogival archway of the campanile, to the right of the Duomo, eighteenth-century inscriptions record four visits of Pope Benedict XIII, and an eruption of Vesuvius. On the side wall nearest the church there is a tombstone of G. C. Dulto, who died in AD 557.

Inside the restored interior of the Duomo there are a fine eighth-century pulpit, some very interesting early carvings (several of animals, including a sheep and a lion supporting a stoup hollowed from a Corinthian capital), and a fourteenth-century fresco of the *Madonna and Child*. Of the eighteen columns of the nave, most are from classical buildings, some possibly from a Roman temple of Jupiter Tifatino which is known to have existed near by.

Behind the Duomo (through the arch of the campanile) is the Gothic thirteenth-century church of the **Annunziata.** The entrance has an eighteenth-century porch.

From Caserta an attractive and interesting day's excursion can be made via Maddaloni and the valley of the Caudine Forks to S. Agata de' Goti, and back by way of the Valle di Maddaloni. From the Corso Trieste we take the Via Appia which runs along the foot of Monte S. Michele to **Maddaloni.** Perched high above the town are the ruins of a castle and two towers. Maddaloni, a market-town with growing industries but architecturally of little interest, stands near the site of Roman Calatia, which was destroyed by the Saracens in 826, the inhabitants finding refuge on Monte S. Michele. In 1465 it became a fief of the Neapolitan Carafas who took the title of Dukes of Maddaloni.

Beyond the town the Via Appia passes through richly fertile country and then enters the **Caudine Forks,** the defile which is traditionally held to have been the scene of the shaming defeat of the Romans by the Samnites during the second Samnite War in 321 BC. Some Samnites in the guise of shepherds lured a Roman army encamped at Calatia to a spot where they found the defile blocked with felled trees and boulders and defended by the Samnites. On retreating, the Romans found their rear similarly blocked and occupied. They surrendered, were stripped of their arms, insulted, and finally suffered to depart after passing under the yoke. Local place names record the incident. However, if Livy's description

of the locality of the disaster is accurate, it hardly fits the landscape around us, and some authorities suggest the narrow valley
of the River Isclero, north of S. Agata de' Goti, as a more likely
site.

Shortly after the railway crossing outside Arpaia we turn left out
of the Via Appia and take the road through Airola to S. Agata de'
Goti. Past Moiano the road winds up around the northern flank of
Monte Mainiti or Maineto, with beautiful views over the valley of
the River Isclero; then it descends to cross its tributary, the River
Riello, and enters **S. Agata de' Goti.**

The origins of the town are lost in obscurity, but its position is
striking, perched between two rivers, the Martorano and Riello.

We arrive in the Largo Annunziata, so called from the Gothic
church of the **Annunziata** on the right. This church is being de-
baroqued and work has revealed some interesting fifteenth-century
frescoes. (If closed, the keys are held by the nuns in the adjoining
Ospedale Civile S. Giovanni di Dio, which was founded by the
Gerosolimitani in 1229.) The *Last Judgment* and *Christ in Glory* on the
wall of the main entrance, as well as the *Annunciation* in the apse, with
its beautiful predellas, are thought to be of the school of Andrea
Vanni. When the stucco has been finally removed we shall be able
to see the original structure of the church; the apsidal end is of the
early fifteenth century, but the rest of the building is almost certainly
earlier. The main doorway, with its low-relief of the *Annunciation*, is
late Renaissance work.

The Largo Annunziata is part of a large irregular piazza whose
various parts bear different names. On the left is the church of
S. Menna, dedicated to the hermit saint of Monte Taburno, whose
relics were brought here after his death in 579. The present church,
which was built by the Norman Count Robert of Capua, was
consecrated in 1114. It has recently been restored, not altogether
happily. Under the portico the original doorway has been retained,
and the arches of the nave are supported by antique columns. There
are remains of early frescoes; but of particular interest is the geo-
metrical mosaic floor which was laid at the beginning of the twelfth
century. Beyond the church, on the left, is the Viale Vittorio Emanuele III which leads to the bridge over the River Martorano, from
which there are some spectacular views.

Back in the piazza, we see the remains of the Gothic **Castello,** and
a curious cylindrical tower which stands alone. This was used as a
prison. A short way along the Via del Duomo, which cuts the town
in two, past the little church of S. Angelo dell' Addolorata, with its

bell-tower, we come to the church of *S. Francesco,* originally of the thirteenth century but rebuilt in the eighteenth. It has an interesting tomb of Ludovico Artus, Count of S. Agata, who died in 1370, and fragments of a triptych by Angelillo Arcuccio of Naples, unfortunately repainted in 1782. The desiccated corpse of Ludovico Artus has been removed from the tomb and is kept in a chest in the sacristy.

Farther along the Via del Duomo, where it opens into the Piazza Umberto I, is a monument to S. Alfonso de' Liguori (1696–1787), who was bishop of S. Agata and is known for his doctrine of 'equiprobabilism' which, very roughly, says that in the case of moral problems we may always follow the more indulgent authorities whenever they are as good, 'or nearly as good', as those in opposition. No wonder they made him a saint!

Immediately following is the Piazza S. Alfonso, with the wide portico of the Duomo forming a continuation of the Via del Duomo. The *Duomo,* dedicated to the Assunta, arose originally in the tenth century, was rebuilt at the beginning of the twelfth, but (like so many other churches in the South) was 'restored' in the eighteenth and nineteenth centuries. The columns of the portico are from ancient buildings, and the Romanesque arch of the main doorway is contemporary with that of S. Menna, but the interior is overlaid with tasteless baroque stucco-work. In the presbytery there are remains of a mosaic pavement, similar to that at S. Menna, and the ceiling of the crypt is supported by ancient columns. Note the curious elongated capitals (one in the body of the crypt and four in the altar recess), with their twelfth-century (?) carvings, which recall those of the cloister of S. Sofia in Benevento (see p. 131). These may be Lombard, but to me they suggest Sicilian-Saracenic influence.

We leave S. Agata de' Goti by the Viale Vittorio Emanuele III, which crosses the Martorano and runs north-west, following the valley of the Isclero through cultivated hilly country, to join the Via Sannitica, the main road between Naples and Campobasso in the Molise. Here we turn left into the wooded Vallone Capitone, with Monte Longano on our left and Monte Calvi on the right, and run in a south-westerly direction for Maddaloni, passing under Vanvittelli's great aqueduct at Ponte della Valle. From Maddaloni we turn right in the Via Appia for Caserta.

Sixth-century mosaics—S. Maria Capua Vetere—the cult of Mithras

S. Maria Capua Vetere lies just west of Caserta, on the Via Appia, two miles from modern Capua. Among houses and modern factories along the Via Appia stand the remains of Roman funerary monuments, the two most famous of which are known as La Conocchia (near the turning for S. Prisco) and the Carceri Vecchie (just outside S. Maria). The latter was thought to be an ancient prison for gladiators, but was in fact a repository for burial urns—the largest of its kind in Campania. In the last century a small chapel (La Madonna della Libera) was built in the upper drum.

A mile before S. Maria Capua Vetere two roads on the right lead to the near-by hamlet of **S. Prisco.** Almost at the end of the main street, which is very narrow, we turn to the left, and immediately on the right stands the church of S. Prisco, whose uninspired façade and campanile were designed by Vanvitelli. Inside, however, is the fascinating **chapel of S. Matrona,** a beautiful example of Hellenistic art which miraculously survived the Saracen raids of the ninth century. S. Prisco was traditionally one of seventy-two disciples who accompanied St Peter to Italy and was created bishop of Capua. After his death he was recognized as a saint, and his shrine became a place of pilgrimage. Among the pilgrims was Matrona, Princess of Lusitania, who built this chapel, then outside the old basilica. It contains Matrona's own tomb, a simple and beautiful Roman bath. But the greatest interest lies in the chapel's beautiful sixth-century mosaics: against a deep blue background stand palm branches and vine tendrils bearing bunches of grapes in vases of gold. Doves appear among the vines. Over the entrance door is the figure of the Redeemer, and on the walls were the symbols of the four Evangelists, but St Mark has been destroyed to make way for a window. A city labelled Bethlehem is also represented.

Ancient Capua passed through all the usual vicissitudes (in 343 BC Livy described it as '*urbs maxima opulentissimaque Italiae*') before the Saracens destroyed almost all of it in AD 840. **S. Maria Capua Vetere,** which today stands on its site, grew up later around the surviving basilican church of S. Maria Maggiore, from which it took its name. Its most important Roman remains are the amphitheatre and a sanctuary of Mithras (Mithraeum). In the nineteenth century S. Maria was a gay garrison town and many of the buildings still have the charm and flavour of the period. Today the city is becoming one of the most important centres of the Terra di Lavoro and has roughly double the population of modern Capua.

We enter the city by the Corso Umberto I and on the left in the Piazza S. Pietro is the church of *S. Pietro in Corpo,* which was built over a basilica of the time of Constantine and contains some columns of the ancient building. A short way on we turn left in the Corso Garibaldi. Here, on the right, is the pleasant nineteenth-century *Teatro Comunale.* Beyond the Piazza Mazzini the Corso, which now becomes the Via Mazzocchi, brings us to the Piazza Matteotti and the *cathedral church of the Collegiata di S. Maria.*

The original church was built in 432 over early Christian catacombs; it was added to in 787 by the Lombard Prince Arechi II, who built the beautiful S. Sofia at Benevento (see p. 131). He added the two outer naves, so that the church now has five aisles, separated by 51 ancient columns. Subsequent baroque and last-century alterations and additions have given us the present somewhat sombre and heavy interior. There is a good Renaissance ciborium in the chapel at the end of the right nave.

On the left-hand side of the Piazza Matteotti is the Ristorante del Faust, which I can especially recommend. Too often restaurants in Campania, outside Naples, fail to produce anything but 'hotel food'; but here the excellent local produce is used and the dishes are perfectly cooked and served. The local wines are excellent, and there are also a few rooms to let, which are simple, clean—and cheap.

It is easy for the visitor to lose his way in S. Maria, so it is perhaps wiser to return by the way we came to the Corso Umberto I, and then turn left (past the massive prison) for the *Anfiteatro Capuano,* which stands on the right at the end of the long Piazza I Ottobre 1860 (admission to amphitheatre and to the Mithraeum, 9.0 a.m. to an hour before sunset).

The amphitheatre, built in travertine and brick by Augustus and restored by Hadrian, was the greatest in Italy before the building of the Flavian Colosseum in Rome. It measures 185 by 152 yards, as compared with the Colosseum's 205 yards by 170. In spite of constant spoliation, the ruins that remain are imposing.

At the entrance we pick up the guide (obligatory) who will conduct us to the *Mithraeum.* This grotto was only discovered in 1922, and is one of the best-preserved sanctuaries in existence of the Persian god Mithras, that serious rival to early Christianity. The cult of Mithras was usually carried out in a small underground sanctuary such as this, and symbolically it represented the world, with the stars

114

frescoed on the vault suggesting the heaven to which the initiate aspired.

Frescoes around the walls are thought to indicate the seven stages in initiation. On the end wall is a splendid representation of *Mithras slaying the bull.* The scene is similar to the relief found on the Capitol in Rome and now in the Louvre. The stone runnels and trough on the right suggest that actual sacrifices of a bull were performed here—possibly followed by the immersion, or aspersion, of the initiate.

To leave S. Maria Capua Vetere for the newer Capua, we return to the Corso Umberto I and turn left. A little way on we see the ruins of the *Arch of Hadrian* that formerly spanned the Appian Way; only the brickwork remains, but it was once faced with marble. An inscription records Garibaldi's victory at the battle of the Volturno, 1860. The Via Appia brings us in less than two miles to Capua, which we enter past the Porta Napoli.

Capua—the Duomo—the Museo Campano—S. Angelo in Formis

Capua was founded on the site of Roman Casilinum, at the point on the Via Appia where a Roman bridge spanned the Volturno, by the Lombard Count Lando in 856 as a refuge for his subjects dispersed after the destruction of Old Capua by the Saracens. This bridge was a casualty of the Second World War, but much of the damage has now been made good; even the busts have been replaced round the wall of the gardens of the Villa Comunale.

From Caserta and S. Maria Capua Vetere the Via Appia, changing its name to the Corso Appio, cuts straight through Capua, opening out on the right, at the town's centre, to form the Piazza dei Giudici. Here, facing us, is the sixteenth-century façade of the *Palazzo del Municipio,* with the seven large heads which once served as keystones of the arches in the amphitheatre at S. Maria Capua Vetere built into the wall. Next to the palazzo is the thirteenth-century church of *S. Eligio,* rebuilt in 1747, which contains a wooden Madonna of the fifteenth century, the work of Pietro Alamanno, one of the best of the wood-carvers employed by the Aragonese of Naples. Adjoining the church is the *Arch of S. Eligio,* also thirteenth-century, sometimes known as the Arco Mazzocchi after the eighteenth-century antiquarian Alessio Mazzocchi who first excavated Pompeii.

On our right, the Via Duomo leads from the piazza, past the

115

Duomo, to join the Via Roma under an arch of the building which houses the Museo Campano (see p. 117). The ***Duomo,*** dedicated to SS. Stefano e Agata, was founded by Bishop Landulf, brother of Count Lando, in the same year as the migration to Capua. It has been many times restored, the last only recently, after heavy bombing in 1943. Fortunately the beautiful ninth-century campanile escaped serious damage—built into its sides can be seen fragments of classical and medieval marbles. The basilican Duomo possesses a magnificent thirteenth-century paschal candlestick, one of the most beautiful of its kind. In the fourth chapel on the right (built and dedicated to S. Lucia by Ferdinand I of Aragon) is a triptych of the *Madonna and Child with SS. Stefano and Lucia* against a background of gold, by Antoniazzo Romano (1489). The presbytery steps lead down to the restored crypt, in the centre of which is a little chapel with some remains of mosaic on its outside walls, and inside, Matteo Bottiglieri's *Dead Christ* (1742) in white marble.

In the sacristy are some of the Duomo's treasures: among them an Exultet, with miniatures of the eleventh century; Saracenic crystal, and works of Gothic goldsmiths and those of the Byzantine-influenced school of Montecassino.

To the left of the Duomo a passageway leads to a busy and colourful market. Crossing this, we come to the new Ponte Romano over the River Volturno, and on the farther side are the remains of the Emperor Frederick II's famous ***Capuan Gate*** (1239) which he himself is said to have designed in conscious imitation of the Romans. Some of its sculptured heads are now in the Museo Campano. We can return by the second of the bridges, the Ponte Nuovo, and taking the Via Gran Quartiere and then its continuation, the Via Palasciano, past the barracks and gardens of the Villa Comunale, arrive at the ***Porta Napoli,*** a marble archway in the Tuscan-Doric style, with motifs of trophies of arms, built at the end of the fifteenth century. A short way on we re-encounter the Corso Appio.

Almost immediately on the right is the Via Giovanni Andreozzi, leading to the remains of the immense Palace of the Norman Princes or ***Castello delle Pietre,*** the latter name deriving from the great blocks of stone which the Norman builders removed from the Anfiteatro Campano. The castle was begun at the end of the eleventh century, and was later enlarged and strengthened by the Emperor Frederick II. Continuing, by way of the Via Principi Normanni (past the little church of S. Salvatore Piccolo, with its Lombard inscription and remains of Byzantine frescoes), we arrive at the

Corso Gran Priorato di Malta. The last house on the right before the
Corso has a Roman low-relief built in its wall, and opposite it is the
church of **S. Marcello Maggiore,** originally of the ninth century
but rebuilt in 1113 and subsequently several times restored. The
beautiful doorway is an interesting amalgam of early styles. The
pilasters, with their scenes from the Old Testament, were probably
from the rebuilding in 1113, and are by Lombard sculptors working
under French influence. On high is an eagle, possibly from a thirteenth-century pulpit.

We turn left in the Via Gran Priorato di Malta, which leads
back under an arch to the Via Duomo. This part of the town is full
of ancient churches, medieval courts and palaces: Roman, Lombard,
Gothic, Catalan—a fascinating efflorescence of styles in stonework.
The last street on the left in Via Malta, the Via Ettore Fieramosca,
brings us back to the Piazza dei Giudici. Half way along, on the left,
is the interesting **Palazzo Fieramosca**; built originally by Giovanni
di Durazzo, son of King Charles II of Anjou (the lilies of France can
be seen above the Gothic doorway), it passed in 1487 to Rinaldo
Fieramosca, the father of the celebrated champion of the Challenge
of Barletta (see p. 273). The building, which is in sore need of
restoration, was much altered at the time of the Renaissance, but in
the courtyard we can get some idea of its earlier form. The tower
on the right was also part of the original fourteenth-century structure.

The **Museo Campano** is one of the best provincial museums of
Southern Italy, and well worth a visit. It is housed in the (partly)
fifteenth-century Palazzo Antignano. One of the two gateways in the
Via Roma is built in a curious, ornate Catalan-Gothic style of the
late 1400's (admission, July 20th–September 15th 8.30 a.m.–
2.0 p.m.; rest of the year 9.0 a.m.–1.0 p.m. and 2.0–5.0 p.m.).

The votive statues of *deae matres* from the sanctuary of the Mater
Matuta, the early Italic goddess of fecundity and maternity (some
authorities associated her with Juno), found in 1845 near S. Maria
Capua Vetere, are particularly interesting. There are other beautiful
figurines of the Tanagra type, some astonishingly graceful Etruscan
bronzes, a Byzantine plaque in low-relief of two horses facing each
other, a fine collection of ceramics, and three excellent examples of
Roman mosaic. One room is devoted to the famous Romanesque
sculpture from Frederick's Capuan Gate. Beside the huge heads of
Capua Fidelis and *Jove* is a portrait of the poet and scholar *Piero delle
Vigne* (1190–*ca.* 1249). From humble origins delle Vigne rose to be
the Emperor's 'Lieutenant-General'; then, falling into suspicion, he

was brutally blinded and led around as a captive in Frederick's train, which included his harem and menagerie. The picture gallery includes paintings of the fifteenth-century Neapolitan school.

For **S. Angelo in Formis** we take the Via Roma (leaving the Museo Campano on our right) and turn left outside the town to follow the bend in the Volturno. A chapel at this point commemorates the treachery of Cesare Borgia in 1501, when 5000 men of Capua were seized and slain in cold blood during a truce. On July 24th, the anniversary of the massacre, the bell of the Duomo in Capua still tolls in memory of the dead.

The road crosses the plain, passing over the Autostrada del Sole, and reaches the village of S. Angelo in Formis at the junction with the main road from Capua Vetere. The basilica of S. Angelo in Formis stands on the hillside behind the village and is approached through an arch, the so-called *Arco di Diana,* which has a memorial to the Battle of the Volturno in 1860 when Garibaldi, with about half the number of troops, routed a formidable Bourbon army of some 40,000 men after the fall of Naples.

The *basilica of S. Angelo in Formis* is one of the most interesting and beautiful churches in Campania, both for its architecture and for its Byzantine-influenced frescoes. It is built on the site of a temple of Diana Tifatina, the federal sanctuary of the Campanian peoples, and takes its name 'in Formis' from the aqueducts (*formae*), which once carried water from Monte Tifata to Capua. In 1072 Richard, Prince of Capua, gave the existing church and monastery to the famous Abbot Desiderio of Montecassino, who built the church we now see. In form it is basilican, with three circular apses, preceded by a portico in the Norman-Sicilian style. The five arches of the portico are supported on stumpy columns surmounted by ancient Corinthian capitals. Note, too, the fluted base of the column on the right. These are fragments from the Temple of Diana. The doorway in white marble is classical; the architrave bears an inscription to Abbot Desiderio. In the lunette is a magnificent half-figure of *St Michael*, Byzantine in its formality and richness of colour, and probably of the late eleventh century; the *Madonna orante*, dressed as an empress (above the door), may be a little later; the repainted figures of saints in the lunettes on either side are possibly of the thirteenth century.

Inside the church the walls are painted with a wonderful display of frescoes by the school of Montecassino.

On the right of the church is the campanile, the lower portion built with blocks of stone from the Temple of Diana; the upper storey in a lovely warm-coloured brick. It is believed to have been the prototype for the campanili of Campania.

Excursions from Caserta—Teano—Roccamonfina—Sessa Aurunca—Carinola—Ventaroli

From Caserta a round trip of about eighty-five miles takes us through the ancient Samnite countryside of the valleys of the upper Volturno and its tributary, the Calore, to **Piedimonte d'Alife,** with two interesting early fifteenth-century churches, and the heights of the Monti del Matese with magnificent views, good fishing (trout, carp and eel) in the Lake of Matese, and shooting in the adjoining marshes. The pretty little town of **Telese** is busy from June to October on account of its medicinal baths. It takes its name from Samnite Telesia, whose ruins near by are at present being excavated.

Another very pleasant day trip from Caserta, of little more than seventy miles, is through the beautiful countryside to the north-west of the city. We leave Caserta by the Via Appia, and five miles beyond Capua, where the road forks, we follow the SS 6 (Casilina) straight on. On our right, set on the foothills of Monte Maggiore, stands **Calvi Vecchia,** a village built on the site of the ancient city of Cales, belonging to the Aruncians, and famous in Roman times for its black glazed *vasi caleni.*

On the right in the town, beyond the ruins of the fourteenth-century castello, is the ***Duomo*** founded in the ninth century by Count Pandulf of Calvi (the name Pandulf was confusingly common among the Lombards). Although in the restoration of 1452 much was altered, the three apsidal ends are original. It contains a damaged twelfth-century pulpit, raised on two lions, with mosaics and sculptured ornament, and a fine episcopal throne, also with lions predominant. The street opposite the Duomo takes us (on the left of the Via Casilina) to the excavations of ancient Cales, near the autostrada, where we can see remains of the forum, baths, and theatre, and a temple of imperial times.

At the Bivio di Torricella we turn left for **Teano,** standing among trees on the high ground above the fertile valley of the Savone, under the woods of volcanic Roccamonfina and Monte Santa Croce (3000 ft). Teano was known to the ancients as Teanum Sidicinum, a city of the Sidicini, a people possibly of Oscan origin. More recently it was a feud of the Gaetani family of Sermoneta. It was on the outskirts of Teano that Garibaldi, victorious on the Volturno, met King Vittorio Emanuele II on October 26th, 1860.

At the end of the avenue of plane trees, just before the built-up area, a path to the right (it begins at a house called Villa Emma) leads down through rich gardens and orchards to the yet unex-cavated ruins of a vast **Roman amphitheatre.** Peasants have built their dwellings among the arches. In the vicinity have been found remains of pre-Roman buildings, as well as four temples of the Hellenistic period. At the beginning of the Empire Teanum became a favourite place of *villeggiatura* for the Roman nobility and there were many luxurious private villas on the slopes towards the River Savone.

In Roman and later in medieval times the main part of the town was on the heights above. We drive up into the Piazza del Duomo, which is surrounded on three sides by the Duomo, the Bishop's Palace and the Seminario. The **Duomo** was founded in 1116, rebuilt to the designs of Andrea Vaccaro in 1630, and has recently been restored after bomb damage in 1943. In the atrium there are two Roman sphinxes in red granite, and fragments of both ancient and medieval monuments have been set in the wall. The church is a well-proportioned basilica, with the three naves divided by columns of grey granite, some of them taken, with their Corinthian capitals, from Roman buildings. The fine thirteenth-century pulpit has been reconstituted.

Teano was badly hit by the last war, but there are many interest-ing bits of medieval churches and old palaces in its winding narrow streets—and a curious little arched building enclosing a waterfall. From the Duomo we take the Corso Vittorio Emanuele (one of the *cardines* of Roman Teanum) to the Piazza Umberto I, the centre of the town; on the right is a continuation of the square, known as the Piazza della Vittoria, where the Palazzo Fondi stands on the site of the ancient acropolis—parts of the walls can be seen in the garden. Just off the Piazza Umberto I, in the Via S. Benedetto, is the church of **S. Benedetto,** which was founded as early as the eighth century. After the destruction of the monastery of Montecassino by the Saracens in 883, the monks fled here to the monastery adjoining the church, bringing with them their precious autograph copy of the *Rule of St Benedict.* Thirteen years later most of the document was lost in a fire.

We leave the centre of Teano by the Via Porta Roma for the beautiful road to Roccamonfina and Sessa Aurunca. As it winds up the side of the extinct volcano of Roccamonfina, breaks in the magnificent chestnut woods give us views over the rich volcanic countryside towards Monte Massico, famous from Roman times for vineyards which produced the Massic and Falernian wines.

At the junction with the road from Sessa Aurunca to Rocca-monfina we turn right, and almost immediately enter this charming hillside town. **Roccamonfina** would be a perfect centre for those who enjoy walking, since at 2000 ft the climate is delightful in the height of summer and the paths through the chestnut and acacia woods have some unbelievably beautiful views. Alas, the town has no inns and only rather primitive lodgings.

At the end of the long Piazza Nicola Amore stands the baroque church of the Collegiata. Opposite this (on the left) is the road to the *sanctuary of Maria SS. dei Lattani,* which winds up for two miles through the woods, past the village of Gallo. To the right of the entrance to the sanctuary stands a chestnut tree, said to have been planted by S. Bernardino of Siena, who in the course of his preaching journeys throughout Italy founded the monastery in the early fifteenth century. Inside the courtyard is the *hermitage of S. Bernardino,* much restored (by order of Mussolini), but showing the original *quattrocento* loggias. The Franciscans will not allow women visitors to the monastery, but they may enter the church. The early wooden doors are bolted by an ingenious locking system, also in wood, made in 1508. There are some remains of fifteenth-century frescoes, and opposite them is the *chapel of the Virgin of Lattani,* with a very early (perhaps before AD 1000) polychrome figure of the *Madonna and Child* on the altar.

The road continues through the beautiful chestnut woods beyond the monastery to the recently reconstructed Capella di S. Bernar-dino, built (it is said) on the site of the Saint's original chapel. Past the wireless station there is a wonderful view towards the Volturno.

Returning to the road junction outside Roccamonfina, we take the road (straight on) to **Sessa Aurunca,** skirting the southern flank of the ancient crater, until we see on our right its highest point, Monte S. Croce. The road descends into a rolling cultivated countryside of vines, olives and fruit trees, with views of Monte Massico, the sea and (on the right) the valley of the Garigliano, with the silver cupola of the nuclear power-station beside the river. Ahead of us, on a spur, stands Sessa Aurunca.

This was Suessa, capital of the Arunci, and its origins go back as far as the eighth to seventh centuries BC. It became a *municipium* in 90 BC and was a flourishing city at the time of Augustus, with baths, theatre, a splendid cryptoportico, and temples, one of them to the tutelary deity of the city, Hercules. As we enter the town we see remains of the **castle,** with its high square tower; farther on we come to Piazza XX Settembre, on which stands the medieval **Palazzo Ducale,** rebuilt (it is thought) on the ancient Temple of Hercules, next to the town hall. On the side of the square is the baroque church of the **Annunziata,** shaped like a Greek cross, with a green and yellow tiled cupola. From the left-hand corner of the piazza we come to another smaller piazza with the pleasant fountain of Hercules slaying the Nemean Lion. From here the Corso Lucilio, called after the Roman poet and satirist Caius Lucilius (born in Suessa about 180 BC), runs down to the Porta Cappuccini, corresponding to the old *cardo maximus*. There are many medieval houses in Sessa, including some of the fifteenth-century Durazzo period, and others incorporating Roman remains, but we shall limit ourselves to a visit to the interesting Duomo.

Some way down the Corso, on the left, we take the narrow Via Delio which brings us out in the Piazza del Duomo. The Romanesque **cathedral church of S. Pietro** was rebuilt from an earlier edifice in 1180; there are records of a bishop of Sessa from the end of the fifth century. In form it is a basilica, two rows of nine columns (of diverse materials and shapes, but all from Roman buildings) separating the three naves. Other ancient stonework and columns are built into the walls and in the crypt. The three doors are approached through a thirteenth-century *pronaos* or portico of three arches, the central one lightly pointed, the others rounded. We see here the Romanesque use of animals as consoles supporting pillars or arches—a practice very common in the churches of Apulia. In the portico the archivolt, which springs from consoles depicting *Samson and the Lion* and *the Drunkenness of Noah*, has sculptured *Scenes from the life of St Paul*. The architrave to the middle doorway is formed from a piece of Roman sculpture, with masks and two panthers facing a vase from which comes a vine branch and tendrils. (There is an identical piece over the gateway to the Bishop's Palace, immediately on the left of the Duomo.) In the lunette is a low-relief of *Christ blessing between SS. Peter and Paul* on a background of mosaic.

The interior was baroqued over in the eighteenth century. On the floor of the central nave are remains of the original twelfth-century mosaic paving, but the mosaics which claim our attention are of the following century: those of the beautiful pulpit, the paschal candle, the organ loft, and the fragment of *Jonah and the Whale* in the right of the nave before the transept. This lovely work was begun probably about 1250 by one Pellegrino and finished by another Taddeo. On
122

the base of the candelabrum stand joyous figures, one with a flower in his hand; the Latin inscription above ends with the words: 'Praise be to Peregrine who sculptured such things; everywhere he reflected the hallowed light. O God, accept our song.'

Outside the Porta Cappuccini a road encircles the town, and from the parapet here we can look over the remains of Roman Suessa: baths and the vast theatre surrounded by its cryptoportico. Other remains of the Roman town are well worth a visit: the Ponte degli Aurunci ('Ponte Ronaco' to the locals) lies some two miles from the town just off the Via Appia, which we join from the Porta Cappuccini.

Returning to the Via Appia, and continuing straight on, we come to the village of Cascano, just beyond which we turn right and take the winding country road for the charming, anachronistic little town of **Carinola,** with its interesting remains of fifteenth-century Catalan-Gothic architecture. This was once the fief of that Petrucci who was executed in Naples for his part in the Barons' Conspiracy against Ferrante of Aragon. On the left as we enter the town are the massive ruins of the fifteenth-century castle or **Ducal Palace.** A few yards after the beginning of the street, on the right, is the **Casa Martullo,** much damaged by wartime bombing and now revealing the open stairway in its courtyard, one of the finest pieces of Catalan-Gothic building in Italy. A little farther on is another fifteenth-century house, the **Casa Novelli,** with a low Catalan arch over the doorway, and contemporary windows. Beyond the piazza formed by the intersection of the Corso Umberto I, we come to the little Piazza Vescovado, with the eleventh-century **Duomo** beside its majolica-capped campanile (the upper portion was rebuilt in the eighteenth century). Roman remains were used in the campanile and church. The church is closed at the moment for repairs, but when it is completed we shall be able to see the Cistercian-Gothic additions to the primitive church and the marble tomb of the founder, the lesser known bishop St Bernard, who died in 1109. Early examples of the Romanesque use of animals as supports can be seen in the elephants and lions on the central doorway. The della Robbiaesque figures in colour-glazed ceramic high on the façade above the portico were placed there in the eighteenth century; they were formerly in the church.

We depart by way of the Corso Umberto I and, almost directly after leaving the built-up area, turn left along a delightful country road for **Ventaroli.** Leaving the car by the eighteenth-century clock tower in the village, we take the lane directly opposite (on the right), for the basilica, first asking at the house on the left of the entrance to the lane for the key. The church of **S. Maria in Foro Claudio** is about two hundred yards away among the fields. It was built in the eleventh century. The entrance is through a Renaissance doorway and down some steps. The twelfth-century frescoes in the central apse should be compared with those at S. Angelo in Formis; they are possibly by a local follower of the school of Montecassino. Most of the other paintings are of a later date, but the remains of a *Last Judgment* on the right-hand wall are worth noticing, with figures of craftsmen—butcher, shoemaker, smith, apothecary, etc. On the same wall a piece of Roman sculpture depicting a boar hunt has been built in. To the right of the entrance the *Madonna and Child with Saints* (fifteenth-century) is signed by the artists Nicola de Belarducci and his collaborator Antonio, both from Carinola. Another fresco shows two bishops blessing in the Greek manner.

From Ventaroli we come again in less than a mile to the Via Appia and retrace our route to Caserta.

CHAPTER 8

Central and Eastern Campania

Maps: I, p.104; II, p.126

Benevento

The round trip by car from Naples to Benevento, thence to Avellino (with a visit to the famous Sanctuary of Montevergine), and back by way of Nola and Cimitile is only about one hundred miles, but there is too much to cover in a single day. Benevento is on the main road from Naples to Foggia and could be visited *en route* to Northern Apulia. Similarly, one of the branches of the new Autostrada del Sole will pass by Nola and Avellino on its way to Bari and Brindisi in southern Apulia. However, the round trip we are suggesting, taking two or three days with stops overnight at Benevento or Avellino, where there are adequate hotels, has much to recommend it.

For Benevento we leave Naples from the Piazza Garibaldi, taking the Corso Garibaldi northwards to its junction with the Via Casanova, where we turn right and proceed straight on. On the hillside to the left is the Camposanto di Poggioreale, where the horrible conditions of the interment of Neapolitan paupers so distressed the Victorians. The bodies were thrown into a vault (one for each day of the year), covered with quicklime, and the stone slab replaced for twelve months. At the annual re-opening of the vault the osseous residue provided an excellent manure.

After five miles we fork left on the SS 162, crossing the verdant Terra di Lavoro for the market town of Acerra, and proceed via Cancello and Arienzo, lying just to the south of the Via Appia which we shortly join. Here we turn right and pass the traditional site of the Caudine Forks (see p. 110).

We cross the Caudine valley, dominated on the north by Monte Taburno, and follow the road to Montesarchio, after which the Via Appia skirts the foothills of Monte Mauro, descending into the valley of the River Corvo. Just before the turning for Castelpoto and the bridge over the Corvo there stands on the left of the road a seven-

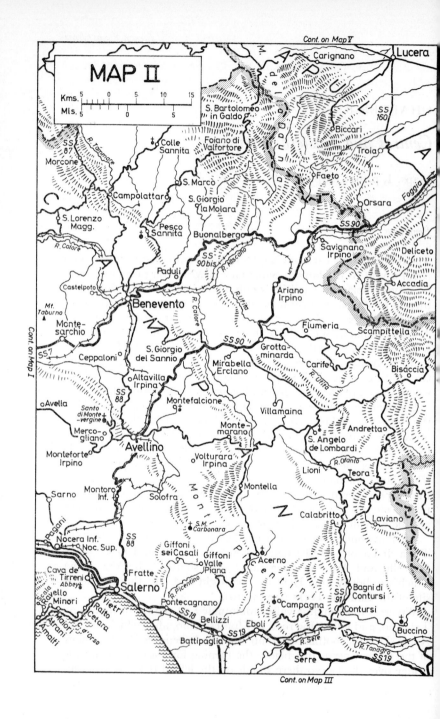

MAP II

Kms. 5 0 5 10 15
Mls. 5 0 5

Lucera
Carignano
S. Bartolomeo in Galdo
Biccari
SS 160
Colle Sannita
Foiano di Valfortore
Troia
SS 87
Morcone
R. Tammaro
Faeto
S. Marco
Campolattaro
S. Giorgio la Molara
Orsara
S. Lorenzo Magg.
Pesco Sannita
Buonalbergo
SS 90
Foggia
R. Calore
A
Savignano Irpino
Deliceto
SS 90bis
Paduli
R. Miscano
Accadia
Castelpoto
Ariano Irpino
Benevento
R. Ufita
Scampitella
Mt. Taburno
Monte-sarchio
R. Calore
Flumeria
SS 7
Ceppaloni
S. Giorgio del Sannio
SS 90
Grotta minarda
Carife
Bisaccia
Mirabella Erclano
R. Ufita
Altavilla Irpina
Avella
SS 88
Montefalcione
Villamaina
Santo di Monte-vergine
Monte-marano
Andretta
Merco-gliano
Avellino
S. Angelo de Lombardi
R. Ofanto
Monteforte Irpino
Volturara Irpina
Lioni
Teora
Sarno
Montoro Inf.
Solofra
Montella
Calabritto
Laviano
Pagani
Nocera Inf.
Noc. Sup.
SS 88
S.M. Carbonara
Acerno
Bagni di Contursi
Cava de Tirreni
Abbey
Fratte
Giffoni sei Casali
Giffoni Valle Piana
SS 91
Contursi
Scala
Ravello
Minori
Salerno
R. Picentino
Campagna
Buccino
Raito
Vietri
Pontecagnano
SS 18
Cetara
C. d'Orso
Bellizzi
Eboli
SS 19
R. Sele
Maiori
Atrani
Amalfi
Battipaglia
Serre
R. Tanagro
SS 19

teenth-century epitaph marking the boundary of the ancient Duchy of Benevento, and from the top of the hill we can see the city ahead, encircled by mountains. After crossing the River Sabato, we enter the town by the Via Porta Rufina, and then turn left (past the market) into the Via Gaetano Rummo, which brings us to the Piazza Orsini and the cathedral.

Benevento, the provincial capital, is one of the oldest cities in Italy, having been founded according to tradition by Diomedes or by Auson, the son of Ulysses and Circe. Its origin may well have been Greek, for, as a principal Samnite town, it carried the inscription *Malies* on its coins, thought to be the Oscan or Samnite rendering of *Maloenton* ('the return of the flocks'), and later Latinized to *Maluentum* or *Maleventum*. Excavations have yielded pottery and bronze objects of the eighth and seventh century BC. In 268 BC a Roman colony was planted there and the name of the city changed to the more auspicious Beneventum. Although it was twice sacked by Hannibal, Beneventum later grew in importance through its position as a junction of the Via Appia with the Via Latina and, in imperial times, as the starting-point of Trajan's road to the Apulian sea-coast, which began at the still existing Arch of Trajan.

Map II
p. 126

Benevento suffered with the rest of Italy from the barbarian invasions which broke up the Roman Empire in the west. However, in 571 it was taken by the Lombards, and for the five hundred years of their remarkable rule was, first as the Duchy, then the Principality of Benevento, usually the leading power in Southern Italy. In 1077 it came into the hands of the Church, and with brief intermissions it remained a papal enclave in the Kingdom of Naples until the unification of Italy in 1860. In 1799 the 'liberating' French occupied the city and made off with the treasures of the Duomo and the Monte di Pietà. In 1805 Napoleon created Talleyrand Prince of Benevento, and it was governed in his name by procurators until 1815, when it was restored to the Church. In 1943 the city was badly damaged by aerial bombardment; more than sixty-five per cent of the houses were destroyed, and the Duomo received direct hits.

The pleasantly aromatic yellow liqueur, Strega, is distilled at Benevento. Its name recalls the ancient legend of the dance of witches (*streghe*) in the valley of the Sabato.

Of the thirteenth-century **Duomo** the campanile, part of the façade, and the crypt have survived the bombing. The façade shows Pisan influence and consists of two tiers of irregular arcades, the blind arches of the lower order being surmounted by a more deeply recessed upper arcade, in which are set the three rose windows over the main doorway. In the recess on the right is the statue known as *the Cavalier*, possibly from a thirteenth-century tomb. The carved stone animals on the consoles and cornice are in the Lombard tradition, but the carving on the jambs and lintel of the main portal suggest a Byzantine influence, and are thought to be the thirteenth-century work of a certain Master Rogerio, who perhaps also built the campanile in 1279. On the campanile seventeen funerary figures from Roman tombs are effectively used as a decorative frieze, and on its left-hand wall is another Roman carving of a wild boar adorned with a sacrificial stole, which has become an emblem of the city.

The reconstructed interior of the Duomo is spacious and light, but impersonal. On either side of the ambones are entrances to the primitive crypt which contains some remains of frescoes of the fourteenth century.

The famous bronze doors of the Duomo, badly damaged in the war, have been placed in the **Biblioteca Capitolare** in the rebuilt Archbishop's Palace, which is entered from the Piazza Orsini, to the left of the cathedral. These doors are supposedly of Byzantine workmanship, but they appear to me to be local Lombard work. We know that the doors of Troia cathedral were made between 1119–27 by Oderisio of Benevento, and already in these there is a departure from the Byzantine tradition. If we accept the date *ca.* 1191 for the Benevento doors, it may well be that a local school carried on the development.

Also in the library are some beautiful examples of manuscripts written and decorated in the 'Beneventan style' (eighth to ninth centuries), as well as the so-called Chair of S. Barbato (eleventh century) and *objets d'art*, including the golden rose given by Pope Benedict XIII. In the reading-room there is a striking statue of this vigorous pope who, born Piero Francesco Orsini, became Archbishop of Benevento in 1686 and administered his diocese with conspicuous ability for thirty-eight years until elected pope in 1724. His work in rebuilding the city after the disastrous earthquakes of 1688 and 1702, when there was hardly a building that had not suffered, earned him the title of *Alter Conditor Urbis*, the second founder of the city.

From the Piazza Duomo in front of the cathedral the Corso Vittorio Emanuele descends to the River Calore, which is crossed by the impressive new bridge, the **Ponte Luigi Vanvitelli**. From the parapet of the Via Posillipo (to the left before the bridge) we can overlook the modern industrial suburb where, in 1266, one of

Above A Roman aqueduct on the island of Ischia.

Right The 11th c. interior of the basilica of S. Angelo in Formis near Capua, one of the most interesting and beautiful churches of Campania on account of its architecture and its Byzantine-influenced frescoes, painted in the 13th c. by the Benedictine school of Montecassino.

The clock-tower presides over the busy Piazza Umberto I, Capri, which is also
the terminus for the funicular from the Marina Grande. Known simply as
'the Piazza', the little square presents an intriguing microcosm of island life.
Here the workaday Capresi mingle with a cosmopolitan crowd of the rich, the
famous, the notorious, the beautiful – and the lookers-on.

the decisive battles in Neapolitan history was fought, during which the Hohenstaufen Manfred (Dante describes him: '*Biondo era*' and '*bello e di gentile aspetto* . . .') lost his kingdom and his life to Charles of Anjou, called in by Popes Urban IV and Clement IV.

Behind us, to the left of the Via Posillipo, wartime bombing has revealed the site of the Roman baths. The road curves to the left and almost immediately on our right opens the broad Viale S. Lorenzo, terminating in the nineteenth-century church of the **Madonna delle Grazie,** a building designed in the neo-classical style by Francesco Coppola in 1837. It contains, above the high altar, a much renovated wooden statue of the *Madonna*, attributed to Giovanni da Nola. At the beginning of the Viale, on our right, stands the *statue of the Bue Apis*, an ancient Egyptian work from the Roman temple of Isis, placed here in 1629. Opposite the beginning of the Viale, on the corners of the Corso Dante, are two baroque palaces. We turn right into the Via Torre della Catena, so called from the tower that remains (together with a gate, the Porta Arsa) of the Lombard city walls.

In front of the Porta Arsa a road leads down, crossing the railway line, past the little ruined church of SS. Cosma e Damiano, to the **Ponte Leproso,** the Roman bridge which carried the Via Appia across the River Sabato and into the city. Four of the five arches are original.

Back on the Via Torre della Catena we follow it to the right, beside the water-meadows of the Sabato, until an opening on the left brings us to the well-preserved **Roman theatre.** This was begun under the Emperor Hadrian and enlarged by Caracalla between AD 200–210 to hold 20,000 spectators (admission, daily from 9.0 a.m. until sunset). Recently restored and transformed, the theatre is now used for musical performances and stage representations. Outside the theatre, the Via Bosco Lucarelli leads back to the Porta Arsa; we follow this and take the first street on the right, which brings us through the eighteenth-century Rione S. Filippo to the church of **S. Filippo,** built by Pope Benedict XIII in 1727. From here the narrow Via S. Filippo takes us (right) to the Piazza Manfredi di Svevia, with the remains of a Roman arch of the period following the Emperor Trajan, now known as the **Arco del Sacramento.** Around us are other Roman remains from what was the centre of ancient Beneventum. By the Via Carlo Torre we return along the right flank of the cathedral to the Piazza Duomo.

The main street of Benevento, the Corso Garibaldi, runs in a slight ascent from the Piazza Duomo to the Piazza IV Novembre.

A short way up the Corso, on the right, is the **Palazzo Paolo V,** now the Municipio, built at the end of the sixteenth century, and next to it the church of the **Carmine** (or of S. Anna), restored to its eighteenth-century lines. Facing the church, in the little piazza called after the Beneventum-born Roman jurist, Paulus Aemilius Papianus, stands one of the two red granite *obelisks* from the Roman Temple of Isis—the other is in the Museo del Sannio. The hieroglyphics, which are translated into Latin and Greek on the base, tell of its having been erected by Lucillus Rufus (in AD 88) in front of Domitian's temple in honour of Isis, 'the divine mother, the morning star, queen of the gods, lady of heaven . . .'

Directly opposite the Piazza Roma (on the right of the Corso) the Via Traiano leads to a piazza flanked with eighteenth-century palaces and the famous **Arch of Trajan,** one of the best preserved of Roman commemorative arches. Built in Parian marble, it stands over fifty feet in height. The work was begun in AD 114, the year Trajan set out on the Parthian campaign, and the arch marks the start of the new Via Traiana. Reliefs represent scenes from the Emperor's life, as well as mythological and symbolical figures. The arch was later incorporated in the walls of the city, and was known popularly as the Port' Aurea. Parts of the remains of these Lombard fortifications can be seen in the Via del Pomerio (to the left of the arch); this street and its continuation in the Viale dei Rettori formed the natural boundary of the ancient city. Just beyond the arch in the Via S. Pasquale, on the left, is the church of **S. Ilario a Port' Aurea,** a most interesting Lombard structure of the late sixth or early seventh centuries, badly in need of repair.

Continuing up the Corso we see on the right the basilica of **S. Bartolomeo,** rebuilt by Pope Benedict XIII in 1729 on the site of the older church destroyed by the earthquake of 1702. Here, under the high altar, are preserved the bones of the Apostle St Bartholomew. The bishop's throne and canopy and the figures of saints above the near-by stalls are fine examples of early eighteenth-century woodcarving.

Farther on the Corso opens out into the Piazza G. Matteotti, a quiet square with an eighteenth-century house and garden on the left, at the end of which we see the truncated façade of one of the most fascinating churches in Campania, **S. Sofia.** An inscription on the wall reminds us that it was originally called Piazza Carlo Maurizio, after Prince Talleyrand. It was to him that the little fountain with its lions and obelisk was dedicated in 1808, and it was at his suggestion that the present Museo del Sannio was founded in

1806. Three of the four sections into which the museum is divided
are housed in the former monastery attached to S. Sofia; the historical section is in the Rocca dei Rettori.

The church of S. Sofia was begun by Gisulph II and completed by
Arechi II in 762. It was rebuilt after earthquakes to the original plan
in 990, and again in 1688, except that on this occasion the *pronaos* was
not replaced. The main doorway, flanked by two antique columns,
is of the thirteenth century; in the lunette above is *Christ enthroned
between the Virgin and St Mercurius*, with an unknown abbot kneeling.
The interior is delightful; the intricate play of warm brick arches
supported on the Corinthian capitals of ancient columns and on
Lombard pilasters is achieved by a daring ground plan, half circular
(with three round apses) and half stellar-pointed. The hexagonal
drum is supported on the inner circle of columns, and round this is
inscribed a decagon of pilasters, with a strange and most suggestive
interplay of vaulting. In two of the apses are remains of eighth-
century frescoes, illustrating *the Story of Zaccariah.*

The adjoining mid-twelfth-century **cloisters** are as surprising
and as beautiful as the church, showing how fruitful was the consolidation of S. Italy and Sicily under the Normans in the intermingling of architectural and sculptural styles. Here, the elegance
of the Moorish horseshoe arches raised on their slender columns is
matched by the vigour and inventiveness of the Lombard carving,
especially on the curious trapezoidal arch-supports above the
capitals.

The monastery buildings have been well converted to display the
interesting collections of antiques (particularly of the Samnite
territories), medals, ceramics, sculpture, paintings and drawings of
the **Museo del Sannio** (admission, daily 9.0 a.m.–1.0 p.m.;
closed on Mondays; historical section in the Rocca dei Rettori, the
same).

The **Rocca dei Rettori** (or 'the Castello', as it is commonly
called), a short way up the Corso Garibaldi from the Piazza
Matteotti, consists of two buildings: the older tower, on the left,
built in 1321 from the ruins of a Lombard fortress, itself incorporating a Roman construction, parts of which have been revealed in
recent restoration; and the section to the right, which was built in
the eighteenth century as the seat of the Apostolic delegation. In the
square in front of the Rocca is the medieval *Lion of the Castello*,
raised (1640) in honour of Pope Urban VIII on two roughly but
intricately ornamented pedestals of the late period of Roman
decadence. The figure of *Trajan* in the re-entrant by the door to the

131

museum is a modern bronze copy of an ancient statue. The historical section of the Museo del Sannio has an important and varied collection of documents connected with the city's history from the fifteenth to the nineteenth centuries, including interesting records of the periods of Talleyrand's rule and of the Risorgimento.

Beyond the Castello the Villa Comunale, laid out with fine trees and flower-beds, offers a wide view over the Valley of the Sabato.

Avellino—the Sanctuary of Montevergine—a famous painting and a pilgrimage

From Benevento two principal roads lead over the Neapolitan Apennines to Foggia and Northern Apulia. We shall take the more interesting route, the Via Appia (SS 7) and then the SS 90, leaving Benevento by the continuation of the Corso Garibaldi from the Piazza IV Novembre, the Viale degli Atlantici. The Via Appia leaves the SS 90 *bis* outside the city.

Crossing the fertile hills which separate the valleys of the Sabato and the Calore, it passes through the village of S. Giorgio del Sannio and meets the SS 90 (delle Puglie) just before crossing over the Calore. The Via Appia now loops back to Avellino, and we continue up the SS 90. The countryside through which the SS 90 now passes, the ancient lands of the Hirpini, has been much subject to earthquakes, the last being in August 1962. A branch road leads to the Pass of Mirabella. Beyond Grottaminarda the road crosses the River

Map II
p. 126
Ufita and climbs through hilly countryside to **Ariano Irpino,** a popular summer resort. Earthquakes have damaged all the churches here, as well as the Norman castle which was many times restored until it fell again in 1732. After Ariano Irpino the road crosses the bare uplands of Camporeale and joins the SS 90 *bis* from Benevento. It then follows the valley of the River Cervaro, crosses into Apulia near the station for Orsara, and comes down into the flat plain of the Capitanata, which it traverses by a straight road to Foggia (see chapter 14).

Map II
p. 126
Avellino lies twenty-one miles due south of Benevento by the SS 88, which follows the valley of the Sabato through fertile wooded country of farms and small villages. The city, the provincial capital since 1806, lies in an arcadian hollow among the mountains, at the junction of the tributaries of the Sabato. Earthquakes have destroyed much of the old city, but it has a clean, modern appearance, and its delightful position compensates for its lack of architectural interest.

The original Hirpinian city of Abellinum was near the village of Atripalda (some two and a half miles to the east), where modern excavations have made some important discoveries. On the destruction of their city in the ninth century by the Lombards the survivors moved to the present site. It was in the cathedral that Roger II was invested in 1130 by the antipope Anacletus as the first Norman King of Sicily. During the sixteenth and seventeenth centuries Avellino was fortunate in its feudal rulers. Artists and poets, among them Tasso, were received in the castello, and later, the little court of Prince Marino II of the Caracciolo family (his father had been created Prince of Avellino in 1581 for his part in the defeat of the Turks at Lepanto) was renowned for the splendour of its social, intellectual and artistic life. Caracciolo founded one of those curiously named 'academies' so popular at the time; his was called the Accademia dei Dogliosi ('the Grieved Ones'), and one of its best-known members was the Neapolitan story-teller Giambattista Basile. The architect Cosimo Fanzago was another of the circle, and some of his works have survived the earthquakes. The castle, alas, has not; but some of Caracciolo's furniture and his sixteenth-century Flemish tapestries can be seen—or will be, if the latter ever come back from being repaired in Naples—in the Abbot of Montevergine's Palace of Loreto (see p. 134).

From the modern centre of the city, the Piazza della Libertà, the Via Giuseppe Nappi leads to the little Piazza Amendola, with its **Palazzo della Dogana** (today a cinema), decorated with antique statues and busts, one of which is of Prince Marino I. This medieval building was restored in 1657 to Fanzago's designs; his also is the monument to Charles II of Habsburg in front of the palace, and also the clock-tower near by. From the piazza, to the right, the curving Via Umberto I takes us down to the seventeenth-century church of **S. Maria di Costantinopoli,** opposite the baroque *fountain of Bellerophon.* (The church has a fifteenth-century fresco of the *Madonna and Child* over the high altar.) Behind the fountain some steps, the Gradelle delle Fontana, lead up through the oldest parts of the city to the Via Seminario; turning left here, we come to the much rebuilt Duomo, of little interest.

The collections of antiquities which form the **Museo Irpino** still await the construction of a new building near the Villa Comunale in the Via Roma; this will eventually house the Museo and the Biblioteca Provinciale 'Capone', at present in the eighteenth-century Palazzo di Giustizia (formerly the Palazzo Caracciolo) in the Piazza della Libertà.

The Companion Guide to Southern Italy

From Avellino the visitor to the famous **sanctuary of Montevergine** follows the Corso Vittorio Emanuele and its continuation
in the beautiful avenue of plane trees, the Viale Italia, until at the
beginning of the SS 7 *bis* for Naples he turns right at the signpost for
Mercogliano. Those who come direct from Naples usually turn left
at the crossroads of Taverna del Pezzente, and meet the Avellino–
Mercogliano road a little before Mercogliano—where we must turn
right (towards Avellino) for the **Abbot's Palace of Loreto,** which
stands above the road on the left at a short distance from the junction.

The palace, the winter residence of the Abbot and the monks of
Montevergine (only some five or six remain at the sanctuary above
to face the rigours of winter at the height of 4165 ft), was built in 1735
by the architect Domenico Antonio Vaccaro, who designed the
delightful cloisters of the Clarisse in Naples. Permission to visit is
given at the lobby on the left of the entrance, opposite the pharmacy
stocked with eighteenth-century ceramic jars. The palace has
splendid examples of Vaccaro's use of billowing curves in the stairs
and wide corridors. The abbot's drawing-room retains the period
furniture. In the muniment room we can see some of the original
tiles in polychrome majolica. The precious library of documents
going back to the twelfth century has modern shelving and cata-
loguing and photographic apparatus. Among the volumes on show
I saw a beautiful fifteenth-century French *Book of Hours*.

From Mercogliano, a pleasant shaded village with a restaurant at
the Albergo Valente, a lift takes visitors to the sanctuary. The views
from the lift, from the good road which winds up among the chestnuts and beeches, and from the top are marvellous.

The **monastery** was begun in 1119 by St William of Vercelli on
the site of a ruined temple of Cybele; under the Normans and the
Angevins both the abbey of Montevergine and the monastic order
of Verginians, also founded by St William, were high in the royal
favour. The famous painting of the *Madonna and Child* (the *Mamma
schiavona* as it is popularly known) over the main altar in the sanctuary was given in 1310 by Catherine of Valois, titular Empress of
Constantinople, who is buried here with her son, the unlucky Louis
of Taranto (second husband of Queen Giovanna I of Naples). The
head of the Madonna in this beautiful picture is Byzantine work from
Constantinople, though the credulous believe it to be by St Luke; the
rest is by Montano di Arezzo, and was painted for Catherine in 1310.

The pilgrimages to Montevergine at Whitsun or for the Nativity
of the Virgin on September 8th are peculiarly Neapolitan festivals,

garish, noisy, half pagan and wholly popular, with a street of shack-like booths set up near the piazza. The rooms in the church where the votive offerings are displayed may shock the northerner. There are representations in silver of cured hearts, lungs, breasts (like bicycle-bells), limbs—but no genitals (unlike the pagan Romans, as we can see in the Museo Campana); and on the walls hang crude paintings of operations and accidents between Cellophane bags containing first communion and bridal dresses and switches of human hair. Refreshments are served by monks in the bar, where the pilgrim may buy various liqueurs and sweetmeats prepared by the religious.

Cimitile—St Paulinus of Nola—Nola

For Nola and Naples we return to the junction with the SS 7 *bis* at Taverna del Pezzente and turn right. Beyond Monteforte Irpino, Mugnano del Cardinale and Baiano, lies on our right the market town of **Avella,** interesting for the near-by ruins of Roman Abella and for its picturesque, somewhat dirty and crowded appearance—very much how these Campanian towns and villages must have appeared a century ago. From Avella comes the French word for hazelnuts, *avelines,* which grow abundantly hereabouts.

Map II
p. 126

    Cimitile, on the right of the road, should on no account be missed. Midway down the very narrow main street, the Corso Umberto I, we see on the right a small piazza or cul-de-sac where the church of *S. Felice in Pincis* stands. Nowhere, not even in Rome, is one so aware of the transition from paganism to Christianity as here among this complex of recently excavated buildings. Cimitile was the cemetery of Roman Nola and it was on this spot that the Nolans in the fourth century buried their first bishop, the Syrian S. Felice, and other Christian martyrs. In the church we can see the intricate structural interweaving of Roman and early Christian basilicas, catacombs, churches and prisons, on different levels and with mosaics and sculptures of many periods. (The key is at the house on the left of the entrance; tip.)

Map I
p. 104

    Closely connected with Cimitile is St Paulinus of Nola (353–413), the pupil of the delightful old pagan Ausonius, and friend and correspondent of St Ambrose and St Augustine. Paulinus was born in Bordeaux. In 379, as *consularis* in Campania, he visited the grave here of St Felix, was converted to Christianity, and began what became a lifetime of devotion to the Saint's memory. Years later he returned as priest; and with his wife, who had now become his sister Therasia, spent his large fortune in acts of charity, on a tomb for the relics of St Felix, the cathedral at Nola, and a much-needed aqueduct. His fame spread, and pilgrims arrived in great numbers. In 409 he was appointed bishop of Nola. He died shortly after the death of his friend, St Augustine, in 413. Paulinus is said to have invented church bells, which are known as *campana* from their Campanian origin. The Saint's feast day (June 22nd) in Nola is a most spectacular affair.

Map I
p. 104 We leave Cimitile by continuing in the Corso Umberto I to where it meets the main Naples–Nola road; there we turn left to **Nola.** The origin of the town is very ancient; it is thought to have been founded by Oscans and later to have come into the possession of the Etruscans, before falling to the Samnites. Like other early Campanian towns, it became Hellenized, and during the Second Samnite War was taken by the Romans. And here in AD 14 the Emperor Augustus died in the arms of his wife Livia.

Nola was the birthplace of Giovanni Marigliano, commonly known as Giovanni da Nola (1488–1558), the sculptor; and of the philosopher Giordano Bruno (1548–1600), who was burnt at the stake in the Campo dei Fiori in Rome on the orders of the Inquisition.

The centre of the modern town is the Piazza del Duomo. The **cathedral church of S. Felice** was gutted by fire in 1861 and rebuilt between 1878 and 1909. (If the main doors are closed, the church can be entered through the sacristy from the street to the right.) On the inner wall of the main entrance is a lively representation of the fire of 1861. The reliefs on the pulpit are said to be an early work of Giovanni da Nola, who is buried here in the chapel of St Paulinus (on the left), which also contains the bones of the Saint. Undoubtedly the most interesting part of the Duomo is the ancient crypt, built on the ruins of a temple of Jupiter and consecrated by St Felix himself. On the wall to the right at the foot of the stairs is a stone with an incised cross and symbols of the eighth century. Above is an eleventh-century relief of *Christ and the Apostles*. On the opposite side of the crypt is the resting-place of St Felix, whose remains were moved here from Cimitile. From his bones there flows five times a year, by means of a silver conduit, the miraculous 'manna'.

Outside the Duomo to the right of the piazza is the Caffè Azzurro, whose proprietor, Signor Ruggiero, is one of the rare southern Italians to know anything of the history or antiquities of his city.

From the café, to the right, runs the Via Giordano Bruno, and on the same side of the street is the Renaissance *Palazzo Covoni* (*ca.* 1500), the lower portions of which are built from Roman remains. To the left of the Piazza Giordano Bruno, farther on, is the fine *Palazzo Orsini,* built in 1461 by Orso Orsini, whose family were lords of Nola. Facing the palazzo is the Gothic church of *S. Biagio.* Here in the sacristy behind the church is a tomb of the Albertini family, attributed by some to Giovanni da Nola or the little-known Neapolitan sculptor Annibale Caccavello (*ca.* 1515–*ca.* 70). Near by, in the passage and stairway, are some remains of fourteenth- to fifteenth-century frescoes.

If we return to the Piazza del Duomo and take the street to the left of the Municipio, we come, in the Via S. Chiara, to the convent and restored fourteenth-century *chapel* dedicated to St Clare. (The Municipio faces the Duomo and contains in the courtyard four rather rough Roman statues, which formerly stood in the piazza.) The French nuns are delighted to show the chapel to visitors. The good frescoes are contemporary with the building. In the convent parlour the ceiling was painted by the eighteenth-century Neapolitan painter Angelo Mozzillo, who painted a number of churches in the neighbourhood of Nola.

For Naples we return to the junction with the road for Cimitile and pass Marigliano and Pomigliano d'Arco, near the foot of the northern slope of Monte Somma-Vesuvius. A little farther on we meet the SS 162 from Benevento and, retracing the first part of our round trip, arrive in Naples.

CHAPTER 9

Procida, Ischia and Capri

Map: I, p.104

The islands of Procida and Ischia, lying to the west of the Bay of
Naples and separated from each other and from Cape Misenum only
by narrow channels, appear to be appendices to the Phlegraean
Fields. The conical shape of Monte Epomeo on Ischia at once
reminds the visitor of its volcanic origin; as does the submerged
crater which today forms Porto d'Ischia. On Procida the sea has
entered and partly destroyed four craters of basaltic tufa and pumice
stone, converting them into bays. The little island of Vivara, which
adjoins Procida to the west, represents a fifth crater.

Throughout the year there are frequent services to the islands by
steamer (*piroscafo*) from Naples (Molo Beverello), provided by SPAN
and other lines. In the summer months sailings are greatly increased
and there is a daily service connecting Ischia with Capri and
Sorrento. Cars can be transported from Naples, but most people use
the car-ferry from Pozzuoli. (The passenger service from Pozzuoli is
also considerably cheaper than that from Naples.) Furthermore, the
traveller arriving by air at Capodichino can fly direct by helicopter
(ELIVIE) in 15 minutes to Casamicciola on Ischia. Another helicopter
service leaves from the Calata Beverello in Naples. Half-way
between air and sea travel are the *aliscafi* (hydroplanes). The
crossing from Mergellina to Porto d'Ischia by *aliscafo* takes half an
hour, but neither this nor the helicopter calls at Procida.

Procida—the market-garden of Naples

The houses facing the port of **Procida,** the Marina Grande, have a
distinctly oriental appearance, which comes partly from their gay
colours, partly from their interesting shapes. They give the impression of having been modelled rather than 'constructed', the effect of

the traditional practice of beating the wet plaster with which they are covered, so that all sharp angles are softened and one is conscious only of curves, half curves and rounded corners. These houses on Procida, with others on Capri, are some of the best remaining examples of this very ancient Campanian craft.

Historically, Procida and Ischia have been closely associated with the fortunes of Naples. In Hohenstaufen and Angevin times Procida was a fief of the celebrated Giovanni da Procida; from 1339 to 1529 it belonged to the Cossa family, and subsequently, until 1743, to the d'Avalos. Ferdinand I and IV used it as a hunting reserve and prohibited cats on the island since they also appeared to enjoy the destruction of its many rabbits. When the king visited Procida, a man-of-war was kept on patrol off the coast as a precaution against a sudden foray from the corsairs. Procida was occupied three times by the English during the Napoleonic struggles; their interference at the time of the short-lived Parthenopean Republic still rankles among Neapolitans and is therefore better left in the decency of oblivion.

Many legends have grown up around the life of Giovanni da Procida (*ca.* 1210–*ca.* 98). Boccaccio makes him the hero of a romantic tale in the *Decameron* (Fifth Day, Novella VI) and credits him with commendable assiduity in the pursuit of his beloved, a certain Restituta Bolgaro of Ischia. 'Not a day passed but he would go to Ischia to see her, and frequently in the night; if he could not get a boat, he would swim over, though it was only to please himself with the sight of her house . . .' What precise part Giovanni played in fanning the fires of revolt against the French which culminated in the massacre known as the Sicilian Vespers (March 30th, 1282) is uncertain, but what does seem well established is that he was one of the most important members of the conspiracy in support of the Aragonese heirs of the Hohenstaufen, and one of the most able and influential diplomats of his time.

Because of its volcanic soil the vegetation of the island is exceedingly rich, and Procida is in effect a market-garden for Naples, producing great quantities of high-quality fruit, particularly oranges and lemons, grapes and melons. The 10,000 Procidani live by this produce or by fishing; they also have a reputation as skilled and intrepid mariners and find employment on the ocean-going liners.

Procida has not been developed to receive large numbers of tourists in the way that Capri has or, more recently, Ischia; but it is a most attractive place for a quiet holiday. There is only one hotel,

Le Arcate, which is simple but comfortable and pleasantly placed overlooking the Marina Corricella, to the east of the island. Visitors may also find lodgings in private houses or in *locande* (establishments with rather primitive rooms to let). There is good bathing here or at the Lido di Procida, and also at the Marina di Chiaiolella, on a bay to the south-west, partly enclosed by the little island of Vivara. Vivara, which is the property of the Commune, is uninhabited and is let privately for the shooting—rabbits mostly. Procida itself is well provided with roads and lanes and is ideally suited for walking. There are a few cars and some buses on the island but the main means of transport is the *carrozzella*—no longer the charming horse-drawn vehicle, with its tasselled awning as protection from the sun, but its modern descendant, a two-seated adaptation of a motor-scooter.

The castle which appears prominently on the high eastern end of the island is, alas, a prison.

Ischia—a tour of the island

Leaving the port of Procida the ship rounds the Punta di Pioppeto, the northernmost point of the island, and ahead lies **Ischia** revealed in the full impressiveness of its soaring contour and brilliant emerald colouring. To the Greeks the island was known as Pithecusa ('Ape-land'), though the Romans seemed to think they also called it Arime or Inarime. Virgil refers to it thus in the *Aeneid*, but the Romans more usually called it Aenaria, a corruption derived from the Greek for 'wine', which suggests that even at that date its wine was good. In the Middle Ages, however, it was known as Iscla, a corruption of *insula*, island, which in turn became in Neapolitan Ischia. Ischia is highly volcanic, and although Monte Epomeo now appears extinct, the island owes its many thermal and medicinal springs to this source, as well as its active *fumarole*. The last violent earthquake, in 1883, practically destroyed the town of Casamicciola, and some three thousand persons lost their lives in the space of fifteen seconds.

By reason of its strategic position at the entry to the Bay of Naples, Ischia has been the scene of political contention from the time of its occupation by Hieron of Syracuse after the defeat of the Etruscans at the battle of Cumae in 474 BC—Pindar sang of these exploits in the *First Pythian Ode*—to its capture by the English squadron under Troubridge during the Napoleonic Wars. In 1438 Alfonso of Aragon expelled all the male inhabitants and married off the women to his

Catalans. Ischia suffered greatly at the hands of the corsairs, particularly from the raids of Barbarossa and Dragut (1543–52); the solid, round look-out towers, like the Torrione at Forio, are reminders of the ever-present threat from those scourges of the Mediterranean. In 1543 Barbarossa carried off four thousand of the islanders, and as late as 1796 six men from Forio, who had gone to cut wood on the island of Ventotene, were captured and enslaved by Barbary pirates.

A painting at the palace of Caserta by a German, Philip Hackert (1737–1807), shows a charming scene on the lake of Ischia, with the Casino Reale on the hill among the trees, and in the background the undamaged Aragon Castello at Ponte. Today the scene at **Porto d'Ischia** is very different. The steamer passes through a canal cut through the lip of the volcano into the crater lake which forms an artificial harbour—the laudable work of King 'Bomba' in 1853—and today the main street of Porto d'Ischia, the Via Roma and its continuation in the Via Vittoria Colonna, is lined with boutiques and fashionable shops.

The modern town of **Ischia,** which depends almost entirely on the tourist trade, stretches for about a mile in a south-easterly direction from the port along the fine sandy beach. It was only after the opening of the port of Ischia in 1854 that this part came to be built, and since the last war the great influx of visitors has transformed the pleasant, rather sleepy, town into a gay, sophisticated holiday resort. Many of the island's villas and hotels stand here among the trees of the celebrated *pineta*, whose pines have flourished on the volcanic soil resulting from the last eruption in 1302, when the lava flow (known as the *lava dell' Arso*) reached the sea, forming the Punta Molina, which separates the Lido from the Spiaggia dei Pescatori at **Ischia Ponte.** The older town, still inhabited largely by fishermen and poorer folk, was at Ponte, which takes its name from the causeway built by Alfonso il Magnanimo in 1438 to connect his island fortress with the mainland.

The picturesque pile of the ***Castello*** at Ponte (it was severely damaged by the English bombardments of 1806 and 1809) is inseparably associated with its most distinguished occupant, the poetess Vittoria Colonna (1490–1547). Here, on December 27th, 1509, in the now ruined fourteenth-century cathedral, she married Ferrante d'Avalos, Marchese di Pescara, the equivocal military commander in the pay of Charles V. During her husband's prolonged absences and after his death in 1525 Vittoria Colonna spent much time on Ischia, employing herself in study, poetry and correspondence with many of the leading spirits of the time. The Castello is now private property but parts of it are open to the public.

From the Piazza del Redentore by the landing-stage of Porto d'Ischia, beyond the last-century church of S. Maria di Portosalvo, the Via Baldassarre Cossa brings us to the station for the chairlift for **Montagnone.** From here we have a fine view over Porto: to the left of the circular basin, beyond the Villa Masturzi, appear the trees of the Park of Remembrance on the point, which is artificially prolonged in the breakwater and lighthouse. To the left of this again, but hidden by the hill from our view, is the little Spiaggia degl' Inglesi —I have never been able to find out why it is called this; perhaps some memory of the English occupation in the early 1800's? On the right of the harbour, above the line of buildings on the quayside, is the Punta S. Pietro, with the Aquarium and the chiesetta of S. Pietro a Pantaniello on the wooded heights. Then farther right, facing Vivara and Procida, is the Lido, and behind the beach the villas and hotels among the greens of the umbrella pines. Ahead of us, over the blue waters of Canale d'Ischia, lies the mainland, rising towards Monte Grillo, with the white houses of Torregaveta and Monte di Procida clearly discernible.

A good motor road encircles the island, linking the most important towns and villages, and offering a variety of beautiful scenery. We leave Porto d'Ischia by the Via Baldassarre Cossa, which immediately climbs steeply and gives some fine views back towards Porto and over the channel to the Phlegraean Fields. On our right we pass the little cemetery of Casamicciola; it would be hard to imagine a more beautiful setting. Near the village of Perrone we can see ahead of us the white houses of the town itself, with Lacco Ameno beyond.

Casamicciola Terme consists of a low-lying quarter which spreads itself along the sea, and a higher part behind, with villas and the well-known thermal establishments among gardens and vineyards. The town, rebuilt after the earthquake, contains little of architectural interest. It was at Casamicciola, in the delightful old Villa Piseni (now re-named Villa Ibsen), with its rose-garden and trellis overlooking the sea, that Henrik Ibsen wrote much of *Peer Gynt* in the summer of 1867.

The white wines of Ischia—the best is called Epomeo—can be very good indeed, but very few of them find their way unadulterated on to the market, and the visitor will have to exercise some ingenuity in order to find something better than those usually offered as

Epomeo. I was fortunate to discover some years ago a wine produced by a peasant-fisherman near the village of Succhivo on the south of the island, which was one of the best *vini da pasto* I have ever tasted. It was light in colour, fragrant, had a delicate flavour, and was of a good alcoholic content. There is also a less common red Epomeo. The finest of these wines are perhaps those produced on the slopes of Epomeo itself around the Villa Piromallo on the south-west of Ischia, towards the Punta Imperatore.

From Casamicciola a secondary road, which passes the Observatory on the Grande Sentinella (there is a good view from this point), leads along the high ground and across the spurs on the foothills of Monte Epomeo to Forio. The coast road brings us to the seaside and thermal resort of **Lacco Ameno.** (Lacco adopted its epithet Ameno —'pleasant, agreeable'—only in 1863.) The mineral springs here are managed in connection with the hotels and are among the most radio-active in Italy. The Hotel Regina Isabella and Sporting, is the most luxuriously appointed on the island—and its charges are commensurate. The curious shaped rock to the right of the jetty is known as *Il Fungo*, the Mushroom.

The first Greek colonists in the western seas migrated here from Chalcis, Eretria and Cyme in Euboea, according to Eusebius, in 1050 BC, but modern authorities tend to place the settlement in the eighth or seventh centuries. These settlers had their acropolis on Monte Vico, to the north-west of Lacco, and their town in the valley of S. Montano at the foot of the hill. Excavations here in 1952 discovered evidence of this from Greek tombs of the seventh century. It may be that other settlers followed at a later date, since the tradition holds that the founders of Cumae on the mainland moved from Pithecusa on account of the earthquakes. In Roman times the town was known as Heraclium, possibly from the important cult of the hero around the Bay of Naples.

It was here, on May 17th, 304, that an event occurred which is still remembered by the inhabitants and celebrated with a profusion of illuminated arches, brass bands and pyrotechnics. On that date a boat was miraculously wafted into the beautiful bay of S. Montano, bearing the remains of the virgin martyr S. Restituta from North Africa. At the end of the eighth century her body was removed to the Duomo in Naples, which was renamed after her, but to the Ischians she has remained patron of the island. The **sanctuary of S. Restituta** at Lacco Ameno consists of two churches, the modern one of the last century, with a façade of 1910, and the older building on the right, which arose in 1036 on a palaeochristian basilica and was restored in the fourteenth century and rebuilt in 1707. We can see in the recently opened crypt something of this original church of the fourth to fifth centuries, together with other antiquities discovered on the spot, and relics of S. Restituta.

The road ascends after Lacco Ameno and then makes a sharp left-hand turn. Here, through the gateway of the Villa Mezza Torre on the rocky headland between Punta Cornacchia and Punta di Caruso, a road leads down to the delightful Lido di S. Montano, a beautiful sandy beach enclosed between wooded hills. A short way beyond this turning the road begins to descend; ahead of us we see the vine-covered foothills of the western flanks of Epomeo and the white houses of Forio grouped around its circular watch-tower. The road then runs down to the coast, passing on the right the track to the beach of Montevergine—or S. Francesco as it is more usually known, from the monastery on the hill above.

Forio is a small town, the centre of the Epomeo wine-growing district. We are immediately aware, as soon as we enter the little Piazza Luca Balsofiore, with its domed church of S. Gaetano on the right, of a different atmosphere, of an individuality in the architecture of its colour-washed houses and churches, which distinguishes it from other towns on Ischia. On the left of the piazza a short street brings us to a crossroads, on the corner of which stands the baroque church of *S. Maria di Loreto* (originally of the fourteenth century), its twin towers capped with majolica tiles. Turning right, we come to the Piazza Matteotti. Here, at the tables of the Bar International, by the somewhat makeshift fountain, is as good a spot as any to observe the cosmopolitan cross-currents of Forian life. It is an intriguing scene.

Opposite, a lane leads through to the *Torrione,* the tower built in 1480 by King Ferrante as a defence against the corsairs. There is a little museum in the tower. Beyond the Torrione the lane descends, past an interesting baroque palace, to the beach and to the restaurant da Filippo 'Il Saturnino'. (I can recommend the lobster here in particular. Another good place to eat, in the style of Bologna, is the restaurant of that name at 35 Via Matteo Verde—from the Piazza Matteotti go straight on past S. Maria di Loreto; the Bologna is on the right.)

Continuing along the Piazza Matteotti, away from S. Maria, we come to the Municipio and the seventeenth-century church of S. Francesco and, beyond, the headland on which stands the picturesque little whitewashed church of the *Soccorso.* Inset in the walls and on the free-standing cross are some beautiful (eighteenth-

The Charterhouse of Padula, one of the most important monuments of Southern Italy, was founded in 1306 but the existing building, constructed like the Escorial on the plan of St Lawrence's gridiron, is baroque. The elliptical staircase (1761) leads to a gallery above the arcades of the Great Cloister where the monks exercised in bad weather.

Mosaic pulpits.
Above Sicilian and Byzantine motifs are combined in this 12th c. example from Salerno cathedral.
Left Nicola Rufolo of Ravello commissioned this one for Ravello cathedral. The work was executed in 1272 by Nicolo di Bartolomeo da Foggia.

century?) majolica tiles, and within the church the walls are hung with crude but touching *ex-votos* of mariners and emigrants. From the Punta del Soccorso can sometimes be seen at sunset (I have never seen them) the curious and unexplained 'green rays' over the sea.

To resume our circuit of the island, we leave Forio by the Via Matteo Verde and then bear right through the vineyards which spread along the lower slopes of Monte Epomeo in continuous waves of green, to be repeated higher up the mountain by the chestnut trees. On our right we can see below us the fine stretch of sand of the Spiaggia di Citara as far as the rocks of the Punta dell' Imperatore, the south-western extremity of the island. To the left, shortly before we reach the village of Panza, stands the red-ochred Villa Piromallo. From Panza a road leads down through rich orchards and vineyards to Succhivo, and beyond it to the stopping-place for buses and cars for S. Angelo.

The final stage to **S. Angelo** is by footpath, and your luggage will be 'looked after' by a struggling crowd of chattering boys. This pleasant fishing village, the last of the island's seaside resorts to be opened up for tourists, is built on the cliffside and around the little piazza and port. Joined to the mainland by a narrow spit of sand is a lofty hill of solid trachite lava whose summit is crowned by the ruins of a tower which was destroyed by the English during the French Wars. A path climbing up the hillside behind the village takes us to the magnificent *Spiaggia dei Maronti.* Those who go there by boat from the harbour will miss the *fumarole* issuing jets of steam beside the path. Along the beach two openings in the cliffs lead to active mineral springs which were used by the Romans. At the eastern end of the Maronti beach a road is being constructed to give access to it from Testaccio and Barano.

Leaving Panza, the road climbs to **Serrara Fontana,** presenting us with wonderful views over intensively cultivated hillsides broken by ravines, S. Angelo and its tower-topped crag, and Capri away in the distance. We continue to climb to **Fontana,** the highest village on the island. This is the usual starting-point for the ascent to the summit of **Monte Epomeo,** which takes something under an hour. The path begins near the post-office and leads up, with an ever-widening panorama, to the Eremo and little church of *S. Nicola* (1459) just below the summit. Inside the church, in the chapel of the Crucifix, is the tomb of Giuseppe d'Argut, the Flemish governor of Ischia under Charles III of Bourbon. One day, when he was pursuing some military deserters, he was saved from death by his prayers to

S. Nicola. He retired from the King's service here, with twelve companions, and enlarged the hermitage (1754), where he ended his days.

The view from the top of Monte Epomeo has a range of some sixty to seventy miles. I am told—and I keep promising myself to do it—that it is an unforgettable experience to spend a moonlight summer's night on Epomeo.

After Fontana the road descends (notice the caves, *cellai,* cut in the tufa to store the wine), and passing through Buonopane, we come to **Barano d'Ischia,** set in an enchanting position among the vineyards. Beyond this we have a magnificent view of the Bay of Naples. At Piedimonte we leave on our left a road through Fiaiano to Porto d'Ischia, and at the junction beyond Molara take the left fork. This descends the Rio Carbone, crosses the *lava dell' Arso* (as the Via M. Mazzella), and finally reaches Porto d'Ischia in the Piazza degli Eroi.

Capri

Few places as limited in extent as **Capri** have had so many words poured out on them in ecstatic description: the natural beauties of the island, the antiquities, architecture, flora and fauna, the exhilarating effects of the magical 'air of Capri', the eccentricities of the expatriates, and the love-lives of visiting celebrities. Yet no traveller in the South of Italy will willingly bypass Capri if he has once tasted its compelling fascination. We can safely leave the charm to look after itself, and what follows is an account of what should not be missed rather than what precisely will be seen.

There is a frequent steamer service from Naples—departing from the Molo Beverello under the Castel Nuovo. In the summer months the morning SPAN boat goes on from Capri to Positano and Amalfi; and another service links Sorrento, Capri and Ischia. There are weekday car ferry services from Naples to Capri from the Immacolatella Vecchia to the east of the Molo Beverello. *Aliscafi* from Mergellina take only half an hour. Travellers who wish to use the ELIVIE helicopter service from Capodichino will need to book beforehand through a tourist agency.

Roman emperors and Barbary corsairs

Capri is small. It is under 4 miles in length, some 1¾ miles at its widest, and has an area of about 5½ square miles. Once it was joined to the mainland—even now only three miles of water (the Bocca Piccola) separate Il Capo on the east of the island from the Punta della Campanella on the mainland—and it is geologically a calcareous prolongation of the Sorrentine peninsula. The ten miles of the island's precipitous coastline, which offers few points of easy access and presents an appearance of almost forbidding grandeur, have been cut into by natural processes to form a number of beautiful caves—there are said to be sixty-five of them, the Blue Grotto being the most famous—and fantastically shaped rocks like the Faraglioni on the south-east point of the island. Its ten thousand residents live mostly in three localities: around the port of the Marina Grande; in the town of Capri, 450 ft above the port; and at Anacapri, the village on the western plateau, 935 ft above the sea.

Capri was inhabited as early as the palæolithic age. It was almost certainly settled by Greeks, but when they arrived is uncertain. Nor has the origin of its name been satisfactorily explained. From 336 BC Capri belonged to Naples and, with the rest of Campania, became increasingly Romanized. Augustus is reported to have visited it in 29 BC on his return to Italy from his victory over Antony and Cleopatra at Actium. Suetonius tells us that the Emperor was much attracted to Capri from the first, not only by its peculiar Greekness but also by the fortunate augury which greeted his arrival, when a withered holm-oak suddenly burst into leaf. This led him to exchange the larger and more productive Ischia with the Neapolitans for Capri.

During the forty years Augustus came to Capri he built aqueducts, temples and several villas or palaces, as well as repairing the stone steps which joined Capri and Anacapri. Vestiges of the original work are still visible. It is also possible that the so-called Villa Jovis was Augustus's work; but this magnificent palace which became the second Palatine of imperial Rome was more likely built by Tiberius. Timberio, as the Capresi call Tiberius, spent the last ten years of his life on Capri, settling there at the advanced age of sixty-seven. However, his age did not spare him from the strictures of Roman historians—Tacitus and Suetonius in particular—who accused him of every sort of cruelty and crime, and of indulging his perverse lusts in the infamous 'orgy of Capri'.

In the Middle Ages Capri was a fief of the Arcucci family. The island suffered much damage from the raids of corsairs, especially from Barbarossa who in 1535 destroyed the castello at Anacapri, the ruin of which is now called after him; and Dragut, who sacked and burnt the Certosa in 1553. Under the Bourbons the islanders were encouraged to undertake their own defence against these sea-marauders by forming a regular militia. (Ferdinand I and IV used to visit the island for the quail shooting in the spring.) At the time of the Napoleonic Wars Capri was the scene of several actions between the English and the French, which resulted in severe damage to many of the remaining classical buildings. In May 1806 an English force overpowered the French garrison and fortified the island. Two French attempts to recapture it under Joseph Bonaparte were foiled, but finally in October 1808 King Murat attacked it in strength and forced the English to capitulate.

The town of Capri

Visitors usually land at the artificially protected Marina Grande on the north of the island and take the funicular up to the **town of Capri.** It can also be reached by steps, the Via S. Francesco, which start from the quayside some two hundred yards to the left of the funicular station; or by carriage-road, the Via Cristoforo Colombo, to the right of the station. If we go up by road, on the right (near the Albergo Bristol) we pass the footpath which leads to the scanty ruins of the *Palazzo a Mare*—perhaps the first residence built by Augustus—and to the better preserved Roman remains known as the *Baths of Tiberius,* which are more likely storehouses or offices overlooking the imperial port. The road then curves to the east, and just before the church of S. Costanzo, also to the right, is the beginning of the ancient steps to Anacapri—there are more than five hundred of them—the *Scala Fenicia,* which are misnamed, since they were originally built not by Phoenicians but by the Greeks to connect the port with Anacapri, before being rebuilt by Augustus.

The church of the patron saint of the island, **S. Costanzo** (once Patriarch of Constantinople, his remains were transported here at the time of the iconoclastic controversy and brought miraculous deliverance to the Capresi from the Saracen attack of AD 881), was built in the eleventh century in the shape of a Greek cross enclosed in a rectangle. Four ancient columns from a Roman villa support the curious Byzantine dome, and another four were removed in 1750 by Charles III of Bourbon for his new palace at Caserta. The church was enlarged and restored about 1330, and the main doorway is from this period.

The road climbs between villas among the vineyards and orange and lemon groves to a crossroads, the Bivio di Capri (the Quattro Venti); to the right is the road to Anacapri, straight ahead that for the Marina Piccola. We take the Via Roma, to the left, which brings us to the terrace of the funicular station and the Piazza Umberto I (usually known as 'the Piazza' *tout court*), the animated centre of Capri.

The small irregular **piazza of Capri** presents in microcosm an intriguing spectacle of the island's life. The setting is colourful but not architecturally remarkable. Here, at one time or other during the day or night, you will see, mingling with the workaday Capresi, a cosmopolitan crowd of the rich, the famous, the notorious, the distinguished, the beautiful (of both sexes)—and the lookers-on.

It was in the eighteenth century that Capri first began to draw to its hospitable hills artists, intellectuals, expatriates and eccentrics. One of the earliest was the Marquis de Sade, who was provided with letters of introduction to the island's authorities by the unsuspecting King Ferdinand I and IV. De Sade was fascinated by the debaucheries of Timberio and used his experiences on Capri as material for his novel *Juliette*. And after the 'discovery' of the Blue Grotto in 1826 the beauty of the island became well-known in European literature. In 1808 a landslide had obliterated one of Capri's main scenic attractions, the Grotta Oscura, which had been often described by travellers as the site of some of Timberio's worst excesses. The lawyer-hotelier Don Giuseppe Pagano decided that this deficiency should be made good, and on August 26th, 1826, he arranged for two visiting German painters to 'discover' the Blue Grotto (see p. 155), which was well-known to all the islanders and to many others; indeed, as the Grotto Gradola it is marked on a map of Capri published in the Venetian Coronelli's *Isolario* as early as 1696.

Until the First World War the Germans and the English accounted for the bulk of the foreign residents or visitors on Capri, but after the abortive St Petersburg rising in 1905 Capri also became the place of exile for a famous colony of Russian revolutionaries. Gorky took over the Villa Behring, which he renamed 'Red House', as a School of Revolutionary technique, with Lenin, Lunacharsky and himself as directors. Others in the circle included Plekhanov, the magnificent bass singer Chaliapin, and Tchaikovsky. Indeed, the list of those who have made Capri their home or have stayed there for some time would include many of the most famous names in the last half-century.

The piazzetta of modern Capri was the centre of the ancient Greek city (fifth to fourth centuries BC), and remains of a megalithic wall, which continued south-west to the heights of Castiglione and formed the fortified acropolis, can be seen built into the houses by the funicular station. And in the narrow (often vaulted) streets—the *viuzze*—off the piazza we can see something of the medieval building styles which are so characteristic of Capri: the use of half domes on roofs, the arcaded terraces, loggias and shaded pergolas. Inside the church of **S. Stefano,** which was rebuilt at the end of the seventeenth century in a style of eastern-influenced baroque, a pavement in inlaid polychrome marble from Tiberius's Villa Jovis has been laid in front of the high altar. Next to S. Stefano, on the right, is the **Palazzo Cerio,** constructed from the castle of Queen Giovanna I, which was on this site. The Palazzo Cerio houses a museum and a library, a collection of Capriana which was begun in the last century by Ignazio Cerio and augmented by his son, the writer Edwin Cerio.

Walks from Capri—famous look-out points

The visitor to Capri who finds pleasure in the juxtaposition of the primitive and the sophisticated will find much to beguile him in the streets leading off the piazza, and he will do best just to follow where his instinct leads. But there are several walks in the neighbourhood which it would be foolish to forgo. The first is a short one of about twenty minutes to the ruins of the medieval **castle of the Castiglione,** an outlook 820 ft above the Marina Piccola. From the piazza we take the steps by S. Stefano and turn right into the curious vaulted thoroughfare of the Via Madre Serafina. Past the church of S. Teresa and after a further vaulted tract, we turn right from the steps which lead to another viewpoint, the **Belvedere Cannone,** and follow the narrow *stradetta*, which almost immediately turns left, then brings us through vineyards to the castle of the Castiglione. From here another path leads down (with some difficulty) to the **Grotta del Castiglione,** which was inhabited in prehistoric times and transformed into a *nymphaeum* by the Romans.

For the **Certosa di S. Giacomo** and the **Parco Augusto** we take the Via Vittorio Emanuele III, the street of fashionable shops which leads out of the piazza under the arch on the left of S. Stefano. At the famous Albergo Quisisana we turn right in the Via Frederico Serena and continue as far as the junction. The road to the right, the Via Matteotti, brings us to the public gardens called after the Emperor Augustus. At this point begins a paved pathway built at the expense of the German armament king, Friedrich Krupp, which descends, with magnificent views, to meet the roadway from Capri to the Marina Piccola. To the left the road brings us shortly to the entrance to the Certosa.

Count Giacomo Arcucci began the building of the Charterhouse in 1371 on the site of a villa of Tiberius, using as his model the Certosa di S. Martino in Naples. In 1386, on losing royal favour (he had been secretary to Giovanna I), he retired here, and died in 1397. Subsequently the buildings were devastated by the Saracens (Dragut himself captured the monastery in 1553) and allowed to fall into ruin after the suppression of the Carthusians in 1807. The two cloisters—the smaller of the fifteenth century, the larger a century later—and the Gothic church have now been repaired. The church retains its original doorway with the figures in low relief of *S. Bruno* and *S. Giacomo*; and in the lunette above there is a fresco, possibly by the Sienese painter Andrea Vanni (*ca.* 1332–1414), which shows the *Madonna and Child with adoring figures,* among them Arcucci and Queen Giovanna.

The Via Cammarelle, flanked with expensive shops, runs to the left of the Albergo Quisisana. Where the road narrows, we follow, on the left, the Via Tragara, which leads among the villas and gardens on the slopes of Monte Tuoro to the Punta Tragara. In about 20 minutes we come out on the **belvedere di Tragara,** with a fine view of the Faraglioni and the Marina Piccola. From here we can descend by the Via Faraglioni (a further 20 minutes) to the little port of **Tragara,** where there are Roman remains. The rock which rises in front of us was formerly the haunt of a species of seal, *Leptonyx monachus* (now probably extinct), from which it derives its name, '*Il Monacone*'. On the near-by Faraglioni rocks are found a rare species of seagull and the famous blue lizard (*Lacerta caerulea faraglionensis*). The flora of Capri is also of the greatest interest to the botanist: some 850 species and 133 varieties have been found here, many of them coming from Roman gardens.

We may return to Capri by way of the Via Pizzolungo, which brings us after a series of magnificent views to the **Grotta de Matromania.** This large cave, with its semi-circular apse, shows traces of the elaborate decoration carried out by the Romans when they converted it into a sanctuary of Cybele, the Mater Magna, whence its name. Steps take us up to a little terrace with a bar, and from here we may go down to the *Arco Naturale,* a picturesque archway formed in the limestone rock by slow erosion. Returning to the *piazzaletto*, we make our way back to Capri up the Via Arco Naturale and then the Via Matromania. At the crossroads we can take either the Via Sopramonte, to the right, or the more direct Via Croce.

For the Palazzo di Timberio, as the local inhabitants call Tiberius's Villa Jovis, we take the Via Croce to the crossroad and continue straight on in the Via Tiberio; leaving on our right the Via Matromania, we pass the charming little church of *S. Michele* (or S. Croce) which was built at the end of the fourteenth century in the typical Capriot style of architecture. Our way takes us through the gardens of villas, orchards and olive-groves, to the *Pharos,* the lighthouse or signal tower, built most probably in the Augustan age and afterwards damaged by earthquake. Beyond this on the clifftop is the notorious *Salto di Tiberio,* where the Emperor is said to have forced his unhappy victims to take an aerial flight into eternity.

The *Villa Jovis* (admission, 9.0 a.m. until an hour before sunset) once extended with its gardens, promenades, stairways, terraces and buildings over the whole of the north-eastern promontory. The ruins which we see give us a very inadequate idea of the palatial imperial residence mentioned by Suetonius and Pliny.

Anacapri

For centuries there was rivalry and fierce enmity between the citizens of Capri and those of Anacapri. As late as 1782 their feuds made it necessary for Ferdinand I and IV to appoint a military governor of the island. Those differences no longer exist, but the ancient gateway at the top of the Scala Fenicia is still called the Porta della Differenzia. These steps were the only means of communication with Anacapri until the carriageway was built in 1877.

There is a frequent bus service between Capri and Anacapri, the buses leaving Capri from the Via Roma near the funicular station. We can also take a bus to the favourite bathing-place of Capri, the **Marina Piccola.** The road descends from the crossroads at the Torre Quattro Venti, first under the precipitous southern slopes of Monte Solaro, then in a series of curves to finish shortly beyond the junction with the Strada Krupp in the little square in front of the church of S. Andrea. The popularity of the Marina Piccola has come about only in the present century: facing due south, it is protected from the north wind, the *tramontano*, and its setting is most beautiful.

From the Quattro Venti, the Anacapri road climbs rapidly through vineyards in a general north-westerly direction, but soon the cultivated vegetation yields to the characteristic Caprese *macchia* of stunted evergreens—cystus, myrtle, juniper, holm-oak, carob, lentisk, heather—a wild pot-pourri which in the hot sun gives off a pungent scent. Beyond the statue of Our Lady of Lourdes the road forms a kind of prolonged terrace over the sea, and near the chapel of S. Antonio the Scala Fenicia crosses it and continues up to the Porta della Differenzia and the Castello Barbarossa, which stands behind the Villa S. Michele on the high ground above us.

Anacapri is a village of great charm and tranquillity set among gardens and vineyards on a flattish ledge at the north-western foot of Monte Solaro. Anacapri's striking difference in appearance from Capri comes partly from the more open nature of the terrain and partly from the architecture of the villas themselves, which is distinctly oriental. We enter by the Via G. Orlandi, which almost at once opens out into the Piazza della Vittoria. From here visitors may take the chairlift to the summit of Monte Solaro. From the left of the piazza the Via S. Michele leads back to the famous *Villa S. Michele,* built by the Swedish doctor and writer Axel Munthe (1857–1949) near the chapel dedicated to the Saint and on the ruins of a Roman villa (admission, 10.0 a.m.–12.0 noon; 2.0–4.0 p.m.). There is a fine view from the terrace over the Marina Grande to the Sorrentine peninsula and the Bay of Naples. From the Via S. Michele a track leads to the ruins of the medieval citadel destroyed by Barbarossa in 1535.

Returning to the Piazza della Vittoria, we continue along the Via Orlandi. At No. 42 is the *Museo della Torre* which has a collection of arms and ancient sculpture found in the vicinity. Past the museum, on the right, the Via S. Nicola brings us to the eighteenth-century church of *S. Michele*—or of the Terrestrial Paradise, so-called from the majolica pavement showing *the Garden of Eden* and *the Expulsion of Adam and Eve*, the work of Leonardo Chiaiese (1761) from the designs of D. A. Vaccaro. Back on the Via Orlandi we arrive at the Piazza Armando Diaz, with its pleasantly baroque parish church of *S. Sofia,* which was medieval in origin, then rebuilt in 1510 and enlarged in 1870. Beyond the Parrochiale the road forks, the right-hand branch leading to Damecuta and the Blue Grotto, the left to the adjoining village of Caprile, really an extension of Anacapri.

Excursions from Anacapri

The district around Anacapri offers pleasant walking to the more energetic visitor. Instead of taking the chairlift to the top of **Monte Solaro,** he may prefer to follow the steep path which begins about 200 yards along the Via S. Michele (sign on the right). In about three-quarters of an hour—a short way past the remains of the English fortifications of 1806—he will come to a little chapel. The path to the left leads (in about 20 minutes) to the fourteenth-century *sanctuary of S. Maria Cetrella,* which stands 1423 ft above the Marina Piccola with a splendid view of the Gulf of Salerno. For Monte Solaro we continue straight on from the chapel and the summit is reached in about another quarter of an hour. As can be imagined, the view from this height (1932 ft) rivals that from Monte Epomeo. The inner man may be restored at the Ristorante La Canzone del Cielo.

Another excursion may be made on foot to the **plateau of Migliara** (about 40 minutes) and back by the Torre della Guardia and **Materita** (a further hour and a quarter). From the Piazza della Vittoria a short street on the left brings us to ancient Strada della Migliara, which begins at the Scala Fenicia and finishes at the Belvedere di Migliara. A track to the right takes us on to the Torre della Guardia overlooking the Punta Carena and the lighthouse, the south-western extremity of the island. From here we return by a path which takes us by the *Torre Materita,* built in the sixteenth century by the Carthusians as a protection against Saracen raids, and abandoned when the Certosa was suppressed by the French. It was restored at the beginning of this century by Axel Munthe, who used to retire there when the press of sight-seers became unbearable at the Villa S. Michele. It was at Materita that he wrote his famous *Story of San Michele* and the manuscript can now be seen, together with other relics and possessions (admission, 11.0 a.m.–1.0 p.m., 2.30–5.0 p.m.; closed Mondays).

By the new road it is a distance of two and a half miles to the piazzetta above the Blue Grotto, passing on the way Mulino a Vento and the *Torre di Damecuta* (signposted). Next to the medieval Tower of Damecuta (twelfth century), which was part of the island's protection against the corsairs, are the excavated ruins of another imperial *Roman villa*—if we believe the historians there were twelve of these Augusto-Tiberian palaces (for the size of

154

the Villa Jovis and this at Damecuta suggest they were palaces rather than villas) dedicated to the twelve major deities of the Roman pantheon. From here there is a splendid view of Ischia and the whole Bay of Naples. The road then descends to the little piazza above the Blue Grotto.

It is more usual to visit the famous **Blue Grotto** by motor-boat from the Marina Grande, the trip taking about an hour and a half. Gradual subsidence of the coast has caused the sun's rays to enter from an opening below the sea, filling the cave with a filtered blue light and making objects below the surface appear a luminous silver. It is best seen, therefore, about noon. Since the entrance is only four feet high, the grotto can be visited comfortably only on a calm day.

Capri is extremely well provided with hotels and *pensioni*, from the luxurious Albergo Quisisana and others of the first category to those of a more modest kind. Prices on the whole are high, and the visitor should be forewarned.

Restaurants are numerous and of varying quality and prices. Many of these are close to the piazza in Capri—La Pigna, for example, 30 Via Lo Palazzo, which is the only one on the island to have had a Michelin star for several years. Here the specialities are ravioli, lobster *al forno*, a *suprême* of chicken with mushrooms, and a genuine Capri red wine.

CHAPTER 10

The Sorrentine Peninsula and the Costiera Amalfitana

Maps: I, p.104; II, p.126

Castellammare di Stabia—Gragnano—Vico Equense—Sorrento

The drive along the coast from Castellammare di Stabia to Sorrento, from there over the wedge-shaped watershed which divides the Gulf of Naples from the Gulf of Salerno, and then along the precipitous Costiera Amalfitana, must surely be among the most beautiful on this earth—and the scenery is miraculously still unspoilt. Ideally the drive should be made in both directions.

For Sorrento, it is advisable to take the autostrada from Naples to Castellammare di Stabia rather than the old SS 18 which is full of interest but almost intolerable (except on a Sunday morning) by reason of the traffic in the densely populated areas through which it passes. At Pompei-Scavi we branch right from the autostrada for Salerno, and a quick run brings us to the city and port of **Castellammare di Stabia** at the foot of the wooded slopes of Monte Faito.

Map I
p. 104

The origins of the ancient city of Stabiae are very obscure; it may have been in turn a Greek, Etruscan and Samnite possession before falling to the Romans in 340 BC. In the Social War Stabiae sided with the Italians against Rome but was taken and destroyed by Sulla in 89 BC. The rebuilt city was finally overwhelmed in the eruption of AD 79. The ancient site was somewhat to the north-east of Castellammare on the rising ground known as Varano, where recent excavations have revealed two large Roman villas among the fields near the Grotto of S. Biagio (this also possibly of pagan origin).

The waters of Castellammare, the ***Terme Stabiane,*** have been famous since Roman times. (The Terme are in the Piazza Amendola near the port.) Over one hundred treatments are undertaken by a qualified staff who direct the application of the waters from twenty-eight mineral springs.

Opposite the Terme Stabiane in the Piazza Amendola are the
156

Naval Shipyards and Arsenal, built by Sir John Acton for Ferdinand I and IV in 1783; shipbuilding is still an important part of the city's economy. We turn right and take the Via Brin and its continuation, the Via Bonito (called after the eighteenth-century painter, Giuseppe Bonito, a native of Castellammare), to the gardens of the Villa Comunale by the sea. Here at the farther end of the Piazza del Municipio (the Municipio was formerly the Palazzo Farnese) stands the **Duomo,** originally of the sixteenth century but much altered at the end of the last century. Behind the Duomo, next to the Stazione Circumvesuviana, is the station for the cable railway to the top of Monte Faito. From the square in front of the Stazione the Via Regina Margherita brings us to the new Strada Panoramica to Sorrento, where we turn right.

A short distance on the left is the road to **Gragnano,** the town which has given the generic name for the well-known red wines produced in this district. This road, an alternative route to Amalfi, climbs up the slopes of the Monti Lattari, through vineyards and woods, crossing the spur (by means of a tunnel) a little to the east of Monte S. Angelo a Tre Pizzi, the highest peak in the Monti Lattari, and coming out into the fertile temperate uplands of Agerola. After a magnificent view over the Bay of Salerno, the road rapidly descends by a series of hairpin bends to Vettica on the coast road about $1\frac{1}{2}$ miles west of Amalfi.

Map I
p. 104

Less than a mile past the road for Gragnano a turning on the left brings us to the toll-road to Monte Faito and the beginning of the avenue of holm-oaks leading to the **Villa Quisisana**—'Here-one-gets-well'—the name given to the royal villa by Ferdinand I and IV who restored it in 1820. It was built originally by Robert of Anjou in 1310, and is full of memories of Angevins, Aragonese and Bourbons, but it has been turned into the Albergo Reale e Quisisana, and is today a most dilapidated and depressing place. Leaves fall from the magnolias for lack of water; gone are the fountains that once gave freshness to the delightfully wooded park.

The view from the **belvedere of Monte Faito** (3600 ft) is magnificent, with the almost unbroken green of the Piano di Sorrento below, Capri beyond, and the Bays of Naples and Salerno. At this height the air can be chilly in the evening, even in summer; but the drive is best at sunset, for often the day-mist will clear at that time or be suffused with a beautiful golden light. There are several restaurants and the return journey can be made by the new panoramic road to Vico Equense.

From the Villa Quisisana we rejoin the Strada Panoramica for

157

The Companion Guide to Southern Italy

Map I
p. 104

Sorrento. In less than half a mile, on the right of the road, stand the ruins of the *Angevin castle,* rebuilt in 1266 by Charles I of Anjou. The original ninth-century castle was raised to protect the mineral springs against Saracen raids; from this Castrum ad Mare de Stabiis comes the present name of Castellammare di Stabia.

From here there is a pleasant run along the coastal Via Sorrentina to the seaside resort of **Vico Equense** on the site of the Roman town of Aequana, which was destroyed by the Goths. The modern town owes its foundation in 1285 to Charles II of Anjou. At Seiana a road leads down to the little beach of Marina di Equa. As the Via Sorrentina rounds the Punta Scutolo and begins to descend, before us lies the wonderfully fertile **Piano di Sorrento,** a natural terrace some 300 ft high, falling for the most part in sheer cliffs to the Bay of Naples, an unbroken expanse of luxuriant green except for the white walls of villas, the church towers and domes capped with multi-coloured majolica.

The richness of the soil and the mildness of the climate (it is some degrees cooler in summer than Naples) have made the plain of Sorrento one vast delectable garden of orange- and lemon-grovesand vineyards, of walnut and fruit trees (figs, cherries and pomegranates) and tropical flowers. From Roman times it has attracted those who sought peace and quiet among surroundings which enchanted and restored.

From Meta, a popular resort where the road branches left for Positano and Amalfi (see p. 162), the built-up area becomes almost continuous and the high walls of villas limit our view of the sea. In the orange-groves the curious little cabins high among the trees contain slats to protect the orange trees from frosts. At **S. Agnello** we may leave the Via Sorrentina and approach Sorrento by the lower road among villas and gardens overlooking the sea. In the village on the right of the main Piazza Matteotti is the Piazza S. Agnello, with its baroque church and statue (1909) of the Saint. From there the Via Cappuccini leads down to the beach of the Cappuccini; but we turn left in the Corso Crawford (so called from the Villa Crawford, where the popular American novelist F. Marion Crawford died in 1909), past the beautifully placed Albergo Cocumella, built in a former convent. Continuing in the Via Rota we reach a T-junction, and bearing right in the Via Califano, arrive at the entrance to the *Museo Correale* (admission, June–July, 9.30 a.m.–12.30 p.m. and 5.0–7.0 p.m.; August–September, 9.30 a.m.–12.30 p.m. and 4.0–6.0 p.m.; October–May, 9.30 a.m.–2.0 p.m.; Sundays, 9.30 a.m.–12.30 p.m.; closed Tuesdays).

158

The museum is housed in an eighteenth-century palace, which was left to the Municipality, together with its contents, by Alfredo Correale, Duke of Terranova, and his painter-brother Pompeo. It is set among gardens and has a charming belvedere, with a view of the Bay of Naples and Mount Vesuvius. The museum contains one of the few paintings in the Kingdom of that macabre painter Salvator Rosa, and a fine collection of the School of Posillipo, including thirty-seven landscapes by Giacinto Gigante. There are also interesting collections of period furniture, porcelain, sculpture and the inlaid woodwork (*tarsia*) for which Sorrento is still famous.

From the museum the Via Correale brings us to the Piazza Tasso, the principal square of the city, with its statues of the city's patron, S. Antonino, and its most celebrated son, the poet Torquato Tasso (1544–95).

Sorrento still has something essentially nineteenth-century about it, and not only in its comfortable, old-fashioned hotels. With Capri and Amalfi, it became *the* winter resort for northerners—particularly literary northerners. Here Ibsen came from Ischia to finish *Peer Gynt* in 1867. Nine years later, during a walk on the hills above Sorrento, Wagner confessed to Nietzsche that he had written *Parsifal* as an expression of his own religious conviction, thereby confirming Nietzsche's suspicions of Wagner's sincerity. And just outside Sorrento, on the road to Massalubrense, stands the villa where Maxim Gorky lived from 1924–33.

Map I
p. 104

Parts of the Sorrentine peninsula were inhabited during the neolithic age. The name Surrentum is said rather poetically to derive from the sirens who lured sailors to their deaths. Certainly the Li Galli group, just round the Punta Campanella, were known to Virgil as the abode of the Sirens, and Odysseus himself was said to have founded a temple to Athena on the tip of the promontory. Sorrento may well have been an unimportant Greek town; but in imperial days it became, with Baia and Capri, a favourite resort of rich Romans.

From the Piazza Tasso we look down over a narrow crevice, and see the Via L. de Maio winding 160 ft below to the Piccola Marina and the landing-place for steamers to Naples and Capri. The ground-plan of the Roman city is cut in two by the Corso Italia, the principal shopping street; but the narrow streets to the right and left of the Corso follow the usual *decumani* and *cardines*. Behind the cathedral, the **city walls,** which were built in the sixteenth century after a Saracen raid, are raised on Roman foundations, and the remains of the arch are those of the Porta Meridiana of the Roman town.

Furthermore, in the cliffs beneath the Albergo Bellevue Syrene in the Piazza della Vittoria (this hotel, by the way, has a lift down to its own lido) can be seen the ruins of the **Temple of Venus,** where Virgil, who was in Sorrento with the Emperor Augustus, dedicated a marble figure of Love as a votive offering for the successful completion of his *Aeneid*.

From the north-west corner of the Piazza Tasso the beginning of the Via L. de Maio leads to the irregularly-shaped Piazza S. Antonino (S. Anthony the Abbot), the saint who escaped to Sorrento from the Lombards and who is buried here (d. 830) in the crypt of the church dedicated to him, on the right of the square. Next to the church is the Palazzo Comunale, once a monastery of the Theatines; and opposite is the post-office, on the left of which is the narrow Via Grazie, which takes its name from the pleasant little church of the Dominicans on the right. This street and the first to the right, the Vico Grazie, which we follow, have some most interesting fifteenth- and sixteenth-century houses and doorways. We come out into the Piazza F. Saverio Gargiulo, where (again on the right) are the church and convent of **S. Francesco.** Through a doorway we enter the beautiful little fourteenth-century cloister, now partly occupied by the School of Art. Two sides are of triple saracenic-pointed and the other two of rounded arches raised on hexagonal columns, with most interesting capitals.

From the gardens of the near-by Villa Comunale there is a splendid view of the bay and Vesuvius beyond. The Via Vittorio Veneto runs from the Villa to the Piazza della Vittoria, and from here a steep and tortuous footpath descends to the Marina Grande. At the beginning of the street, among gardens on the cliff edge, is the **Albergo Imperiale Tramontano,** which incorporates part of the house where Torquato Tasso was born and spent his early years.

Tasso's father, Bernardo, a noble from Bergamo, was a courtier in the service of the Prince of Salerno. When the Prince for some reason fell foul of the Spanish government in Naples, the Tassos shared in his ruin and left Sorrento. In 1557 Bernardo Tasso found a new appointment at the court of Urbino, and the good-looking and intelligent Torquato joined in the studies and diversions of Francesco Maria della Rovere, the heir to the duchy of Urbino. At eighteen the publication of his epic poem *Rinaldo* brought Tasso immediate fame and he became a member of the cultivated court of the d'Este of Ferrara and the particular intimate of the princesses Lucrezia and Leonora. There followed in 1573 and 1574 the pastoral drama *Aminta* and the epic *Gerusalemme Liberata*, which revealed him as a poet of the highest order. But about this time the signs became more frequent that he was suffering from some form of paranoia. The record of his so-called 'imprisonments' by the Duke (who seems to have been genuinely intent on his welfare), his escapes and wanderings on foot throughout Italy, is both ludicrous and tragic. In 1594, when his fortunes appeared to be about to take a turn for the better, Tasso was invited to Rome to receive the crown of laurels (which had earlier been bestowed on Petrarch); but here again the fates were against him, for he died before receiving the crown, at the convent of S. Onofrio on the Janiculum.

Tasso's sister Cornelia's house, the **Casa Sersale** (she had married into a noble Sorrentine family of that name), is reached by the Via Tasso, which runs from the Piazza della Vittoria to the Corso. Tasso visited his sister here on his escape from Ferrara. Beyond the baroque church of S. Paolo (early eighteenth century) we turn right, in the Vico S. Nicola; a short way along, the house, No. 29, is recognized by its imposing doorway *a bugne* and little balcony. Inside, the vaulted ceiling of 1615 is frescoed with coats-of-arms and military trophies.

Returning to the Via Tasso, we continue towards the Corso and take the first narrow street on our left, the Via S. Cesareo, to where it meets the Via Reginaldo Giuliani. Here stands the **Sedile Dominova,** a fifteenth-century open loggia (the majolica-tiled cupola is of two centuries later), one of the two *sedili* where the nobles of Sorrento met to conduct their affairs. Inside are the coats-of-arms of the families belonging to the *sedile.* The Via Reginaldo Giuliani brings us back to the Corso opposite the Duomo, with its campanile and the adjoining Archbishop's Palace.

The ancient **Duomo** was rebuilt in the fifteenth century (a doorway on the right, of 1479, shows the arms of Aragon), but the façade is modern Gothic of the beginning of this century. The archbishop's throne was made in 1573, using ancient marbles, two columns of which are of *giallo antico.* The woodwork of the choir stalls is an interesting example of Sorrentine marquetry.

The Sorrentine peninsula—Massalubrense

Visitors with more time on their hands will want to explore the villages among the hills, bays and headlands at the extremity of the **Sorrentine peninsula.** For this we take the Corso d'Italia and continue past the turning on the left for the new Strada del Nastro

Azzurro. At a bend of the road, on the right, just before the village of Capo di Sorrento stands the *Villa Il Sorito,* where Gorky lived—looking prosperously bourgeois for the home of a revolutionary writer. Beyond this, again on the right, a narrow lane paved in grey-black *piperno* leads down to the sea and to the ruins of the **Roman villa of Pollio Felix.** Unless your car is very small, it is better to walk—it is difficult to pass other traffic or even to turn. Particularly interesting is the little bay which was incorporated perhaps as a *nymphaeum* or bathing-pool in the Roman buildings—these remains were known erroneously to the local inhabitants of Capo as the 'baths of Queen Giovanna'. In certain lights the colours of the water and of the rocks beneath are remarkable.

Map I
p. 104

Massalubrense is becoming popular as a seaside resort, but it suffers with the other towns and villages of this coast from a lack of first-class bathing facilities—bathing is to be had, of course (here at the Marina della Lobra), but the bays are small, not always easily accessible, and rocky. It was at a villa near Massalubrense that King Joachim Murat in 1808 watched the French troops successfully assault Capri.

Map I
p. 104

From Massalubrense one road leads past Pastena to the pleasant little town of **S. Agata sui due Golfi**—shortly beyond which it meets the Strada del Nastro Azzurro. Another road passes Marciano and Termini (from the latter a track descends to the Punta Campanella); after Termini it continues, high among the hills, through Metrano to S. Agata. All this region is delightful to walk over, but not in the height of summer, as much of it is arid and treeless, and the heat can be intense. At the *Punta Campanella* once stood the temple to Athena, supposedly raised by Odysseus; and near by is the *Torre Minerva,* built by King Robert of Anjou in 1335 (restored in 1566), where a bell was placed to give warning of the approach of the Saracens. It is from this that the point takes its name.

Positano—the Sbarco dei Saraceni

From Sorrento there are two routes to Positano and Amalfi: by returning to Meta and taking the Via Amalfitana; or by the new Strada del Nastro Azzurro, which winds up over the rocky watershed, with fine views of the Bay of Naples, Capri and the Bay of Salerno, to meet the Via Amalfitana at the Colli S. Pietro.

Beyond Colli S. Pietro the road descends in sweeping curves among olive groves, with splendid views over the Bay of Salerno, the islands of li Galli and the Costiera Amalfitana from the extremity of the Sorrentine peninsula to Capo Sottile. When we round the Punta Germano, we see **Positano** ahead, its white and pink houses falling in terraces among the green of gardens, apparently right to the water's edge. A short way beyond the Belvedere di Positano, we turn off the coast road and descend the narrow one-way Viale Roma for the centre of Positano and the car-park near the Municipio. Fortunately the beach is not accessible to cars, and this has the advantage of preserving the older parts of the town, with their narrow streets and stone steps overhung with vines and flowering creepers. And what an enchanting place it is; even its popularity has not spoilt its charm.

Map I
p. 104

Positano was a Roman town and may owe its name to the Posidii, a family of freedmen of the Claudian age. In the early Middle Ages it grew in prominence and became a rival in maritime trade to its neighbour Amalfi. Since the war it has become (like S. Stefano) one of the smartest and most cosmopolitan of Italian bathing resorts, in its *mores* perhaps the modern equivalent of ancient Baiae. The shingle beach is not large; but by boat one can go to bathe off the rocks or from the near-by coves.

Just before we reach the steps at the bottom of the Via Garibaldi, which brings us to the beach and the famous café-restaurant of the Buca di Bacco, a gateway on the left of the alley opens on to a courtyard. Within, we see the façade and colonnade of a baroque villa, the garden bright with bougainvillea and hibiscus.

From the Buca di Bacco I watched, many years ago, the spectacular *Sbarco dei Saraceni,* which takes place on the second Sunday of August in commemoration of the defeat of a Saracen attack from the sea. All the lights in the town were extinguished, and out of the velvety darkness the 'infidels' attacked from the sea. Flares and explosions marked the progress of the combat on the shore until the heroic 'Christians' finally got the upper hand and drove the Saracens back to their boats. Then gradually from all the houses on the hillside sprang tiny pin-points of flame, as thousands of candles were lit on terraces and roof-tops. Church bells rang out and a band struck up in the general rejoicing at so splendid a triumph of the Christian faith.

After Positano the Via Amalfitana continues its tortuous course, bearing now in a more southerly direction to round **Capo Sottile.** From this height the view back towards Positano and beyond is magnificent. Shortly before the village of Vettica Maggiore, to the right of the road and built in the cliff-side, is the Albergo Tritone.

Its position is incomparably beautiful and tranquil, and on the storeyed terraces are two swimming-pools and a restaurant.

Beyond Capo Sottile the road hugs the cliff face, passing through a series of tunnels. There is striking grandeur in this stretch of the coast; the precipitous mountainside is cut into by gorges of barren, jagged rock which, far below, form little sandy bays dotted with groups of fishermen's houses. Shortly after Praiano we cross a viaduct over the impressive Vallone di Furore, and ahead, on the tip of Capo di Conca stands a martello tower, raised in the sixteenth century against the corsairs. At the Ristorante La Conca Azzurra is the entrance to the lift and stairs for the **Grotta di Smeraldo,** named after the peculiar greenness of its light (admission, April–September 9.30 a.m.–5.0 p.m., October–March 10.0 a.m.–4.0 p.m.). The cave was once dry, but the whole of this coast has altered considerably even in the last few centuries, and interesting submerged formations of stalactites and stalagmites can be seen in the filtered and reflected emerald light.

Amalfi—maritime power—the Duomo—Atrani

After some impressive views of the whole of the Amalfi coast as far as Capo d'Orso, the landscape becomes gradually more cultivated, with olive groves, vines and terraces of lemon pergolas. Ahead we catch a glimpse of the tiled cupolas and pink houses of **Amalfi,** and on the hilltops appear ruined towers, monasteries and villas. As we enter Amalfi, we see on the hill-face to the left the famous Albergo Cappuccini, built in a former Cistercian monastery, founded in 1212. Passing through a tunnel, we come out in the Via M. Camera, which brings us just beyond the Gothic remains of the ancient Arsenal of the Republic to the Piazza Flavio Gioia, an open space, gay with flower-beds and tropical palms, bordering on the sea. The birthplace of Flavio Gioia, who is said to have invented the mariner's compass in 1302, is disputed between Positano and Amalfi, but the point is academic, for it seems that he never existed. Nevertheless, sailors from this area were certainly the first Europeans to employ the lodestone at sea.

Map I
p. 104

Amalfi has preserved much of the peculiar charm that made it one of the most favoured wintering places of our Victorian and Edwardian grandparents. Its origin is uncertain; not until the eighth century does Amalfi appear in documents with any frequency. It was then nominally under the Byzantine emperors, but after 786, when it successfully resisted the attacks of Arechi, the Lombard prince of Benevento, Amalfi became virtually an independent republic with its own elected Doges.

The period of its splendour, when it was the strongest sea-power in the Mediterranean and the largest arsenal in the world, lasted until it fell to the Norman Roger II in 1131. A few years later Amalfi, together with its territories of Ravello, Atrani, Maiori and Minori, was sacked by its maritime rivals the Pisans, who carried off the precious copy of Justinian's *Pandects*. By the irony of history this book was removed later by Pisa's own conquerors, the Florentines, and today is in the Biblioteca Laurenziana in Florence. At the height of the Republic's power there were colonies of Amalfitan merchants in all the principal cities of Italy and in all important parts of the Levant; their trading rules, set out in the *Tavole Amalfitane*, were the recognized maritime laws of the Mediterranean until 1570. In Jerusalem they founded hospitals and churches, one of which, dedicated to St John, was reconstituted about 1087 by Fra Gerardo Sasso (who was born at Scala in the territory of Amalfi) and became the well-known Order of St John of Jerusalem, or the Knights Hospitallers.

From the Piazza Flavio Gioia a short street (away from the sea) brings us almost immediately to the Piazza del Duomo, in the centre of which is the baroque (1760) fountain of S. Andrea. On the right, preceded by a high flight of steps and an atrium, is the **cathedral church of S. Andrea**, which contains beneath the high altar in the crypt remains of the apostle St Andrew (all except his head, which was carried off in the fifteenth century by Pope Pius II for the Vatican). The Duomo was rebuilt in the Norman-Saracenic style in 1203, and has been many times restored since. The façade was completely reconstructed at the end of the last century, but the earlier form has been preserved; decorated with multi-coloured stonework, its atrium is composed of Saracenic arches, also richly decorated. The proportions of the three central arches are particularly fine. In the typanum is a mosaic after the design of Domenico Morelli (1826–1901), showing *Christ in Glory*. To the left of the Duomo, and out of alignment with it, stands the original campanile of the early church, crowned with a drum and four turrets, a profusion of interlaced decorative arches in yellow and green tile-work.

The frescoes on either side of the main door and in the lunette above were also painted from the designs of Morelli. The fine bronze doors were made in Constantinople in 1066 for Pantaleone di Mauro Comite, the head of the Amalfitan colony there; he (or his son) also presented similar doors to S. Salvatore at Atrani and to the sanctuary at Monte S. Angelo. It is a pity that the interior of the church has been baroqued over in the eighteenth century, thus hiding the antique columns, although the rich ceiling may be admired by some. At the beginning of the choir stand two ancient columns from Paestum, and beside them two candelabra in mosaic. The *ambones* near the high altar are also decorated in mosaics of the twelfth to thirteenth centuries. On the right a stairway descends to the crypt, where St Andrew lies buried beneath the altar designed by Domenico Fontana (1543–1607). The large statue of the Saint, the work of Naccherino (1550–1622), was the gift of Philip III of Spain. The other two statues, of S. Stefano and S. Lorenzo, are by Pietro Bernini (1562–1629). From the bones of St Andrew, which were brought here in 1208 from Constantinople (or perhaps from Patras), there exudes an oily substance, called by the faithful 'manna' and considered to have miraculous powers.

From the left of the atrium we proceed to the delightful *Cloister of Paradise* (admission, 8.0 a.m.–7.0 p.m.), a jewel of Saracenic-inspired architecture, built in 1266 by the archbishop as a cemetery for the illustrious dead of Amalfi. Around the cloisters have been brought together pieces of ancient and medieval sculpture.

From the Piazza del Duomo we may take the Via Genova and its continuation, the Via Capuano, and explore some of the oldest parts of the town to either side, where the covered streets and steps sometimes give the impression of corridors and stairs in some vast medieval palace. Farther on we find ourselves in the Valle dei Mulini, so called from the water-mills where paper was once manufactured—the first of their kind, it is said, in Europe. There is a very pleasant and picturesque walk of about an hour up the valley to the Mulino Rovinato.

The Corso Roma runs as a wide esplanade parallel with the sea and lido from the Piazza Flavio Gioia to the Via Amendola. On it stands the *Municipio,* where in a small museum (admission 9.0 a.m. –2.0 p.m., closed Sundays) is kept a late copy of the *Tavole Amalfitane.* This was found in Austria and redeemed in 1929; the script suggests that the copy was made in the fifteenth or early sixteenth centuries, but the formulation of the laws and usages may be as early as the end of the eleventh century. The Via Amendola brings us to the cape on which stands an old watch-tower, the Torre di Amalfi, now an annexe to the Albergo Luna across the road. This hotel, like the Cappuccini, is a converted monastery, in this case a Franciscan one, said to have been founded by St Francis himself, and both should be visited for their charming cloisters. It was at the Luna that Ibsen wrote *A Doll's House* in 1879. Looking back from this point there is a fine view of Amalfi, before we turn the promontory for Atrani.

Atrani was until the sixteenth century the aristocratic quarter of Amalfi, and it was here in the church of *S. Salvatore de Bireto* that the Doges received the biretta at their installation and were often buried. The church, founded in 940, was completely restored in 1810, fortunately preserving (besides the bronze doors of 1087) some twelfth-century carving in the jambs of the main doorway and a most interesting piece in the right nave, where the symbols of peacocks, palms, birds and sirens suggest the influence of Byzantium. At Castiglione, a scattered village adjoining Atrani, is the road-junction for Ravello.

Map II
p. 126

Ravello—S. Pantaleone—Klingsor's magic garden—S. Giovanni del Toro —Scala

The wild and romantic setting of the little hilltop town of **Ravello,** built on a high ridge between the Valle del Dragone and that of Reginna, provides a dramatic background for its churches, palaces and villas and for the intimate charm of its hanging gardens. And Ravello has something further to offer—for I consider the Caruso Belvedere, in the medieval Palazzo d'Afflitto, to be the most delightful hotel that it has been my fortune to find in all Southern Italy.

Map II
p. 126

There is no historical record of Ravello before the ninth century, when we hear of it as being subject to Amalfi. After two centuries it rebelled in favour of King Roger, who came to its rescue in the first attack of the Pisans against the Republic of Amalfi in 1135; but in their second attack two years later Ravello was destroyed. It reached the height of its mercantile prosperity in the thirteenth century, when the inhabitants are said to have numbered 36,000. The Rufolo family, one of whom is mentioned by Boccaccio in the *Decameron*, as 'not being content with the riches he possessed', was only one of the many princely, merchant, warrior and ecclesiastical families who brought renown to the city. The Norman-Saracenic architecture, which we see at its best in the Palazzo Rufolo, is evidence of the links with Sicily and the Orient.

The road from Castiglione, which at one stage passes under a long pergola of vines completely covering the road, brings us up to the twelfth-century church of *S. Maria a Gradillo,* where the captain-general of the city once took office. Here a road with a sharp bend to the left branches off for the Piazza Fontana Moresca, so called from its fountain, which was in fact only constructed in the eighteenth century from pieces of medieval sculpture. In the Piazza Moresca is the Albergo Parsifal, converted from a thirteenth-century Augustinian monastery. However, if we continue straight on, we come under the Gothic ruins of the *Castello* (thirteenth century) and arrive in the Piazza Vescovado, the centre of the town. On the left rises the *cathedral church of S. Pantaleone,* the patron of Ravello, built in 1086 by Orso Papirio, the first bishop of Ravello. Standing back on the right of the church is the beautiful thirteenth-century *campanile.* The *bronze doors,* with fifty-four panels representing the *Story of the Passion,* as well as saints and warriors, were made in 1179 by Barisanus of Trani, who is also responsible for the doors of the Duomo at Trani and the north door of Monreale in Sicily.

On the right of the central nave stands the magnificent *pulpit,* one of the most beautiful examples of mosaic work in the South. This was executed in 1272 by Nicolò di Bartolomeo da Foggia for Nicola Rufolo. Underneath the pulpit, which is raised on six graceful barley-sugar columns in mosaic supported by lions, is a triptych of the *Madonna and Child with the Baptist and St Nicholas of Bari.* This was in the Rufolo chapel. The cornices and capitals of the pulpit are all richly carved, and the panels of the front, stairway and sides have bold designs of interlaced circles in brightly coloured mosaic. At the entrance to the stairs (facing the choir) two figures in low relief appear above the trilobate opening. These are almost certainly by Nicolò di Bartolomeo; but the identity of the sculptor of the majestic bust of an unidentified woman with a diadem and long drop-earrings, which has been placed on the parapet, remains uncertain.

Opposite the pulpit is another example of early mosaic work in the *ambo* (1130), which depicts, in the fashion of the Campanian artists, Jonah being swallowed and regurgitated by an extraordinary winged whale. In the *chapel of S. Pantaleone,* to the left of the high altar, is an ampoule of the Saint's blood which is said to liquefy on the anniversary of his martyrdom on July 27th, 290. Here in the Duomo mass was celebrated in 1156 by the only Englishman to become pope, Nicholas Breakspeare, who as Adrian IV was visiting Ravello.

On the corner of the piazza to the right of the Duomo is the square-towered gateway to the *Palazzo Rufolo,* a romantic conglomeration of medieval buildings set in beautifully kept gardens, where Richard Wagner, on May 26th, 1880, is said to have conceived the idea for the magic garden of Klingsor in *Parsifal* (admission, daily

168

8.0 a.m.–4.0 p.m.). Beneath the arched gateway, in the corners, are four carved stone figures, two of them representing the virtues of *Charity* and *Hospitality*. Parts of the palazzo go back as far as the eleventh century, but in the main it is of the thirteenth century, when it was in the possession of the Rufolos. By 1851 it had fallen into a sad state of ruin, but was bought from the d'Afflitto family by a Scotsman, F. N. Reid, who restored it and whose family still own it. The little Moorish court of two superimposed arcades decorated with graceful encrusted arabesques is particularly lovely. From the garden terrace below the house there is a fine view of the coastline and cultivated landscape towards Capo d'Orso.

To the right of the entrance to the Palazzo Rufolo the Via S. Francesco brings us past the church and monastery of S. Francesco (traditionally believed to have been founded by the Saint in 1222—there is an interesting early cloister) to the Via S. Chiara, where there is also a thirteenth-century convent attached to the rebuilt church (eighteenth century). From here steps lead to the *Villa Cimbrone* (admission 8.0 a.m.–4.0 p.m.), the house and gardens standing in a magnificent position at the end of the spur on which Ravello is built. The villa itself has been largely reconstructed, using ancient stonework, and there is a pleasant little courtyard; but the old gardens and the view from the belvedere are really beautiful.

Back in the Piazza Vescovado a street to the left of the Palazzo Rufolo leads down under a tunnel to the newly-constructed Strada Panoramica. At this point, steps on the left, the Via S. Giovanni del Toro, bring us up past many interesting old palaces (one of them, formerly the Palazzo Sasso, is now the Albergo Palumbo) to the recently restored church of *S. Giovanni del Toro,* in the piazza of that name opposite the Albergo Caruso. S. Giovanni was built in 1065 and was for long the church of the Ravellese nobility whose palaces were grouped in the quarter around the little piazza. In the interior, which is divided into nave and aisles by eight ancient columns, there is another beautiful pulpit, built in the twelfth century by Alfano da Termoli, with brilliant mosaic and decorative motifs of birds and the usual representation of *Jonah and the whale*. Note the most effective use of saucers of Islamic majolica in the design on the stairway. Note also the carving on the capitals and the curious bases to the columns. The fine frescoes are of the fourteenth century. On the left of the church in the chapel of the Coppola is a stucco figure of *St Catherine of Alexandria* (found in 1895) also of the fourteenth century and possibly by Tino di Camaino. On the opposite side of

169

the church we descend to the deep crypt, formed of three apses, where there are more frescoes by followers of Pietro Cavallini.

The entrance doorway to the Albergo Caruso is composed of pieces of sculpture from the destroyed church of S. Eustachio at **Scala.** It is a pleasant walk of just over a mile to this little town, once the rival of Ravello, which we see facing us on the hillside over the Valle di Dragone. There in the twelfth-century *cathedral of S. Lorenzo* is kept a jewelled mitre, presented by King Charles I of Anjou. In the year 1270 Charles was on his way to the help of St Louis of France against the Saracens, when his fleet was struck by a severe storm. Sailors from Scala prayed successfully for S. Lorenzo's intercession, and the king in recognition bestowed this mitre on the bishop. One of the leading families of Scala was that of Coppola; Antonio Coppola was among those nobles treacherously seized and put to death by King Ferrante in the Barons' Conspiracy of 1468.

Map II
p. 126

Minori—Maiori—Raito—Vietri

From Castiglione the road continues closer to the shore, doubles the point on which rises the square Torre dello Scarpariello, and runs down to the seaside resort of **Minori.** This whole region is famous for its delicious lemons. Try a *spremuta limone.* The lemons are grown on terraces which are often set so steep in the cliff-side that one wonders how they were built. The white wine produced in the valleys behind is also excellent. Formerly these towns were known as Reginna Maior and Minor; both were subject to the Republic of Amalfi, and at the latter were important shipyards and arsenals.

Map II
p. 126

The road climbs to round the point on which rises the Torre del Mezzacapo, and then descends to the pleasant and increasingly popular resort of **Maiori** which stands at the mouth of the valley of Tramonti. Much of the good wine of the district is produced from the vineyards in this valley; and through it too runs the road from Maiori up over the mountains behind (the Valico della Torre Chiunzi) to Pagani and Angri on the Naples–Salerno road. From the public gardens on the foreshore the Corso Reginna Maior runs inland towards the valley on either side of the River Reginna, whose banks have now been walled in. (High on the right of the valley appear the ruins of the Piccolomini *castle of S. Nicola*—fifteenth century.) A short way up the Corso a flight of steps brings us to the church of *S. Maria a Mare,* which was founded in the twelfth century but rebuilt many times, the last occasion being in 1836.

Map II
p. 126

170

Among the treasures of this church is an alabaster low-relief depicting *Scenes from the Life of Mary*. This is English work of the fifteenth century, and I have been unable to find out how it came here.

The road begins to rise again as we leave Maiori. On the farthest point of the bay stands the seventeenth-century Torre Normanna, which has now been converted into a pleasantly-placed restaurant. (There are also a few rooms to let, and good bathing in the cove below.) From now on the road continues to rise, skirting the precipitous rocky flanks of Monte Demanio, with wonderful views of the coast behind us, until we reach the Capo d'Orso, where there is a tolerable restaurant. Beyond the cape the Bay of Salerno comes into view, and the scenery now is wild and impressive.

The road between Maiori and Cetara requires careful driving, particularly by those travelling west. The deep gutters cut on the landward side of the road can easily cause trouble for an unwary motorist.

Cetara is a small fishing village, beautifully situated on its little bay; and by a curious fortune it has not been developed for tourists. After Cetara the road again climbs, and from the heights we have views of Salerno and the plain towards Paestum, with the blue mountains behind—the Monti Picentini and Alburni. As we approach Vietri, we see picturesquely set in terraces high up on the hillside on our left the white houses of **Raito** (the new Albergo Raito has a magnificent view), and tourist shops by the roadside display pottery, majolica tiles and ware from the famous manufacturers of Vietri. From where the Raito road turns off on the left, we look down on the beach umbrellas of the Marina di Vietri, and across the Vallone Bonea to **Vietri** itself, grouped around the majolica-domed church of S Giovanni.

Map II
p. 126

Map II
p. 126

Map II
p. 126

On the right-hand side of the piazzetta of Vietri sul Mare, which forms a kind of belvedere, there was until recently a balustrade with high pillars tiled with beautiful Victorian majolica. On the left of this a house with some good baroque stucco-work reminds us of another art now lost. We take the narrow one-way street in front of this house, and signs direct us through this populous and pleasant town, with its shops, factories and art school all connected with the ceramics industry, to the Tirrena Inferiore road (SS 18) from Naples and Cava de' Tirreni to Salerno. From the junction we descend, overlooking the port and city, and passing on the right the Albergo Lloyds Baia, arrive at Salerno.

CHAPTER 11

The Salernitano

Maps: II, p.126; III, p.182

A palaeochristian round church—Cava de' Tirreni—Abbey of the Trinity of Cava

Most motorists travelling south from Naples to Salerno today will avail themselves of the splendid autostrada which is now completed as far as the outskirts of Salerno, where there is a gap before it continues on the southern side of the town. After passing Mount Vesuvius and the excavations of ancient Pompeii, it begins to cross the fertile *ager Sarnensis* of the Romans, then, beyond the junction for Castellammare and Sorrento, we turn away from the Bay of Naples and enter the Agro Nocerino, the fertile land lying between the high wooded slopes of the Monti Lattari and the ranges of hills to the east. This is some of the richest land in Southern Italy.

On the right stands **Angri,** from which a road leads up to the Valico di Chiunzi, to come down the other side of the mountains on the Costiera Amalfitana at Maiori. It was near Angri in AD 553 that the formidable eunuch Narses won back Italy for the Emperor Justinian from the Goths.

Map II
p. 126 At the next turn-off we may leave the autostrada for Pagani and the two Noceras (Inferiore and Superiore). **Pagani** stands about a mile to the west of Nocera Inferiore, and in the basilican baroque church of S. Alfonso, next door to the monastery founded by the Saint, lies the body of S. Alfonso de' Liguori, the amiable bishop of S. Agata de' Goti (see p. 112).

Map II
p. 126 **Nocera Inferiore** is a centre for the distribution, canning and exporting of the produce (especially tomatoes) of the Agro Nocerino. It has little of architectural importance, though its origin is very ancient. From here the SS 18 leads (with a view on the right of the sixteenth-century sanctuary of S. Maria di Monte Albino) to **Nocera Superiore.** About a mile farther on, we turn left, cross the canal, and come to one of the most architecturally interesting of

172

Italian palaeochristian round churches, **S. Maria Maggiore** or the **Rotonda.** It is thought that this was built originally as a baptistery (like the Baptistery of Constantine in Rome or that of Ravenna), but the date of construction is uncertain, authorities generally placing it in the fourth or fifth centuries (Banister Fletcher dates it as early as AD 350, making it contemporaneous with S. Costanza in Rome). It stands some way below the present level of the street, is 80 ft in diameter, and its egg-shaped stone vaulting (circular from the exterior and covered by a tiled roof) is raised on thirty pairs of antique columns, above a large octagonal font. There are some remains of frescoes in a bad state—but note the cross and letters *alpha* and *omega* carved on the marble panels of the font. The cupola was rebuilt after it collapsed during the last eruption of Vesuvius in 1944.

Instead of returning to the autostrada, we may continue on the SS 18 to the attractive town of **Cava de' Tirreni.** The cylindrical towers on the hillsides are still occasionally used for a curious method of netting wood-pigeons, which is thought to go back to Lombard times. Finely-meshed nets are strung across the narrow parts of the valleys, and into these the pigeons fly, following whitewashed stones that the *cacciatori* throw down into the valleys from the towers.

Map II
p. 126

Cava is a pleasant, prosperous little town. The basis of its prosperity came in the Middle Ages from its connection with the near-by abbey of the Trinity of Cava, when the town was ceded to the abbots by the Lombard Prince Gisulph II. Freed from customs dues at its port at Vietri, Cava carried on an important trade, especially in silk. The abbey's ships, with a monk always as captain or pilot (rather like a Christian commissar), were prominent for centuries in the maritime trade of the Mediterranean.

The Corso Italia, the main street of Cava, is flanked by dark stone porticoes reminiscent of Bologna, and opens out into the Piazza Vittorio Emanuele III with its neo-classic Duomo. From the Piazza Roma beside the Duomo, the Via Rosario Senatore leads to the **Abbey of the Trinity of Cava** (about 2 miles). At the village of Corpo di Cava we turn left under the ancient walls (on which in a romantic position stands the old hostelry of Michele Scapolatiello) and, skirting the town, come shortly to the piazza in front of the entrance to the abbey, which is built on the side of a rocky, wooded ravine.

The abbey, the most celebrated monastery in Italy after Montecassino, was founded between 1011 and 1015 by St Alferius, a member of the noble Lombard Pappacarbone family from Salerno.

The young Alferius, on a diplomatic mission to the Emperor of Germany, fell dangerously ill and was nursed by St Odillon, a monk from Cluny. On his return to Salerno he retired to this spot, where he lived in a cave and soon became remarkable for his piety. Waimar III of Salerno gave him the lands of Cava for his monastery, and the church was consecrated by Pope Urban II in 1092. Alferius is said to have died at the age of one hundred and twenty.

As we face the abbey, on the right is the baroque campanile of 1622. The Roman baroque façade of the church was reconstructed in a grey volcanic stone to the designs of Giovanni del Gaizo, when enlargements and repairs were carried out in the second half of the eighteenth century. Much of the fresco-work in the atrium and in the church itself is modern. There are a fine *ambo* and paschal candlestick in Cosmatesque mosaic, the former being reconstituted from the original twelfth-century fragments at the end of last century. On the right of the church is the cave in which St Alferius lived. Among the various relics here is a piece of the True Cross contained in an eleventh-century Byzantine reliquary.

On the left of the church is the entrance to the **Benedictine monastery** (admission, weekdays 9.0 a.m.–12.30 p.m.; holidays 9.0–11.0 a.m.; a guide accompanies visitors). The chapter-house was restored in 1632 and has frescoes of that period. Its inlaid wooden stalls are reputed to have been designed by Andrea da Salerno and the paving in majolica tiles is of the late eighteenth century. The thirteenth-century Little Cloister, off it, is interesting. Pairs of short columns in different marbles support rounded arches on elongated stilt-blocks which betray a Byzantine influence. Here, and near by in the early chapter-house and Cappella del Crocifisso, we can see the juxtaposition of Greek, Lombard-Romanesque and Gothic elements, and the classical sarcophagi add to the effect. In another adjacent chapel is a beautiful marble *paliotto* from the altar consecrated by Pope Urban in 1092. Descending to the so-called Lombard crypt, once used as a cemetery for monks and illustrious laity, we pass the tomb of Queen Sibylla, wife of the Norman Roger II of Sicily.

The **Museum, Archives and Library** are now housed in what were the guest-rooms in the Middle Ages. The museum contains classical and medieval antiquities, some valuable religious works of art, and paintings (several by fifteenth-century Florentines). The precious collection of Lombard and Norman manuscripts in the archives makes the abbey one of the most important repositories in Italy of documents of this period. Among the most interesting are a

Bible, written in the Visigothic hand by the monk Danila in the ninth century; the *Codex Legum Langobardorum*, the oldest of the three known digests of ancient Lombard Law (eleventh century); and an early eleventh- to twelfth-century copy of the *De Temporibus* of the Venerable Bede.

We return to the village of Corpo di Cava and the terrace of the Albergo Scapolatiello, passing on the way the little monument to Urban II (1892). Before the First World War Augustus Hare described this hotel as 'tolerable'. It is much more than that, and it would be a perfect place to stay for those who wish to explore on foot this beautiful, wooded countryside.

There are remains of a medieval aqueduct at La Molina, the village lower down the valley on the SS 18, but we return direct to the autostrada, which from now on coasts along the steep sides of Monte S. Liberatore with magnificent views over the Bay of Salerno. Still on the heights, we leave the autostrada proper for the centre of Salerno. A tunnel is under construction which will connect the autostrada west of Salerno with the south-eastern section that now runs from Fratte, just north of the city, to Battipaglia, but at present one has to go through Salerno.

Salerno—an early medical school—the old city—the Duomo—the Museo del Duomo—the Museo Provinciale

Salerno, the capital of the southernmost province of Campania, consists of an old quarter, typical of ancient Mediterranean coastal towns, more modern quarters stretching along the shore, and new suburbs built since the war on the hills behind. The city is very ancient, though it is probable that the original Etrusco-Campanian town was situated somewhat inland around Fratte, in the valley through which the SS 88 leads up among the mountains to Avellino. Many objects from a recently excavated necropolis of the sixth to fifth century BC can be seen in the Museo Provinciale. The name Salernum, by which the Roman colony was known, may be derived from its position on the salt sea (*sal*), where the River Irnus (today Irno) enters it. The city suffered the usual vicissitudes in the struggles between Goths and Byzantines, and in AD 646 was annexed by the Lombards to the Duchy of Benevento. Two hundred years later it broke away and established itself as a separate state under its own Lombard Princes. In 1077 during one of the continual raids by the Saracens the Norman Robert Guiscard (a relative by marriage

Map II
p. 126

of the ruling Prince Gisulph) took Salerno and made the city into the capital of the kingdom he was carving for himself in Southern Italy. In 1127 the capital was transferred to Palermo.

Salerno enjoyed its greatest period of brilliance between the eleventh and thirteenth centuries (although it was sacked and partly destroyed by the Emperor Henry VI in 1194), chiefly because of the fame of its celebrated School of Medicine, the Scuola Medica Salernitana. The schools of Salerno—philosophy, theology and law were also taught—effectively formed the first European university. The Medical School was already described as 'ancient' in a codex of AD 846, and was said to have been founded by a Greek, a Roman, an Arab and a Jew, so cosmopolitan were the professors and students there. It seems likely from an early description of the town as an *urbs graeca* that Graeco-Roman civilization persisted in Salerno and was perhaps even sustained by the Lombards, but the *Civitas Hippocratica*, as it became known, reached the zenith of its fame when Constantine the African (d. 1087) lectured there, bringing with him Latin translations of the Arabic developments of medical science. When they were being persecuted elsewhere, Jewish doctors were prominent at Salerno; and the schools, which had a distinctly secular flavour, admitted both sexes as pupils and professors. St Thomas Aquinas declared Salerno to be as pre-eminent in medicine as Paris was in science and theology and Bologna in law.

Crusaders returning from the Holy Land often stopped at Salerno to consult the doctors, and the practical prescriptions of the school were known throughout Europe in a curious and remarkably unscientific poem in Leonine Latin verses, dictated, it is said, for a certain *Rex Anglorum*. But by the end of the thirteenth century the school's great days were over, though it lingered on, to be finally suppressed by King Joachim Murat in 1812.

The small **port of Salerno**, which was once repaired and enlarged by the enigmatic Giovanni da Procida (see p. 139), lies at the western end of the city. From May to September tourist steamers sail from here to Amalfi, Positano and Capri. Behind it are the gardens of the Villa Comunale, and to the left stands the nineteenth-century Teatro Verdi, decorated with paintings by Domenico Morelli and others. Opposite this the Piazza Amendola opens out with its grandiose fascist Prefettura and Palazzo di Città. From the south side of the Villa Comunale, near the Jolly Hotel, begins the Lungomare Trieste, a broad esplanade that runs along the foreshore to the beach, open-air swimming-pool and public tennis courts; and parallel with the Lungomare is the main street

176

of Salerno, the Via Roma, and its continuation, the Corso Giuseppe Garibaldi.

To the north of the Villa Comunale we see the back of the church of *SS. Annunziata,* with its theatrical pink-washed campanile in the eighteenth-century baroque style of Ferdinando Sanfelice. The entrance to the church is in Via Porta Catena and this is a good point to begin our exploration of the oldest and most interesting parts of the city. A short way brings us to an enchanting little piazza, once a market-place, the *Sedile del Campo,* with its dolphin fountain—the Fontana dei Delfini. At the farther side of the piazza are some remains of the Lombard *Porta Rateprandi,* and among the doorways of different periods is one in the corner on the right by Sanfelice, the entrance to the former Palazzo Genovesi. From the left of the square the Via Porta Rateprandi brings us to the little church of *S. Andrea* (rebuilt in the eighteenth century), with an original twelfth-century campanile where Ippolito di Pastena in 1647 sounded the tocsin to call the people to revolt against the Spaniards.

The Via Dogana Vecchia and its prolongation, the busy Via dei Mercanti, bring us under the vaulted *Arco di Arechi,* the remains of a palace built by a Lombard prince in the eighth century. All this region, especially round the Via dei Canali on the left, reveals a fascinating amalgam of architectural bits and pieces of many periods, built into palaces, houses, shops and workshops.

The Via dei Mercanti, the main shopping centre of the old town, is crossed by the Via del Duomo. (Try the fresh cakes, pastries and biscuits cooked on the premises of the old family firm of Pantaleone, 73–5 Via dei Mercanti.) Turning right in the Via Duomo, we come to the baroque church of *S. Giorgio,* which has frescoes by Solimena (1630–1716) and some paintings by the best-known of local artists, Andrea Sabatini, called more usually Andrea da Salerno (1490–1530). Retracing our steps and continuing up the hill, we arrive at the most remarkable of all the monuments of Salerno, the magnificent *cathedral of St Matthew,* founded in 845 and rebuilt by Robert Guiscard between 1076 and 1085.

To the right of the Duomo, the Via Roberto Guiscardo separates it from the *Bishop's Palace.* The palace wall facing the cathedral has been stripped recently to reveal its thirteenth-century arcading and opposite it rises the Romanesque early twelfth-century campanile of the Duomo.

At the foot of the steps in the Via Duomo, where it joins the Via Roberto Guiscardo, an entrance brings us to a series of vaulted rooms, now used as offices, which are said to have been ancient class-rooms of the **old Medical School**. Ramped steps lead up to the Romanesque Porta dei Leoni, called after the two crouching lions that flank it, and out of this opens the beautiful *atrium,* formed by classical columns supporting Arabo-Sicilian arches on high stilt-blocks, the whole surmounted by an elegant loggia. Around this portico are Roman sarcophagi, converted in medieval times into tombs for celebrated personages. In a room on the right St Thomas Aquinas is said to have lectured on philosophy and theology. The centre of the court, where a granite fountain and basin of the classical age now stand, was once occupied by a great porphyry *vasca,* removed by Ferdinand I and IV for his new Villa Comunale in Naples.

The **main entrance** to the church is preceded by a baroque portico, above which is a statue of *St Matthew between two saints* (1733), the work of the Salernitan sculptor Matteo Bottiglieri. High up on the façade a marble band records that the church was built and dedicated to St Matthew, apostle and evangelist, the patron of Salerno, by Robert at his own expense. The central doorway is original, with rich Romanesque decoration (note an inscription in Armenian low down on the left jamb). The doors are later, and were cast in Constantinople in 1099; the figures were once encrusted with gems, and the silver of the *niello*-work has been removed. The fresco in the lunette above is of the eleventh century. Inside the church, in the corresponding lunette, is a thirteenth-century mosaic representing *St Matthew.*

The Duomo suffered greatly in the earthquake of 1688, and perhaps quite as much at the hands of the restorers; the transept is now out of alignment and the floor rises towards the east. The two beautiful *ambones* and the paschal candlestick are twelfth-century work, showing both Arabo-Sicilian and Byzantine motifs in their decoration; compare them with those at Ravello and Amalfi. On the right of the church, against the wall of the choir, is the tomb of Roger Borsa (d. 1111), Robert Guiscard's son—his remains were placed in a Roman sarcophagus depicting Dionysius and Ariadne. From here we enter the transept, the east wall being composed of three apses, containing restored eleventh-century and modern mosaics.

The apse on the right was decorated by Giovanni da Procida and is known as the **Cappella delle Crociate** (knights on their way to the Crusades were blessed here) or the **Cappella di Gregorio VII,** from the tomb of the pope which lies beneath the altar. On the right

is the third-century sarcophagus (beneath a stone recording Giovanni da Procida's reconstruction of the port of Salerno at the time of
King Manfred), where the papal saint's bones formerly lay. The
great Hildebrand, as Gregory was more commonly known, was
driven from Rome and the papal throne by the Emperor Henry IV
in 1084, to die the following year as a guest in Salerno of Robert
Guiscard. His dying words were said to have been: 'I loved justice,
I hated iniquity, and for this reason I die in exile.' In 1606 he was
canonized by Pope Paul V.

In the central apse stands the throne of Gregory VII, used in the
consecration of the church in 1084, and opposite the seventeenth-
century pulpit is the archbishop's baroque throne with seven steps
like a papal throne, a concession by Gregory. From the left of the
transept a door leads to the sacristy and the Museo del Duomo (the
principal entrance to the latter is from the Via Mons. Monterisi on
the left flank of the Duomo.) At the end of the left aisle is the
monument to Queen Margherita (wife of Charles III of Durazzo),
who died in Salerno in 1412. This is by Antonio Baboccio, whose
carving we have seen in Naples in the portal of the Duomo, S.
Giovanni dei Pappacoda and at S. Chiara.

Crossing the church we enter the *crypt,* noticing the little Roman
low-relief in the wall of a ship being unloaded. The walls and
pilasters of the crypt are richly decorated in polychrome marbles by
Domenico Fontana in the baroque taste of the early seventeenth
century, and the vaulted ceiling frescoes of about the same period
are by Corenzio. Beneath the altar are the remains of St Matthew,
brought here from Capaccio in 954 by Prince Gisulph. The two
bronze statues of the Saint are by the Florentine Naccherino. To the
right of the central apse stands a block of stone on which three
Salernitan martyrs are said to have been decapitated—SS. Fortuna-
to, Caio and Ante.

The *Museo del Duomo* (admission, weekdays 9.0 a.m.–12.0
noon; Sunday 10.0 a.m.–1.0 p.m.) has among its collection several
exhibits of outstanding interest: particularly a *paliotto* (altar-front)
and an *Exultet.* The former consists of fifty-four scenes (four others
are in foreign museums) from the Old and New Testaments, carved
in ivory by various artists of the twelfth century. The treatment shows
traces of styles as different as Byzantine, Provençal, Romanesque and
Sicilian-Arabic. Two paintings have been removed here from
churches in Eboli: one, the *Crucifixion* (second half of the fourteenth
century), is attributed to Roberto Oderisi, a follower of Giotto,
whose work we have seen in the church of the Incoronata in Naples;

179

and the other, the *Coronation of the Virgin,* is by the so-called Maestro dell' Incoronazione di Eboli (mid-fifteenth century). The beautiful *Exultet* is on parchment, with miniatures of the thirteenth century. A cross inlaid with gems was a gift of Robert Guiscard.

The Via Roberto Guiscard (for those with time, the *Episcopio* is worth a visit for its Gothic thirteenth-century *salone,* with arches raised on ancient columns from Paestum) brings us to Via Antonio Genovesi in which we turn left, and then almost immediately right in the Via S. Benedetto, for the recently-opened *Museo Provinciale* which, when it is completed, will occupy the whole site of the old Benedictine monastery. The portion to the right of the street, which is now open to the public, has been imaginatively constructed to incorporate some of the arches of the royal palace of the Normans, the Castelnuovo, built to replace the Lombard castle whose ruins still dominate the city on a hill to the north. (It was from the latter castle, built over a Roman fortification, that Robert Guiscard ousted the last Lombard Prince Gisulph in 1077.) The royal palace in turn incorporated parts of the ancient Lombard atrium in front of the Romanesque church of S. Benedetto, as well as portions of the original Lombard eighth-century city defences.

The museum will eventually display exhibits in chronological order from the excavations now in progress in the Agro Picentino (the area between the Rivers Sarno and Sele) and as far south as Capo Palinuro. Some of the discoveries from local burial grounds date possibly from the ninth century BC, and are archaeologically extremely important. The fine bronze *head of Apollo,* which is of Hellenistic workmanship of the first century BC, was found by fishermen off the coast in 1930.

The Via S. Benedetto leads into the Via Velia, where we turn right. The Via Velia is in turn crossed by the Corso Vittorio Emanuele: to the left we have modern prosperous Salerno, a wide street of banks and large departmental stores; to the right, beyond the piazza of the Sedile di Portanova, is the beginning of the Via dei Mercanti and the old town. A short way down the hill there is a lively produce market on the right, and behind rises the *Porta Nuova,* once the eastern gate of the city, erected in the sixteenth century but rebuilt in 1752, and surmounted by a benign statue of St Matthew.

Pontecagnano—the British Military Cemetery—Battipaglia

We leave Salerno by the Lungomare Guglielmo Marconi to join the
SS 18. The autostrada is now finished as far as Battipaglia, but the
delays at the Fratte entrance-exit north of Salerno, as well as the
interest of the SS 18, make the latter a preferable route.

Passing through the rapidly growing suburbs and new industrial
area, we round Monte Giovi and come out on the rich plain around
the town of **Pontecagnano.** Shortly after the road crosses the River
Picentino at the entrance to the town, a cul-de-sac on the left brings
us to a restaurant which delights in the name of the Roxy Club.
Here, both the Neapolitan *pizzas* and their *prosciutto crudo* are
excellent. The *pizzas* are immense, and are better shared. I recommend a white San Severo wine from Apulia to accompany them. Map II
p. 126

The road runs away from the sea and there are views of Monte
Alburno ahead. Outside the town of Bellizzi there is a **British
Military Cemetery,** with nearly two thousand graves of those who
died in the Salerno landings of 1943, and on a hill on the left, above
the town of Battipaglia, is the toy-castle residence of the Princes
Strongoli Pignatelli. The castle was Norman in origin (1194), but
was completely restored inside and out in 1920. **Battipaglia** was
founded as recently as 1858 by Ferdinand II, when this whole
district was a wild malaria-infested scrubland supporting only herds
of buffaloes. The transformation into rich farmland and orchards is
the result of a closely integrated system of drainage and irrigation.
Battipaglia is famous for its *mozzarella*, a white cream-cheese made
from buffalo milk; it is also the road and rail junction for communication through Eboli with Potenza and the Basilicata, and down the
Vallo di Diano through Lagonegro to Calabria. Map II
p. 126

Links with Greece—Paestum

The southernmost district of the province of Salerno consists of the
mountainous tract of the Cilento, bounded on the east by the fertile
Vallo di Diano and to the west by the sea, with its marvellous
coastline of wooded hills and cultivated valleys separating beaches
of the purest golden sand. Small, primitive-looking fishing villages,
whose inhabitants carry on age-old trades, are linked by a corniche
road with unrivalled views. All along the coast are traces of the

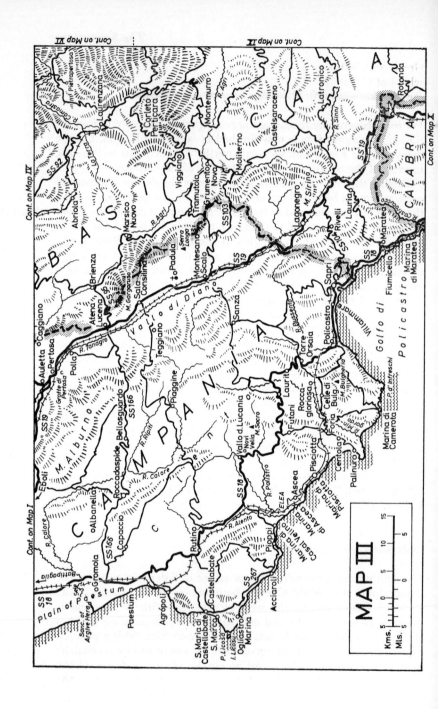

Cont. on Map X

MAP III

Kms. 5   0   5   10   15
Mls. 5   0   5   10

BASILICATA

CALABRIA

Comoncello   Pietrapertosa   Laurenzana
SS 92   La Lera   La Lera
Corleto   R. Agri
Perticara
Abriola   Montemurro
Castelsaraceno
Marsico   Viggiano   Moliterno   Latronico   SS 19
Nuovo   R. Agri   R. Sinni   Rotonda
Brienza   Sarra   Tramutola   Grumento   Castelsaraceno
M. Gorgarus   Loca   Novo   SS103
Atena   Salala   Padula   Montesano   M. Sirino   Lauria   SS 19
Lucena   Consilina   Scalo   Lagonegro   SS 106
SS 92   Rivelli   SS
SS 19   Valle di Diano   SS   Sapri   18
Auletta   Caggiano   19   Policastro
Pertosa   Bussento   Policastro   Marina   Golfo di
R. Tanagro   Teggiano   Torre   Maratea   di Fiumicello
Grotte di   Polla   Orsaia   Villammar   di Maratea
Pertosa   Sanza
Eboli   Piaggine   Laurit   Policastro
SS 19   M. Alburno   Rocca-   Futani   gloriosa   Marina di
R. calore   SS166   Foria   Camerota
R. Ripiti   Celle di   M.Bulgheria
Battipaglia   Roccadaspide   Bellosguardo   Bulg.   Piscio   R.Mingardo
SS 18   SS166   CAMPANIA   Futani   parto   P.d'Infreschi
Capaccio   R. Calore   Centola   Marina di
o   Vallo d. Lucania   Foria   Camerota
Plain of   Albanella   Novi   Pisciotta   Palinuro
Paestum   Velia M. Sacro
Sanc. of   Gromola   SS 18   VELIA   Marina di
Argive Hera   Rutino   Ascea   Pisciotta
Paestum   R. Palistro   ELEA
Agropoli   R. Alento   Marina di
P.Licosa   Casal Velino   Ascea
S. Maria di   S. Marco   Castellabate   Pioppi
Castellabate   L.Licosa   SS   Acciaroli
Ogliastro   267
Marina

R. Sele

Greek civilization which made ancient Elea the philosophical school of Hellas; the flora, too, recalls the wild flowers and herbs of the Greek mainland. This sixty-mile stretch of coast from Agropoli (the name itself Greek), south to the Punta Licosa, where the siren Leucosia found her watery grave; Cape Palinuro, where Palinurus, the helmsman of Aeneas, was swept overboard and drowned—all this hitherto untouched riviera is rapidly being developed with hotels and *pensioni*, and will soon provide some of the most attractive of all the Italian seaside resorts.

From Battipaglia there are two main roads leading south to Calabria: the more direct SS 19 (delle Calabrie) which runs for part of the way down the beautiful Vallo di Diano (the route to be followed by the new Autostrada del Sole), and the longer but fascinating coast road, the SS 18 (Tirrena Inferiore) which we shall follow first.

At Battipaglia we bypass the town; the road runs almost due south through lands reclaimed from malarial swamps, now largely parcelled out in small-holdings. This triangular Plain of Paestum (or of the Sele), with its base on the twenty miles of sandy seashore and its apex in the pass beyond Eboli, was a fiercely fought battlefield in the last war, when the Allies made the successful 'Salerno landing'.

Shortly after crossing the railway line we come to the broad River Sele. A little more than a mile farther on (beyond the station for Albanella), a road on the right, signposted Gromola, leads among orchards and white houses to the **sanctuary of the Argive Hera** by the mouth of the Sele. The ruins are a little difficult to find, but ask for '*Il Santuario Greco*'; nor is there much to be seen on the actual site, for the valuable sculptures have been removed to the museum at Paestum; but legend says that the temple dedicated to the Argive Hera was founded by Jason and the Argonauts. It was probably built on a spot already sanctified to the Mother-Goddess, at the same time as that of Poseidonia (Paestum). Poseidonia was founded as an offshoot of the Achaean town of Sybaris about the middle of the seventh century BC, and this would also account for the prominence given in Paestum to the very ancient cult of Hera of Argos, which was a strongly Achaean cult (as we can see from the part she played in siding with the Greeks in the siege of Troy).

The SS 18 soon reaches the ancient walls of **Paestum,** and we enter the enceinte by the Porta Aurea. Excavations of a necropolis at the Masseria Gaudo (which lies near the large farmhouse— Map III p. 182

masseria—to the right of the Salerno-Agropoli road, about a mile north-west of Paestum) have revealed pottery which suggests that the inhabitants had connections with Asia Minor as early as 2400–1900 BC. Vases similar to the curiously shaped black ones now in the Paestum Museum have been found only in the earliest of the cities on the site of Troy.

Since it had no acropolis, Poseidonia depended for its defence on the strength of its *walls,* which are some three miles in circumference, to allow the city's flocks and herds to be brought within the enclosure in times of danger. Much of the walls still stand, including the four main gateways—the Porta Aurea, by which we arrived; the southern Porta della Giustizia; the eastern Porta della Sirena (so called from a figure of a siren, almost obliterated, over the arch); and the Porta della Marina—in many ways the best preserved—on the west, facing the sea.

The walls reveal Paestum's earliest history. The lowest courses, constructed of large blocks of limestone, are those of the original Greek city which carried on a flourishing trade with the Etruscans and the rich lands to the north. Then, about 400 BC, Poseidonia was conquered by the Italiot Lucanians, who added to the walls, italianized the name to Paistom or Paistos, and substituted bronze coins for the beautiful silver coins showing Poseidon in the act of hurling a trident. In 273 BC the city fell to the Romans, who further strengthened the fortifications, adding some of the present towers. Paestum, as the Romans knew it, became once more a flourishing city, with baths, forum, temples and an amphitheatre. It was famous in antiquity for its violets and roses (Virgil mentions them), which were used in a lucrative scent industry. The Alexandrine writer Athenaeus tells us how the inhabitants of Paestum always remembered their Greek origins and once a year used to call on the gods by their Greek names, inviting them to share in a sacrificial meal, weeping as they remembered that they had once been Greeks.

Paestum declined with the Roman Empire, and through the ravages of malaria. A small Christian community struggled on, until in the ninth century Saracen raids drove them to seek refuge at Capaccio Vecchio. They took with them the body of St Matthew, which a citizen called Gavinus had somehow acquired in 370. It was removed to Salerno cathedral in 954 by Prince Gisulph I. Later the Normans despoiled many of the temples of Paestum, carrying off columns and marbles for the rebuilding of the Duomo at Salerno. By the eighteenth century all but the three main temples were buried beneath a tangled mass of vegetation.

The main entrance to the excavations is from the SS 18 (admission, daily 9.0 a.m. until an hour before sunset; the museum closes at 4.0 p.m.). Immediately opposite are two magnificent temples of local limestone—marble was rare in Southern Italy—which are still confusingly referred to by the names originally bestowed on them by the archaeologists of the eighteenth century. The archaic Doric *Basilica* (as it is known) on the left, the southernmost of the temples, is also the earliest, possibly about 565 BC. Within, the building was divided down the middle by a row of eight columns, of which three remain, and recent discoveries of votive offerings suggest that it was dedicated to Hera. In front of the temple is a large rectangular sacrificial altar, and next to it the pit into which the remains of the sacrifices were cast.

To the right of the basilica stands the misnamed **Temple of Poseidon** or Neptune, a magnificent building in the fully-developed Dorian style of the mid-fifth century BC. This lovely building is the most perfect specimen of Doric temple architecture in existence. The many votive offerings found in the vicinity suggest it too was dedicated to the Argive Hera. In front of it stand the remains of two altars.

If we pass through the temple in the direction of the sea and cross the intervening lawn, we come to the *cardo maximus* which runs north from the Porta della Giustizia on our left (part of the gate is incorporated in the Ristorante di Nettuna), past the crossing with the *decumanus maximus*, and thence by the Via Sacra to the third of the great temples of Paestum. At the crossing of *cardo* and *decumanus*, to our right, is the area of the *forum,* showing remains of the Lucanian and Roman periods built over the more ancient *agora* of the Greek city. Farther to the east is the Roman **amphitheatre,** now cut in two by the main road.

Excavations are in progress on the west side of the *cardo* and Via Sacra, in an area apparently of shops and private dwellings. Beyond the forum, on the right of the Via Sacra, stands a very ancient **subterranean chapel.** The precious collection of objects found intact within it and now in the museum suggests it too was dedicated to Hera.

The third of the large temples, erroneously called the **Temple of Ceres** (in fact it was dedicated to Athene), was built at some time between the two southern temples, about 528 BC. Its lobby had Ionic capitals (two are preserved in the museum), and this temple was therefore one of the earliest examples of the mixing of the orders in the ancient world. It was used in the early Middle Ages as a Christian church, and there are three Christian tombs.

To the east of the temple a gate takes us across the SS 18 to the excellent modern ***Museum,*** whose treasures range from prehistoric until Roman times. To the left of the museum, and slightly behind it, stands the church of the ***Annunziata,*** from which the removal of baroque accretions has revealed the original palaeo-christian basilica. It may be as early as the eighth century.

From the SS 18 a road leads outside the southern wall of the ancient city, passing the Ristorante del Nettuno and the Autostello (pleasantly set among trees by a stream) to the rapidly developing Lido di Pesto. There is a fine view from the near-by medieval watch-tower, the Torre di Paestum, and good bathing at the sandy Lido della Sirena.

Agropoli—S. Maria di Castellabate—Palinuro

A few miles south of Paestum there is a turning on the right off the SS 18 for the coast road (SS 267) for Agropoli, Castellabate and Palinuro. The SS 18 is the more direct route to the summer bathing Map III p. 182 resort of **Sapri,** but the alternative route, though longer and rougher, is really magnificent. (One word of warning: all this area is subject to frequent landslides; they are usually quickly marked with warning-signs FRANA, but the authorities are often rather dilatory in repairing them.)

As the SS 267 reaches the sea near Torre di S. Mario, a repaired and inhabited martello tower, a new road on the right leads to the Map III p. 182 Lido of Paestum. Ahead of us, on its promontory, stands **Agropoli,** the old town grouped around the ruined castello on the hill, and the newer town (*un paese evoluto*—a go-ahead town, as the natives are proud to assert) built round the piazza through which our road runs.

Although the name is Greek, Agropoli was Byzantine in origin, possibly founded as late as the fifth century AD. (This would rule out the legend that St Paul landed here on his way to Pozzuoli and left the imprint of his foot, which the pious used to point out to the credulous.) It was captured by the Saracens who were finally expelled in 1028, and like most of the coastal towns it suffered from raids by corsairs—it was destroyed by Barbarossa in 1535, and again by sea-marauders in 1630.

Agropoli has two (only fair) beaches and a comfortable hotel, the Carola, as well as other accommodation. There is a pleasant walk up through the old town (which has some charming nineteenth-century villas) to the ruins of the *castle,* built by the Byzantines and strengthened by the Aragonese. Today there are orchards and gardens within the ramparts. Some Arabic writing over one of the portals recalls the Saracen domination.

From Agropoli the road runs inland, past arcaded farmhouses, to avoid Monte Tresino, and then, with enchanting views, down to the coast again at **S. Maria di Castellabate,** an attractive and popular seaside resort. Castellabate, perched high on the hillside, was built in 1120 as a fortified castle for the Abbots of La Cava de' Tirreni— hence its name. A lucrative trade was carried on by the monks in their ships (called *saette*) from the two small near-by ports now called **S. Maria** and **S. Marco.** A beautiful sandy beach joins these two seaside villages, and the road up to Castellabate leaves the SS 267 midway between them. In a splendid position, overlooking the beach, is the modern Grand Hotel S. Maria. Other hotels are in the course of construction, and this will certainly become one of the most popular seaside resorts.

Map III p. 182

Map III p. 182

S. Marco is the base for the fishing fleet. The catch is immediately packed in ice and transported to Naples by lorries, so that one can seldom buy here the enormous *aragosta* (lobster) for which this coast is famed. Beside the modern mole at S. Marco foundations of Roman structures can be seen beneath the sea. And from here there is a beautiful walk of about two miles through orchards and fields to the **Punta Licosa.** On a clear day Capri and the whole Amalfi coast can be seen. There are also ruins, perhaps of a Roman villa, off the island of Licosa, with its modern lighthouse. The point itself was known to the Romans as *Enipeum* or *Posidium promontorium*, and the island was called after the Siren Leucosia. The property beyond the point is private.

From the turning off for S. Marco the SS 267 veers inland to avoid Monte Licosa, rejoining the coast again at Agnone and following the shoreline through the small, pleasant resort of **Accia-roli,** once much favoured by Ernest Hemingway, where the Hotel La Scogliera may be recommended. The coast at the little resort of **Pioppi** is rather rocky, but there are sandy stretches nearer the **Marina di Casal Velino.** Here the road turns inland to cross the fertile plain watered by the River Alento. At the road-junction, the road to the left leads to the SS 18, but we turn right, and, doubling back towards the coast, see ahead on the spur of the hill the tower of **Velia.** Beyond the spur, across the railway on the left, are the partly excavated *ruins* of the ancient Greek city of Elea.

Map III p. 182

Elea, an Ionic colony of the Phocaeans, was founded in 536 BC, and was famous in antiquity for its school of philosophy, known as the Eleatic, of which Parmenides and Zeno were the most prominent members. It remained a town of some importance under the Romans, and Cicero often visited his friend Trebatius at his villa there. Horace, too, was advised by his doctor to undergo a treatment of sea-bathing at Elea. Excavations have revealed Roman baths, parts of the surrounding walls, and the foundations of a temple (near the present tower on the hill) on what was the ancient acropolis.

Map III p. 182 After Velia the road passes, on the right, the turning for the **Marina di Ascea,** a seaside resort with good bathing, and then climbs among groves of magnificent olives to the village of Ascea. From here to Pisciotta the scenery is very fine, though there is as yet no adequate provision for tourists.

At S. Caterina a road is under construction which will follow the coast to Palinuro and on to the Marina di Camerota, but at present the road turns away from the sea to cross the rather dreary valley of the River Lambro.

To reach Palinuro, we turn right at the crossroads outside Foria, and continue on the high ground between the Rivers Lambro and Mingardo through the picturesque village of **Centola.** From Centola the road descends, with wonderful views, to the village of Palinuro.

Map III p. 182 **Palinuro** has something of a South of France atmosphere about it. There are good sandy beaches, including the Marina di Molpa on the southern side of the headland; and all this coast from Capo di Palinuro to the Marina di Camerota, and beyond the Punta degl' Infreschi towards Sapri, is studded with caves. Some, like the Grotta Azzurra at Palinuro, are very beautiful and accessible only from the sea, so one must bargain with the boatmen. Speleologists have found bones of animals of the quaternary period (*bos, cervus elaphus*, etc.), and remains which show that the caves were inhabited by man in the Stone Age.

Excavations to the north-east of the village of Palinuro have revealed that there was a settlement there in the sixth century BC— possibly of an indigenous people who had come under Hellenistic influence, perhaps from Sybaris. Silver coins found here depict a wild boar and the legend *Pal-Mol*, suggesting that Palinurus was joined politically with near-by Molpa.

The Grotte di Pertosa—Teggiano—the Certosa di Padula

The alternative—more customary—route to Calabria, the SS 19, runs through Eboli, and from the junction just before Auletta, where the SS 94 branches left for Potenza, we follow the course of the River Tanagro. A couple of miles past the village of Pertosa, we come to another road-junction, with several small *ristoranti* catering for visitors to the celebrated **Grotte di Pertosa**. These caves, which are among the most spectacular in Southern Italy, are entered from the car-park a short way along the road to the right (admission, 9.0 a.m.–5.30 p.m.; tickets at the *Biglietteria* on the left of the park). A warning: even in the summer the caves can be very cold.

Regaining the SS 19 we continue our ascent until, after the Ponte di Campestrino, we see before us the luxuriant **Vallo di Diano,** an elongated hollow (once a prehistoric lake) enclosed by wooded mountains. As the road descends to the valley, the town of Polla is on our right. An inscription by the roadside recalls the Consul P. Popilius who in 123 BC built the Via Popilia from Capua to Reggio Calabria. Near by was the Roman town of Forum Popilii; but the Roman remains in the Vallo di Diano are too numerous to record individually here.

Map III p. 182

A few miles farther on we come to a crossroads: the road to the left, the SS 95, passes through Atena Lucana for Brienza and Potenza. Shortly afterwards a road on the right leads to **Teggiano**, which merits a detour. A Roman city of great antiquity, Tegianum is believed to have been destroyed by Alaric the Goth in 410 AD. The new town which rose on the ruins was known as Dianum, whence Diano, which gave its name to the valley. Its present name was adopted only in 1862. In the castle Antonello Sanseverino, one of the rebellious barons, was unsuccessfully besieged by Frederick of Aragon. The cathedral and a number of Romanesque, Gothic and Aragonese churches and cloisters make Teggiano a fascinating town for the medievalist.

Map III p. 182

Back on the SS 19 we cross the Canale dei Pioppi, and shortly beyond the railway level-crossing come to the turning on the left for Padula and its famous Charterhouse, one of the most important monuments in the South of Italy. The **Certosa di Padula** was founded by Tommaso Sanseverino in 1306; but the predominant style of architecture is baroque, of the end of the seventeenth and early eighteenth centuries. The plan of the vast complex of buildings,

189

like the Escurial, represents St Lawrence's gridiron. (Visitors are accompanied by a guide: tip.) The Certosa served as a prisoner-of-war camp in the last war, and at the moment it is being restored to house a museum of local antiquities and serve as a cultural centre for conferences and students.

The entrance is by way of a courtyard, two sides of which were occupied with stables and domestic offices. At the farther end is the rather clumsy baroque entrance façade, built in 1718. A passage leads to a pleasant frescoed cloister (1561), with guest-rooms leading off the first-floor loggia. On the right of this is the entrance to the church (originally Gothic but baroqued over), through doors with low-reliefs of *Scenes from the Life of S. Lorenzo* (1374). The choir-stalls are of magnificent inlaid wood. The altar is of blue and black marbles and mother-of-pearl. From the left we pass into the chapter-house, and from there, next to the old cemetery (reconstructed as a cloister in the eighteenth century), to the chapel containing the sixteenth-century tomb of the founder. The refectory is entered from the cemetery cloisters, as are also the splendid monastery kitchens and cellars. Here, it is said, the monks once cooked an omelette composed of a thousand eggs for the Emperor Charles V, who was a guest of the Prior after his victorious return from the capture of Tunis in 1535.

The library is reached by a curious corkscrew staircase. The floor is paved with beautiful eighteenth-century majolica tiles. Windows look out over the Prior's cloister and the individual loggias and gardens of the monks' cells, which are entered from the magnificent Great Cloister of 1690. Each cell had a study or workroom on the floor above, three or four rooms below, and a loggia to meditate in. In the north-west corner of the cloister an elliptical stairway (1761) leads to a gallery above the arcades, where the monks could exercise.

Beyond the Certosa in the town of Padula is the church of the SS. Annunziata, where two hundred revolutionaries are buried, victims of the ill-fated uprising against the Bourbons in the Cilento in 1857.

The valley now begins to close in; on the right are the wooded flanks of Monte Cervati; behind Padula rises the Serra Longa; and ahead of us lie the mountains which form the boundary with Lucania (Basilicata). The SS 19 begins to rise beyond the River Porcile, which marks the termination of the Vallo di Diano, and at the Stretto Gauro we enter Basilicata.

CHAPTER 12

Potenza and its Environs

Map: IV, p.192

Basilicata, or **Lucania,** forms a rough-shaped wedge between Southern Campania and Apulia, with its base to the south in the Pollino range, which separates it from Calabria. It possesses a short sea-board on the Tyrrhenian Sea in the Gulf of Policastro, with the increasingly fashionable resort of Maratea; and another on the eastern Ionian coast in the Gulf of Taranto. To the west, the mountains of the Lucanian Apennines make access difficult; farther east the high land falls into hilly country which is divided into a number of more or less parallel valleys by the Rivers Bradano, Basento and Basentello; farther east still the country takes on the character of the limestone hills, with outcrops of rock and profound gorges (*gravine*), of the Apulian Murge. Here, particularly, deforestation has led to considerable erosion of the clay soil, leaving scarred hillsides, boulders and escarpments of calcareous stone.

The names Basilicata and Lucania are both used. Lucania is the older and is derived from a very early, perhaps indigenous people who were driven south by the Samnite conquests. With modern Calabria, it formed Augustus's III Regio (Lucania et Bruttii). Following the reconquest of the toe of Italy from the Lombards and Saracens by the Eastern imperial armies of Nicephorus Phocas at the end of the tenth century, these regions were governed by a *basilikos*. The name Basilicata appeared first in a document in 1175, and was that adopted by the conquering Normans. Despite efforts to have the earlier name reintroduced during the Bourbon period, and after the reunification of Italy, 'Lucania' was only restored to official use in 1932. This is the poorest region in Italy, and although tourist facilities are improving, visitors should be warned that they will not always come upon efficient and comfortable hotels except in the provincial capitals.

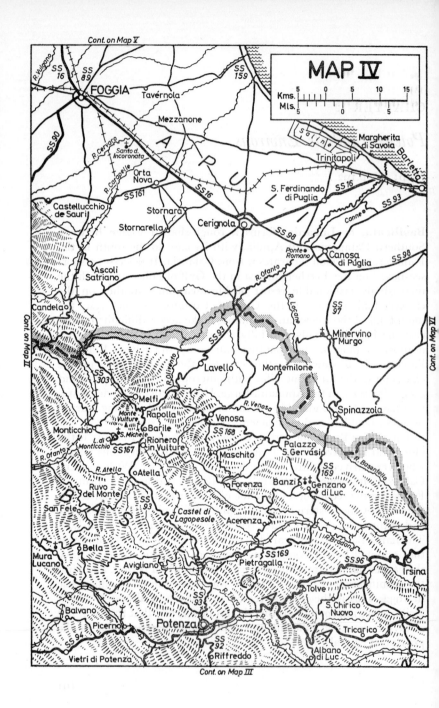

Cont. on Map V

MAP IV

Kms.
Mls.

5   0   5   10   15

Cont. on Map II

Cont. on Map VI

Cont. on Map III

R. Vulgano
SS 16
SS 89
FOGGIA
Tavérnola
Mezzanone
SS 159
Saline
Margherita di Savoia
Barletta
SS 90
R. Cervaro
Santo d. Incoronata
Trinitapoli
Orta Nova
SS 161
S. Ferdinando di Puglia
SS 16
SS 93
Castellucchio de Sauri
R. Carapelle
Stornara
Stornarella
Cerignola
SS 98
Canne
Ponte Romano
Canosa di Púglia
SS 98
Ascoli Satriano
R. Ofanto
R. Locone
SS 97
Candelao
SS 93
Minervino Murgo
SS 303
R. Olivento
Lavello
Montemilone
Melfi
R. Venosa
Spinazzola
Monte Vulture
Rapolla
Barile
Venosa
Monticchio
S. Michele
Rionero in Vulture
SS 168
Palazzo S. Gervásio
R. Bosentello
L. di Monticchio
SS 167
Maschito
SS 169
R. Ofanto
R. Atella
oAtella
Forenza
Banzi
Genzano di Luc.
Ruvo del Monte
R. Fiumarella
San Fele
SS 93
Castel di Lagopesole
Acerenza
R. Bradano
Bella
Mura Lucano
Avigliano
Pietragalla
SS 169
SS 96
Irsina
Balvano
Picerno
SS 93
Potenza
R. Tiera
Tolve
S. Chirico Nuovo
Tricarico
SS 94
R. Basento
SS 92
Riffreddo
Albano di Luc.
Vietri di Potenza

A P U L I A

B A S
I L I C A T A

Routes to Potenza

The shortest and most convenient route (which is more or less that followed by the railway) from Naples to Potenza is via Salerno, Battipaglia and Auletta. There is also a more northern route via Avellino and thence along the Via Appia (SS 7) to Potenza. The Via Appia is winding and mountainous for much of the way, but it allows us to visit the historically interesting little town of **Muro Lucano,** standing against the overhanging walls of the mountain at the southern end of its artificial lake. There are many Roman remains in the vicinity (including a bridge of the second century BC in the *contrada pianello*) and the town is thought to have been built on or near the site of Roman Numistrum, where in 210 BC the consul M. Claudius Marcellus resisted the attacks of Hannibal. And in the *castle* here—its remains can still be visited—the unfortunate Queen Giovanna I was supposedly strangled in 1382 (see p. 228). The Queen's body was taken back to Naples lashed to the back of a mule, and then exposed in S. Chiara. In the much restored *cathedral* is a painting by the Fleming Cornelius Smet (1589), known as the *Picture of Queen Giovanna*, which was given to the church by the painter as an act of repentance. About half a mile north-west of the town, on the road to Bella, stands the interesting little church of *S. Maria di Capodigiano* (or of the Madonna delle Grazie) built at the end of the twelfth century or beginning of the thirteenth by the locally born Maestro Sarolo, whose work we can see at S. Maria di Pierno near Atella, and in the campanile of the cathedral at Rapolla.

Potenza

The city of **Potenza,** one of the two provincial capitals of Lucania, has grown rapidly in the last fifteen years. The highest provincial capital on the mainland of Italy (2675 ft) gives one the impression that every building is of recent construction. And in fact earthquakes and bombing in the last war have left very little of historical or aesthetic interest. Potenza is an important centre of road and rail communication. The streets and squares are clean, but the churches and palazzi lack interest and it would hardly be worth a stop if there were adequate hotels to be found elsewhere in the region.

From the Piazza Matteotti, one of the two main squares of the city, buses leave for the **Provincial Museum** in the Via Piemonte, to the north of the old town in the Rione S. Maria (admission, weekdays 9.0 a.m.–1.0 p.m.; Sundays 10.0 a.m.–12.0 noon). Most interesting are its archaeological sections, which contain prehistoric finds from the province as well as objects from the excavations at Grumento, Metaponto, Garaguso, and Roman Potentia.

Some nine miles south of Potenza on the SS 92 is the summer resort of **Rifreddo,** standing among oak woods 3770 ft above sea-level. Its position gives the newly opened Hotel Rifreddo an advantage over the Grande Albergo in Potenza.

The cathedral of Acerenza—Castel di Lagopesole—Atella— Laghi di Monticchio

From Potenza the SS 93, which runs north then north-east to link up with Foggia and the towns of northern Apulia, passes through some of the most beautiful and historically and architecturally important parts of Basilicata. We leave the city by the Via Appia (SS 7), which we follow to the road-junction under the high ground of Monticchio. Here the SS 93 branches right. At the Quandrivio di S. Nicola, the road to the right, the SS 169, is an alternative route to northern Apulia via the important rail and road centre of Spinazzola.

Those who are interested in church architecture should take this road to visit the hillside town of **Acerenza** and its splendid cathedral which, with the cathedral at Aversa and the abbey in near-by Venosa (see pp. 105 and 201), have been described as 'the purest examples of true Gothic to be found south of the Alps'.

Acerenza (ancient Acheruntia) was taken by the Romans as early as 318 BC. Totila captured the town and made it a Gothic outpost against attacks by Byzantines and Lombards. The Byzantines gained possession of it, only to be ousted in turn by the Normans. The original plan (*ca.* 1080) of the **cathedral of the Assunta and S. Canio** we owe to the Normans, and its construction appears to be the work of French architects, for it resembles churches of Auvergne, Poitou and Caen in the use of the *chevet*, which we have already seen at Aversa. The style is rather French Romanesque than Gothic, and the church is seen at its best from the rear.

Rebuilt after 1281, it retained its earlier form; the façade suffered some alteration in 1524, and the right campanile was restored in 1554. The fine central doorway is possibly Angevin work of 1281, but some authorities claim that the portals here and at Monopoli
194

set the style for the churches of Apulia. Unfortunately there remains only one angelic bust of the original archivolt; the columns which supported this structure have survived and rest on curious groups of men and monkeys—Lombard or French, it is difficult to say. The crypt is interesting, and the sacristan will show visitors the marble bust of Julian the Apostate, which was removed from its place of honour on the façade after it was discovered to have been erroneously taken for a portrait of the saintly Bishop Canio.

From the Quadrivio di S. Nicola the SS 93 runs north through countryside which was once desolate but is now being brought under cultivation. Ahead of us we can make out the imposing mass of the **Castel di Lagopesole,** and behind, the slopes of Monte Vulture. We turn right into the main street of the poor village at the foot of the hill on which the **castle** stands. In 1242 the Emperor Frederick II began to build this hunting lodge in what was then thick wooded country abounding in game. Lagopesole was one of the Emperor's favourite residences, and it was there that he spent the last summer of his life. However, the building was not complete at his death in 1250. His son Manfred lived in the castle, and after his death at the hands of Charles of Anjou Manfred's wife Elena was imprisoned there. The early Angevins used Lagopesole occasionally as a summer retreat, but in 1416 Queen Giovanna II gave it, together with Melfi and Atella, to her lover Ser Gianni Caracciolo, and it remained in his family until 1530 when the Emperor Charles V presented it finally to the still existing Neapolitan branch of the Genovese family of Doria.

What immediately strikes the visitor as he climbs up to the castle's entrance is the almost complete absence of external windows. This was a common feature of Frederick's buildings; what windows there were, usually opened on to inner courts. It is difficult to picture the original gateway façade at Lagopesole, since the central portion between the two west-facing abutments has collapsed and been repaired, a round arch now partly masking the Saracenic pointed arch of the portal. The wooden doors may be as early as the fourteenth century. We look straight through, beneath a further pointed archway, to the entrance to the chapel on the far side of the great courtyard. The design of this doorway is curious: a well-proportioned rectangular opening is recessed in a much higher pointed Saracenic arch, bordered by dog-toothing; and the whole is set in a frame capped by the triangular arch which Frederick used elsewhere—for example, in the main entrance to his famous Castel del Monte.

To the right of the chapel door stairways lead to the smaller courtyard, where the small inner keep, with its single arched window, stands completely isolated. In the wall-face above the window are two remarkable carved heads. The head of the woman shows a competent sculptor's hand. The man's features have suffered decay, but we can make out the crown and—an odd addition—his ass's ears. The people of Avigliano, in a popular song, ascribed ass's ears to the Emperor Frederick Barbarossa; but it is a mystery why his grandson should have represented him in this fashion.

Back in the great court we see opposite us on the north side the stairway and windows of the Queen's apartments. It appears that the King had his quarters on the side of the entrance facing west over the vast forest that once extended towards Monte S. Croce.

From Lagopesole the road descends into the valley of the River Atella, with extensive views. At a crossing with the road from Muro Lucano we can turn right and climb the hill to the little town of **Atella,** which is interesting for its Duomo and medieval remains. The road crosses the town and joins the main road again on the north. In the centre of Atella is a public garden, at the farther end of which stands the fourteenth-century *cathedral of S. Maria.* Its pleasant façade, flanked on the left by a squat, square campanile, is transitional in style, containing both Romanesque and Gothic elements. The baroqued interior is of little interest. Farther along the street we come to the remains of the *Castello,* with its cylindrical towers. In the vicinity of the neighbouring piazza the buildings incorporate doorways and windows of the Angevin period. At the end of the town a street on the right brings us to the cemetery and the church of *S. Lucia,* another Angevin building (1389), but subsequently rebuilt. The earthquake of 1851 brought down a wall in the original apse and revealed a contemporary fresco, which shows the *Guardian Madonna* in the act of protecting human sinners with her cloak from the arrows of a wrathful God. The sinners include a pope, a king, a queen and a bishop.

From near-by Rionero in Vulture an excursion through beautiful country can be made to Monte Vulture and the Lakes of Monticchio. A good road, SS 167, runs westward from the SS 93 along the southern slopes of the mountain, with fine views to the south over the River Atella. **Monte Vulture,** an extinct volcano, is the only volcano to the east of the Apennines, and is remarkable for its flora and fauna: a naturalist's paradise. The road climbs what was the lip of the crater and descends through the Bosco di Monticchio, a magnificent forest of great trees beneath which grow all manner of shrubs and creepers, to the narrow strip of land which separates the two **Laghi di Monticchio,** the Piccolo (to our right) and the Grande. On the north-eastern side of the little lake we see the white buildings of the abbey of S. Michele di Monticchio among the thick woods beneath Monte Vulture. If plans materialize, visitors will eventually be able to take a funicular to the summit, to enjoy a view which extends over much of Lucania and Apulia.

There are restaurants on the narrow tongue of land between the lakes, and a short way on, to the left, stand the ivy-covered ruins of the eleventh- or twelfth-century Benedictine *abbey of S. Ippolito.* A road to the right leads up to the Albergo Casina ai Laghi and the entrance to the *abbey of S. Michele.* From this height there is a magnificent panorama over the woods and lakes towards the valley of the River Ofanto. The original abbey was built by the Benedictines over a celebrated grotto which earlier formed part of the habitation of an enclave of Basilian hermits. In 1059 it was consecrated by Pope Nicholas II, but a little later the Benedictines abandoned S. Michele and built S. Ippolito below. However, malaria forced them to return to S. Michele. After a short period of suppression the abbey came into the hands of the Capuchins in 1608. The present building was erected at the end of the eighteenth century, incorporating behind the high altar of its baroque church the original grotto, the chapel of S. Michele. On the wall facing the entrance is a *deisis*—Christ represented praying between the Virgin and John the Baptist; on each of the side walls are *three figures of Apostles*; in the vaulting is *an eagle with a halo* holding a roll in its beak, probably signifying St John the Evangelist. These Byzantine frescoes are possibly as early as the ninth century.

Returning to the road, we continue round the north end of the Lago Grande to the village of Monticchio. Here we fork right and, running along the northern slopes of Monte Vulture, arrive at the Sorgente Gaudianello, the springs and bottling station from which comes the *acqua minerale Monticchio*, one of the best of Italian table-waters. From here it is a pleasant run over hills covered with woods, olive-groves and vineyards to the interesting town of Melfi.

Melfi—Rapolla

For the more direct route to Melfi we leave Rionero in Vulture by the SS 93, cross the railway and enter the small town of **Barile,** settled in the Middle Ages by Albanians and still retaining many of

The Companion Guide to Southern Italy

their ancient customs. On Good Friday the inhabitants put on a medieval version of Our Lord's Passion. (The wines of this district are perhaps the best in Lucania: Aglianico di Vulture (red, 12–13°), Malvasia di Vulture (12–14°, pale yellow, semi-sweet) and Moscato di Vulture (12–15°), the last two being dessert wines.) Shortly beyond the town we pass the fifteenth-century *sanctuary of S. Maria di Costantinopoli* in which there is a much-venerated Byzantine painting of the Madonna, also of the fifteenth century.

The road winds among a countryside clearly volcanic in origin, with caves cut in the tufa. Many of these served as habitations until quite recently, but are now used to store the wine. Looking back at Monte Vulture, we can see the cross which crowns its summit. On the outskirts of Rapolla a road on the left, the SS 303, branches off for Melfi and Avellino.

As one approaches **Melfi,** one is struck by its medieval appearance: the vast bulk of its castle and city walls, built on top of what was a subordinate volcanic cone of Monte Vulture. Although Melfi's origin is pre-Roman, the town owes its historical importance to the Normans, to whom it surrendered in 1041. At their parliament held in Melfi two years later William Bras-de-fer was recognized as Count of Apulia, and in 1057, Robert Guiscard succeeded William's sons Drogo and Humphrey as Count of Apulia and leader of the Normans.

In 1059 Pope Nicholas II held a council at Melfi and invested Robert Guiscard with his lands, styling him 'by the grace of God and St Peter Duke of Apulia and Calabria and, with their help, hereafter of Sicily'. In 1089 Pope Urban II convoked here another council to debate whether to embark on the First Crusade. The Emperor Frederick II chose Melfi as the city from which he promulgated in 1231 the famous *Constitutiones Augustales*, a code of laws and regulations described as 'the fullest and most adequate body of legislation promulgated by any western ruler since Charlemagne', which limited the powers of the barons (even then the curse of the South) and gave certain privileges to the representatives of the towns, who were also called to the 'parliament'.

In spite of the damage done by a long series of earthquakes, Melfi has much to remind us of the presence of Normans and Swabians in Southern Italy. We enter by the Porta Venosina erected by Frederick. Higher up in the town, in the Piazza del Duomo, stands the *cathedral church of the Assunta,* which was begun in 1155—or in 1153, if it was contemporaneous with the campanile, the date of which is given in the inscription on its base. The church has been rebuilt and
198

restored several times, and in the restoration after the earthquake of 1930, a Byzantine-type fresco of the *Madonna and Child enthroned with two angels* was revealed. The campanile has interesting decoration in dark lava; the gryphon was the emblem of the Norman ruling house and has been adopted in the present armorial bearings of the municipality of Melfi. Roman stonework was incorporated in the building; and about ten feet above the top of the steps on the left-hand side is a curious horseshoe mark in the stone.

Also in the Piazza del Duomo is the ***Episcopio*** (the Archbishop's Palace), where the authorities have placed the beautiful ***Roman sarcophagus*** from Rapolla, formerly kept in the Municipio (admission by ringing for the porter: tip). This impressive piece of funeral statuary was discovered near Rapolla in 1856, and would appear to be from the first century AD, during the reign of Claudius or Nero. The recumbent figure of the young woman has her head supported by pillows. Below a frieze of tritons and marine monsters, on each long side stand in relief five gods, goddesses or heroes enclosed in architectural niches separated by spiral columns.

At the highest point of the town stands the ***Castello*** begun by the Normans, rebuilt by Charles of Anjou in 1278–81, altered by Andrea Doria (who received the town in fief from the Emperor Charles V), and repaired many times after earthquake damage. It has been closed for some years for further restoration. The castle was the seat of four papal councils at the end of the eleventh century, and it was from his royal residence here that the Emperor Frederick II issued his constitutions. The side of the irregular-shaped building nearest the town is defended by a moat with a drawbridge; the earlier entrance was on the farther side. From the hills there is a fine view back towards Monte Vulture.

Melfi has only one hotel, the Albergo Bellapanella.

Throughout this district caves and grottoes have been excavated in the tufaceous rock; some of these were used as shrines or chapels. Off the Rapolla road, about half a mile from Melfi station, the ***grotto-church of S. Margharita*** lies to the left of the road beyond the cemetery, whence it is approached by a footpath. The church has interesting restored remains of thirteenth-century frescoes covering the walls and the vaulted ceiling.

Rapolla also has a very medieval appearance, with its maze of steep alleyways between the conglomeration of houses. The town has medicinal waters, but more interesting are its cathedral and the church of S. Lucia. The ***Duomo,*** which was completely rebuilt in 1253, has suffered from earthquakes and was last restored in the

199

'thirties. It possesses a good Romanesque portal. Next to it stands the earlier campanile built to the designs of Maestro Sarolo in 1209. The two low-reliefs of the *Annunciation* (which shows the influence of Byzantine ivory carvings) and of *Original Sin* are also by him. From the balustrade by the cathedral we can look out over the rooftops to the valley beyond.

Below is the interesting church of **S. Lucia,** originally the cathedral of Rapolla, built by the Normans on the model of Byzantine churches. The interior shows the simplicity of early church design: rectangular in form, with a single central apse, the barrel-vaulted nave is supported by square pillars, with two elliptical cupolas between the second and fifth arches. This simplicity is echoed in the façade, which is featureless save for the high rounded arch of the main doorway.

The SS 93 skirts the town and runs down the valley with caves cut into its sides. After a few miles we come to a road junction where the SS 168 branches right for Venosa, Palazzo S. Gervasio and, crossing the border into Apulia, Spinazzola. The SS 93 continues north-east to Lavello, then traverses the lower countryside watered by the River Ofanto and passes into Apulia, to Canosa di Puglia (see p. 278).

The birthplace of Horace—the Abbey of the Trinity

Venosa, the ancient Roman city of Venusia, was the birthplace (65–8 BC) of the poet Horace (Horatius Flaccus). The 'house of Horace' is, as that authority on the spurious, Norman Douglas, put it, about 'as genuine as that of Juliet in Verona or the Mansion of Loreto'. The poet is also remembered by an indifferent nineteenth-century statue in the piazza called after him. However, another ruin from antiquity may be genuine. This is the **tomb of Claudius Marcellus,** the opponent of Hannibal and the victor of Syracuse, who was ambushed and killed near Venosa in 208 BC.

The Saracens took the city in 851 and held it for fifteen years. Under the Normans, and their Swabian successors, Venosa became a city of importance once more, and it was here that Charles I of Anjou founded one of the earliest known military hospitals. Later Venosa was held in fief by some of the leading families of the King-dom—the Sanseverino, Orsini and del Balzo. It was Piero del Balzo who in 1470 began the cathedral and built the castello which we see today.

The Royal Palace at Caserta has been called 'the overwhelmingly impressive swan-song of Italian baroque'. It was designed by the Dutch architect Vanvitelli to rival Versailles. The Hall of the Guard on the first floor gives some idea of its magnificence.

Opposite, above Looking towards the Royal Palace from the park. The water for the artificial lakes is brought by a series of tunnels and aqueducts from Monte Taburno, twenty-five miles away. *Opposite, below* The Arch of Trajan at Benevento, one of the best-preserved Roman commemorative arches. It was begun in AD 114, is of Parian marble, and over 50ft in height. The reliefs represent scenes from the Emperor's life. *Above* Benevento's Roman theatre was begun under Hadrian and enlarged by Caracalla to hold 20,000 spectators. It is now used for musical performances and stage representations. *Below* The elegance of Moorish arches on slender columns is matched by vigorous and inventive Lombard carving in the 12th c. cloister of S. Sofia.

Amalfi cathedral claims to possess the remains of the Apostle St Andrew. It was rebuilt in the Norman-Saracenic style in 1203. The façade and atrium, reconstructed in the last century, preserve the earlier form.

But pride of place must go to the ruins of the great ***abbey of the Trinity***. This stands to the north-east close to the road to the railway station and opposite the excavations of the Roman amphitheatre. Masonry from Roman buildings was extensively used for the abbey (as we learn from many inscriptions) and for other churches and dwellings in the town. The impressive ruins consist of an older church, which held the tombs of the Norman royal house, and behind, the beautiful abbey church which was never completed.

The old church, which was begun by Count Drogo and entrusted to the Benedictines before his death in 1051, was built over a palaeo-christian edifice, which in turn is thought to have arisen from a temple of Hymenaeus, the ancient god of marriage. It was con-secrated in 1059 by Pope Nicholas II. Robert Guiscard buried here the remains of his half-brothers, William Bras-de-fer, Drogo (who was assassinated at Venosa on the feast of S. Lorenzo) and Hum-phrey, and his own divorced first wife Alberada. When Robert died in Corfu in 1085, his body was also interred with those of his family. Only the tomb of Alberada has survived, on the left of the church.

The enlargement of the abbey was initiated by the Benedictines about 1135, but the troubled times which followed and the vastness of the undertaking were too much for the remaining monks. In 1297 Pope Benedict VIII gave the abbey to the Hospitallers of St John of Jerusalem, but they too failed to proceed with the building, prefer-ring to use Drogo's smaller church. On the walls of the latter are some interesting frescoes: beneath the portraits of *Pope Nicholas* and *St Catherine of Siena*, is a *Pietà* which has been attributed by Bernhard Berenson to Roberto Oderisi (second half of the fourteenth century).

The beautiful apsidal end of the unfinished abbey, with its three deambulatory chapels, suggest that here too—as at Aversa and Acerenza—the Normans called in French architects to design the church rather than use the local Lombard builders.

Farther down the road to the station, cut in the tufa to the left of the road, are Jewish Catacombs, possibly of the third to fifth centuries AD.

CHAPTER 13

Matera and its Environs

Maps: III, p.182; IV, p.192; VI, p.238

The route to Matera—Tricarico—Miglionico

Matera, the capital of the second of Lucania's two provinces, lies due east of Potenza near the Apulian border. The most usual route from Naples is the SS 19 and 94 to Potenza, and then the SS 7, the Via Appia, which runs on to Taranto and Brindisi. The Via Appia crosses into the province of Matera at the turning on the left for S. Chirico Nuovo. From here we run along the watershed between the Rivers Bradano and Basento, with an extensive panorama to the north and south. Below us, Tricarico comes into view, looking, like so many of the towns of Northern Lucania, straight out of the Middle Ages.

Map IV p. 192 **Tricarico** was a Byzantine town and the seat of a bishop as early as 968. The most ancient part, which is known as Civ ità, has a nucleus of buildings called the Rabatana, which suggests, as does the architecture, that the Saracens possessed the town and fortified it at some time between the tenth and twelfth centuries. The *cathedral* was built by Robert Guiscard, but has suffered rebuilding and restoration; the campanile, however, is of the thirteenth century. Inside is a monumental baroque tomb of Bishop Diomede Carafa (1639); and a piece of a Roman sarcophagus of the third century AD has been placed in the sacristy. Other churches are worth visiting: *S. Chiara* (built in 1322, but restored in the sixteenth century and subsequently) and its adjoining monastery, which has an Aragonese round tower; *S. Francesco* (fourteenth-century but rebuilt in 1882) where the portal and parts of the structure are original; *S. Antonio da Padova,* with a doorway of the Durazzo period (1491) and in the monastery next door a statue of the Saint of the same date. The *Episcopio* and several of the near-by palaces have points of interest. Of the Norman *castle* nothing remains except the tower, and even this was perhaps rebuilt by the Aragon-

202

ese. To the north the town overlooks the valley of the River Bilioso, a tributary of the Bradano.

The road continues, through the lower hills between the river valleys, to Miglionico. Since the war a dam has been built across the Bradano, and the vast reservoir is now being used to irrigate formerly barren land over a wide area of the province. (The plans of this land reclamation scheme can be seen in the offices of the Consorzio della Bonifica at Matera.)

Miglionico, it is claimed, was founded by Milo, the athlete-hero of Croton; but its early history is obscure. As we enter the town, we see on the right the Sanseverino castle, now inhabited by a number of poor families. This is the celebrated *Castello della Congiura,* called after a meeting here in 1481 in the Sala del Malconsiglio (the Hall of Ill Counsel) of the disaffected barons of the Kingdom under the presidency of the Duke of Sanseverino.

Map VI
p. 238

Miglionico has several churches with interesting Romanesque, Gothic and Renaissance features, as well as private houses of all periods. In the church of *S. Francesco* there is a polyptych by Cima da Conegliano (1459–1517), the only example (to my knowledge) of this fine Venetian master in Southern Italy.

Matera—opéra bouffe—the Sassi Barisano e Caveoso—the Duomo—hypogea-churches

Shortly after Miglionico the road turns and runs north-east, crossing the River Bradano below the new dam. The country here is monotonous, but has a certain wild grandeur—erosion of the low limestone hills forming the characteristic ravines or *gravine*. We pass on our right the Capuchin monastery and the junction with the SS 175, and enter **Matera** by the Via Lucana.

Map VI
p. 238

The city is built on the precipitous edge of the ravine of the River Gravina di Matera, parts of the town being separated by the rocky valleys known as the Sassi Barisano and Caveoso. In these *sassi* many of the dwellings have been cut out of the rock-face, and present a terraced conglomeration of cave-like houses connected by narrow alleys and steep stone steps. Archaeological evidence of the foundation of Matera, though it is still a matter of dispute, shows that the city is very ancient, certainly extending back to palaeolithic times. It was later much influenced by the Greek civilization of the Ionian coast. Pliny calls the inhabitants of the district Mateolani, and it may be that Matera is derived from Mateola, the name of their capital. From Roman times until the coming of the Normans in 1064 the city's history is one long record of subjection and devastation: it was occupied in turn by Pyrrhus and Hannibal, and suffered greatly in the Social Wars; sacked by the Goths, it recovered only to be taken by the Lombards and annexed to the Duchy of Benevento; it was destroyed by the Franks, and again in 867 by the imperial troops who drove out its Saracen captors; these latter reoccupied it in 937, finally destroying it completely in 994, when they killed all the male inhabitants and enslaved the women. The Byzantines restored the city, but by this time the citizens had taken to the caves. In 1133 Matera passed into the royal domain; but at the end of the fifteenth century Ferdinand II of Aragon gave it in fief to Count Giovanni Carlo Tramontano, who began the *castle,* the unfinished towers of which we see today on the hill to the west of the town. Count Tramontano's rule did not last long, for the citizens, driven to revolt by his oppression, slew him in front of the cathedral in 1514. Later Matera was held by the Orsini family, until it redeemed itself from feudal ties in 1638. From 1663 until 1806 it was the capital of Basilicata, when Potenza, as more centrally placed, succeeded it. In 1927 the region was divided into the present two provincial administrations.

It would seem a far cry from the *sassi* of Matera to the aristocratic splendour of pre-revolutionary Paris; yet the popular *opéra bouffe* owed much to Egidio Romoaldo Duni, a native of Matera. Duni was born in 1708, studied music in Naples, and achieved success as a composer of opera in London and Paris, before he settled in Paris in his late thirties. There he, and other composers like Grétry, adapted the Neapolitan comic opera to French taste. He enjoyed immense popularity before his death in Paris in 1775.

The centre of Matera, the Piazza Vittorio Veneto, is reached by continuing in the Via Lucana and then turning right in the Via Roma; or by forking right in the Via Ridola just after we enter the city. On the east side of the piazza, at the beginning of the Via S. Biagio, stands the Romanesque church of *S. Domenico.* To the right of the Via S. Biagio is the little church of *Mater Domini,* built in the eighteenth century by the Knights of Malta, with its curious bell-tower and emblem of the Maltese cross. Farther up the street, which at this point opens out into a *largo,* is the very interesting church of *S. Giovanni Battista,* which is entered through a beautiful Romanesque doorway (1204) on the right side of the church, the main entrance from the former monastery having been incorporated in the adaptation of the monastery as a prison. Its delicate foliate

decoration is pure Byzantine in inspiration, and within the rectangular door-recess a Saracenic arch adds to the complex, but
perfect blending, of styles.

This portal resembles strongly that of SS. Nicolò e Cataldo at
Lecce (see p. 334), and the resemblance is increased when we enter
the church. SS. Nicolò e Cataldo is some twenty years earlier than
S. Giovanni; yet both buildings show a harmonious fusion of French
and Saracenic elements with those of Apulian-Romanesque, and
suggest that their architect was trained in Burgundy.

The Via S. Biagio is continued in the Via S. Cesarea as far as a
crossing; here the Via d'Addosio, on the right, descends to the little
piazza in front of the church of S. Agostino, allowing us a fine view
over the Sasso Barisano towards the spur on which rises the cathedral.
S. Agostino, which stands on the edge of the ravine at the north-
eastern extremity of the city, was built over the earlier church of S.
Guglielmo in 1594 and rebuilt in 1750. In the sacristy there is a
fourteenth-century painting in the Byzantine manner, known as the
Madonna della Bruna (there is another of the same name in the
cathedral). By a door to the left of the main altar we descend through
a passage cut in the rock to a chapel dripping with water. This is
part of the old church of S. Guglielmo, on the walls of which are the
remains of frescoes.

The Via d'Addosio takes us down into the Sasso Barisano; at the
bottom the Via S. Antonio Abate leads to the beginning of the
Strada Panoramica dei Sassi which winds along the edge of the
ravine, east of the hill crowned by the Duomo, to the Sasso Caveoso.
Here, at the foot of the conical mass of rock known as Monte Errone
or Montirone, is the baroque-restored church of *S. Pietro Caveoso,*
and next door the *school* founded by St John Bosco. On the western
side of Monte Errone, which we can climb among deserted houses
now falling into decay, is the little church of *S. Maria de Idris,* cut,
like so many of the churches in the vicinity of Matera, from the solid
rock. The epithet 'de Idris' is a popular mistake arising from an
early fresco which depicts the Madonna with two pitchers beside her;
the original title was 'Odigitria', that is, 'Protectress of the Road'.
At the rear of the church is another church, a *hypogeum,* or place for
interment of the dead, which is known as *S. Pietro Monte Errone*
and may be as early as the eighth century. In both churches there
are traces of frescoes, some unmistakably Byzantine.

Continuing in the Strada Panoramica, we come to the Via
Casalnuovo, which brings us up to the Via Ridola at the point where
it opens out into a piazzetta in front of the Chiesa de Carmelo

(1608). From the balustrade here there is a good view of the Sasso Caveoso and Monte Errone. A short way on, to the left of the Via Ridola, stands the former monastery of S. Chiara (1698) which today houses an interesting **archaeological collection.** The prehistoric sections are particularly valuable for the light they throw on the earliest civilizations of Southern Italy (admission, weekdays 9.0 a.m.–12.0 noon, 3.0–5.0 p.m.; Sundays 9.0–11.0 a.m.).

Farther along the Via Ridola, on the same side, is the baroque church of the **Purgatorio** (1770), with the grim *memento mori* decorations of skulls usual on such churches in the South. Opposite is the Albergo Italia, one of the two 'adequate' hotels in Matera. The other is the Jolly.

We turn right beyond the Italia in the Via S. Francesco which brings us almost immediately to the church of **S. Francesco.** The structure of the early church, which was given to St Francis of Assisi during his lifetime (*ca.* 1218), has been hidden beneath the baroque accretions of 1670. This Franciscan church was itself built over a much earlier *hypogeum* dedicated to SS. Peter and Paul. From the third chapel on the left we can descend to the remains of this first church, which contains some interesting frescoes of the eleventh century. Admirers of Bartolomeo Vivarini (1450–99) can see here nine panels from a polyptych, set in the organ *cantoria.*

From the right of the church we come to the Via Duomo, which leads up through a fascinating quarter of old palaces to the Piazza del Duomo and the cathedral. The **Duomo,** begun in 1268, is a good example of later Apulian-Romanesque and shows the typical Lombard construction of a high nave, with the characteristic arched corbel-table, flanked by lower aisles. Typically Lombard too is the use of animals as supports for columns, particularly in doorways and windows. The fine rose window is supported by figures of angels and surmounted by that of St. Michael. Above the main doorway is a sculptured group of the *Madonna and Child* (a representation of the popular Madonna della Bruna) *between SS. Peter and Paul.* Most interesting is the second of the two doorways on the right, the Portal of the Lions. The campanile has been spoilt by the later addition of an upper storey and pyramidal top.

The inside of the Duomo, in spite of baroquing, is still impressive, and the columns of the nave (some are from ancient temples at Metaponto) have good capitals. The choir of inlaid wood is the work of Tantino d'Ariano (1453); and the chapels contain sculpture and paintings by local artists, which include a crib in polychrome stonework by Altobello Persio (1534). Over the first altar on the left is the Byzantine-inspired fresco of the *Madonna della Bruna* (thirteenth century), surrounded by inlaid marbles and heads of angels (1627). And two altars away is a painting of the *Madonna and Child with S. Anne*, attributed to the little-known Polish artist Sebastian Maieski (1632). Farther along the left side of the church a doorway takes us to a courtyard in which is the Romanesque church of **S. Maria di Costantinopoli.** In the lunette above the fine doorway is a thirteenth-century representation of the triumphal car of the Madonna della Bruna entering the cathedral, which is of interest for the evidence it gives of the early date of the **Festa (or Sagra) della Madonna della Bruna** on July 2nd.

According to popular tradition this festa was begun by the notorious Count Tramontano; but it seems inherently unlikely. *Bruna* is derived from a medieval term for a cuirass or hauberk, and the festival more probably originated to commemorate some victory of the Materani over the infidels. It certainly has a very military character: a band of mounted clergy and citizens in armour accompany the statue of the Madonna, which is carried on a triumphal car three times around the Piazza del Duomo—the *tre giri*—before the car is smashed and the pieces carried off by the townsfolk as precious relics.

Round Matera are many **hypogea-churches** cut in the rock. The best known are S. Barbara, the Vaglia and the Palomba. **S. Barbara** is reached by a path, which descends to the Gravina di Matera from the SS 7, just before the convent of the Cappuccini that we passed as we entered the city from the south. The church, distinctly Byzantine in inspiration, has some thirteenth-century frescoes: one of *a landscape with shepherds*, *a Madonna*, and *the two St Barbaras.*

The other two churches are to the north of the city, which we leave by the continuation of the Via Appia (SS 7). After a little over a mile we take the SS 99, which branches left for Altamura. Here we come shortly to the church of **S. Maria della Valle** or Balea, or popularly **La Vaglia,** cut from the tufa in 1280 to the designs of Maestro Leonio di Taranto. The interior of four aisles has remains of seventeenth-century frescoes. Near by is another hypogeum-church known as the **Cristo alla Gravinella,** the façade of which was rebuilt in the seventeenth century, when the ancient frescoes were repainted.

We return to the crossroads and, following the Via Appia beyond the bridge over the gravina, shortly come to a path on the right which takes us to the brink of the ravine. Here, picturesquely set on its heights, is the church of the **Spirito Santo,** known more frequently as **La Palomba.** The Romanesque façade, with its rose window, has over the portal a fifteenth-century low-relief figure of the *Madonna della Palomba,* from which comes the popular name for the little church.

An alternative route to Matera—Grumento Nova—Stigliano—Pisticci— land reclamation

An alternative route to Matera, some sixty miles longer via the Vallo di Diano, leaves the SS 19 at Montesano Scalo where the SS 103 begins immediately to climb the beautifully wooded slopes to the south of Serra Longa. We pass into Lucania at the Sella Cessuta (3400 ft), and come shortly to the small town of **Moliterno** with the ruins of a castle, built by the Normans over an earlier Lombard fortress, on its beetling rock. The road descends into the fertile Valley of Grumento, skirting the foothills of Monte di Saponara; a road to the left leads up to Grumento Nova, which overlooks the confluence of the River Sciaura, on our left, with the River Agri.

Map III
p. 182

Grumento Nova, which was known as Saponara di Grumento until 1932, was founded by survivors from ancient Grumentum, destroyed finally by the Saracens about 1000. In 1497 the fief of Saponara was granted to Ugo Sanseverino by Frederick of Aragon as a reward for his loyalty. Ugo had three sons, and in 1516 their jealous uncle poisoned these inconvenient heirs. Visitors to Naples may see in the Sanseverino family chapel in the church of SS. Severino and Sossio the monument, designed by Giovanni da Nola, which the boys' mother erected in their memory. She herself lies in a simple tomb at their feet.

Map III
p. 182

The site of ancient Grumentum is on the high ground on the farther side of the River Sciaura, about half a mile from the road. Excavations are now in progress. Records of the city date from the Second Punic War; under its walls the Consul C. Claudius Nero inflicted a severe defeat on Hannibal in 207 BC. It suffered greatly in the Social Wars, but later became a *municipium*, until finally destroyed by the Saracens. In 1820 the beautiful so-called 'Siri Bronzes' were found on the site; they have been in the British Museum since 1833.

Beyond Grumento the road climbs again to over 3000 ft before it crosses the SS 92 from Potenza at Corleto Perticara. It continues its tortuous course among the mountains until we see ahead of us, beautifully situated on its high hill, the ancient town of **Stigliano,**

Map VI
p. 238

208

once a fief of the important Colonna family. The origin of the town is obscure; possibly it was one of the centres of the Lucani. The municipal crest proudly shows the figure of Tullius Hostilius, the third king of Rome. From the ruins of the castello at the top of the town there is a fine panorama. Near the small market in the centre of Stigliano is the fifteenth-century church of *S. Antonio,* which has a curious baroque façade *a bugne* (1763); its campanile is capped by almost an onion cupola.

After Stigliano the road descends through a desolate-looking countryside until, a few miles beyond the village of Craco, we come to a junction (the Bivio Craco). The right-hand fork goes past the town of Montalbano Ionico to meet the Via Ionica at Scanzano.

For Matera we branch left on the SS 176. High on the hill to our right we see the houses of **Pisticci,** which is reached by a road of hairpin bends. Today the town's prosperity comes from the land reclamation works which are transforming the valley of the River Basento between the railway stations for Pisticci and Ferrandina. The aperitif Amaro Lucano is manufactured in the town. The women of Pisticci and Stigliano both have a sombre and almost nun-like traditional dress: a longish black skirt is worn below a black bodice relieved by a white blouse with elaborately puffed and frilled sleeves, and a black shawl covers the head and crosses over the breast.

Map VI
p. 238

The road between Stazione di Pisticci and the junction of the SS 176 and the Via Appia near Miglionico (where we turn right for Matera) has been newly constructed, following the discovery of natural gas (methane) near Ferrandina in 1959. The gas will supply local industries, which are to be built around Stazione di Pisticci, and will also be piped to other regions of Lucania and Apulia for industrial use. This discovery, combined with the water from the Bradano reservoir, has transformed the whole area. Visitors who care to see what irrigation can do, should make a diversion to Metaponto, near the mouth of the Bradano, where land which was only a few years ago unproductive waste is now parcelled out in rich cornfields and orchards, each farm with its neat white homestead.

CHAPTER 14

Foggia and its Province

Maps: IV, p.192; II, p.126; V, p.222

History of Apulia

The region of **Apulia,** lying to the east of the Apennines, forms the entire 'heel' of Italy from its northern 'spur' in the Gargano promontory to its southernmost tip in Cape S. Maria di Leuca. Topographically the region falls into well-marked divisions. In the north there are the mountains of the Gargano, which in Monte Calvo reach a height of 3463 ft. Between these and those offshoots of the Apennines known collectively as the Monti della Daunia lies the great plain (Il Tavoliere) of the Capitanata, stretching as far south as the River Ofanto—the most extensive tract of flat country in Italy. South again come the *murge* of the so-called Terra di Bari, a series of upland plateaux, nowhere much more than 1000 ft above sea-level, descending in terraces towards the Adriatic coast. Finally there is the Salentine peninsula, which again consists of low murge, characterized by numerous outcrops of rock in the red soil, with a restricted area of plain, the Tavoliere di Lecce. The region is divided into five provinces: Foggia, Bari, Brindisi, Taranto and Lecce.

In comparison with other parts of Italy Apulia is still little known to the tourist, either from other countries or even from northern Italy. Hotel accommodation is very restricted, and although it is being rapidly increased visitors are recommended to stay either at a provincial capital or a well-known resort. Fortunately the capitals are the best centres from which to explore, and furthermore, they are all on or within very easy reach of the sea; the most distant, Foggia, being only some twenty miles from the excellent beach at Siponto. Those who do not care for the heat should avoid Apulia in July or August, since much of it is low-lying and, with the exception of the beaches of the northern Gargano and of the Tremiti Islands, similar to North Africa in climate.

210

Apulia is for me one of the most fascinating of all the Italian regions for the austere beauty of its landscape, its history, the magnificence of its churches and castles, for the exotic, oriental appearance of many of its gleaming white towns and the unexpectedness of a city like Lecce, for the excellence of its wine and fruit, and for the character of its people.

When the Dorian Greeks founded Taras (Taranto) at the end of the eighth century BC, they found people already in possession of Apulia whom they called Iapigi—possibly of the same Illyrian stock as the Iapudi of Dalmatia. (The name Apulia is possibly a Latin rendering of this.) Three main branches of the Iapigi seem to have been distinguished: the Dauni, who inhabited the Capitanata; the Peucezi in the central region (what is today the Terra di Bari); and the Messapi of the Salentine Peninsula. To make things more confusing, the Romans further divided the Messapi into the Salentini and the Calabri.

In Greek mythology Diomedes came to Daunia after the destruction of Troy, helped the king against the Messapians, and married his daughter. Diomedes was the legendary founder of Argyrippa, later called Arpi, the ruins of which lie a few miles north of Foggia. One story tells of Diomedes's death on the Tremiti Islands, where he and his companions were turned into the herons that still live there, the birds of Diomedes.

After the failure of King Pyrrhus of Epirus to render effective aid to the Tarentines against the growing power of Rome, and the surrender of the city in 272 BC, many of the cities of Apulia allied themselves with Rome. Even Hannibal's disastrous defeat of the Roman army at Cannae (near Barletta) in 216 BC failed to prevent the ultimate settlement of Apulia as a Roman province. When Rome turned to the conquest of the East, the ports of Apulia, linked directly with the capital by the Via Appia and later the Via Traiana, became of paramount importance. In the administrative division of Italy under Augustus, Apulia and Calabria (the Salentine peninsula, not present-day Calabria) became the II Region. Aerial photography has shown how the fertile plain of the Capitanata was laid out by the Romans as a chess-board of roads, canals and allotments—whence the name Tavoliere.

During the downfall of the Roman Empire of the West Apulia shared in the general decay of social and economic life. From the time of the establishment of the Lombard Duchy of Benevento (AD 590) until the subjection of the last cities of Apulia in 1071 to the rule of the Norman Duke Robert Guiscard, the region suffered from continuous wars between Lombards and Byzantines. In 843 the Saracens, called in by the Lombards, took Bari; and thenceforth their ferocious raids added to the general deterioration, which the intervention of Frankish kings and German emperors did little to diminish.

It was under the Norman kings and their Hohenstaufen successors that Apulia recovered stability and embarked on the wonderful flowering of culture which we associate with the architecture of Apulian-Romanesque. From the First Crusade in 1096 until the last (the Eighth) in 1270, the ports of Apulia drew immense profits from traffic with the Levant. John of Salisbury describes a dinner he attended in 1155 in Canosa di Puglia which lasted from two in the afternoon until six the following morning, the tables laden with delicacies from Constantinople, Cairo, Alexandria, Palestine, Syria, Phoenicia and Tripoli. A visit to the Castel del Monte, though it is today but a ruined shell of its original splendour, will show us the sophisticated luxury in which the Emperor Frederick II lived. This prosperity continued under the first of the Angevins.

It was the rise of the feudal nobility, and the intervention of foreign powers in the struggles for the throne of Naples, culminating in the long Spanish vice-regal domination, that reduced Apulia to one of the poorest regions in Italy. Its lands became a battlefield between the French and the Spaniards; its trade fell into the hands of Venetians, Genovese or Florentines. In 1480 the Turks took Otranto and slew its male inhabitants; in 1680 they sacked and burnt Manfredonia. By the eighteenth century the formerly rich plains served only as winter pasturage for flocks of sheep which were driven down from the mountains. In 1799 the towns of Apulia were sacked by the Sanfedisti, and for decades afterwards outlying farms (*masserie*) were subject to the extortions of brigands. Even late last century the land around S. Severo, which now produces one of the best Italian white wines, was described as a desert.

Only in the period between the last wars was the problem of restoring prosperity to Apulia seriously tackled. The Acquedotto Pugliese—one of the greatest irrigation schemes in existence—which brings water from near the source of the River Sele on the western side of the Apennines, was finally completed in 1939. But the greatest progress in land reformation, industrial development and the provision of social services has been made since the Second World War. In 1901 Bari had a population of 78,000; today it is still growing rapidly, with a population in excess of 320,000, the second largest city in Southern Italy.

Foggia—a miraculous icon—the Cathedral and Civic Museum—ritual abduction

Foggia, the capital of the Capitanata, is the centre of communica-   Map IV
tions for northern Apulia. It is reached from Naples by rail and by   p. 192
the SS 90 (delle Puglie). From the north the SS 16 (Adriatica) turns
inland from the Adriatic shortly after Termoli, crosses the Capitanata to Foggia, and goes on to Brindisi and Otranto. Foggia is completely modern in appearance; it was rebuilt after being almost
totally destroyed by the earthquake of 1731, and again after the last
war, when some 70 per cent of its buildings suffered from aerial
bombardment.

After the mysterious disappearance of Diomedes's city of Arpi, the
survivors seem to have existed as nomadic shepherds. A little village
grew up around a tavern, Borgo del Gufo, at the crossroads a short
way south of ruined Arpi, and legend has it that it was near this spot
on the night of August 13th, 1073, that some of these itinerant *pastori*
beheld three flames burning on the surface of a marsh. There they
found an object wrapped in seven veils, which was discovered to be a
painting of the Virgin—the Byzantine icon which today is venerated
in the cathedral. The cult of the *Icona Vetere*, or the *Madonna dei
Sette Veli*, drew together the dispersed survivors of Arpi, and they and
other nomads founded here the city of Foggia. The name is apparently derived from *fovea*, which either refers to the low-lying site or to
the ditches then (and subsequently) used for storing grain.

With the consolidation of Norman power Foggia grew in importance; in 1170 William the Good began the cathedral. But the
true founder of the city's greatness in the Middle Ages was the
Emperor Frederick II, who in 1220 built the enclosing walls and
began his sumptuous palace, the wonder of the age. The architect
was the celebrated Bartolomeo da Foggia. He and (his son?) Nicola
(or Nicolò) di Bartolomeo da Foggia and Gualtiero da Foggia were
the leading sculptors in the school of artists formed by the Emperor.
So impressive were the halls, courtyards, statues, covered walks,
artificial lakes and fountains of the palace at Foggia that after the
siege of Cortenuova Frederick ordered the captured Lombard
knights to be conducted through them, in order that they might see
with their own eyes the brilliant civilization of the imperial Hohenstaufen.

Although the capital of the Kingdom was Palermo, between his

213

return from Germany as Emperor in 1220 and his death thirty years later, Frederick spent only four years away from Apulia. There may have been good political reasons for this, but his main reasons were perhaps more personal: he loved the Apulian countryside, once declaring 'that it was no ignoble thing to be called "a man from Apulia".'

Foggia is admirably placed for the exploration of northern Apulia. It is well provided with a wide selection of hotels, including the 1st category Palace Hotel Sarti. The railway station has a more than passable Buffet Stazione. There are some good local wines, among them the excellent white San Severo, the pleasant *rosato* from Cerignola, and the full-bodied reds of the Gargano. Apulia's roast kid (*capretto ripieno al forno*) and stuffed aubergines (*melanzane ripiene*) should be tried; and as a dessert the *pancielli d'uva passula*, little aromatic packets of vine leaves containing dried raisins.

The **cathedral of S. Maria Icona Vetere** lies just off the Piazza del Lago, which commemorates the shepherds' discovery of the icon. The crypt and parts of the lower external walls of the present Duomo are Norman; the rest, like the campanile, is baroque, following reconstruction after the earthquake of 1731. The bombardment of 1943 has revealed some interesting arcading and reliefs above a doorway on the left flank, which seem to be an early-fourteenth-century refacing that suggests a distinctly Pisan influence. In a chapel to the right of the chancel is kept the Byzantine painting of the *Madonna of the Seven Veils*. The crypt has been restored but its original shape retained. The round arches in the centre are supported on short columns of conglomerate from the Gargano, with delicately carved capitals, believed to be the work of Nicola di Bartolomeo da Foggia.

Near the cathedral, at Piazza de Sanctis 88, is the **Palazzo de Rosa,** with an open loggia above, one of the few Renaissance palaces in the city. Nothing now remains of the Emperor's palace but a doorway on the right side of the Palazzo Arpi in the adjacent Piazza Vincenzo Negri. A rounded arch resting on carved eagles which serve as consoles (said to be the work of Bartolomeo da Foggia) surrounds an early inscription. The palazzo houses the **Musei Civici** (admission, weekdays 9.0 a.m.–1.0 p.m.; closed holidays), which consist of sections devoted to archaeology, science, history, popular traditions, as well as a collection of mementoes of Umberto Giordano, the Foggian composer (1867–1948). The art gallery has paintings of the nineteenth and twentieth centuries, mostly by local artists, but also some by the School of Posillipo. In the entrance hall are a mosaic of marine animals from the excavations of ancient Arpi, and a relief which was perhaps part of a tomb. This was found near the Duomo and is thought by some to represent the Emperor Frederick, whose heart was kept in a casket in the cathedral until it was destroyed in the earthquake of 1731.

The central arch of the *Porta Arpana,* or the Porta Grande, off the Piazza Negri, is all that survives of Frederick's city walls.

On the northern outskirts of the city, in the district known as **Borgo Croci,** live some hundred families who, in race, appearance, dress and customs, are quite distinct from the Foggians. These people are called *Terrazzani,* 'of the earth, earthy'. A proud, independent, self-employed people, who up to now have refused to be assimilated in the city's life, they live by gleaning, poaching, and gathering snails, frogs, wild chicory, asparagus and herbs in the countryside, which they sell in the markets. Their traditions, and the peculiar quality of their music, particularly their laments, suggest that they are descendants of the Saracens of Lucera who escaped the massacre ordered by Charles II of Anjou, and wandered for centuries as nomadic pariahs, until the restriction of pasturage in the last century drove them to adopt a more settled form of life. One of their customs seems to confirm this origin. They marry young, and although the marriage is subsequently celebrated in church and at the Municipio, these rites are preceded by a ritual abduction. The young man borrows a small cart and, with several companions as witnesses, goes late at night to the house of his beloved. There he sings her a serenade, and furtively the girl runs from the house and climbs into the cart. The companions melt away in the darkness, and according to Terrazzano custom the couple are married from the moment the girl mounts the cart.

Lucera—Luceria Saracenorum—a Hohenstaufen palace

A comfortable half-day's expedition by car from Foggia can encompass the two interesting hill-towns of Lucera and Troia. There is also a bus service to these towns, and a frequent electric train service to Lucera.

Lucera stands on a hill above the Tavoliere, eleven miles north-west of Foggia by the SS 17. The Via Lucera runs almost straight across the plain, climbs up to the *circonvallazione*, which follows the line of the encircling walls built by Robert of Anjou, and, passing under a gateway, enters the Corso Garibaldi. To the north-east are

Map II
p. 126

the mountains of the Gargano, to the west the Apennines, and the town of Troia away to the south-west visible on its lofty spur.

In origin Lucera was an ancient city of the Daunians, the legendary founder being the indefatigable Diomedes who deposited there the palladium that he had carried off after the capture of Troy. From the time of the Samnite Wars, right through the Punic and Social Wars, Luceria, as it was then known, was a loyal ally of Rome. In 314 BC it became a *colonia iuris latini*. Cicero speaks of it as among the most flourishing cities of Italy, and in imperial times it enjoyed great prosperity, with splendid buildings, baths and the amphitheatre which we see today. Under the Lombards it was capital of a region or *gastaldo*; and as such it was captured and destroyed by the Byzantine Emperor Constans II in AD 663. The Normans gained possession of the city about the year 1070.

The Emperor Frederick II made Lucera into one of the strongest fortresses in Italy. Here, between 1224 and 1246, he kept numbers of rebellious Saracen soldiers from Sicily under his surveillance. The wisdom and tolerance with which the 'sultan of Lucera', as his Guelf enemies called him, treated thousands of these men and their families—he allowed them to build mosques and follow their own customs and trades—won the Saracens' loyalty to the house of Hohenstaufen. They later supported Frederick's legitimized son Manfred against Charles of Anjou, and, after Manfred's death at Benevento, rallied to the support of the young Conradin. After Conradin's defeat in 1268, Charles turned his attention to the Saracens of Lucera, who were ultimately forced to surrender in 1269. Finally, in August 1300, Charles II gave orders for those who would not abjure their faith and their loyalty to the Hohenstaufen to be put to the sword. Their mosques were razed to the ground and Luceria Saracenorum became the most Christian Città di S. Maria.

The hand of the supplanting Angevins is everywhere in evidence today—in the city walls and gates, the splendid fortifications of the citadel, and the churches. The **Duomo,** begun by Charles II in 1300 on the site of the principal Saracenic mosque, is unquestionably French in style. The characteristic Lombard form of high nave and lower aisles is masked by the simple front, with its three Gothic portals, its rose and pointed windows. The two columns of *verde antico* which support the canopy of the central doorway are Roman. The apsidal end (thought to be the only part of the building attributable to Charles's architect Pierre d'Agincourt) shows at once the northern influence in the prominent buttresses and the high lancet windows. Inside, the height of the nave with its soaring

216

pointed arches is most impressive. The high altar is formed from a stone table from the Castel Fiorentino, the last residence of the 'baptized sultan'. Over the main altar in the left transept is a late-fourteenth-century wood-carving (painted in the following century) of the *Madonna della Vittoria*, commemorating the victory of the Angevins over the Hohenstaufen. The pulpit has been constructed from the tomb (1560) of the noble Lucerian family of Scassa.

Opposite the cathedral is the elegant eighteenth-century **Episcopio,** flanked on the left by the **Palazzo Lombardi** of the same period. The Piazza Salandra, the centre of the city, lies at the rear of the cathedral, and we pass on the way the impressive exterior of the sacristy, which was added by the Aragonese in the fifteenth century. The Via de Nicastri brings us shortly to the **Museo Civico Fiorelli,** housed in the palace of the Marchesi de Nicastri (admission, Sunday 10.0 a.m.–12.0 noon; on other days apply to the Biblioteca Civica in the Municipio. For this, take the first street on the right, off the Via de Nicastri, the Via Amendola, which leads to the Corso Garibaldi. The Municipio stands almost opposite.)

The museum contains interesting local material. Of particular interest are the local terracottas, which include a fine bust of *Proserpine* (third or second century BC); the *Marine Venus*, a first-century copy of a statue of the school of Praxiteles; and some portrait busts and masks, including (in Room IV) the head of a Negro in grey limestone. In the museum and elsewhere in Lucera there are reminders of the Neapolitan scholar, journalist and politician, Ruggero Bonghi (1825–95), whose surname would have delighted Edward Lear.

For the **Roman amphitheatre** we follow the Via de Nicastri and its continuation in the Via Vitagliani to the end; if we turn left here, and then almost immediately right, we come out on the Via Napoleone Battaglia, part of the *circonvallazione*. Here we turn left, and after about two hundred yards arrive at the entrance of the Viale Augusto, which leads to the amphitheatre. This is the earliest amphitheatre known to have been dedicated to the Emperor Augustus. Inscriptions state that it was erected by M. Vecilius Campus, a magistrate (*duovir iure dicundo*), in honour of Caesar Augustus and the colony of Luceria. The two principal entrances, at either end of the main axis, have been restored to reveal the fine proportions of the doorway, their Ionic-capped columns supporting the architrave and pediment, within which is a shield crossed by a javelin.

The **Castello** stands on a spur to the north-west of the town; it is well named 'the key of Apulia'. From the narrow end of the Piazza Duomo, we cross the Piazza Nocelli and take the Via Bovio and the Via Frederico II to the Piazza Matteotti. (A short distance to the right along the Via S. Domenico, which we cross, lies the Piazza Tribunale and the church of *S. Francesco,* a beautiful example of Angevin architecture, contemporary with the Duomo.) The public gardens here form a belvedere from which we have a magnificent view.

As we approach the fortress from the Piazza Matteotti, we come to the ditch cut through the hill by Charles I of Anjou as protection from attack from the town side. The fortress wall above appears to be in a state of perfect preservation. Behind the circular Torre del Leone, and forming part of the north-east wall, are the remains of the Hohenstaufen palace. The *enceinte,* which is roughly pent-agonal in plan, is enclosed by walls interspersed with twenty-four towers, the perimeter being over half a mile in extent. It gives us some impression of the commanding strength of the fortress that Charles built to control the Capitanata.

Of the splendid palace-stronghold built by the Emperor Frederick inside the enclosure little remains save the base—vertical, then sloping—and a section of the curved vaulting, the ribs of which appear to act as buttresses to the inner wall. In 1790 the authorities blew up the palace for material to build a new Tribunale at Lucera (at that time capital of the Region of the Molise and the Capitanata). Luckily a French artist, Jean-Louis Desprez, had made a drawing of it a few years earlier for the book on Southern Italy published by the Abbé Saint-Non. Round an inner courtyard with fountains playing ran a series of magnificent second-floor apartments. The two lower floors probably contained the treasury and imperial mint, and workshops for the household.

Excavations have revealed a great catchment-area, with a com-plex of tanks and conduits for the storage of rainwater. Foundations of a building have also been found in the centre of the enclosure; this may be the Franciscan church which Charles II raised here.

Troia—the Duomo

Map II
p. 126

From Lucera, it is a run of eleven miles almost due south by the SS 160 over the plain to the little hill town of **Troia**. Troia is built on the site of the ancient Aecae, which in imperial times became known as Colonia Augusta Apula. The later town was founded on the ruins of the first by the Catapan Basilios Bogianos in 1019 as a Byzantine fortress against the Lombards. Troia fell to the Normans in 1066, and later appears to have been governed by a succession of powerful bishops, one of whom, Walter II, was chancellor to the Hohenstaufen Emperor Henry VI and regent during the minority of his son Frederick II. Possibly the Troian bishops became too independent, for Frederick destroyed the town in 1229.

Nevertheless, it was to these bishops that we owe the splendid *Duomo,* one of the most harmonious examples of the blending of Romanesque styles in Apulia: Lombard, Byzantine, Saracenic and Pisan. The Duomo was begun in 1093 on the site of an earlier church; but progress was delayed, so that the lower portions are of the early twelfth century and the upper structure of the thirteenth. This delay partly accounts for the diversity of styles in the extraordinary façade. The blind arcading (continued in the flanks and rear of the church) is distinctly Pisan, even down to the lozenge and circular recesses under the rounded arches. (This Pisan influence can be seen again in the churches of Siponto and in S. Maria Maggiore at Monte S. Angelo.) In the upper storey, above the deep cornice, is a fantastic display of essentially Lombard sculpture around a remarkable rose window. Projecting lions serve as consoles or as heads to columns; and above them two bulls (or maybe cows) seem to have half freed themselves from the façade to fly out over the piazza. The design of the window itself is most intricate, and the openwork designs in stone between the radials suggest Saracenic models.

The carving of capitals and architrave of the central doorway is clearly Byzantine. However, the beautiful bronze doors, the work of Oderisio da Benevento (1119), who is also responsible for the doors (1127) on the right flank of the church, are much less Byzantine in influence than those of other contemporary workers in bronze. Some panels are incised, but others are in powerful high-relief. On the left flank, in the lunette above the doorway, are figures in low-relief of *Christ between two angels,* which have some affinity with the lunette above the doorway of S. Leonardo di Siponto. At the rear of the church the semi-circular apse retains the characteristic Lombard form, although the round arches are supported on a rather unusual arrangement of superimposed columns. Around the two central columns two lions peep. Above there is a graceful rose window.

Inside the church recent restoration and the removal of baroque accretions allow us to enjoy the beauty of its proportions and of the contrasting textures of highly finished columns against the matt

surface of white stonework. The chapels of the transept remain
perfect examples of the degeneracy of baroque. On the left of the
nave stands an exquisitely carved pulpit (1169) which came from the
near-by church of S. Basilio, a Romanesque foundation earlier than
that of the Duomo. The sacristan will show visitors the interesting
treasury on request. The design and carving both inside and outside
the Duomo are remarkably powerful. We shall see this again in
many of the churches and castles of Apulia.

*S. Giovanni Rotondo—ancient Sipontum—Manfredonia—Monte S. Angelo
—the Sanctuary of the Archangel St Michael*

There are several ways of exploring the Gargano peninsula from
Foggia. However, since most visitors to Apulia will want to see the
famous Sanctuary of Monte S. Angelo, we shall describe the direct
route first. For Manfredonia we leave Foggia from the Piazza Piano
della Croce by the Via S. Lazzaro, and take to the SS 89 (Garganica).
After a couple of miles a provincial road branches left for S. Marco
in Lamis, and about two miles along this road, on the outskirts of the
village of Arpi Nova, are the excavations of *Arpi,* the largest city of
ancient Daunia. The site was only discovered by accident in 1939,
and recent digging has brought to light Roman buildings of the
third to second centuries BC; the mosaic pavement from one of these
is in the Foggia Museum, together with red-figured Apulian vases
of an earlier period from tombs found in the vicinity.

The Statale runs in a straight line through a rather desolate
countryside, with few trees and scattered *masserie,* and ahead of us
the mountains of Gargano appear as a solid wall of barren pale-grey
rock. Shortly after crossing the River Candelaro, the SS 273
branches left for **S. Giovanni Rotondo,** a small country town which
has grown considerably in recent years as a place of pilgrimage to the
Capuchin convent of S. Maria delle Grazie, and the headquarters
of the saintly Padre Pio. This remarkable man drew the faithful and
their funds from all over the world by his asceticism, his works of
charity, and his reputed possession of the stigmata; and the crowds
of pilgrims and tourists have resulted in a number of new hotels,
restaurants and shops for their reception. Thousands believe in the
miracles Father Pio performed; his extraordinary devotion was
certainly evident to those who attended his early-morning mass. But
he made light of his great reputation, and his conversation was down
to earth, full of common sense and flashes of wit. He died in 1968.

Map V
p. 222

S. Giovanni Rotondo was on the old pilgrim road to the Sanctuary of St Michael of Monte S. Angelo and derives its name from the very ancient circular baptistery to the east of the town, known as the Chiesetta di S. Giovanni or simply the **Rotonda.** It is thought to occupy the site of an ancient temple of Janus, possibly the oldest of Italian gods. On the right of the Rotonda is the fourteenth-century church of S. Onofrio, the interior of which has been completely restored in 'medieval' style. The Viale dei Cappuccini, lined with hotels and *pensioni*, brings us to the convent and the two churches dedicated to **S. Maria delle Grazie**; the older was consecrated in 1629; the larger one beside it was built recently with funds raised by Padre Pio. From S. Giovanni Rotondo the SS 272 runs east to Monte S. Angelo.

From the *bivio* for S. Giovanni the SS 89 climbs some low hills and shortly, on the right, we see the abbey church of **S. Leonardo di Siponto.** The church dates from the end of the eleventh or beginning of the twelfth century. In 1261 the monastery passed from the Canons Regular of St Augustine to the Teutonic Knights, who later built the hospital, the ruins of which we see today. Some time after 1450 it was raised to the dignity of an abbey, and from the seventeenth century until its suppression under Murat it was held by the Franciscans. Abandoned for over a century, the church was restored and re-dedicated in 1950.

S. Leonardo shows clearly the interpenetration of eastern and western styles. The influence of Tuscan builders, which we saw at Troia, is again in evidence in the arcading and the apsidal ends, while the two hexagonal domes are more reminiscent of the east. The magnificent portal on the left of the church shows a fine blending of Byzantine decoration with Apulian-Romanesque. The delicacy of the Byzantine motifs and carving is well illustrated in the door-jambs and the broad band which surrounds the lunette; although figures of men appear together with animals and fabulous creatures (a concession to Lombard taste), they form a pattern among the meandering vine leaves and tendrils which is immediately recognizable as Byzantine. And the lunette itself, which shows *Christ in Glory* between two supporting angels, could have been copied from an oriental ivory plaque. The exquisite carving of the capitals (*Balaam and the Ass* on the left, *the Three Magi* on the right), if western in spirit, is still tied to eastern forms. It is only in the two figures above the door (particularly in the monk on the right) that we see the freedom of the western artist from the Byzantine tradition. Inside, the barrel vault of the nave and the curvature of the aisle vaults suggest that

221

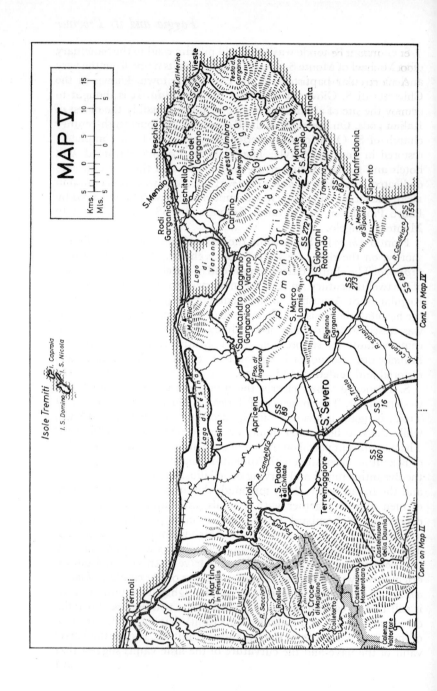

MAP V

Kms. 5 0 5 10 15
Mls. 5 0 5 10 15

Isole Tremiti
I. S. Domino   I. Capraia
I. S. Nicola

Térmoli

S. Martino in Pensilis

Ururi

R. Saccione

Rotello

S. Croce di Magliano

Casacalenda

Castelnuovo della Daunia

Castelnuovo Monterotaro

Calenza Vattofore

Serracapriola

Apricena

Lesina

Lago di Lésina

S. Paolo di Civitate

R. Candelaro

Terremaggiore

S. Severo

R. Friolo

SS 89

SS 16

SS 160

Lago di Varano

Rodi Garganico

S. Menaio

Ischitello

Vico del Gargano

Peschici

M. d'Elio

Sannicandro Garganico

Cagnano Varano

S. Marco in Lamis

Pso. di Ingarano

Carpino

foresta Umbra

Albergo

Testa d. Gargano

Trieste

S. M. di Merino

SS 89

promontorio del Gargano

Rignano Garganico

S. Giovanni Rotondo

SS 273

SS 272

Monte S. Angelo

Mattinata

Taverna

SS 89

S. Maria di Siponto

Manfredonia

Siponto

R. Candelaro

SS 159

R. Salsola

R. Celone

R. Celone

Cont. on Map IV

Cont. on Map II

French influence was also at work here. Over the altar is a painted wooden crucifix (1220–30), much restored.

A short way beyond the church we catch sight of the sea on our right, and ahead of us, where the mountains fall away to the coast, shine the white buildings of Manfredonia. Less than a mile past the junction with the SS 159 from Barletta, almost opposite the turning for the modern Lido di Siponto and close to the church of S. Maria, a granite column with a Byzantine capital marks the site of ancient *Sipontum,* of which some blocks of the city walls alone remain. Some palaeochristian catacombs cut in the rock have been found among the villas of the Lido—one is near the office of the Consorzio della Bonifica.

Sipontum, the port for the Daunian city of Arpi, was captured by Hannibal and later retaken by the Romans, who settled a colony there in 194 BC. The inhabitants were early converted to Christianity, and Siponto became one of the most important dioceses in Apulia. The city was long contested by the Greeks and Lombards, but fell to the Normans in 1039. South of Siponto there were in antiquity a series of lakes or lagoons, some open to the sea, which the Romans worked as salt-beds. These still exist to the north of Margherita di Savoia, and are the largest in Europe. But the silting up of the river mouths and the gradual sinking of the land turned most of them into pestilential marshes. An earthquake, or succession of earthquakes in 1223, destroyed Siponto, and King Manfred moved the survivors to a healthier spot, where in 1256 he founded the city which bears his name. With malaria now a thing of the past, and with a fine sandy beach, Siponto has developed since the war into a popular seaside resort.

The church of *S. Maria di Siponto* was built at the beginning of the eleventh century over an earlier church, which today remains as a crypt, occupying the same area as the upper church. In S. Maria we find a similar intermingling of oriental and western styles as in S. Leonardo. Like eastern churches it is square in plan, with a central cupola; the external walls, however, are a beautiful variant of Pisan blind-arcading, the rounded arches supported on columns with richly ornamented capitals. The lozenges which we saw at Troia are repeated here. Much of this work was probably added in the restoration carried out in 1117. The main portal has a deep archivolt which is raised on free-standing columns supported on lions.

The blind arcades of the exterior are repeated within on three sides. (If the church is closed, the key is with the sacristan in the house next door.) Pointed arches spring from four prominent square pilasters; above, four columns support the cupola and the eight small arches of the lantern. The circular chapel to the right of the main altar in the apse is a later addition. The crypt, in addition to the four columns corresponding to the pilasters above, contains sixteen other columns, some of them from ancient buildings, with Corinthian or Byzantine capitals; these form a Greek cross. Over the altar are the carved figures of the *Madonna and Child*; the workmanship is medieval but the colouring has been crudely restored.

Recent excavations to the left of the church have uncovered the remains of an early Christian basilica which, from an inscription found on the site and now in Naples Museum, seems to have been built on a temple of Diana. Tombs dating from pre-Roman times until the destruction of medieval Siponto have been found in the vicinity.

Map V
p. 222 Charles I of Anjou, after Manfred's death, wished to re-name **Manfredonia** Sipontum Novellum, but the inhabitants resisted the change. As we enter the city we see one of the five remaining circular towers of the walls which Charles raised.

Manfredonia, a market and commercial centre, has a small but active port and fishing fleet. Boats leave from the port twice or three times a week for the Tremiti Islands via Vieste, Peschici and Rodi Garganico, a voyage of five hours, with beautiful and varied coastal scenery against a background of mountains. The town itself has few features of interest, little of the early building having survived the Turkish invasion of the seventeenth century. From the main street, the Corso Manfredi, the Via Campanile (on the left) leads to the Piazza del Duomo and the **cathedral,** built by Archbishop Orsini (later Pope Benedict XIII) in 1680 to replace the destroyed Gothic church. The Via Arcivescovado brings us to the Piazza del Popolo, where in the church of **S. Domenico** parts of the earlier Cappella della Maddalena, built by Charles II of Anjou in 1294–99, have been retained, including the original doorway. The interior contains portions of the early structure and some contemporary frescoes. In a niche beneath a fresco of the *Pietà*, human skulls provide a *memento mori*. At the rear of the main altar is a marble group of the *Madonna and Child* by an unknown early-sixteenth-century sculptor. Next door, the former **convent of S. Domenico** (seventeenth-century), which has a pleasant open loggia, is now occupied by offices.

The Corso Manfredi ends at the **Castello,** which was begun by Manfred but owes much to the Angevin military architect Pierre d'Agincourt. The outer walls were added later by the Aragonese, with the exception of the side facing the town; this was constructed in the sixteenth century. The castle was finally forced to surrender when the city was taken and burnt by the Turks in 1620; the defenders of the castle were among the few who escaped with their lives, but were nevertheless carried off into captivity.

Beyond Manfredonia the road begins to ascend. At the hamlet of Taverna a steep and rough road winds up to Monte S. Angelo; it is better to continue on the SS 89 to the Bivio la Cavola and take the SS 89 *bis*. The road climbs steeply up the side of the Valley of Carbonara with magnificent views over the terraced, limestone countryside and the white houses of Mattinata on the coast below, to the milky-blue surface of the Adriatic. Nearer the top of the ridge, an unbelievable panorama opens out to the south.

We enter the town of **Monte S. Angelo** by the Via Manfredi which, winding up the hill, with various changes of name, brings us to the gateway in the Via Reale Basilica of the *sanctuary of the Archangel St Michael,* flanked by the lofty hexagonal campanile of Charles I of Anjou (1273). The town owes its existence from the fifth century entirely to the sanctuary which, as one of the oldest and most celebrated in Europe, is the goal of multitudes of pilgrims, particularly on the Feasts of St Michael (May 8th and September 29th), when the town fills with the faithful, many wearing their colourful traditional dress. According to the legend, the Archangel appeared three times in person to St Laurence, Bishop of Siponto, on May 8th, 490, 491 and 493, in front of a cavern (now built into the sanctuary), where he left the imprint of his foot. His words to St Laurence are inscribed over the doorway: '*Ubi saxa panduntur ibi peccata hominum dimittuntur. Haec est domus specialis in qua noxialis quaeque actio diluitur*—Where the rocks are thrown open, there men's sins are forgiven. This is no ordinary house; here all sinful actions are washed away.' The sanctuary soon became a place of pilgrimage, and the Lombards of Benevento made it their national shrine. Sacked by the Byzantines in 657 and twice by the Saracens (in 869 and 920), it was here that the Normans are said to have foreseen a successful entry into the tangled political situation in Southern Italy. The cult of St Michael would have had close association for them with Mont St Michel in Normandy, and at the time of the Crusades the sanctuary became an obligatory stopping-point on the way to the Holy Land. Much of the building that we see today is the work of the Angevins.

The entrance is by way of an atrium, which is in surprisingly good taste for the date when it was built—1865—and follows the lines of

Map V
p. 222

the much earlier right-hand portal, the work of Simeone da Monte S. Angelo (1395). In the lunette is his low-relief of the *Madonna between SS. Peter and Paul*. High in the centre of the façade is the youthful figure of *St Michael*. From the entrance lobby, where sacred objects are sold (made here under a privilege granted by the Aragonese), steps lead down to the shrine. We enter through the Porta del Toro—why it should be called after a bull, I do not know—into the open *atrio interno*, where the Romanesque doorway of the basilica faces us, with, above it, the words of St Michael. The beautiful bronze doors in Byzantine niello-work depict *Scenes from the Old and New Testaments*. An inscription tells us that Pantaleon of Amalfi presented the doors, which were made in the imperial city of Constantinople and were placed here in 1076. The donor 'asks and abjures' that those in charge of the shrine shall clean the doors at least once a year in the prescribed fashion, so that they remain bright and shining.

The doors open into the Gothic structure of Charles of Anjou (1273). Immediately on our right is the altar of St Francis of Assisi beneath which is a 'T' said to have been traced on the rock by the Saint. Beyond this is the opening of the cavern, the **Grotta dell' Arcangelo,** with (to the right) the altar of S. Michele and an alabaster statue of the Saint, attributed to Andrea Sansovino (1460–1529). The twelfth-century episcopal chair of Leo II, archbishop of Siponto and Monte S. Angelo, is a remarkable piece of work, resting on two lions, with Byzantine decoration on its back and a relief of *St Michael* on the right-hand side.

The altar on the left of the Grotta dell' Arcangelo is dedicated to the Madonna; behind this is a well whose water, drunk by the faithful from a silver stoup, is held to have miraculous powers. At the far end of the Angevin chapel, opposite the entrance doorway, is the baroque (1690) Cappella del Sacramento; and on the outer side, facing the Valley of Carbonara, are two further chapels. The chapel nearer the doorway has inlaid choir-stalls of the early seventeenth century, and the Cappella delle Reliquie contains some interesting relics, among them an icon on copper of St Michael which may date from the end of the fifth century, an eleventh-century statue of Our Lord and a cross in delicate silver tracery, the gift of the Emperor Frederick II.

Opposite the campanile at the gates of the sanctuary some steps lead down from the Largo Tomba di Rotari to the ruined façade (on the left) of the late-twelfth-century church of **S. Pietro.** (If the church is not open, the key is with the custodian, Via Reale Basilica

78.) The decoration of the rose window is formed by the interlacing of four figures of sirens. Inside, roses grow where the body of the church formerly stood; all that remains of the structure is the vast apse. A doorway to the left of the apse leads to the interior of the curious building known as the **Tomba di Rotari,** the exterior of which towers above houses, ruins, and the façade of S. Maria Maggiore to the right. The name comes from a misreading of an inscription which tells us that it was built by Pagano di Parma and one Rodelgrimo of Monte S. Angelo. It has been variously held to have been a campanile, a baptistery or a mausoleum. Its date is almost certainly about the end of the twelfth century. Over the doorway are some interesting carvings in low-relief of the *Passion*, and there is evidence that they come from sculptors trained in the schools of Southern France, possibly in Toulouse. Within, the capitals of the columns supporting the pointed arches show *Scenes from the Old and New Testaments*. The square ground-plan of the building is converted by the use of squinches to an octagon at the level of the windows, above which a roughly elliptical cornice of curious figures (two are of *Luxury*) takes the asymmetrical cupola.

The church of **S. Maria Maggiore** next door is at a lower level and is entered by a portal from the street. Here again, as at Troia and Siponto, the blind arcading and lozenges in the façade clearly indicate Pisan influence. This part of the church was built by Archbishop Leo II of Siponto in the early twelfth century. The interior, consisting of a nave and two aisles separated by pilasters with interesting capitals, and a single apse, was rebuilt about 1170 by a priest Benedetto. The beautiful main doorway (1198) was added, according to an inscription, by a 'second' Benedetto. Particularly fine is the lunette in low-relief showing the *Madonna and Child between two angels*.

For the **castle,** which overlooks both the town and the surrounding countryside, we return to the Via Reale Basilica and continue up it until steps on the right bring us to the bare rocky eminence on which stand the impressive ruins of this fortress begun by Robert Guiscard, continued by Frederick II, and added to under the Aragonese. Wandering through the desolate halls and empty rooms, we remember that here the Emperor Frederick brought his brilliant retinue, among them Bianca Lancia, his beloved mistress and the mother of the unfortunate Manfred.

In the lower town there are several interesting early churches, some in ruins. In the Via Verdi is the Angevin **S. Benedetto**; next door, the so-called **Ospizio della Regina Giovanna** (fourteenth-century); farther along, in the Via S. Antonio, the disused twelfth-century *S. Antonio Abate*; and, returning to the Via Verdi and taking (on the left) the Via Raffaelo Cassa and the Via S. Oronzo, the church of *S. Francesco d'Assisi* (on the right of the entrance is a sarcophagus, supposed to contain the remains of Queen Giovanna I, who was murdered in Muro Lucano in 1382).

Foresta Umbra—the best white wine in Southern Italy—and the best duck-shooting

Map V
p. 222 For the **Foresta Umbra** the road leaves Monte S. Angelo from the Piazzale della Basilica and runs along the southern slope of the Valle di Carbonara, before descending by a series of loops, with fine views of the valley and grey mountains beyond. At a road junction we turn off to the right: the SS 272 goes on to S. Giovanni Rotondo and to San Severo. Our road climbs up the farther side of the valley, the landscape becoming more and more dreary and, after a turning on our left for Carpino, even more rocky and savage. The geological structure of the Gargano—it is of the same composition as the mountains of Dalmatia—consists of eroded limestone, honeycombed with fissures and caves, so that in places rainwater disappears below the surface, to appear elsewhere as variable springs. It is this that accounts for the surprising change after the Masseria Azzarone, when we enter the magnificent woods of the Foresta Umbra.

In the Emperor Frederick's time the forests were more extensive than today; however, the State is now controlling the planting and felling of the trees. At a height of over 2000 ft above sea level and in the shade of oaks and beech the air is delightfully fresh; in fact, it can be distinctly chilly even in late spring. Horace wrote of the north winds which belabour the oak-woods of the Gargano and strip the ash of its leaves:

Aut aquilonibus
Querceta Gargani laborant
Et foliis viduantur orni . . .

In the depths of the forest is the Albergo Rifugio Foresta Umbra, which has fifteen bedrooms and is a delightful place to spend a night or two. On the last Sunday of July crowds in traditional costume come here from all over Apulia and elsewhere to take part in the Sagra della Foresta, a festival of popular music and dances begun in 1948 under the auspices of the Provincial Tourist Board.

After a pleasant descent through woods and countryside cultivated with olives, vines and orange trees, we pass the village of Vico del Gargano, where we leave on our left the road to Ischitella and reach the northern coast of the Gargano peninsula to join the SS 89 just east of S. Menaio.

Other pleasant day trips around the Gargano from Foggia take in the beaches and fishing villages which are justly becoming well known to tourists as the Riviera del Gargano. We leave the city by the Via S. Severo to join the SS 16 (Adriatica), which runs north-west over the cultivated Tavoliere. Near San Severo we can see how the Apulians grow their vines. Regularly spaced long lines of wires bear the carefully pruned branches, so that the grape clusters are suspended at a height from the ground.

San Severo is an important market and commercial centre. The origin of the city is ancient, but a disastrous earthquake in 1627 destroyed much of the older part, and baroque and modern rebuilding has not added anything worthy of note. From 1578 until 1809 the feudal lords were the family of Sangro di Torremaggiore, who took the title of Principi di Sansevero, and built themselves the fantastic Cappella Sansevero in Naples. The eleventh-century *cathedral* has been completely baroqued, and of the city's churches, only *S. Severino* (in the Via Fraccacreta, on the left of the Municipio) retains something of its Romanesque (twelfth-century) form, including a decorated doorway and a pleasant rose window.

Map V
p. 222

For the oenophile San Severo will make up for its lack of architectural interest by the excellence of its wine, particularly the white; but there is also a good rosé. San Severo is a dry white wine, light in colour and with a fresh bouquet, and of a strength between 11° and 13°. With the exception of wines from a few individual vineyards (near Forio on Ischia, for example, or at Ravello), San Severo is probably the best white wine in the South of Italy.

A privately owned railway joins San Severo with Peschici on the north-east coast, the journey taking about two hours. The train climbs along the flanks of the mountains of Gargano, for much of the way close to the road. From the Stazione Peschici–Calenella there is a bus service to Peschici and Vieste.

From San Severo, we take the SS 89 (Garganica) north-east to the foothills of the western end of the mountainous regions of the Gargano, and the town of **Apricena.** The road bypasses the town to the east, but admirers of the Emperor Frederick may like to make a diversion to see the remains of his hunting lodge, which were incorporated in the present Palazzo Baronale (1658) when it was

Map V
p. 222

rebuilt after the earthquake of 1627 that destroyed the town. Frederick had a particular affection for Apricena, and frequently hunted in the woods which at that time appear to have covered the slopes that today are so bare and arid. It may have been here and in the Daunian Lakes near by that he made his studies of the migratory habits of birds which he published in his *De Arte Venandi cum Avibus*, a book remarkable for its accurate observations, one of the earliest of its kind since antiquity. We know too of an order Frederick gave to a certain Riccardo di Pulcaro, whose estates presumably included these lakes, 'that he see that Berardo, our court cook, has some good fish from Lesina and others of the best to be found, so that he can prepare for us the *aschipecia*.' This was fish fried in oil and served with mint and vinegar.

After Apricena the road climbs bare foothills until it crosses the railway line at the Passo di Ingarano and reveals an ever-widening view over the mountains of Daunia and the Molise, the Lago di Lesina below, and beyond it to the north, the Tremiti Islands. A more level stretch of cultivated countryside brings us to **Sanni-candro Garganico,** a market town built round the fifteenth-century castle of the della Marra family. The road now runs along the heights and turns the spur from which Monte lo Sfrizzo runs out to Monte d'Elio, separating the two Daunian Lakes: the **Lago di Lesina** on the left and, to the east, the **Lago di Varano.** The Lago di Lesina, Pliny's *Lacus Pantanus*, is a shallow sheet of water (at the deepest no more than five feet) running parallel to the sea and separated from it by a sandy spit. About thirteen miles in extent, it is under two miles across at its widest point. The Lago di Varano is slightly larger in area, and trapezoidal in shape; it is sixteen feet deep in places. Both are exceedingly rich in fish—Lesina abounds in eels— and in the autumn and winter months sportsmen come from all over Italy for the excellent duck-shooting along the reedy eastern shores of the lakes.

Map V
p. 222

Cagnano Varano, a village built on the side of a rocky valley, is the centre for the surrounding countryside and for the fishing. From here the road descends to cross the Piano di Carpino, where irrigation allows the rich land to be used to produce fine crops of corn, and early fruit and vegetables. At the beginning of the straight stretch of road, a short track on the right leads to the ruins of some Roman baths. Finds of Roman lamps, bronze implements and vases in the vicinity suggest that this may be the site of ancient Uria, mentioned by Strabo and Pliny. A provincial road on the right runs up through thick olive-groves to the village of **Carpino,** with some

Map V
p. 222

230

early churches and the remains of a della Marra castle, and then continues to climb up over the mountains to join the road from Monte S. Angelo to the Foresta Umbra.

Shortly after this turning, another road on the right leads up to the beautifully placed village of **Ischitella,** the birthplace of the celebrated legal historian Pietro Giannone (1676–1748), to whose work Gibbon owed so deep a debt. As the Statale winds over the hills among the olives, there are views ahead to Rodi Garganico on its promontory.

Map V
p. 222

Although there are small bathing-places on the long stretches of sand to the west, the Riviera Garganica proper, with its beautiful sandy beaches and wooded hinterland, extends eastwards from Rodi to the Testa del Gargano beyond Vieste, and includes the popular Tremiti Islands. This coast, and the Tremiti group, are being developed to provide for the increasing number of visitors, both Italian and foreign, who have discovered in them a riviera perhaps second to none in Italy.

All around **Rodi,** from Ischitella to S. Menaio, is one immense citrus grove, so that the air is scented with the blossom. The town, which is said to have been founded by Greeks from Rhodes—whence its name—stands high above the sea, stone steps between houses and gardens of orange trees leading down to the beach. In a house known as the Torretta del Re Joachim Murat sought refuge after the fall of Napoleon.

Map V
p. 222

The Tremiti Islands—the abbey of S. Nicola

The *motonave* from Manfredonia calls at the port of Rodi three times a week for the **Tremiti Islands.** (There is another service to the islands from Termoli.) The group consists of three islands, S. Nicola, S. Domino and Capraia (only the first two are inhabited), and some rocks, of which Cretaccio and La Vecchia are the most important. Geologically the Tremiti are part of the Gargano peninsula. The *motonave* drops anchor in a sheltered roadstead between S. Domino, green with pine woods, and the little port and stone walls of S. Nicola; ahead lies the bare yellow rock of Cretaccio and beside it, iron-grey, stands the smaller rock of La Vecchia. Passengers are brought ashore in boats.

Map V
p. 222

To the Romans these were the *Insulae Diomedeae*, the resting-place of the Greek hero after his labours in founding all the cities of Daunia, whose tomb was watched over by his former companions, transformed into wheeling sea-birds by the will of Aphrodite. Augustus banished his niece Julia there, and she lived for twenty years until her death on S. Domino, then known as Trimerus or Tremitis, whence the present name of the group. The language spoken on the islands today is Neapolitan, not one of the Apulian dialects, because the majority of the islanders are in fact descendants of Neapolitans settled here in 1843 by Ferdinand II of the Two Sicilies.

The legend of the founding of a church on **S. Nicola** comes from an early-sixteenth-century *Cronaca*. It seems that in the first years of the fourth century a saintly man betook himself here, to what was then described as a 'singular refuge of the Corsair Robbers of the Sea'. His mode of life evidently found favour in heaven, for in the course of time the Virgin Mary appeared to him. She bade him dig in the ground; there he would find treasure; with this he was to take ship to Constantinople and acquire everything necessary to build a temple to her glory. For some reason or other the good man ignored the Virgin's commands; so she appeared again, this time 'with altered visage and eyes flashing imperiously, reproving him with bitter words'. He dug in the ground and soon found some vases filled with gold and—an archaeological discovery of the first importance—the gilded crown of Diomedes. In the course of one night he made the journey to Constantinople. There he loaded a ship with building materials, hired workmen, returned to S. Nicola and built the church, the fame of which (and of his own miracles) quickly reached the ends of the earth.

The first historical record of the *abbey of S. Nicola* is from the eighth century, when it was in the possession of the Benedictines of Montecassino. From them it gained its autonomy, but later passed to the Cistercians and from them to the Canons Regular of the Lateran. It suffered much from attacks by corsairs (in one foray in the thirteenth century all the monks were massacred and the abbey laid waste), and it became in time a fortress as much as a religious foundation. By the eighteenth century the great fortunes of the abbey had declined, and it was suppressed by Ferdinand IV of Naples in 1783. From 1792 until 1943 the buildings were used as prisons, first for common convicts, then, after 1926, for those in disfavour with Mussolini.

Bertaux described the abbey of S. Nicola as a 'Montecassino set in the middle of the sea', and the visitor who lands at the Marina and makes his way up the walled approach and through the gateways into the fortified town will see everywhere examples of the material splendour and military strength of this monastic fortress. The church of **S. Maria a Mare,** founded by the Benedictines in 1045, was reconstructed in the fourteenth and again in the fifteenth centuries, when the present façade was built. The pleasant Renaissance doorway (1473) is the joint work of Andrea Alessi of Durazzo and the Florentine Nicolò di Giovanni Cocari. The interior of the church has a painted eighteenth-century ceiling and an interesting floor, much of which is paved in the original eleventh-century polychrome mosaic, revealing a strong Byzantine influence. Over the main altar is an early-fifteenth-century Venetian polyptych in gilded wood, with figures of the *Virgin and saints*; and in a side chapel is a Byzantine painting of the *Crucifixion*, possibly from the twelfth century.

The warrior-monks of S. Nicola used to look on the island of **S. Domino** as the Garden of Eden; and the contrast with their own bare island is certainly remarkable. S. Domino, only 1¾ miles in length and no more than a mile in breadth, rises to a height of 280 ft in the pine-clad Hill of the Hermit in the south-west of the island. Its broken coastline has delightful small bays and inlets and a series of caves which rival those of Capri—among them the Grotta delle Viole (on the south-east), the Grotta del Bue Marino (on the south-west) and the Grotta delle Rondinelle (on the west, near the bay known as the Cala degl' Inglesi). This cave was used by the English fleet in the Napoleonic Wars, when they landed on S. Domino and shelled the Murat forces on S. Nicola. Both the bathing and the underwater fishing from these islands are marvellous; their shores provide a real marine paradise. The islands are only now being opened up for the tourist, and their natural beauty and tranquillity are yet unspoilt.

Beautifully placed on the east side of S. Domino, with a view over the Adriatic to the mountains of the Gargano, is the recently built Hotel Eden. Other hotels and *pensioni* are in course of construction. For campers there is the Campeggio Sociale of the Touring Club Italiano above the Cala degl' Inglesi.

The Riviera Garganica—Peschici—Vieste

After skirting Rodi Garganico the SS 89 comes down to run along the shore. Inland from the beach of fine sand the countryside is green with citrus groves and pine woods, and the gardens of the villas which are now springing up along the whole riviera. **S. Menaio,** the lido for Vico del Gargano, clusters around the well-preserved

Map V
p. 222

233

tower, built by the Spanish Viceroy in 1606 as a part of the system of coastal defences against the Turks—between Peschici and Vieste there are a number of similar *torrioni*. The magnificent Pineta Marzini covers the hills behind the beach, and under the shade of these pines is the Tendopoli ('Tent-town') of the Ente Provinciale per il Turismo, where well-equipped tents may be hired. The Italian Automobile Club has recently taken over the Autostello Bellariva, which lies between the Statale and the beach, rather close to the railway.

From S. Menaio the road continues in the Pineta, turns the promontory of Coppa Marzini, and veers inland to cross the Piana di Calenella. Beyond the Stazione Calenella–Peschici, the terminus of the railway (buses connect with Peschici and Vieste), the road climbs to round the promontory of Monte Pucci. In the pine-woods by the beach at Calenella there is the Villaggio Turistico 'Macchia di Mare', with huts and tents for hire at very reasonable prices, and restaurant, bar and other facilities on the site. On the hill to the right some palaeochristian cave-tombs (*hypogea*), have recently been excavated, dating possibly from the middle of the fourth to the beginning of the sixth century. From the crest of Monte Pucci, below the belvedere, there is another Spanish defence tower, and on the rocks beneath, a *trabucco*, a great net, raised and lowered by windlasses, to catch the *cefali* and *spigole* which are prolific off the point.

To the east of another fine stretch of sand, the fishing village of **Peschici** rises on a rocky cliff, its houses grouped behind the medieval Castello (rebuilt in the seventeenth century). Peschici, a port of call for the Manfredonia–Tremiti service, also has great possibilities as a seaside resort, and a coast road is planned to connect it with Vieste, passing the Campeggio Manacore, another attractive newly-built village with restaurant and other services. Close by is the recently opened Albergo Gusmay, and other hotels are planned or are already in course of construction. Important archaeological discoveries have been made in the vicinity, throwing light on the civilization of the Italic peoples at the beginning of the sixth century BC.

Map V
p. 222

The Statale turns south after Peschici, leaving (just beyond the town, on the right) a turning for the ruins of the abbey church of S. Maria di Calena, which was founded in the ninth century and suppressed in 1780. The road then winds among the pine-clad hills and crosses the River Macchia; just beyond this, at the sawmill of Mandrione, a road on the left leads to the Sanctuary of S. Maria di

234

Merino and the recently excavated Roman ruins of Merinum which was destroyed by the Saracens in 914. Near by, on the beach, the unfortunate Pope Celestine V (see p. 55) was captured in 1294. Beyond Mandrione, in groves of magnificent olive-trees, we meet the Statale from Manfredonia; then, bearing left, enter Vieste.

Vieste, a fishing-port and seaside resort, is the most eastern town of the Gargano. Its origin is uncertain but undoubtedly ancient, as is attested by the discovery of Graeco-Apulian vases, remains of megalithic walls, and a burial ground of the third century BC. The *castle* above the town was built by Frederick II, but was restored in the sixteenth to seventeenth centuries. Today it is a lighthouse station of the Italian Navy. The town suffered terribly at the hands of corsairs; in 1554 Dragut landed there and massacred many of the townsfolk in and around the Duomo, before departing with seven thousand captives. The ***Duomo,*** dedicated to S. Maria Oreta, which stands below the castle, shows some of the original Romanesque structure in the left wall. The ceiling is crudely painted in unusual blacks and browns.

Map V
p. 222

Vieste has two excellent sandy beaches, S. Lorenzo to the north-west and the Spiaggia del Castello to the south. Just off the latter is the curiously shaped lofty rock known as the Pizzimunno, and behind runs a road which will ultimately follow the line of the coast south to Mattinata. About six miles from Vieste a completed section of the road brings us to the newly-built Hotel del Faro at the Testa del Gargano, the extreme easterly point of the 'spur'.

After Vieste, the SS 89 leaves the coast and climbs into the mountains. The run south to Manfredonia is extraordinarily beautiful, with magnificent views of the sea and the green and white landscape around Mattinata. Less than a mile beyond the village we come to the turning for Monte S. Angelo.

From Foggia to Barletta and Bari

The route for Barletta from the Gargano follows the SS 89 to Siponto, three miles south of Manfredonia, and then the SS 159 which branches off to run parallel with the shoreline through a countryside which has been partially reclaimed from marshes. This area was once the Lago di Salpi, parts of which still exist as lagoons and, farther south near Margherita di Savoia, as extremely productive salt-pans. Shortly after Margherita di Savoia we meet the SS 16 (Adriatica) from Foggia, then cross the River Ofanto, which forms the boundary between the provinces of Bari and Foggia, and a brief run of five miles brings us to Barletta (see p. 271 *et seq.*).

However, the most usual route from Foggia to Barletta and Bari is by the SS 16 (Adriatica), which leaves the city to the south-east, and runs in a straight line across the flat Tavoliere to a bridge over the River Cervaro. Just beyond the river a road on the right leads to the popular *sanctuary of the Incoronata.* The shrine used to stand surrounded by woods in which the Emperor Frederick delighted to hunt; today the woods have practically disappeared and the ancient sanctuary has been replaced by modern buildings (1958). Farther on, we come, again on the right, to the junction with the SS 161, which runs through Orta Nova to meet the SS 90 from Benevento to Foggia (see p. 132). The road begins to ascend and we see ahead of us the high cupola of the cathedral of Cerignola.

Map IV
p. 192 Founded perhaps as a staging-post of the Via Traiana, **Cerignola** is today an important agricultural centre for the southern districts of the Tavoliere, but the city has few buildings of interest. Near Cerignola in 1503 the Spaniards under Gonsalvo di Cordova fought the decisive battle against the French, in which the French commander, the Duc de Nemours, lost his life and the French were driven from the Kingdom.

The modern *cathedral,* in a bastard Tuscan-Apulian-Romanesque style, has over the altar at the end of the right aisle a Byzantine-inspired painting of the *Madonna di Ripalta*, found in 1172 in a cave by the River Ofanto. In a house in the street named after him (it is shown by a commemorative plaque) Mascagni, the composer from Leghorn, composed *Cavalleria Rusticana*, which was produced with resounding success in Rome in 1890. From Cerignola the SS 16 turns north-east to meet the SS 159 from Manfredonia.

CHAPTER 15

Bari and the Terra di Bari

Maps: IV, p.192; VI, p.238

Bari

Bari, the capital of Apulia, is probably the best centre from which to explore the region. Centrally placed and on the sea, it is admirably served by road, rail and air communication with the rest of the country.

Map VI p. 238

Bari has excellent hotels of all categories, including three of the first category, the Palace, the Oriente, and the delle Nazioni which overlooks the sea on the Lungomare N. Sauro. Among several good restaurants we may single out the Sirenetta a Mare, also on the sea, about five miles south of the city on the road to Mola di Bari.

The newer sections of the city resemble those of any other progressive Italian city, but the old quarters are left intact. It is to the Città Vecchia, occupying the little promontory between the Old and New Ports, that the visitor must go to discover the history of this ancient city in the warren of colourful streets, the magnificent churches and the Castello of the Emperor Frederick II.

Evidence for the existence here of a Bronze Age settlement has come from finds in the Piazza S. Pietro near the tip of the promontory. Bari does not appear to have been a Greek outpost, although the Peucezi, who made it one of their centres, came early under Hellenic influence. With the extension of Roman power in Southern Italy, and later in Greece and Asia Minor, Barium enjoyed a long period of commercial prosperity. However, from the time of the barbarian invasions until the establishment of the Norman kingdom Bari was caught up in the incessant struggle between Lombards and Byzantines, with the intervention of emperors and popes, Saracens and Normans. It was held by the Saracens for forty years, until liberated by the Emperor Lewis II in 870. After the loss of Sicily to the Saracens, Bari became the capital of the Byzantine 'Theme of Lombardy', under a Strategos who was in 975 promoted as the

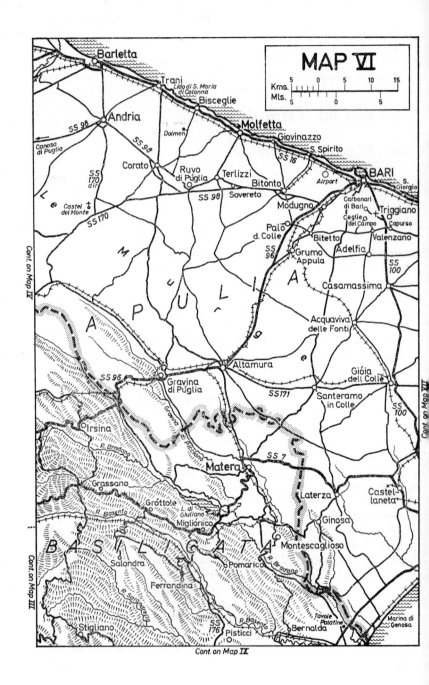

MAP VI

Kms.
Mls.

Barletta

Trani
Lido di S. Maria
di Colonna
Bisceglie

Andria
SS 98
Molfetta
Giovinazzo
S. Spirito
SS 16

Canosa
di Puglia

SS 98
Corato
Ruvo
di Puglia
Terlizzi
Dolmen
Bitonto
Sovereto
SS 98
Airport
BARI
S. Giorgio

SS 170
dir

Castel
del Monte
SS 170
Modugno
Palo
d. Colle
Bitetto
Carbonari
di Bari
Ceglie
del Campo
Triggiano
Capurso
Valenzano

Grumo
Appula
SS 96
Adelfia
SS 100

A P U L I A

Casamassima

Acquaviva
delle Fonti

Altamura

Gióia
dell Colle

SS 96
Gravina
di Puglia
SS171
Santeramo
in Colle
SS 100

Irsina

R. Bradano

Gravina di Picciano

SS 7

Matera

Grassano

Gróttole
L. di
Giuliano
Miglionico

Laterza
Castel-
laneta

Ginosa

R. Basento

B A S I L I C A T A

Salandra

Pomarico
Montescaglioso

R. Bradano

Ferrandina

R. Salandrella

Stigliano
SS
176
Pisticci
R. Basento
Bernalda
Tavole
Palatine
Marina di
Genosa

Cont. on Map IV

Cont. on Map III

Cont. on Map IX

Cont. on Map VII

'Catapan of Italy'. With the assistance of the Normans, Melo freed the city from Byzantine rule and proclaimed himself Duke. The Normans gradually asserted their ascendancy and finally Bari fell to Robert Guiscard in 1071. The Crusades brought wealth and fame to the ports of the Adriatic.

On May 9th, 1087, a ship berthed at the port of Bari, bearing, we are told, the remains of St Nicholas, Bishop of Myra in Asia Minor, which had been stolen by (precisely) forty-seven sailors of Bari. While historians are silent about the earthly activities of the saintly bishop, hagiographers have been busy. So Nicholas is the patron saint of children, sailors and Holy Russia, and later became Santa Claus—an American corruption of the 'San Nicolaas' of their early Dutch colonists. The acquisition of the relics of so popular a saint (there are more than four hundred churches dedicated to him in Protestant England) was a great stimulus to the religious life of Bari: his body was buried in the newly-constructed crypt below the present church of S. Nicola, and there in 1089 Pope Urban came to consecrate its resting-place and to hold a Council, in which St Anselm of Canterbury ably defended Western orthodoxy against the beliefs of the Eastern Church concerning the Trinity.

In 1156 the town rose against the Normans, and as a reprisal William the Bad razed it to the ground with the exception of the shrine of St Nicholas. The Emperor Frederick II, however, built the Castello and improved the port. After a period of decline under the later Angevins, Bari was given by the Aragonese to the Sforzas, and enjoyed a season of splendour as the court of Isabella d'Aragona and her daughter Bona. On the latter's death in 1558 it passed into the Kingdom of Naples. In 1808 King Joachim Murat made it the provincial capital in place of Trani, and it was he who inaugurated the modern city on the plans of Bourbon architects. After the union of Italy the city began steadily to expand, and the population has quadrupled since 1901. Intellectually Bari holds a high place in the South of Italy. Since 1930 the Fiera del Levante has been held annually in September; an important fair for the exchange of goods between European markets and those of the Near and Far East.

The Castello—an episode in the life of St Francis

The Corso Vittorio Emanuele divides the old city from the new, running eastwards from the Piazza Garibaldi to the Piazza degli Eroi del Mare on the reconstructed **Old Port,** an artificial shelter

crowded with small vessels of every variety. South-east of the Molo
S. Nicola begins the broad marine esplanade of the Lungomare
Nazario Sauro, and south of the Piazza degli Eroi del Mare runs the
Corso Cavour, an important shopping street with the principal
banks and the ornate Teatro Petruzzelli (1898). Northwards,
beyond the Cinema-Teatro Margherita, a building of tomato-
coloured stucco backing on to the port, the Lungomare Imperatore
Augusto leads to the wide esplanade which now separates the
promontory from the sea.

Leaving the Old Port behind us, we take the Corso Vittorio
Emanuele and come shortly to the Piazza della Libertà, with the
Municipio and adjoining Teatro Piccinni on the left and, facing it,
the Prefettura. To the left of the Prefettura lies the Piazza Massari,
with its monument to one of Bari's most celebrated sons, the composer Nicola Piccinni (1728–1800).

To the right the Piazza Massari adjoins the Piazza Frederico II di
Svevia, bounded to the north by the moat and massive ramparts of
the *Castello*. The earlier structure—of which we see from the piazza
the two square towers *a bugne* and the connecting southern wall—
was built on the foundations of a Norman and Byzantine fortress by
the Emperor Frederick II between 1233 and 1240. The ramparts,
with their knife-edge corner-angles, which enclose Frederick's castle
on its three landward sides, are sixteenth-century work of the Sforza
period (admission, weekdays 8.0 a.m.–1.0 p.m.; Sundays 9.0 a.m.–
1.0 p.m.). The bridge over the moat leads through a vaulted portico
to the courtyard separating the outer walls from Frederick's palace.
The doorway to the inner court is just beyond the square Torre dei
Minorenne, and its Saracenic archway is richly carved, though worn
with age. The skilful carving of the capitals in the vaulted lobby and
loggia which bring us to the great court is possibly the work of a
Melo da Stiglione, who signs his name on the capital composed of
eagles and griffins. Note the curious console formed by eight faces
on the side wall. Work is still in progress to free the interior from
later accretions, and restore the fine proportions of the Hohenstaufen
building. In some of the rooms, which retain the original vaulting and decoration of the imperial eagle, are displayed early pieces
of Apulian sculpture, as well as paintings by the Vivarini and
others.

During the restorations in 1950 a stone was discovered carrying an
inscription in Latin: 'Here Francis, dressed in an ash-grey robe,
subdued with fire a lascivious girl temptress, who resembled a fierce
Hydra. In this castle he who with prudent flames extinguished
240

Above The Tremiti Islands, off the Gargano peninsula, are of bare limestone. The abbey of S. Nicola on one of the two inhabited islands has been described as 'Montecassino set in the middle of the sea'. Superb bathing and underwater fishing help to make the island's shores a marine paradise.

Right Stalactites and stalagmites of coloured alabaster adorn the Grotte di Castellano near Conversano, the most spectacular and comprehensive of all Italian caves.

The 12th c. west doorway of Trani cathedral is one of the masterpieces of the Apulian-Romanesque style. The crisply cut, stylized foliage of the archivolts contrasts with the Lombard work on the jambs. The bronze doors themselves date from 1175.

Venus born of the sea (who close to the sea assailed him), by his strength made impregnable the retreat of chastity.' In 1220 St Francis of Assisi returned from Egypt, where he had tried to convert the Sultan Al-Kamil, and the Holy Land, and was a guest of the Emperor Frederick. The Emperor apparently introduced a beautiful girl into his guest's room and watched through the key-hole to see what would happen. St Francis gallantly offered to lie with the 'lascivious temptress' on condition that she join him on the floor, where he had prepared a bed of live coals from the brazier. The girl declined the Saint's invitation, and Frederick was so impressed by St Francis's behaviour that he sent her away and spent the night in deep conversation with the Saint.

From the entrance to the castle we continue in the Piazza Frederico II and, crossing into the old quarters by the church of S. Giacomo, come to the Piazza dell' Odegitria (a reminder of the city's Byzantine past) and the Cathedral dedicated to S. Sabino.

The Apulian-Romanesque style

The whole question of the influences and of the schools of architects and sculptors employed in building the magnificent churches of Apulia—and of the precise elements that go to form the style, or rather styles, known as Apulian-Romanesque—is a vexed one. Even the experts differ. However, the visitor unfamiliar with the variety and richness of architecture and sculptural decoration that make the Apulian churches one of the glories of Italian medieval art, will need some guidance, and for him, perhaps, the following notes will not be out of place.

One finds a similar flowering of creative energy in eleventh- and twelfth-century France and England, and in parts of Germany such as the valley of the Rhine, as well as in Lombardy and Tuscany. In Italy the establishment of a strong kingdom in the South by the Normans and their Hohenstaufen and Angevin successors meant that architects, sculptors and artisans were able to travel about more freely and to discover new techniques, forms and styles. Workshops moved from place to place, especially along the popular pilgrim routes, stopping where there was a demand. In the South, classical models, which had reached the country first through Byzantium, continued to inspire stone carvers with the decorative motifs of acanthus leaves, meandering vine tendrils, animals and birds. Later, Roman portraiture and sarcophagi were to play their part. The small domed churches of S. Marco at Rossano and La Cattolica at Stilo provide examples of the Byzantine influence on ecclesiastical architecture in contemporary Italy, and the domes continued to be employed in later buildings such as the cathedral of Molfetta.

The Lombard influence was strong—in sculpture it would be better described as the Lombard-French element. It was Lombard sculpture that caused St Bernard of Clairvaux (1090–1153) to remonstrate: 'Then, in the cloisters, right under the eyes of the brothers as they read and meditate—what business there have these ridiculous monstrosities, this indecent magnificence and this magnificent indecency? What business there have these foul apes, these savage lions, these monstrous centaurs, these tigers, these fighting men, these hunters blowing horns? Under one head are seen several bodies, and again on a single body several heads. Here is a quadruped ending in a snake, and there a fish with the head and breasts of a beast suckling its young . . . For God's sake, if you have no shame over this foolery, have at least some care for the cost of it!'

Architecturally, the Lombards contributed to Southern churches the high central nave flanked with the two lower aisles, the arched corbel-table below the roof, and, to a lesser extent, the triform apsidal ends. Another typical Lombard feature are the beautiful lateral galleries formed of open arcades, and it is also possible that they were responsible for the magnificent rose windows which are so much in evidence in Apulia.

The final supremacy of the Normans in Southern Italy and Sicily at the end of the eleventh century brought fresh influences from central France and Normandy which resulted in a grandeur of plan and execution not attempted since Roman times (in a journey through France Pope Urban II consecrated some twenty new abbey churches, far larger than any built hitherto). The Benedictines, and in particular the great Desiderius, Abbot of Montecassino, were mainly responsible for the building of these great abbey churches. Tuscan craftsmen were also employed in northern Apulia, and took the churches of Pisa as their model. From Sicily oriental, Saracenic features were transmitted—interlaced arches, the pointed Saracenic arch, and eastern decorative motifs.

Apulian-Romanesque, then, consists of a blending and flowering of all these diverse elements into a brilliant aesthetic homogeneity. With the sophisticated Emperor Frederick II there came a return to classical Roman models, and a new refinement in the planning and decoration of his 'palaces of solace'. Later still, the Angevins were to construct their castles according to the military science of the day and their churches in the developed Gothic style; but by this time the great period of Apulian-Romanesque was over.

The Cathedral—S. Nicola—the Museo Storico—the Pinacoteca Provinciale —the Archaeological Museum

In Bari's **cathedral** and the church of S. Nicola we have two splendid examples of Apulian-Romanesque, thanks to the intelligent authorities who have stripped these churches and others in the region of hideous baroque accretions, and restored them to their original simplicity. The Duomo, begun in 1170 to replace the Byzantine structure demolished by William III in 1156, is basilican in plan, with shallow transepts surmounted by an octagonal drum— an oriental feature. The three doors of the west front are all that remain from the baroque additions of the eighteenth century. The high nave and lower aisles with their arched corbel-tables are Lombard, as are the grotesque animals on the corbels and protruding from the deeply recessed archivolt above the rose window. A Byzantine-inspired frieze on the exterior separates the large window from a smaller one above it. On the left (north) flank a deep blind arcade supports an elegant gallery. Beyond the doorway, with its Byzantine carving, is the **Trulla,** a circular building begun in 1618 on the foundations of a baptistery destroyed in 1156. The walls of the transepts and of the east end form an organic whole, since the rounded apses have been masked by the wall which joins the corner towers—we shall see this unusual feature again in the church of S. Nicola. Of the two towers only one remains, a tall graceful campanile—the other collapsed in the earthquake of 1613. The central eastern window is interesting: a rounded canopy rests on two sphinxes, these in turn being supported by slender columns borne by two lions on consoles. The beautifully articulated carving shows a strong Byzantine influence. Note, too, the powerful figures of birds by the lower windows of the transepts.

The carefully restored interior has a solemn austere beauty. The pulpit, ciborium and episcopal throne have all been reconstructed from fragments of the originals. On the floor of the nave are remains of a fourteenth-century pavement in polychrome marble, with a rose design similar to that of the western window. On the left, at the end of the nave, an entrance leads to the twelve-sided Trulla: it is used as the sacristy. Ask here to see the Archives, which include a beautiful eleventh-century *Exultet* roll on parchment. The script is Beneventan and the illumination Byzantine. From either side of the nave-end stairs lead down to the crypt, which was baroqued in the eighteenth century. Under the altar lie the remains of S. Sabino, Bishop of Canosa, brought to Bari in 872. Above is a much repainted Byzantine icon of the *Madonna,* reputed to be the work of St Luke.

From the left of the Duomo we take the narrow Strada del Carmine and its continuation in the Via delle Cruciate (the Street of the Crusades). This whole quarter is most attractive, with arches and alley-ways between the old houses, shops and workrooms, and crowds of children. Beyond the church of *S. Marco* (with the symbol of St Mark on the window), built in the twelfth century by the colony of Venetian merchants, we arrive, on the right, at the *Arco di S. Nicola,* an Angevin structure of the fourteenth century leading into the piazza of the church of S. Nicola. On the left of the arch stands the little early-eleventh-century church of *S. Gregorio,* singularly pure in style, with three rounded apsidal ends. In the church is a statue of S. Nicola, which is carried to his own church opposite on April 29th, at the beginning of the 'Sagra di S. Nicola'. On the farther side of the arch is the reconstructed *Portico dei Pellegrini,* with various pieces of sculpture.

The church of *S. Nicola,* the first of the great Norman churches in Apulia and a prototype of Apulian-Romanesque, stands surrounded by four courts, once the site of the palace of the Byzantine Catapan. The crypt, begun by the Abbot Elia in 1087 for the reception of the Saint's relics, was consecrated by Pope Urban two years later; the church itself appears to have been completed by 1105, but its consecration did not take place, for some reason, until 1197 when Bishop Corrado of Hildesheim officiated in the presence, it is believed, of the Emperor Henry VI. In plan the church is a basilica, with a transept slightly wider than the nave and aisles, and the rounded apses masked externally by a wall similar to that of the Duomo. Originally it had four towers, but the two eastern ones collapsed in an earthquake; of the remaining truncated western towers, that on the right, known as the Torre del Catapano, may have belonged to an earlier building.

The west end is simple and severe, two piers supported on classical columns separating the lofty nave from the aisles. The central gable-end has a sharper angle than is usual, and the roofs of the aisles slope more gently. Under the small eye-window the façade is pierced by slim round-arched windows in pairs, and below them by single openings. The *main doorway,* an interesting, typical Apulian-

244

Romanesque portal, has a triangular canopy supported on classical capitals by slender hexagonal columns, these borne by two magnificently stylized bulls on consoles. The door-jambs, arch, archivolt and spandrels are covered with low-relief carving in a diversity of styles; Arabic, Byzantine and classical. Two inscriptions on either side of the doorway record the consecration of the church, its privileges and immunities. The names 'Ansaldo' and 'An. de Fumarello', also cut in the stone, refer to a master sculptor and (possibly) the architect.

The exterior sides of the church as far as the transept are deeply recessed by round-arched arcades, above which runs a beautiful gallery; above this again we see the wall of the nave, with rounded window openings, blind arcading and a corbel-table of similar round arches—the whole a Romanesque masterpiece of subtle spacing and proportions. Two doorways on each flank give access to the aisles, the first on the left side being the celebrated *Porta dei Leoni,* the semi-circular stilted arch richly carved with a lively scene of knights on horseback, suggesting French origins. The arch springs from two curious blocks, carved in low-relief and thought to represent Months. On the white wall of the restored east end is a window which was probably the model for the similar window in the Duomo. Below, an early fifteenth-century low-relief depicts *the miracles of S. Nicola.*

In the *interior,* the three transverse arches, placed here in 1451 to give additional structural support, immediately draw our attention to the fact that the main axis of the church is out of alignment with the east and west ends. The richly gilded and painted ceiling is by Carlo Rosa of Aquila (1661). To the right of the main door, beneath a painting of *S. Girolamo* by an unknown follower of the sixteenth-century Venetian school, is the Renaissance tomb of the Canon Giovanni Bonn (1510). Beyond, on the ground floor of the Torre del Catapano, is the *treasury,* which contains many objects of interest.

Through the arches of the *iconostasis* (note the fine capitals) separating the nave from the transept, can be seen an unusually beautiful ciborium (tabernacle), one of the earliest in Apulia (1150), and the model for many others. Four columns of antique *breccia,* with exquisitely carved capitals, support the architrave on which short columns raise a two-tiered canopy in the form of a hexagonal pyramid. In the centre of the architrave facing the nave is a small copper and enamel plaque, showing S. Nicola crowning King Roger. Art historians have variously attributed this to Byzantine or Limousin craftsmen, or to local artists influenced by one of these. Perhaps

245

a more likely guess is that it came from twelfth- or thirteenth-century Sicilian workshops. (Roger was not in fact crowned at Bari but in Palermo on December 25th, 1130.) Behind the altar in the central apse backed by the monument to Bona Sforza (1593), with the original pavement of oriental mosaic, is the splendid *episcopal chair*. The frame of the seat is of Byzantine inlay, the sides Saracenic, and the figures supporting it Lombard in style. Two slaves struggle under the weight, and the overseer (in the centre) lends a helping hand. At the rear two lionesses play menacingly with terrified men.

Above the twelfth-century altar in the apse on the right is a fine painting by Bartolomeo Vivarini (signed and dated 1476) of the *Madonna and Four Saints*; in the lunette, a *Pietà* with S. Francesco and S. Nicola. On the wall are some fourteenth-century frescoes, revealed in the recent restoration. Over the altar on the south wall of the transept is the '*Black*' *S. Nicola* (seventeenth-century), much venerated by the local people. Steps lead up to the *sacristy,* which contains precious relics and a Byzantine icon almost completely overlaid with silver, presented by the King of Serbia at the beginning of the fourteenth century. Over the altar in the left-hand apse is an interesting triptych of the *Madonna and Child between St John the Evangelist and S. Nicola*, a work of the sixteenth-century Cretan school of icon-painters, possibly by Rico da Candia. At the north end of the transept is the altar in embossed silverwork (1684) by the Neapolitans Domenico Martinelli and Ennio Avitabile, depicting *Scenes from the Legend of S. Nicola*.

Stairways at the end of the aisles lead down to the *crypt.* Let in the wall of the stairs on the right of the church is the tomb of Bishop Elia, a fourth-century Roman sarcophagus of four panels with three-quarter-length male figures; above is an inscription in good lettering. Opposite the entrance below is a truncated column of porphyry, enclosed in an iron cage. Legend has it that the Saint saw the stone beside the Tiber in Rome, blessed it and told it to betake itself to Myra. This it did; then in 1089 it miraculously turned up here, when a column was lacking to complete the crypt. The columns, and their interesting capitals, are worth noticing. The bones of S. Nicola, conserved beneath the twelfth-century altar, distil a 'Holy Manna', with miraculous properties.

On the left of S. Nicola, and to the rear of S. Gregorio, the Largo Urbano II leads us through a passageway to the Lungomare Cristoforo Colombo. In the Largo, at No. 2, is the *Museo Storico,* containing collections of arms, curios, mementoes, documents and photographs, chiefly concerning the First World War (admission,

8.0 a.m.–1.0 p.m.; 4.30–7.30 p.m.; closed Fridays). The walk through the old quarter of S. Nicola to the Piazza S. Pietro is full of interest; but visitors with less time on their hands should certainly not miss the Piazza Mercantile, the centre of the Città Vecchia. We take the street behind the apsidal end of S. Nicola to the Corte del Catapano and, passing under two arches, follow the Strada Palazzo di Città, a narrow way with some interesting old houses (e.g. Nos. 37 and 29).

In an opening to the left stands the church of *S. Agostino,* or S. Anna, as it is more commonly called, rebuilt by the Milanese colony in 1508 and revealing in its façade fragments of an older church. From here, slightly left, we take the Via Fragigena (the 'Street of the French') which brings us to the picturesque *Piazza Mercantile.* To the left is the *Sedile dei Nobili,* with an open loggia and clock-tower, the gathering-place of the noble families who conducted the city's affairs. Below, in the piazza, a column and a lion (the stone rubbed smooth with age) are raised on a circular base of four steps. This is the *Colonna della Giustizia,* a pillory where bankrupts were exposed to public reproof and a reminder that Bari's life depended on trade. Opposite the Sedile, in the narrow Vico Fiscardi, is the house in which Piccinni was born in 1728. The open-air markets are continued in the adjoining Piazza del Ferrarese, so called from the colony of merchants of Ferrara who lived here in the seventeenth century. Crossing the piazza and continuing south, we arrive at the Corso Vittorio Emanuele and the Piazza degli Eroi del Mare.

From the Piazza Eroi we take the Lungomare Nazario Sauro for the *Pinacoteca Provinciale,* which occupies the top floor of the grandiose Palazzo della Provincia—some two hundred yards beyond the *Rotonda,* the semi-circular belvedere on the sea. The art gallery contains paintings by the Vivarini, Giovanni Bellini, Veronese, Tintoretto and Bordone. There are also landscapes by Poussin and Corot, a battle scene by Salvator Rosa, and a representative collection of the School of Posillipo. A section of the gallery is devoted to figures from eighteenth-century Neapolitan cribs.

For the *Archaeological Museum,* which is housed together with the main building of Bari University in the impressive Palazzo Ateneo (1868), we take the broad Corso Cavour from the Piazza degli Eroi del Mare as far as the Via Petronio Petroni, where we turn right; beyond the gardens and trees of the Piazza Umberto I stands the Palazzo Ateneo. The Museo Archeologico is on the first floor, reached from the main entrance by crossing the courtyard and climbing the grand staircase (admission 9.0 a.m.–2.0 p.m.; closed Mondays). The collection of vases and material from excavations in Apulia is the most valuable in the region for the knowledge it provides not only of ancient Peucezia (the present province of Bari) but also of Daunia (Foggia) and Messapia (the Salento). It will eventually be moved to a more commodious setting.

Giovinazzo—Molfetta—Bisceglie

The towns round Bari, both along the coast (particularly to the north-west) and in the hinterland, are so rich in architectural and historic interest that the visitor can easily suffer from an indigestible surfeit. The itineraries below should therefore be followed with discretion; it will probably be better to split them up.

One trip takes us up the coast to Bisceglie, inland to the Castel del Monte, and back to Bari via Ruvo di Puglia and Bitonto—a journey of about seventy-five miles. We leave Bari by the Via Adriatica (SS 16). In just under two miles a turning on the right leads to the permanent site of the Fiera del Levante, and a little farther on the turning for the lido for Bari, the fine sandy beach of S. Francesco all' Arena, well provided with seaside amenities. This part of the coast has few good beaches, and long stretches of low rock which make bathing difficult except from a boat. After passing the road for Bari airport, and the promontory at S. Spirito with its many villas, the road runs parallel with the coast through the countryside

Map VI
p. 238

to the small port of **Giovinazzo.**

Built on an ancient site—possibly of Netium or Natiolum— Giovinazzo has some light mechanical industry and workshops for dressing the local marble. The church of **S. Domenico** stands in the spacious central Piazza Vittorio Emanuele II, opposite the Municipio and the Palazzo del Marchese di Rende with its Doric colonnade. Within, there is an interesting work by Lorenzo Lotto (1542), originally part of a triptych, showing the seated figure of *S. Felice.* At the end of the Piazza Umberto I, on the right of the Municipio, are the old city gates, known as the *Arco di Traiano* from the four Roman milestones of the ancient Via Traiana which support the pointed medieval arches. From the little Piazza Costantinopoli, beyond the gateway, the Via Cattedrale brings us to the sea-shore and the Duomo.

The *Duomo,* which was begun in the twelfth century but not consecrated until 1283, has suffered much alteration; nevertheless

248

the east end shows the typical Apulian-Romanesque enclosure of the apse by a wall linking the two square corner towers. Of these, the taller southern one is original, but the other had to be rebuilt at the end of the seventeenth century. The entrance of the church, the south flank, is reached by a high double flight of steps, and the portal has a richly carved archivolt enclosing a rose window with a representation of *the Mystic Lamb* in low-relief. The primitive simplicity of the interior has been hideously baroqued over. From the left aisle a stairway descends to the crypt (if closed, the sacristan will open it on request), which is raised on ten pillars with interesting Romanesque capitals in a variety of designs.

Above the high altar is a Byzantine-inspired early-fourteenth-century painting, the *Madonna di Corsignano*, which has replaced *the Redeemer* or *the Risen Christ*, now hanging on the right of the chancel. The attribution of *the Redeemer* has been the matter of much debate; it undoubtedly has marked affinities with the painting of the same subject by Paolo Serafini (*fl.* 1387) in Barletta cathedral. Treasures in the **sacristy** include a *cassetta-reliquiario* of tenth- or eleventh-century Byzantine workmanship, and a French (possibly Provençal) reliquary-cross of the late fifteenth century, bearing the Orsini arms —the cross itself is a later addition.

If we return to the Piazza Costantinopoli and take the Via Santo Spirito, we come to the medieval church of **Spirito Santo** (1385). The exterior is Gothic, with oriental influence in the cupolas; inside, only the pointed arch remains of the early building. Here again is a Byzantine-type *Madonna and Child* by the Cretan painter Angelo Bizamano (*fl.* 1518–32). The picturesque alleyways of the old town reveal many medieval towers, palaces and courts.

Beyond Giovinazzo the road skirts the sea and brings us to the prosperous commercial and industrial centre of **Molfetta.** Its port shelters a large fishing fleet, and there is an important wholesale fish market. We enter Molfetta by the Via Tenente M. Fiorino and arrive at the Piazza Garibaldi, with the gardens of the Villa Comunale (or Garibaldi), on the right and, to our left, the Gothic-style *guglia* of the Calvario (1856), behind which stands the church of **S. Bernardino** (1451, but rebuilt 1585); if the church is closed, the key can be obtained from the hospital next door. S. Bernardino has two paintings by the little-known Flemish artist Gaspar Hovic (*ca.* 1550–1613) and a triptych by Tuccio di Andria (*fl.* 1487–8), an interesting painter who was influenced by the contemporary Tuscan schools as well as the Flemish.

Behind the Villa Comunale on the sea side of the piazza, the

Map VI
p. 238

Corso Dante opens out into the Piazza Mazzini; to the north of this, on a little promontory, stands the tight-packed cluster of houses and alleyways of the old town, with the Duomo Vecchio. The **new cathedral of the Assunta,** which was built in the seventeenth century and raised to its present rank in 1785, is on the left of the Corso; an impressive building both without and within, and typical of southern baroque. Among its paintings are an *Assumption* by the local painter Corrado Giaquinto (1703–65), a *Visitation* by the popular Carlo Rosa (*ca.* 1678), and a curious *Dormitio Virginis* by an anonymous southern painter of the sixteenth century. The sacristy has, among other objects of value, a beautiful calendar and missal illuminated by Giovanni di Francia (*fl.* 1405–48). Almost opposite the cathedral a short street leads to the Largo Municipale and the baroque Palazzo di Città backing on to the sea.

From the Piazza Mazzini, with the little church of S. Stefano (thirteenth century, but rebuilt 1586) on the left, we arrive at the port; straight ahead lies the Banchina S. Domenico and the fish-market; to the right the Banchina Seminario brings us to the **Duomo Vecchio,** one of the most unusual of Apulian-Romanesque cathedrals. From the port we see its two eastern towers and the three polygonal drums capped with pyramidal roofs at different levels which cover the cupolas. In few of these southern churches can we see so clearly the diversity of elements that constitute Apulian-Romanesque. Here, in the plan of the Duomo and in the cupolas it is the Byzantine influence that is uppermost; but the fecundity of ideas and imaginative fusion of the oriental with the local tradition is astonishing. The cathedral was begun about 1150 but was not completed until over a century later. (The west end was, in fact, never completed; two towers were begun but rise no higher than the nave.) The east end shows the same masking of the apse that we find at Bari and Giovinazzo. The interlaced blind arcading is Saracenic; the projecting lion supports of the circular window arch are Lombard, as are the carvings on the consoles. On the northern flank the chapel of S. Giuliano was added in the fourteenth century. The entrance—by way of the Bishop's Palace on the southern side of the church—is through an eighteenth-century doorway beneath a window and two niches of the Renaissance.

If the exterior of the Duomo lacks the graceful lines of the Bari churches and especially of the cathedral of Bitonto, the interior comes as a revelation. Four great cruciform pilasters with embedded half-columns divide the church into nave, aisles and transept. At the east end a large semi-circular apse is flanked by two niches. Our gaze is attracted upwards to the light coming from the windows of the three cupolas, and is arrested by the complexity of the symmetrical and asymmetrical forms. This, the greatest of the Apulian domed churches, is a magnificent harmonious blending of the architecture of the east and west. In the decoration of capitals and consoles we see the local craftsman's hand, but what of the carving on the stoup on the right of the entrance? This meeting of man and fish reflects perhaps some distant memory of Hellenistic art, here in Apulia never completely forgotten.

The old town is divided by a straight street, the Via Marte, like the backbone of a sole, with narrow alleys off it forming the lateral bones. The origin of Molfetta is unknown, though near by at Pulo there were certainly Stone Age settlements. The town was first known as Melfi, and documents from the twelfth to the sixteenth century refer to it as Melficta. By the time of the Hohenstaufen and the Angevins it was of such importance as to have its customs and privileges recorded in the *Libro Rosso*, kept today at the Pontifico Seminario Apulo in the Viale Pio XI to the east of the town. It was destroyed by French troops in 1529, during the wars between the Emperor Charles V and François I, and passed into feudal hands.

From the south side of the Villa Garibaldi we continue straight on and, crossing the Piazza Vittorio Emanuele, take the Via S. Pansini and its continuation in the Via Madonna dei Martiri. Shortly after the latter is joined on the right by the street from the port, the Piazza S. Francesco opens out on the left. We turn left here into the Via S. Francesco for the neolithic *necropolis of Pulo di Molfetta,* turning left again at the end, then almost immediately right into the Via Poggioreale. This country road brings us in about half a mile to a vast overgrown *doline*, a cavity formed by erosion in the limestone, which resembles a disused quarry. There are storeys of caves cut in the rock face, dwellings of prehistoric men; excavations both here and in the near-by necropolis have brought to light pieces of primitive pottery and implements, now in the archaeological museum at Bari.

Back at the Piazza S. Francesco, we turn left into the Via Adriatica. On the right a short road leads down to the shore, with the ruins of the ancient **Ospedale dei Crociati** (1095) and the restored church of the **Madonna dei Martiri,** founded in 1162. Above the high altar is the Byzantine painting of the Madonna which gives the name to the church; according to the legend, this was brought from Constantinople in 1188.

The Statale winds among olive groves and vineyards; here and to

Map VI
p. 238

the north, a sweet white dessert wine is produced, going by the generic name of Moscato di Trani and reaching the formidable alcoholic strength of 17°. Then, through market gardens, orchards, and citrus groves, we come to the market town of **Bisceglie**. Founded in the early Middle Ages, Bisceglie was first mentioned in historical records when it was taken by Robert Guiscard in the second half of the eleventh century and bestowed in fief on Count Pietro of Trani. Under the Normans it became an important centre and port, with fortified walls and towers, and it continued to prosper under the Hohenstaufen and Angevins, the latter granting the feudal rights to the Provençal del Balzos. From them the town passed to Don Alfonso d'Aragona who, as the Duke of Bisceglie, married (as her second husband) Lucrezia Borgia. There is a small lido to the right of the port and other beaches to the north-west of the town, but there is only one hotel, the Albergo Commercio.

In the old parts of Bisceglie behind the port are some interesting medieval houses and churches. From the large Piazza Vittorio Emanuele II, the modern centre of the town, we take the Via Imbriani to the Piazza Margherita di Savoia; from there we follow the Corso Umberto I with its covered-in market. The Via S. Margherita, on the right, brings us to the little late-twelfth-century church of *S. Margherita,* one of the best-preserved of the smaller Apulian-Romanesque churches, set back from the street in a court-yard on the left. (If the gate and church are closed, the key is at the Ufficio della Polizia Urbana in the Piazza Margherita di Savoia.) On the left flank of the church are several thirteenth-century tombs of various members of the Falcone family, one of whom, Falco, an imperial judge under Henry VI of Hohenstaufen, founded the church in 1197. The monument of the Falcone children (1276), is by one of the best-known sculptors of the period, Anseramo di Trani (*fl.* 1240–76), whose work we shall see again at Terlizzi. The interior of S. Margherita has a single nave with a cupola and rounded apse. Over the remains of an altar on the right is a canopy supported on columns, resting on two lions.

Continuing on the Corso Umberto, we come on the left to the Largo Castello. This is the beginning of the medieval town proper, with its narrow alleys and houses of rusticated stonework. A short way along the Via Tupputi we pass under the Arco S. Adoneo on the right and reach the church of *S. Adoneo,* which was begun in 1074 and is typical of the period, with its gabled end and circular window surrounded by four lions and a statue of the Saint on consoles. To the right of the doorway is the tomb of the church's founder, Bartolomeo.

The interior of the church has been spoilt by later additions; the font, however, is medieval. The private house to the left of S. Adoneo has a fifteenth-century façade in diamond *bugne*. Returning to the Via Tupputi, we shortly turn right again in the Via Cardinale dell' Olio. This brings us to the **cathedral,** which was begun by Count Pietro in 1073 but was not consecrated until 1295. The thirteenth-century façade has a richly carved central doorway, Romanesque windows and corbel table. The original rose window was replaced by a baroque one, subsequently restored. On the right flank a portal raised on two antique columns is the usual entrance to the church, the interior of which has been baroqued. The carved choir stalls, which came from the suppressed Benedictine monastery of S. Maria dei Miracoli near Andria, each carry representations of two prominent members of the Order; St Benedict himself is in the sacristy. From the Duomo one can walk down to the little port, with the fishing-boats drawn up on the shore near the ruined bastion of a Spanish fort.

Castel del Monte

From Bisceglie the Via Adriatica continues along the coast to Trani and Barletta. But for Castel del Monte we leave Bisceglie by the Corato road to the right of the railway station in the newer part of the town, reached from the Piazza Vittorio Emanuele II. Just over two miles from Bisceglie a signpost points to a track to one of the largest **dolmens** known. This prehistoric stone structure, possibly a funerary monument, stands among the olives about half a mile from the road. An open *dromos* of flat stones leads up to the *cella*, which is covered by a single large stone. There are other similar constructions in the district, known in the Middle Ages as Tavole dei Paladini, a reference to the legend of the Knights of the Round Table.

Our road climbs to a crossroads where we turn right; two miles farther on we come to the road from Ruvo di Puglia; here we again turn right and shortly after enter **Corato,** an important centre for the wine and olive oil trades, built around a medieval hub which retains some old houses and churches. Turning left in the circular road and taking the fourth road, again on our left, we cross the SS 98 and continue over the low hills until we join the SS 170. From time to time we see ahead of us on the summit of a low conical hill the regular shape of Castel del Monte, its colour blending with the pale, dry landscape. At the Masseria Castello we turn right in the SS 170 *dir*

Map VI
p. 238

for Andria and Barletta, and soon after, left, into the drive which brings us up to the Ostello di Federico and the Ristorante Taverna Sforza beneath the castle.

All through the South of Italy we glean but a shadowy impression of the creators of its magnificent medieval past—even of Robert Guiscard; in Apulia, however, we gradually become aware of the actual presence of that great figure of the late Middle Ages, the Emperor Frederick II, and nowhere more acutely than here in his last and most sophisticated 'place of solace', the **Castel del Monte**. Two descriptions perhaps sum the man up: his own, as simply 'the man from Apulia'; the other, as *'stupor mundi et immutator mirabilis*— the amazement of the world and a marvellous innovator'. This mixture of simplicity and magnificence in Castel del Monte gives support to the tradition that the Emperor designed it himself, though today the magnificence requires some effort of imagination, for those splendid rooms are now empty shells, desecrated by idle visitors. But Castel del Monte nevertheless remains one of the finest examples of secular architecture of the European Middle Ages, reproducing the practicality and elegance of the classical age or the Arab world, and anticipating the developments of the Renaissance villa. As we approach, the building appears smaller and its honey-coloured walls less regular than from a distance. But regular it is in design, with octagonal towers—formerly somewhat higher than they are today—standing at each angle of a perfect octagon.

The Castel del Monte—or the Castel di S. Maria del Monte, as it was first known, after a Benedictine monastery near by—was begun by Frederick about 1240. An imperial edict of January 22nd of that year orders Roberto di Montefuscolo, his Justiciar for the Capitanata, to collect materials for the castle 'that it is Our wish to erect *apud Sanctam Mariam*'. It is not known whether the castle was in fact completed at Frederick's death in 1250, but the three young sons of Frederick's successor Manfred were imprisoned in the Castel del Monte after his death. Their development from boyhood to manhood was marked by an increase in the weight of the chains and fetters which bound them. After thirty years the survivors, Henry and Frederick, were transferred to the Castel dell' Ovo in Naples. Frederick managed to escape on the journey, and made his way to the courts of England, Germany, Aragon and Castile, but no one was interested in the Hohenstaufen cause; rejected and humiliated, he appears again in Egypt, then is lost to sight. Enfeebled and blind, Henry died in Naples. In the fourteenth century the Castel was the scene of several brilliant weddings of the del Balzo family. Later it belonged to the Carafa Dukes of Ruvo, and in 1799 was fortified against the Sanfedisti. At this time it appears still to have possessed much of its marbling and sculpture; but in the troubled period that saw the fall of the Bourbons and the unification of Italy Castel del Monte became the haunt of brigands and a shelter for shepherds. It was redeemed from complete destruction by the State in 1876, and is now being restored as a national monument (admission, summer 9.0 a.m.–12.0 noon; 3.0–6.0 p.m.; winter 9.0 a.m.–12.0 noon; 1.0–4.0 p.m.).

The **main entrance** of *breccia* marble faces east (there is another, simpler entrance in the rear) and is approached by a double ramp of steps. The design shows a conscious attempt to revive the classical architecture of the triumphal arch. However, this classical element cannot prevail against the Gothic, which is apparent in the elongated proportion of the whole façade and the acute angle of the pediment, quite apart from the pointed arch of the doorway that might even be taken for Saracenic. Graceful columns carry two Romanesque lions (the one on the left has almost disappeared), from which the arch springs. Within, the plain lintel is borne by two sturdy columns; between the columns there is a channelling to take the portcullis. Above the doorway is an elegant Gothic window.

Rooms I and II (rooms are numbered successively from the right of the entrance) form a vestibule. The **ground floor** consists of eight similar rooms, trapezoid in shape, corresponding to the external walls and those of the interior courtyard. Four half-columns of *breccia*, with boldly carved capitals of a leaf pattern, support the Gothic rib-vaulting; in some rooms there are remains of the conical canopy of the fireplace. From the vestibule we go out through a Saracenic-arched doorway into the **courtyard,** in the centre of which water once played in a marble pool. Above are three well-proportioned Romanesque apertures, serving both as windows and doors on to the wooden gallery that formerly encircled the court. Above a doorway on the right to Room IV is a fragment of a finely sculptured figure of a horseman, riding straight out from the wall-face. The downstairs rooms have access to towers which either contain stairs (only those from Rooms V and VIII are at present in use) or one of the castle's lavatories, with an air vent and a system of flushing fed by water from the roof—perhaps the earliest example that we have of such sanitary arrangements since antiquity.

In Room VII, from which a door opens on to the court, the keystone of the vaulting is carved in a low-relief representation of a faun's head with a garland of vine leaves. From Room VIII the corkscrew stone staircase brings us to the **upper floor,** where the room-plan corresponds precisely to that below, except that the communicating doors are arranged differently. On the ceiling above the stairs in the tower the vault-ribs rest on consoles supported by grotesque figures of naked men; other heads form consoles in the tower off Room IV.

Turning to the right at the top of the stairway, we pass into the so-called **Throne Room,** typical of the elegance of the Emperor's living quarters: two windows (the external one with marble steps and window-seats) give ample illumination; the ribbed vaults spring from stylized leaf capitals raised on a cluster of three graceful columns in pale pink or blue marble; the keystone is again the head of a faun; a mosaic pavement originally covered the floor; the walls were faced with marble up to the cornice, and above it (in the lunettes formed by the arched vaulting) with alternate courses of limestone and *opus reticulatum*—the first example of this work since classical times. This room is immediately over the main entrance; in the niches beside the front window are provisions for raising and lowering the portcullis. Frederick would have furnished these apartments with oriental rugs, cushions, Saracenic silks, rare pieces of classical sculpture, and books.

Room VIII, with its fireplace, lavatory and access to the roof terraces (now closed), may have been the Emperor's bedroom. It is possible that he kept his falcons and rare birds in specially built aviaries on the terrace, as described in his *De Arte Venandi*. The roofing was originally built with a slope both outwards and inwards; the outward slope supplied water for the lavatories by a system of tanks and conduits, the inner provided water for the basin in the court.

Ruvo di Puglia—Terlizzi—the Cathedral of Bitonto

We return to Bari via Ruvo di Puglia, Terlizzi and Bitonto. From Castel del Monte we retrace the SS 170 but leave on our left the turning for Corato, continuing over the crossing with the SS 378 and turning left shortly after in the SS 98 from Andria and Canosa di Puglia. We enter **Ruvo di Puglia** (which stands to the left of the Statale) at the large Piazza Giovanni Bovio.

Map VI
p. 238

In antiquity Ruvo was celebrated for its vases; it was one of the chief centres for the manufacture of what became known as 'Apulian' ware. As a leading city of the Peucezi, Rhyps (or Rhybasteinon, in

256

Above S. Nicola di Bari, the first of the great Norman churches in Apulia and a prototype of Apulian-Romanesque, was completed in 1105.
Below The south side, with its recessed arcade, gallery and blind arcading, reveals the subtle spacing and proportions of this style.

Bari, the second largest city of Southern Italy. *Above* Panorama showing the Old Port. *Below left* Pots and pans for sale in the old quarter of S. Nicola. *Right* A street in the old quarter.

its Greek form) came early in the fifth century BC into contact with the Hellenic cities of Magna Graecia. The number of Attic and Corinthian black and red figure vases found there would indicate that workshops of Greek potters and vase painters were early established at Ruvo, and that local work was based on Greek models. Geometric designs such as those produced in near-by Canosa, which were common among the early Italiot peoples, were also used at Ruvo. However, the characteristic Apulian vases were something very different. Deriving from the Attic red figures on a black ground, they gradually lost the sharpness and delicacy of the graphic line of the originals and became increasingly more impressionistic. Finally the earlier freshness declined into flashy baroque.

Under the Romans Rubi became a *municipium* and an important station on the Via Traiana. The town may have been destroyed by the Goths in 463, but its prosperity revived in the Norman and Hohenstaufen periods and Frederick II provided it with fortifications. From 1510 until the end of feudalism in 1806, Ruvo was a fief of the Carafas. Today it exports excellent table grapes and olive oil from the rich surrounding countryside.

The **Museo Jatta,** founded at the beginning of the last century by Giovanni Jatta and housed in the family palazzo, is on the Piazza Giovanni Bovio, at No. 35. This contains a magnificent collection of more than 1700 vases of Greek and local provenance. Particularly good is the Attic krater in the centre of Room IV; this beautiful work, representing the death of Talos, the bronze giant who guarded Crete and fell to the Argonauts by the charms of Medea, was possibly painted by the Athenian Meidias at the end of the fifth century BC. (Admission 10.0 a.m.–12.0 noon; 4.0–6.0 p.m.; and by personal application to the proprietors.)

To the north of the piazza are the medieval quarters of the town. Taking the Via Menotti Garibaldi, we turn left into the Via Cattedrale and arrive at the piazza with its late Romanesque **cathedral,** and, to the right of it, isolated from the church, the older campanile. The building, in a dark grey stone, was begun at the end of the twelfth century and completed about 1237; later additions were made at the end of the thirteenth century. The design of the façade is unusual, even allowing for the many divergences from the norm of Bari in Apulian-Romanesque cathedrals, and not altogether happy in its proportions. The surface is also unrelieved by pilasters, so that the prominent rose window bears little relation to the three portals. The four half-pillars and the blind arcading above these doorways indicate that a portico was planned here. The arched corbel-table is a distinctive feature of the façade (it is continued on the right flank).

The rounded central doorway consists of four bands of beautiful carving (in which Byzantine, Saracenic and classical motifs are harmoniously fused), surmounted by an archivolt springing from two magnificent sphinxes with heads of men between their paws. These rest on slender free-standing columns borne on the backs of lions, which have weathered so that they now resemble a pair of performing seals. Two crouching human figures support the lions. A further sphinx crowns the archivolt, in which *the Eternal Father* appears flanked by the figures of saints; and beneath this are *the Mystic Lamb* and the *symbols of the four Evangelists*.

The interior, which has been restored to its earlier form, is basilican in plan, with three semi-circular apses, the high central nave looking almost Gothic. Only two of the side chapels—added perhaps as late as the sixteenth century—have been left open. A gallery, resting on consoles of animals and humans, runs along the sides of the church and the inner wall of the west end. The nave and transepts are covered by a wooden ceiling. The ciborium is modern, designed in the Romanesque style by the Roman architect Ettore Bernich. In the right transept are some frescoes of the *Madonna* and *St Sebastian* and of other saints, possibly by a fifteenth-century follower of Giovanni di Francia. There is also a painting by the Sienese Marco Pino (1525–88), and over the altar in the right-hand apse a *Madonna and Child* by an unknown early sixteenth-century artist.

In the Piazza G. Matteotti, off the Via Cattedrale, are the remains of a **castle,** the headquarters of the French army in 1503; it was from here that the thirteen French knights set out for the famous Challenge of Barletta (see p. 273). We leave Ruvo by the Via Roma, and a short stretch of straight road brings us to Terlizzi.

Map VI
p. 238 Another rich agricultural centre, **Terlizzi,** although of ancient foundation, possesses few buildings of interest. However, a doorway from the destroyed cathedral has been preserved, the work of the thirteenth-century sculptor, Anseramo di Trani, on the right-hand side of the Oratorio della Madonna del Rosario, next to the Chiesa del Purgatorio in the Largo Plebiscito. The main interest lies in the low-relief scenes on the lintel (*Annunciation, Journey of the Magi, Nativity* and *Crucifixion*) and in the rendering of the *Last Supper* in the lunette: the figures of Christ (on the left) and the disciples are shown seated around a table laid with food and wine. The work appeals for its human, homely, down-to-earth qualities.

From the Piazza Plebiscito we take the Corso Vittorio Emanuele

258

and, leaving Terlizzi, cross a terraced countryside broken by little valleys known locally as *lame* (a *lama* is a blade), to meet the SS 98 again at Sovereto. A straight run due east brings us to the interesting town of **Bitonto,** an agricultural centre with fascinating medieval streets and Renaissance palaces and one of the most beautiful cathedrals in Apulia. Archaeological discoveries in the vicinity, which include coins with the superscription 'Butontinon', show that Bitonto was an important settlement of the Peucezi as early as the fourth century BC. Under the Romans Butontum or Butuntum was a staging-post on the Via Traiana, with the privileges of a *municipium*. Sacked by the Catapan Zaccariah in 975, it must have regained prosperity rapidly after the Norman conquest of Southern Italy to be able to embark on the building of so large a cathedral in 1175. To the north-west of the town the troops of Charles III of Bourbon, commanded by the Count of Montemar, defeated the Austrians on May 26th 1734, putting an end to the vice-regal government and re-establishing the Kingdom of Naples.

Map VI
p. 238

We enter Bitonto by the Via Ammiraglio Vacca; at the Piazza L. della Noce we turn right in the Via G. Matteotti, which brings us to an open space at the centre of the town, with the Piazza Margherita di Savoia on our left and the Piazza Marconi ahead of us. The large round *tower* was erected probably *ca.* 1370 as part of the city's defences to the north-east; the walls would have run south to the edge of the Lama di Macina, north-west along the Via Matteotti, then south again to the *lama*, thus enclosing the medieval town. On the right of the tower is one of the old gates, the **Porta Baresana,** and beyond it lies the Piazza Cavour with the baroque church of **S. Gaetano** (1609). At the bottom of the piazza, to the right of the decayed Palazzo Sylos Calo, we take the narrow, busy Via Giandonato Rogadeo. Beyond the church of the **Purgatorio,** with its *memento mori* of human skeletons, we pass under two arches, the second of which is decorated with the armorial bearings of old noble families of Bitonto. On the left is the chapel of one of these families, the **Cappella Rogadeo.** Shortly after, a street on the right brings us out into the Piazza Cattedrale, with its baroque **Guglia dell' Immacolata** and the towering grey mass of the Duomo.

In the **Duomo** dedicated to S. Valentino we see the perfect culmination of that variety of Apulian-Romanesque style of which S. Nicola of Bari is the prototype. One explanation for the homogeneity of structure and ornament may lie in the fact that only twenty-five years elapsed between its foundation and its completion in the year 1200 (though the bands of stonework above the lateral

doorways and the imposts on the pilasters of the façade show that a
portico was originally intended). Deep pilasters separate the nave-
end from that of the aisles; a cornice of draught-board design caps
these pilasters, the pattern repeated above the arches of the corbel-
tables, and continued along the flanks. The pitch of the roofing of
the nave, triforium and wings (that on the right over the open
gallery) is subtly varied. The relation of the openings is equally
successful. High beneath the gable is a magnificent rose window,
with a deep and richly decorated archivolt springing from two
projecting animals on columns. Below this are a pair of double-
arched windows with linking archivolts; and these are flanked on the
same level by the similar, though less ornate, end-windows of the
triforium. Finally, the proportions of the three round-arched doorways relate perfectly to the disposition of the window openings in the
surface area.

The beautiful **central doorway** is composed of two bands of
carving on the jambs and round the head of the arch, the inner with
a delightful pattern of animals amid meandering tendrils, the outer,
more formally, with interlaced tendrils and rosettes. To the side,
slim columns are supported by lions on consoles; the Corinthian
capitals serve as rests for two griffins with feathers like laminated
petals, which bear the imposts of the archivolt. This in turn is
decorated with an exquisitely carved design of acanthus leaves.
Above stands a pelican. On the lintel are representations in low-
relief of the *Annunciation*, *Visitation*, *Epiphany*, and *Presentation in the
Temple*; and in the tympanum a group of seven figures depicts the
Descent into Limbo.

On the right flank are arcades, six deep, and beyond them, in the
transept and the masking wall of the apsidal end, the design is
continued in blind arcading, each main arcade being divided into
two by pilasters as in Bari. The doorway in the last arcade before the
transept (with a sculptured Crucifix in the lunette) is known as the
Porta dell' Scomunica. A superb gallery or loggia runs the length of
the nave, with a pilaster above each pier of the arcade, and five
elegant columns in the intervals supporting double rounded arches.
Because of the depth of the voussoirs, the capitals are elongated
inwards, their surface carved in beautiful designs of foliage and
animals, with Saracenic, Byzantine and Lombard elements in
heterogeneous exuberance. Above this again, four Romanesque
windows give light to the nave. In the transept two orders of pairs of
double-arched windows are surmounted by the beautiful rose
window, again with a deep canopy and projecting animals. The two

central windows of the apsidal end are interesting; the lower one bears a close resemblance to the apse windows of the Duomo and S. Nicola of Bari, with animal supports, free-standing columns, and richly carved archivolt. But most curious is the large window above, where a cluster of short columns raise a deep rounded arch; the influence here is decidedly Saracenic.

The *interior* has had all its trappings removed and the stonework cleaned, so that the full glory of the rounded Romanesque forms can now be seen. The capitals of the pillars and pilasters of the nave are particularly fine. On closer inspection the rich classical regularity of the carving reveals animals and heads of men among the stylized foliage—a typical piece of Lombard fantasy.

On the first pilaster on the left of the nave are the remains of a contemporary fresco of a bishop; the whole interior was once covered with frescoes. On the right, the baptismal font is cut from a single block of stone. Farther along on the same side stands the beautiful *pulpit,* which was put together from fragments of the original tabernacle and high altar by Gualtiero da Foggia in 1240. The magnificent *ambo,* which an inscription tells us is the work of 'Nicolaus sacerdos et magister' (1229), stands against the pilaster at the beginning of the crossing. The semi-circular central section projects between two open-work panels and is divided into decorative squares enclosing roses and studded with polychrome marbles; the puny figure of a man supports a majestic eagle against whose head rests the marble lectern. On the side of the steps at the rear are the doll-like figures of a king and queen and two youths, believed by some to represent the Emperor Frederick II and his family.

At the end of the right aisle a stairway leads to the splendid *crypt.* On a pilaster there are two curious reliefs; an old man serves as a console, and above him at the foot of the shaft is another male figure, with two tails for legs, holding in his hand what appears to be a paint brush. I have been unable to discover the significance of this fantastic being. The crypt which, like the transept, has three apses, is sustained by thirty columns with interesting capitals. There are some remains of fourteenth-century frescoes.

On the left side of the church, opposite the Porta dell' Scomunica, a doorway brings us out into the courtyard of the Bishop's palace. When I was last there the yard contained some good pieces of Romanesque carving among the heaps of rubble.

There are some fascinating medieval churches and palaces in the maze of streets of the old town, among them the *Palace of the Sylos Labini family,* which has been declared a national monument. From the Piazza Duomo we take the Via Antonio Planelli; at No. 51, on the right, is a Catalan-Gothic gateway which opens into the courtyard of the fifteenth-century palace. Facing us is a triple round-arched portico and loggia, with a Renaissance balustrade divided into panels of low-relief carving, except the end panels which contain busts of youths in scalloped niches. In the panel next to the niche on the left, a very feminine figure with a dagger has below it the inscription 'Scipio Africanus'. The work has all the freshness and charm of the early Renaissance, a period of which there are few examples in the deep South.

From the Piazza Marconi the short Via Volta brings us to the *circonvallazione*, in which we turn right and descend to cross the Ponte del Carmine, then continue straight on in the SS 98. At Modugno we join the SS 96 from Altamura and Matera, and crossing the rich countryside, quickly reach the outskirts of Bari, which we enter by the Via Francesco Crispi.

Trani—the only Romanesque portico in Apulia—the Cathedral

Map VI
p. 238

From Bari, we continue for a few miles along the SS 16 (Adriatica) beyond Bisceglie (see p. 252) for the attractive town of **Trani**. On the latter stages the road is lined with limestone workshops, the *pietra* or *marmo di Trani*, much used as facings for buildings. Coming from Barletta, we turn right at the entrance to the town in the Piazza Indipendenza and take the Corso Vittorio Emanuele as far as the well laid out piazza of the same name. Here we turn left in the Via Cavour, which leads from the railway station to the Piazza Plebiscito and to the gardens of the Villa Comunale on the sea.

The first reference to Turenum or Tirenum is from the third or fourth centuries of the Christian era. The destruction of Canosa di Puglia by the Saracens in 872 encouraged the development of the town and port, which became extremely prosperous as a free commune under the Normans, benefiting greatly from the trade which accompanied the Crusades, and rivalling both Barletta and Bari. If we can accept the (rather doubtful) date of their promulgation as 1063, Trani's code of maritime laws, the *Ordinamenta Maris*, are contemporaneous with the more famous *Tavole Amalfitane*. Trani reached the peak of its medieval prosperity under the Emperor Frederick II, who built the castle and strengthened the port defences. With his usual freedom from contemporary prejudices, Frederick placed in the hands of the Jews of Trani the monopoly of the manufacture of silk, which had been introduced from Sicily by Roger the Norman. The city's decline during the Angevin period was accelerated by internecine family feuds. At the end of the fifteenth and the beginning of the sixteenth centuries Trani was pawned to the Venetians by the Aragonese kings of Naples. The existence of literary academies kept alive some spark of intellectual independence during the seventeenth and eighteenth centuries, which lighted up in 1799 when the middle and upper classes sided with the Parthenopean Republic. The people, however, rose against them, and overthrew the revolutionary government; the city was then besieged by the French forces under General Broussier, who finally took it, and sacked and burnt it in April 1799. Today, Trani has a small coastal trade: its chief commercial assets lie in the local production of wine (especially the well-known Moscato di Trani) and of marble.

On the right of the Piazza Plebiscito is the church of **S. Domenico,** a medieval structure possibly of the Angevin period but practically rebuilt in 1763. Some of the original work in the windows on the left flank of the church and in the campanile can be seen from the gardens of the Villa Comunale. The **Villa Comunale** itself has been laid out on what were in the Middle Ages the walls and fortifications guarding the entrance to the port. A shaded walk to the right, past six milestones from the ancient Via Traiana, brings us to the balustraded end of the terrace from where there is a good view southeast to the point of Capo Colonna with its Benedictine abbey and cluster of white villas. At the farther end of the gardens we look back towards the old quarters of the town and follow the curve of the port to its extremity, where Trani cathedral, one of the most surprising and beautiful of all Apulian-Romanesque churches, rises like some baronial castle in Normandy.

From the Piazza Plebiscito the short Via Tiepolo brings us to the Via Statuti Marittimi; here, facing the port, is the baroque church of the **Carmine,** and, on the left, the impressive eighteenth-century **Palazzo Quercia.** Beyond the palace, the Via Statuti Marittimi, bearing slightly to the left, passes under an arch and joins the narrow Via Ognissanti in the heart of the old town. Shortly after the junction we come to the early twelfth-century Romanesque church of **Ognissanti** on the right. The church is unique in Apulia in having the **original portico** (in this case a double one), following the model of Desiderius's church of Montecassino. (In Apulia many of the great cathedrals were designed to include the portico, but either it was never built or, as in the Duomo of Trani, it has not survived.) Ognissanti was erected by the Templars in the courtyard

263

of their hospital, and was used by them until the suppression of the Order in 1312.

The vaulting of the portico is raised on ancient columns. Particularly interesting are the capitals of the columns on either side of the beautiful central doorway, that on the right showing a primitive representation of *St Michael slaying the dragon.* The carving on pilasters beside the door-jambs and continued in the archivolt displays an intricate interweaving of animal and plant motifs. Above, in the lunette, are two rectangular panels of the *Annunciation* in low-relief. The tympana and archivolts of the lateral doorways are also richly carved. The interior consists of a nave and two aisles separated by majestic columns and ending in rounded apses. Over the altar to the right of the high altar is a *Madonna and Child,* possibly the work of a sixteenth-century Cretan painter, Rico da Candia. The sculptured relief of the *Crucifixion* over the altar to the left is interesting. The formality of the folds of Mary's dress and the stylized attitude of her hands and head are quite unlike the mellow (almost soft) plasticity of the clothing and bodies of both St John and Christ, suggesting that this early fourteenth-century work was from an Apulian workshop, where late Byzantine influences were giving way to a return to classical naturalness and the developments of Nicola Pisano.

A short way beyond the church an alleyway leads down to the port; from here we can see the east end of Ognissanti, formed by the three rounded apses. That on the left has above it a double-arched window, in turn surmounted by an open belfry and the central apse has a beautifully decorated window with projecting figures of animals. Farther along the Via Ognissanti, we pass the baroque church of **S. Teresa,** next door to which is a rare southern example of a late Gothic town house, the **Palazzo Caccetta,** built in 1458 by a rich merchant. Only two years later the Aragonese deprived him of his luxurious palace, with its fine rooms and porticoed courtyard. When Trani was pledged to the Venetians by Ferdinand II, it was in the Palazzo Caccetta that their governors resided.

Beyond the Palazzo Caccetta the Via Ognissanti opens out into the Piazza Trieste; here we bear to the left, away from the port, into the Piazza Sacra R. Udienza, and thence, again on the left, into the Piazza C. Battisti where the Municipio faces us. A short street on the right of the building takes us past the **Arcivescovado,** which has been the Archbishop's palace since 1414, and brings us out on to the broad Piazza Duomo where, right on the edge of the sea, the **cathedral church of S. Nicola Pellegrino** stands, overtopped by its soaring campanile: a dazzling brilliance of white stone, triumphantly answering the challenge of the beautiful site. An inscription on the lower part of the campanile reads, 'Nicolaus sacerdos et proto-magister', possibly the same man who was responsible for the beautiful *ambo* at Bitonto in 1229. Besides designing the lower storeys of the campanile, Nicolaus probably also had a hand in the magnificent decoration of the church itself.

On May 20th, 1094, Nicholas the Pilgrim from Livadia in Greece fell unconscious in front of the church of S. Maria della Scala; carried to the near-by hospital, he died on June 2nd. Two years later he was canonized by Pope Urban II and was chosen by the people of Trani as their patron. The new crypt, begun in 1096, cut across the apsidal end of S. Maria, and was intended to receive the Saint's relics. The church of S. Maria is mentioned from the seventh century, and was itself built over the even earlier Ipogeo di S. Leucio, now some five feet below sea-level. Above these edifices rose the present cathedral, which was built mainly between 1159 and 1186, and completed about the middle of the thirteenth century.

From the wide piazza, our first impression of the cathedral is one of light—a *hieron anaduomenon*, a temple rising from the sea, with a façade of the utmost simplicity and elegance.

The **campanile,** too, is one of the most perfect in Apulia. Above the high Saracenic archway at street level are five storeys surmounted by a hexagonal belfry and pyramid. The first two storeys, the work of Nicolaus, are pierced by double-arched windows; each successive upper floor carries one more later Gothic window-arch than the storey below. In 1954 subsidence threatened the structure, which was taken down and rebuilt with the original materials. Like many Apulian-Romanesque roofs, those over the aisles have a step down at their extremities. The upper portions are bounded by a narrow cornice of leaves and beading, and the gable end has a single rounded window. The rose window is surrounded by six animals on projecting consoles, and below this are three simple Romanesque windows, the central one larger and more ornately carved than the other two, and flanked by two delightful toy elephants on consoles, which once supported columns under the lions. The ground level of the cathedral is some sixteen feet above the surface of the piazza. A double ramp of steps leads up to a terrace, both steps and terrace covering the atrium of the earlier church of S. Maria below. The lower portion of the façade has nine blind arcades raised on half columns, the central (larger) arcade forming the single doorway. From the fragments of arches springing from the columns beside the portal, and from the remaining bases for columns on the outer side of the terrace, it is clear that a portico was originally planned. Some authorities believe that it was built and collapsed in 1719.

On the right flank of the church the massive pilasters of the deep arcading are used almost like buttresses. Animals project from the wall face. In the transept above the now familiar pairs of shallow blind arcades, two Romanesque round windows are surmounted by a beautiful rose window below a deep and richly decorated cornice. The east end dispenses with the usual Apulian-Romanesque enclosing wall masking the apsidal ends, and the perfect proportions of the cluster of high semi-circular apses is remarkable; like lofty round-towers, with their plain conical caps, they suggest the fortified châteaux of medieval France. Two windows open in each, and the wider central apse has a large and finely carved window-frame crowned and flanked by animals on consoles.

The carving of the ***western portal*** is one of the masterpieces of Apulian workmanship. The four archivolts on either side of the doorway are crisply cut in an ornately stylized pattern of foliage, with an inner band of rosary beads. The doorway has no lintel or tympanum; the jambs rest on the rear portions of fierce lions (the animal on the right has its paw on a man it is about to devour; that on the left is struggling to the death with a snake and a dragon). Here the Lombard element is in the ascendant; but in the carving on the outside and the inner side of jambs and arch we see other influences at work; and above, in the magnificent archivolt, a Byzantine pattern of iris flowers and deeply incised meandering tendrils is woven around curious figures, where the fantasy of the northern artists has full play. A female centaur clutches a hare in one hand, while with the other she reaches up to pluck a bunch of grapes as she gallops along. A naked man holds by the tail a bird which is grasping his foot in its powerful beak. The panels in the door-jambs consist of representations of mythological and biblical scenes— *the Sacrifice of Isaac, Jacob wrestling with the Angel,* and *Jacob's Dream.*

And here at Trani this wealth of magnificent carving surrounds the original ***bronze doors,*** the first (1175) of the three existing examples of the work of Barisano da Trani—the others are in the Duomo of Ravello and at Monreale in Sicily. In the plastic treatment of the figures on his panels Barisano has departed from the traditional Byzantine manner, and is reaching out for the realism found in classical models, culminating later in the Florentine doors of Andrea Pisano. In the panel above the door-knocker on the right, next to the beautiful *Deposition,* we see the pigmy figure of Barisano kneeling at the feet of S. Nicola.

In the *interior* of the cathedral recent restoration has revealed the spacious austerity of the original structure. In the shape of a Latin cross, the nave is separated from the aisles by pairs of columns (unique in Apulia), and nothing impedes the sweep of the eye over these rounded forms to the airy transept and towering central apse. By stairways at the end of the aisles we descend to the *crypt of S. Nicola,* with its high forest of columns and their beautiful capitals. The relics of the Saint, for which the crypt was erected, were transferred to the church of S. Giacomo (see below) during restoration to the crypt, but will presumably be returned. There are plans to hang here the interesting Byzantine-inspired painting of *S. Nicola the Pilgrim and the Story of his Life*, a fourteenth-century work flanked by sixteen panels with scenes of the Saint's earthly pilgrimage. The cathedral *treasury* also contains an illuminated Neapolitan missal of the fourteenth century, and a curious ivory *altarolo*, thought to be French work of the same period.

From the crypt we pass to the seventh-century church of *S. Maria della Scala,* occupying the space under the nave of the Duomo, which is raised on columns of granite and oriental marble possibly from Roman ruins at Canosa di Puglia. There are remains of frescoes on the left of the church, and of particular interest to art historians is the fresco of the *Madonna between two saints* above the Gothic tomb of Passapepe Lambertini (thirteenth- or early four-teenth-century) on the right. This is now believed to be by Giovanni di Francia (*ca.* 1405–48). By a stairway on the left we descend to the very early *hypogeum of S. Leucio,* built to house the relics of the Saint. This consists of a corridor surrounding a small cell, in which a few years ago I saw a mound of human skulls and bones.

If we continue along the shore from the Piazza Duomo, we come, beyond the Palazzo del Tribunale, to the Piazza Re Manfredi, with the *Castello* built by Frederick II in 1233 and added to under the Angevins by the celebrated military architect Pierre d'Agincourt, who died in Trani in 1310. Today the castle is a prison. At the far end of the piazza from the sea front we take the Via Diego Alvarez, and a short way along, on the left, come to the little church of *S. Giacomo,* which has an interesting Apulian-Romanesque exterior. The interior, which was gutted by fire in 1902, has been restored. From the choir we descend to the crypt, where the tomb of S. Nicola Pellegrino lies during restoration work in the cathedral. Beyond S. Giacomo we turn left into the Via Mario Pagano, a twisting narrow street which cuts through the heart of the old town and is joined in the triangular Piazza della Libertà by the Via Ognissanti.

Just before the piazza, on the right, stand the churches of *S. Andrea* and *S. Francesco,* which both reveal a strong Byzantine tradition in their ground-plan of a Greek cross and their cupolas.

S. Andrea was built in the eleventh century but has lost its original façade; nevertheless, it retains its primitive shape, with three semi-circular apses and a single cupola, round within, but consisting externally of a square drum covered with a pyramid. Classical stonework (probably from Canosa) used in the construction of the church can be seen in the bases of the half columns in the walls and the inscription from a milestone of the time of Constantine in the first column on the right. S. Francesco was begun by the Benedic-tines in 1176 and consecrated to the Trinity in 1184; in the sixteenth century it came into the possession of the Franciscans and was rededicated. The exterior of S. Francesco shows the early form, with its three oriental cupolas and its simply adorned façade. Inside, baroque decoration overlays much of the primitive austerity.

The old streets and piazzas, churches, palaces and period houses of Trani are attractive, and about a mile south-east of the town, on Map VI p. 238 the farther side of Capo Colonna, is the **Lido of S. Maria di Colonna,** with a long narrow stretch of good sand, easily reached by bus. On the way to the point, along the esplanade of the Lungomare Cristoforo Colombo, there are a number of seaside *trattorias* special-izing in locally-caught fish: the Scialla Cristoforo Colombo, for example, which is built out over the sea.

The *abbey of S. Maria di Colonna* was begun by the Benedic-tines in 1104, when building of the new cathedral of S. Nicola forced them to vacate their church of S. Maria della Scala. Parts of the church and former monastery (which was taken over by the Franciscans in 1427 until its dissolution in 1867), date from the original construction. On the edge of the bay to the west of the point is the Sorgente di Cristo, a spring with reputed laxative properties. To the east is the popular **Spiaggia di S. Maria di Colonna.** In recent years a suburb of villas has arisen along the foreshore and in the regularly planned streets behind, including a number of small *pensioni,* among them the Pensione il Paese del Sole. Trani itself has a Jolly Hotel, the Motel Autocomfort (with restaurant), and three very plain hotels, without restaurants: the Italia, the Adriatico, and the Romagna.

Andria

For the important agricultural centre of **Andria,** south-west of
Trani, we leave Trani by the road at the north-western extremity of
the Corso Vittorio Emanuele, and climb the murge, the low hills
where many of the quarries for the celebrated *pietra di Trani* are
located. From Barletta we take the SS 170 *dir*, which continues on
through a rather featureless countryside to Castel del Monte.

Map VI
p. 238

In Roman times there was a posting-station (called Rudae or
Budae) on the Via Traiana near the present city, but the earliest
historical record of Andria comes from the end of the ninth century,
when we hear of the *loco Andre* as being a possession of the Counts of
Trani. The town rose rapidly in importance under the Normans and
Hohenstaufen, especially under the Emperor Frederick II who
granted it fiscal immunities and was later to praise its loyalty. In the
cathedral lie buried two of Frederick's wives. The Angevins raised
Andria to the status of a duchy, granting it in fief to the del Balzo
family. After a brief possession by Gonsalvo di Cordova, the duchy
was held by the Carafas from 1552 until the close of the eighteenth
century. Yet it was a Carafa, the young Ettore, who joined the
French at the time of the Parthenopean Republic and took a leading
part in the siege of the city, which had remained loyal to the Bourbons. He later paid the price for putting his liberal ideals into action
on the scaffold in the Piazza del Mercato in Naples. The blood-
thirsty scenes when Andria was taken by the French on March 23rd,
1799, were to be repeated at Trani, and by the Sanfedisti at Altamura.

The Barletta road enters the city by the Via Francesco Ferrucci,
which will bring us to the Piazza Vittorio Emanuele, the centre of
the old town. However, we may turn right in the circular road at the
beginning of the built-up area for the ***Porta S. Andrea,*** the only
surviving medieval gate (but transformed in 1593), where Frederick
II's tribute to Andria's loyalty is inscribed: *Imperator Fredericus ad
Andrianos—Andria fidelis nostris affixa medullis.* Continuing in the Via
Porta Nuova, we come to the Piazza Ettore Carafa, from which the
Via S. Maria Vetere leads to the church of that name. In the
convent attached to the church are three paintings from a polyptych
by Antonio Vivarini (1467); the remaining parts are in the Bari
Provincial Gallery. From the Piazza Carafa the Via Porta la Barra
brings us to the church of ***S. Agostino,*** with a remarkable fourteenth-

century Gothic portal. The church was founded in 1230 by the Teutonic Knights, but was transferred to the Augustinians in 1316. Standing isolated on the pavement in front of the doorway are two stumpy antique columns with medieval capitals. The broad decorated bands which form the jambs and lightly pointed arch are contained within a rectilinear frame. Their rich carving is mostly in low-relief, with the unusual exception of the outermost band which consists of bold ribbons enclosing at regular intervals square panels with formalized floral motifs. In the lunette, *Christ heralded by angels* appears between S. Remigio and S. Leonardo, a characterless piece of carving. The interior of the church has been baroqued.

On the left of S. Agostino the Via Flavio Giugno leads down to the church of **S. Maria di Porta Santa,** a fifteenth-century church with a Renaissance doorway, in the pilasters of which are two medallions said to represent *the Emperor Frederick and his son Manfred.* Opposite S. Maria, we take the Via Porta Santa; beyond the archway we turn left in the Via Flavia de Excelis, passing (on the left) the medieval Palazzo Sgaramella; thence, by way of the Via La Corte and, to the right, the Via Vaglio, we arrive in the Piazza Vittorio Emanuele. On one side of the piazza is the flank of the **Palazzo Ducale,** which is entered from the adjoining Piazza La Corte. The Carafa Dukes altered and enlarged the medieval structure at the end of the sixteenth century, and again two hundred years later. From the piazza the Via Corrado IV di Svevia brings us to the church of **S. Domenico,** begun in 1398 by the Orsini wife of Duke Francesco I del Balzo, but subsequently much altered. In the sacristy is a powerfully realistic bust of *Francesco II* by Francesco Laurana (1472), depicting this shrewd and unscrupulous del Balzo in the habit of a tertiary; his mummified remains are conserved beneath.

From the Piazza La Corte we pass to the adjacent Piazza Duomo, with the **cathedral of the Assunta** and its fine campanile, begun in 1118 (the first storey is from this time) and added to from the thirteenth to the fifteenth century. The fabric of the Duomo is of many periods, from the ninth- or tenth-century crypt to the façade with its atrium-portico designed by Frederico Santacroce in 1844. Restoration of the interior has been going on for several years. The great Gothic arch of the choir was built by the local architect Alessandro Guadagno in 1365. Off the left transept is the Cappella di S. Riccardo, where the Italian champions of the Challenge of Barletta are said to have prayed for victory on their way to the combat (see p. 273). S. Riccardo, the patron saint of Andria, was an Englishman who, according to tradition, arrived here in 492 and became the town's first bishop. In the treasury is a reliquary containing the Saint's bones, and a statue of him in silver. Among other works of art in the Duomo are a Byzantine-type painting of the *Madonna and Child*, thought to be the work of a Tuscan artist of *ca.* 1275, and a very striking crucifix in painted wood, possibly by a thirteenth-century Spanish carver.

The stairs at the beginning of the right-hand aisle lead down to the crypt, which is basilican in form, with a semi-circular apse, and preceded by an atrium. Two plain slabs cover the tombs which are traditionally believed to be those of two of the wives of the Emperor Frederick II—Yolande of Jerusalem and Isabella of England. One of the remaining frescoes shows *Christ blessing* in the Greek manner.

Not far from the cathedral is the church of **S. Francesco,** begun in 1230 and completed by Bonanno da Barletta in 1346, but transformed in the eighteenth century. Two Gothic doorways remain, one with a band of enclosed square panels with rose decorations similar to that of S. Agostino.

For Canosa di Puglia we leave Andria by the Via Annunziata. The road crosses a countryside of low hills with vineyards and olive-groves, passing the large building of the Agricultural Institute, the Podere Papparicotta. At several points we have glimpses of the sea and of the Castel del Monte away to the south. Then from the hilltop we see ahead of us the white buildings of Canosa (see p. 278 *et seq.*).

Barletta—the only contemporary likeness of Frederick II—the Challenge of Barletta—the Duomo

I have a long-standing affection for **Barletta,** a market-town and port full of reminders of the Crusades, of Richard Cœur de Lion, the Emperor Frederick II, and Manfred. It also has a good bathing beach, the Spiaggia di Levante, just beyond the massive bulwarks of the castle. Barletta, which was probably colonized from Illyria, on the opposite coast of the Adriatic, was variously known to the ancients as Bardulum, Barduli, Bardulos or Baretum. In Roman times it was the port for the rich hinterland around Canosa di Puglia. Under the Normans it became an important trading post and fortress, its population increased by the inhabitants of near-by Canne after Robert Guiscard's destruction of that city in 1083. Before leaving Barletta for the Holy Land in 1228, Frederick II, that

Map VI
p. 238

271

successful though excommunicated crusader, proclaimed there his son Henry as heir, the same Henry who later revolted against his father and rode his horse over a cliff at Martirano in Calabria. Barletta was also the favourite residence of the ill-fated Manfred, Frederick's legitimized son by Bianca Lancia. As early as 1345 an English traveller writes of the beauty of the women of Barletta in their black silk cloaks.

In the centre of the town, at the junction of the Corso Vittorio Emanuele with the Corso Garibaldi, is the church of S. Sepolcro. On the left flank of S. Sepolcro, the level of which is some feet below that of the street, stands the bronze *statue of the Colossus*. This crude but impressive figure (it is 16 ft high) is now usually considered to be a fourth-century representation of the Emperor Valentinian, and a good specimen of those colossal imperial statues so popular at the close of antiquity. It was looted from Constantinople in the thirteenth century by Venetian sailors who were then shipwrecked off Barletta. Found lying on the beach, it was presented to the Dominicans of Manfredonia, who apparently cut off the hands and legs to use for their church bells. In 1491 these mutilations were made good by the Neapolitan sculptor Fabio Alfano, and the statue placed where it now stands.

S. Sepolcro is perhaps the earliest example of the use of predominantly Gothic forms in Southern Italy. It was built at the end of the thirteenth century, incorporating an older edifice of customary basilican plan. The central bay was once covered with an octagonal lantern and spire, which collapsed in the earthquake of 1731. An arcaded atrium, of which the bases of the pillars alone remain, formerly preceded the entrance. Inside we are confronted with an unusual narthex, the nave being seen through the wide span of a pointed arch. The font, immediately to the right, is also of the thirteenth century. Both the nave and aisles have high Gothic arches, and the aisles are covered by pointed groined vaults. In the left-hand aisle is a painting of the Madonna. Its Byzantine influence is seen again in the remains of the thirteenth-century frescoes in the apsidal end.

On the same side of the Corso Vittorio Emanuele, about a hundred yards away from the Colossus, is one of the many charming theatres found in these former Neapolitan provinces, the **Communal Theatre Giuseppe Curci** (a musician of Barletta, 1808–77). It was built in the last century in the 'classical' style by Frederico Santacroce, the architect who designed the atrium of the cathedral at Andria. The stuccoed façade, with its high niches enclosing busts of

Above The octagonal Castel del Monte, favourite castle of the Emperor Frederick II, was built *ca* 1240. *Below left* The main entrance, of marble, represents an attempt to revive the classical architecture of the triumphal arch, but it is overmastered by the Gothic elements of the elongated proportions, pointed arches and elegant window. *Right* In the Castello of Gioia del Colle is the so-called throne of Frederick II.

Right The façade of Troia cathedral is a harmonious blending of Lombard sculpture, Byzantine capitals, Saracenic window-tracery and Pisan arcading.

Below Detail of high relief from the bronze doors, 1119.

musical celebrities, is very attractive, as is the arcade on the left, running the whole depth of the theatre, with its beautifully proportioned doorways and tiered galleries.

Retracing our steps past the Colossus, we turn left into the Corso Garibaldi. On the right is the damaged baroque church of S. Domenico, and opposite the seventeenth-century palace of the Counts of Lesina, now the Bank of Naples. At this point the Via Cavour opens out to the right and on either side we can see arched doorways and windows from medieval palaces retained in later buildings. These were once the counting-houses of Florentine bankers who linked Barletta with their agents in Bruges, Antwerp and Lombard Street. A few steps from the Corso Garibaldi, again on the right, is the **Communal Museum and Picture Gallery** (admission, weekdays 9.0 a.m.–1.0 p.m., 5.0–7.0 p.m.; Sundays 9.0 a.m.–12.0 noon), which houses an interesting collection of paintings, including work by Barletta artists and members of the Schools of Naples, Posillipo and Portici. It also contains a bust of the Emperor Frederick II, the only contemporary likeness we have, which even in its mutilated state conveys something of the enigmatic character of that remarkable man.

Continuing along the Corso Garibaldi in the direction of the port, we see ahead of us, on the corner of the now narrower street, one of the best-preserved Gothic palaces in Barletta, the **Palazzo Bonelli,** built in 1324 in the reign of Robert the Wise of Anjou. The courtyard within is surrounded by an arcade, which supports a gallery above. Opposite is the baroque church of the Purgatorio.

At the next crossroad the Via Duomo leads to the cathedral and to the church of S. Andrea, but we shall first turn left into the little Piazza della Disfida. On the left is a Gothic palace with two pointed-arched doorways: the hostelry, the **Cantina della Disfida,** whose cellars were in the Middle Ages the scene of the famous **Challenge of Barletta.** The French under the Duke of Nemours and the Spaniards led by Gonsalvo di Cordova, 'il Gran Capitano', were in Italy for the purpose of dispossessing the successors of Alfonso il Magnanimo of their Neapolitan Kingdom. They had fallen out among themselves, and in February 1503, Gonsalvo was being besieged in Barletta by Nemours. During a sortie under the city walls, a band of Italians fighting alongside the Spaniards inflicted a sharp defeat on the French, and some French knights were taken prisoner, among them Guy de la Motte. According to the custom, the prisoners were entertained by their captors, and at a vinous gathering in the tavern La Motte loudly expressed his opinion that all Italians were faithless, ignorant of the use of arms, despicable soldiers, and traitors. With Ettore Fieramosca as their leader, the Italians demanded satisfaction. It is said that the French chose thirteen combatants on each side, and fixed on February 13th as the date of combat because of the widely-held belief that Italians were cravenly superstitious. The fight was to be on neutral ground, and for this reason the farm of *S. Elia,* just off the road leading from Andria to Corato, was chosen, as being under the jurisdiction of Trani, at that time in the possession of Venice. (A signpost directs the motorist up a paved track to the stone memorial—rebuilt in 1846—that marks the spot where the Challenge took place.) One of the two umpires was the Frenchman Bayard, the 'chevalier sans peur et sans reproche'.

The result was an overwhelming defeat of the French, their humiliation made even more bitter by being led back as prisoners to Barletta, since in their arrogance they had neglected to bring with them the agreed ransom in case of capture. At the Porta S. Leonardo the victors were met by a procession bearing from the cathedral Paolo Serafini da Modena's marvellous painting of the Virgin and Child, known henceforth as the *Madonna della Disfida.*

The cellars of the Cantina have been restored, but the attempt to reconstruct the medieval appearance by a collection of contemporary utensils and furnishings is not very convincing. A plaster group (1866) of the kind enjoyed by Victorian medievalists, the work of Achille Stocchi, shows Fieramosca striking down the Frenchman La Motte. Around the walls hang the armorial bearings of the thirteen Italian champions of the Challenge. At the rear the cellars descend to an even greater depth; to the right a shaft connected the kitchens with the palace above.

If we turn left on leaving the Cantina, and continue along the Via Cialdini, we see on the right the seventeenth-century palace of the Monte di Pietà, next door to the damaged church of the Jesuits (1630). A few yards farther on is another baroque palace in the very different style of some eighty years earlier, the **Palazzo della Marra.** The prominent Marra family settled in Barletta in 1170 in the wake of Frederick Barbarossa, but had died out by the end of the eighteenth century. The sadly neglected palace has a doorway with fantastically carved consoles above, reminiscent of the work of Leccean sculptors. The internal courtyard is surrounded by superimposed arcades, richly decorated with allegorical statues.

In the streets leading back from the Via Cialdini towards the Corso Vittorio Emanuele there are many old palaces: some with

274

pointed-arched doorways, some of the Renaissance, and some later. In their central courts may be seen several examples of open stairways, the work of the Neapolitan school of Sanfelice or of architects directly influenced by it. However, for the moment we shall turn away from this quarter and take the opposite direction towards the port.

The **Porta Marina,** the monumental gateway at the entrance to the port, was built in 1751 by Charles III of Bourbon through the now long since demolished city walls. From here the ramparts and bastions of the *castle* can be seen. Rebuilt in the thirteenth century by Frederick II on an earlier Norman fortress, it was long known as the Castello Svevo; the four corner bastions were added by Charles V in 1532–7, when he remodelled the older structure. In the lunettes of three Saracenic arched windows in the courtyard (to the left as one enters) is the Hohenstaufen eagle in low-relief. The castle was shelled by Austrian warships in the First World War.

From the Jolly Hotel in the garden in front of the castle, it is a short walk to the *cathedral of S. Maria Maggiore*; the street passes under the fine campanile. The Duomo of Barletta sums up both the architectural and historical associations with the Crusaders in Apulia during the Middle Ages. From the front, one is immediately aware of the height of the nave, with its large circular window, compared with that of the aisles. The windows and doorways are richly carved with animals and grotesque figures. (Some have deciphered in these Lombardo-Byzantine carvings a cryptogram alluding to Richard Cœur de Lion and William the Good of Sicily.) The two lateral doors are ogival, but the central one was rebuilt after 1500 in the Renaissance style. Above the left-hand doorway is a eulogy in medieval Latin to its royal donor, Richard Cœur de Lion. The older Romanesque parts of the building, including the sacristy, can best be seen from the small piazza on the right-hand side of the church.

Facing the Duomo and separated only by the narrow street, is the **Palazzo Santacroce,** with one well-preserved pointed-arched doorway. And on the other side of the Via Duomo are the time-worn doors of the little **oratory of S. Pietro** (rebuilt in 1595), which has inside an early *quattrocento* painting of the *Dead Christ and Scenes of the Passion*, attributed by some authorities to Giovanni di Francia.

On entering the Duomo we are again struck by the height of the nave. The first four arches are from the earlier Apulian-Romanesque basilica, begun by Simiacca of Barletta in 1150. The columns supporting these arches are antique and have fine capitals; above,

275

the triforium of coupled arches is also the work of Norman builders. Massive nave piers mark the beginning of the Gothic extension of 1307, under the Angevins; the ambulatory and polygonal apse were added in the developed French Gothic style of the early fifteenth century. The pulpit (*ca.* 1260) on the right is supported by four slender columns; two further columns have been removed and now stand beside the bishop's throne. The tabernacle over the high altar is a good nineteenth-century reconstruction of an earlier one, dismantled in the seventeenth century. Just before the steps to the ambulatory on the right are two small low-reliefs let into the wall by the sacristy door—*Christ's Entry into Jerusalem* and *the Last Supper*, fragments from the original Romanesque central doorway. Round the apse are tombstones of ecclesiastics. Barletta was the seat of the Archbishops of Nazareth from 1291, when the Franks abandoned Syria, until the see was abolished in 1818. In the central niche of the apse hangs Serafini's beautiful *Madonna della Disfida*, painted in 1387. There is a painting of the Redeemer on the reverse, which is not visible. Near by is one of the few works known of the painter Giovanni di Francia, a strange picture of the *Trinity and the Dormition of the Virgin*; there is also a painting of the *Madonna* by Giovanni in the art gallery.

Outside the cathedral we take the Via Duomo, returning towards the centre of the town, to the crossroads. Here we turn right in the Via S. Andrea, which brings us almost immediately to the much frequented little church of **S. Andrea,** built in the twelfth century and known as Il Salvatore until it was enlarged in 1528. The Romanesque doorway, although much mutilated, is of great interest and beauty. In the Byzantine carving we see the last of the long Hellenic heritage in the sharp-cut foliage and vine tendrils meandering round peacocks, eagles and gentle animals. The low-relief in the lunette above the door shows *Christ blessing between the Madonna and St John the Baptist* (thirteenth century). The inscription below tells us that this is the work of Simeon of Ragusa, then living in Trani.

If the front door to the church is closed, there is a door at the far end on the right. Inside, in the first chapel on the right is a rather poor painting, the *Madonna of the Angels*, by the Lucanian Mattia Preti, considered by some to be the last of the important seventeenth-century Neapolitans. The adjoining chapel contains sepulchres of the Fraggiani family, with hard-headed effigies. On either side of the main altar are two sculptured figures, that on the left of *St Michael*; that on the right, of *St John the Baptist*, a fine piece of simple, strong carving. In the chapel to the right of the high altar are twenty-seven busts of saints in gilded wood, possibly Neapolitan work of the seventeenth century. The sacristy has a fine *cassone*, two paintings of the *Madonna* (one Byzantine and the other by Cristoforo da Lendinara who died in 1491), and, above all, a beautiful *Madonna and Child* by Alvise Vivarini, signed and dated 1483.

The battlefield of Cannae

A pleasant excursion from Barletta to Canosa di Puglia may be combined with a visit to the battlefield of **Cannae.** We leave the centre of the city by the Corso Garibaldi and its continuation in the Via Imbriani; beyond the railway line this becomes the Via di Canosa and then the SS 93 (Apulo–Lucana). A turning on the right for **Canne della Battaglia** leads between hedges of rosemary to the Map IV p. 192 recently discovered *Christian cemetery* and *Apulian village.* About one hundred yards before the archaeological area, a large menhir of the Bronze Age stands in a field on the left, the most northern menhir yet found in Apulia. It appears that the village was of some importance between the sixth and third centuries BC; was probably destroyed in the battle of 216 BC, and remained abandoned until it became a burial ground (the graves grouped around a small church) in the Middle Ages. The new Viale Panoramico takes us shortly to the Antiquarium and the excavations of the Citadel of Cannae. Beyond the Antiquarium the road goes on to the railway station of Canne della Battaglia, in the vicinity of which are the remains of a Roman villa-farm.

From the high ground, before the murge fall away to the valley of the River Ofanto (the Aufidus of the ancients), we look out over the Tavoliere to the north, bounded by the mountains of the Gargano. Authorities differ over the precise site of the battle, one of the most famous in antiquity; but it seems likely that the main action took place near where we are standing, on the flat and rising ground to the south of the Ofanto.

On the outbreak of the Second Punic War in 218 BC, Hannibal, eluding the troops of Scipio, crossed over the Alps, and to the consternation of the Romans, carried the war into Italy. After the crushing defeat of a large army in the vicinity of Lake Trasimene in the spring of 217 the road to Rome lay open. Hannibal, however, marched south into Apulia, where he could find ample supplies of corn and new mounts for his cavalry, and only in August 216 was the reinforced Roman army ready to attack. Hannibal placed his light troops in the centre, with instructions to retire before the heavy-armed legionaries. The Roman charge on the centre carried them too far, whereupon the heavy troops on the Carthaginian wings turned inwards on the unprotected Roman flanks. The Numidian cavalry then fell upon the rear, and the encirclement was complete. Out of an army of between 50–80,000 men, the Romans lost 25–50,000 dead and some 10,000 prisoners. Only 4,000 succeeded in escaping to Canosa. With the whole of Southern Italy in his power, Hannibal could have again marched on Rome; but once more he let the occasion slip. Livy wrote of the Romans: 'No other people would have been able to survive so great a disaster.'

In the *Antiquarium* there are plans of the battle, and archaeological material from the excavations of the Roman town, the newly-discovered Apulian village and the medieval necropolis. The collection of vases includes some neolithic ones painted in geometric designs, among the earliest to have been found in Italy.

Canosa di Puglia—the Cathedral and Bohemond's tomb

Map IV
p. 192 Returning to the SS 93, we resume our run to **Canosa di Puglia,** built on a hill from which there are wide views over the Tavoliere and the valley of the River Ofanto. Canusion (Latin Canusium), founded according to the legend by Diomedes, may well have had a Greek origin; certainly the citizens were still bilingual at the time of Augustus, and their coins were inscribed in Greek. After its occupation by the consul L. Plautius in 318 BC Canusium became a Roman ally, and as such it welcomed the Roman survivors from Cannae. It owed its prosperity at this time to the production of vases and the trade in wool; some idea of Canusian wealth and elegance can be gained from the objects found in graves, among them an exquisite golden diadem set with coloured stones and enamels, now in the Taranto Museum. As a staging-post on the Via Traiana, Canusa retained its importance, and in the fourth century AD became the capital of the region and seat of the governor, the *corrector Apuliae et Calabriae*. The appointment of a bishop in 374 makes it the oldest diocese in Apulia. Destroyed by the Saracens in 835, it was rebuilt but never regained its earlier position, and the ecclesiastical and political hegemony passed to Bari.

In the centre of the town, on the Piazza S. Sabino, is the *cathedral of S. Sabino,* dedicated to the memory of a sixth-century bishop of Canosa. The church was begun about the middle of the eleventh
278

century in a predominantly Byzantine style; it is therefore one of the oldest of existing Apulian cathedrals, belonging to the first phase of Apulian-Romanesque before Byzantine models had been transformed by influences from the north. This is best seen from the gardens of the Villa Comunale, on the right of the Duomo, since the façade and front sections are later additions carried out from the seventeenth to the last century. From the gardens we can see the characteristic domes and, below the level of the balustrade, the strikingly oriental tomb of Bohemond. The structure of the original church begins beyond the third arcade from the main doorway. The five cupolas are raised on free-standing monolithic columns of *verde antico*, *cipollino* and granite, from ancient Canusium. Inside on the left stands the tall, rather primitive pulpit, built by Archdeacon Acceptus about 1050, but reconstructed in 1905, showing in its decoration both Byzantine and Arab sources. The ciborium in the centre of the crossing is a modern imitation. Behind it in the deep semi-circular apse of the original building (the smaller apse on the left is later) the earlier canons' seats have been covered over in the reconstruction of 1905. The bishop's throne shows that the sculptor Romualdus (1078–89) was still leaning heavily on Byzantine and Saracenic models—even the sturdy elephants which support the seat are highly formalized. Inscribed verses offer the occupant of the chair a prescription for ordering his earthly life so that he will achieve a heavenly throne.

On the left of the church is the **tomb of S. Sabino.** The **treasury** contains a curious cross-reliquary; the cross itself appears to be Byzantine work and older than the emaciated figure of Christ, which may be a local thirteenth-century copy of a Spanish crucifix. Another curiosity is the liturgical fan (*flabello liturgico*) which, according to the local tradition, belonged to S. Sabino. This beautiful object, with its finely carved handle and fan of gaily painted parchment, came from the Ukraine, but the work seems undeniably Arabic. From either of the side aisles we descend into the unusually deep **crypt,** its roof raised on tall columns with antique capitals. A door at the end of the right transept brings us to a courtyard and the **tomb of Bohemond** against the wall of the Duomo. The courtyard also contains two columns, pieces of Roman and medieval sculpture and inscriptions, and the remains of a Hellenic torso.

Bohemond, a son of Robert Guiscard by Alberada, his first wife (later repudiated), was the Prince of Antioch, in which city he died in 1111; at his own request his mother buried him at Canosa, and built this oriental mausoleum: a veritable *turbeh funéraire*, of the kind erected in front of a mosque. Square in plan, with a small semi-circular apse at its east end, it is surmounted by an octagonal drum containing a round-arched window on each outer face, and covered by a low egg-shaped dome. The blind arcading of the walls is supported on pilasters and consoles. Particularly fine are the solid bronze doors by Roger of Melfi. Here again we see a combined Byzantine-Mohammedan inspiration in the decoration of the two leaves which compose the door: the right-hand leaf is divided into four panels, of which the two middle show Byzantine figures that once were inlaid with silver; the upper and lower panels have raised circular discs of Arabic interlaced motifs. The leaf on the left has three similar decorative circles, the centre containing a door-knocker in the form of a lion-head mask. The inscriptions recall Bohemond's virtues and the name of the artist. The interior is plain; the cupola is formed by the use of pendentives; the tombstone is inscribed simply BOAMUNDUS.

Among the trees and flower-beds of the gardens of the Villa Comunale are a number of Roman sculptural remains, some from the amphitheatre. A classical column was raised here in 1958 in memory of Scipio Africanus, who is said to have sworn an oath in Canusium never to rest until he had wiped out the disgrace of Cannae (he finally defeated Hannibal in Africa in 202 BC). From the Villa the Corso S. Sabino runs up to the Piazza della Repubblica, with its column of the Immacolata, erected in 1750. The piazza opens out on the right to the Piazza Martiri della Libertà, with the Municipio housed in a former Franciscan monastery. From the piazza we may ascend by way of the Via Trieste e Trento to the ruins of the medieval castle, built on what was in classical times the city's acropolis. From here there opens out a wide panorama.

Back in the Piazza della Repubblica, we take the Corso Garibaldi (to the right), turn left in the Via Carlo Alberto, then right again in the Via Generale Cadorna, and arrive in the zone of the ***Ipogei Lagastra.*** These, the largest of the many funerary chambers in Canosa (several of which are now built over) may have been constructed as early as the fourth century BC, but were used again in later times. A custodian will show visitors over them (tip). The Ipogei Lagastra were excavated in 1843, and contained skeletons, some with traces of their gold-embroidered dresses, lying on beds of gilded bronze with objects of adornment and practical use on marble tables or on the floor beside them. The rock faces and roofs were often decorated, and we can still see the painted stucco on columns and in one room a *trompe l'œil* communicating doorway. The richness
280

of the jewellery, vases and glassware found in these tombs gives some idea of the luxury of Roman Canusium.

From the Via Trieste e Trento the Via Varrone, curving down the hill, brings us to the SS 98 for Cerignola, which runs beside the ancient Via Traiana. On our left, a short way past the railway crossing, is a **Roman arch** of the second century AD, the brick remains of which were formerly faced with marble. The Via Traiana was once flanked by tombs and funerary monuments, some of which still remain, such as the so-called **Torre Casieri,** beyond the arch, the **mausoleum** of the Augustan age a little farther on, and still farther, the **Monumento Bagnoli** of the second century AD, which has recently been restored. Just over a mile from Canosa, to the left of the modern bridge over the River Ofanto, is the **Ponte Romano,** partly rebuilt in the Middle Ages. And outside Canosa, to the south-east, off the Andria road, a very early Byzantine basilican church dedicated to **S. Leucio** has recently been discovered; built largely with Roman stonework, it is at the moment being excavated and restored.

CHAPTER 16

The Murge

Maps: VI, p.238; VII, p.292

The *murge* are the low limestone hills (for the most part between 1000 and 1500 ft in height) which occupy the central area of Apulia, south of the River Ofanto and north of the isthmus between Taranto and Brindisi. On the west they run into Basilicata as far as the valleys of the Rivers Basentello and Bradano; on the east they fall as terraces to the Adriatic Sea. In the north-west and west the horizon appears flat, but the land is cut by deep ravines (*gravine*) formed by the erosion of the limestone; the shallow, whitish soil, which grows some light wheat and provides a scanty pasturage, is pitted with outcrops of rock, fully deserving the name of *Puglia petrosa*—stony Apulia. The south-eastern area, the so-called *murge dei trulli*, is very different, especially the area between Conversano, Alberobello, Fasano and Locorotondo; here erosion has furnished a rich rust-coloured topsoil, as fertile as the coastal terraces, and covered with luxurious vegetation; only the presence of caves, such as those of Castellana and Putignano, reveals the limestone beneath.

Altamura—Gravina di Puglia

One interesting expedition from Bari takes us to Altamura, Gravina di Puglia, Gioia del Colle and back via Acquaviva delle Fonti. For Altamura and Gravina di Puglia we take the SS 96 (Barese), which crosses the arid western uplands before passing into Basilicata to join the Via Appia at the Bivio di Tricarico, and continuing to Potenza. We leave Bari by the Via Francesco Crispi, and at the small town of Modugno turn off left for **Bitetto** which has an interesting Apulian-Romanesque *cathedral,* erected in the eleventh century and added to by Lillo di Barletta in 1335, as we learn from an inscription above the central doorway. It is a curious group of buildings; the façade appears unaltered, but to the left stands a

Map VI
p. 238

282

baroque campanile of 1764, and behind it and to the right of the nave rise two lofty domes, the larger of them covered with yellow and green patterned tilework. The central portal has a finely decorated architrave and archivolt supported on columns borne by two lions. The lunette contains a low-relief *Madonna and Child with two angels* which suggests a Provençal influence. Christ appears among his Apostles on the lintel, and the jambs have representations of scenes from his life. The interior has been horribly baroqued. In the streets off the piazza we find fragments of the medieval walls, with their towers, some interesting doorways of early dwellings, and the Casa Fazio (in Via Leonese), once the property of the Knights of Malta.

From Bitetto we return to the Statale at **Palo del Colle,** a country town with an old quarter on the higher ground around the cathedral, known as Terra di Palo, as distinct from the more modern Borgo. The *cathedral of S. Maria della Porta* was erected in the twelfth century, but was modified and partly rebuilt in the sixteenth. The façade follows the style of S. Nicola di Bari (see p. 244), with the exception of the doorways which are in the style of the Renaissance. Built into the left transept and forming part of the original Romanesque structure is the high and graceful campanile, one of the most elegant of its kind, the model for several others in the region. The interior of the church has recently been partly restored. In the near-by Piazza S. Croce are some interesting *palaces,* particularly those of the Princes Filamarino della Rocca and the della Mura family. Map VI p. 238

After Palo del Colle the road continues to climb the steps of the murge through dull countryside, the vineyards, olive groves and clumps of oak giving way at higher levels to desolate patches of cornland and rough pasturage. **Altamura,** standing on a hill of the high murge some 1500 ft above sea-level, can be seen in the distance. In 1799 Altamura witnessed some of the worst atrocities of the Sanfedisti. Having enthusiastically sided with the Parthenopean Republic and refused to surrender to the army of Cardinal Ruffo, the town was finally taken and put to sack, amid fearful scenes of carnage, looting and arson. Map VI p. 238

The present city owes its foundation to the 'baptized sultan', the Emperor Frederick II, who in 1230 brought here a mixed population of Greeks, Italians and Jews with promises of municipal privileges. The ancient town of the Peucezi, the origins of which were prehistoric, was destroyed and depopulated by the Saracens possibly in the ninth century. Large stretches of the fifth-century BC walls still exist, as well as two gates and sections of the Angevin fortifications. In the eighteenth century Altamura had a certain intellectual pre-eminence in Apulia and possessed its own university from 1748 until the disaster of 1799. Today it is a market town and commercial centre with a few light industries. In the old quarters there are some notable buildings, particularly the cathedral, one of the very few churches raised by Frederick II.

We enter Altamura by way of the Piazza Unità d'Italia and the medieval Porta di Bari, on the left of which are some remains of the late thirteenth-century walls. On the right of the piazza the Viale Regina Margherita runs down to the station, and a short way along the avenue (again to the right) is a section of the megalithic walls of the earlier city. Through the gateway we arrive in the Corso Frederico II di Svevia, the principal artery of the old quarter, which brings us to the Piazza del Duomo. Between the Porta di Bari and the Duomo is the attractively simple little church of **S. Nicolo dei Greci,** built in the thirteenth century by Frederick's Greek subjects, where the liturgy was conducted according to the Greek rite until 1601. The Gothic doorway is decorated with carvings of *Scenes from the Old and New Testaments*.

The Piazza del Duomo has a monument to the martyrs of 1799, and is flanked by the south-east wall of the **cathedral of the Assunta,** one of the four palatine basilicas of Apulia (the others are S. Nicola di Bari and the cathedrals of Barletta and Acquaviva delle Fonti). The building, begun by Frederick in 1228 (or 1232), was much damaged by earthquake in 1316 and subsequently rebuilt; but the greatest structural alteration was made in 1534, when the church was reorientated, the main portal and rose window being carefully dismantled and replaced in their present position, which was previously the apsidal end. The two campanili were erected in the same century, but their baroque onion domes and pinnacles were added in 1729. The loggia between the towers, with its figure of the *Assunta,* is also baroque. The original Gothic window from the apse is now seen in the left-hand section of the façade, next to the three armorial bearings (the central *stemma* is that of the Emperor Charles V). The beautiful rose window is deeply recessed, with three bands of ornate carving, the rays of short columns terminating in a rich interweaving of fretted stonework.

The main portal, somewhat later in date than the rose window (possibly early fourteenth-century), is reputed to be the most richly decorated of all the Apulian doorways. The majestic lions which support the outer pair of the four columns raising the deep canopy, were restored in 1534 by Maestro Antonio di Andria. The internal band of deeply incised carving which forms the door-jambs and the lightly pointed Gothic arch, consists of intertwined leafage springing from two vases held by human figures. In the lintel is a representation of the *Last Supper*; above, in the lunette, are the *Madonna and Child with two angels*. The external band of carving shows a marvellous series of *Scenes from the Life of Christ*, from the Annunciation to the Day of Pentecost.

The flank of the church is still primarily Romanesque, although the windows beneath the round-arched arcading are pointed. The doorway, the Porta Angioina, is called after Robert of Anjou who built it, and whose arms appear above beside the Gothic inscription. The transept, built during the sixteenth-century alterations, is lit by two Gothic windows from the original façade.

In the vast and sombre interior, later redecoration has not entirely concealed the Romanesque and Gothic forms. The chapels and sacristy contain a number of rather indifferent paintings. The pulpit, episcopal chair and choir stalls in inlaid wood (1543) are the work of an obscure carver, Colantonio Bonafede.

In the Corso Frederico II, just beyond the Duomo, stands part of a building from the former University of Altamura. The University is also remembered in the **Palazzo degli Studi,** farther up the Corso in the Piazza Zanardelli; today this houses the archives, library and **Museo Civico** (admission, weekdays 8.0 a.m.–1.0 p.m.; 4.0–6.0 p.m.). The museum contains considerable archaeological material found in the neighbourhood of the city—jewellery and ceramics from the Stone and Bronze Ages, as well as Greek and Apulian ware. There is also a beautiful ark-like box (*cofanetto*), a reliquary of gilt and enamel from the thirteenth-century workshops of Limoges.

For Gravina di Puglia by the SS 96 we leave the city by the Via Vittorio Veneto, passing on the right the turning for Corato and Trani, and cross the rolling countryside which the *bonifica* is transforming for the cultivation of wheat. A short way before Gravina we see on the hillside to the right the ruins of a castle or **hunting lodge of Frederick II,** which was supposedly built by the Florentine architect and sculptor Fuccio in 1230. The last stage of the road to Gravina follows the track of the ancient Via Appia.

Gravina di Puglia, a market and commercial town, is set in a wild, picturesque position on the edge of the deep and rocky ravine which gives it its name (Civitas Gravinae). The hill of Botromagno, on the west side of the *gravina* from the present town, was inhabited

Map VI
p. 238

in the Bronze Age, and later became an important centre of the Peucezi, known as Sides or Sidion. During the barbarian invasions the old town was destroyed and the inhabitants were forced to live in caves in the *gravina*, which many continued to occupy even after a new town began to rise in the fifth century on the east side of the ravine. The Saracens took Gravina in 970; then for more than ten years the unfortunate inhabitants were involved in siege and attack, until in 983 the Saracens finally destroyed the town and slaughtered the townsfolk. Gravina was occupied by the Normans in 1041, becoming a county under Humphrey de Hauteville. In 1420 the turbulent Roman family of Orsini became lords of the town and district, which they held from 1453 until the abolition of feudalism in the Kingdom of Naples in 1807.

The old quarters of winding streets and steep steps are on our right as we enter from Altamura. The centre of the town lies around the Piazza della Repubblica, with its baroque Palazzo Orsini. From the piazza we take the Corso Matteotti to the Piazza Notar Domenico (called after a fourteenth-century lawyer and chronicler of Gravina), where beyond the fish-market stands the curiously decorated church of the **Purgatorio.** There is a *memento mori* of skeletons on the tympanum above the doorway. The three columns supported by bears refer to the building of the church by the Orsini in 1649. In the interior, the third chapel on the right contains the tomb of Ferdinand III Orsini, erected in 1660 by his widow. Lovers of baroque painting will admire several works by the Orsini court painter Francesco Guarino (1611–54). The *Annunciation* is typical of the taste of the age.

To the left of the church, at the beginning of the ancient street which leads down to the Rione Fondovico, is the **Biblioteca Finya,** founded by Cardinal Angelo Finy (1669–1743), and claimed (wrongly) to be the oldest library in Apulia. (For the key enquire from the sacristan of the cathedral.) Before descending into the Rione Fondovico, we continue past the Purgatorio to the Piazza Benedetto XIII, flanked by the right-hand wall of the **Duomo dell' Assunta.** Although work on the cathedral was begun in 1092, subsequent enlargement and alterations, particularly in the fifteenth century, have left us what is virtually a Renaissance building with Romanesque and Gothic remains. The campanile was raised in 1698 by Cardinal Vincenzo Maria Orsini, later Pope Benedict XIII, who was responsible for some of the unfortunate embellishments of the interior. Restoration has, however, been going on. A window on the left gives us a fine view out over the *gravina*. On the right wall, near the usual entrance doorway, is a curious sixteenth-century low-relief, *the Presentation of Mary in the Temple.*

Back at the Biblioteca Finya, we take the narrow street down into the Rione Fondovico, which brings us to the grotto church of **S. Michele,** the mother church of Gravina, excavated entirely in the rock face. The church is still used to celebrate mass on the feasts of St Michael—May 8th and September 29th. (If the sacristan is absent, a child will fetch him for a small consideration.) In a corner are heaped the bones of the victims of the Saracen attack in 983. There is a further stack of these in the adjoining **Grotta di S. Marco,** which is reached by a way that affords us an excellent view of the *gravina* and of the caves cut in the tufa. An even better view is to be had by returning to the Piazza Notar Domenico and taking the Via Ambrazzo d'Ales to the right of the Purgatorio; this brings us (on the left) to the Via Michele Calderoni, at the bottom of which is a bridge crossing the *gravina,* one of the deepest of its kind.

From the Via Ambrazzo d'Ales we take the Via Lelio Orsini to the **Museo Pomarici Santomasi,** given to the town, together with the palace, by the Barone Ettore Pomarici Santomasi in 1917 (admission every day on request to the keeper in residence). One room has been left intact, with its *ottocento* decoration and furniture. Other rooms on the ground floor show archaeological material excavated from neighbouring sites; a numismatic collection; and one of folk-lore. The Art Gallery has a lovely *Madonna and Child* by Guarini, and also paintings of the Neapolitan School of the sixteenth to eighteenth centuries. Upstairs, the library contains some 20,000 volumes.

On the left of the Palazzo Santomasi the Via S. Giovanni Evangelista and the Via Abate Clemente bring us to the little fifteenth-century church of **S. Sofia,** which has a fine tomb of Angela Castriota Scanderbeg, the Albanian wife of Duke Ferdinand I Orsini, who died in 1518. The monument is attributed to a follower of the Spanish sculptor Bartolomeo Ordonez, who was working in Naples about this time. A street on the left of S. Sofia leads to the Renaissance church of **S. Francesco** (the campanile is 1766), which contains an interesting painting, *Adoration of the Magi (ca.* 1530), signed by Sebastiano Pisano.

Two further churches are worth a visit. The church of the **Madonna delle Grazie** by the railway station has a most extra-ordinary façade (1602). The then Bishop of Gravina had the façade decorated with his own crest carved in the tufa: three castellated towers, surmounted by a great eagle with outstretched wings, its body incorporating the rose window. The other church, the **Grotta** *di S. Vito Vecchio,* is on the outskirts of the town and is reached by the Via S. Vito from the Piazza Pellicciari. On the walls of the nave and apse of this little chapel are some remarkable frescoes. On the left, *the Marys at the Tomb* dates from the beginning of the fourteenth century; the *Enthroned Christ* in the apse and the figures of *saints* may be of the previous century.

Gioia del Colle—Acquaviva delle Fonti

From Gravina di Puglia we return to Altamura and take the SS 171
Map VI   to the market town of **Santeramo in Colle.** Saint Erasmus on the
p. 238   Hill—the name is derived from its patron saint—was the birthplace
of Francesco Netti, a well-known painter connected with the last-century schools of Naples. From the central Piazza Dottore Simone, the Via Roma (on the right of the Municipio) brings us to the baroque church of **S. Erasmo** (1701), opposite the ducal palace with its façade *a bugne* of 1576. The church has fragments of a doorway by Francesco Laurana, who appears to have worked here (*ca.* 1473) on his return from Sicily. The most important fragment, and almost certainly by Laurana, is the low-relief *Madonna and Child* from the lunette, which is over the second altar on the right. The others, two pilasters with a representation of the *Annunciation*, on the left of the choir, may have come from members of his workshop.

A further run across the hills brings us to the important centre of
Map VI   **Gioia del Colle** on a saddle between the north-western murge and
p. 238   the *murge dei trulli.* The neighbourhood was inhabited from pre-historic times; two settlements of the Peucezi have been excavated, but records of the modern town go back only to 1085; for several centuries Gioia was a feud of the Acquaviva of Conversano. Today it is a centre of communications and has a number of small factories for the manufacture of the famous *mozzarella* cheese, and for furniture and footwear. Architecturally, Gioia del Colle possesses one of the best preserved of the Emperor Frederick's hunting lodges or castles.

The **Castello,** of regular courses of brown stonework *a bugne,* rises impressively above the acacias in the piazza. It was begun by the son of Count Drogo de Hauteville in 1090, and added to by King Roger, but the planning of courtyards and rooms and the decoration of the windows (especially the small eye-windows in the south-eastern tower, which are distinctly Mohammedan in inspiration) reveal the hand of Frederick II, and there would be more to show had not
288

Above Balaam and the Ass, as they appear on a capital of the main portal of the early 12th c. abbey of S. Leonardo di Siponto.
Below The 15th c. Palazzo Sylos Labini at Bitonto is a national monument. The beautiful balustrade with its low-relief carvings is one of the few examples of early Renaissance architecture in the deep South.

Above Peaceful Lago di Cecita, an artificial lake in the Sila Greca in Calabria, is part of the great hydro-electric scheme for Southern Italy. *Below* Street in Alberobello, with the distinctive conical roofs of *trulli* houses, a feature of the region. Their origin is obscure but ancient, although most existing *trulli* are of recent date.

'restoration' and rebuilding at the beginning of the century falsified much of the interior. We enter from the west, and passing through a vaulted lobby, where two columns have fine capitals by Melo da Stigliano (whose work we have seen in the Castello at Bari) and Finarro da Canosa, come out into the courtyard. An open stairway leads to the loggia, which has been much restored. The so-called throne room has at one end a throne which is certainly not authentic. Frederick's own private quarters may be the rooms directly above the kitchen. In the kitchen an enormous oven may perhaps be original.

Around the adjoining Piazza dei Martiri del 1799 lie the medieval parts of Gioia, with busy narrow streets and old houses and courts. The town now has a single hotel, the recently constructed Jolly.

From Gioia del Colle a road continues due east via Noci to Alberobello in the centre of the '*trulli* region'; and the SS 100, which joins Bari with Taranto, runs south-east to Taranto via Mottola. We, however, return to Bari by way of the historic town of **Acqua-** Map VI
viva delle Fonti, which has a fine cathedral. p. 238

The secondary road branches left from the SS 100 on the northern outskirts of Gioia. The region in the immediate vicinity of Acquaviva delle Fonti is richly cultivated, because the subterranean limestone allows a plentiful supply of easily accessible water—hence *delle Fonti*. We enter Acquaviva by the Via G. Maselli Campagna, passing on our right the Chiesetta del Carmine, with its cupola resembling the cone of a *trullo*.

The earliest town, which arose possibly about the seventh century AD, was twice destroyed by the Saracens. After falling to the Normans, who built a castle, Acquaviva became the feud of some of the most illustrious families in the Kingdom: the Provençal del Balzo; the Acquaviva d'Aragona, Counts of Conversano; Prospero Colonna; the Spinelli, and finally the de Mari, who had the title of Princes. The de Mari built the **Palazzo del Principe** at the end of the seventeenth century. Today the Municipio, it retains the towers from the earlier castle. The façade, facing the Piazza dei Martiri del 1799, has the ground floor *a bugne*; above is an open loggia, and beneath the roof runs a decorative course of masks and niches.

Near by is the elegant **cathedral of St Eustace,** in the style of the Lombard Renaissance, a successful sixteenth-century transforma- tion of the twelfth-century Norman building, retaining much of the original structure. The surface of the façade is broken horizontally by two cornices divided vertically into three sections by bold pil- asters; above this a single wide gable, with a prominent cresting, is capped at the apex by a statue of the Madonna and Child and at each end by the figure of a saint. The high central doorway has a broken pediment supported by freestanding fluted columns borne by two large Romanesque lions. In the lunette is a sculptured low-relief of *St Eustace with the stag*. The two lateral doors are lower, and have niches framed in classical pilasters and pediments. Over the central portal is a beautiful rose window of delicate Renaissance tracery. On the left wall of the church the plain surface is relieved by pilasters and a decorative frieze. A rose window opens in the transept, and below it two pairs of lightly pointed Gothic windows. The apsidal end is lit by a single window of the sixteenth century or later. At the corners are two campanili, that on the right modelled on the Romanesque belfry of the Duomo at Palo del Colle.

The crypt is from the original church (although the decoration is nineteenth-century), and the central altar has a beautiful *paliotto* in silver by an unknown artist. This silversmith may also be responsible for the exquisite central figure of St Eustace and the stag on the cathedral's precious sixteenth-century processional cross of Neapolitan workmanship. The sacristan will show this to visitors on request. The *paliotto* of the left-hand altar is of 1753.

Map VI
p. 238

After Acquaviva delle Fonti the road descends to the villages of Adelfia and **Valenzano,** where we may make a diversion to the church of *Ognissanti.* Set among fields about a mile to the east of Valenzano, it is reached by turning right in the centre of Valenzano into the Via Tufaro. Erected by the Benedictines in 1061, nearly a century before the much grander Duomo di Molfetta, this simple little building (recently restored) is one of the earliest of the Apulian-Romanesque three-domed churches. Of the original narthex only the right-hand arcade has survived; from this, three round-arched portals (the larger central doorway decorated with bold rosary-beading) gave access to the nave and two aisles. From the outside the cupolas are masked by plain walls; within they are seen to be raised on pendentives over the nave. There is no transept, the nave and aisles ending in rounded apses.

From Valenzano our road crosses the fertile countryside round the adjoining villages of Ceglie del Campo and Carbonara di Bari, and enters Bari by the Corso Sicilia.

Another interesting day's excursion from Bari is to Alberobello and
Locorotondo in the *murge dei trulli*; thence to the hill resort of Selva
di Fasano, and back to Bari by the SS 16 (Adriatica) via the coastal
towns of Monopoli, Polignano a Mare and Mola di Bari. The rich
countryside of the *murge dei trulli* is striking after the bare, often
desolate high murge of the north-west. It is broken up into many
small-holdings of olive groves, vineyards and orchards separated by
low stone walls, one proprietor often cultivating a number of widely
dispersed plots. The inhabitants live mainly in scattered white *case
coloniche* or the characteristic *trulli* which give their name to the
district.

The *trulli* are found over a wide area and their origin is obscure,
though certainly ancient. They may be connected with the prehistoric *specchie* of the Salento region, but the *nuraghi* of Sardinia have
important differences. The *trullo* is usually circular in plan (though
interconnected series of *trulli* are common, sometimes with straight
walls, forming a house and its outbuildings), with a conical roof
capped by a finial which is almost invariably whitewashed. The
walls, too, may be whitewashed, but the roof is left in the natural
stone and decorated with hieroglyphs, frequently the cross in varying
shapes, or some other, even magical, symbol. The thick walls and
roofing are constructed without mortar of thin, regular courses of
local limestone. Inside, there is usually a square living-room, with
small annexes off it. Few of the existing *trulli* are older than the last
century, but the characteristic shape is adapted to modern require-
ments, so that all the rooms of a house, including the bathroom, are
formed from separate *trulli*. And there are even *trullo*-shaped churches,
and *trulli* hotels.

Leaving Bari by the Corso Cavour, we bear left (after the passage
under the railway) in the Via Extramurale Giuseppe Captuzzi, and
almost immediately turn right into the Via Giovanni Amendola,
which brings us past the new university buildings and on to the
SS 100 for Gioia del Colle. The road runs in a straight line through a
district famous for its dessert grapes until it reaches the crossroads
for Triggiano and Carbonara di Bari. Less than a mile along the
right-hand road is the **British Military Cemetery,** where more
than 2,000 dead from the Second World War lie buried. At the

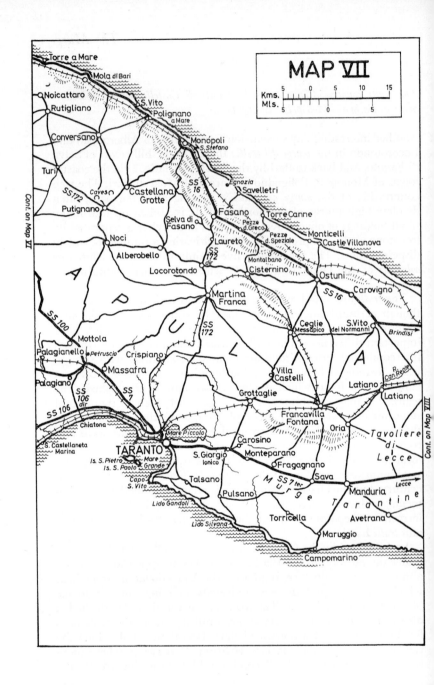

MAP VII

Kms.
Mls.

Torre a Mare
Mola di Bari
Noicattaro
Rutigliano
S. Vito
Polignano a Mare
Conversano
Monópoli
S. Stefano
Turi
SS 172
Caves
Castellana Grotte
SS 16
Egnazia
Savelletri
Putignano
Fasano
Torre Canne
Selva di Fasano
Pezze d. Greco
Monticelli
Noci
Laureto
Pezze d. Speziale
Castle Villanova
Alberobello
SS 172 dir
Montalbano
Locorotondo
Cisternino
Ostuni
Carovigno
Martina Franca
SS 16
A P U L I A
SS 172
Ceglie Messapico
S. Vito dei Normanni
Brindisi
SS 100
Mottola
Villa Castelli
Latiano
R. Can Reale
Palagianello
Petruscio
Crispiano
Latiano
Palagiano
Massafra
Grottaglie
SS 106 dir
SS 7
Francavilla Fontana
Oria
Tavoliere di Lecce
SS 106
Chiatona
Mare Piccolo
Carosino
S. Castellaneta Marina
TARANTO
Is. S. Pietro
Is. S. Paolo
Mare Grande
S. Giorgio Ionico
Monteparano
Fragagnano
Sava
Lecce
Capo S. Vito
Talsano
Pulsano
Murge
SS 7 ter
Manduria
Lido Gandoli
Torricella
Avetrana
Lido Silvana
Tarantine
Maruggio
Campomarino

Cont. on Map VI

Cont. on Map VIII

village of Capurso we turn left off the SS 100 into the Via Madonna del Pozzo and pass through an intensely cultivated district of fine vineyards to reach the market town of **Noicattaro.** Of very ancient origin (excavations have yielded grave material of the seventh to sixth centuries BC), the town was called Noia (boredom) until 1863. In the chiesa Madre (early thirteenth-century but much altered) there is an *ostensorio* in silver, typical of the late fifteenth-century Neapolitan workshops. Beyond the town stretch more vineyards, the vines strung high '*a tendoni*'.

Map VII
p. 292

A couple of miles farther on, the town of **Rutigliano** is built on the site of a settlement of the Peucezi. On the Piazza C. Battisti in the old quarters stands the ***Torre,*** the remaining tower of an eleventh-century Norman castle. The Via Porta Castello leads us, past two palaces with their façades *a bugne*, to the church of *S. Maria della Colonna.* The church, which was begun by the Norman Count Hugo and consecrated in 1108, has a main doorway and another portal on the left flank in the thirteenth-century Apulian-Romanesque style. The campanile is also early, except for the baroque onion dome. The church possesses two interesting paintings, a *Madonna* by an unknown thirteenth-century Byzantine-inspired artist, and a beautiful polyptych of the *Madonna and Child*, with the *Resurrection* above, flanked by *saints*. Berenson ascribed this to Antonio Vivarini (*ca.* 1460), one of the finest examples of the Vivarini to be found in the South.

Map VII
p. 292

After Rutigliano the road continues through this pleasant, fertile countryside. Less than a mile before Conversano, we see on the right the medieval church and ex-abbey of *S. Maria dell' Isola,* the burial place of some of the Acquaviva family. The custodian lives in the house at the rear of the church. Palma Giovane, a Venetian painter almost as popular with the churches and monasteries of Apulia as the Vivarini, has here a *S. Girolamo* of about 1610. The monumental tomb of Giulio Antonio Acquaviva (killed in 1481 fighting against the Turks at Otranto), and of his wife, was carried out in the following century by Nunzio Barba of S. Pietro a Galatina. Near by are the kneeling figures of Giulio Antonio's son, Andrea Matteo, and his wife. In the adjoining cloister the monastery well has good baroque ironwork.

Conversano, today a thriving market town, is built on a spur of the murge some 700 ft above the sea, with wide views over the coastal plain towards Mola di Bari, Polignano and Monopoli. Conversano probably occupies the site of the Peucezian city of Norba; the remains of the megalithic walls suggest that it was an important

Map VII
p. 292

centre earlier than the fourth century BC. Changing masters several times during the struggle between Byzantines and Lombards, Cupersanum, as it was then known, was wrested from the Lombard Princes of Salerno by the Normans, its first count being Geoffrey, nephew of Robert Guiscard. From 1508 until 1801 Conversano was in the possession of the Acquaviva d'Aragona.

Passing the gardens of the Villa Garibaldi on the right, we come up into the Piazza del Castello, dominated by the well-preserved *castle*. This was begun by the Normans and added to in the following centuries, the last main additions being made by Dorotea Acquaviva in 1710. The entrance (from the Piazza della Concilazione) is through the Countess Dorothy's Renaissance gateway and courtyard, with a pleasant portico and loggia above. Several families occupy the castle; the *appartamento signorile*, which may be visited on request, has a frescoed ceiling in the Sala dell' Alcova by the Neapolitan painter Paolo Finoglia (1590–1645, at Conversano), or a follower. Finoglia also painted twelve *Scenes from Gerusalemme Liberata* for the castle, now in Rome in the Manzolino Collection. On the right of the Piazza della Concilazione is the Apulian-Romanesque *cathedral*. Originally of the eleventh to twelfth centuries, it was altered at the end of the fourteenth, suffered from a disastrous fire in 1912, and has been well restored. The façade is of the fourteenth century, but follows S. Nicola di Bari with a high central nave and rose window, and the characteristic portals. Opposite the cathedral is a lane leading to a medieval house which has an ogival window in the Saracenic style; in the courtyard under the arches there is another window, the remains of what was possibly a thirteenth- or fourteenth-century dwelling.

In the street behind the cathedral we come to a statue of *St Benedict* on a column at the corner of a crossing. Here we take the Via S. Benedetto on the left, and come shortly to the entrance of the famous church and convent of *S. Benedetto* under a baroque campanile. The foundation of this ancient institution, of which there are documentary records since the ninth century, is ascribed to S. Mauro, the disciple of S. Benedict. When, for some unexplained reason, the monks fled on the downfall of the Hohenstaufen, their place was taken by nuns of the same Order in 1266. The abbess became in time a feudal grandee in her own right, and for centuries, in spite of strong opposition, exercised feudal and ecclesiastical jurisdiction equal to that of the bishop, not only over the clergy and townspeople but also over a large area of the countryside. Nor was she without supporters, for when King Murat transferred the abbess's rights to the bishop of Conversano in 1810, her admirers referred to him as 'the monster of Apulia'.

The structure of the church is ninth-century; however, the main doorway on the left-hand side of the building is sixteenth-century (incorporating the Romanesque lions of the earlier portal), and the central cupola dates from restoration done in 1658. The unusual frieze in rough mosaic-work is part of the original decoration. Within, the fabric of the early church is overlaid with rich seventeenth-century baroque. Among the artists represented here are Paolo Finoglia (his *S. Benedetto and S. Savino* hangs over the main altar), Carlo Rosa (*Crucifixion* and *Baptism*) and the somewhat earlier Cretan painter, Michele Damasceno (*fl.* 1573–88), who decorated the church of S. Giorgio dei Greci in Venice. Here he has a *Madonna del Rosario.*

To the right of the entrance to the church is the **convent.** The Sisters will show visitors the pleasant cloister and the crypt to the earliest church, which was destroyed by the Saracens in 841. The cloister, which has been recently restored and in part rebuilt, is very similar to that of S. Benedetto in Brindisi (*ca.* 1080).

Descending the Rampa di S. Benedetto, we see on the right part of the megalithic walls. Through the near-by gate we take the Via Arringo, then the Via Municipio (passing the Arco della Gabella of 1338), and arrive in the Piazza Umberto I, from which the Corso Umberto I brings us to the church of **SS. Cosmas and Damiano.** (If closed, the key may be obtained at the convent next door.) Admirers of seventeenth-century baroque should not miss this church, with its extraordinary display of stucco, gilding, frescoes, marbles and paintings by Paolo Finoglia and other members of his circle.

After leaving Conversano the broken terrain reveals the limestone structure of these murge. On a hill to the right of the road stands the ***Torre del Castiglione,*** marking the site of a medieval fortified town, inhabited until the end of the fifteenth century. The fourteenth-century walls are in places raised on rough blocks of the Pelasgian type; these, together with discoveries from excavations, suggest that there was a settlement of the Peucezi here from as early as the sixth century BC. At the entrance to the town of **Castellana Grotte** we turn right just before the level-crossing for the ***Grotte di Castellana,*** the most comprehensive and spectacular of all Italian caves, with beautiful stalactites and stalagmites of coloured alabaster. The usual visit—as far as the Precipice—takes about an hour; the full journey to the miraculous Grotta Bianca, a distance of nearly a

Map VII
p. 292

mile, requires more than two hours. (Admission, every day from May 1st to September 30th, at 9, 10, 11, 12, 2.30, 3.30, 4.30 and 6; for the rest of the year at 10.30, 12, 3.30 and 4.30.)

On the piazzale at the entrance to the caves are the Autostello and the Locanda Matarrese, both clean, modern establishments. At near-by Castellana, which was for nearly a century after 1267 under the civil and ecclesiastical jurisdiction of the abbesses of S. Benedetto di Conversano, there are several adequate *ristoranti*. The old quarters of Castellana have narrow, winding streets with scrupulously clean, whitewashed houses, many of which have pleasant terraces, stairways and little balconies of simple local ironwork.

From the Grotte we return to the Castellana–Putignano road where we turn right. The first of the *trulli* appear before we reach **Putignano,** an ancient town of the Peucezi, which from 1358–1808 was in the possession of the Knights of Malta. The town has a number of early churches and palaces, but most have been spoilt by restoration. The church of **S. Pietro,** on the Piazza Plebiscito, begun in 1158 but rebuilt in 1474 and again some hundred and fifty years later, has a rose window and Gothic doorway. The baroqued interior has three paintings attributed to Luca Giordano (1632–1705), and statues of *S. Giuseppe, the Madonna* and *St Peter* by Stefano da Putignano (early sixteenth century), a vigorous second-rate sculptor. To the west of the town, on the *circumvallazione* near the hospital, are the attractive gardens of the **Villa Karusio.**

Map VII p. 292

A road runs south from Putignano to the town of **Noci,** appropriately named, for there are many almond trees in the neighbourhood and the nuts are excellent. However, we turn left into the SS 172 (dei Trulli) through a landscape increasingly studded with *trulli,* and climb steadily to a height of over 1300 ft before entering **Alberobello,** the centre of the *trulli* country. The town seems not to have an ancient origin. In former times the district was covered with oak woods (the name is derived from Silva Arboris Belli), belonging to the Acquaviva of Conversano; and the village apparently owed its prosperity to the initiative of members of this family, particularly Count Gian Girolamo II who in 1635 erected a mill and tavern near his villa. Today, the successor to the tavern is the Hotel dei Trulli, a miniature village of twenty-three *trulli* on the edge of the *zona monumentale*—this is a quarter, comprising Rioni Monti and Via Piccola, entirely composed of *trulli,* which has been declared a national monument.

Map VII p. 292

Still following the SS 172, we cross an undulating countryside
296

dotted with white *trulli* to **Locorotondo,** situated on the top of a hill from which there are splendid views. The houses in Locorotondo have high stepped gables, and the buildings themselves are often high, reminding one of Edinburgh tenements except for the white-wash. In the Via Cavour is the *Chiesa La Greca,* erected by Piero del Balzo, Prince of Taranto, a rather lifeless late-Gothic building recently restored. The nave and aisles are divided by pointed arches on pilasters and half-columns with interesting capitals and bases. In the corner to the left of the altar is the statue of a del Balzo, kneeling in full armour.

Map VII p. 292

From Locorotondo the SS 172 goes on to Martina Franca (see p. 318), from where it crosses the less fertile murge southwards towards the Ionian coast and, skirting the Mar Piccolo, enters Taranto by the Via Napoli. However, our route takes us north on the 172 *dir* to the village of Laureto, one of the resorts in an area that is becoming increasingly popular as a place of *villeggiatura*. About a mile beyond Laureto we turn left off the Statale for **Selva di Fasano,** perhaps the best known of these resorts. Beautifully placed on a spur of the murge 1300 ft above sea level, Selva di Fasano has fine views across the uplands of the *murge dei trulli*, and eastwards over the coastal plain to the sea. It boasts a Casino Municipale, with *sale di gioco*, a ballroom and refreshment bar. There are no hotels at the moment, but several *pensioni*, among them the Villa Paradiso, the Miramonti and the Trullo d'Oro. At this height it is degrees cooler than on the coast, yet these resorts are only some seven miles from the sea and within easy reach of the thermal spa of Torre Canne (see p. 302).

Map VII p. 292

The road from Selva di Fasano has magnificent views as it winds down the terraced hillsides of the murge to the plain. **Fasano** is a pleasant, pretty little town in the province of Brindisi, once the property of the Knights of Malta who have left their distinctive cross on several buildings. From Fasano we take the SS 16 (Adriatica), which crosses the coastal strip to the north-west through groves of ancient olives. We approach the sea at **Monopoli,** a town engaged in commerce, light industry and fishing, with a modern quarter of broad streets and squares and an interesting old town around the port.

Map VII p. 292

The centre of the town is the wide Piazza Vittorio Emanuele, planted with holm-oaks. From one side of the piazza there opens out the Largo Plebiscito, with the baroque church of S. Francesco (1742) on the left, and the near-by Municipio. Opposite the latter we take the Via S. Domenico to the church of *S. Domenico,* which has an elegant Renaissance façade, a pleasant doorway and rose window, and possesses one of the better examples of Palma Giovane's Apulian work, *the Miracle of Soriano*, painted probably in the first years of the seventeenth century. Beyond the church, at No. 73, is the entrance to the **crypt of the Madonna del Soccorso.** In a niche in the wall are three stone figures, two in an attitude of prayer and one supporting a console; these are attributed to the sculptor Stefano da Putignano (*ca.* 1500), parts of a lost group representing the *Madonna del Rosario*. Within the crypt is a much-repainted fresco of the *Madonna and Child*.

Taking, on the right of the Via S. Domenico, the Via S. Angelo, and then, again on the right, the Via Garibaldi, we come out in the picturesque little Piazza Garibaldi. Above the fish-market and arcade through to the port on the right is a pleasant eighteenth-century *palazzo* housing the Biblioteca Comunale. In the centre of the piazza is the former theatre. On the left the Via Amalfitana brings us shortly to the charming little church of **S. Maria Amalfitana,** erected in the early twelfth century (in what was then their quarter) by traders from Amalfi. In the fifteenth century, Gothic additions were made, and later a baroque façade was added. Recent restorations give us a better idea of the earlier building. The pillars dividing the nave from the aisles have fine Romanesque capitals. Near the main doorway slits in the stonework mark the limits of the original façade. By a stairway on the right we descend to the crypt, the primitive Basilian *laura*; here on the left and behind the altar the lower level of the floor is covered with sea-water. At the end of the right aisle a door leads to a small courtyard, from where we may see the interesting rounded apsidal ends. The Apulian-Romanesque central apse, with its slender half-columns, its grotesque consoles and fine window, shows predominantly Lombard elements.

From the Piazza Garibaldi we pass through the arch to the port. On the right a Venetian palazzo has an arched loggia overlooking the basin. On the promontory stands the **Castello** (now a prison), erected by Frederick II and subsequently rebuilt and strengthened, especially in the sixteenth century when the Emperor Charles V reinforced the city's fortifications against the Turks. Leaving the port, we may take the winding, narrow Via Pintor Mameli between whitewashed houses, and then bear left for the cathedral. Alternatively, we take the Via S. Domenico to the Piazza XX Settembre, then left for the adjoining Piazza Vescovado, and from this the Via Cattedrale, which opens out into a piazzetta on which stands the grey façade of the eighteenth-century **cathedral,** claimed to be among the most notable baroque churches in Apulia. The original church, founded in 1107, was completely rebuilt from 1742–70.

Reflections of the earlier prosperity of Monopoli, the cathedral and the **Bishop's Palace** contain a number of paintings and precious objects. Over the first altar on the right in the cathedral is a *S. Michele* by Palma Giovane; in the right transept is his *Madonna in Glory with S. Rocco and S. Sebastiano*; there are also two further paintings by his hand, *the Fall of the Rebel Angels* and *the Coronation of the Virgin*, the latter in the Vescovado. Among other Venetian works in the Bishop's palace are a *Madonna and Saints* by Veronese and a *S. Girolamo* attributed to Lazzaro Bastiani (1430–1512). Other artists represented include Marco Pino of Siena (1525–87) and Paolo Finoglia. Antonio Verrio of Lecce (who was court painter to Charles II from 1672–1707; there are examples of his work at Hampton Court) has two canvases. Artists of the Neapolitan school are represented, and Bardellino (1731–1806) has a painting of *the Arrival of the Madonna della Madia* in the apse, which shows the miraculous arrival on a raft of the Byzantine painting of the *Madonna della Madia*, the much-venerated thirteenth-century icon which hangs near by. In the Sala del Capitolo, where the cathedral chapter meets, is another Byzantine-inspired *Madonna*.

The cathedral possesses a rare treasure in an exquisite mid-tenth-century **reliquary of the True Cross**, possibly from Constantinople. A small rectangular chest has two doors in front which open to form a triptych; the central panel shows the Crucifixion, and the side panels the figures of St Peter and St Paul, all on a ground of gilded silver, the figures being depicted in *cloisonné* enamels, in which shades of clear blue predominate. Other precious objects include a processional cross from a sixteenth-century Neapolitan workshop; the four evangelists are represented in high relief on the arms of the cross, with the Crucifixion; on the reverse is the figure of the Virgin Mary.

In the sacristy is some of the stone carving from the main doorway to the Romanesque building, important for the study of the development of sculpture in Apulia. Unlike most of the work in Monopoli, which is Byzantine-inspired, this sculpture shows unmistakably the hand of masons either from Lombardy or, probably, from the workshops of southern France—perhaps Toulouse. The archivolt of the heads of angels may well have been the model for the portal of the Duomo at Acerenza. A capital shows *Daniel in the Lions' Den*. But most remarkable of all is the carving on the architrave, which is decorated with scenes representing *the Descent from the Cross*, *the Marys at the Tomb*, and *Christ in the Underworld*. On the left, Luxury is shown as a naked woman, her body wreathed with snakes who nibble her breasts; on the right, a venerable bearded man sits writing with a curious spectator looking over his shoulder.

The coast to the north-west of Monopoli presents a fractured rocky frontier to the sea, with a few small sandy coves. There are a number of caves in the cliff face, some, such as those at Polignano, forming great caverns. The SS 16, running north-west parallel to the shore, crosses a series of gullies (*lame*) cut by the rush of the seasonal rains from the murge to the sea. The town of **Polignano a Mare** has its older, medieval quarters built right on the cliff-edge, some 70 ft above the surface of the Adriatic. The origins of Polignano are obscure; it may have been built on the site of Greek Neapolis, since coins of that city have been found in the vicinity.

Map VII
p. 292

The town boasts a modern hotel, the Grotta Palazzese, built in a magnificent position overlooking the sea and directly above the best-known of the many local caves, after which it is named. A stairway from the hotel leads down to the ***Grotta Palazzese,*** which has been transformed into a majestic ballroom with a circular tiled dancing floor. The near-by Ristorante Sportelli also enables one to enjoy the magnificent view.

In the Piazza Vittorio Emanuele stands the ***Chiesa Matrice,*** a Gothic church (1295) which has been much altered, with a main doorway of the late Renaissance. The five panels of a polyptych in the left transept are signed Bartolomeo Vivarini and dated 1472, but experts believe they are by his assistants. The sculptor Stefano da Putignano is represented by a *Pietà*, a *Madonna and Child* and a *Presepio*. In the treasury is a beautiful ring, an emerald in an elaborate setting of fauns and masks in gold and enamels, considered to be late-sixteenth-century Tuscan work, possibly in the tradition of Benvenuto Cellini. The near-by church of **S. Antonio** contains paintings of some interest. The *Madonna and Child with S. Vito and S. Biagio* is by the painter from Padua known as Padovanino (1588–1648). The coat-of-arms at the bottom of the picture shows that it was presented by Rodolavic from Dubrovnik, a feudal lord of Polignano. The large canvas of *the Virgin with Franciscan Saints* (1599) is by the Flemish painter Gaspar Hovic.

Leaving Polignano a Mare by the SS 16, we cross a deep *lama* and arrive shortly at a crossroads. On the right is the fortress-like building which incorporates the church of the former Benedictine **abbey of S. Vito,** standing on the rocky coast. At intervals along the shore stand look-out towers, some in ruins but others kept in repair—sixteenth-century precautions against Turkish sea-marauders.

Ahead of us on its promontory stands **Mola di Bari,** the white houses with their flat roofs grouped around the *Castello,* built by Charles of Anjou in 1278 but much altered and strengthened in the sixteenth century by the Emperor Charles V. Map VII
p. 292

At the centre of the town, the Piazza Roma, the more modern quarters meet the old. By the Via Veneto, on the left, we enter the medieval town, and come almost immediately to the *cathedral of S. Nicola,* an interesting example of how the Romanesque-Gothic style (*ca.* 1260) was carried on into the Renaissance, with major alterations made to the building from 1545–64. Below the original rose window the Renaissance doorway is flanked by columns based on two Romanesque grotesques; in another portal on the left of the church the columns are borne on the customary lions. The interior, too, shows the commingling of styles; the round arches of the nave are raised on Corinthian capitals, and above the classical frieze is a curious clerestory. Over the first altar on the left is an interesting fourteenth-century *Madonna and Child* in the Byzantine tradition. In the right-hand aisle the baptismal font is raised on a plinth decorated with dancing *putti.* The statue of *S. Sebastiano* is by Stefano da Putignano.

A short run brings us to the bathing resort of **Torre a Mare,** which has a sandy beach and some caves, including the Grotta della Regina. We follow the broken coastline, passing the village of S. Giorgio alla Marina with its villas and market gardens, and approach the built-up area on the outskirts of Bari, which we enter by the Corso Sonnino and the Lungomare Nazario Sauro. Map VII
p. 292

CHAPTER 17

Brindisi and its Province

Maps: VII, p.292; VIII, p.330

When Horace travelled to Brundisium in 37 BC in company with Virgil, Maecenas and some amusing companions (the account of the journey he gives in *Satires* 1,6), the party went not by the more direct route of the Via Appia, which had been continued from Capua in the second century BC to link Rome with its most important port in the Adriatic, but the more leisurely way through Benevento, Canosa, Bari and Egnazia. The road from Canosa on was then known as the Via Egnatiae; subsequently the route from Benevento to Brindisi was rebuilt by the Emperor Trajan and the road renamed Via Traiana. Today the main roads from Central and Northern Italy to Brindisi, the SS 7 (Appia) and the SS 16 (Adriatica) follow in the main the course laid down by Roman engineers.

Bari to Brindisi—Ostuni—some early frescoes

From Bari the SS 16 runs along the low rocky coast as far as Monopoli (see chapter 16). After passing through the fishing village of Savelletri, it reaches the seaside resort and medicinal spa of **Torre Canne.** The modern Albergo Terme and the two mineral springs for the treatment of liver and gynaecological complaints are set in a park. There is also the Pensione La Primula. South of the lighthouse on the point is a stretch of good sandy beach ideal for bathing.

Map VII p. 292

Beyond Monopoli the SS 16 turns almost due south towards the foothills of the murge, enters Fasano (see p. 297), and then proceeds south-east (with glimpses of Selva and Laureto), passing the villages of Pezze di Greco, Pezze di Speziale and Montalbano. Just before Speziale the Statale is crossed by a provincial road running from the fascinating little hill-top town of **Cisternino** to Torre Canne. These towns and villages have an increasingly oriental appearance; the houses are low, with flat roofs, and are painted a dazzling white. One of the most characteristic and attractive of them is **Ostuni,** ahead of us on its three hills. The white houses of the old quarter on the highest hill gleam against the burnt brown of the countryside and of the walls of the convents and churches.

Map VII
p. 292

Of Messapian origin, Ostuni is first mentioned in the tenth century, when it became the seat of a Byzantine bishop. Taken by the Normans in 1071, it was later held in fief in turn by the ruling houses of Lecce, Taranto and Bari; in 1639 it came into the possession of the Zevallos family, with whom it remained until the beginning of the last century. Today it is a clean, prosperous-looking town engaged in the wine and oil trade and in the manufacture of the locally grown tobacco. The Corso Mazzini brings us to the centre of the town, the triangular Piazza della Libertà, attractive in its irregularity, the different levels of the buildings and the variety of the architecture. At the end of the piazza rises the baroque Guglia di S. Oronzo (1771); and near by are several interesting churches. From the piazza we take the Via P. Vincenti, which winds up into the old town, past narrow alleyways, arches, steps and balconies. From the Piazzetta del Moro we ascend by the Via G. Petrarolo and come on the left to the Monastero delle Carmelitane and next to it the baroque church of **S. Maria Maddalena,** with a cupola of polychrome majolica. Beyond it, we pass under an arch and come out into a piazza at the highest point of Ostuni, on which stands the strange but beautiful late Gothic **cathedral.**

Work was begun on the church in 1435—the year the last Angevin, René of Lorraine, came to the throne of Naples—but the building was not completed until between 1470 and 1495, when their Aragonese successors were well established in the Kingdom. These dates may account for the distinctly Spanish flavour of the Gothic; the boldness of the curving ends, concave over the gable, convex over the aisles, seems to prefigure the baroque. However, the three ogival doorways, the two 'eye' windows, the magnificent rose window, and the decoration (particularly the highly ornate crowning) are all unmistakably Gothic. There are also two strange little gazebo-like structures terminating the gable above the projecting Apulian-Romanesque lions. The interior has *settecento* decoration. In the last of the baroque chapels on the right is a *Madonna and Child with Saints* (*ca.* 1610) by Palma Giovane.

At the end of the piazza, where the Episcopio is joined to the Seminario by an arcaded loggia (1750), we pass under an arch and

303

take the Vico Castello on the right, which runs along the wall of the bishop's palace and the ruins of the Castello, erected in 1198 by Godfrey, Count of Lecce, and partly demolished in 1559. We come out on a belvedere from which we can appreciate Ostuni's impregnable position, the houses in places incorporating the remains of the Aragonese ramparts. There is also a magnificent view over the coastal plain to the blue waters of the Adriatic.

At Ostuni they bake a delectable *pizza*, which I first came on in a baker's in the Via Petrarolo. The area around the villages Monticelli and Castel Villanova is scheduled for development as the lido for Ostuni.

For Brindisi we leave Ostuni by the Corso Vittorio Emanuele for the SS 16. About a mile from the town we see on the left the Gothic façade of the church of **S. Maria la Nova** (1561). Formed from a natural cave, the church contains traces of fifteenth-century frescoes. The Statale passes south of Carovigno, then runs in a straight line to **S. Vito dei Normanni,** a settlement founded in the Middle Ages by a colony of Slav refugees, and known until 1865 as S. Vito degli Schiavoni. Its fifteenth-century Castello has had considerable later alterations; the wall of its square tower is pockmarked by gunfire.

Map VII
p. 292

Beyond S. Vito dei Normanni the Statale crosses a cultivated plain, and shortly before the loop over the railway at the Stazione di S. Vito, a poorly-marked rough road on the left leads in under a mile to the *Grotta di S. Biagio.* For this cave-church we follow the track as far as the white group of buildings of the Masseria Iannuzzo. Just before this another track curves to the right up a shallow valley, and a short way along, a rough wooden door in the hillside, again on the right, opens into the Grotta di S. Biagio. It is a miracle that any of the frescoes should have survived; nothing appears to have been done to preserve them. Authorities differ in dating the paintings; an inscription above the door attributes them to a Master Daniel in 1197, but they are thought to be at least a century later. The subjects include *the Presentation in the Temple, Annunciation,* a re-painted *Flight into Egypt, Entry into Jerusalem, Christos Pantocrator* (with symbols of the Evangelists) and the figures of *two prophets* and of *various saints.* The inscriptions are in Greek.

The *Grotta di S. Giovanni* is near the Masseria Cafaro, about a mile and a half along a track to the right of the Statale, immediately before the loop where it crosses the railway. Here the inscriptions on the frescoes are in Latin, but the frescoes themselves may be earlier than those of S. Biagio. The majestic *Archangel Michael,* dressed as an

Leccean baroque. *Above left* Well in the courtyard of the Seminary.
Right Façade of SS. Niccolò e Cataldo.
Below left Façade of S. Chiara.
Right Well in the cloister of SS. Niccolò e Cataldo.

Lecce's contributions to art and letters have earned her the titles of 'the Florence of the baroque' and 'the Apulian Athens'.

By the ruins of the Roman amphitheatre (*below*) stands the Sedile (*above*), former meeting-place of the civic authorities. It was built in 1592.

Eastern emperor, is in the Byzantine manner of the eleventh century, and may have been painted a century before the other portraits.

As we draw near Brindisi, the flat landscape is dominated by the great 'amphitheatre' of steel girders of the American Air Force base. Leaving the bypass on our right, we continue on and meet the provincial coast road, where we turn right and, rounding the western arm of the harbour, the Seno di Ponente, pass Tancred's Fountain as we ascend and enter the city.

Taranto to Brindisi—Francavilla Fontana—Oria

For Brindisi and the Salentine peninsula (the heel of Italy) we leave Taranto by the Via Appia (SS 7), which is reached from the Città Nuova by the Via G. Mazzini and its continuation in the Via C. Battisti. The road runs due east, to the south of the Mare Piccolo, and ahead of us are the low hills of the Murge Tarentine. After passing on the left the secondary road which joins the SS 7 with the SS 172 for Martina Franca the Statale begins to climb gently through a countryside planted with olives and vines, to the outskirts of the village of S. Giorgio Ionico, and turns abruptly north-east for Grottaglie.

As we approach **Grottaglie,** ahead of us on a hill, the country becomes richer. The town is a prosperous centre for ceramics. In the narrow alleys below the *Castello* (built in the fourteenth century by Grottaglie's feudal lords, the bishops of Taranto) are the potters' workshops. In the centre of the town, the Piazza Regina Margherita, rises the *Chiesa Matrice,* with its cupola of majolica tiles over the Cappella del Rosario (1709) to the right of the façade. The church, which was founded at the end of the eleventh or beginning of the twelfth century, has retained its Apulian-Romanesque doorway, although the façade was rebuilt in 1379. The much altered interior contains a painting of the *Madonna del Rosario* by Paolo de Matteis (1662–1728) and, in the fourth chapel on the left, a Renaissance relief of the *Annunciation* by an unknown hand.

Map VII
p. 292

Beyond Grottaglie the Via Appia crosses into the province of Brindisi and runs due east to **Francavilla Fontana.**

Map VII
p. 292

Built on an ancient Messapian site, the town owes its rise in the Middle Ages to Philip I of Anjou, Prince of Taranto, who is said to have found a miraculous icon of the Madonna near a fountain in 1310—hence the name Fontana. The 'Francavilla' refers to the fiscal immunities granted by Philip to those who settled in his new town. The Acquaviva Counts of Conversano and the Imperiali Princes of Francavilla were the most powerful of the feudal magnates in Southern Apulia. The palaces in these Apulian towns show the opulence in which they lived.

Entering the town through the Porta del Carmine, we find ourselves in the Via Roma, which is flanked by some fine seventeenth- and eighteenth-century palaces, among them No. 27, the Palazzo Giannuzzi-Carissimo, in brown stone with an imposing balcony. Farther on, in the streets off the Piazza Umberto, are other interesting palaces, especially the fourteenth-century Palazzo de Argentina-Leo (Via S. Giovanni 12), which has a loggia richly decorated in carved stonework. Beyond in the Via Umberto I we come to the princely **Palazzo Imperiali,** begun in 1450 by Giovanni Antonio Orsini, added to by the Bonifacio in 1536 and again by the Imperiali at the beginning of the eighteenth century. On the right of the building four french windows enclosed in baroque arcading open on to a rather ponderous balcony, the balustrade of which is topped by four clusters of globular lamps. The *settecento* portal gives access to a large courtyard, with a loggia raised on a columned arcade. Since 1821 the palace has been the seat of the Municipio, and permission is given to visit the Sala del Consiglio which is reached by a grand double stairway. The room shows the arms of the Imperiali over the fireplace, and contains some paintings of the sixteenth to eighteenth centuries, including a pleasant *St Agnes and the Lamb* by the Neapolitan painter Pacecco de Rosa.

It is well worth making a short diversion from Francavilla Fontana to the town of **Oria.** From the crossroads on the Via S. Francesco d'Assisi outside the Porta del Carmine a secondary road runs southeast through the Tavoliere di Lecce. After crossing the railway for Brindisi, we see ahead of us the castle of Oria crowning the hills on which the town is built. Hyria or Uria was one of the chief Messapian towns, and even in the time of Strabo (latter half of first century BC) the royal palace and temples still existed. It suffered the customary vicissitudes of other centres of Apulia in the struggles that followed the break-up of the Western Empire; it was taken by the Goths, Byzantines, Lombards, the Frankish Emperor Lewis II, and was finally sacked by the Saracens in 925. Later it became part of the possessions of the Princes of Taranto, and was again caught up in the dynastic struggles of the later Angevin period and in the Franco-Spanish wars.

Map VII
p. 292

We enter under the fourteenth-century Porta degli Ebrei and
306

come to the Piazza Cattedrale, with a modern statue of Constantine (Mario Sabatelli, 1924) and the baroque **cathedral,** rebuilt in 1750 in a warm brown stone and capped by a dome in multi-coloured majolica. The piazza stands on the southern side of the hill just within the limits of the defence walls, part of which remain (with a cylindrical tower, the Torre Palomba) behind the cathedral. From the left of the church we take the narrow Via Castello which leads up between high walls to the **Castello,** begun in 1227 by the Emperor Frederick II and enlarged under the first Angevins, possibly by their famous military architect Pierre d'Agincourt. The castle was restored in 1933 (admission, October 1st–March 31st, 10.0 a.m.– 12.0 noon, 2.0–4.0 p.m.; April 1st–September 30th, 9.0 a.m.– 12.0 noon, 4.0–7.0 p.m.).

The plan of the castle and grounds is roughly triangular, occupying the site of the Messapian acropolis. As we approach the entrance we see first the square tower, which was the keep of the Hohenstaufen structure; then follow two Angevin cylindrical towers, the first (beyond which is the present entrance) known as the Torre del Cavaliere, and the other, the Torre del Salto, forming the south-east angle of the walls. Within the *enceinte*, beyond the gravelled walks and gardens of the Piazza d'Armi, the Torre del Sperone forms the apex of the triangle. To the left, in the corner past the massive square tower (behind a well) a pointed-arch doorway, partly below the ground level, led to the original main entrance. An external stairway round the Torre del Cavaliere brings us to a large vaulted chamber in which is housed the Martini Carissimo collection of antiquities. Through other rooms we climb to the terrace from which there is a splendid view of the Tavoliere di Lecce, the Murge Tarentine and the distant Ionian Sea.

The north-western side consists of the Palazzo del Castellano, many times restored but still revealing parts of the earlier structure. In the south-eastern corner, among the cypresses at the foot of the Torre del Salto, steps lead down to the interesting little **crypt of SS. Crisanto and Daria,** in the form of a Greek cross; this is thought to be ninth century or possibly earlier. Among the faded remains of frescoes are those (repainted) of the saints to whom the church is dedicated. On the other side of the east wall of the Castello is the park of Montalbano, created by the bishops of Oria. Descending the Via del Castello and bearing left, we come to the Piazza S. Croce, the town's centre, with the former Palazzo Martini Carissimo, now the Municipio.

From Francavilla Fontana we resume our eastward journey on the

Map VII
p. 292

Via Appia, though vines and olives prevent our seeing much beyond the road. **Latiano** is a small country town with a Palazzo Comunale which was once another Imperiali mansion. The prosperous market town of **Mesagne** is the distributive centre for the local products of this rich countryside—wine, table grapes, olives and tobacco.

Leaving Mesagne by the Via Brindisi, we follow the final stretch of the Via Appia Antica, running parallel to the railway. As we approach the capital, little villas appear among the vineyards and orchards. We cross the bypass of the SS 16 from Bari to Lecce, and after the level-crossing to the left of the railway station, come to the remains of the walls of Charles V and the pointed-arched Porta Mesagne (thirteenth-century), the entrance to the city of Brindisi.

Brindisi—the Cathedral—Libraries and Museums—S. Benedetto

Map VIII
p. 330

Another Messapian foundation, **Brindisi** seems to have been a port for trade between the Apulian and Illyrian peoples as early as the seventh to sixth centuries BC. The name is said to be derived from the Messapian word *brunda* (or *brendon*), meaning 'stag's head', a reference to the shape of its harbour. The Greek name of Brentesion became Latinized to Brundisium after the Romans occupied the city in 266 BC and developed it as a naval base. Even after the defeat of Cannae (216 BC) Brundisium refused to come to terms with Hannibal, and for its loyalty the city was later made a *municipium* and a free port.

With Roman successes in the East, and the extension of the Via Appia in the second century BC, Brindisi took over from Taranto as principal port for the Orient. During the events which ended in the establishment of the principate, Julius Caesar very nearly managed to block Pompey in Brindisi 49 BC, and the following year he sailed from Brindisi with his legions to defeat Pompey at the Battle of Pharsalia. Nine years later Octavian and Mark Antony signed a truce at Brindisi, which was known as the *foedus brundisinum* and postponed Octavian's final victory over Antony and Cleopatra until September, 31 BC at Actium. It was here, once again on Saturnian land, that Virgil died on September 21st, 19 BC. Taking the unfinished manuscript of the *Aeneid* with him, he had sailed for Greece to meet Augustus who was on his way home from an official visit to Asia Minor. At Megara the poet became ill, but returning in the Emperor's suite, he reached Brundisium and died three days later. He had requested that the incomplete draft of his epic be destroyed at his death. However, on the authority of Augustus, the work was edited and published, with the express instructions 'that nothing should be added and that only superfluities should be expunged'.

Brindisi shared the fate of other Apulian towns in the early Middle Ages: Goths, Byzantines, Lombards and Saracens laid it waste; the Emperor Lewis II destroyed it. In 1071 it fell to Robert Guiscard. During the Crusades its prosperity began to revive, and the Emperor Frederick II, seeing the strategic importance of its port, built the Castello and granted the town the right to levy customs. These advantages were continued under the early Angevins, but Brindisi suffered in the dynastic disturbances that marked the end of the French house. The attacks of the Turkish allies of the Venetians against the Aragonese (Otranto was sacked in 1480) led to the construction of the fortress on the island of S. Andrea in the outer harbour and the complete blocking of the narrow channel which joins this with the inner basins, an action fatal to Brindisi's maritime existence. In the Spanish vice-regal period the town's fortunes fell to their lowest ebb.

On the initiative of Ferdinand IV of Bourbon in 1775 Andrea Pigonati was employed to clear the channel which today bears his name, and drain the pestiferous marshes, and this led to the rebirth of Brindisi's sea trade. The opening of the Suez Canal in 1869 brought new life to the port, and during the First World War Brindisi was the base for Allied naval operations in the Adriatic and eastern Mediterranean, as it was later for Mussolini's attacks on Ethiopia, Albania and Greece. The city was occupied by Allied troops on September 10th, 1943; the same day King Victor Emmanuel fled here from Rome, and it became the seat of Marshal Badoglio's interim government until February 1944, when the government was transferred to Salerno.

Brindisi was made a provincial capital in 1927, and has expanded rapidly in the last twenty years. Today it is the port for the motor-ferry service to Corfu and Igoumenitsa in Greece, and is also connected by regular services with Venice, Patras, the Piraeus and the Near and Far East. There are direct rail services from Rome and Naples via Bari and Benevento; from Reggio Calabria via Taranto. There are daily air services with Bari and Rome, and weekly flights to and from London. The Montecatini refinery is one of the largest works of its kind in Italy, and other industries include the canning of locally grown fruit and vegetables, and the production of artificial manures. There is a choice of hotels of all categories, and there are good bathing beaches in the vicinity.

The centre of the city is the adjoining Piazzas del Popolo and della Vittoria, the former constructed by the junction of the three main arteries, the Corso Umberto I, the Corso Roma and the Corso Garibaldi. The Corso Garibaldi runs down to the Piazza Vittorio Emanuele, with its gardens and palms and fountain of dolphins on the edge of the harbour, and to the right the Stazione Marittima, the quay for the car-ferries for Greece and the rail terminus.

The Piazza della Vittoria has a fountain composed from fragments of ancient and medieval stonework by the Spanish governor, Pedro de Torres, in 1618. At the far end of the square the short Piazza Sedile opens out into the larger Piazza G. Matteotti with the Municipio. In the near-by Via G. B. Casimiro destruction of some buildings in 1958 revealed extensive Roman ruins. Continuing north from the Piazza, we take the Via Duomo, passing the present seat of the Tribunale at No. 20 on the right, occupying the fine seventeenth-century Palazzo Granafei-Nervegna.

On the left of the Piazza Duomo, at the beginning of the Via Tarantini, is the Loggia Balsamo, its arches supported on curiously carved consoles, part of a fourteenth-century Angevin palace. At the other end of the piazza rises the eighteenth-century façade of the Duomo. But first we take the Via Colonne, which passes under the pointed arch of the baroque campanile and brings us to a belvedere. Here the **terminal column of the Via Appia Antica** stands, together with the base of another similar column which collapsed in 1528 and was removed to Lecce, where it now supports the bronze statue of that city's patron, S. Oronzo. The remaining column, of fine African *cipollino*, rests on a square base, with an inscription of the Byzantine governor, Lupos Protospata, who rebuilt the city in the tenth century. The magnificent white marble capital, depicting the figures of Jupiter, Mars, Neptune and tritons, has a circular plinth above it, which perhaps once supported a statue. On the wall of a house near by an inscription records Virgil's death at Brindisi.

From the top of the steps of the Salita Colonne we have a fine view of the harbour. On the opposite shore rises the **Monumento al Marinaio,** the memorial to Italian seamen erected in 1933 in the form of a gigantic ship's rudder standing 173 ft above the sea. This may be reached by a ferry which leaves from the Viale Regina Margherita, the esplanade immediately below us (to the left). A lift takes visitors to the summit of the monument, from which there is a splendid panorama of sea and city (open 9.0 a.m.–12.0 noon, 2.0–6.0 p.m.).

We return to the Piazza Duomo. Of the original **cathedral,** which was begun in 1140 and saw in 1225 the festivities that attended the marriage of the Emperor Frederick II with Yolande of Jerusalem, little remains, since the church was demolished in the earthquake of 1743 and rebuilt three years later. Restoration in 1957 has brought to light sections of a mosaic pavement of birds and animals behind the high altar and to the left of the choir, including an ass thoughtfully chewing its own tail. To the left of the Duomo is the **Portico dei Cavalieri Templari,** the fourteenth-century portion consisting of two arches raised on sturdy pilasters, and a single squat column with a Byzantine-inspired capital. The continuation of the arcading is modern. Beneath the portico are some carved capitals from the destroyed eleventh-century church of S. Andrea dell' Isola, as well as stonework from the Norman cathedral.

In the courtyard behind are the entrances to the **Provincial Library** (8.0 a.m.–12.0 noon, 4.0–8.0 p.m.; closed Saturday afternoon) and to the **Museo Archeologico Provinciale 'Francesco Ribezzo'.** The museum is admirably laid out and contains Messapian, Greek and Roman vases, statuary, mosaics and inscriptions. There is also a particularly good numismatic collection, which includes some gold coins of Frederick II. Across the piazza in the eighteenth-century Seminario is the **Biblioteca Arcivescovile 'De Leo',** founded in 1798, and containing a *Commentary on the Prophet Isaiah,* claimed to be by Alexander Hayles, the Englishman who was educated in the early thirteenth century at the celebrated abbey of Hayles in Gloucestershire. Known to his contemporaries by the grandiloquent titles of the 'Irrefragable Doctor', the 'Monarch of Theologians' or the 'Fountain of Life', he was one of the most celebrated professors at the University of Paris, where he died in 1245. Very few copies of his *Commentary* exist—if indeed it is his and not that of Alexander of Alexandria (1270–1314)—one being at the Ambrosian Library in Milan and another at the University of Leipzig.

From the Piazza Duomo we take the Via Tarantini and its continuation in the Via Santabarbara; here a short street on the left, the Via S. Giovanni, brings us to the round church of **S. Giovanni al Sepolcro.** Built possibly as a baptistery by the Knights Templar in the eleventh century, it subsequently passed to the Knights of the Holy Sepulchre. The doorway is preceded by a canopy raised on two columns with carved capitals, supported on two much worn Romanesque lions. The lintel and jambs are decorated with carving. In the interior eight columns of *cipollino* and granite (some of the capitals come from antique buildings) raised a cupola which has collapsed and is now replaced by a tiled roof. On the walls are remains of fourteenth-century frescoes.

Returning to the Via Santabarbara and continuing along it, we come shortly on the left to the Via S. Benedetto, which leads to the lovely church and cloister of **S. Benedetto,** which have recently been well restored. On the south portal of the church the architrave shows low-relief carvings of men fighting strange animals, a powerful piece of work which seems to reveal an Assyrian inspiration. The monastery was founded in 1080 and the cloister is of the same period. However, the dating of the church presents certain problems: the ground plan is similar to that of S. Francesco at Trani, begun in 1176, but where the roofing of the nave at Trani is formed by three cupolas, here it is roofed by rib-vaulting, with barrel-vaulting over the equally high aisles. The charming simple cloister is surrounded by a portico with a low parapet on which slim tapering columns support flat 'crutch' capitals; some of these have delicately carved designs of formalized Byzantine motifs.

If we continue in the Via Benedetto and then turn right in the Via Carmine, we come to the Porta Mesagne. In the Via Cristoforo Colombo to the left of the gate are the remains of a system of Roman waterworks. To the right, the Via C. Colombo and its prolongation in the Via Vittoria brings us to the massive **Castello Svevo,** today the headquarters of the Comando Militare Marittimo. The original fortress, commanding the Seno di Ponente, was begun by the Emperor Frederick II in 1227, and consists of the inner keep with its angle-towers. Outside Frederick's fortress Ferdinand I of Aragon added in 1481 a further system of walls and circular towers, the whole being strengthened by the Emperor Charles V when he built the city walls (parts of which we still see) in 1550.

There are other buildings of interest in the southern part of the city. From the south side of the Piazza del Popolo the short Via Pozzo Traiano brings us to the Via S. Lucia. Here, turning right, we find the church of **S. Lucia** on the corner of the Via Lata, of Romanesque origin but very much rebuilt. The nave is separated from the aisles by pilasters raising Gothic arches. On the walls are the faded remains of medieval frescoes. A stairway in the right aisle (enquire of the sacristan) descends to the eleventh-century Basilian crypt which contains some interesting Byzantine frescoes: the *Madonna enthroned* and *Mary Magdalen* (both of the twelfth century), and *S. Nicola and other saints* (thirteenth- to fourteenth-century).

Following the Via Lata and then turning left in the Via Porta di Lecce, we arrive at the impressive gateway of that name restored by the Emperor Charles V and incorporated in the city walls. Just before the gate, steps on the left bring us to the Chiesa del Cristo or, as it is more usually known, the **Chiesa del Crocifisso**—this after a much venerated Crucifix, a fine, expressive piece of wood-carving possibly by a thirteenth-century German artist. The church, begun in 1230 by Frate Nicola Paglia, anticipates the better-known church of S. Maria del Casale in the use of courses of different coloured stone in its façade, and also in the round-arched blind arcading in the gable end. The beautiful rose window consists of simple radials with outer circles of delicate carving, surmounted by a deep and ornate archivolt. In a niche to the right of the entrance is a statue in painted wood of the *Madonna and Child Enthroned*, a thirteenth-century work that seems to show a French influence.

Tancred's Fountain—S. Maria del Casale

For the beautiful church of S. Maria del Casale, just under two miles from the town centre, we take the Via C. Colombo and join the SS 16 for Bari, until the latter turns due west at the extremity of the Seno di Ponente. Shortly before the road curves to round the arm of the harbour we see on the left the **Fontana di Tancredi.** It appears that there was a Roman fountain here, which was rebuilt in 1192 by Tancred, the last of the reigning Norman kings, to commemorate the wedding of his son Roger with Urania of Constantinople. It was restored in 1540. The tradition is that the Crusaders used the fountain trough to water their horses while waiting for transport to the Holy Land. Leaving the SS 16 on the left, we continue in the Via Ettore Ciciriello to the crossroads on which stands the Youth Hostel. From here we take the Via Benedetto Brin to the football-ground, where we turn left in the Via S. Maria del Casale.

The church of **S. Maria del Casale,** founded in 1320 by Philip of Anjou, Prince of Taranto, is built in a transitional style between Romanesque and Gothic. The simple façade is decorated with geometric patterns in shades of honey-coloured stone. The central doorway is surmounted by a prominent canopy, with a round trefoliated opening and blind arches similar to those of the gable end. Above this is a single pointed-arched window. Within, one is impressed by the harmony of the pale colours of the frescoes. On the wall of the entrance is a great *Last Judgment*, the signed work of Rinaldo da Taranto (beginning of the fourteenth century). The frescoes on the walls of nave, transepts and east end—the *Annuncia-*

313

tion, Crucifixion, Christ Enthroned among Angels and various *saints*—
appear to be by several hands, for they show different influences:
Byzantine, Gothic, even Giottesque. During the summer months
there is usually an attendant present; at other seasons it is advisable
for visitors to enquire first at the offices of the Ente Provinciale per
il Turismo in the Viale Regina Margherita.

For the Salentine peninsula we leave Brindisi through the Porta Lecce
on the SS 16, which crosses the railway line and passes the cemetery,
where there are graves of officers and men of the British Navy who
lost their lives in the First World War. Running parallel with the
railway, the Statale crosses the Tavoliere di Lecce to the small town
of S. Pietro Vernotico. Shortly after it passes into the province of
Lecce, and enters the important wine-producing district of Squinzano. Joined on the right by the SS 7 *ter* from Taranto, the Statale
enters Lecce by the Via d'Aurio.

CHAPTER 18

Taranto and its Province

Maps: VI, p.238; VII, p.292

In Roman times Taranto lay on the Via Appia, on the route between Rome and Brindisi, the principal port for the Roman provinces in Macedonia, Asia Minor and Egypt. Standing at the head of the gulf which bears its name, Taranto is today an important centre of communications, and, with La Spezia, one of the two chief Italian naval bases.

Matera to Taranto—Massafra—cave-churches

Coming from Matera to Taranto the SS 7 runs first among the hills of the murge. In summer the land here gives the appearance of arid and rocky desolation. Shortly after crossing into Apulia, the road reaches a height of some 1200 ft, then descends to cross a viaduct, and continue through rather dull countryside to the small town of **Laterza,** built on the edge of a ravine.

Map VI p. 238

Leaving Laterza, we first cross a rocky and barren tract in a north-easterly direction, then run in an almost straight line—passing on the left the Masseria del Vecchio—as far as the Cappella Madonna del Carmine, where a road branches left for the SS 100 from Gioia del Colle. Here the Via Appia turns south and descends.

Castellaneta is also built on the edge of a *gravina*; it is in fact almost surrounded by one of the deepest of them, a fearsome ravine of grey rock with scattered bushes of prickly pear, reaching a depth of more than a thousand feet. The Largo Umberto I ends in a balustraded terrace from which there is a magnificent view. The *cathedral of the Assunta,* in the oldest part of the town, stands on a kind of promontory on the very brow of the *gravina.* Erected in the thirteenth century, the earliest structure has been almost entirely obliterated, inside and out, by the eighteenth-century reconstruction, the squat campanile to the left alone retaining its Romanesque

Map VI p. 238

315

form. On the right of the choir is a fine polyptych by Girolamo da Santacroce, who came possibly from Bergamo, and died in Venice in 1556. Some of the panels are missing. On the left of the cathedral an alleyway leads to a gate (if closed, apply to the sacristan), from the farther side of which there is an awe-inspiring view of the *gravina*.

After descending into the Gravina di Castellaneta, the Statale climbs the farther side, soon crosses the Gravina di Palagianello, and reaches the turning for the village of Palagianello. Bypassing the village of Palagiano, the road swings north-east (with a view of Mottola on its hill on our left), and almost immediately arrives at the junction with the SS 106 *dir*, an alternative route to Taranto.

On the SS 7 we continue to the junction with the SS 100 from Gioia del Colle and Bari, where we turn right and, through a countryside planted with olives and furrowed with *gravine*, come to one of the most extraordinary of these cliff-edge towns, **Massafra.** The town is built astride the Gravina di S. Marco, the old quarter of Terra, to the west, being joined with the more modern Borgo on the east of the ravine by two lofty bridges.

Map VII
p. 292

On the outskirts of the town, near the crossroads, stands on the right the *Cappella di S. Lucia,* a tenth-century Byzantine chapel which retains parts of the original building, including the two cupolas, rounded inside but covered externally by square-based pyramids. Above us on our left as we continue on the Via Appia is the lower of the two viaducts spanning the Gravina di S. Marco; the old town lies grouped around the castle, and to the east are the modern flat-topped houses of the Borgo. At the next crossroads we turn left and, climbing up with a magnificent view as far as Taranto and the Ionian Sea, enter the new town. From the Piazza Vittorio Emanuele we take the Corso Roosevelt and cross over the *gravina* by the lower viaduct, the Ponte Vecchio, to the centre of the old town, the Piazza Garibaldi, with the Municipio and offices of the Tourist Association Pro Loco.

In the sides of the ravine, among the boulders, clefts and man-made terraces with their bushes of prickly pear, you will see the entrances of the numerous *caves* for which the neighbourhood of Massafra is famous. People have carried on a trogloditic existence here from earliest medieval times until our own days. During the barbaric invasions which broke up the Roman Empire in the West, the destruction of their homes forced the local inhabitants to take to holes in the tufa, which they enlarged to accommodate their families and a few animals. Groups of Basilian hermits also took up their abode here, and it is to them primarily that we owe the many existing crypt-churches. These are well worth visiting, and enquiries at the Association Pro Loco will produce descriptive booklets and, if you are lucky, a guide.

The best-preserved of these cave-churches is the ***Chiesa-Cripta di S. Marco***. Its date is unknown, but it is at least as early as the thirteenth century. We enter through a vestibule which once served as a baptistery, the font being the deep cavity on the left. On the right is a fresco of *St Mark*. The church itself, which is nearly fifty feet in length, has two apsidal ends and is divided by pilasters into nave and aisles. There are some rough carvings and inscriptions in Greek and Latin. The right apse is separated from the aisle by a parapet which was used as a pulpit. The walls have openings which possibly served as *arcosolia*; of the frescoes which once adorned them, moisture has destroyed all except the thirteenth-century figures of the medieval *SS. Cosmas and Damian*.

The ***Cripta di S. Leonardo,*** thought to be of the fourteenth century, also has *arcosolia* and a number of frescoes, some well-preserved. The ***Cappella-Cripta della Candelora*** has an interesting collection of frescoes from the thirteenth century onwards, including a well-preserved *Presentation in the Temple*. The ***sanctuary of the Madonna della Scala*** (so called from the 125 steps which lead down to it) was built over the primitive cave-churches in 1731. Above the main altar is a twelfth- or thirteenth-century fresco from the Basilian crypt beneath: the *Madonna and Child with two kneeling dogs*. Next to the sanctuary is the partly ruined ***Cripta della Buona Nuova***. Above the altar are a *Madonna della Buona Nuova* (thirteenth century) and a more than life-size *Christos Pantocrator*. From the entrance to the sanctuary we descend to one of the earliest of the cave-churches (it is thought to be of the eighth or ninth century), basilican in form, and with numerous crosses cut in the stone.

Back in the Piazza Garibaldi, the Via Lopizzo brings us to the ***Castello***. The original fortress was rebuilt and altered by the Pappacoda family, who were the feudal lords of Massafra from 1497 until 1633, when the feud passed to the powerful Imperiali, who also added to the castle. Crossing the courtyard, where a ramp bears right under the escarpment, we follow this and its continuation in the Via la Terra to the church of ***S. Lorenzo*** (1533), built in a rampart of the Castello. From the terrace below one looks out over the coastal plain to Taranto and the curving shoreline of the Ionian Sea.

After Massafra the Via Appia runs in a straight line to Taranto. As we approach Taranto, we can see the results of modern irrigation

317

and also recent industrial developments. We are joined on the right by the SS 106 from Reggio Calabria, and on the left by the SS 172 from Martina Franca; then, crossing the railway line, we enter Taranto by the Via Napoli.

Bari to Taranto—Martina Franca—a taste of southern baroque architecture

From Bari to Taranto there are two principal routes (with variants). The first of these is the SS 100 through Gioia del Colle. (For the first section see pp. 291 and 289.) After leaving Gioia, the Statale runs south-east, crossing the infertile Piano di Gaudella, until ahead of us, like a hill fortress, we see the outline of Mottola. As we draw nearer to **Mottola** a wonderful panorama opens out, extending from the southern slopes of the murge to the curve of the Gulf of Taranto and as far west as the Sila Mountains in Calabria.

Map VII
p. 292

From Mottola the road descends rapidly, with fine views towards the Ionian Sea. On the left is the deep Gravina di Petruscio; opposite the ruins of the Torre Petruscio a path leads down into the ravine, where we find the cave-village of **Petruscio,** the date of which is uncertain, but probably contemporaneous with the crypts of Massafra. A short run over this broken terrain brings us to the junction with the SS 7, the Via Appia, and Taranto.

The variants to this route from Bari bring us through the *murge dei trulli,* a countryside fascinating both for its landscape and for its towns, to Locorotondo on the border between the provinces of Bari and Taranto (see p. 291 *et seq.*). From Locorotondo the SS 172 crosses the picturesque and fertile Valle d'Itria. To the left we see the clustered houses of Cisternino in the province of Brindisi; ahead of us high on the hilltop is Martina Franca.

Map VII
p. 292

The origins of **Martina Franca** go back to the tenth century when a village of refugees from Saracen raids on Taranto was founded on Monte S. Martino, on a site possibly already inhabited by Basilian hermits. The epithet Franca refers to the fiscal immunities and incentives granted by Philip of Anjou, Prince of Taranto, at the beginning of the fourteenth century. Later in the same century the town was fortified with walls and a castle by Raimondello Orsini. In 1506 Martina Franca was given in feud to a branch of the powerful Neapolitan family of Caracciolo, who held it, despite a serious rebellion of the inhabitants led by a blacksmith appropriately named Capo di Ferro in 1646, until the extinction of the line in 1827. The

318

district is noted for its strong white wine (*bianco neutro di Martina*), used in the fortification of other wines, particularly *spumanti*, and in the preparation of vermouth. There is also an important annual fair here every autumn at which locally bred horses, mules and donkeys, the *razza murgese*, are shown and sold. Apulian mules are extremely fine. The wealth gained in these lucrative pursuits enabled the citizens to build Martina Franca's charming baroque and rococo town houses in the late seventeenth and eighteenth centuries.

It is still a charming, prosperous, well-kept town today with a pleasant hotel, the Albergo Semeraro, in the Piazzetta S. Antonio, close to the Villa Comunale (formerly the gardens of the Convent delle Grazie) and the town centre, the Piazza XX Settembre. (There is another hotel, the Albergo Olimpo, Via Taranto.) Also on the Piazzetta is the church of *S. Antonio,* a fifteenth-century Gothic structure beneath its baroque surface, which has a *Madonna della Grazie* by the once well-known but now almost forgotten local painter, Leonardo Olivieri (*ca.* 1690–*ca.* 1745). He was sent to Naples to the studio of Solimena by Cardinal Caracciolo, and his popularity is demonstrated by the number of his works in the province of Taranto.

From the piazza we pass through the Porta S. Antonio (1764), surmounted by an equestrian statue of the city's patron St Martin, into the triangular Piazza Roma, with its fountain of dolphins. The *Municipio,* once the Ducal Palace, faces on to the piazza. Erected by Duke Petracone V Carracciolo in 1669 and attributed by some to Bernini, it is a handsome building with a fine baroque ironwork balcony running its entire length. The ducal apartments on the first floor are now used for municipal purposes. Some of the rooms are decorated with extraordinary paintings by Domenico Carella, an eighteenth-century local artist; the mayor's rooms have inexpert portraits of the Caracciolo family.

The narrow and winding Corso Vittorio Emanuele takes us, past some baroque and rococo palaces, to the fantastic collegiate church of *S. Martino* (1747–75) and next to it, on the left, the *Palazzo della Corte* (1759–62) and the *Torre dell' Orologio* (1734). The group of buildings is an interesting example of Southern Italian *settecento* baroque architecture. On the right of S. Martino is the restored late Romanesque-Gothic campanile from the earlier church (fifteenth-century). The main doorway, with its representation of *St Martin and the beggar*, is a foretaste of the richly adorned interior.

From here we proceed to the Piazza Plebiscito and its continuation in the old market-place, now the Piazza Garibaldi. From the left of the Piazza Plebiscito runs the Via Cavour, flanked by charming *settecento* (and earlier) town houses. The whole quarter repays exploration. At the farther end of the Piazza Garibaldi the Via Principe Umberto, on the right, brings us to the baroque church of **S. Domenico** (1760), and, beyond the Conservatorio di S. Maria della Misericordia, to the **Porta S. Maria.** From here we turn left in the Via Pergolesi for the **Villa del Carmine** and a magnificent view from its balustrade of the Valle d'Itria.

Back in the Piazza Garibaldi, we take the Via Alighieri to where it joins the Via Ciaia, on which rises the façade *a bugne*, with its open campanile, of the fifteenth-century church of **S. Vito dei Greci.** The Via Alighieri is continued in the Via Manzoni, which has some fascinating smaller houses, with terraces, outside stairways, and pleasant doorways and balconies.

Map VII
p. 292

Leaving Martina Franca by way of the modern suburbs to the south of the old town, the SS 172 runs for some miles in a straight line alongside the railway, through a countryside whose fertility gradually diminishes as we approach the southern edge of the murge. A turning on the right leads to the village of **Crispiano** which stands on an ancient, perhaps Greek, site, with some frescoed Basilian cave-churches. As we descend the last of the foothills of the murge we see ahead of us the Ionian Sea and Taranto across the lagoon of the Mare Piccolo. For those who wish to bypass Taranto and continue on to Lecce, there is a secondary road on the left which rounds the northern and eastern shores of the Mare Piccolo to meet the SS 7 just before S. Giorgio Ionico.

Taranto—Dorian Greeks from Sparta—the Città Vecchia—the Città Nuova —the Museo Nazionale—the tarantella—Holy Week Ceremonies—beaches

Map VII
p. 292

The city of **Taranto** stands partly on the mainland and partly on an artificial island formed by cutting through the narrow peninsula that once almost closed the inner 'sea', the Mare Piccolo, from the outer 'sea', the Mare Grande (or Mar Piccolo and Mar Grande). The Mare Grande is separated from the open sea by the Isole Cheradi, the islands of S. Pietro and S. Paolo. The area around the railway station and the new industrial suburbs to the west is known as the Borgo, and a bridge, the Ponte di Porta Napoli, links this with the Città Vecchia. This is in turn connected by a swing bridge

320

Above left Byzantine frescoes in the 11th c. Basilian crypt of S. Lucia, Brindisi.

Above right The beautiful 15th c. rose window in the cathedral of Otranto.

Right Thought to be a 4th c. representation of the Emperor Valentinian, the 16ft high bronze Colossus at Barletta came originally from Constantinople.

Above The swing bridge at Taranto links the old and new cities.
Below The Museo Nazionale contains magnificent Greek and Roman collections. Here a vase and a marble head hint at the riches to be seen.

over the navigable canal with the modern quarters of the Città Nuova.

The oldest habitation was probably the quarter of the Borgo near the railway station known as Lo Scoglio del Tonno; archaeological finds here, including Mycenaean pottery, show that the inhabitants (possibly Iapygians or Messapians) had trading relations with the main centres of Aegean culture as early as the end of the second millennium BC. But the decisive event in the development of the settlement was the coming of the Greeks, traditionally in 706 BC. Taras—the name may be Messapian—was the only colony ever established by Dorian Greeks from Sparta. During the war with Messenia the Spartans were absent from home for many years and the legend tells how the women in the interval formed connections with the Helots. The children born of these unions, known as Partheniae—'maidens' children'—conspired against the state and were expelled. The oracle directed them to settle at Taras, which they did under the leadership of the hero Phalanthus, who was later represented on their beautiful coins, riding on a dolphin. The prosperity of the new colony came from its position, the plentiful supply of fish, wine, fruit and salt, and the development of industries such as pottery and the manufacture of woollen stuffs, which were dyed with the purple obtained from the shellfish, the murex.

Taras enjoyed its period of greatest splendour under the enlightened leadership of Archytas in the mid-fourth century BC. Archytas seems to typify the ideal man of the democratic Greek city-states. Re-elected year after year to almost autocratic authority, he is said never to have abused it. As a general he was unbeaten. His studies in mathematics included dissertations on the different kinds of progression, on the nature of infinity, and a solution to the problem of the duplication of the cube. Plato corresponded with him and visited him; it was Archytas who persuaded Plato to visit Dionysius the Elder of Syracuse, and, when Plato's life was endangered, successfully intervened on his behalf.

The sophisticated elegance of Greek Tarentine life may be seen in the exhibits at the Museo Nazionale. Today, Taranto has a population of 200,000; in Archytas's time 300,000 inhabitants lived within a ten-mile circuit of walls. Until the time of Archytas the Greek city was probably on what is now the island of the Città Vecchia, with a defensive wall where the Canale Navigabile was later cut (this, together with the Castello, was part of Ferdinand of Aragon's defences constructed in 1481 against the Turks). Outside the walls was the necropolis, which has yielded precious objects now in the

Museo Nazionale, but this area has been entirely built over since the
Naval Arsenal was begun in 1883. In later Greek and Roman days
the overcrowding of the city necessitated the removal of the walls to
a position much farther east, and the founding of a new necropolis
outside them.

After Archytas's death in 365 BC the Tarentines relied on mercenaries, particularly from the Greek mainland, in their almost
constant warfare with the local peoples. In 281 BC the Romans broke
the treaty they had made with the Tarentines during the Second
Samnite War, whereby no Roman ship was to sail beyond the
Lacinian promontory (Capo Colonna near Crotone); and in the
ensuing war the Tarentines called on the assistance of King Pyrrhus
of Epirus. However, in 272 BC the Epirote garrison surrendered the
city to the Romans. In 212 Taranto rebelled against Rome and sided
with Hannibal, only to be captured and sacked three years later by
Fabius Maximus. The immense booty carried off by the victorious
Romans was a foretaste of their later systematic pillage of the art
treasures of ancient Hellas. 'Molle Tarentum' was how the Romans
still described it in the imperial age; but Horace had high praise for
Taranto: 'Dearest of all to me is that corner of the earth which
yields not to Hymettus for its honey, nor for its olive to green
Venafrum; whose heaven grants a long springtime and warmth in
winter, and in the sunny hollows Bacchus fosters a vintage noble as
Falernian . . .' (*Odes*).

Today there are very few classical remains in Taranto, but for
information and for permission to visit the excavated sites apply to
the Soprintendenza alle Antichità, Via Cavour 10.

After the downfall of the Roman Empire in the West Taranto was
caught up in the struggles between Byzantines and the Lombard
Dukes of Benevento, and devastated by Saracen raids, particularly
that of 927 when the city was practically destroyed. In 967 it was
retaken by the Emperor Nicephorus Phocas and made into a bastion
of Byzantine rule until its capture by Robert Guiscard in 1063.
From then on, except for a period in the fourteenth and early
fifteenth centuries when it was in the possession of the del Balzo-
Orsini, it was an appendage of the ruling house of the Kingdom of
Naples.

During the Napoleonic Wars its strategic position against the
English Mediterranean fleet was recognized by the French, and
Marshal Soult in 1801 set to work to fortify it, employing as one of
the military engineers an artillery officer, Choderlos de Laclos,
better known to posterity as the author of *Les Liaisons Dangereuses*.

After crossing from the Borgo to the **Città Vecchia** by the Ponte di Porta Napoli, we turn right into the Corso Vittorio Emanuele II. The Corso, flanked on the left by *palazzi*, is open to the sea; from the height of the esplanade we look over out the Porto Mercantile to the low forms of the Isole Cheradi. The construction of the Suez Canal did much for the port of Taranto, but it has always had a serious rival in Brindisi. At the east end of the island we cross the Piazza del Municipio for the bridge over the canal and the hotels of the Città Nuova (Taranto is well provided with hotels of all categories). On the right of the piazza stands Frederick of Aragon's **Castello,** incorporating in its cylindrical towers and curtain walls the fabric of earlier buildings. Today it is occupied by the Italian Navy, but permission will be given to visit the restored **Cappella di S. Leonardo** (sixteenth century). On the other side of the piazza rises the Municipio (1886) and to the right of it in the corner of the square is the beginning of the narrow Via Duomo. The whole island is a warren of narrow alleys, and is traversed by four roughly parallel streets: the Corso Vittorio Emanuele II on the Mar Grande, the Via Duomo, the Via di Mezzo and the Via Garibaldi, where the fishermen's boats are drawn up on the Mar Piccolo.

Almost immediately on the right of the Via Duomo is the **oratorio della SS. Trinità**, with the remains of the **Doric temple** in the courtyard (if closed, apply for the key at the shop next door). A little farther on, the Via Paisiello on the left brings us to the house in which one of the most celebrated eighteenth-century composers of Neapolitan opera, Giovanni Paisiello, was born. His delightful *Barber of Seville* has had the misfortune to be superseded by the later version of Rossini. The **Duomo** is dedicated to the seventh-century Irishman, St. Cathal of Munster (Italianized to S. Cataldo), who, returning from a pilgrimage to the Holy Land, was persuaded by the Tarentines to remain as their bishop. The present church, founded in 1071 on the site of an earlier building, has been many times altered and restored, but the worst of the baroque accretions have recently been removed, with the inexplicable exception of the façade of 1713. From the outside the sides and the transepts have a simple decoration of blind arcading; the circular Byzantine drum (with a shallow conical roof at the crossing) is interesting, and has blind arcades supported by slim columns. The unimaginative campanile of 1413 has been rebuilt in the recent restoration.

On the left of the entrance is the vestibule-baptistery, containing a font covered by a canopy (1571) resting on antique columns, and the seventeenth-century tomb of Archbishop Tommaso Caracciolo.

The interior is basilican in form, with a raised transept, the nave separated from the aisles by columns of antique marble supporting rounded arches. Notice the capital of the second column on the left, which is purely Byzantine in inspiration, with birds pecking among the foliage. The gilded ceiling of 1713, which shows *S. Cataldo with Maria Immacolata*, has been retained, as has the baroque Cappella di S. Cataldo on the right of the apse, behind the ornate bronze and iron-work—that 'jovial nightmare in stone', as Norman Douglas described it. The cupola is decorated with frescoes by Paolo de Matteis (also in 1713). Here at the altar are preserved the relics of S. Cataldo; the statue of the Saint is by the Neapolitan Vincenzo Catello (1892). On the right of the church we descend to the crypt, passing an altar with a low-relief in stucco of the *Madonna and Child*, thought to be by Tommaso Fiamberti from Como (*fl.* 1498–1524). The crypt, with its low vaulting (unexpected, lightly-pointed arches borne on stumpy columns), has been likened to an early Christian catacomb; and the sarcophagi and remains of frescoes support the comparison.

A short way beyond the cathedral, at the end of the Via Duomo, we turn right and come to the church of **S. Domenico Maggiore,** which is approached by high double steps of the baroque period. The church itself was built at the end of the eleventh century, but was remodelled in the Gothic style in 1302; the main portal, with its deep archivolt and the graceful rose window above are from this Angevin reconstruction. Among the church's paintings are a *Circumcision* by Marco Pino of Siena (a replica of the picture is in the Gesù Vecchio in Naples), the *Virgin and Saints* by L. A. Olivieri of Martina Franca, and the *Dream of St Joseph* by Corrado Giaquinto (1703–65).

If we continue north from S. Domenico we come to the Piazza Fontana on the Mar Piccolo, with the Ponte Porta Napoli on our left and the crowded, lively Via Giuseppe Garibaldi on the right, separating the conglomeration of ancient buildings, pierced by narrow *viuzze*, from all the activity of the waterfront. Strings of mussels (*cozze*), oysters (*ostriche*) and other shellfish are displayed in the Mercato Frutti di Mare. The stakes in the Mar Piccolo are used in the culture of these shellfish for which Taranto is traditionally famous. Near by are two of the best restaurants for fish from Taranto's inland sea: the Pesce Fritto, Via Cariati 46; and Al Gambero across the channel in the Borgo, Vico del Ponte 4. At Gambero's the specialities include *risotto* or *spaghetti Gambero*, *zuppa di pesce*, and lobster cooked on a spit (*gambero allo spiedo*). Try with the

324

last-named a bottle of San Severo or white Castel del Monte, or perhaps a Torre Giulia.

Crossing from the old city to the **Città Nuova** by the swing-bridge over the Canale Navigabile and then continuing straight on, we come shortly to the Piazza Archita—or, rather, to that part of it (laid out in gardens and palms) known as the Villa Garibaldi. Beyond the Via Cavour, on the farther side of the piazza, is the imposing bulk of the **Palazzo degli Uffici,** which houses a secondary school, the law-courts, and the meteorological observatory. On the north side of the Villa Garibaldi, on the corner of the Corso Umberto and the Via Cavour, is the **Museo Nazionale,** occupying what was once part of the Convent of the Padri Alcantarini (admission, November 1st–April 20th, 9.30 a.m.–4.0 p.m.; May 1st–October 31st, 8.0 a.m.–1.30 p.m. and 3.30–7.0 p.m.).

Nothing conveys more vividly the glory of Magna Graecia than a visit to the magnificent collection of antiquities in the National Museum. The art of the earliest Italic peoples is also illustrated, and the effect on local production brought about by the coming of the Greeks. The ground-floor rooms represent the indigenous inhabitants of Southern Italy: the Messapians in the Gallery of the Provinces of Taranto, Brindisi and Lecce; the Peucezi in the Gallery of the Province of Bari; the Daunians in the Gallery of the Province of Foggia; and two smaller sections are given to the Lucanians and the Bruttians of (modern) Calabria.

The main rooms of the first floor, the Taranto Section, consist largely of objects found in the necropolis of the city. Rooms I and II contain Greek sculpture, including a beautiful *head of Aphrodite* of the mid-fourth century BC, and a funerary *stele*. In Room IV is a sarcophagus cut from a single block of stone and covered by a gabled top with palmettes at the corners, which shows the original decoration in red, blue, green and gold. Within is the skeleton of a young athlete of the late sixth century BC, with a magnificent set of white teeth.

Rooms V–XI contain the fine collections of vases discovered in the necropolis under the Città Nuova, grouped according to date and provenance. Two most beautiful cups, decorated inside with sporting tunny fish and dolphins and outside with a circle of birds, are paradoxically from philistine Sparta.

Room XII, the Gallery of the Jewellery, has beautiful gold and enamel work and the marvellous funerary objects from Canosa di Puglia, especially the diadem consisting of a garland of gold leaves with flowers of delicately coloured stones and enamels.

The remaining space on this floor is occupied by the terracottas, for which Taranto was justly famous. On the second floor two rooms have been arranged to illustrate the prehistoric civilizations of Apulia and Lucania.

The modern suburbs of Taranto have little of architectural interest, and some of the official buildings of the fascist period are hideous. On the northern side of the peninsula the Via Roma leads to the gardens of the Villa Peripato, from which we have a wide view out across the naval dockyards and waters of the Mar Piccolo to the enfolding range of the murge.

Taranto has given its name to a species of large spider (*Lycosa tarantula*), whose bite was reputed to induce a contagious hysteria which was apparently prevalent in Southern Apulia, especially in the seventeenth century. All that remains to us of the heady therapeutic dancing ritual designed to counteract the effects is the graceful (but bowdlerized) modern version of the traditional tarantella.

However, another Tarentine custom (this one from at least as early as the sixteenth century) has not been allowed to perish. Taranto's curious and colourful ceremonies during Holy Week draw great crowds of reverent spectators. From Maundy Thursday until Easter Sunday the four Confraternities (of the Carmines—known to the people as the 'pardoned ones', the *Perdune*; the Spirito Santo or Nome di Dio; the SS. Rosario; and the Addolorata) process slowly from church to church, bare-footed and dressed in medieval attire, and bearing with them the signs of Our Lord's suffering and death. Most impressive are the white-cowled figures (with slits for eye-holes), leaning on their white staves as they follow the *Truccalande* in slow-moving procession through the darkened streets of the Città Vecchia.

Unlike other provincial capitals in Apulia, Taranto is fortunate in her beaches. Within easy reach of the city to the west are the Lido Azzurro, the Lido Venere, the Lido Impero at Chiatona and the Marina di Ginosa. And southwards towards Capo S. Vito and beyond, are a number of excellent beaches connected by bus services from the Viale Virgilio. Praia a Mare and Marechiaro lie this side of the cape, and beyond the lighthouse is the little sandy cove of the Lido Bruno. Farther to the south-east, along the old road to Gallipoli which hugs the broken coastline, are the Lido Gandoli and the Lido Silvano.

Manduria—Messapian remains—Pliny's Well

From Taranto the Lecce road, the SS 7 *ter* (Salentina), branches right from the Via Appia (SS 7) at S. Giorgio Ionico and passes through the monotonous rolling landscape of the Murge Tarentine, and the villages of Monteparano, Fragagnano and Sava. From here a short run brings us to the interesting town of **Manduria.**

Map VII p. 292

The centre of the town is the triangular Piazza Garibaldi, where the majestic *Palazzo Imperiali* (1709) stands facing us, with its great doorway, and its balcony running the entire length of the façade. On the right is the eighteenth-century baroque church of the Carmine and the adjoining convent, now occupied by the Municipio. Here, on the first floor, is the *Biblioteca 'Marco Gatti',* containing works by local authors, studies of Messapian archaeology, and some rare first editions of early medical books. The librarian will show visitors (9.0 a.m.–1.0 p.m.) his collection of Mandurian antiquities, which include undeciphered Messapian inscriptions, some Saracenic copper cauldrons, and curious pyramid-shaped objects in terracotta with incised Messapian characters—possibly seals. On the left of the Palazzo Imperiali the Via Mercanti brings us to the *Duomo,* a building originally Romanesque but showing Gothic, Renaissance, baroque and recent additions and alterations. Opposite the cathedral an archway leads to the medieval *ghetto* with its windowless houses.

From the Piazza Garibaldi, the Lecce road to the right of the Palazzo Imperiali brings us to the Piazza Vittorio Emanuele. In the piazza and the streets off it are several interesting baroque palazzi, with pleasant balconies and loggias. Just outside the town we turn left into the new Viale Panoramico, which crosses the railway by a causeway and bridge. A short way beyond the bridge a gateway cuts through the megalithic walls of ancient Manduria, thought by some to be the Porta Lupiae (Lecce). The city was surrounded by three walls, dating from the fifth to the third centuries BC, with a circumference of about three and a half miles. Outside the outer wall by the Porta Lupiae and to the north a number of graves have been excavated in the *tufa*. Note the shells of oysters and other *frutti del mare*, which were embedded in the soft stone. Continuing to the right along the inside of the walls, we come to a second gate with an extensive necropolis outside it. From here a track on the left brings us to the walled enclosure surrounding *Pliny's Well* (Fonte Pliniano), so called from having been described by Pliny the Elder in his Natural History in AD 77: 'In the Salentine territory, near the town of Manduria, there is a well full to the brim, the level of which is not lowered by drawing off water nor raised by pouring it in.'

The almond tree growing inside a circular wall is the legendary tree (today on Manduria's civic crest) on which the victorious Messapians used to hang almonds of gold. Close by, steps lead down into a large cool cavern and Pliny's Well. Today the water, which is fed from another underground cistern, flows into a cavity outside the well. The cistern explains Pliny's comment on the water-level.

From Manduria we cross a countryside devoid of particular interest, and after meeting the SS 16 from Brindisi, enter the provincial capital of Lecce.

CHAPTER 19

Lecce and the Salentine Peninsula

Map: VIII, p.330

Lecce—Southern Italy's baroque city—ancient origins—Tancred—
SS. Nicolò e Cataldo—Leccese churches

Nothing could be more surprising than the presence at one of the furthermost extremities of Italy of a city such as **Lecce** with its early eighteenth-century sophistication and elegance. The architecture is predominantly baroque, but baroque merging into rococo, rococo into a 'classical' Georgian. Even a little pavilion in the style of the Second Empire finds its place naturally in this setting.

The road from Taranto enters the city under the **triumphal arch** erected (1548) in honour of the Emperor Charles V, the founder of the city as we see it today. Just before the gateway, at the junction with the wide tree-lined boulevard which encircles the city, stands an obelisk with reliefs of dolphins holding fish in their mouths, raised by King Ferdinand I and IV of the Two Sicilies early in the last century. The old sections of the city were enclosed within walls and bastions by Charles V between 1539 and 1548, when he employed the Leccese architect Gianjacopo dell' Acaya to improve the fortifications and to remodel the castle, built by one of the French family of Brienne, Counts of Lecce, two centuries earlier. The only portion of the wall still standing is on the side of the city by which we enter. Three of the city's gates, however, remain; a fourth, the Porta S. Martino, was demolished in 1826 to make way for the gardens behind the Prefettura.

Inside the arch, on the right, at the beginning of the Via G. Palmieri, stands the little church of **S. Maria della Porta** (rebuilt 1855 on a sixteenth-century site), with its attractive majolica dome. A few yards farther, on the opposite side of the narrow street, is the **Teatro Paisiello,** with a good 1870 façade. Originally the Teatro Nuovo, it was built privately in 1758 (only twenty-one years after Naples's San Carlo) and is said to be one of the oldest playhouses in

329

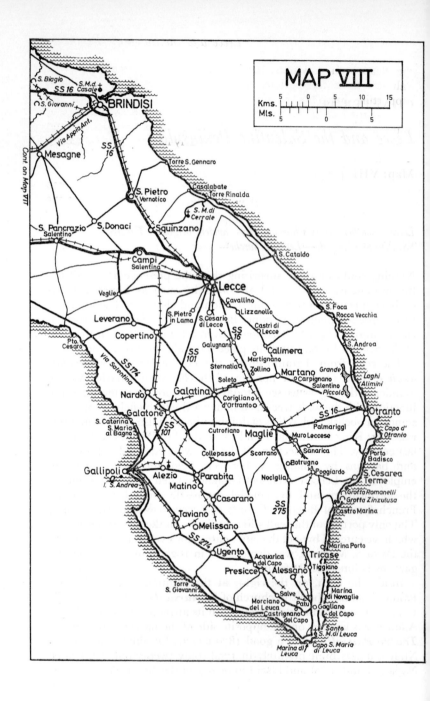

MAP VIII

Kms.
Mls.

S. Biagio
S.M.d. Casale
SS 16
S. Giovanni
BRINDISI

Via Appia Ant.
Mesagne
SS 16

Torre S. Gennaro
Casalabate
S. Pietro
Vernotico
Torre Rinalda
S.M. di Cerrale

S. Pancrazio
Salentino
S. Donaci
Squinzano

Campi
Salentina

S. Cataldo

Lecce

Veglie
Cavallino
S. Pietro
in Lama
Lizzanello
S. Foca
Rocca Vecchia
S. Cesario
di Lecce
Castri di
Lecce
SS 16

Leverano

Copertino

Galugnano
SS 101

Calimera

S. Andrea

Pto.
Cesaro

Via Salentina
SS 174

Martignano
Sternatia
Zollino
Martano
Carpignano
Salentino
Grande
Laghi
Alimini

Nardò
Galatina
Soleto
Piccolo

Corigliano
d'Ortranto

Galatone
SS 101
S. Caterina
S. Maria
al Bagno

Cutrofiano
Maglie
Muro Leccese
Palmariggi
SS 16
Otranto
Capo d'
Otranto

Collepasso
Scorrano
Sanarica
Botrugno
Poggiardo
Porto
Badisco

Gallipoli
I. S. Andrea
Alezio
Matino
Parabita
Nociglia
S. Cesarea
Terme
Grotta Romanelli
Grotta Zinzulusa
Castro Marina

Casarano
SS 275

Taviano
Melissano
SS 274
Marina Porto

Ugento
Acquarica
del Capo
Tricase
Tiggiano

Presicce
Alessano

Torre
S. Giovanni
Salve
Morciano
del Leuca
Patù
Marina
di Novaglie
Gagliano
del Capo
Castrignano
del Capo
Santo
S. M. di Leuca
Marina di
Leuca
Capo S. Maria
di Leuca

Cont. on Map VII

the Neapolitan provinces. Several of the small palaces in Via G. Palmieri have the curious carved stone brackets (or consoles), supporting balconies of stone or graceful ironwork, which are peculiar to much of the baroque architecture, both ecclesiastical and domestic, in Lecce. (Examples of these palaces are to be found everywhere in the old town, but particularly fine ones can be seen in Via Leonardo Prato, Via Palazzo dei Conti and the Corso Vittorio Emanuele.)

Lecce is a monument to the mason's art. The warm stone which paves the streets is continued without break in the façades of the houses, cut so clean-edged as to resemble stucco. On all sides there is a harmony of golden sandstone—from the paving up through every form of embellishment to the upright pineapple forming a finial or the aerial figure of a saint against a blue expanse of sky. When it is freshly quarried this stone is cream in colour and easy to work; exposed to the weather it hardens and gradually takes on its warm shades of honey-gold. It does not appear to suffer with age.

Four tall palm trees and a date-palm in the little piazza opening from the left of Via Palmieri remind us that geographically we are not far from Africa. Near this piazzetta, on the same side of the street, is a seventeenth-century house, the *Palazzo Palmieri,* with curious trefoiled openings between the ground-floor windows, and delicate wrought-iron balconies. Here King Joachim Murat stayed on a visit to Lecce. A tablet on the last house on the right records the birth there of the historian Michelangelo Schipa. Lecce's contributions in the field of arts and letters have earned her the titles of the 'Florence of Baroque Art' or the 'Apulian Athens'.

Before us is the magnificent, extravagantly ornamental entrance, built for Bishop Sozi-Carafa in the middle of the eighteenth century, to the wide expanse of the *Piazza del Duomo.* Berenson considered there was no cathedral close to equal this in Italy, perhaps on the Continent. In the piazza is the *cathedral of S. Oronzo,* built (1659–70) by Giuseppe Zimbalo to replace an earlier church. The interior is mainly eighteenth-century work—for example, the choir and baptistery—but much of the marble was placed here in the last century after being removed from suppressed convents in Napoleonic times. The campanile on the left of the square is also Zimbalo's work; built in 1661–2, it is 227 ft in height. To the right of the cathedral, and set back from it, is the *Bishop's Palace* (Vescovado), with its graceful loggia. The palace was originally built by Geronimo Giudano in 1420–8, at which time its ground-floor was occupied by shops and the annual fair took place in the piazza in front of it.

The present baroque appearance derives from its rebuilding in 1632, and it was extensively remodelled again by the diocesan authorities in 1874. The **Ecclesiastical Seminary** (Seminario Vescovile) on the right-hand side of the piazza was designed by Zimbalo's pupil, Giuseppe Cino, and built (1694–1709) for two Pignatelli brothers, both Bishops of Lecce. In its courtyard is a charming well, also by Cino, the decoration rich and bold.

Leaving the Piazza del Duomo by the main entrance, we turn right in the Corso Vittorio Emanuele, one of the city's main shopping streets, which leads from the Porta Rudiae to the Piazza S. Oronzo. A short way along, on the left, is the church of *S. Irene* (1591–1639). This church and the Jesuit church of the **Buon Consiglio** (or del Gesù, 1575) in the Via Rubichi, just off Piazza S. Oronzo, are two of the earliest and least florid of the baroque churches in Lecce, both having much in common with contemporary Roman architecture. Their altars, however, are ornately decorated in the prevailing Leccese style of Spanish influence. Above the main door of S. Irene is a statue of the Saint carved by Mauro Manieri, the only example we have of his work. A few yards farther on we come into the wide space of the Piazza S. Oronzo, the centre of the city. By the partly excavated ruins of the Roman amphitheatre stands the **Sedile,** the former meeting-place of the civic authorities, built by the Sindaco Pier Mocenigo in 1592. Adjoining it on the right is the little chapel of the colony of Venetian merchants in Lecce, dedicated to their patron *S. Marco* (1543), with the lion of St Mark in a lunette over the doorway. But it is the bronze statue of the city's saint, S. Oronzo, on his lofty marble column that dominates the square. This Roman column was one of the pair which marked the end of the Via Appia on the waterside at Brindisi, and was brought here in 1681. The plinth on which it stands was designed by Zimbalo.

Publius Orontius, one of the earliest Christian martyrs, was said to have been a rich and aristocratic follower of the Pythagorean schools which still flourished at that time in Magna Graecia. In AD 57 Orontius was out hunting when he met a traveller named Justus who had that day landed at Otranto from Corinth, bearing an epistle from St Paul to the Romans. The hospitable Orontius invited him to his house, and within forty-eight hours was converted to the Christian faith. On his return from his mission to Rome Justus took Orontius with him to Corinth, where St Paul, impressed by his character and zeal, appointed him Bishop of Lecce. Both Orontius and Justus are said to have suffered martyrdom together outside Lecce during one of Nero's persecutions, either in AD 66 or 68.

The origins of Lecce are very ancient; almost certainly of Messapian foundation like the near-by Rusce (Latin *Rudiae*), it seems that it came early under Greek influence. Tradition says that both towns were founded by the Messapian King Malennius, son of Daunus, whose daughter Euippa married the Cretan Idomeneus on his return from Troy. Over the Porta Rudiae, the gate leading to Rusce, are four statues representing these personages. To the Romans Lecce was known as Lupiae; its importance as a Roman colony seems to have increased as its neighbour Rudiae declined. It was at Rudiae, just west of Lecce, that Quintus Ennius, the 'father of Latin poetry' (*'ingenio maximus, arte rudis'*, according to Ovid) was born in 239 BC, descended from the old Messapian nobility. The city now lies buried under the fields, awaiting excavation. Recently an ox broke through the ceiling of a lofty room while ploughing. On one of its walls was an inscription in characters very similar to Greek, but so far their interpretation has baffled scholars.

Until the beginning of the present century it was believed that the two towns were joined by underground passages. Digging under the Piazza S. Oronzo revealed a network of stone alleyways and vaults, but these turned out to be part of the remains of a Roman amphitheatre of the second century AD. Not far from the Piazza S. Oronzo the ruins of a theatre are further testimony to the importance of the city in Roman times. (Incidentally, it was at Lecce in 44 BC that Octavius, on returning from the East, heard of his uncle's assassination and was first acclaimed Emperor.) To reach the theatre, we take the short Via Augusto Imperatore to the little Piazza Vittorio Emanuele II, where a grandiloquent statue of the King stands, dressed in baggy trousers. At the end of the square is the unfinished rococo façade of the church of **S. Chiara** (1687). The decoration of the altars in S. Chiara shows the deeply incised carving characteristic of Lecce work; here vine tendrils entwine heads of *putti* in a bacchanalian riot of ornamentation. To the left of S. Chiara runs the Via Arte della Cartapesta, so called because the craft of making papier-mâché figures of saints was once carried on here. A short street, the first on the right in Via Arte Cartapesta, leads behind S. Chiara to the little Roman theatre, well below the present street-level.

If we continue along the Via Arte Cartapesta, we arrive at the Via del Palazzo dei Conti di Lecce, and in the corner, at the other end of the piazzetta at the junction of these streets, can be seen, partly set back and obscured by other buildings, all that remains of the *palace of the Counts of Lecce*. During the Dark Ages the city suffered greatly from the wars, when Goths and Lombards were trying to wrest these lands from the eastern Emperors in Constantinople. As early as the eighth century the Saracens first appeared on these shores which they were to harass for more than a thousand years. In 1055 the Normans finally overthrew Byzantine rule, and Geoffrey (or Godfrey), son of Tancred de Hauteville, became the first Count of Lecce. The line of Hauteville counts came to an end with another Tancred, King of Sicily, in 1194; and in 1200 the city passed into the power of the French family of Brienne, with the marriage of Tancred's daughter Albiria to Walter III of Brienne. Finally, in 1463, the more or less independent County of Lecce became merged in the Kingdom of Naples when Isabella of Brienne married Ferdinand of Aragon.

The memorial that the last Tancred left to Lecce was described by Gregorovius as 'the most beautiful and most characteristic monument of Norman art, and the one which gives the most perfect impression of classic simplicity and symmetry'—the church of SS. Niccolò e Cataldo. The romantic circumstances of Tancred's birth became the theme of many medieval poems. Roger, Duke of Apulia, the eldest son of King Roger II of Sicily, had been sent by his father to the court of his kinsman Robert IV, Count of Lecce, to be trained in all the refinements of chivalry. Trade had followed in the wake of the crusaders, and Robert's court at Lecce was one of the most brilliant of the time. Robert had a daughter Sibylla, famed for her beauty, and the young Roger fell deeply in love with her. They somehow managed to keep their liaison secret until the birth of a second child, Tancred, when Roger was found to be suffering from an incurable disease. Recalled by his father to Palermo, he confessed his love for Sibylla and obtained the King's consent to marry her by proxy, but before the event was solemnized he died. After his death King Roger drove Count Robert from the country, giving Lecce over to the depredations of his troops.

The church of **SS. Nicolò and Cataldo** is outside the city walls. From King Ferdinand's obelisk with the dolphins we take the Via Nicola, which leads to a four-columned portico with a heavy architrave, the entrance to the Campo Santo. In the cemetery a cypress-lined walk ends in front of the church. Henri Bertaux described SS. Nicolò and Cataldo as 'a Burgundian church of Leccese stone in a shell of Greek-Apulian architecture'. But this does not do justice to the variety of styles, since the façade, save for Tancred's beautiful Romanesque doorway, is baroque of great charm (Cino, 1710) and

334

the internal arches show a Saracenic influence similar to those of the contemporary cathedral at Monreale in Sicily. The success of these Cluniac builders is best appreciated inside the church. Although it is small, the delicate clusters of columns and Saracenic arches give an impression of soaring height. The single tomb is that of Ascanio Grandi, the seventeenth-century Leccese poet whose interminable *Tancred* once had a great vogue among southern audiences. Another fine Romanesque portal leads to the cloisters of the monastery, now a hospital for the aged poor.

Lecce has at least three good hotels, and others which, though more modest, are clean and comfortable. The Risorgimento in Via Augusto Imperatore and the Patria in Piazzetta Riccardi both have an almost Edwardian air with their marbles and mirrors and offer the visitors old-fashioned comfort and service. There is also the more modern Albergo Jolly in Via Reggimento Fanteria. Lecce makes an ideal headquarters from which to explore the Salentine peninsula, and is only seven miles from the excellent Lido of S. Cataldo.

Since it is impossible here to comment in detail on the architectural richness of Lecce, it may help to bear in mind the periods during which the more outstanding churches and palaces were built. The first period, 1539–91, represents the peaceful years under the Emperor Charles V, when conditions first allowed trade to flourish in Lecce. The earliest church within the walls has recently been desecrated and now houses a workshop, a curious quirk in a city so proud of its monuments. This is *S. Sebastiano* (1520), on the corner of Via G. Paladini, directly behind the Duomo, a Renaissance-type chapel of Florentine simplicity with a little rose window, similar in design to the two other small churches of this period, *dell' Assunzione* (or S. Elisabetta), in Via G. Libertini, and *S. Marco,* in Piazza S. Oronzo. The **triumphal arch** and the **castle** are also of this early period. And in 1549 work was begun on the fantastic *S. Croce,* which was, however, not completed until 1697. The building carried out by the great monastic orders brought the baroque style to the city. Besides S. Croce, there are *S. Teresa* (1569) in Via G. Libertini, the *Gesù* or *Buon Consiglio* (1575), and *S. Irene* (1591). Then there is a gap in church building for some sixty years, with the exception of *S. Maria delle Grazie* (1606) in the Piazza S. Oronzo, and the church of the *Scalze* (1630) in Via Beccerie Vecchie. These years marked the unrest against Spanish rule in the Kingdom of Naples, culminating in Masaniello's revolt in 1647.

The second great period marks the height of baroque and rococo

335

in Lecce, with the work of Zimbalo and his pupil Cino, a period roughly contemporaneous with that of Sir Christopher Wren. During these years the Leccean painter Antonio Verrio was working in England. Horace Walpole says that he had the amiable habit of incorporating portraits of his enemies in the large murals he painted at Hampton Court, Chatsworth and elsewhere. Many of the *palaces* were built about this time. Of the churches, *S. Angelo* (1663) in Via Manfredi is perhaps more rococo than baroque—there can be no strict delineation of the terms. And not far from S. Angelo in Via Umberto I is the splendid *Prefettura* (1646) adjoining S. Croce. (The Prefettura houses the *museum,* founded by the Duke of Castromediano, which contains, among antiquities, paintings, and *objets de vertu,* the chains worn by the Duke during his twelve years' imprisonment under Ferdinand I and IV.) The buildings in the Piazza del Duomo are all of this period. And three further churches are worth visiting: the *Rosario* (1691–1728) in Via G. Libertini, the cloisters of which have been taken over as a tobacco manufactory (Leccean snuff has been famous since the time of Napoleon, who would use no other); the extraordinary *S. Matteo* (1700) in Via dei Perroni, and the whimsical church of the *Carmine* in Piazza Tancredi, the last being Cino's final *jeu d'esprit.* By the time the *Porta S. Biagio* was built in 1774, much of the creative force of Leccean baroque was already extinguished, but the city has been fortunate in that, with the exception of some crude fascist office blocks near the Piazza S. Oronzo, later building has not spoilt its beauty.

The heel of Italy

The southernmost districts of the heel of Italy—the province of Lecce—have until recently drawn only the more hardy travellers, archaeologists mostly, or ethnologists and zoologists attracted by the important discoveries of evidence of animal existence from the quaternary period and of prehistoric men in caves such as the Grotte Romanelli and Zinzulusa. However, we can also find plenty of remains from the succeeding civilizations: Messapian, Greek, Roman, Byzantine—and above all, feudal. Every town and practically every village, even the smallest, can show a baronial castle or palace, and many are still lived in. Yet only in recent years have rational plans of assistance begun to make good the ravages of time. For this district has suffered more than any other from Saracen

Above The three semi-circular apses of the 11th c. Basilian monastery church of Patirion, near Rossano, show Byzantine influence. So do the five cupolas of the church of La Cattolica at Stilo (*below*). Stilo was the southern centre for Basilian monks and hermits in Calabria as Rossano was the northern one.

Left The base of one of the two terminal columns of the Via Appia Antica at Brindisi. In Roman Brundisium Virgil died, and from its port Caesar sailed to defeat Pompey at Pharsalia in 48 BC.

Below Castor and Pollux once fought in defence of the ancient city of Locri, whose extensive ruins now lie among farmland.

raids, large-scale Turkish invasions, and attacks from Algerian corsairs; and also from more natural disabilities such as malaria and a chronic lack of water.

The Apulian Aqueduct, one of the largest systems of the kind in the world, conveying water from the upper reaches of the River Sele on the Tyrrhenian slopes of the Apennines, was completed in 1939. Today, new roads are being constructed and existing ones asphalted; vast areas of formerly malarial swamp-land reclaimed, trees planted and important national monuments repaired. But there are still few good hotels and pensions outside Lecce.

Maglie—Alessano—Capo S. Maria di Leuca

The most direct route from Lecce to Capo S. Maria di Leuca, the southernmost point of the peninsula, is via Maglie. Leaving the Piazza Roma outside the Porta S. Biagio by the Via di Leuca, we come to the SS 16 (Adriatica), which runs through arid, treeless country in a south-easterly direction until, with a slight ascent, the land becomes more fertile and we reach the crossroads at Galugnano. From here on the cultivation is of olives, figs and some fields of grain, interspersed with rocky, uncultivated tracts. The VC painted on stone walls of buildings signifies that the owner has paid his dues for the services of the *vigili campestri*, watchmen to protect against theft of crops or livestock. Just beyond the turning on the left for Martignano and Calimera is the village of **Sternatia,** standing just off the Statale to the right. This is one of the many Albanian or Greek towns in the district; the inhabitants retained the Greek rites until the seventeenth century, and in several villages a dialect of Greek origin is still spoken. Sternatia has an eighteenth-century Palazzo Marchesale of the Granafei family, and a parish church of the same period with a baroque campanile modelled on that of Lecce cathedral.

Zollino is another of these Albanian-Greek villages, founded by refugees in the Middle Ages. At the next crossing, the road on the left goes to Martano, and that to the right to Soleto and Galatina. Ahead of us is the water-tower of the Apulian Aqueduct, and beyond it and more to the right, the *campanile of Soleto* (see p. 341), reputed the most perfect of its kind in Southern Apulia. At the next crossroads we may make a very brief diversion to visit **Corigliano d'Otranto,** one of the main centres of the Grecia Salentina, where Greek is still fairly common. On the left, as we enter the town, is the church of *S. Nicola,* the façade of which has a sixteenth-century Renaissance doorway which was left in the rebuilding of the church in 1743, presumably after the earthquake of that year, which did much damage in these parts. The campanile was begun in 1465, in imitation of that of Soleto, but was not finished. A little farther on, in the Piazza S. Nicola, is the baroque *Palazzo Comi*; and in a private house near by is the so-called *Arco dei Luchetti* (1497), a low-sprung archway with carving of classical, Byzantine and Mohammedan inspiration. From the piazza the Via Alighieri leads to the impressive *Castello de' Monti,* which successfully resisted Turkish attacks after the capture of Otranto in 1480. The four cylindrical corner towers were added shortly after; and in 1667 the building was embellished with the present baroque façade, with a balcony and niches between the windows.

Back on the Statale we cross the railway line and enter **Maglie,** a busy centre where the inhabitants carry on such traditional industries as the making of lace, furniture, ornamental ironwork and woven baskets. There is a popular market on Saturdays. Maglie still has a very *settecento* air. The Via Roma is flanked by baroque palaces, and in the Piazza del Municipio, the town centre, with its monument to Francesca Capece whose wealth was devoted to the instruction of the poor, stand the fine *Palazzo Capece* (now a school) and the *Municipio.* The latter building provisionally houses the *Palaeontological Museum* which consists of fossils of animals of the pleistocene period, discovered in 1957 in caves near S. Sidero, to the north-west of the town.

From Maglie the SS 16 turns almost due east to finish its long course at Otranto. A provincial road joins Maglie with Galatone to the west, and for the south we take the SS 275 (di S. Maria di Leuca), leaving on our left the turning for the spa and bathing resort of S. Cesarea Terme (see p. 351).

Beyond Nociglia the road continues to rise, and runs between some fine olive groves and the occasional vineyard and tobacco plantation, until it enters **Alessano,** a town built at the foot of the Serra dei Cianci, the highest of these Salentine hills, which seldom exceed 500 ft. Alessano was the seat of the Bishop of Leuca from the tenth century until 1818, and it has several interesting buildings, among them the *Collegiata* (1762), the *Palazzo Gonzaga* (sixteenth-century) and the *Palazzo dei Sangiovanni* (1536). At the village of Montesardo, about a mile beyond Alessano, we arrive at the summit of the Serra, with views of the sea on either side; on clear days the mountains of Albania can be seen to the east across

338

the Strait of Otranto. After crossing the railway line near the station for Gagliano-Leuca, and meeting (on the left) the road from Tricase, we bypass the village of Gagliano del Capo. Shortly after, the Statale is joined by the road for Salve and Gallipoli. To the left stands the convent and church of **S. Francesco,** built by the Castriota Scanderbeg family in 1613, on the site of an earlier church destroyed by the Turks. It now belongs to the Trinitarian Fathers. As the road descends, we catch sight ahead of the little bay enclosed by the Punta Meliso to the east and the southernmost tip, Punta Ristola, to the west. The road then forks, the left-hand branch leading to the Capo S. Maria di Leuca, the right descending to the **Marina di Leuca,** a seaside resort with villas and two *pensioni*—the Rizieri and the Minerva—and a 1st category hotel, the Albergo L'Approdo.

Capo S. Maria di Leuca, the *Iapygium promontorium* or *Sallentinum promontorium* of the ancients, is a conspicuous cliff of white limestone, the Greek *leukos*, 'white', giving its name to the earliest settlement there. A Roman column commemorates the completion of the Apulian Aqueduct (1939), the end of which is so constructed that when there is an abundance of water (there seldom is), it falls as a cascade to the sea. Steps lead up to the piazza in front of the **sanctuary of S. Maria di Leuca** (or *in Finibus Terrae* —'Land's End'), with its Corinthian column erected in 1694 by Filiberto Aierbo d'Aragona to mark the spot where St Peter traditionally preached. The church is reputed to stand on the site of a temple of Minerva mentioned by Strabo, and contains on the right of the doorway an ancient altar which may have come from the pagan building. The sanctuary is much visited by pilgrims; the popular legend being that it is the first step to Paradise, and the souls of those who have not made the pilgrimage in their lifetime must needs do so after death.

You can visit the lighthouse on the Punta Meliso. Around the rocky coast are a number of caves, best visited from a boat which can be hired in the port. There are some conducted tours in the season; otherwise a bargain has to be struck.

Galatina—a gem of medieval architecture—Soleto—Galatone—Nardò—Copertino

From Lecce a pleasant day-trip can be made to a group of neighbouring towns which offer outstanding examples of medieval and baroque architecture. Leaving the city from the Piazza Roma, we take the Viale Francesco lo Re and its continuation in the Via B. Realino, which passes under the railway and heads almost due south for **S. Cesario di Lecce.** Here the *Municipio* was formerly the Palazzo Ducale of the Marulli family, who reconstructed it, giving it its present façade, with the statues, in the seventeenth century. The parish church near by in the Piazza Garibaldi is of the last century. In a street to the rear of the church is the restored fourteenth-century church of *S. Giovanni Battista,* which has some almost effaced early frescoes.

From S. Cesario the road cuts straight across the countryside, cultivated with tobacco, vines and olives, to the town of **Galatina,** one of the larger towns of the Salento, important for the production of the excellent wine of the district. Apulia produces more than one-sixth of all Italian wine, the chief vineyards being found here on the Ionian side of the Salentine peninsula, the Tavoliere di Lecce, the Terra di Bari, and north of Foggia in the white-wine-producing area of S. Severo. Galatina's church of S. Caterina is a gem of medieval architecture worth a journey for itself alone.

The centre of the town is the Piazza Alighieri, planted with palms and pines, which adjoins the Piazza S. Pietro, and the *Parrochiale* dedicated to SS. Peter and Paul, a baroque edifice begun in 1633. On the right of the church, we take the Via Vittorio Emanuele, then (on the right) the Via Umberto I, which brings us to the Franciscan church of *S. Caterina di Alessandria,* built between 1384 and 1391 by Raimondello del Balzo Orsini, one of the most powerful barons in the Angevin Kingdom. His son, Giovanni Antonio Orsini, added the octagonal Gothic chapel behind the apse.

The *façade* is not wholly successful; the central section, with its finely proportioned rounded doorway, rose window and trifoliate blind arches of the gable end, is flanked by the similar but lower gables of the outer aisles, which have their doorways out of align-ment with the apexes of the gable ends. And this lack of symmetry is not balanced by their small eye-windows. The design and decoration of the *central portal* show the strength of the Apulian-Romanesque tradition. Two slender columns based on lions (much worn) sup-port two sphinx-like figures on the carved capitals from which the archivolt springs. Within are three bands of intricate carving in low-relief, the two innermost bands of Byzantine inspiration. Above the rounded arches is a classical pediment. Most effective are the figures of *Christ and the Apostles* which form the lintel.

If the church is not open the street to the right brings us (with views of the transept and the octagonal chapel behind the apse) to the entrance gate of the **monastery,** where the monks willingly admit visitors (a donation can be given to the church funds). Inside the church the nave is separated from the double aisles by low pointed arches, the ribs of the Gothic vaulting springing from clusters of columns and pilasters with interestingly varied capitals. But it is the frescoes that cover the walls and arches which are so fascinating and reveal so much of medieval art and life. In some of these proud youthful figures we see not so much portraits of saints, but rather the glorification of northern feudalism. We know the name of only one of the artists who worked here; under the fourth arch of the right aisle the figure of *S. Antonio* is signed and dated Francesco de Arecio, 1435. But it may well be the work of followers of Paolo Serafini of Modena, whose *Madonna* and *Redeemer* are in the Duomo of Barletta.

Against the left wall of the chancel is the tomb of Raimondello del Balzo Orsini, the figure of the deceased represented twice, once lying in the habit of a Franciscan, and again kneeling. His son, Giovanni Antonio, is buried in the chapel which he built behind the apse. The **treasury** contains precious objects, some given by Raimondello on his return from the Holy Land: a thirteenth-century Byzantine mosaic of the Redeemer set on wood and framed in silver-gilt; a chalice of gilded copper, possibly of late fourteenth- or early fifteenth-century Apulian workmanship; a Byzantine icon of the Madonna. The church also possesses a marble high-relief of the *Madonna and Child* by an unknown sixteenth-century Tuscan sculptor.

Before going to to Galatone, a visit should be made to **Soleto,** two miles to the east of Galatina. Soleto was one of the possessions of Raimondello, and here too he has left his mark in the beautiful campanile of the parish church of **S. Maria Assunta** (rebuilt 1770). The Guglia di Raimondello, as it is sometimes called, was begun in 1397 and completed by Giovanni Antonio Orsini after his father's death. The architect of this perfect blending of Romanesque and Gothic forms was Francesco Colaci di Surbo.

From the left of the church the Via Donato Perrino brings us to the Piazza Castello, from which, taking the Via Regina Margherita, then, on the left, the Via Ospedale Carrozini, we arrive at the *chapel of S. Stefano* (or of S. Sofia as it is also known). The Romanesque-Gothic façade is of 1347, but the rest of the fabric may be a century earlier, if the styles of the frescoes which cover the walls are an indication. An inscription in Greek, now gone, gave the date

341

of some of the frescoes as the year 6855 from the creation of the world, that is, AD 1347. However, the frescoes in the apse and the adjacent walls seem to belong to an earlier period than the others. On the entrance wall is a Byzantine-inspired *Last Judgment*. Note the *Crucifixion* on the wall to the left, where two men in the light workaday dress of warm climates nail Our Lord to the Cross.

Near by in the Via Tafuri is the Renaissance-style house in which the doctor and philosopher Matteo Tafuri (1492–1548) was born. The mural inscription may be translated 'I am humble and humility is enough for me, but I will become a dragon should someone touch me.'

Leaving Soleto, we retrace our tracks to Galatina, and to the south of the town take the provincial road which runs south-west to **Galatone,** a prosperous country town in a countryside noted for its vineyards. The town successfully withstood an attack by Giovanni Antonio Orsini in 1434, but was sacked by the Turks in 1480, and four years later was taken by the Venetians. Opposite the castle rises the sumptuous baroque façade of the *santuario del Crocifisso della Pietà,* built by Brother Nicola da Lequile between 1696 and 1710. The decoration of the interior is no less ornate than the exterior would lead one to expect.

The Via Convento brings us to the Piazza Municipio where, beside the Municipio, is another baroque church, *S. Sebastiano* (1612 but restored in 1712). The Renaissance-style doorway is decorated with a 'classical' frieze depicting the *Triumph of Constantine.* From the piazza the Via Chiesa leads to a third of these baroque churches, the *Chiesa Matrice,* which was begun in 1574 and its façade completed in 1595. Taking the Via S. Demetrio and continuing in the Via S. Sebastiano, we come on the right to the Via Galateo, where at No. 14 the humanist Antonio de Ferrariis (1444–1517) was born, known as 'Il Galateo'—'old Galateus', as Norman Douglas affectionately called him. The Via S. Sebastiano ends at the medieval gateway in the walls of the old town.

We leave Galatone by the SS 174 (Salentina) and a short run to the north-west brings us to the prosperous market and commercial town of **Nardò,** after Lecce the most populous centre of the province.

The centre of the city is the picturesque Piazza A. Salandra, designed as if it were an opulent stage-setting for some *settecento* opera. In the centre of the piazza is the fantastic Guglia dell' Immacolata (1769). The white *Palazzo della Pretura,* which was rebuilt in 1772 after the earthquake of 1743, is a genial expression of florid baroque, verging on the rococo. Above a well-proportioned open arcade, the first floor consists of two pairs of windows flanking a central loggia, separated by highly ornate pilasters. The decoration is of shells, scrolls and bizarre curves. Near by is a modern fountain with a bull in the central niche. On one side of the square an early baroque chapel is now used for communal purposes; the other sides are faced with buildings with deeply recessed loggias, above which the skyline is broken by the irregular silhouettes of church ends and campanili.

In the adjoining piazza stands the church of **S. Domenico,** built in the sixteenth century but restored after the 1743 earthquake. It too is quite fantastic, with extraordinary herms and caryatids in a confusion of over-ornamentation. The street on the right of the church leads to the baroque church of **S. Giuseppe,** from which by the Via Lata we come to the **Municipio** in the Piazza Diaz. This was formerly the castello of the Acquaviva Dukes of Conversano, who held Nardò from 1497; erected by Giovanni Antonio Acquaviva at the end of the fifteenth century (the massive cylindrical towers are original), it has subsequently been unhappily added to and restored. From the Municipio the Corso Galliano brings us past the round towers of the medieval walls to the curious little building known as the **Osanna,** called after a word of the inscription which tells us that it was built by two town officials in 1603. Octagonal in plan, with eight columns supporting Gothic-inspired arches, and a domed roof surrounded by little pinnacles, it is strange that these medieval architectural features should have persisted so late.

Returning to the Piazza A. Salandra, and taking the Via Duomo, we arrive shortly at the interesting **cathedral,** which was begun in 1090 by the Benedictines on the site of a Basilian church. It was partly rebuilt in 1230 after an earthquake, enlarged in the following century, a baroque façade and decorations to the interior were added in 1721, and it was wisely restored inside to the earlier style at the end of last century. From outside the church we can see the blind arcading of the early edifice, and the thirteenth-century apsidal ends. Within, the arches on the left of the nave are pointed (thirteenth-century), those on the right being the usual rounded Romanesque. Over the first altar in the right aisle and the third in the left are two paintings—once attributed to Sanfelice, but now considered to be more likely by L. A. Olivieri of Martina Franca. The *S. Michele* over the third altar on the right is reputed to be by Solimena. Above the second altar on the left is the so-called 'Black Crucifix', traditionally held to have come from a Basilian monastery

343

and to have sweated blood when the Saracens tried to carry it off. It is more likely to be of Catalan workmanship, possibly of the thirteenth century. In the *Chronicon Neretinum* (*ca.* 1368) an account is given of a miracle performed by a crucifix in 1255, and the reference may well be to the Black Crucifix of the Duomo.

On the inside of the aisle pilasters and on the walls are a number of fine frescoes of the thirteenth to fifteenth centuries; and the chancel, which is entered under a pointed arch, has been frescoed by the nineteenth-century Sienese painter Cesare Maccari.

We leave Nardò by the provincial road for Copertino, running almost due north through a country of fine vineyards. At the time of the *vendemmia* in late September and early October one sees the great tuns of grapes carried on high-wheeled (often painted) carts drawn by handsome spirited horses. **Copertino** is a country town mostly concerned with wine production. From the centre of the town, the Piazza Umberto I, the Via Margherita di Savoia leads to the Collegiata or church of the *Madonna delle Nevi,* with its ponderous baroque campanile (1597–1603). The church was founded in 1088, but has undergone several alterations, not the least damaging being that of 1707. On the left flank the Renaissance doorway (1506?) has been heavily overpainted. In the interior are several paintings by the Copertinese Gianserio Strafella (*fl.* 1560–77), who was traditionally held to have been a pupil of Raphael and Michelangelo; but it is unlikely that he went north of Naples. Here his *Deposition* is interesting; the other paintings of saints less so. In the left aisle is a monument to Tristano Chiaromonte who died in 1460.

We follow the Via Margherita di Savoia, then, turning left in the Via Giuseppe Desa, arrive at the baroque church of *S. Giuseppe da Copertino* (1754), dedicated to the Saint (1603–33) whose gift of levitation so intrigued Norman Douglas. The house in which S. Giuseppe was born is opposite the church.

The principal monument of Copertino is the impressive *Castello,* erected in 1540 by Evangelista Menga for Alfonso Castriota, to enclose the earlier Angevin building. Preceded by a colour-washed gateway, the main entrance across the moat is in the form of a triumphal arch, decorated with low-relief carvings which include medallions representing the lords of Copertino from the Norman Godfrey to the Emperor Charles V and the Castriota. Through a vaulted passage we enter the irregular courtyard, where parts of the Angevin structure can be seen. On the left behind a well is a pleasant loggia; to the right stands the chapel of St Mark, containing some sixteenth-century tombs.

From Copertino we follow the provincial road through olive groves and some tobacco plantations and vineyards to the village of S. Pietro in Lama; thence it is but a short run to Lecce.

Lecce to Otranto

There are plans under way for a new road to follow the whole coastline of the 'heel' from Brindisi through Otranto to S. Maria di Leuca, and thence north along the Ionian shore to Gallipoli. Much of this has already been built. From Brindisi the road will join the sea at Torre S. Gennaro and, crossing into the province of Lecce, will pass through the fishing village of Casalabate to Torre Rinalda. (The 'Torre' in so many of the place names along the Adriatic shore comes from the towers erected against the Turks and corsairs—many of them, though in a ruined condition, still to be seen.)

From Lecce we take the SS 16 in the direction of Brindisi as far as **Squinzano,** and there turn right for **Torre Rinalda,** crossing rather desolate countryside to the Masseria Cerrate. The farm buildings to the right of the road enclose the interesting remains of the twelfth-century church of *S. Maria delle Cerrate,* which was founded by the Norman Tancred when he was Count of Lecce. The legend relates that Tancred, while hunting here, had a vision of the Virgin appearing between the antlers of a stag—whence the name Cervate or Cerrate. The simple façade has a rose window and a richly carved portal, with high-relief representations of *St Michael, the Nativity, the Baptism of Christ* and, among others, that of *a monk in prayer.* On the left of the church are the remains of a boldly conceived portico, with rounded arches borne on high columns. Near by stands a rectangular Renaissance well. The capitals of the columns which separate the nave from the aisles show good Romanesque carving. The high altar was covered by a canopy (1269), with an inscription in Greek. Among the frescoes are a fifteenth-century *St George and the Dragon* and an *Annunciation*; on the left the *Virgin* shows the persistence of Byzantine influence in these regions as late as the sixteenth century.

Just under two miles north of the farm (reached by a track) is the *Specchia Calone,* one of the many curious heaps of stones to be found in the Salento—dating from prehistoric times, their purpose has never been satisfactorily explained.

After Torre Rinalda the road runs south-east along the coast and then turns inland until it meets the loop in the direct route from

Lecce to the resort of **S. Cataldo.** This seaside resort, with its fine sandy beach (rare in these parts) and its *pineta*, has one hotel, the Albergo Bella Vista and a camping place under the pine trees (enquiries to the Ente Provinciale per il Turismo, Viale Gallipoli 39, Lecce). Just south of the little fishing village we see the large stone blocks which once formed part of the mole of Porto Adriano, the Roman port founded by the Emperor Hadrian in AD 130. From S. Cataldo the road follows the rocky coast, passing through Torre Specchia Ruggeri and S. Foca, to Roca Vecchia.

Roca Vecchia, with its few houses and the remains of a castle erected in the fourteenth century by Walter of Brienne against the pirates, is built on a Messapian site, which has been systematically excavated since 1928 and has yielded many of the vases now in the Lecce Museum. There are tracts of the walls of the fourth and third centuries BC, remains of a gateway and two square towers, as well as other constructions towards the port, and numerous graves. Crossing the viaduct over the road leading down to the bay of Torre dell' Orso, we come to the fishing village of S. Andrea, and enter the district of the land-reclamation which is rapidly transforming all the countryside north of Otranto. Our road passes between the sea and the **Laghi di Alimini,** two shallow lakes joined by a canal, which are particularly prolific in fish and water birds. The pine woods here make the lakes an attractive place for picnickers. After meeting the SS 16, we run down into Otranto.

Alternative routes to Otranto

From Lecce there are two main routes to Otranto, the usual (though not the shortest) being via Maglie on the SS 16 (Adriatica). The alternative provincial road takes us through a region known as Grecia, from the number of colonies of Greek refugees who settled there in the Middle Ages. In some villages a Greek dialect is still spoken. We leave Lecce on the SS 16, but shortly after the city outskirts branch left for Cavallino. From Cavallino we take the road for Lizzanello, and beyond Lizzanello we leave Castri di Lecce on our left, and arrive at **Calimera,** whose name reveals its Greek origin. In the public gardens stands an Attic funerary *stele* of the fourth century BC, the gift of the municipality of Athens in 1960. The Greek inscription reads: 'You are not a stranger here in Calimera.' A straight run, with the Serra di Martignano on our right, brings us to another town founded by Greeks in the eighth or ninth
346

century, **Martano,** which has a fifteenth-century Castello with two cylindrical towers.

We leave Martano by a road running south-east across a desolate countryside. Shortly on the left, stands **Carpignano Salentino,** also of Greek origin, with a palazzo, once owned by the Orsini, adjacent to the Parrocchiale (1574). Near by, in the Piazza Madonna delle Grazie, is the *Cripta delle SS. Cristina and Marina,* a double church cut out of the tufa, the left-hand section dedicated to S. Marina, that on the right to S. Cristina. The interesting Byzantine frescoes include some of the oldest of their kind to be found in Apulia. On a pilaster are represented *SS. Teodoro, Nicola and Cristina*; these are of the twelfth century. Two recesses in the wall to the right contain figures of the *Enthroned Christ*, signed and dated 'Eustathios 1020' and 'Theophilaktos 959'; beside them is an *Annunciation* also of the tenth century.

After Carpignano the road crosses an arid and undulating region of scattered olives and poorly cultivated fields. Then on our left we catch sight of the Lago Alimini Piccolo and the coast beyond, before we cross the railway line and come out on the SS 16, by which we enter **Otranto.**

Otranto—the sack of 1480—the Cathedral—routes to S. Cesarea Terme—prehistoric remains—caves

Hydruntum, so called from the stream which enters the sea there (now known as the Idro) was a Greek city, founded possibly by the Tarentines. (The inhabitants still refer to themselves as Idruntini.) Standing at the mouth of the Adriatic, and separated from the Illyrian coast by little more than forty miles of water, now known as the Strait of Otranto, Hydruntum was in antiquity one of the leading ports for the movement between Italy and Greece and Asia Minor. In the days of imperial Rome Otranto was eclipsed by its rival Brindisi, but under the Byzantines it became the capital of the region still known as the Terra d'Otranto. The city was, like Taranto and Bari, one of the Byzantine centres of resistance to the Normans, only falling to Robert Guiscard in 1068. At the period of the Crusades its port shared in the general activity and traded extensively with Venice and the Levant.

Otranto had suffered much from Saracen raids, but in 1480 a blow was struck from which it never recovered. In their struggle with the Aragonese of Naples the Venetians called on the assistance of the

Turkish forces of Mohammed II. At dawn on July 28th, 1480, the citizens of Otranto observed the sails of a great fleet bearing north. The alarm was given, but it was first thought that the destination of the flotilla was Brindisi or Bari. Suddenly the fleet wheeled and made for Otranto. There was little time to prepare for defence; those who elected to stay were hurriedly brought within the walls; the gates were locked, and when the Turkish commander, Achmed Giedik, called on the city to surrender, the keys were defiantly thrown into the sea. After three days of intense bombardment the walls were breached, but the citizens fought on for another twelve days in the hope of outside help; finally, when this was seen to be vain, the survivors surrendered on August 11th. The bishop, Stefano Pendinelli, the clergy and those (mostly women and children) who had taken refuge in the cathedral were massacred. It was said that in all some twelve thousand persons lost their lives. But what has left the greatest impression on posterity was the behaviour of the eight hundred wounded prisoners remaining. On the near-by Hill of Minerva they were drawn up before the Turkish commander and the executioner, and promised their lives if they abjured their faith. Not one recanted. In the chapel of S. Maria dei Martiri, which today stands on the hill, at the end of the lists of the Christians who died is the name Belar Bey, the executioner. It is said that he refused to continue his bloody work, confessed himself a Christian, and was put to death with the others.

The Turks were not driven from their foothold in Apulia until Alfonso, Duke of Calabria retook Otranto in September 1481. The Aragonese re-fortified the city, but it never regained its prosperity. The countryside was depopulated, the marshes became malarial, and even today Otranto is a small town with some interesting monuments, an indifferent beach, and a small port for its fishing fleet and the car-ferry for Corfu and Igoumenitsa.

After the recapture of Otranto, Ferdinand of Aragon set about fortifying it against fresh attacks with walls and the **Castello** (1485–98), the Castle of Otranto of Horace Walpole's 'goblin tale which thrilled so many a bosom', as Sir Walter Scott described it. However, there is nothing 'Gothick' about its solemn impressiveness, with its great round towers—incidentally, the arms over the main doorway are not those of the Neapolitan house of Aragon but of the Emperor Charles V. We enter the old town by two gateways, firstly the Porta di Terra, and then through the Torre Alfonsina (1483) in the opening between its cylindrical defence towers. By the Via

348

Alfonso d'Aragona and, to the right, the Via Basilica, we come to the piazza with the **cathedral of the Annunziata.** Begun by the Normans in 1080, it was restored in 1481 (the Turks used it as a stable) and again in recent years, when the baroque excrescences were removed. The simple façade has a fine rose window (fifteenth-century) and an ornate but effective baroque portal of 1764.

Within, the church is in the form of a basilica, the nave being separated from the aisles by fourteen columns of diverse marbles, some antique, with interesting capitals. But the outstanding feature of the cathedral is the magnificent **mosaic pavement,** executed about 1165 by one Pantaleone. It consists of a *Tree of Life* extending the length of the nave, with representations of *the Months, Adam and Eve, Cain and Abel, Noah's Ark, the Tower of Babel, Alexander the Great* and *King Arthur.* In the intertwining of branches appear birds, animals and fishes, both natural and mythological—an extraordinary feat of imagination, decorative ingenuity, and perseverance. On the walls are faded remains of frescoes. To the right of the chancel the chapel of the Martyrs, recently glassed in, contains the bones of many of the victims of 1480. One used to be seen with an arrow protruding from his eye socket. Beneath the altar is kept the stone block on which the executions took place. On the pavement in front of the chapel is another mosaic placed there by command of Ferdinand I of Aragon.

By stairways in the aisles we descend to the crypt, consecrated in 1088 and restored a few years ago, unfortunately with a new paving, the too shiny surface of which diminishes the effect of the beautiful columns and capitals and the frescoes. The columns are of different marbles, some fluted or decorated with carving in low-relief; the capitals, too, show an astonishing variety of forms. Much of the stonework comes from ancient buildings, both classical and Byzantine.

We return by the Via Basilica to the Largo Cavour, which forms a terrace overlooking the sea. From here the Corso Garibaldi takes us past a house, No. 41, the **Casa Arcella,** which has incorporated in its doorway an altar with an inscription dedicating it to the Emperor Marcus Aurelius and his adopted brother, Lucius Verus, who may have set out from Otranto on their expedition against the Parthians in AD 162. Beyond this, the Via S. Pietro leads up to the little Byzantine church of **S. Pietro,** built in the tenth or eleventh century in the shape of a Greek cross inscribed in a square, with three rounded apses. (If the church is closed, enquiries should be made to the sacristan of the cathedral.) The arms of the cross have barrel vaults, supported on short columns; above the crossing is a rounded cupola. On the walls are frescoes, mostly of Byzantine inspiration.

Leaving the town by the Castello we take the road to the left which climbs up to the Hill of Minerva, so called presumably from an ancient temple to the goddess. Here steps lead up to the church of *S. Maria dei Martiri*; half way up the steps there is a little chapel on the right, marking the spot where the executions took place, and opposite it a column commemorating the conversion of Belar Bey. In the baroqued interior of the church, on the left of the entrance, an inscription tells of the siege and massacre. Four lists on the walls record the names of those who died at that time or in the recapture of the town in 1481; among them names of some of the proudest families in the kingdom.

From Otranto south to S. Cesarea Terme we have the choice of two roads. The first, the Provinciale, after passing the Hill of Minerva, crosses the savage, rocky promontory which forms the easternmost point of Italy, the **Capo d'Otranto.** On the cliff edge are the ruins of the Torre del Serpe, the tower which figures on the town's coat-of-arms. To the right of the road stand the remains of the Basilian *abbey of S. Nicola di Casole,* founded between the fifth and the eighth centuries, and destroyed by the Turks in 1480. On a clear day there is a splendid view over the Strait of Otranto to Albania, and, away to the right, the pale outline of Corfu. We meet the main road, the SS 173 (delle Terme Salentine), the alternative route, near the little cove of **Porto Badisco.** This is the spot where, according to some authorities (though others would place it farther south, near Castro), Aeneas and his companions first beheld the land they were to inhabit, as described by Virgil in the *Aeneid*: *Iamque rubescebat stellis Aurora fugatis* . . . 'And now the stars had fled and Dawn came up blushing, when far off we made out the indistinct hills and low Italian coast. "Italy!" Achates was first to shout; "Italy!" with joyful cry his companions proclaimed.'

There is a majesty in this wild fractured coastline. The Statale winds among a lonely desolation of barren rock, and then descends to the bathing resort and spa of S. Cesarea Terme, strikingly oriental in appearance with the Moorish-looking Palazzo Sticchi on the promontory.

From Lecce the quickest route to S. Cesarea is via Maglie (for the first section see p. 337 *et seq.*). Leaving Maglie on the SS 275 for S. Maria di Leuca, and on the outskirts of the town bearing left in the Provinciale, we come shortly to **Muro Leccese.** In the central Piazza del Popolo stand two baroque churches, the Chiesa dell'

Immacolata (1778) and the Parrocchiale dell' Annunziata (1680), the latter containing a number of paintings from the sixteenth to the nineteenth centuries. Also in the piazza is the Palazzo Principesco, once the dwelling of the feudal lords. South-east of Muro Leccese lies the village of **Sanarica,** which has a baroque Sanctuary of the Madonna di Sanarica (1716) and a Palazzo Ducale of the Basurto family. Continuing to the south-east through a countryside of olives and some cereal crops, we come to the market town of **Poggiardo.** Between the balustraded eighteenth-century Palazzo Ducale dei Guarini and the rococo Parrocchiale (façade of 1728) a narrow alleyway brings us to the Via della Chiesa; here we turn right and a short distance along, in the middle of the street, an iron trap-door opens into the Basilian Cripta di S. Maria, discovered quite by chance in 1929. Unfortunately the important frescoes have been removed to Rome for restoration.

We leave Poggiardo past the park of the Villa Episcopo, its entrance flanked by little gazebos. (The bishops of Castro sought refuge here after the destruction of that town by the Turks in 1537. The see was merged with that of Otranto in 1818.) On the outskirts of the village of **Vitigliano,** by the road junction to the left, is the *Cisternale,* a deep cistern built roughly in large stone blocks. Its use has been much disputed—it may have been for the conservation of water or simply a burial place; nor is its age certain, for some authorities reject the theory that it is Messapian. Beyond the village the road ascends to cross the Serra di Cerfignano before descending in loops to the sea at **S. Cesarea Terme.**

The sulphur-bearing waters of the state-owned spa of S. Cesarea, which rise from four natural springs in caves in the cliffs, are taken in conjunction with mud and marine baths. The cure for rheumatism is considered particularly successful. One of the two main establishments is in the *Grotta di S. Cesarea,* the cave where the patron saint of the town is said to have escaped from the incestuous embraces of her demented father. There are two hotels, the Albergo Palazzo and the Hotel La Salute, and a large open-air swimming pool. On the hill behind the town there is a pleasant *pineta,* with fine views over the Strait of Otranto.

From S. Cesarea it is an excursion of about an hour by boat to visit the *Grotta Romanelli,* a cave which is of the greatest importance to palaeontologists for its fossilized remains of animals of the quaternary period. The climatic changes which have taken place are shown by fossils of animals of hot climates (elephant, hippopotamus and rhinoceros) and those of cold conditions (goats and birds of

351

the northern steppes). Representations of men and animals have been found on the walls of the cave, some painted in red ochre; they are the only palaeolithic paintings to have been discovered on the Italian mainland. (For permission to visit the cave, apply at the Municipio.) Although this and other caves in the vicinity can be reached from the Castro road, it is perhaps pleasanter to visit them by water. A little to the south is the *Grotta Zinzulusa,* of great interest to biologists since it harbours several species of tiny crustaceans which exist nowhere else in Italy, their presence suggesting that at some very early epoch Apulia was joined to the mainland across the Adriatic.

Farther south still are the *Grotta Rotondella,* the *Grotta Rotonda* and the *Grotta Piccionara,* all worth a visit for the strangeness and beauty of their formation and the colours of rock and water.

From S. Cesarea Terme we continue south along the magnificent coast on the Provinciale, leaving first, on the left, a track for the Grotta Romanelli, then shortly after, a road which leads to a belvedere above the Grotta Zinzulusa (admission, 10.0 a.m.–6.0 p.m.; refreshments). Rounding the promontory, we reach **Castro Marina,** the little fishing-port for Castro, an interesting small town built possibly on the site of the ancient Castra Minervae, beautifully placed on the hill behind. Of the Romanesque cathedral (twelfth century) there remain some of the façade, the two side doorways and the transept. Inside, a tenth-century Byzantine church has been incorporated in the left aisle. There is a magnificent view from the walls of sea and coast, out over the terraces of holm-oaks and olives.

Continuing on the *litoranea,* we pass the fishing village of Torre d'Andrano and come to the little port and resort of **Tricase Marina** (or Marina Porto). The new coast road now continues to Marina di Novaglie, and will eventually go right down to Capo S. Maria di Leuca. However, we shall take the older route from Marina Porto to the market town of **Tricase.**

In the Piazza Vittorio Emanuele is the grandiose Palazzo Gallone, a fourteenth-century castle to which the corner towers and the loggia on the right were added in the sixteenth century. The Chiesa Matrice, a baroque structure of 1770, contains two paintings by Palma Giovane (1544–1628), a *Deposition* and an *Immacolata,* as well as a work by a follower of Veronese, the *Virgin and saints.* Opposite stands the church of S. Domenico (1678), which was formerly attached to a monastery. The church of S. Angelo (1624) reflects the change of style from that of the Renaissance to baroque.

Gallipoli, from the Greek *Kallipolis* – 'beautiful city', was a centre of Byzantinism until it fell to the Normans in 1071. In 1560 these attractively weathered classical reliefs were assembled to form the Fontana Ellenistica in the main street.

Robert Guiscard rebuilt the castle at S. Severina which dominates the wild Calabrian countryside. The castle was further extended and reinforced in 1496.

After we leave Tricase southwards, the road continues to rise to about 400 ft between Caprarica del Capo, the next village, and Tiggiano. Leaving Corsano on our left, we join the SS 275 just before the turning for Gagliano del Capo, and proceed to Capo S. Maria di Leuca.

The Ionian coast—Casarano—Gallipoli

The western, Ionian side of the Salentine peninsula is more fertile than the Adriatic littoral. From S. Maria di Leuca we cross an agricultural countryside to the prosperous town of Gallipoli. When the proposed coastal road is completed, it will follow closely the rocky shoreline, passing through some small resorts which will need development before they can cater for tourists. At **Torre S. Giovanni** (4 miles south-west of Ugento), there are the remains of the Roman port of Uzentum. However, the SS 274, which runs farther inland, offers the visitor a number of interesting small towns and villages, notably Casarano, which lies due north of Ugento and is well worth the diversion from the direct route to Gallipoli.

The provincial road from Ugento meets another from Taviano and Melissano and crosses the railway on the outskirts of **Casarano.** Near by is the church of *Casaranello* or *S. Maria della Croce,* with a simple façade opened by a small fourteenth-century rose window. (The key is with the custodian next door; tip.) The earliest part of the church is the transept, which is covered by a barrel vault and has a cupola raised on pendentives. The nave and aisles, also barrel-vaulted, are from the reconstruction of the thirteenth and fourteenth centuries. Among the frescoes here is a portrait of *Urban V* (pope 1362–70) on the second pillar on the right. The frescoes depicting the *Life of St Catherine* and *Episodes from the New Testament* appear to be of the thirteenth century, and that over the altar, *S. Maria della Croce,* of a century later. But the most precious of these works of art are the fifth-century *mosaics*: the Cross against a background of stars in the cupola, and the most lively representation of birds, fish, rabbits and ducks among geometric designs in the chancel. These mosaics are the only palaeochristian ones to be found in Apulia.

Gallipoli (from the Greek *Kallipolis,* 'beautiful city') is thought to have been founded by the Tarentines. According to Pliny, the Latin name for the *municipium* was Anxa, but this would appear more likely to have been Messapian. Sacked by the Vandals in 460 and by

Totila in 542, Gallipoli was a centre of Byzantinism until it fell to the Normans in 1071. It succeeded in repelling the Turks in 1480; three years later, however, it was taken by the Venetians, but they only held it for four months. The fortified town was sufficiently strong to withstand a bombardment by the English and Bourbon fleets in 1809.

Today, it consists of two parts; the ancient Città on the island and the modern Borgo on the promontory to which it is joined by a bridge of 1603, flanked by another for the railway and port traffic. In appearance Gallipoli, and indeed the whole district, has a distinctly Greek air, partly perhaps from the low, flat-roofed, colour-washed houses—white mostly, but pinks also and even pale blue. The town owes much of its prosperity to its trade in oil, wine and table grapes. Before the First World War quantities of olive oil were shipped to Russia for the icon lamps. Today the port is used principally by local fishing vessels or coastal traders. The proximity of excellent sandy beaches has brought increased tourist traffic in recent years. There is a Jolly Hotel and at S. Giovanni, a resort just to the south, the Albergo Lido S. Giovanni.

The Corso Roma, running east to west through the Borgo, brings us to the building of the Comando del Porto, to the left of which stands the **Fontana Ellenistica,** a fountain composed of much-worn classical reliefs (1560). From here we look out over the southern of the two harbours, the Seno del Canneto, to the Città, with the mass of the **Castello** and its prolongation in the round-towered Rivellino (1522). The polygonal section of the castle is the early Byzantine fortress, which was added to by Charles I of Anjou and reinforced in the sixteenth century.

We cross by the old bridge and come to the Piazza Mercato under the walls of the castle. From here we take the Via Antonietta de Pace, the main street which cuts the old city from east to west. A short way along (passing some interesting *palazzi*) we arrive, on the left, at the **cathedral of S. Agata** (1630–96), its baroque façade in a dark stone somewhat burdened with statues. Within the church is a gallery of baroque paintings, for the most part by local artists.

Continuing along the Via de Pace, we come (on the right) to the **Municipio** and then to the **Biblioteca,** the latter building housing also the little **Museo Civico** (admission, 10.0 a.m.–12.0 noon), which has a miscellaneous collection of antiquities and curiosities, including Messapian sarcophagi and vases, the vertebrae of a whale and some foetuses in bottles. Most curious of all is a model of a coffin containing figures of a man and woman—'To show that a man

354

lasts longer,' my courteous guide explained to me. Sure enough the model showed the woman as a skeleton, while the man had only two gaping holes in his belly. (Is this an echo of the medical teaching of Galen?) At the western extremity of the Città stands the church of *S. Francesco* (late seventeenth century), which possesses another example of the *realismo* of the people of Gallipoli in the wooden carvings of the *Two Thieves* by Vespasiano Genuino (second half of sixteenth century). The narrow streets are full of interest, human and architectural; and a walk around the Riviera, formed by the removal of the encircling walls, is rewarding for its view of the island of S. Andrea and of the coastline, and in clear weather, the mountains of Calabria.

CHAPTER 20

The Ionian Coast

Maps: IX, p.357; X, p.368; XI, p.372

Cities of Magna Graecia—Metaponto—Heracleia—Sybaris—Corigliano
Calabro—Rossano

From Taranto we cross the Ponte di Napoli and continue in the Via
Napoli until beyond the railway line we fork left from the Via Appia
into the SS 106 (Via Ionica). Once outside the built-up area both
road and rail follow the curve of the shoreline for almost the entire
journey, separated from the sea by sand dunes covered with a thick
undergrowth of *macchia*—lentisk and a form of cistus and maritime
pine. The countryside here has been greatly improved by post-war
drainage and irrigation and is now rich with citrus-groves, vineyards
and olives. Inland on the hills we can see the white buildings of
Massafra and Mottola. South-eastwards, beyond the Isole Cheradi,
the coastline of the Murge Tarentine fades into the distance.

On the left a number of roads lead down to developing seaside
resorts: the Lido di Taranto, Chiatona, S. Castellaneta Marina and
(just before we enter Basilicata) the Marina di Ginosa. At most of
these there are camping sites, and the next few years may see hotels.
Crossing the River Bradano, which forms the provincial boundary
between Taranto and Matera and between the regions of Apulia and
Basilicata, we come to the ruins known as **Tavole Palatine** and the
Map IX
p. 357 recently constructed **Antiquarium of Metaponto** (1961). Visit the
Antiquarium first, for it has excellent maps and diagrams of the
whole extensive area which was occupied by the ancient city of
Metapontion. The Tavole Palatine—a Doric temple of the sixth
century BC, possibly dedicated to Hera—was situated in a suburb
some distance from the main city and its port.

Metapontion was founded by the Achaeans *ca.* 690–80 BC as an
outpost to prevent the spread of the Dorian Tarentines. They raised
horses and grew cereals on the rich land (the beautiful coins show an
356

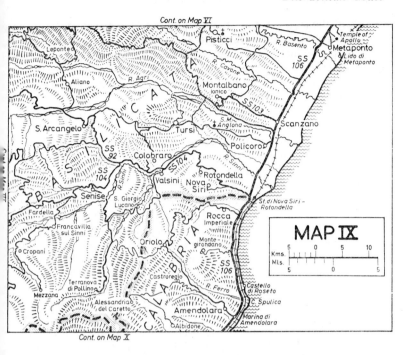

Cont. on Map VI

Cont. on Map X

ear of barley). Pythagoras, the mathematician and religious teacher, retired to Metapontion, when he and his followers were driven out of Croton along with the oligarchical faction which he supported. Metapontion thus became a centre of Pythagorean ideas. During the Second Punic War Hannibal made the city his headquarters from 210 BC until he retired from Italy three years later, evacuating some of the leading citizens with him. It was a flourishing Roman *municipium*, but began to decay in the imperial age and was finally destroyed by the Saracens. The low-lying countryside soon became practically uninhabitable because of malaria, and only since the last war has the *bonifica* restored the region to the fertility it enjoyed in antiquity.

Not far from the Antiquarium we come to the junction with the SS 175. To visit the ruins of the **agora,** the **temple of Apollo Lycius** and the **theatre,** we turn left in this (passing fifth-century tombs on the right near the Casa Ricotta), until we come to the crossroads shortly before the railway station. Here we turn left again in a road running parallel with the line, and after about a mile

357

arrive at the ruins. Aerial photography has shown that much of the area between the Rivers Bradano and Basento was occupied by the city proper (which was connected by a canal with its port) and by outlying suburbs or villas and farmsteads. Archaeologically, it is a misfortune that the bull-dozers of the *bonifica* have scattered the tombs before they could be examined.

Beyond Metaponto station, the junction of a line to Naples and (by changing at Ferrandina) to Matera, a short road brings us to the excellent sandy beach of the **Lido of Metaponto.** From May to October there is a well-equipped camping-site here.

Map IX
p. 357

The road crosses the River Basento and, running almost straight through cultivated fields, with the lofty Monte Pollino range ahead, comes to the village of Scanzano. Here the SS 103 branches off to cross the mountains and descend into the Vallo di Diano at Montesano. Shortly after, we cross the River Agri and come to **Policoro.** Near by is the site of ancient *Heracleia,* a colony founded by the Tarentines in 432 BC (thereby driving a wedge between the Achaean cities to the north and south). It was at Heracleia that the Roman legions were defeated in 280 BC, overcome by the elephants of King Pyrrhus of Epirus. Pyrrhus had been called in by the Tarentines to check the growing power of Rome, but he is reported to have declared that another victory at such cost would lose him the war.

After the River Sinni, the foothills approach the sea; and at **Stazione di Nova Siri-Rotondella** we pass from Basilicata into Calabria. From here the SS 104 turns off for Sapri on the Tyrrhenian Sea, with the SS 92 branching off it for Potenza. Our own road and the railway now hug the coast for some twenty miles, until we round Cape Spulico and enter the alluvial plain of Sybaris, watered by the Rivers Coscile and Crati (the ancient Crathis), and bounded on the north by the Pollino Mountains, on the west by the foothills of the Catena Costiera of the Tyrrhenian seaboard, and on the south by the Sila Greca. This fertile plain, once so malarial, is now richly cultivated with cereal crops and orange-groves. Just after Villapiana Lido the SS 105 runs west to Castrovillari, the important market-town for the district and the centre of communications (see p. 391). The Statale Ionica and the railway bear away from the sea to the **Stazione di Sibari.**

Map IX
p. 357

Map X
p. 368

In the last few years archaeologists claim to have located the site of the destroyed city of *Sybaris,* buried under as much as twenty feet of alluvial deposit on the tree-lined Crati. Before its destruction in 510 BC, ancient Sybaris was one of the richest and most populous cities of Greece. It has been suggested that it was at least four times

358

as large as its colony Paestum, with a circuit of about twelve miles, a population within its walls of more than 100,000, and a total population in its territory of some half a million. As at Metapontion, there may have been outlying suburbs, extensive villas and farmsteads.

Sybaris was said to have been founded by Is, a citizen of Achaean Helice in the north of the Peloponnese, who arrived with a band of Achaean Troezenians in 720 BC. Its lands were rich (the bull on its beautiful coins signifies its fertility), but it was the trade which passed through the city that made its wealth proverbial. Goods from Asia Minor were brought here, conveyed overland to its Tyrrhenian colonies of Laos, Scidros and Poseidonia (Paestum), and exchanged for luxuries from Etruria. The luxury and soft-living of the Sybarites were exaggerated by their less fortunate contemporaries, and the anecdotes that emerged, the *Sybaritakoi logoi*, are perhaps more amusing than accurate. In fact, life in Sybaris seems to have included sensible arrangements for a hot climate: streets and roads were lined with trees for shade, no noisy trades were permitted in the city, there were public baths (the first in antiquity), freedom between the sexes, and pleasure was taken in dress, food and wine.

In the battle between Sybaris and its fellow-Achaean neighbour Croton, which was fought in 501 BC near the river today known as the Trionto, the Crotonians, under their general the famous athlete Milo, were completely victorious. Sybaris was destroyed, and the River Crathis was diverted to overwhelm it.

At the Bivio Favella the SS 106 *bis* branches right for Castrovillari and Cosenza, and a short way on, again on the right, is the turning for S. Demetrio Corone and the Sila Greca (see p. 397). The curious building with the hybrid Moorish architecture on the right is the ruined summer palace of the Sanseverino family. The road begins to climb among olive groves, with views over the coastal plain, the seaside resort of Marina Schiavonia and the long sweep of the shoreline, until we come to the pleasant town of **Corigliano Calabro.** Map X p. 368

The winding road up to the town passes on the left the church of *St Anthony of Padua,* with its cupola and cupolettas in polychrome majolica, and leads to the main street, the Via Roma, passing under what might be taken for a Roman aqueduct. This is actually medieval in origin and supplied water for the castle; now it is used as a footbridge joining the high ground on either side of the Via Roma. We come almost immediately to the little Piazza del Popolo, the animated centre of the town. Corigliano has an elegant eighteenth-century air, with its stuccoed façades painted in different colours and

359

ornamented with ox-heads, fish and flowing designs in low-relief stucco. A narrow street to the right brings us to the *Castello,* with its cylindrical towers and drawbridge, rebuilt in 1490 and subsequently many times restored. Since 1828 it has been in the possession of the Compagna family, who have turned it into a sort of domestic science college, run by nuns. Visitors are not usually admitted. There is a fine view from the adjoining parapet. On the left is the church of *S. Pietro,* gaily baroqued in pale blue and white. In the church are two interesting fifteenth-century paintings from Patirion, copies of Byzantine work of the twelfth century. On one side is represented the *Madonna and Child* with the subscription in Greek attributing to her the guardianship of the streets—*odegitria.* On the reverse is the *Crucifixion.*

Back on the Statale Ionica we come after about four miles to the turning on the right for the ruins of the *monastery of Patirion* and the beautiful church of *S. Maria del Patir* (or Patire—'Father'). A narrow road, built by Austrian prisoners of the First World War, leads up through the woods of holm-oak to this remote upland plateau. The Basilian monastery was founded by the Blessed Bartolomeo di Simeri (the 'Father') *ca.* 1100, perhaps on the site of a more ancient hermitage, as there were many such groups of anchorites in these parts. It grew steadily in fame and riches, and was visited by many pilgrims. The monastery was suppressed in 1806, and earthquake damage has joined with time to effect its ruin. The church, however, has been restored. In form it is basilican, with three semicircular apses, each composed of blind arcading, with the remains of a circular decorative motif under the arch. In the interior there are portions of early paving in *opus sectile* depicting a centaur, unicorn, panther and other animals. The main portal is ogival (fifteenth century), surmounted by a modern round window and, above, an older one. To the left of the church some of the rounded arches of the sixteenth-century monastic cloisters are still standing.

From the turning for Patirion a run of some three miles brings us to the junction with the SS 177, the road which leads over the Sila Greca via Rossano, Longobucco and the Lake of Cecita to Cosenza.

Map X
p. 368 It is worth making a diversion here to visit the little town of **Rossano,** which stands on a hill overlooking a ravine, three miles south of the junction.

Rossano was the birthplace of St Nilus (910–1005), the founder of the Basilian monastery of Grottaferrata in the Alban Hills near Rome—one of the two monasteries in Italy which, to my knowledge, still follow the Rule set up in the East by St Basil (*ca.* 360); the other is at S. Basile near Castrovillari. St Benedict (480–543), who was the founder of Western monasticism, referred his monks to 'the Rule of our holy father Basil'. According to Lenormant, the edict of Leo the Isaurian (726) which banned the use of images in the Eastern Church, was the cause of some 50,000 priests, monks and laymen of the Orthodox faith fleeing to Calabria. The names are known of ninety-seven monasteries of the Basilian Rule which were founded about this time in Calabria alone. Byzantinism was always strong in the South of Italy, and Rossano was one of the chief centres.

The eighth to ninth centuries saw the arrival of more Greek-speaking refugees from Sicily and elsewhere, as the result of the Arab invasions. In the fifteenth century, after the death of Scanderbeg, many of his Albanian followers accompanied his son, Giovanni Castriota, into exile rather than submit to the Turks. And in succeeding centuries both Greeks and Albanians were granted lands in some of the wildest parts of Southern Italy, particularly in Calabria, where they have maintained many of their traditions and even their language to this day. The Sila Greca, and such towns and villages as Spezzano Albanese, S. Demetrio Corone, S. Sofia d'Epiro, and a score of others, bear witness to the origin of the inhabitants. In their churches the Greek rite is followed, but they are in communion with Rome. Rossano's heritage is distinctly Byzantine; between the eighth and twelfth centuries it was the most important town of northern Calabria.

The Via Garibaldi brings us to the centre of the town, the Piazza Cavour. At the beginning of the Via Garibaldi, the Passeggiata di S. Stefano offers a magnificent view of the Gulf of Taranto. From the Piazza Cavour we descend by a ramp to the **cathedral of the Assunta.** Rossano was seriously damaged by an earthquake in 1836, and the façade of the Duomo is modern (1914). The interior is much decorated, especially the ceilings of the chapels; the chandeliers which hang low between the arches of the nave suggest Eastern churches. In a baroque shrine in the nave is the much venerated fresco on stone of the *Madonna and Child*. This Byzantine painting, known as the 'Madonna Achiropita', surpasses even the works of the indefatigable St Luke, for it is *acheiropoieta*, that is, not painted by hand at all. It was, however, touched up in 1929—this time presumably by human agency. On the right of the church we pass through the sacristy to the **museum,** which among other treasures contains the celebrated *Codex Purpureus Rossanensis* (sixth or seventh century). This beautiful work is the only pre-eighth-century Greek testament extant that contains pictures illustrating the life of Christ.

Returning to the Via Garibaldi, we cross the town to its extreme south-east limit on the edge of the ravine. Here we come to the little church of **S. Marco** which, together with the Cattolica of Stilo, is one of the two finest examples of Byzantine architecture in Calabria. S. Marco was built in the ninth century; its form is that of a Greek cross inscribed in a square. Three palm trees by the entrance add to the Eastern appearance of its five little cupolas. In the interior the light comes from windows in these cupolas and from the curious circular aperture of opaque glass in the lower window frames. A piece of early mosaic found in the restoration of 1931 has been hung on the wall to the left of the altar. A door on the right leads to a terrace overlooking the gorge.

At one time this *gorge* at Rossano was a veritable Thebaid, from the great number of hermits or anchorites who inhabited the many caves which are still to be seen. This must have been before the time of St Nilus; we learn that there were fourteen monasteries in the vicinity of Rossano, of which Patirion was the most famous.

We return to the SS 106 (for the route from Rossano to Cosenza see pp. 398-9), and run for some miles due east along the olive-covered foothills, with occasional views of the Ionian sea and, ahead, the lighthouse of Capo Trionto. At **Cariati,** with its little fishing port and beach, the SS 108 *ter* branches inland and we cross the boundary between the provinces of Cosenza and Catanzaro formed by the River Fiumenica.

Map X
p. 368

Crotone—Capo Colonna—Rocella—Squillace—Lido di Copanello and Soverato

The road now runs south along the shore, past Torre Melissa, to the station for Strongoli, the town itself being five miles inland. We cross the River Neto and enter the region known as the Marchesato, for many years the broad lands of the Ruffo family. Shortly after the Bivio Passovecchio and the SS 107 for S. Severina and S. Giovanni in Fiore, we turn off the main road, to the left, for the important centre of **Crotone.**

Map XI
p. 372

To the classical scholar the names of these once flourishing cities of Magna Graecia are full of nostalgia. The Achaean colony of **Croton** was founded *ca.* 710 BC to the north of the Lacinian Promontory (now the Capo Colonna) on the advice of the Delphic oracle, and the earliest incuse coins of Croton show the Delphic tripod, with Apollo shooting the Python. The city was sited on the

362

only port on the Ionian coast between Taranto and Reggio, as its successor is today. It does not seem to have been materially very rich, yet it was to become in the sixth and fifth centuries BC the most powerful state in Magna Graecia. The fame of its athletes and its medical school spread over the whole of Hellas at this period, Crotonian athletes won the stadion at Olympia seven times in the eight contests between 508 and 480. Earlier, in 532, Milo, whose athletic prowess became legendary, won the first of his six successive victories.

Pythagoras, fleeing from the tyranny of Polycrates in his native land of Samos, arrived in Croton about 540. Besides his mathematical studies and his collaboration with the already established medical school of Croton, he was a religious teacher and a powerful influence in local politics. However, not long after the defeat of Sybaris, whose side he took in the war, Pythagoras was forced by a democratic insurrection to leave Croton for Metapontion, where he died. Some fifty of his followers were burnt to death in the house of Milo, who was one of his disciples.

Both medical school and the philosophico-mathematical school continued to flourish; the study of medicine may have owed something to the training of the athletes in the *palaestra*. The Crotonian women, too, were famous for their beauty. The painter Zeuxis is said to have been allowed to choose five of the most beautiful girls of Croton for his picture of Helen of Troy to be hung in the Temple of Hera—so that from their various excellences 'he might transfer the truth of life to a mute image.'

In 389 BC Croton, with other Achaean foundations, fell to Dionysius the Elder of Syracuse. In 277 BC it was conquered by the Romans and began to decline. Croton sided with Hannibal, who wintered there, and it was from its port that he finally sailed back to Carthage in 207, after slaughtering on the shore thousands of Italian mercenaries who had refused to follow him. At the fall of the Empire Croton was a backward provincial city. Its fortunes began to look up again only after 1284, when Charles of Anjou gave it in fief to Pietro Ruffo, Count of Catanzaro, who made it the chief town of his 'Marquisate'. In recent times the establishment of the great Montecatini industrial works and the extension of its port facilities, together with the eradication of malaria, have lifted it out of the misery and sloth in which Gissing found it in 1897.

Crotone was known as Cotrone from Norman times until 1928—the corruption coming, no doubt, from the ignorance of Robert Guiscard and his Normans of the classical authors; they were busy with more material matters. The town has several modest hotels as well as the Albergo Bologna. There are good bathing beaches near by. Crotone is best avoided at the height of summer, when the heat, dust and absence of trees can be trying.

From the central piazza the Via Vittoria leads to the Piazza Duomo and the cathedral. In the *Duomo,* a building of no architectural pretentions (Crotone suffered damage in the 1783 earthquake), is the Byzantine *'Black' Madonna,* or the *Madonna di Capocolonna* (above the altar on the right). The sacristan (tip) has to roll down by means of a crank the heavy gilded screen which covers the much-venerated painting. On the second Sunday in May the picture is carried, with much pomp, to the sanctuary on Capo Colonna, where it is said to have been brought from the East when the country was converted to Christianity. The following night it is brought back by sea, accompanied by a long procession of boats, and escorted by torchlight from the port to the cathedral.

Behind the Duomo rises the older part of the town, the street-names recalling its Greek heritage: Via Pitagora, Via Menelao, Via Milo, etc. Through these we climb to what was the acropolis, now covered by the *castle* built by Don Pedro de Toledo against the corsairs, using in its construction much of the ancient stonework. From it, or the gardens next door, there is a good view. In the castle enclosure is the *Museo Civico* (admission 10.0 a.m.–1.0 p.m.; if not open, the key may be obtained from the Municipio, which entails a walk back to the centre of the town. It is thus advisable to enquire there first). The museum contains an interesting collection of ancient coins and other objects.

The trip to **Capo Colonna** used to be made by boat, but there is now a quite adequate road, which passes the cemetery and runs along the shore and over the low hills to the spot where one remaining Doric column commemorates the most famous meeting-place of all Greeks in Magna Graecia, the Temple and Sanctuary of Hera Lacinia, raised on a shrine dedicated by Hercules himself as he returned with the bulls of Geryon. At the beginning of the sixteenth century forty-eight columns were said to have been still standing, but they were taken by an appropriately named Bishop Lucifer to build his palace, and, when this fell in the earthquake of 1783, to strengthen the mole of the port.

Resuming our journey south on the Statale Ionica, we turn away from the sea to climb the bare hilly country, which in the summer and autumn has a certain austere beauty. Just beyond Cutro the SS 109 branches right, and makes an attractive detour to Catanzaro, passing through Petilia Policastro, and thence along the southern flanks of the Sila Piccola, through pleasant country to Taverna and the SS 109 *bis* (see chapter 24). The Statale Ionica joins the sea again just before the village of Steccato, and follows the coast past the seaside resort of Cropani Marina to **Catanzaro Lido,** which has a good beach, and restaurants, but only one rather poor hotel. This is the road and rail junction for the provincial capital of Catanzaro, which stands on its commanding position nine miles inland (see chapter 24).

Map XI
p. 372

After crossing the River Corace, we see ahead the village of **Roccella.** Here, among the olive trees to the right of the road, are the interesting ruins of the church of the ***Roccelletta del Vescovo di Squillace,*** which was, after the cathedral at Gerace, the largest church in Calabria. Basilican in form and built in a reddish Roman-type brick, the date of its construction has given rise to much discussion among the authorities. Lenormant placed it very early indeed; others attributed it to the sixth century; but the prevailing opinion seems now to regard it as Romanesque of about the eleventh century.

Just before the attractive Lido di Copanello, the SS 181 leads up on the right to **Squillace** on its rocky crag and over the mountains to Maida. Squillace is today of little interest architecturally, except for the ruins of its (originally Norman) castle. The Duomo, which stands at a lower level to the left of the principal piazza, was rebuilt after the earthquake of 1795.

The **Lido di Copanello** challenges its neighbour, **Soverato,** eight miles to the south, for the tourist brochure title of 'pearl of the Ionian'. It lies just north of the Punta (or Coscia) di Staletti, a hilly headland over which the road passes and whose shores are broken into granite cliffs and little sandy coves. Here, as at Soverato, there is excellent bathing, as well as underwater fishing. However, there is, yet again, little accommodation for the tourist—a single Motel with only nine bedrooms—though Soverato has two very modest hotels, the S. Vincenza, and the Scalamandre, both on the Corso Umberto.

Map XI
p. 372

The coast road runs through olive groves, passing several small villages, to Badolato Marina, and from there through rather desolate hills to the River Assi at Punta Stilo, the boundary between the provinces of Catanzaro and Reggio. Immediately after is Monasterace Marina and from there a run of 83 miles to Reggio Calabria (see chapter 22).

CHAPTER 21

The Tyrrhenian Coast

Maps: III, p.182; X, p.368; XI, p.372; XII, p.380

Calabria and the beginnings of 'Italy'

Calabria, in the toe of Italy, lying between the Tyrrhenian and Ionian Seas, is less rich in monuments or works of art than Campania or Apulia, but this is compensated for by the variety and beauty of its natural scenery. On the west, the Tyrrhenian coast, it is traversed as far south as the Vale of Maida by a chain of mountains, the Catena Costiera. The Pollino range forms its northern boundary with Lucania; farther south it is crossed laterally by the three divisions of the mountains of La Sila (the Sila Greca, Sila Grande, and Sila Piccola); and in the extreme south rise the Appennino Calabrese, terminating in the heights of Aspromonte behind Reggio Calabria. Large tracts of these mountains are covered by forests, and the cultivated areas are for the most part restricted to the few plains or river valleys or terraced hillsides. On the Ionian coast the indiscriminate felling of trees in the past has led to serious erosion.

The name 'Calabria' was applied by the ancients to the heel of Italy, the toe being then known as the lands of the Bruttii (or Bruttium), after the indigenous peoples. 'Calabria' was first applied to the western region by the Byzantines about the seventh century AD.

Possibly in the second millennium BC, certainly by early in the first, Greek traders had penetrated the western seas and set up trading ports with the inhabitants. (The sacral, religious foundations of these Greek cities, which stretched along the Italian shore from Taranto to Cyme, in Sicily, and on the Mediterranean coasts of France and Spain, came much later.) The Greek colonists introduced both the vine and olive to Italy, and by the time of Pythagoras (sixth century BC) these prosperous western colonies were referred to collectively as 'Great Greece', Magna Graecia. A century later the Greeks of Southern Italy had become known, in contrast with the

366

natives, as *Italiotai* or *Italikoi*. According to the legend, Italos, grandson of Odysseus and Penelope, seized the toe of Italy and introduced into his new kingdom the order, science and customs of the Greeks. By the fourth century BC 'Italy' consisted of an area south of a line between Scalea and Metaponto, but by the following century the Romans had adopted 'Italia' as a name for the whole peninsula. Through the cities of Magna Graecia flowed that Hellenic culture which has left such an indelible imprint on our western civilization.

As we have seen on p. 183, there are two main routes from Naples to Reggio Calabria—the SS 18 and 19. The latter, after Lagonegro, crosses the mountainous tract of western Lucania, through Mormanno and Morano Calabro to the important town of Castrovillari beneath Monte Pollino. It then crosses the upper reaches of the plain of Sybaris to Spezzano Albanese, and from there follows the valley of the River Crati to Cosenza, one of the three provincial capitals of Calabria (the others are Catanzaro and Reggio). About ten miles south of Cosenza we leave the SS 19, which goes on to Catanzaro, and turn right in the SS 108, which brings us down to the coast to join the SS 18 to Reggio just south of Amantea. This is the route which the new Autostrada del Sole will take, and there is already a stretch open which bypasses Cosenza to the west and joins the SS 108 south of the town.

Most tourists, however, will want to travel by the magnificently scenic coast road south from **Sapri.** Beyond Sapri the SS 18 leaves Campania and crosses the short Tyrrhenian coastline of Basilicata, running high along the cliff-face of Capo Bianco. At Fiumicello, with **Maratea** standing on the hillside above, is the Albergo Santavenere (which takes its name from the ancient watch-tower), one of the most luxurious of all southern hotels. The stretch of coast below Maratea is becoming deservedly fashionable and popular as a seaside resort, with good hotels and pensioni—and even night-clubs. The fishing, both surface and underwater, is particularly good here.

In **Maratea Inferiore** (once known simply as Borgo) the church of S. Maria Maggiore has an interesting fifteenth-century doorway in carved sandstone, with marble figures of angels. The more ancient upper town (formerly differentiated as Castello) was a feud of the Carafas of Policastro. In the parish church there is a ciborium of 1518, which depicts four angels in an architectural setting.

Beyond Marina di Maratea the road turns from the sea and, after crossing the River Castrocucco (or Noce) and its tributary, the Fiumarella, enters Calabria. Shortly after, we come to **Praia a Mare,** a rapidly expanding seaside resort with a long stretch of

Map III
p. 182

Map III
p. 182

Map X
p. 368

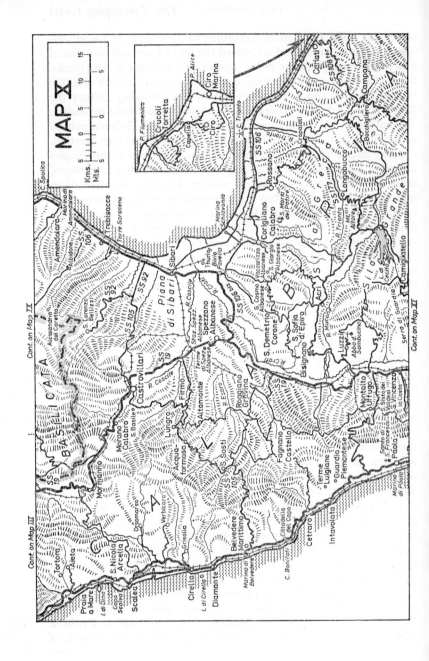

beach, and, just offshore, the **Isola di Dino,** which is well worth a visit for its caves, especially the Grotta Azzurra. Behind the town, on the side of Monte Vingiolo, is the *sanctuary of the Madonna della Grotta,* a somewhat dingy, unprepossessing cavern, reached by a flight of steps and much frequented by pilgrims.

After Praia the road first skirts the sea, then, past S. Nicola Arcella on its little cove, rises to cross the Capo Scalea to the town of that name, so called from the steps (*scalea*) which lead up through narrow streets to its ruined castle. **Scalea** is picturesquely situated but is architecturally disappointing. However, in the church of *S. Nicola* there is a fourteenth-century tomb of the Angevin admiral Ademaro Romano, in a chapel of the same period. The five sculptured panels of the *virgin saints* suggest a Pisan influence.   Map X p. 368

At the mouth of the River Lao a few miles farther on, stood the ancient Greek colony of *Laos,* possibly originally Lucanian, but later one of the dependencies of Sybaris. Before its destruction in 510 BC (when some of the survivors settled here), Sybaris owed much of its famed wealth to its trade with Miletus in Asia Minor, and Laos was its *entrepôt.* Later Laos fell to the Lucanians and was destroyed. The Roman city of Lavinium which rose near by perhaps resuscitated its original name. Above **Cirella** (where there is a good Autostella) we can see on the hill the deserted ruins of Cirella Vecchia, completely destroyed by bombardment from a French fleet in 1806. Offshore is the little **Isola di Cirella,** also with ruined remains. At the pleasant little town of **Diamante** the road forms an esplanade overlooking the sea, and south of the town there are good sandy beaches.   Map X p. 368

Ahead of us, in a beautiful position on its hill, is **Belvedere Marittimo,** which is reached by a road from its Marina. The town is dominated by a medieval castle. Over the main doorway of the *Chiesa Matrice* is a low-relief of the *Madonna and Child* of fifteenth-century Tuscan workmanship. Between Belvedere and the little resort of Cittadella di Capo Bonifati, to the left of the road stand the picturesque ruins of the Castello del Principe, with its cylindrical towers. The town of **Cetraro,** once the property of the abbey of Montecassino, is a market and commercial centre for the villages in the hills behind. In the church of the *Retiro* there are three statues by the little-known sculptor from Carrara, G. D. Mazzola (1544–77); these are of the *Madonna and Child* and *two Franciscan saints.*   Map X p. 368

After the village of Intavolata a road leads up to the sulphur springs of the **Terme Luigiane**—the turning for Guardia Piemontese is a little farther south. **Guardia Piemontese** was settled by   Map X p. 368

Waldensians from Piedmont at the time of the Emperor Frederick II. This town, with others near by—S. Vincenzo la Costa, S. Sisto dei Valdesi and Montalto Uffugo—is said to have given refuge to some 10,000 of these Protestants, until the Inquisition caught up with them in 1560–61, when a Crusade led by the future Pope Pius V exterminated the heretics with relentless cruelty. Their head, Luigi Pascale, was burned alive at Guardia. The local dialect has many words of Franco-Provençal origin.

The road continues along the hillside, with views over the cultivated coastal strip and the town, marina and little port of **Paola**.

Map X
p. 368 Just north of the town is the ***santuario di S. Francesco,*** built in 1453 by S. Francesco di Paola, the founder of the Minims—the '*minimi*', the least in the house of the Lord—the strictest order of the Franciscans, whose motto is *Caritas*. The sanctuary is preceded by a wide drive, bounded on the left by the River Isca and on the right by a long wing of offices and the monastic library (1779). Ahead of us is the main entrance to the monastery, the two lower storeys in the style of the Renaissance (1452—restored in 1555, after being sacked by corsairs), and surmounted by baroque pinnacles. In the interior, to the right, is the late-Renaissance chapel which contains some relics of the Saint, an ornate altar and an interesting painting of *the two SS. Francesco* of the sixteenth-century Neapolitan school. The pleasant cloister (fifteenth to sixteenth centuries) has some remains of rather poor frescoes.

Paola, the town itself, is partly built on a spur, and consists of an upper and a lower town. The Marina is a little farther south. In the lower town there is a delightful example of baroque scene-painting in the piazza before the church of the Madonna di Montevergine with its ornate façade and archway. The colours of the painted stucco have faded, and in the evening light the little square has all the charm of a theatrical setting.

The well-graded road from Paola over the mountains to Cosenza has magnificent views, which can also be enjoyed from the little rack-and-pinion railway that connects the two towns.

We leave Paola past the Castello of the Spinelli, who were the leading feudal family here and in the region just to the north. In the Map XI
p. 372 castle at **S. Lucido**, some five miles south of Paola, was born a prominent member of one of the most powerful of all Calabrian families—the future Cardinal Fabrizio Ruffo (1763–1832), whose bands of Sanfedisti, recruited among the lawless peasantry of these wild mountains and almost inaccessible valleys, restored King Ferdinand I and IV to his throne in June 1799.

The Statale and the railway line run along the narrow strip of coast between mountains and sea, gravel alternating with sandy beaches, to the pleasant little town of **Amantea** which, like Paola, has an upper and lower town. Towards the upper town is the beautiful little fifteenth-century church of *S. Bernardino da Siena.* Above the pointed-arched portico on the façade there is a fifteenth-century cross made from brightly-coloured plates of majolica (we have already seen majolica similarly used in the cathedral of Carinola in Northern Campania, and plates of Persian ware in the pulpit of S. Giovanni del Toro at Ravello). A Renaissance doorway on the right formerly gave access to the Oratorio della Confraternità dei Nobili; now the cloisters have been adapted for use as a school. In the church there is a marble group of the *Madonna and Child* (1505) by Antonello Gagini, one of a Lombard family of sculptors extensively represented in the South of Italy.

Map XI
p. 372

At Campora S. Giovanni we meet the SS 108 from Cosenza; and shortly after crossing the River Savuto, the SS 18 *dir* for Nocera Terinese and Nicastro. From the latter we can join the SS 19 *dir* from S. Eufemia Lamezia to the provincial capital of Catanzaro and the Ionian coast.

From Cape Suvero we have a splendid view south over the Gulf of S. Eufemia, with Stromboli standing out among the Lipari Islands (the Aeolian Islands of the Greeks). We now enter the richly cultivated *bonifica* of the plain of S. Eufemia. This is the narrowest point of the Calabrian peninsula (about 19 miles as the crow flies), and across it the ancient Greek Croton communicated with the now vanished cities of Terina and Temesa on the Tyrrhenian shore. On the south side of the valley stands the little town of **Maida,** which gives its name to the London suburb of Maida Vale in commemoration of Sir John Stuart's victory there over the French on July 4th, 1806. (For the road connections from S. Eufemia Lamezia see p. 404.)

Map XI
p. 372

Since Calabria was the scene for so much of the fighting for the Kingdom of Naples during the Napoleonic Wars, it is worth turning at this point to the brief summary of the main events to be found in Appendix 3.

Pizzo—Vibo Valentia

At Ponte Angitola we meet a branch of the 19 *dir* for Catanzaro, and shortly after, the SS 110 for Serra S. Bruno. There are fine views

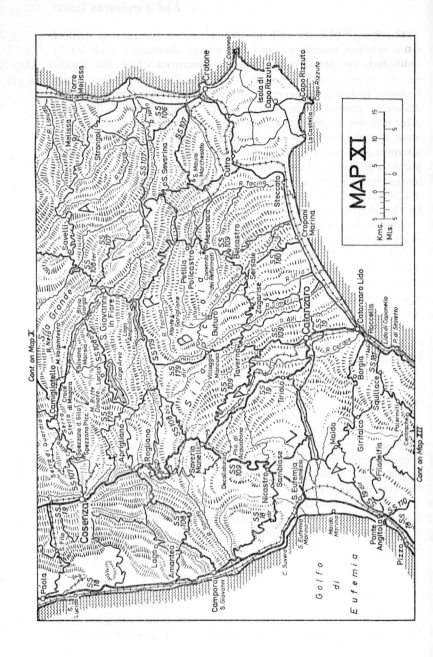

Cont. on Map X

Cont. on Map XII

MAP XI

Kms. 5   0   5   10   15
Mls. 5   0   5

Paola

S. Lucido

Cosenza

SS 18
SS S. Filo 19
SS 107

Serra di Guardia

M. Volpintesta
Camigliatello
Serra S. Croce
SS 107
Spezzano d. Sila
Spezzano Picc.

Silvana Mansio
Silla Grande
M. Botte
M. Donato, Lorica
SS 108
Bivio
Gorga

R. Neto
R. Volpintesta

Savelli

S. Severina

SS 107
SS 108 ter
S. Giovanni in Fiore

Lago Arvo
Lago Ampollino

SS 108 bis

Aprigliano

Rogliano

Lago Savuto

Amantea

SS 18
SS 108

Campora
S. Giovanni

C. Suvero

Golfo di Eufemia

S. Eufemia Marina
Maida Marina

Ponte Angitola

Pizzo

SS 18
SS 19 dir
SS 19
SS 110

SS 179
SS 179

R. Tacina
Monte
Gariglione
Governo dei Riformati

Petilia Policastro

Mesoraca
S. Mauro Marchesato

Cutro

Crotone

C. Colonna

Isola di Capo Rizzuto
La Castella
Capo Rizzuto

Torre Melissa
Melissa
Strongoli
R. Lipuda
SS 106
SS 107
R. Nicà
R. Vitravo

SS 109
Belcastro
Sersale
Steccato
Cropani Marina

SS 180
R. Crocchio

Zagarise
R. Simeri
R. Alli
Taverna
R. Uria
SS 109
SS 109

SS 179
Villaggio Mancuso
Buturo

Silaca

Sila

Pso. di Acquabona
Savelli Marelli
SS 109
Decollatura
Nicastro
Sambiase
S. Eufemia Lamezia

Tiriolo
Borgia
SS 19

Catanzaro
SS 19
R. Corace
Roccella
Catanzaro Lido
Lido di Capanello
P. di Staletto

Squillace
SS 181
Girifalco
Filadelfia
Palermiti
Centrache

Maida
SS 19 dir

over the Gulf of S. Eufemia and the town of **Pizzo** ahead, perched
on its dominant rock. Pizzo is probably medieval in origin, but its
buildings have suffered much from earthquakes. From April until
July it is one of the centres for fishing for tunny and swordfish.

Map XI
p. 372

Pizzo has its small niche in history, for it was there, on October
8th, 1815, that Joachim Murat landed to raise what he thought were
his loyal subjects in an attempt to regain his throne. He received no
response at all to his harangue in the public square; instead, the
Bourbon officer commanding the district was quickly informed of his
arrival, and Murat was captured. Naples was informed by sema-
phore, and the order came back that he was to be court-martialled
and condemned as a public enemy. On October 13th he was found
guilty and sentenced to be shot. He was buried in an unknown grave
in the Collegiata di S. Giorgio, the baroque church (1662) which we
see near the piazza.

The *Castello,* built by Ferdinand I of Aragon in 1486, may be
visited; it is today used as a Youth Hostel.

Vibo Valentia is a go-ahead, prosperous town in a beautiful
position on the Tavolato del Poro, 1800 ft above the sea, with fine
views towards the Lipari Islands and Sicily. The town has grown up
near the Greek city of Hipponion, founded by the Locrians possibly
in the fifth century BC. Its fortunes fluctuated until a Roman colony
was established there in 192 BC, when the town became known as
Vibo Valentia and quickly grew in importance, so that Cicero, who
visited it, could speak of it as an *'illustre et nobile municipium'*. During
the Byzantine dominion of Southern Italy the town was 're-hellenized', but was twice (in 850 and 983) taken and sacked by the
Saracens. Its true re-founder was the Emperor Frederick II in 1235,
who gave it the name of Monteleone, which it retained until it
reverted to Vibo Valentia as recently as 1928. Under Murat, with a
population of 20,000, it was the capital of the province and headquarters for his proposed attack on Sicily; but after the return of the
Bourbons it was punished for its liberal ideas, its population reduced
to 8,000, and the provincial capital shifted to Catanzaro.

Map XII
p. 380

From the Statale we take (on the left) the Via Garibaldi which
rises to the piazza of the same name, the centre of the city, flanked
on the farther side by some imposing palaces. To the left runs the
Corso Umberto I and half-way along on the right is the rather
dilapidated little *Teatro Vibonese,* once the church of S. Giuseppe,
but transformed for more mundane uses by Murat. Below the Corso
on the other side are the fine gardens of the Villa Regina Margherita.
At the end of the Corso, where it is met by the Via Vittorio Veneto,

stands the church of the **Collegiata,** of very early foundation, perhaps ninth century, but completely rebuilt in 1680–1723 after earthquake damage. The façade, with its two campanili, was reconstructed in 1852.

The interior of the Collegiata has to be seen to be believed: decorations of white and pink stucco are a background for statuary in cream and white marble. Over the high altar is a marble group, the *Madonna della Neve*, which appears to be a copy of that by Santacroce in the church of S. Anna dei Lombardi in Naples—possibly by the master himself. The figures of *St Luke* and the *Madonna and Child* in the right transept are attributed to two brothers of the Gagini family (*ca.* 1536). Undoubtedly the most striking piece in the church is the altar in the left transept, of fine dark marbles, including the rare Calabrian *verde*. The figures of the *Magdalen ascending to Heaven*, the *Madonna and Child* (Madonna della Grazia) and the somewhat effeminate *St John the Evangelist*, are by Antonello Gagini, the father of the brothers mentioned above. The bronze figures of angels and cherubs are part of a large ciborium executed by Cosimo Fanzago in 1631 for the Charterhouse at Serra S. Bruno. In a chapel on the left is a fine early (fifteenth-century?) crucifix. The paintings over the altars in the first two chapels on the right have been attributed to the school of the Florentine Salviati (1510–63).

To visit some of the few remaining ruins of Greek **Hipponion,** we take the road on the right of the Collegiata. After about a quarter of a mile a narrow road on the right leads up to the cemetery on the hill. At the last bend before the entrance to the cemetery, we can see parts of the lower courses of the ancient walls of the city. The visit is worth while for the panorama alone.

Returning to the Corso Umberto I, we continue on past the Piazza Garibaldi, and in Via Pasquale Galluppi come to the much deteriorated Renaissance church of **S. Michele** (1519), which is thought by some to be by the Sienese architect Baldassare Peruzzi (1481–1537). The campanile is later (1671).

Higher up the hill (behind the Piazza Garibaldi), which is crowned with the ruins of its Norman castle from which there is an excellent view, are two palaces which have private collections of antiquities (some from ancient Hipponion). Those who wish to visit these must write beforehand to the directors of the **Palazzo Cordopatri** and the **Palazzo Capialbi.**

Map XII
p. 380 The SS 182 leads up over the mountains, among fine woods, to Serra S. Bruno (see p. 411), passing through **Soriano,** where there are the ruins of the monastery of S. Domenico (see p. 413). From

374

Serra S. Bruno the SS 110 passes through magnificent forests and descends via Stilo (see p. 388) to the Ionian sea.

Tropea—Mileto—the Plain of Gioia—Scilla

Tropea, Parghelia and Briatico, the seaside resorts on the peninsula which ends in Capo Vaticano, are still almost completely without hotel accommodation. For Tropaea, instead of the coast road through Briatico, we may follow the SS 18 some five miles south of Vibo, turn right by the disused aerodrome, and cross the pleasantly rolling countryside by a road which Murat planted with white poplars. **Tropea** is perched on the edge of a sheer cliff overlooking the sea. Its palaces and churches, especially the exquisite cathedral, have much to offer; the bathing is excellent, and the climate delightful, even in winter. Unfortunately its one 4th category hotel is near the railway station, some way from the beaches.

Map XII p. 380

The centre of the town is the Piazza Ercole—a reminder that Tropea was the Portus Herculis of the Romans. On it stands the old Seggio (or Sedile) de' Nobili, where the nobility once foregathered to discuss municipal affairs. Although the town was taken and occupied for a time by the Saracens, it flourished under the Angevins and Aragonese, and its ships contributed much to Don John of Austria's victory over the Turks at Lepanto in 1571. The statue near by is of Pasquale Galluppi—a philosophic member of a prominent local family. At the end of the piazza a belvedere overlooks the beautiful beach of the Mare Piccolo, with its Lido S. Leonardo, and the villa-like church of *S. Maria dell' Isola,* on a rocky promontory to the left.

The Via Roma takes us from the piazza to the *Duomo,* an eleventh-century Norman structure which has been splendidly restored to the original simplicity of its basilican form. The nave and two aisles have semi-circular apses, and there is a good modern timbered ceiling. On the right is the private chapel of the Galluppi family, with some baroque tombs, and in the next chapel the 'Black Crucifix'—a powerful piece of carving in wood, possibly of the fifteenth century. In the passage leading to the sacristy and chapter-house on the right is a beautiful tomb of a brother and sister, presumably by one of the Gagini. Round the walls of the chapter-house hang 'portraits' of all the bishops of Tropea since 499—some of them seem to bear a curious family likeness. In another chapel on the right of the church, there is a portrait of a Franciscan with an interesting

375

trompe l'œil effect. A doorway by the sacristy (note the rather crude early low-relief on the outside) leads into a little court.

Over the altar at the end of the right aisle is a fine *Madonna and Child* ('*Madonna del Popolo*'), thought to be the work of Fazio Gagini (1555); and above the high altar, covered by a silver screen, is a striking Byzantine-looking painting, the *Madonna di Romania*, of uncertain date and provenance. In the chapel to the left is a beautiful Tuscan fifteenth-century ciborium with 'Ave Maria' in Roman and Greek characters; and above, another sixteenth-century statue, the *Madonna della Libertà*.

Outside, the cathedral is joined to the **Bishop's Palace** by a Gothic portico which contains more sixteenth-century statues—of *St Peter, St Paul, the Madonna, a Franciscan*, etc. In the palace there is a chapel with frescoes of 1486. In the Largo S. Michele the **Palazzo Toraldo** contains a collection of early Christian inscriptions, considered to be the finest in Calabria.

Map XII
p. 380

Resuming our journey south, we return to the SS 18 and turn right for **Mileto,** an uninteresting town of mainly one-storeyed buildings erected after the disastrous earthquake of 1783, and rebuilt after those of 1905 and 1908. The Norman town of Mileto, which King Roger (1137–54) made the capital of the region, lies to the east of the present town; it is reached from the country road to the hamlet of S. Giovanni. Among the ruins of the *abbey of the Trinity* are fragments of marbles from the ancient Temple of Proserpine at Vibo. Near here in 1190 King Richard Cœur de Lion, on his way from Salerno to Reggio, was set on by the inhabitants for stealing a hawk and narrowly escaped death at their hands.

Map XII
p. 380

The road descends, with views over the Plain of Gioia to the mountains of Aspromonte behind. Just beyond the boundary between the provinces of Catanzaro and Reggio a signposted road on the right leads to **Nicotera,** an old town built on a hill, with magnificent views over the sea, the coast and the green plain of Gioia. The cathedral has a *Madonna della Grazia* by Antonello Gagini, some fragments of low-reliefs in a chapel on the left of the high altar, and a much venerated wooden crucifix. There is a good sandy beach at Nicotera Marina.

Map XII
p. 380

The Plain of Gioia, or of Rosarno (but usually called simply La Piana) is one of the principal olive-growing districts of Italy. The trees grow to such an immense size in the perfect conditions that picking presents difficulties. The main centres are **Rosarno** and **Gioia Tauro,** the latter a somewhat sprawling town built, it is thought, on or near the site of ancient Metauron, a colony of the

Locrians. From Gioia the SS 111 crosses the mountains to Locri on the Ionian seaboard.

After crossing this fertile plain, the SS 18 ascends with extensive views over the Strait of Messina to **Palmi,** a prosperous town which, like so many others in this region, has suffered much from earthquakes. For the town and its beautiful beaches we have to leave the Statale and drive down for about two miles between vineyards and olive groves. There are only very simple hotels at Palmi but one can lunch pleasantly at the small *trattoria* right on the beach of the Marinella, among the fishermen's huts and the boats drawn up on the shore. To our left the bay is closed by a little rocky island with a single windswept olive tree.

Map XII
p. 380

Just south of Palmi, a road on the right brings us in a few minutes to the **belvedere of Monte S. Elia,** a diversion well worth making for the splendid view. On a clear day you can see the two famous volcanoes—Etna in mountainous Sicily to the south and Stromboli out at sea to the north-west.

The vineyards, terraced on the steep slopes, increase around **Bagnara Calabra.** This town has been several times destroyed by earthquakes, most recently in 1908. It is one of the best places for fishing for swordfish (*pesce spada*) in the spring and early summer. There are two small *pensioni*, the Castello Emmarita and the Reginella. The former was once a residence of the Ruffo family.

Map XII
p. 380

From just east of Bagnara a stretch of autostrada has now been completed as far as Archi, a few miles north of Reggio. **Scilla** stands partly round the castle on its famous rock (once the property of the Ruffos, now a Youth Hostel), and partly on the two bays on either side. The nearer side as we approach is inhabited mostly by fishermen, with the main beach on the farther side. Beside the castle is the recently rebuilt church of the Immacolata, to which was formerly annexed a famous Basilian monastery.

Map XII
p. 380

Homer writes in the *Odyssey* of the narrow dangerous strait through which the hero and his men would have to pass, homeward bound for Ithaca from the siege of Troy. 'For on one side lay Scylla and on the other divine Charybdis sucked down terrifyingly the salt water of the sea.' From Scilla to the Punto del Faro on the Sicilian shore is about four miles, and the waters of the strait do at times appear strangely agitated. The *faro* (lighthouse) was the dividing point for the Kingdom of the 'Two Sicilies', *cis* and *ultra pharum*— i.e. on this side of and beyond the lighthouse. On the beach, the Marina Grande, there is now an excellent, modern hotel, Matteo a Mare. The cooking is good, especially of the local fish; and one can eat outside on the terrace overlooking the beach, the sea, and Sicily beyond; an enchanting spot.

Beyond Scilla the road comes down to Villa S. Giovanni where the train- and car-ferries leave for Messina, whose white houses we can see opposite against blue mountains. The Statale now runs along a narrow coastal strip through luxuriant orange-groves, palms and prickly pear. Then the built-up area becomes almost continuous as we pass through the seaside resorts of Catona and Gallico Marina, and finally enter the straight, modern-looking streets of Reggio Calabria.

CHAPTER 22

Reggio di Calabria and its Environs

Map: XII, p.380

Reggio—Scenes from the Life of Persephone

The *Castor and Pollux* bearing St Paul to Pozzuoli put in to Syracuse in Sicily for three days—'then we coasted round the further shore, and so arrived at Rhegium. When we had spent a day there a south wind blew up, and we made Puteoli on the second day out' (*Acts*). A little more than a generation before the apostle's visit (about AD 23) the geographer Strabo had described Reggio, Taranto and Naples as being the only three cities of Italy which retained the customs, habits and language of the Greeks—all the rest had become Romanized. After Cumae, **Reggio** is the oldest Greek settlement on the Italian mainland. The date of its foundation by Chalcidians of Euboea is not certain, but was possibly about 730 BC.

Some Messanians exiled from the Peloponnese were also involved in the foundation of Rhegion. They formed the ruling class, and one of them, Anaxilas, became tyrant of the city in 494 BC and invited more Messanian settlers to Rhegion. In 396 BC Rhegion was taken and sacked by Dionysius the Elder, tyrant of Syracuse; but later restored. In 280 BC, fearing both Pyrrhus and the Carthaginians, Rhegion allied itself with Rome, in whose fortunes it henceforth shared. Rhegium, as the Romans called it, became a *municipium* in 89 BC, and under the Roman policy of securing the loyalty of the Greek cities, was allowed many privileges—including the retention of its customs and language. In the break-up of the Roman Empire, Reggio was destroyed by Alaric, and subsequently by Totila in AD 549. The Byzantine Emperors promoted it to be the metropolitan city of the newly designated area of Calabria, with its bishop of the Eastern rites. Reggio was re-hellenized by the Byzantines, and in spite of its temporary capture by the Saracens in the tenth century, remained Byzantine until it fell to the Normans.

Reggio was captured by Roger in 1059, and the last Saracen

MAP XII

Kms. 5 0 5 10 15
Mls. 5 0 5

stronghold in Sicily fell to him in 1091, five years after his half-brother Robert Guiscard's death. Count Roger held Calabria and Sicily until his death in 1101, when he was succeeded by his son Roger II. It was this Roger who consolidated the Norman possessions and founded the dynasty in Southern Italy and Sicily, being recognized by the Pope in 1130 as 'King of Sicily, Apulia and Calabria, help and shield of the Christians'. The 'baptized sultan', as Roger was called by his enemies—he shared the title with his great Swabian successor, the Emperor Frederick II—lived with his harem in oriental splendour at his capital of Palermo until his death in 1154.

Architecturally Reggio has little to offer, for since antiquity men have joined with earthquakes to destroy it. In 1543 Barbarossa burnt it; in the next fifty years it was devastated four times by corsairs; earthquakes in 1783 and 1811 reduced it to ruins; and finally, in 1908, the Messina earthquake left hardly a house standing and killed 5000 of Reggio's 35,000 inhabitants. Today it is an undistinguished city of low buildings, for the most part constructed of reinforced concrete.

There are, however, the remains of the *Aragonese castle* on the hill, and opposite it in the Piazza del Castello the re-built *Chiesa degli Ottimati* has a cosmatesque pavement of the Norman period and four columns from the destroyed Byzantine church. In the Lungomare (the esplanade by the sea) there are some *remains of the Greek walls*—near the Post Office—and of the *Roman baths.* Off the Corso, in the Piazza del Duomo, stands the ugly rebuilt *cathedral,* preceded by two statues of *St Paul* and *St Stephen of Nicaea,* the first bishop of Reggio. These are the work of Francesco Ierace (1854–1937). An inscription recalls the apostle to the gentiles, '*Circumlegentes devenimus Rhegium . . .*' Inside, on the right of the entrance, an inscribed stone of Spanish vice-regal days from the destroyed cathedral is an eloquent reminder of the horror and destruction of the 1908 earthquake. Farther along the Corso, towards the Piazza Garibaldi on which stands the Central Station, we come to the *gardens of the Villa Comunale,* with a fine collection of exotic flowering plants and trees. From the terrace there is a splendid view over the Strait to the Sicilian shore.

Nevertheless, despite architectural poverty, the town's beautiful position and good hotels make it an excellent centre from which to explore the toe of Italy.

Reggio's *Museo Nazionale della Magna Grecia* is housed in a modern building where the Lungomare meets the Corso, towards the port and lido at the northern end of the city. Unfortunately the rearranging of the exhibits, which has been going on for some years now, is not yet complete; but visitors will be admitted on application at the door, preferably in the mornings.

The two centralized museums of Reggio and Taranto contain immensely valuable collections relating to life in the ancient Greek cities of Magna Graecia, and in both the arrangement of the objects is imaginative and up-to-date. At Reggio the *pinakes* (small terracotta plaques in low-relief) from a votive deposit at Locri are especially interesting. They were produced in Locri between 480–50 BC, and are unique in presenting us with mythical scenes from the life of Persephone-Kore, which have no record in the literary tradition, though the cult was pursued throughout South Italy and Sicily.

Behind the Museo Nazionale the Viale Genoese Zerbi takes us to the Lido and to the port, the Stazione Marittima. The less populated beaches of Gallico Marina and Catona are within easy reach by bus or train. From the port there is both a ferry service (the train-car-ferry goes from Villa S. Giovanni) and a hydroplane service to Messina. From Messina trips can be made to the Lipari Islands and to the attractive resort of Taormina under Etna.

Gambarie—where Garibaldi was captured—Seminara—Melito di Porto Salvo

There are a number of good day excursions which can be made from Reggio. Two excellent ones take in the village of Gambarie, a popular summer resort and centre for winter skiing, which stands north-east of Reggio where the Apennines end in the heights of Aspromonte.

For the first of these we return on the SS 18 to Gallico, where we turn right on the SS 184, and almost immediately start to climb. Extensive views open below of the rich coastal plain north of Reggio and the Strait and Messina at the foot of the Monti Peloritani. The citrus-groves that cover the plain and the valleys through which we pass grow oranges, lemons, tangerines and mandarins, and *citrus bergamia* is also cultivated, from which the oil known as bergamot is extracted for making scent and eau-de-cologne. This fruit is grown nowhere else. South of Reggio, and especially around the village of Brancaleone on the eastern side of the 'toe', jasmine is also cultivated for its use in scent manufacture.

As we get higher the olives become less frequent and the woods increase. In the villages the upper floors of the houses are sometimes built of wood (or even corrugated iron), often with ironwork balconies from which hang pots or baskets of flowers. **S. Stefano** was the birthplace of perhaps the last of the famous Calabrian brigands, Musolino, who, after shooting a number of police and informers at the beginning of this century, was caught, brought to trial and sentenced to thirty years' imprisonment on Elba. His name was a household word among the local peasantry, and he was said never to have refused money to the poor.

Neat well-to-do villas and bungalows announce the outskirts of **Gambarie** and the crossroads for Melito to the south and Delianuova to the north. Ahead of us is the chair-lift for the ski-slope on the side of Montalto, the highest peak of Aspromonte. Gambarie has three hotels, the Grande Albergo Gambarie, the Excelsio, and the Del Turista. For summer visitors there are some excellent walks, including a long and steep haul by mule-track to the statue of Our Redeemer which crowns Montalto. From the summit a track descends for a further twelve miles in a north-easterly direction through wooded valleys to the picturesquely situated Norman-Basilian *sanctuary of S. Maria di Polsi.* Other tracks lead south to meet the main road from Melito to Gambarie.

Turning left at the crossroads at Gambarie on the road for Delianuova, we cross an upland plateau, and after a few miles a signpost on the right directs us through the woods to the *Forestali* and the so-called *Mausoleum of Garibaldi,* the scene of the hero's capture by government troops on August 29th, 1862, when he raised an army of 3000 volunteers with the call of '*Roma o morte*' in an unsuccessful attempt to incorporate Rome and the Papal States in United Italy. In fact, Rome was not 'liberated' until 1870.

At the crossroads before Delianuova, which we can see on the hillside, we meet the SS 112 from Bagnara Calabra on the Tyrrhenian to Bovalino Marina on the Ionian Sea (about 63 miles from coast to coast). Here we turn left for Sinopoli, but before reaching the village turn into a minor road on the right which takes us through the hamlets of S. Procopio and Melicuca to the town of Seminara.

Seminara, founded in about the fifth century AD by refugees from Taurianum, was one of the strongest fortresses in Calabria during the Middle Ages; and at the end of the fifteenth century it was given in feud by Ferdinand II to the Spinelli family. Later it was a fief of the Ruffos. Battles that took place here at the end of the fifteenth century during the struggle between the French and

Spaniards for the Kingdom are commemorated in some low-reliefs from a destroyed Spinelli monument (Seminara has suffered badly from earthquakes), now housed in the Sede Comunale on the corner of the main square, the Piazza Vittoria. On the front wall are two feudal *stemmi* (armorial bearings) with that of the Municipio, the latter depicting S. Mercurio slaying Julian the Apostate. Two of the reliefs are on the walls of the entrance hall and another pair on the stairway.

By a street to the left of the Sede Comunale we come to the **santuario della Madonna dei Bogeri,** which has a venerated twelfth- or thirteenth-century *Madonna and Child.* We can climb up behind the main altar to view this rather pathetic object. On the left of the main doorway the Tuscan sixteenth-century font, reconstructed after earthquake damage, stands next to a *Madonna and Child* which is similar in style to the near-by figure of the *Magdalen* by the Messinese sculptor Rinaldo Bonanno (active 1577–91). Note the two vigorous statues of *St Peter* (the head has been badly replaced) and *St Paul* by an unknown artist.

If we continue along the street to the left of the church for about a hundred yards and then turn left, we come to the rebuilt church of **S. Marco,** which has some interesting reliefs and carvings, including a *Madonna and Child,* possibly by Antonello Gagini but showing perhaps the influence of his master Francesco Laurana, whose work we have seen on Alfonso il Magnanimo's triumphal arch in Naples.

Seminara was the birthplace in the fourteenth century of that versatile religious figure, Barlaam, who tried in vain to teach Petrarch Greek and later provoked the Hesychast controversy. The schism between the Catholic and the Eastern Church took place in 1054, but Southern Italy had many Basilian monasteries which still followed St Basil's rule for the Eastern church. Barlaam, as Abbot of the Basilian monastery of S. Salvatore in Constantinople, had discovered that some of the monks on Mount Athos were seeking God in the contemplation of their navels. His relentless logic led him to denounce the views of these so-called *Umbilicanimi* as leading straight to polytheism—the postulation of two eternal substances, a visible and an invisible God. When the Eastern Emperor was finally called in to decide this important point, things went against Barlaam, so that he retracted and fled to Calabria, where he afterwards became a bishop in the Roman Church.

From Seminara we descend to the coast near Palmi and thence follow the SS 18 back to Reggio.

For the alternative route to Aspromonte we leave Reggio by the

SS 106 (Ionica), the road which rounds the toe and then skirts the Ionian Sea to Taranto. When the road ascends to round the Punta di Pellaro the views over the Strait are particularly fine. Just before the village of S. Elia a road leads inland to **Montebello Ionico** beyond the curious village of **Pentedattilo,** built beneath a vast outcropping of precipitous rock, from which it derives its Greek name meaning 'five fingers'.

A short way beyond the turning for Montebello we come to the southernmost town of the toe of Italy, **Melito di Porto Salvo,** famous for the two landings made here in 1860 and 1862 by Garibaldi. For Gambarie we turn left in the SS 183, following the river-course (often dry and stony in summer, but after rain a raging torrent) of the Melito. This southern promontory was known as Leukopetra by the Greeks from the whitish appearance of the land from out at sea. The road continues to loop its way up the mountain-side, until we come out on to a high upland plateau with incomparable views over the Strait and Sicily. At the crossroads at Gambarie we turn left and return, via the village of S. Stefano, to the coast at Gallico, and thence back to Reggio.

The Ionian coast—Gerace—ancient Locri—Stilo

When the SS 106 from Reggio to Taranto rounds Capo Spartivento (the Heracleum Promontorium of the Romans) and bears north-east we become fully aware for the first time of the Ionian Sea. We come first to **Brancaleone Marina,** the seaside village for the town on the hill. Road and rail follow the contour of the shore. Inland rise the mountains, with broken valleys running down to the coastal plain, which is planted with vines, fruit trees and bergamot oranges. There are long stretches of beautiful sand, but few of the seaside resorts are yet equipped to cater for tourists.

The Greek cities along this coast were some of the most famous in Magna Graecia. The southernmost colony was Locri Epizephyrii. Then followed a string of Achaean colonies, with two Ionian exceptions, and finally in the extreme north, on the gulf which still bears its name, the most celebrated of them all, the Dorian Taras (Tarentum, Taranto).

After Brancaleone, the road bears almost due north, and passing Capo Bruzzano and the town of Bianco, brings us to **Bovalino Marina.** Near the middle of the town, close to the sea, is a simple trattoria with vaulted stone ceilings, delightfully cool in the heat.

From Bovalino Marina the SS 112 crosses the mountains north of Aspromonte for Bagnara Calabra. A diversion can be made here before rejoining the Statale Ionica at Locri. We turn left in the SS 112, then just beyond the mountain village of Piminoro take the SS 111 *dir* on the right, which brings us through Oppido, the epicentre of the 1783 earthquake, to Taurianova, an important centre for the olive-oil industry of the plain of Gioia Tauro. Here we turn right in the SS 111 and shortly after come to Cittanova. As the road climbs to the high Passo del Mercante we see behind us the green olive-covered plain stretching as far as the Tyrrhenian Sea. Then the Ionian Sea comes into view, and we descend to the impregnable town of **Gerace**, perched in a commanding position on its hill and crowned with the ruins of the Norman castle built by King Roger. The ***Duomo,*** which is the largest church in Calabria, was founded in 1045 by Robert Guiscard, restored and enlarged by Frederick II in 1222, and restored again after the earthquake of 1783. We enter the church from the left under an ogival-arched portico. On the right is the entrance to the crypt which is supported by twenty-six columns from ancient Locri. Behind an iron grille is a barrel-vaulted chapel called, after the painting it contains, the Cappella della Madonna della Deitria. This painting is said to have been brought from Constantinople in 1261; if it was, it must have been re-painted at a much later date. On the walls are curious eighteenth-century stucco plaques illustrating the attributes of Our Lady as Queen of Heaven, Star of the Sea, the Mystic Rose, etc.

The church itself is in the form of a Latin cross, with round arches (of differing heights) supported on high stilt-blocks resting on antique columns of granite and marbles—*rosso* and *verde antico*—from Locri. The story is told that Murat wished to remove some of the more precious of these columns, but the citizens revolted and drove away his workmen. Saw marks may still be seen in a column near the present entrance.

Returning to the piazza (in the streets just off it are some houses with remains of Norman-Saracenic windows), we pass under the baroque archway and take the street by the left side of the Duomo. Through a wooden gateway (if locked, apply to the sacristan) we can see the simple ogival façade and main portal of the cathedral. Continuing, we come out on a platform and before us are the impressive ruins of the ***Castello,*** built on a sheer rock. Back at the apsidal end of the Duomo, we take the Via Cavour on the left. Passing the Chiesetta del S. Cuore di Gesù, we arrive at the church of ***S. Francesco,*** built by the Hohenstaufen in 1252 and now in process of restoration. Note the Saracenic influence in the main doorway. Inside is a tomb of Niccolò Ruffo (d. 1372), which suggests the hand of a sculptor connected with the Pisan school. On the right of S. Francesco is the interesting little Norman church of **S. Giovannello.** Leaving the town, we continue, to meet the SS 106 again at **Locri.**

The site of the ancient city of Locri is two miles south of the modern town on the SS 106. The precise date of the founding of Locri is uncertain, but it would appear to have been about the turn of the eighth to seventh centuries BC. About 660, political disagreements which had arisen, possibly between the Greek colonists and the native Sicel element, were resolved by the publication of a written code of laws, attributed to Zaleucus—the first of its kind in any Greek city. These laws were intended to be unalterable; any proposer of changes had to appear before the assembly with a halter round his neck, which was drawn tight if his measure failed to be carried by the majority. In the second half of the sixth century BC a Locrian force of 10,000 men is said to have defeated an army of 130,000 Crotonians on the River Sagra (the modern Allaro)—an event which gave rise to a proverb for something happening contrary to all expectation. The Spartans, to whom the Locrians had appealed for help, sent them the Dioscuri (Castor and Pollux), who fought in scarlet cloaks and mounted on white horses. Dionysius the Younger, expelled from Syracuse, made himself tyrant of Locri in 352, but committed such excesses against the citizens that they rose in revolt in 346 and slew the tyrant and all his family. The city surrendered to Pyrrhus, and in 216, after the battle of Cannae, to the Carthaginians. It was taken by the Romans in 205. The ancient city lingered on until its final destruction by the Saracens in the seventh century AD, when the survivors founded Gerace.

The walls of **ancient Locri** are some four and a half miles in circumference, extending from the sea to the three hills of Castellace, Abadessa and Manella, which are separated by narrow valleys. Much of the extensive site is now occupied by farms, and antiquarians are advised to apply at the museum in modern Locri for guides. Near the sea stood an Ionic temple of the fifth century BC, on which the two marble statues of the Dioscuri and their horses, now in Naples Museum, served as *acroteria* (figures above the pediment at the corners). Farther inland was a Doric temple (Contrada Marafioti) from which the Reggio equestrian figure of one of the Dioscuri came. On the hill Manella was a temple of Athene, and beneath it in the ravine, a celebrated Sanctuary of Persephone. In

387

the area have been discovered both Sicel and Greek burial grounds; in the latter the *pinakes* in Reggio were found.

Modern Locri has a lido and three modest hotels. The *Museo,* with objects from ancient Locri, is worth a visit.

At the **Marina di Gioiosa Ionica** a few miles farther on, a small *Roman theatre* has been excavated at the end of the street on the right of the railway station. Gioiosa Ionica itself, a market centre, stands a few miles inland, and from it a secondary road leads up to the summer resort among the woods at the Pass of Croce Ferrata, some 3500 ft above sea-level. The road continues, winding across the mountains, to Serra S. Bruno.

All along the Ionian coast we see the remains of look-out towers (some constructed from remains of classical buildings), a reminder that these shores were constantly open to attacks from corsairs. **Rocella Ionica** consists of an upper town (now largely depopulated) with its castle built on a precipitous rock, and a modern lower town —the latter possessing a sandy beach and modest hotels. The Castello successfully beat off an attack of the corsair Dragut and its guns inflicted heavy losses on the Saracens' ships. Four miles on we come to Marina di Caulonia, the station for **Caulonia** which is five miles inland. This was known until 1860 as Castel Vetere from the remains of its Byzantine (or Norman) castle. It was probably not, after all, founded by refugees from ancient Caulonia—the site of which has been discovered farther north near the Punta Stilo. It was a feud of the Carafa family from the thirteenth century; and in the Chiesa Madre is the tomb of Tuscan workmanship of Vincenzo Carafa (1488).

We cross the Allaro, the scene of the Locrians' victory over the Crotonians, and just before Monasterace Marina pass the junction of the SS 110 for Stilo, Serra S. Bruno and the Tyrrhenian coast. Just north of Monasterace Marina is the site of the Achaean colony of Caulonia, probably founded by the Crotonians *ca.* 675–50 BC as an outpost against the expansion of their rivals, the Locrians.

Stilo's little Byzantine church of the Cattolica is worth going a long way to see, and since the coastline north of the Punta di Stilo has nothing of outstanding interest, it is well worth making a detour inland by the SS 110 to visit Stilo, also the Bourbon hunting-lodge known after its builder as the Ferdinandea, and the Carthusian abbey at Serra S. Bruno (see p. 412), before returning to the coast at Soverato (a round trip of about 60 miles).

Stilo stands halfway up on the rocky flank of Monte Consolino, with, behind, the forest-covered heights of Monte Pecoraro. The

SS 110 brings us up to the piazza, passing on the left a former monastery of the Liguorini. The statue in the piazza is of Tommaso Campanella, the Dominican philosopher and poet who was born in Stilo in 1568.

For the **Duomo** we take the narrow Via Campanella—it is wiser to leave the car in the piazza—which winds up past the little Piazza Vittorio Emanuele to the Piazza Duomo. The main doorway of the cathedral is from the original early fourteenth-century Gothic structure. On the left of the portal the base of an antique statue has been incorporated in the wall—two feet broken off at the ankle. From the balustrade to the right of the building we can follow the River Stilaro to the sea.

The church of the **Cattolica** stands on the hill above the town, and is approached by taking the main road for Serra S. Bruno, until a new road on the right brings you to the gate of the enclosure. One of the horde of small boys will usually inform the woman who has the keys (tip) of your arrival. The brick and stone of the building have worn to a beautiful warm reddish-brown colour, the brickwork forming patterns, especially in the five cupolas. The date of the church is uncertain but it was possibly built as late as the twelfth century. Stilo was an early centre for Basilian monks and hermits in Southern Calabria, as Rossano was for the Northern region. On the right as you enter are three semi-circular apses, the left of which contains a bell. In Greek on the first column on the right are the words, 'God is the Lord who appeared to us', inscribed in a Greek cross. There are some remains of Byzantine frescoes. This exquisite little church resembles those of the Near East.

CHAPTER 23

Cosenza and the Sila

Maps: III, p.182; X, p.368; XI, p.372

Lagonegro—Morano Calabro—Castrovillari—Altomonte—Spezzano
Albanese—local costume

Cosenza, the most northerly of the three provincial capitals of
Calabria, is the best centre for the exploration of the mountainous
tracts which go by the generic name of La Sila. Travellers from
Naples by train are advised to take the Reggio-Calabria line as far
as Paola and then the rack-and-pinion branch line over the Catena
Costiera to Cosenza.

By road, one can take either the SS 19 (delle Calabrie) or the
Autostrada del Sole (when completed) to Lagonegro, or the SS 18
to Paola (see chapters 11 and 21) and then the SS 107 over the
coastal mountains.

Map III
p. 182

Although **Lagonegro** is in Basilicata, it is convenient to continue
the itinerary from this point. There is something almost Alpine about
the setting and appearance of the town. In the Piazza Grande is the
baroque church of *S. Anna* (1665), and to the right of this a narrow
street brings us to the Via Giuseppe Aldinio, which leads down to
the Piazza del Purgatorio and the old quarter of the town. On the
left, the wide eaves of the *Chiesa del Rosario,* above the fresco of
the *Last Judgment* (Antonio Cascini, 1824), give a distinctly Swiss
impression.

Ahead of us looms the rock on which the *castle* was built—
originally it may have been a Roman watch-tower; latterly, it was
the property of the feudal Counts of Lauria. Steps, replacing the old
drawbridge, bring us up to the Porta di Ferro (once faced with iron),
which was built in 1552 when the citizens freed themselves from their
feudal ties and destroyed the castle—an act that is symbolized by the
stemma here, depicting St Michael slaying the dragon. Higher up,
next the ruins of the castle, is the ninth- to tenth-century church
of *S. Nicola* in which, it is claimed, Mona Lisa del Giocondo—

390

Leonardo's lady of the enigmatic smile—was buried on her death here in 1505.

The Statale continues to wind through the mountains. Beyond the little Lago Sirino—all that remains of a once much bigger lake—the SS 104 branches right for Sapri, and shortly afterwards its eastern section branches left for **Latronico** (in the church of S. Egidio there is an indifferent statue of the Saint, said to be by a follower of Giovanni da Nola), the valley of the River Sinni, and the Ionian coast at Stazione Nova Siri. We pass into Calabria at the bridge over the River S. Primo, with the wooded sides of Monte Pollino on our left, and ahead the village of Mormanno.

Map III
p. 182

The road now crosses the rich upland pastures of Campo Tenese, and comes down into the valley of the River Coscile. On the right is the straggling town of **Morano Calabro** with its baroque church of La Maddalena and the ruins of a Norman castle on the top of a conical hill. At the foot of the town is the beautiful church of *S. Bernardino* (1452 and restored in 1949), built by one of the Sanseverino princes of Bisignano (the key is with the sacristan next door; tip). The Gothic entrance has an original fifteenth-century wooden door. The Venetian-style woodwork of the ceiling is also contemporary with the church. The sacristy is panelled, and also has a ceiling in wood, but later in date. The pride of the church is the exquisite polyptych over the high altar; this is by Bartolomeo Vivarini and is signed and dated 1477. The *Collegiata della Maddalena* in the upper town has a statue of the *Madonna and Child* by Antonello Gagini (1505).

Map X
p. 368

A short run brings us to the pleasant little town of **Castrovillari,** an important centre of communication on the low hills to the south of the Pollino range. Castrovillari possibly had a Roman origin (Castrum Villarum), but the first record of it dates only from the eleventh century. The more modern quarter of the town lacks any particular architectural interest, but south of this is the old town, known as the Città, with a well-preserved *castle* built on the site of an older one by the Aragonese in 1490. Over the main entrance are the arms of Aragon and a Latin inscription which informs us that the castle was built 'for the purpose of holding the citizens to their fidelity'. Opposite stands the Chiesa Madre, and to the left of this is the Via S. Maria del Castello, which winds down through the Città, passing on the right the church of S. Giuliano, with a late Renaissance doorway, and then up to the *sanctuary of S. Maria del Castello*. The story is told that the Norman Count Roger began to build a castle on this commanding height. Every morning

Map X
p. 368

it was found that the work done on the previous day had been destroyed. The mystery was solved when a workman suddenly struck a piece of stone on which was painted a Byzantine-type representation of the Madonna. On the intercession of the bishop and people, Count Roger changed his plans and built here in 1090 a sanctuary to the Madonna of the Castle.

Little of the Norman work remains except for the crypt—for some reason this can no longer be visited, though it contains some remains of Byzantine-inspired frescoes—and the main portal to the upper church from the loggia (entered from the last doorway on the left as we approach from the Città), which is surmounted by curious trilobate apertures suggesting a Sicilian-Saracenic influence. Above the usual entrance to the church, on the road by which we came, is a thirteenth- or fourteenth-century carving of the *Madonna and Child*, possibly by a follower of Tino di Camaino. The venerated picture of the *Madonna del Castello* itself shows much over-painting. The interior has been horribly baroqued in the eighteenth century, and there are also some very indifferent baroque paintings.

Castrovillari is joined by the SS 105 with Belvedere Marittimo on the Tyrrhenian Sea and with Villapiana Lido on the Ionian. It is worth making a little diversion from here to visit what remains of perhaps the finest Angevin church in Calabria, at Altomonte. We leave Castrovillari by the SS 105 to the west, crossing the River Coscile, and pass the village of **S. Basile,** which has one of the two remaining Basilian monasteries in Italy—the other is in the Alban Hills. The winding road brings us first to Firmo, then to Lungro, both settled by Albanians, and a short way before Lungro a secondary road on the left leads up to **Altomonte** on the summit of a hill.

Map X
p. 368

The church of *S. Maria della Consolazione* was erected in 1336, on the site of a Norman edifice, by Filippo Sangineto, Count of Altomonte, Seneschal of Provence and Grand Justiciar of the Kingdom. This beautiful church, with its Gothic architecture, its tombs and early paintings, has been sadly abandoned. Altomonte is a most interesting little town, with churches, ex-conventual buildings and the Pallotta Tower; it retains something of the medieval air of its former feudal days.

Map X
p. 368

For **Spezzano Albanese** we can continue on a secondary road from Altomonte, coming down into the valley of the Rivers Fiumicello and Esaro, tributaries of the Coscile. Beyond the railway line and the bridge over the Esaro we reach a crossroads. Straight ahead the road climbs up to Spezzano, a small, rather drab Italian country town, showing nothing of its Albanian origins except on the occasion of a *festa*, when the women of Spezzano and the other Albanian villages and towns put on their beautiful traditional dress. This consists of a long, full skirt, very high-waisted, in the brightest red, green or blue. Both skirt and apron, which from the front appears as the central panel of the skirt, are heavily edged or embroidered in gold. Above this is worn a white blouse of fine linen, and over the shoulders or head a stole, usually of lace. The different coloured dresses glow like a bed of gorgeous tulips.

Cosenza—an ill-fated expedition—the Duomo—S. Francesco d'Assisi

Just beyond Spezzano, the SS 106 *bis* on the left joins our road with the Via Ionica, SS 106. The SS 19 now enters the wide valley of the River Crati, which narrows to the south, so that at the junction with the road from Paola the mountains appear to hem us in. At the end of the valley, at the confluence of the Rivers Crati and Busento, stands the flourishing city of **Cosenza,** surrounded by mountainous peaks.

Map XI
p. 372

Consentia was the principal city of the ancient Bruttii, but it came early under the influence of the Greek settlements of Magna Graecia. After the Second Punic War it was taken by the Romans in 204 BC, but continued to flourish, especially after the construction of the Via Popilia. Pliny speaks of the excellence of its fruits and wine. In AD 410, Alaric the Visigoth died there on his way back to Sicily after sacking Rome. Tradition has it that he was buried, together with a great quantity of treasure, in what is now the bed of the Busento. The river was then diverted to flow over him, and those who had dug his grave were put to death so that none should reveal where he lay. The city was taken by the Lombards and in the eighth and ninth centuries was the centre of their local administration, subordinate to Salerno. It was twice devastated by Saracens before it fell to Robert Guiscard about 1050, but remained the chief city of northern Calabria. Cosenza enjoyed a period of cultural predominance with the founding of its Academy in the sixteenth century by the grammarian Parrhasius (1470–1534). The most celebrated of its native-born scholars was the philosopher Bernardino Telesio (1509–88), the master of Tommaso Campanella. The Accademia Cosentina still exists.

It was possibly the liberal tradition of its Academy that led Cosenza to play a prominent part in the political opposition to the Bourbons. It was the rising of March 15th, 1844, put down with little difficulty by the troops of King 'Bomba', that brought about the ill-fated expedition of Attilio and Emilio Bandiera, two young Venetian naval officers serving in the Austrian Navy. Persuading a fellow-officer, Domenico Moro, to desert their ship, they landed with a band of nineteen patriots at Cotrone [Crotone] on the night of June 12th, 1844, to raise the standard of Italian liberation in Calabria. But no volunteers rushed to enrol with them; they were betrayed by one of their companions and taken to Cosenza, where they were court-martialled, and nine of them, including the Bandiera brothers and Moro, were condemned to death. A memorial marks the place of their execution near the railway station for Catanzaro.

We enter Cosenza by the Corso Mazzini, through the modern quarters which occupy the level ground in the angle formed by the Rivers Busento and Crati, and arrive at the Piazza XX Settembre, with its statue to Telesio. This piazza adjoins, on the left, the Piazza IV Novembre and the Central Station. To the right is the broad Corso Umberto I. The older, more interesting, parts of the town are across the Busento on the Colle Pancrazio, where a warren of narrow streets leads up to the Castello.

From the Piazza IV Novembre we continue due south to the Ponte S. Domenico, which takes its name from the fifteenth-century church of *S. Domenico* on the left. This retains its original Gothic porch and pleasant rose window, but the interior was badly restored in the eighteenth century. Next door, the former cloisters of the monastery, which are of the same date as the church (1449), are now transformed into barracks, but can be visited. On the left of the entrance are some relics of the Bandiera brothers.

Over the river, on the right of the Piazza Valdese, the Corso Garibaldi begins to wind up the farther side of the Colle Pancrazio, then swings back among the olive groves to the Corso Vittorio Emanuele II and the Castello. On the left, beyond the Jolly Hotel, is the Corso Telesio, which was once the main street of the old city. Cosenza has three 1st category hotels: the Jolly, the Imperiale and Mondial; there are also the Excelsior, Alexander and Principe, and others more modest, and in the country, about eight miles from the city on the SS 107 to Spezzano della Sila, looking over the foothills of the Sila and the valley of Cosenza, is a little modern inn, the Albergo Petite Etoile.

A short way up the Corso Telesio a piazza opens out on the left, backed by the Municipio and flanked on the right by the façade of the *Duomo.* The cathedral, replacing an earlier edifice destroyed by earthquakes, was begun in 1185 in the Romanesque style, but at the beginning of the next century it was completed in the Provençal Gothic manner, which had been brought here by the Cistercians. We have another example of their building in the near-by abbey of Sambucina (see p. 396). The Duomo was consecrated in 1222 and restored in 1947, when many of the baroque accretions were removed to reveal the earlier structure. The mixture of styles can be seen in the interior, where rectangular piers support the rounded Romanesque arches of the nave, with Gothic-pointed windows in the clerestory above them.

In the left transept there is a fine piece of carving by an unknown French sculptor, depicting Isabella of Aragon and her husband King Philip III of France kneeling to adore the Madonna and Child. Isabella died in premature childbirth in 1271 at Cosenza, after falling from her horse into the swollen River Savuto. On the right of the church, near the door leading to the Corso Telesio, is a late-Roman sarcophagus with a representation in low-relief of *Meleager at the Calydonian Hunt*. Behind the Duomo is the **Archbishop's Palace,** where, in the office, is kept the beautiful **reliquary crucifix** presented by Frederick II when he attended the consecration of the Duomo. This exquisite cross, in gold and enamel work with Greek lettering, is Byzantine in style, but may have been produced by the Sicilian workshops which had been set up by King Roger.

If we continue in the Corso, we come to the Piazza XV Marzo, with the Teatro Comunale and the Palazzo del Governo, and beyond it the gardens of the Villa Comunale, which offer a fine view over the valley of the Crati and the foothills of the Sila. The theatre used to house the **Museo Civico,** which has some interesting bronze objects and pottery of the indigenous Bruttians from a necropolis at Torre Mordillo (ninth to eighth century BC). This collection is being moved to the **castle,** which is reached by taking the Via Paradiso and then turning right in the avenue of plane trees which leads up to the Porta Piana. The castle, of Norman origin but much altered by Frederick II, is now being repaired.

To visit the oldest quarters of the town, which retain much of their medieval appearance, we take the Via del Seggio in the Corso Telesio opposite the Duomo, or the near-by Salita Liceo, which begins opposite the Archbishop's palace. The narrow streets run tier upon tier up the hillside—arches, doorways, balconies, terraced gardens, courtyards of every period from the Angevin to the eighteenth century. When we reach the Via Francesco d'Assisi we bear right for the thirteenth-century church of *S. Francesco d'Assisi,* and its monastery. The church was supposedly begun in 1217 by the

Blessed Piero Cathin, the companion of St Francis. The Gothic doorway is the original one, but much else is later.

Inside the church we are at once struck by the hideous pictures. The main altar is backed by eighteenth-century carved woodwork painted in white and gold. To the right of the altar a door leads to the little thirteenth-century Gothic cloister. The sacristy has a carved choir (1505), which shows in its curious figures of animals how the Gothic influence lingered here. The Cappella di S. Caterina on the right of the nave is richly adorned with wood carving and plaster mouldings picked out in gold. On leaving S. Francesco (note the bold arcading of the Palazzo Sambiasi on the left of the church), we descend by alleyways and steps to the Piazza Valdese.

The Sila—Sila Greca—Bisignano—Acri—S. Demetrio Corone

Cosenza is an ideal centre from which to visit the mountainous regions of the **Sila.** The name Sila is a corruption of the Latin *silva*, a forest; the Greeks, and the Romans after them, traded with the Bruttians for timber for ship-building. From the time of the papacy of Gregory the Great (fourth century) many of the churches in Rome were roofed with timber from the Sila, particularly with the Pino della Sila (*Pinus larico*, var. *Calabra*). In the nineteenth century the state-owned forests were ruthlessly cut down, under contract with German companies; today reafforestation goes on apace. For the most northern of the three divisions into which they are conveniently grouped—the **Sila Greca,** so called from the number of Albanian villages—we go north on the SS 19 and after about fifteen miles branch right, near the station, on the Bisignano–Acri road, to cross the river by the Ponte Crati. Shortly after, a road, again on the right, brings us up to the small town of **Luzzi.** The *abbey of Sambucina* stands on an isolated hill not far from Luzzi as the crow flies; but the road, which is much subject to landslides, winds for quite a distance among the hills.

Map X
p. 368

This famous Cistercian abbey was founded in 1141 by Abbot Bruno from the monastery of Chiaravalle near Milan; it became an important religious centre for the Cistercian Rule in Calabria, Apulia, Lucania and Sicily. It was suppressed in 1780. The beautiful central doorway, so lightly pointed as to appear almost rounded, is the original entrance to the primitive church, and was replaced here in 1625 after a landslide had destroyed the main body of the structure. The square Guelf window above it is very curious; unique in

Southern Italy. Strange, too, in the interior is the little rectangular apse. On the wall to the right of this are the remains of a fifteenth-century fresco of the *Madonna and Child*. Behind the church, part of the monastic buildings have been recently restored.

We return through Luzzi to the main road and bear right for **Bisignano,** which is built around a hill and on its jutting-out spurs. The town has been much damaged by earthquakes; the Byzantine-Norman castle is in ruins and the cathedral, which was also Norman, retains little of the original fabric. Bisignano, however, is very ancient; as Besidiae it was occupied by Hannibal, and it was the see of a bishop as early as 743. It became a feud of the Sanseverino family, who derived from it their title of Princes of Bisignano. Beautiful terracotta pots and jugs are made locally.

Map X
p. 368

From Bisignano the road runs along the northern flank of the deep valley of the River Mucone to **Acri.** The town was almost entirely destroyed in the bitter struggle between Sanfedisti and the French in 1806. In the upper town is the former Palazzo Sanseverino (sixteenth-century), now the ***Palazzo Falcone***; and behind it in the square to the right stands the eighteenth-century Palazzo Servidio. On the wall of the Palazzo Falcone which flanks the piazza is a commemorative tablet to Giambattista Falcone who lost his life on the expedition to Sapri in 1857—he was just twenty-one.

Map X
p. 368

> '*They were three hundred, they were young and strong,*
> *And they are dead and gone,*'

in the words, known to every Italian schoolboy, of Mercantini's 'The Gleaner of Sapri'.

A few years ago I was shown over the palazzo by the present owner, the grand-nephew of Giambattista. This vast, decaying palace has two great wings—one for use in summer, the other in winter. In the summer *salone*, where the shutters flap in glassless windows, the frescoed ceiling painted by Federico Zuccari (1543–1609) is hanging in shreds. On the walls are portraits of Giambattista, a brother who put down brigandage in these parts, and a third brother who was a colonel under Garibaldi. Precautions were taken in the family chapel against raids from these brigands. The altar has two columns of polished wood which swing back to disclose an armoury of swords and rifles.

From Acri we take the road north to **S. Demetrio Corone,** a centre of Albanian intellectual life after the founding of its Italo-Albanian College by Ferdinand I of Bourbon in 1794 on the site of a dissolved Basilian monastery. The names of the near-by villages

Map X
p. 368

The Companion Guide to Southern Italy

reveal their Greek or Albanian origin: S. Sofia d'Epiro, S. Cosmo Albanese, Vaccarizzo Albanese, S. Giorgio Albanese. Albanian is spoken by the older people—and in some places, like S. Sofia, Greek—but the inhabitants have become pretty thoroughly Italianized.

To the right of the entrance to the college, facing the road, is the interesting church of **S. Adriano,** built in a warm coloured stone. The exterior has little left of architectural value, but inside it is still one of the most rewarding of Calabrian churches. (If the door to the road is closed, you can enter through the college.) The monastery and church were founded in 955 by St Nilus of Rossano beside the ruins of a chapel of the Eastern saints Adrian and Natalie, but within a few years the buildings were destroyed by the Saracens. The present edifice was begun in 980, and is basilican in plan, with a mixture of Byzantine, Romanesque and Gothic elements; but the structure is predominantly Norman (twelfth-century). On the right of the doorway from the college are some curious low-reliefs in imitation of the head of Medusa. The capitals of the columns which support the ogival Norman-Saracenic arches are of different periods; one is Byzantine and another Corinthian, perhaps coming from Thurioi. There are remains of frescoes under the arches. A Byzantine capital forms the stoup. There is also a bell-shaped stone with carved heads in low-relief of a bearded saint (or does it represent God?) around it, and on top a curious (broken) figure squatting on two animals. The pavement, in *opus sectile* and mosaic, showing lions, snakes and a panther, is Norman. The two sculptured lions, almost shapeless with age, came from the destroyed façade.

The road descends beyond S. Demetrio through white eroded hills, where some wheat is grown in early summer, to meet the Via Ionica near the Moorish-looking ruins of the Sanseverino villa.

Sila Grande—Longobucco—hand-weaving—S. Giovanni in Fiore

For the **Sila Grande** from Cosenza we leave the Piazza IV Novembre and cross to the farther bank of the River Crati, then turn right in the Via Gravina, past the large building of the Law Courts (Tribunale), where the SS 107 makes a sweep to the left and immediately begins to ascend, with beautiful views over the countryside. After a few miles a road on the left goes to the village of **Zumpano,** where there is in the parish church a beautiful triptych by Bartolomeo Vivarini (1450–99). The SS 107 continues to climb, passing

398

through Celico and Spezzano della Sila (or Spezzano Grande, to distinguish it from its neighbour, Spezzano Piccola). After another ten miles we reach the top of the pass, the Valico di Monte Scuro, between the Serra di Guardia to the north, and the Serra Stella. From here there is a magnificent panorama of the Sila Grande and the Sila Greca.

The northern flanks of the Serra Stella, along which the road now descends to the village of Fago del Soldato, obscures the highest peak of the Sila, the Botte Donato. The summer and skiing resort of **Camigliatello Silano** is reminiscent of the lumber towns of New England: the houses and shacks are built of wood or corrugated iron, and timber stands in stacks in clearings of the forest. There are now several hotels.

Map XI
p. 372

At Camigliatello the SS 177 for Rossano branches left from the SS 107, which runs on to the chief town of La Sila, S. Giovanni in Fiore (see p. 400). The Rossano road skirts the southern edge of the Lago di Cecita, then passes on the left the road to Acri and begins to climb in a series of tortuous curves to the pass over Monte Altare. But these bends are nothing to those which we meet beyond the head of the pass, when we descend to Longobucco in the valley of the River Trionto, among scenery of the wildest grandeur. The woods here are some of the finest in Calabria.

Longobucco stands above the gorge of the Trionto, where it begins to widen out to form the valley. Norman Douglas describes in *Old Calabria* a somewhat hazardous scramble from Acri to Longobucco down this savage and precipitous gorge by way of a track which hung suspended, as it were, several hundred feet above the boulder-strewn bottom.

Map X
p. 368

Longobucco is the centre of an ancient and important textile industry. The work is done by women on hand-looms, and the antiquity of the tradition is shown in the designs, which incorporate Saracenic and Byzantine motifs. There is a permanent exhibition of these beautiful, vegetable-dyed carpets, rugs, bedspreads, shawls and materials at the workshops of the Tessitura d'Arte Calabrese, Via Monaci 12, in the upper town.

Off the piazza is the church of the **Assunta,** with its sixteenth-century campanile standing apart. The main portal and the two side doors of the church, which was rebuilt in the eighteenth century, are in a dark basalt-like stone. Note the rather crude low-reliefs of the sun. In the interior is an interesting coloured wood-carving of the *Virgin and Child*, perhaps local work of the fifteenth century.

Turning right at Camigliatello, the SS 107 quite shortly crosses the head-waters of the River Neto (the ancient Neaethus) at the village of Croce di Magara. In the spring the fields and meadows are full of wild flowers and yellow broom. Some miles farther on there is a turning on the right for **Silvana Mansio.** The Albergo Silvana Mansio, a timbered chalet set in a park-like valley, lies about a mile and a half from the main road. This is an ideal headquarters for those who want to explore the countryside on foot. Beyond the hotel a track (passable by car in the summer) crosses the high ground between Monte delle Porcina and Monte Carlomagno, and comes down to the Lago Arvo and the SS 108 *bis*.

Map XI
p. 372

After the turning for Silvana Mansio the SS 107 continues along the valley, between Monte Volpintesta to the north and Monte Carlomagno, to the Bivio Garga, where the SS 108 *bis* branches right for Lake Arvo. **Lorica,** on the northern shores of this artificial lake, is being developed as a tourist resort and possesses four hotels. There are facilities for bathing, boating and trout-fishing in tranquil surroundings where cows graze in the rich meadows by the water's edge.

From the Bivio Garga we come shortly to the principal town of the Sila, **S. Giovanni in Fiore.** The narrow streets and hovels of this town are infinitely depressing, and even the new building is hideous.

Map XI
p. 372

The town of S. Giovanni in Fiore grew up around its famous Monasterium Florense, founded by the Abbot Gioachino da Fiore in 1189, after a pilgrimage to the Holy Land and service as the porter in the Cistercian abbey of Sambucina. Dante wrote of him in the *Paradiso*:

> . . . *and, shining by my side*
> *Joachim the Calabrian Abbot, great*
> *In gift, through whom the spirit prophesied.*

The order was suppressed in 1806; but the church adjoining the monastery, which had been allowed to fall into ruin, was restored in 1928. It stands in the lower part of the town, beyond the central piazza, to the left of the tortuous, narrow main street. The Gothic central doorway is particularly fine.

From S. Giovanni the SS 108 *ter* runs north-east, through Savelli, to descend to the Ionian coast at Cariati. The SS 107 itself continues to S. Severina and Crotone, and a secondary road leads south from S. Giovanni to meet the SS 179 at the eastern end of Lake Ampollino, from where we have a number of alternative routes back to Cosenza or to the SS 19 for Catanzaro.

From Cosenza there is a branch-line of the Calabro-Lucana railway for Catanzaro, which leaves not from the main station in the Piazza IV Novembre, but from the Stazione Casali on the other side of the River Crati. The train climbs and twists among the mountains, hanging at times over vertiginous ravines so deep that one has to stand up to see their bottom from the carriage window.

CHAPTER 24

Catanzaro and its Province

Maps: XI, p.372; XII, p.380

Routes to Catanzaro

After Soveria Mannelli the SS 19 south from Cosenza to Catanzaro runs along the watershed between the River Corace, which finds its outlet in the Ionian Sea, and the headwaters of the River Lamato, which enters the Tyrrhenian just south of S. Eufemia Lamezia. Soon after the town the SS 109 branches right for Nicastro and the Tyrrhenian Coast, an interesting diversion from the more direct route, and a few miles farther on the eastern section of the SS 109 forks left for Taverna and S. Severina. As we approach the charming little town of Tiriolo there are magnificent views of both seas, and south over the Stretta di Catanzaro (the narrowest part of the toe of Italy) to the mountains of the Serre beyond.

Map XI
p. 372 **Tiriolo** is of ancient though uncertain origin. It was certainly Roman, perhaps even an earlier Hellenized town of the native peoples. In 1640 a bronze tablet was found there, with a *senatus-consultum* of 186 BC, mentioned by Livy, forbidding bacchanalian festivals. The beautifully chiselled Hellenistic bronze helmet, now in the museum at Catanzaro, was also discovered at Tiriolo. The women still wear the traditional native dress, and the Tiriolan local variation is one of the most picturesque and colourful in the province. There is an Autostello just south on the Catanzaro road. On the Piazza Italia the little Albergo Belvedere serves good simple meals and has a few bedrooms.

From Tiriolo the road descends with numerous curves and a series of fascinating, varied views, until ahead of us, strikingly situated on a lofty spur, we catch sight of the provincial capital of Catanzaro. The town is reached by crossing the valley of the Fiumarella by the modern single span bridge of reinforced concrete.

The alternative route via Nicastro and the SS 109 takes us through the wooded Conca di Decollatura, the hollow between Monte

Reventino to the west and the Monti Zingari and Contro to the south-east. Every year from September 20th–23rd the 'Cucuzza Fair' is held at the village of Decollatura. The country people congregate in their traditional dress and there is folk-dancing and music. At the Pass of Acquabona several signposted paths on the right lead up through the chestnut- and beech-woods to the summit of Monte Reventino, a climb of about one and a half hours, well worth the effort for the magnificent panorama. As the road descends, the Gulf and Plain of S. Eufemia come into view, and the woods give place to vineyards, olive-groves and cornfields. As we approach Nicastro, we see on its rocky height the ruins of the Norman and Swabian castle where Henry, the rebellious Guelf-minded son of Frederick II, was imprisoned before his mysterious death; he is said to have ridden his horse over a precipice at Martirano, to the north-west of Monte Reventino.

Nicastro is a thriving market town with wide main streets, the centre for a rich countryside producing wine, fruit, vegetables and olive oil. Its light industries, such as the weaving of blankets, rugs and shawls, and the manufacture of pottery from the local red clay, have brought it a certain prosperity in recent years. This prosperity is reflected in the cleanliness of the streets and in the beautiful dresses and proud carriage of its women. To the irreverent, the women of Nicastro resemble nothing so much as a species of gorgeously plumed turkey. The most distinctive feature of the dress in the province of Catanzaro is the bustle. The simplest type—worn every day for work in the house or in the fields by the women of Sambiase and Tiriolo—is a long red skirt (or rather underskirt), showing an inch of white petticoat, and with an elaborately pleated black overskirt drawn back to form a frilled bustle. A black apron is also an essential part of the dress, and a black tasselled mantle or shawl is often worn round the shoulders and crossed over the breast.

Map XI
p. 372

The origins of Nicastro are uncertain; it is thought to have been, like Catanzaro, Byzantine; but it owed its prosperity to the Normans, and, after them, to the Hohenstaufen. Later it was held in fief by two of the greatest families in the Kingdom, the Caracciolo and d'Aquino. In 1799, when the leading noble houses took up the cause of the Parthenopean Republic, the city was sacked by the Sanfedisti of Cardinal Ruffo. Earthquakes and floods increased the destructive toll, and there remains little of architectural or historical interest, save the ruins of the Castello and the older, more picturesque quarters on the castle hill.

Two miles beyond Nicastro to the west, on the SS 18 *dir*, is the

Map XI
p. 372
little town of **Sambiase,** the headquarters of the wine trade; the best red wine of the region takes its generic name from the town. During the *vendemmia* in mid-September the air is heavy with the smell of must; and everywhere, in and around the town, there are donkeys with oval-shaped wooden wine-barrels strapped like panniers on their backs, or great round casks being brought in on high-wheeled carts drawn by splendid white oxen. About three miles north-west of the town are the very ancient mineral springs known as the Terme Caronte.

From Sambiase it is a run of a little over two miles south to meet the Via Tirrenia (the SS 18) at S. Eufemia Lamezia, and from here we can take the new Strada dei Due Mari which crosses the Plain of S. Eufemia—or the Vale of Maida—to Catanzaro and to the Via Ionica (SS 106) at Catanzaro Lido.

Catanzaro—the silk industry—waxworks—the Provincial Museum

Map XI
p. 372
Catanzaro has progressed rapidly since the war. New suburbs, S. Leonardo and Rione Milano, are rising on the hills behind the older sections which stand on the lofty bluff between the gorges of two mountain torrents, the Fiumarella to the west and the Musofalo to the east. Since 1815 Catanzaro has been the provincial capital, replacing the French-sympathizing Monteleone (Vibo Valentia). It owed its foundation to the Byzantines at the end of the ninth century, when the imperial armies under the vigorous Nicephorus Phocas regained Calabria from the Lombards and Saracens. Silk-weaving was introduced very early, either by the Byzantines or, more likely, by the Normans after Robert Guiscard took the town in 1059. Count Roger encouraged the Saracenic silk manufacturers whom he found in Sicily, and settled colonies of them on the mainland. Frederick II gave the Jews the monopoly of dyeing silk at Naples and Capua, and the rights of manufacturing it at Trani. Jews were also engaged in the trade at Catanzaro, and there was a ghetto behind the present Palazzo Fazzari on the left of the Corso Mazzini. The eminence of this silk industry can be gauged by the fact that Catanzarese weavers were called to Tours and Lyons in 1470 to teach the French the secrets of the art. In 1519 the Emperor Charles V granted the Guilds (*consulates*) special statutes, and at the end of the seventeenth century there were more than a thousand looms at work, with five thousand people employed out of a population of sixteen thousand.

404

Robert Guiscard built a castle, remains of which still exist, incorporated in the prison, between the Piazza Matteotti and the Corso Mazzini. Frederick II made Catanzaro part of the great fief that he bestowed on his Grand Marshal Pietro Ruffo, a vast domain, still known as the Marchesato, which stretched north over the hilly country behind Crotone and including the town.

As in so many other towns in Calabria, earthquakes are mainly responsible for the absence of buildings of outstanding merit—one violent shock at the end of the eighteenth century left scarcely a house intact. However, the view towards the Ionian Sea is a compensation for the humdrum architecture.

From the station for the Cosenza line in the upper town the Via Indipendenza runs south to the Piazza Matteotti, whence, changing its name to the Corso Mazzini, it winds as the main artery of the city to the belvedere of the *circumvallazione*, from which there is a fine view, particularly in the early morning and at sunset, over the countryside to Catanzaro Lido eight miles away on the Ionian Sea. At the beginning of the Via Indipendenza the Via Osservanza, on the east, brings us to the little church of the **Osservanza** which has a piece of sculpture by Antonello Gagini, the *Madonna della Ginestra* (1508), and an extraordinary, realistically painted wood carving of *Christ nailed to the cross* (1650) by Fra Giovanni da Reggio. The Via Osservanza continues past the grounds of the Villa Manichini to the public gardens of the Villa Pepe, with a view out over the ravine of the River Musofalo and southwards to the Gulf of Squillace.

Facing us on an angle of the Piazza Matteotti is the crude statue known as the *Cavatore*, from the 'vigorous' figure of a workman swinging his pick at the rock, from which water emerges—symbolic of the harnessing of the streams of La Sila for electric power. At the left of the entrance to the Corso stands the Carcere Giudiziario, the prison built in 1860 over the old Norman castle. The Corso, the most animated street in the city, opens out into the little Piazza Garibaldi. Beyond, on the left, is the neo-classic **Teatro Comunale** (1818) and, next to it, the basilica of the **Immacolata,** rebuilt in 1765 and subsequently several times restored. The Immacolata contains some of the few existing examples of the Neapolitan female painter and modeller, Caterina de Julianis (1695–1742). Groups of these extraordinary figures, modelled in wax and then coloured, stand against painted backgrounds. A short way farther on is the Piazza Grimaldi, the heart of the city.

Continuing along the Corso, on our left is the modern **Palazzo Fazzari,** built by the architect Frederico Andreotti in the fifteenth-century style of his native Florence. Farther along we come to the little Piazza Cavour, with its fountain, and shortly beyond this the Salità dei Tribunali on the right leads up to the baroque church of **S. Domenico** (or del Rosario). In S. Domenico there are a marble statue of the *Madonna and Child* by the early-seventeenth-century Neapolitan sculptor Francesco Cassano and two paintings of the Neapolitan school, the *Madonna of the Victory* (commemorating the naval defeat inflicted on the Turks by Don John of Austria at Lepanto in 1571); and the *Madonna del Rosario* (1615), possibly by Fabrizio Santafede. If we take the street to the right of the church, we arrive almost immediately at the **Duomo** and the Archbishop's Palace. The nineteenth-century cathedral was destroyed by air raids in the last war and has now been rebuilt in a more 'ambitious' form.

Back in the Corso, we take the street to the right of the Central Post Office for the Municipio, the Villa Trieste and the Provincial Museum. The position of the public gardens right on the edge of the ravine of the Musofalo is magnificent.

The **Provincial Museum** stands on the left of the entrance to the Villa Trieste (admission 10.0 a.m.–1.0 p.m. and 4.0–7.0 p.m.). It contains material from the sites of Magna Graecia, including a Hellenistic helmet from Tiriolo, a marble head of a woman in the manner of Scopas, and an Athena in terracotta from Locri. The collection of coins from the mainland of Greece, Asia Minor, Egypt, Magna Graecia and imperial Rome is particularly good. The historical section has documents from the time of the Aragonese, Murat and the Bourbons. The art gallery includes four little landscapes by that late-seventeenth-century Neapolitan swashbuckler, Salvator Rosa.

Returning to the Corso Mazzini and proceeding south, we come to the Piazza Roma with its Victorian funicular station for the Catanzaro–Sala station in the valley. Buses Nos. 9 and 10 also leave for the lido from the terminus in the Via Indipendenza. A little farther on the Corso widens out to end in the *circumvallazione*.

Catanzaro has two 1st category hotels, the Grande Albergo Moderno, and the Jolly; one 2nd category, the Diana; and several 3rd and 4th category ones, as well as a 3rd category pension, the Rosa.

*Sila Piccola—Taverna—works by Mattia Preti—tourist villages—
Mesoraca—S. Severina*

Catanzaro lies just to the south of the mountains of the **Sila Piccola,**
and is only twenty-eight miles from the modern summer resort of the
Villaggio Mancuso (4265 ft), built among the pine trees in the heart
of the Little Sila. We leave Catanzaro by the SS 109 *bis* which runs
almost due north to the junction with the SS 109 from Soveria
Mannelli, then turn right in the SS 109, which winds along the
lower spurs of the Sila Piccola to the village of **Taverna** set on the
hillside.

Map XI
p. 372

The origin of Taverna is ancient, perhaps Greek but more
probably Roman. Its name may derive from a post-stage on the road
(*taberna*, an inn). The earlier town was destroyed by the Saracens,
and a succeeding one by the *condottiere* Francesco Sforza in the wars
of the fifteenth century. Some of the seventeenth-century family
houses, however, have pleasantly proportioned doorways and
balconies in billowing ironwork. The family of Poerio was native to
Taverna (Carlo Poerio was a friend of Gladstone's), but Taverna's
most celebrated son was the painter Mattia Preti (1613–99), the
'Cavaliere Calabrese' who succeeded Ribera as the leader of the
baroque School of Naples. Four of the town's churches contain works
by Preti.

In the centre of the town, where a feeble modern statue of the
artist stands, steps lead down to a tree-shaded piazza and the baroque church of **S. Domenico,** which was formerly the church of a
Dominican monastery. This is virtually an art-gallery almost entirely
devoted to Preti. Over the first altar on the left of the church, the
St John the Baptist has in the right-hand bottom corner a self-portrait
of Preti dressed as a Knight of Malta, with sword and paint-brush.
The painted woodwork of the church furnishings is unusual. On the
right of the main doorway is a good wooden and gesso crucifix
(sixteenth-century?). The paintings in gilt frames on the upper walls
of the church are by the Neapolitan painter Antonio Sarnelli
(1742–93).

A mile beyond the town we come to the junction with the SS 179
dir. The **Villaggio Mancuso,** a few miles up the SS 179 *dir*, stands
on a high plateau in a clearing among the pines. Adjoining it is Il
Rosetto, a village of chalets, and a mile or so to the north is another
resort, Villaggio Racisi. Farther to the east and 1000 ft higher up on

Map XI
p. 372

the wooded slopes of Monte Gariglione is Buturo with magnificent views of the two seas. From the Villaggio Mancuso it is a run of about ten miles to Lake Ampollino, where there is good trout-fishing. Another tourist village is under construction at the eastern end of the lake at the hamlet of Trepido. The shooting is also good—hare and woodcock for the most part, and some wild boar.

Map XI
p. 372
From Taverna, we continue on the SS 109 to **Zagarise.** On the left of the piazza at the top of some steps is the church of *S. Maria Assunta,* which has a finely proportioned Gothic portal and a rose window. The date, 1521, which is carved by the doorway, seems too late. I would place the building of the church at least seventy-five years earlier. The interior has been poorly baroqued and is un-interesting.

At Sersale there is a secondary road to the left for Buturo and a good road, the SS 180, down to the coast, where it meets the Via Ionica just south of Cropani Marina. The SS 109 continues to wind among woods, with views of the mountains and of the hills of the
Map XI
p. 372
Marchesato towards Capo Rizzuto. **Mesoraca** is a pleasant little town built on a high hill between two mountain torrents. A mile before the centre of the town, standing above the road on the left, is the *Convento dei Riformati,* known locally as the 'Ecce homo' from a much-venerated polychrome wooden crucifix. This moving work is attributed to the Franciscan monk Fra Umile da Petralia, who was at the monastery between 1622 and 1633. It is in a framed case above the altar in the chapel on the right of the church. (If the church is closed, ring at the door of the monastery.) Over the high altar is a genial *Madonna and Child* in marble, crowned with silver coronets (1504), by Antonello Gagini.

Mesoraca must be just as poor as other Calabrian small towns such as S. Giovanni in Fiore, but it presents a striking contrast. The inhabitants here usually wear modern dress, yet in a wonderful range of bright colours. The convent church of the *Retiro* at the far end of the town is certainly one of the most curious churches in Calabria. The convent itself is in ruins, destroyed by the earthquake of 1783. The baroque paintings of the late Neapolitan school, with later 'restorations', are extraordinary. The dome, which is painted in the crudest colours, with clouds that resemble boulders, was repaired after damage from earth tremors in 1893 by a member of the prominent Rossi family—the family still exists. Another Rossi gave the paintings in the apse in 1773. In the crypt beneath the church are tombs of ecclesiastics and of the Rossi. Over the altar is one of the worst paintings I have ever beheld in a public place.

408

Mesoraca was the birthplace of the irascible Pope Zosimus (417–418).

A short way beyond the road junction in the village of Foresta we come to a turning on the left for **Petilia Policastro,** which, like Mesoraca, stands high between two torrents from the Sila. Policastro was of Byzantine origin (Polycastron), the addition of Petilia deriving from a mistaken belief that it was built on the site of the Greek settlement of Petelia, which most authorities now place farther north near Strongoli. In the Chiesa del Rosario there is a marble statue of the *Madonna and Child* by a follower of the Gagini. Shortly after leaving the town we reach the junction with the SS 179 from Lake Ampollino, and continue in an easterly direction to meet the SS 107 from S. Giovanni in Fiore and Cosenza. Ahead of us, against the sky, we see **S. Severina** dominating the landscape from its acropolis of grey rock. As we climb round the hill to enter the city we pass on our right the interesting little church of *S. Filomena.* This is of late Byzantine foundation (eleventh- to twelfth-centuries), with Gothic additions. The exterior is oriental in its high semi-circular apse (two smaller apses are contained in the thickness of the walls) and its cupola, which is formed by a cylindrical drum with slender columns, capped by a conical roof of tiles. The ogival-arched lateral doorways are considerably later. The church is built over a crypt which was in fact a second church, known as S. Maria del Pozzo because it was once used as a cistern. Beyond S. Filomena the road ascends to the Piazza del Municipio, the centre of the town.

Map XI p. 372

Map XI p. 372

S. Severina, an important centre of Byzantine influence, was taken and held by the Saracens for twenty-six years, until it was recaptured by Nicephorus Phocas in 866. The town was the birthplace of another saintly Calabrian pope, Zaccarias (741–752). In 1075 S. Severina fell to Robert Guiscard, who rebuilt or strengthened the existing castle. The earthquake of 1783 destroyed the eastern section of the town, demolishing much of the old Byzantine cathedral (remains were incorporated in the seventeenth century into the Chiesa dell' Addolorata) and other churches, the ruins of which are still visible. The inhabitants of S. Severina are poor (there is no hotel), but the Piazza del Municipio is clean, even elegant, in comparison with the wretchedness of S. Giovanni in Fiore. At one end stands the **cathedral church of S. Anastasia,** with its campanile and baptistery to the left. The façade, in a warm coloured stone, has a Gothic central doorway harmoniously enclosed in a Renaissance-style frame. This early Angevin church was built 1274–95, but has been much altered in subsequent restoration. The interior has a

409

seventeenth-century marble pulpit, and the remaining majolica tiles of the paving in the chapel at the end of the right aisle are of the same period. In another chapel on the right is a fine wooden crucifix, possibly as early as the fourteenth century. From the left of the church we pass to the restored Byzantine baptistery, which was built in the eighth or ninth century on the usual circular plan of early baptisteries, but with four alcoves which form a Greek cross. Eight granite columns, taken from classical buildings, support the rounded arches from which rises the cupola, pierced by apertures for light. Note the Greek writing on one of the capitals and the remains of a fifteenth-century fresco on the wall to the left. The original font has been replaced in the centre of the floor.

On the farther side of the piazza is the well-preserved **Castello,** now used as a school. The earlier castle of Robert Guiscard was added to and reinforced in 1496 by Andrea Carafa, Count of Sanseverino, whose family arms are above the entrance. Quadrilateral in plan, with circular towers, its bulk and apparent strength are impressive.

After S. Severina the road bears southerly to the crossroads just north of the village of S. Mauro Marchesato. The road to the left, the shortest route for Crotone, meets the Via Ionica at the Bivio Passovecchio. The right-hand branch takes us to the Via Ionica at Cutro.

Serra S. Bruno—the Charterhouse

From Catanzaro another pleasant excursion can be made through the region of the Calabrian Apennines known as the Serre to the interesting town of Serra S. Bruno. We take first the SS 19 south to Catanzaro Lido, where we turn right in the Via Ionica as far as the road junction with the SS 181 (for Squillace), just before the Lido di Copanello. At this point there is a choice of routes open to us. We may continue on the Via Ionica to Soverato, then turn right in the SS 182 for Chiaravalle Centrale, thus keeping to main roads. Or we may follow a more rewarding route via Squillace, which involves taking narrow roads for some of the way.

Turning away from the coast on the SS 181, we see ahead of us the buildings and ruined castle of Squillace high on an outcrop of granite rock. Just under three miles beyond Squillace we turn left off the Statale into the SS 382 for Chiaravalle, and climb among the olive groves to Palermiti. Beyond the village the road continues its ascent through chestnut woods, then suddenly begins to descend, with fine views over wooded mountains and valleys, to Centrache. It is a delightful run past these upland villages with their cultivated fields among the woods, and here and there open stretches covered in a species of *Erica* from the roots of which pipe bowls are made locally. We join the SS 182 from Soverato at the pleasantly situated little hill town of Chiaravalle. The earthquake of 1783 almost totally destroyed the old town.

The Statale then bears south-west, passing below the villages of Torre di Ruggiero and Cardinale on the left (the latter at the foot of Monte Burilli), and arrives at the junction with the SS 110 from the Ponte Angitola on the Gulf of S. Eufemia. Here we turn left and run along the watershed on which rise the Rivers Mesima and Ancinale, the former flowing into the Tyrrhenian, the latter into the Ionian Sea.

Serra S. Bruno owes its fame to its Charterhouse, the Certosa di S. Stefano del Bosco, founded by the founder of the Carthusian Order itself, St Bruno, who was granted the lands by King Roger the Norman in 1090. The monks' lives of almost complete self-denial were spent in prayer, study and the labour of their hands. The Rule has been modified only in detail; Carthusians can claim that their Order has been 'never reformed, because never deformed'. Map XII p. 380

We enter Serra S. Bruno from the north; the town, which was held in fief by the Certosa until 1765, has a relative prosperity from its craft of wood-working, and presents a cheerful appearance, with its neat houses, often entered from external steps, and its balconies of graceful seventeenth-century ironwork. In the eighteenth and nineteenth centuries Serra, inspired by the work of foreign artists employed by the Carthusians, produced some fine sculptors and engravers, particularly in the Scaramuzzino and Barillari families, whose work may be seen in the town's churches. In the wide main street there are four churches with interesting baroque façades of local granite. The first, on the left, is the **Chiesa Matrice** (1795). This contains four marble statues from the Certosa, with interesting little low-reliefs on their bases, the work of an artist under Flemish influence, who signs himself 'David Müller 1611'. The carved late-eighteenth-century wooden pulpit by a member of the Scaramuzzino family is a good example of the skill of local craftsmen. The two paintings of the sixteenth-century Flemish school in the apse also came from the Certosa.

A short way farther stands the church of the **Addolorata,** almost a text-book example of the strength and weakness of ecclesiastical baroque. This was built in 1794 (although the style is earlier), perhaps to the design of one of the Scaramuzzinos—certainly the family had a hand in its construction. The façade bears scarcely any functional relation to the body of the building; it is purely ornamental. The elliptical form is bold indeed, and the curves, pinnacles, broken lines and the proportions of the apertures and mouldings are arresting; while the pale grey local granite brings all the elements together in a most satisfying way. Inside the church there are bronze statues and coloured marbles from the great ciborium designed for the Certosa by Cosimo Fanzago in 1631. (Other parts of this monumental work are in the church of the Collegiata at Vibo Valentia.) In the destruction of the Charterhouse in the earthquake of 1783 these were buried under the ruins; they were recovered and restored by the Barillari in 1810.

Still farther along the street, on the right, is the church of the **Assunta** (or di S. Giorgio), the baroque façade, with its campanile and clock, masking a thirteenth-century church, the oldest in Serra. Over the high altar is a painting of the *Annunciation*, believed to be a sixteenth-century copy of an earlier work, perhaps contemporary with the church. Continuing, we come to the quarter known as Spineto. Here, over the altar in the parish church of the **Assunta allo Spineto,** is a wood-carving of the Madonna by one of the Barillari family.

The street on the right of the Assunta brings us to the Park of Remembrance, and a poplar-lined avenue leading to the **Certosa di S. Bruno.** Women are not permitted to enter the monastery, and on the morning several years ago when I presented myself at the entrance a white-cowled head with the eyes of an albino eventually answered my ringing to whisper that the lay brother who acted as porter was ill and that it was impossible for me to enter.

As a result of the terrible earthquake of 1783 none of the original buildings of the Certosa di S. Stefano del Bosco remain, and only the façade of the church and cloisters of 1595. New cloisters and chapels, built in a severe style by French architects, were erected only in 1900. The little church of **S. Maria del Bosco** is reached by continuing in the avenue past the Certosa, until we come to a clearing in the woods. Here, S. Bruno lived and died. On Whit Monday the silvered statue and relics of the Saint are brought to this spot, accompanied by crowds of the faithful. The sick bathe in the waters of the lake, which are held to have miraculous healing powers.

There are many pleasant walks round Serra S. Bruno, but the hotel accommodation is poor. Apart from rooms to let in private houses, there is only the modest Albergo Centrale. From the Colle d'Arena, some eight miles to the south-west, there is a wonderful panorama towards Vibo Valentia and Capo Vaticano between the Gulfs of S. Eufemia and Gioia. And to the south-east, off the SS 110, is the Bourbon hunting-lodge of Ferdinandea.

Serra S. Bruno is linked with Vibo Valentia and the Tyrrhenian coast by the SS 182. Some seven or eight miles from Serra, on this road, are the adjoining villages of **Sorianello** and **Soriano Calabro,** between which stand the ruins of a Dominican monastery. (In the Chiesa di S. Giovanni at Sorianello is a wooden crucifix by the same German artist, David Müller, whose work we have seen in the Chiesa Matrice at Serra.) The ***monastery of Soriano,*** once one of the richest and most illustrious houses of the Order in Europe, was founded in 1510, and destroyed by the earthquake of 1659; rebuilt in even grander style, it was overwhelmed in the disaster of 1783. In the new church, constructed in the last century, are paintings of *Benedict XIII* and *Innocent XI* (two of the four monks from Soriano who became Pope) by a follower of Caravaggio. There is also a much venerated painting of *St Dominic*, said to be painted by no human hand (*achiropita*). This miracle seems to have occurred in Naples at the end of the fifteenth or beginning of the sixteenth century.

Map XII
p. 380

Food and Wine

Campania

The cooking in the south of Italy, especially that of Naples (*la cucina napoletana*), is some of the best known in all Italy, and has produced several dishes that are recognized throughout the western world. At its best the food is full of flavour, derived from a plentiful use of fine olive oil, tomatoes, garlic, of such herbs as parsley, basil and wild marjoram (*origano*) and of anchovies and characteristic cheeses; it is rich too in the variety of its brilliant and subtle colours. The food in Naples and other large southern cities can be very rewarding, but in popular tourist resorts and in out of the way places, it is often frankly rather monotonous. It is better to admit this, to avoid disappointment. In this brief account I am not talking of the food in the most expensive hotels, which is of the kind known as 'international', but of the better of the typical dishes found for the most part in good (but not necessarily the most expensive) smaller ristoranti and trattorias.

The usual Italian meal consists of an hors d'œuvre, soup or spaghetti, a main course of meat or fish, vegetables (often eaten as a separate course), followed by cheese, and finally a sweet finish with a *dolce* or fruit. Because of the absence of adequate grazing, meat is not good in the South, the best being from young veal, lamb or kid, killed in the spring or early summer. Fish (including shell-fish) is plentiful and varied; cheeses are fair; and, of course, the fruit and vegetables are excellent.

For the first course (*antipasto*) smoked ham with fresh figs or melon (*prosciutto con fichi, con melone*) is highly recommended. Tomatoes (*pomodori*), artichokes (*carciofi*) or fennel (*finocchio*) are often eaten with an oil and vinegar dressing as a first course. A mixed hors d'œuvre (*antipasto misto*) of salami, anchovies, mussels, clams, tunny, mushrooms, pimentoes in oil, artichoke hearts, olives, etc., can be excellent if prepared on the spot, but dreary if the ingredients have been bottled in brine or vinegar.

The specialities among the soups around the coast of Southern Italy are those made from fish, the best known of which are *zuppa di pesce* (the generic name for a kind of bouillabaisse, which differs from season to season and from place to place), *zuppa di cozze*, made from mussels and *zuppa di vongole* (clams). On Capri the local variant, *zuppa di pesce Caprese*, is produced from

415

a broth made from tomatoes, celery, parsley, garlic, herbs, lemon peel, white wine and olive oil, in which are stewed sliced octopus, inkfish, mussels in their shells, a species of large prawn, and a fish resembling mackerel. This is served with sippets of bread fried in olive oil. *Zuppa di pesce* can be excellent, especially if accompanied by a strong local wine, and is a meal in itself.

Naples is famous for its spaghetti in all forms (*pasta asciutta*) which it exports in large quantities. *Spaghetti* or *maccheroni alla Napoletana* is served with a sauce made from a special plum-shaped tomato and served with cheese. This is also known simply as *al pomodoro*. Spaghetti is cooked quickly, so that it remains firm to the teeth—*al dente*. The various forms of spaghetti are served with a variety of sauces: *alla carbonara*, a Roman version made with bacon and beaten eggs; *alla matriciana*, another Roman dish, with a sauce of salt pork and tomatoes; *alla marinara*, a Neapolitan sauce consisting of tomatoes and garlic cooked in olive oil and flavoured with basil; and *spaghetti alle vongole* or *alle cozze*, in my opinion perhaps the best of the Neapolitan versions, which has a sauce of clams or mussels cooked in olive oil with onions, garlic, tomatoes and parsley. Cheese does not add to the last two dishes. The Neapolitans devour huge quantities of their *maccheroni*; if it is too much, one can ask for a '*mezza porzione*', a half portion.

Another Neapolitan speciality which has recently migrated abroad is the *pizza*, but it does not really travel well, even to other parts of Italy. Outside Naples, the only place where I have eaten a pizza which compared with the local product was at the Roxy in Pontecagnano, south of Salerno. Expert Neapolitan pizza-makers are hired to cook in local resorts during the summer. A peculiar skill is required to beat out with even pats of the hand the leavened dough to form the circular pizza, which is then garnished in different ways with tomatoes, anchovies, capers, garlic, herbs and slices of *mozzarella* (buffalo) cheese. The pizza is then slipped on to a long-handled wooden shovel and placed in the igloo-like oven which is the feature of a *pizzeria*. Within a few minutes it is on the table, crisp, with an appetizing aroma, quite delicious. *Calzoni* are made from the pizza mixture, but they are folded over to form half-moon-shaped envelopes enclosing the savoury filling. Another popular dish made with this buffalo cheese is *mozzarella in carrozza* ('mozzarella in a carriage'), which in its basic form consists of pieces of the cheese placed between two slices of bread, dipped in beaten egg, and then fried in olive oil.

No visitor should miss the Southern Italian fish-markets for the marvellous multicoloured variety of the shell-fish and the bizarre shapes and fantastic colouring of fish—from the little silver-blue anchovies to the gigantic, obscene octopus. We have already referred to the excellence of the mussels and clams. Traditionally the most famous town for oysters (*ostriche*) is Taranto, but they are to be had almost anywhere on the coast. Swordfish (*pesce spada*) and tunny or tuna (*tonno*) can be very good indeed, the best parts of the latter being cuts from the stomach (*ventresca*). They are both excellent grilled (*alla griglia*). One of my favourites is red mullet (*triglia*); dipped in flour and fried in olive oil it retains the fresh tang of the sea, and is a beautiful pink-gold in colour. Other good fish are sea-bass (*spigola*) and *dentice*, a fish which has no English equivalent; these may be roasted (*arrosto*), grilled (*alla griglia*) or boiled (*in bianco*). For some snobbish reason sardines and anchovies (*alici, acciughe*) are only eaten in Naples by the poorer classes; freshly caught and fried they are delicious. Those little monstrosities which are served like rings of guttapercha in a *fritto di pesce* (mixed fried fish)—the *polpi, seppie* and *calamari* (octopus, squid and cuttle- or ink-fish) are much favoured by southerners but are not always acceptable to northern palates. The lobsters (*aragosta*) and *scampi*, however, can be very good indeed.

Beef (*manzo*) and veal (*vitello*) are usually served grilled (*al ferri*) or boiled (*bollito*). A typical Neapolitan recipe is for *bistecca alla pizzaiola*—a powerful dish, but a favourite of mine. The steaks are browned in a pan with a little olive oil and are served with a pungent sauce of fresh tomatoes, garlic, salt, pepper and *origano* (wild marjoram). Because of the toughness of southern meat it is better to try chicken (*pollo arrosto*—roast, or *allo spiedo*—on the spit) or meat from young animals, such as sucking-lamb (*abbacchio al forno*— a typical Roman dish; the lamb, plentifully seasoned with rosemary and garlic, is roasted in the oven) or kid (*capretto*, again roasted, *al forno*). Another popular dish is a *fritto misto*, the contents of which vary, but usually contain brains, sweetbreads, aubergines, mushrooms, *zucchine* (small marrows), cauliflower, etc., fried in a batter in olive oil.

From the rich surrounding countryside of Campania Naples is plentifully supplied with excellent fresh fruit and vegetables. Aubergines and pimentoes constitute a pleasant change from the more usual vegetables. In Naples they serve an aubergine pie (*melanzana parmigiana*)—alternate layers of aubergines (*melanzana*) and *mozzarella*, covered with a sauce of tomatoes and sprinkled with grated Parmesan cheese, baked in the oven. They may also be eaten stuffed (*melanzane ripiene*) with a mixture of anchovies, black olives, parsley, garlic and capers. Pimentoes are also served stuffed in this way (*peperoni ripieni*). *Peperonata* is a stew of pimentoes, tomatoes, onion and garlic—this can be very good. In Naples most ristoranti prepare potato croquettes (*crocchette di patate*) which, made from potatoes, Parmesan or Gruyère cheese, egg, salt and pepper, then rolled in fine breadcrumbs and fried in oil, should not be missed.

Of the cheeses, besides *mozzarella*, *provola* is also produced from buffalo milk, and *provolone*, though a type of the latter can be made from cows' milk. Similar to *provolone* is the curiously shaped *caciocavallo*. *Buttiri* (or *burrini*) is a Calabrian version of *caciocavallo*, in which the cheese encloses a nut of butter. *Provola di pecora* from the Sorrentine district is made from ewes' milk, as is also the well-known *ricotta*.

The Neapolitan *dolci* known as *sfogliatelle* are quite perfect; made of the lightest flaked pastry, they are flavoured with a variety of delicious fillings. The excellent southern fruit needs no comment—nor the fine walnuts from Sorrento, and the water-ices of Naples are justly famous. A pleasant way to finish one's meal is to place a peeled peach in a glass of white wine; the bouquet of the fruit infused with the wine is exquisite. And finally the coffee of Naples is the best in the world.

When Pulcinella thinks of wine, he thinks of *Gragnano* (11°), a deep-coloured red wine, which sometimes has a purple froth, dry and full bodied. But, with the exception of some of the Apulian wines, it is very difficult to generalize about the qualities of a particular wine. Two bottles from the same source can be absolutely dissimilar. The red wines often have a sharp tang, as if from the volcanic nature of the soil, and this can degenerate into a distinct acidity. *Falerno* (both red and white, 12°–14°), the wine so praised in antiquity, is still produced in the Phlegraean Fields and districts to the north, but it is sad to have to admit that either the wine has deteriorated in quality or classical tastes were different from ours. *Lacrima Christi*, too, must owe much to the beauty of its name, which covers white wines (both sweet and dry, 12°–13°) a rosé (12°) and a red (12°). It is grown on the slopes of Vesuvius, which also produces a red wine, *Vesuvio* (10°–12°). Other red wines are *Aglianico* (12°–14°) and *Solopaca*, from the province of Benevento. (There is also a white.) Of the white wines we have *Asprinio* (8°–10°), a light wine with a distinct sparkle, and the famous wines of the island of Ischia, the best being *Epomeo* (11°–12°), which can be very good indeed, a fresh, dry, yellow-coloured wine, with a pleasant bouquet. There is also a good dry red *Epomeo*. The wines of Capri are a myth (except from small privately owned vineyards); I suspect most of it comes from Ischia. At Ravello there are produced two most reliable wines, a white (12°) and a rosé, from the vineyards of Signor Caruso; these are very good, and are exported. On the Amalfi coast, especially around Minori, are found some delicate white wines. In the southern districts of Campania the local wines are only too often scarcely drinkable.

Calabria

High among the regional specialities must come the tunny (tuna) and the swordfish, perhaps best brushed with oil and grilled. Aubergines play a big part in Calabrian culinary usage, an interesting variant being *melanzane al funghetto* (cooked like mushrooms), where the aubergines are diced and seasoned with garlic, parsley, pepper and olive oil. A Calabrian way of serving spaghetti (*alla calabrese*) is with a pungent sauce made from pimentoes. Trout (*trota*) caught in the mountains of the Sila are good, both fried in oil or *in bianco*. *Turiddù* are biscuits made of flour, eggs and almonds and powdered over with sugar. Calabrian wines can be very strong, 15°–16° being common alcoholic strengths. The best-known reds are perhaps *Pellaro* (16°) and *Cirò* (14°–15°), the latter being a favourite of Norman

Douglas—'the purest nectar'. But, speaking of the wine of Calabria, he says that you have 'to pounce upon him at the psychological moment'; I, alas, have made some sadly unrewarding pounces. Cirò has a characteristic flavour which suggests Marsala.

Basilicata

Here the highly flavoured sausages (*salcicce, soppressate*) are a speciality. The trout from Lake Sirino are usually roasted with garlic and parsley, or poached in a court-bouillon and served with olive oil and lemon. *Aglianico di Vulture* (12°–13°) is an agreeable red wine, fresh and full-bodied, with a bouquet.

Apulia

Among the regional specialities of Apulia is *capretto ripieno*, young kid roasted in the oven with herbs and spices. Roast young lamb (*agnello in forno*) is also good. Fish from the Adriatic are considered by some to be superior to those from the western seas. *Cozze alla marinara* is a soup of mussels, flavoured with garlic, parsley (and often pimentoes). A Tarantine speciality are *cozze gratinate*, where the mussels have one shell removed, are covered with fine breadcrumbs, garlic and chopped parsley, sprinkled with oil and then baked. Taranto is famous for its shellfish and especially its oysters, appreciated by the ancients. Particularly good at Taranto (and all along the Adriatic coast) is the *zuppa di pesce*. *Panzerotti* are little envelopes of pasta (like *ravioli*) filled with eggs beaten with cheese (*mozzarella* or *ricotta*), meat, small onions, tomatoes or anchovies, then fried in olive oil.

I have never tasted a poor wine in Apulia; even the smallest wineshop in out of the way villages supplies really first-class wines. The *rossi* of Bari (14°) and Barletta (14°–15°) are robust wines, generous and fruity. From the Gargano, Foggia, Castel del Monte come pleasant red wines (11°–13°), while a particular favourite of mine, *Squinzano* (12°), a light red wine of fine flavour, comes from the district north of Lecce. *Aleatico di Puglia* is a strong (16°–17°), not too sweet, red wine, excellent with dessert. Castel del Monte produces also a rosé and a white wine (11°–13°). Another good rosé, the *Rosato di Salento* (12°–13°) is very similar to Squinzano. Of the whites the palm must go to *San Severo*, a pale straw-coloured wine, deliciously fresh, dry and fragrant (11°–12°). Also good, but not so distinctive, are the white wines which go under the generic name of *Locorotondo* (11°–13°). Among dessert wines are *Malvasia bianca* (13°–15°), a golden wine with a characteristic bouquet, and *Moscato di Trani*, sweet, with an alcoholic content reaching as high as 20°. Moreover, many of the lesser-known local vineyards produce wines in every way as good as these.

APPENDIX 2

Chronological Table

BC		THE GREEKS
ca.	750	Greek settlement on Ischia and Cumae
	721	Traditional date of foundation of Sybaris
	707	Traditional date of foundation of Taranto
	703	Traditional date of foundation of Croton
ca.	700	Traditional date of foundation of Reggio Calabria
6th century		Foundation of Naples (Neapolis-New City) on site of older settlement (Palaeopolis, Parthenope)
525 & 474		Greek victories over Etruscans at Cumae
	510	Sybaris destroyed by Croton

		THE ROMANS
326–304		Second Samnite War
	325	Naples surrenders; becomes ally of Rome
	326	Roman defeat at Caudine Forks
298–290		Third Samnite War. Rome paramount in Campania, Apulia, Lucania
	280	King Pyrrhus of Epirus invited by Taranto to combat Rome
	274	Taranto surrenders to Rome
	267	Reggio falls to Rome
218–201		Second Punic War. Hannibal in Italy
	216	Roman defeat at Cannae

AD		
	61	St Paul lands at Reggio Calabria and Pozzuoli
	79	Destruction of Pompeii and Herculaneum
	476	Romulus Augustulus, last Western Roman Emperor, retired to Naples

		THE BARBARIANS AND BYZANTINES
495–526		Ostrogothic Kingdom of Italy
after 500		Foundation of Abbey of Montecassino
535–40		Belisarius reconquers Southern Italy for Eastern Empire
	543	Gothic invasion under Totila

420

554	Goths defeated by Narses
571	Lombards establish Duchy of Benevento
646	Lombards annex Salerno

THE AUTONOMOUS DUCHY OF NAPLES

763–1139	Naples, nominally Byzantine, ruled by own Dukes
786	Amalfi becomes autonomous
before 800	Foundation of Salerno School of Medicine
ca. 830	Appearance of Saracens
840	Saracens capture Bari
870	Frankish Emperor Louis II frees Bari
871	Defeat of Saracens at Gaeta by Neapolitan admiral Cesario Console
875	Bari seat of Byzantine Catapan

THE NORMANS

1015	Normans at Monte Sant' Angelo
1027	Norman Count Rainulf obtains Aversa
1053	Robert Guiscard defeats Pope Leo IX at Civita
1059	Robert Guiscard acknowledged Duke of Apulia and Calabria by Pope Nicholas II
1060	Count Roger takes Reggio Calabria
1130–54	Roger II (Count of Sicily, 1105; Duke of Apulia and Calabria, 1127; King, 1130)
1139	Naples submits to Roger
1154	William I (the Bad)
1166	William II (the Good)
1189	Tancred
1194	William III (deposed)

THE HOHENSTAUFEN

1194	Henry VI (Roman Emperor)
1197	Frederick II (Emperor)
1224	Foundation of University of Naples
1231	*The Constitutions of Melfi*
1250	Conrad IV (Emperor)
1254	Manfred
1266	Manfred defeated and killed at Benevento
1266	Conradin (beheaded in Naples, 1268)

THE ANGEVINS

1265	Charles I
1282	The Sicilian Vespers
1285	Charles II

1309	Robert (the Wise)
1343	Joan I (deposed)
1381	Charles III of Durazzo
1414	Joan II
1435	René of Lorraine

THE ARAGONESE

1442	Alfonso V (the Magnanimous)
1458	Ferdinand I
1494	Alfonso II (abdicated)
1495	Ferdinand II
1496–1502	Frederick of Altamura

THE SPANISH VICEROYS

1504–7	Gonsalvo di Cordova
1532–3	Pedro de Toledo, Marchese di Villafranca
1616–20	Pedro Giron, Duke d'Ossuna
1647	Revolt of Masaniello

THE AUSTRIAN VICEROYS

1713–34

THE BOURBONS

1734	Charles III of Bourbon
1759	Ferdinand IV (of Naples)
1799	Parthenopean Republic
1799	Reconquest of Southern Italy by Cardinal Ruffo and the Sanfedisti
1799	Restoration of Ferdinand IV
1806	Joseph Bonaparte
1808	Joachim Murat
1815	Restoration of Ferdinand IV (now I of the Two Sicilies)
1825	Francis I
1830	Ferdinand II ('Bomba')
1859	Francis II
1860	Bourbon forces defeated by Garibaldi; Francis abdicates; the Two Sicilies henceforth part of United Italy under House of Savoy

A Note on the Napoleonic Wars and the fall of the Bourbons

It is perhaps worth inserting here a brief summary of the main events of the short-lived Parthenopean Republic, from July 1793 when Naples joined England against republican France, until the fall of the House of Bourbon, with the unification of Italy, in 1861.

On his accession to the Spanish throne in 1759, Charles III (Don Carlos) who had done much for his newly won Kingdom of Naples, was succeeded as ruler of Naples by his eight-year-old son Ferdinand, who in 1768 married the ambitious Austrian Maria Carolina, sister of Queen Marie-Antoinette. Tanucci, his father's prime minister, was dismissed, and under the Queen's direction (with the aid of the new prime minister, Sir John Acton) Neapolitan policy was freed from Spanish influence and aligned with England and Austria. In 1793, the year of the execution of Louis XVI and his Queen, Naples joined in the first coalition against France, but French victories under Bonaparte in Northern Italy caused Ferdinand to sue for peace in 1796. Nelson's defeat of the French fleet in Aboukir Bay in 1798 restored Ferdinand's courage, and he rashly led an attack on Rome, only to beat a hasty and ignominious retreat before the French General Championnet, who forthwith marched on Naples. The King and the royal family embarked on Nelson's ships for the safety of Sicily. The *lazzaroni* of Naples fought desperately for their King and Church against the French; but Championnet entered the city in January 1799, and the so-called Parthenopean Republic was proclaimed. The republic, failing to attract popular support, fell to Cardinal Ruffo and his Calabrian Sanfedisti in June of the same year.

Neapolitan policy, alternately in the hands of Ferdinand and Maria Carolina, veered like a weather-cock before the winds that blew from France. In 1802 the royal family returned to Naples from Sicily, but were forced to flee there again in 1805 when Napoleon marched on the Kingdom and placed his brother Joseph on the throne. Joachim Murat, who succeeded Joseph in 1808, did much for the Kingdom, reforming both the law and the out-dated feudal system. Murat tried to keep his throne after the final defeat of Napoleon, but was worsted at the battle of Tolentino by the Austrians in

1815; and the Congress of Vienna confirmed the return of the Bourbons to Naples.

Ferdinand I and IV of the Two Sicilies (as he was thenceforth entitled) crushed all attempts at constitutional reform, as did his successors, Francis I (1825–30) and Ferdinand II (1830–59). The latter (known as 'Bomba' after his commander Filangieri shelled the rebels in Palermo in 1848), though bigoted, narrow-minded and overbearing, was a good economist, and the country profited under his rule—though not where personal or political liberty were concerned. The fall of the last of the Bourbons of Naples, Francis II (1859–60) was precipitated by an abortive rising in Palermo on April 4th, 1860. Garibaldi, with the connivance of Cavour on behalf of Victor Emmanuel of Savoy, and the sympathetic neutrality of England and France, sailed from Genoa on May 5th with the 'Thousand', and overran Sicily. Then, effecting a surprise landing on the mainland at Melito on August 18th–19th, with only 4500 men, he quickly seized Reggio Calabria, and joining up with guerrilla bands in the Calabrian mountains, marched northwards against the numerically superior but now demoralized Bourbon troops. Garibaldi entered Naples on September 7th, forcing the King and the remnant of this army to fall back on Gaeta, where they held out, even after their defeat on the Volturno on October 1st and 2nd, until February 13th, 1861. A plebiscite on October 21st, 1860, finally proclaimed the Kingdom of the Two Sicilies a part of United Italy.

Readers with a Whiggish turn of mind might like to follow more closely the events in G. M. Trevelyan's still very readable *Garibaldi and the Thousand* and *Garibaldi and the Making of Italy*; those whose bent is more Tory will enjoy Mr Harold Acton's most entertaining two volumes, *The Bourbons of Naples* and *The Last Bourbons of Naples*.

APPENDIX 4

Hotels and pensioni mentioned in the text

For a fuller list consult the Michelin *Italie* and the *Annuario Alberghi d'Italia*

Acciaroli: *La Scogliera* (III).

Agropoli: *Carola* (III).

Alberobello: *Dei Trulli* (I).

Amalfi: *Cappucini Convento* (I); *Luna e Torre Saracena* (I) Via Amendola.

Bagnara Calabra: *Pensione Castella Emmarita* (II); *Pensione Reginella* (II).

Bari: *Delle Nazioni* (I) Lungomare Nazario Sauro; *Palace* (I) Via Lombardi; *Oriente* (II) Corso Cavour.

Barletta: *Jolly* (II).

Bisceglie: *Commercio* (IV).

Capri: *Quisisana* (I).

Castel del Monte: *Ostello di Federico* (III).

Castellana Grotte: *Autostello Aci* (II); *Locanda Matarese*.

Catanzaro: *Grande Albergo Moderno* (I) Piazza G. Matteotti; *Jolly* (I) Via Tedeschi; *Diana* (II) Discesa Piazza Nuova; *Pensione Rosa* (II) Via XX Settembre.

Cava de' Tirreni: *Scapolatiello* (III).

Cirella: *Autostello Aci* (II).

Cosenza: *Imperiale* (I) Viale Trieste; *Jolly* (I) Via Lungo Crati Deseta; *Mondial* (I) Via Molinella; *Alexander* (II) Via Monte San Michele; *Excelsior* (II) Piazza Stazione; *Principe* (II) Via Monte San Michele.

Crotone: *Bologna* (II).

Foggia: *Palace Hotel Sarti* (I) Viale XXIV Maggio.

Gallipoli: *Jolly* (I); at S. Giovanni: *Lido S. Giovanni* (II).

Gambarie: *Grande Albergo Gambarie* (II); *Excelsio* (III); *Del Turista* (IV).

Gioia del Colle: *Jolly*.

Ischia, Lacco Ameno: *Albergo della Regina Isabella—Sporting* (I).

Lecce: *Jolly* (I) Via Reggimento Fanteria; *Patria* (I) Piazzetta G. Riccardi; *Risorgimento Palace* (I) Via Augusto Imperatore.

Maratea: *Santavenere* (I) at Fiumicello.

Marina di Leuca: *L'Approdo* (I); *Pensione Minerva* (II); *Pensione Rizieri* (II).

Martina Franca: *Semeraro* (II) Piazzetta S. Antonio; *Olimpo* (III) Via Taranto.

Matera: *Jolly* (I) Via Roma.

Melfi: *Pensione Bellapanella* (III).

Monte S. Angelo—Foresta Umbra: *Rifugio* (III).

Monticchio Laghi: *Casina ai Laghi* (III).

Naples: *Excelsior* (L) Via Partenope; *Vesuvio* (L) Via Partenope; *Ambassador's Palace Hotel* (I) Via Medina; *Continental* (I) Via Partenope; *De Londres e Ambasciatori* (I) Piazza Municipio; *Majestic* (I) Largo Vasto a Chiaia; *Mediterraneo* (I) Piazza Municipio; *Parker's* (I) Corso Vittorio Emanuele; *Royal* (I) Via Partenope; *S. Lucia* (I) Via Partenope; *Britannique* (II) Corso Vittorio Emanuele; *Pensione Caracciolo* (I) Via Caracciolo; *Pensione Maurice* (I) Via Partenope; *Pensione de Mille* (II) Piazza Amedeo.

Paestum: *Autostello Aci* (II).

Peschici: *Gusmay*.

Polignano a Mare: *Grotta Palazzese* (I).

Potenza: *Grande* (I) Via Bonaventura.

Praiano—near Vettica Maggiore: *Tritone* (II).

Procida: *Le Arcate* (III).

Ravello: *Caruso Belvedere* (II) Palazzo d'Afflitto; *Palumbo* (II) Via S. Giovanni del Toro; *Parsifal* (III) Piazza Moresca.

Rifreddo: *Rifreddo*.

Salerno: *Jolly delle Palme* (I) Lungomare Trieste.

S. Agnello: *Cocumella* (I).

S. Cataldo: *Bella Vista* (IV).

S. Cesarea Terme: *Palazzo* (II); *La Salute* (III).

S. Giovanni: *Albergo Lido S. Giovanni* (II).

S. Maria di Castellabate: *Grand Hotel S. Maria* (II).

Scilla: *Matteo a Mare* (I).

Selva di Fasano: *Paradiso* (II); *Miramonti* (III); *Pensione Trullo d'Oro*.

Serra Pedace—Silvana Mansio: *Silvana Mansio* (II).

Serra S. Bruno: *Centrale* (IV).

Sorrento: *Imperiale Tramontano* (I) Via Vittorio Veneto; *Bellevue Syrene* (II) Piazza della Vittoria.

Soverato: *S. Vincenza* (III) Corso Umberto; *Scalamandre* (IV) Corso Umberto.

Spezzano Piccolo—near Cosenza: *Petite Etoile* (III).

Spiaggia di S. Maria di Colonna: *Pensione il Paese del Sole* (III).

Tiriolo: *Autostello Aci* (III); *Belvedere* Piazza Italia.

Torre Canne: *Terme* (II); *Pensione La Primula* (III).

Trani: *Jolly* (II); *Motel Autoconfort* (III); *Italia* (IV); *Adriatica* (IV); *Romagna* (IV).

Tremiti Islands—San Domino: *Eden* (I).

Vico del Gargano—S. Menaio: *Autostello Aci* (II) Bellariva.

Vietri sul Mare—Raito: *Raito* (I); *Albergo Lloyds Baia* (I).

Vieste—near Pugnochiuso: *Del Faro* (II).

Index of Places

Index of Places

Index of Places

Index of Places

Index of Persons

(Where possible, dates have been inserted for architects, musicians, painters and sculptors)

Acceptus, Archdeacon, 279
Acciaiuoli, Niccolò, 34
Acquaviva family, 288, 289, 293, 294, 296, 306, 343; Andrea Matteo, 293; Dorotea, 294; Gian Girolamo II, 296; Giovanni Antonio, 343; Giulio Antonio, 293
Acton, Sir John, 20, 157
Adrian IV, Pope, 168
Agincourt, Pierre d' (d. 1310), 216, 224, 267, 307
Agrippa, Marcus Vipsanius, 71, 77, 78, 80
Agrippina, Empress, 60, 79
Agrippino, St, 63
Aierba d'Aragona, Filiberto (17th c.), 339
Alamanno, Pietro (15th c.), 115
Alaric, King of the Visigoths, 189, 379, 393
Alba, Antonio Alvarez de Toledo, Duke of (Viceroy of Naples 1622-9), 56
Alberada see Apulia, Countess of
Alessi, Andrea (15th c.), 233
Alexander of Alexandria, 311
Alexander of Tunis, Field Marshal Earl, 109
Alexander Severus, Emperor, 79
Alfano, Fabio (15th c.), 272
Alfano da Termoli (12th c.), 169
Alferius, St, 173-4
Alfonso I of Aragon (King of Naples 1435-58), 23, 29, 106, 140, 141, 273, 384

Alfonso II of Aragon (King of Naples 1494-5), 20, 37, 348
Alfonso de Liguori, St, 112, 172
Al-Kamid, Sultan of Egypt, 241
Altobello, Perso (16th c.), 206
Altomonte, Filippo Sangineto, Count of, 392
Ambrose, St, 135
Anacletus, Anti-Pope, 133
Anaxilas, Tyrant of Reggio, 379
Andrea da Salerno (1490-1530), 174, 179
Andreotti, Federico (15th c.), 405
Andrew of Hungary, 31, 105
Anjou, House of (Kings of Naples 1266-1435), see Charles I, Charles II, Charles III, Giovanna I, Giovanna II, Ladislas and Robert, see also Durazzo and Taranto
Anselm, Archbishop of Canterbury, 239
Anserano di Trani (fl. 1240-76), 252, 258
Antinoüs, 33, 60
Antioch, Bohemond, Prince of, 279-80
Antonello da Messina (ca. 1430-79), 65
Antonio di Andrea (15th c.), 124, 285
Antony, Mark, 15, 77, 147, 308
Appius Claudius Caecus, 13
Apulia, Alberada, Countess of, 279; Drogo, Count of, 198, 201, 288; Humphrey, Count of, 198, 201; Robert Guiscard, Duke of (see Guiscard, Robert); Roger, Duke of, 334; Roger Borsa, Count of, 178;

Index of Persons

Bramantino (Bartolomeo Suardi, *c.a* 1455 - *ca.* 1535), 35, 45
Brancaccio, family of, 46; Cardinal, 46; Scipio, 64
Brienne, family of, 329, 334; Walter, 346; *see also* Lecce, Counts of
Breughel, Jan (1565-1625), 65; Pieter (1530-69), 65
Broussier, General, 263
Bruno, St, 412
Bruno, Giordano, 44, 136
Brutus, Decius Junius, 75

Caccavello, Annibale (*ca.* 1515 - *ca.* 70), 137
Caesar, Julius, 75, 78, 308
Cafaro, Donato (17th c.), 35
Calabria, Alfonso of Aragon, Duke of, *see* Alfonso II
Calabria, Charles of Anjou, Duke of, 39
Calabria, Mary of Valois, Duchess of, 39
Calpurnius, L., 76
Calvi, Pandulf, Count of, 119
Campanella, Tommaso, 389, 393
Canova, Antonio (1757-1822), 22
Capece, Francesca, 338
Capua, Arechi II, Prince of, 114, 131; Lando, Count of, 115, 116; Landulf, Bishop of, 116; Pandolf IV, Prince of, 103; Richard, Prince of, 118; Robert, Count of, 111
Caracalla, Emperor, 59, 129
Caracciolo, family of, 42, 133, 318, 403; Marino I (Prince of Avellino), 133; Marino II (Prince of Avellino), 133; Sergianni, 195; Tommaso (Archbishop of Taranto), 323
Carafa, family of, 20, 42, 53, 110, 225, 255, 257, 269, 270, 318, 367, 388; Andrea (Count of Sanseverino), 410, Anna (Duchess of Medina de Las Torres), 71; Cardinal, 319; Carlo (Bishop of Aversa), 105, 60; Diomede (Count of Maddaloni), 46, 60; Diomede (Bishop of Tricarico), 202; Ettore, 269; Francesco, 45; Petracone V (Duke of Martina Franca), 319; Sozi (Bishop of Lecce), 331; Vincenzo, 388; *see also* Paul IV, Pope

Caravaggio (Michelangelo Merisi, 1569-1609), 45, 46, 413
Carella, Domenico (18th c.), 319
Casale, Gaspare, 31
Casanova, Giovanni Jacopo, 22
Cascini, Antonio (19th c.), 390
Cassano, Francesco (17th c.), 406
Cassius (Gaius Cassius Longinus), 75
Castriota-Scanderbeg, family of, 339; Alfonso, 344; Angela, 287; Giovanni, 361
Catello, Vincenzo (19th c.), 324
Cathin, Blessed Piero, 396
Cavagna, G. B. (16th c.), 46
Cavallini, Pietro (*ca.* 1279-1364), 53, 54, 170
Celebrano, Francesco (18th c.), 43
Celestine V, Pope, 55-6, 235
Cellini, Benvenuto (1500-71), 23, 300
Cerio, Edwin and Ignazio, 150
Chaliapin, F. I. (1873-1938), 149
Charlemagne, Emperor, 198
Charles I of Anjou (King of Naples 1266-85), 23, 29, 33, 43, 44, 48, 51, 129, 158, 170, 195, 199, 200, 216, 218, 224, 225, 226, 301, 354, 363
Charles II of Anjou (King of Naples 1285-1309), 44, 54, 55, 117, 158, 215, 216, 218, 224
Charles III of Anjou-Durazzo (King of Naples 1382-6), 179
Charles II, King of England, 299
Charles II of Habsburg, King of Spain (also King of Naples 1665-1700), 35, 133
Charles III of Bourbon, King of Naples and Sicily 1734-59 (later King of Spain 1759-88), 22, 23, 27-8, 56, 58, 59, 64, 86, 89, 107, 145, 149, 259, 275
Charles V, Emperor (also King of Naples 1516-56), 23, 141, 190, 195, 199, 251, 275, 284, 298, 301, 308, 329, 335, 344, 348
Charles VIII, King of France, 30
Chiaiese, Leonardo (18th c.), 153
Chiaromonte, Tristano, 344
Choderlos de Laclos, Pierre Ambroise François, 322
Cicero, Marcus Tullius, 60, 75, 77, 80, 188, 216, 373

438

439

Index of Persons

Index of Persons

Lenin, V. I., 149
Lenormant, Charles, 361
Leo III, the Isaurian, Emperor, 361
Leonardo da Vinci (1452-1519), 65
Lewis II, Emperor, 237, 306, 309
Lillo di Barletta (14th c.), 282
Livia, Empress, 136
Livy (Titus Livius), 110, 278, 402
Lorrain, Claude (1600-82), 65
Lotto, Lorenzo (ca. 1480-1556), 65, 248
Louis IX (St), King of France, 170
Louis XII, King of France, 35
Lucilius, Caius, 122
Lucullus, Lucius Licinus, 74, 80
Lunacharsky, A. V., 149
Lytton, Edward Bulwer-, 100

Maccari, Cesare (19th c.), 344
Maecenas, 302
Maestro Antonio di Andrea, see Antonio di Andrea
Maestro dell' Incoronazione di Eboli (mid-15th c.), 180
Maestro Leonio di Taranto (13th c.), 207
Maestro Sarola (late 12th and early 13th c.), 193, 200
Maieski, Sebastian (17th c.), 207
Maiuri, Amedeo, 58, 90, 92, 94
Malaparte, Curzio, 17, 31
Malvito, Tommaso (15th-16th c.), 45, 53
Manieri, Mauro (17th c.), 332
Manfred of Hohenstaufen (King of Sicily 1254-66), 129, 179, 195, 216, 223, 224, 227, 254, 271, 272
Manso, Giovanni Battista, Marquis of Villa, 44-5
Mantegna, Andrea (1431-1506), 65
Marcellus, M. Claudius, 193, 200
Marcus Aurelius, Emperor, 349
Margherita of Anjou-Durazzo, Queen of Naples, 179
Maria Carolina of Austria, Queen of Naples, 68, 108
Maria Cristina of Savoy, Queen of Naples, 23
Maria of Anjou (illegitimate daughter of Robert I), 50
Maria of Anjou, Queen of Hungary, 38

Maria of Hungary, Queen of Naples, 54
Marigliano, Giovanni, see Giovanni da Nola
Marino, Giovanni Battista, 44
Marius, Gaius, 78
Marra, family of, 274
Martinelli, Domenico (1650-1718), 246
Martini, Simone (1283-1344), 32, 65
Marullo, family of, 340
Masaccio (Tommaso Guidi, 1402-43), 65
Masaniello, Tommaso, 48, 335
Mascagni, Pietro (1863-1945), 236
Masolino da Panicale (1383-1447), 65
Massa, Donato and Giuseppe, 39
Mazzocchi, Alessio, 94, 115
Mazzola, G. D. (1544-77), 369
Mazzoni, Guido (end of 15th c.), 36, 66
Medici, Lorenzo (the Magnificent), Ruler of Florence, 46, 60
Medina de Las Torres, Ramiro de Guzman, Duke of (Viceroy of Naples 1637-44), 71; see also Carafa, Anna
Medrano, (18th c.), 28, 64, 86
Meidias (5th c. B.C.), 257
Melo da Stiglione (13th c.), 240, 289
Menga, Evangelista (16th c.), 344
Mengs, Anton Raphael (1728-79), 108
Metastasio (Pietro Trapassi, 1698-1782), 28
Michelangelo Buonarroti (1475-1564), 36, 59, 65, 344
Michelozzo (Michelozzo Michelozzi, 1396-1472), 46
Migliaccio, Lucia, see Floridia, Duchess of
Milo of Croton, 203, 359, 363
Milton, John, 44-5
Minutolo, Cardinal Filippo, 53
Mocenigo, Pier (16th c.), 332
Mohammed II, Sultan of Turkey, 348
Montano di Arezzo (14th c.), 134
Montefoscoli, Goffredo di, 82
Montefuscolo, Roberto di, 254
Montemar, Jose Carillo de Albornoy, Count of, 259
Mormile, Iacopo (16th c.), 103
Morelli, Domenico (1826-1901), 26, 66, 165
Moro, Domenico, 394

Index of Persons

446